A World of C

# A World of Chess

*Its Development and
Variations through
Centuries and Civilizations*

JEAN-LOUIS CAZAUX *and*
RICK KNOWLTON

McFarland & Company, Inc., Publishers
*Jefferson, North Carolina*

The present work, *A World of Chess*, with well over 100 variants, is constructed on a solid foundation. The French *L'Odyssée des Jeux d'Échecs*, authored by Jean-Louis Cazaux, published in 2010 by Praxeo Editions, Paris, is the ground upon which the present book is built. Originally conceived as a translation of the French work, this text has been broadly revised, re-organized and augmented with a wealth of new material. But this book owes its greatest debt to the original French edition.

Alexis Beuve, editor of Praxeo, was deeply involved in the publication of *L'Odyssée des Jeux d'Échecs*. His role was indispensible as technical and artistic director, offering improvements, additions and even the original book title. We offer our profound gratitude for his contributions.

We are particularly grateful to Alexis Beuve and Praxeo for authorizing and encouraging the present English publication.

LIBRARY OF CONGRESS CATALOGUING-IN-PUBLICATION DATA

Names: Cazaux, Jean-Louis, author.
Title: A world of chess : its development and variations through centuries and civilizations / Jean-Louis Cazaux and Rick Knowlton.
Description: Jefferson, North Carolina : McFarland & Company, Inc., Publishers, 2017 | Includes bibliographical references and index.
Identifiers: LCCN 2017020887 | ISBN 9780786494279 (softcover : acid free paper) ∞
Subjects: LCSH: Chess—History.
Classification: LCC GV1317 .C39 2017 | DDC 794.109—dc23
LC record available at https://lccn.loc.gov/2017020887

BRITISH LIBRARY CATALOGUING DATA ARE AVAILABLE

ISBN (print) 978-0-7864-9427-9
ISBN (ebook) 978-1-4766-2901-8

© 2017 Jean-Louis Cazaux and Rick Knowlton. All rights reserved

*No part of this book may be reproduced or transmitted in any form or by any means, electronic or mechanical, including photocopying or recording, or by any information storage and retrieval system, without permission in writing from the publisher.*

Front cover: Chess pieces, clockwise from bottom left: Brass Queen, reproduced from Lucas van Leyden's *The Chess Game* (1508); wooden King from a traditional Cambodian set; metal King from a traditional Muslim set, procured in Rajasthan, India; Bishop, reproduced in casting stone and based on the twelfth-century Isle of Lewis chessmen, made by Ivan Simberg of Montreal; seated King from an elaborately detailed set from India; shogi King, simplified one-kanji design, from Japan; and janggi General ("King") from a typical Korean set (photograph by Rick Knowlton)

Printed in the United States of America

Edited by Robert Franklin
Designed by Susan Ham and Robert Franklin
Typeset by Susan Ham

*McFarland & Company, Inc., Publishers*
*Box 611, Jefferson, North Carolina 28640*
*www.mcfarlandpub.com*

Dedicated to the memory of

Harold James Ruthven Murray
whose passion for chess history has inspired
a century of scholars and enthusiasts

and

Robert Charles Bell
who invited us to come and play

# *Acknowledgments*

The writing of this book has spanned more than six years. In this long period, the authors have been supported by several of the most talented experts in various fields of chess culture and history. They are acknowledged here for their proofreading, advice—and friendship, especially Michel Boutin, Manfred Eder, Gianfelice Ferlito, Robert Franklin, Fred Horn, Tomohide Kawasaki, Madoka Kitao and Yaeko Tomita, Erwann Le Pelleter, Morten Lilleøren, Peter Michaelsen, Marc-Antoine Nguyen and Ülrich Schädler.

The authors are also grateful to Lisha Bai, Peter Banaschak, Antonio Barra, John Beasley, Clément Bégnis, Wout Blommers, Hans Bodlaender, Frank Brady, Éric Cheymol, Jérôme Choain, Thierry Depaulis, Ivan Derzhanski, Alan Dewey, Yu Ren Dong, Sean Evans, René Gralla, Michel Guttierez, Leo Ha, Nguyễn Quí Hải, David Howe, Jiří Jákl, Sylvestre Jonquay, Gerhard Josten, Lev Kislyuk, François Leysour de Rohello, Emile Lhomme, Kenneth Lightfoot, Robert Montay-Marsais, Arnold Mayer, Egbert Meissenburg, Alejandro Melchor, Nikolas Axel Mellem, Brigitte Mérigot, Harm-Geert Muller, Sonja Musser, Fabien Osmont, Khoa Pham, Jacques Pineau, Patrice Plain, Rodolfo Pozzi, Gaëtan Prigent, Dermot Rochford, Maria Carmen Romeo, Anthony Saidy, Vabha Sazawal, Samuer Shao, Yasuji Shimizu, Michel Van Langendonkt, Siddarth Wakankar, Maths Winther, Frédéric Wittner and Nathaniel Zoso for their precious help.

Peter Blommers deserves a special note of appreciation: his expertise, broad experience in the field, keen eye for details of language, and steadfast encouragement were indispensible to the completion of the manuscript.

Finally, we are very indebted to the cautious and patient proofreading provided by Gabrielle Lennon Knowlton!

# Table of Contents

*Acknowledgments* vi
*Introduction* 1
*Chess of the World* 2 / *About This Book* 3

## Part I. Chess of the Arabian Nights 7
1. Shatranj 8
2. Muslim Chess Variants 21
3. Timur's Great Chess 30
4. Shatar 39

## Part II. Chess in the Land of Monsoons 47
5. Chaturanga 47
6. Chaturaji 59
7. Large and Giant Indian Chess 64
8. Ouk and Makruk 77
9. Sit-Tu-Yin 85
10. Catur 93

## Part III. Gunpowder on the Chinese Board 98
11. Xiangqi 98
12. Janggi 109
13. Qiguo Xiangxi 116
14. Sanguo Qi 120
15. Banqi 123
16. Doushouqi 125
17. Luzhanqi 131

## Part IV. Generals and Mercenaries of the Rising Sun 142
18. Shogi 143
19. Chu Shogi and Dai Shogi 154
20. Tenjiku Shogi 163
21. Giant Shogis 167
22. Wa Shogi 177
23. Tori Shogi 180
24. Dobutsu Shogi (Let's Catch the Lion!) 183
25. Ko Shogi 188
26. Taikyoku Shogi 194

## Part V. Evolution and Revolution in Europe 198
27. Medieval Chess 199
28. Rithmomachy 211
29. King Alfonso's Games 223
30. Courier Chess 232
31. Gala 237
32. European Chess 240

## Part VI. Chess Out of the Box  250

33. Knighted Chess Variants  251
34. Fairy Pieces on Board  265
35. Chess and War  280
36. Round Chess  284
37. Hexagonal Chess  288
38. Four-Player Chess  295
39. Three-Player Chess  300
40. 3-D Chess  307
41. Extraterrestrial Chess  314
42. Chess960  319

## Part VII. The Origins of Chess  326

43. Legends of the Creation  327
44. The Modern Search Begins  330
45. Approaching the Question from Several Angles  334

*Timeline*  355
*Notes*  359
*Bibliography*  385
*Index*  391

# Introduction

Chess is an engaging game of strategy, familiar to most people, played by many, and mastered by a gifted few. To the player, chess offers an absorbing complex of logical possibilities, moments of intrigue and a seemingly endless call for the full faculties of logic, invention and intuition. Yet many who have come to know this game and have played it with great enthusiasm, and many who have deeply studied and even become skilled in the game's most subtle challenges, have very little idea of the extraordinary cultural advent of chess itself, as it has spread and evolved all over the world for centuries.

Was this game first conceived as a teaching device for an ancient cadre of army generals? Was it contrived by a wise counselor to teach the subtle laws of cause and effect to an impetuous king? Was chess made as a game of gambling stakes, or as a meditative diversion behind the walls of some ancient monastery? Chess has been all of these things, and many more. And though the threads of actual invention become elusive as one traces them ever further back in time, the journey of chess unfolds as a tale of unfathomable proportions. Ever since that spark of chess was first kindled in the human mind, it has spread across humanity like wildfire—permeating tribes and civilizations, enchanting the royalty, exciting workers, soldiers, poets, mystics and scientists.... It has even become an object of art, elaborated and refined by the hands of the finest craftsmen and designers in every corner of the world.

In the West, including Europe and the countless regions of European influence, chess has become firmly defined, with official rules consistently implemented, and playing pieces commonly recognized. With this widespread uniformity, a player in Missouri can easily sit down with a player from Italy, Moscow or Dubai, and engage equally in a game of total familiarity. In their enthusiasm for chess, amateurs and great players alike often think of this as the one great game, unchanged over eons around the globe. But this particular chess that we know so well is just over 500 years old.

If the scope of chess is extended over just a few more borders, to peek back in time or project into the future, a very different view of chess quickly emerges. There are *xiangqi*, the chess of China, and *shogi*, the chess of Japan. Chess, in fact, has been undergoing continual change in playing pieces, boards and rules of play—so much so that a modern player might find the game utterly unrecognizable in a different land or a past era. But with a little knowledge, that player will soon see that—yes—this foreign game with its odd shapes and conventions of play is another cultural and historic working of familiar patterns and a well-known theme. This too is chess.

This book is presented to chess players, game enthusiasts and lovers of cultural history as a broad review of chess as a worldwide human event. We have gathered the most up-to-date historic resources and the most accurate accounts of these divergent games, and put them into a clear and concise context. In some cases, we have endeavored to correct long-held misconceptions in chess history, and have re-envisioned accounts of historic variants in light of the most current research. Several of the chess forms shown here are actually appearing in English print for the first time. Other games presented here are still flourishing in their native lands, providing a cultural access point to any willing new player.

The reader is invited to read herein the legends, histories and discoveries of chess in its many forms, and finally, to learn and play these games, actually experiencing chess as it has come to exist through all humanity.

# *Chess of the World*

Even today, though the game we call chess is played around the world with broad uniformity in rules and chessmen, if you scratch the surface, the diversity of cultural associations begins to shine through. You may be sitting at the same familiar board, playing with a player from France, Germany, India or Russia, but seeing a very different metaphoric array. The piece you know as a Bishop is known as a Fool *(Fou)* to the French player and a Camel *(Umt)* to many Indians. Your Knight is simply a Horse to most non–English players, but to the German, it is a Jumper *(Springer)*. Although the piece being played looks like a castle turret, the Russian knows it to be a Ship *(Ladya)*. We call this piece a "Rook"—which has no special meaning to us, but harkens back many centuries to the original Persian name, *Rukh*.

If you travel to China, Korea, Thailand or Japan, you will find other forms of chess still widely played at every level of society, from barrooms and clubs all the way up to high-level national championships. These other forms of chess are not merely variants of our own familiar game, but complete branches of chess in their own right, with brilliantly conceived rules instituted centuries ago to enhance the game's dynamic intellectual struggle.

Here, we invite the reader to look at chess anew, to look both deeply into the history and evolution of the game and broadly at the many branches of chess as it has been transformed, adapted and remade through every civilization it touched. Chess is not merely a single game with its familiar rules, tournaments and brilliant champions. It began some 1500 years ago, first as one of the world's many strategy board games, but quickly transcending the cultural barriers of diverse civilizations, crossing international boundaries with remarkable fluidity.

Somehow, this new game, with its two monarch Kings flanked by symmetrical forces of various powers and a forward row of foot soldiers, "clicked" with a greater human concept of an ideal strategy game. This game of battle became a conqueror itself, often supplanting other games as the new template for the symbolic intellectual challenge. Chess could be used for gambling, or enjoyed for no stakes at all; it was played on the street as a pastime and by merchants in their travels, even as it was refining the strategic judgment of the royal court, the analytic minds of mathematicians and the meditative minds of cloistered monks. All the while, the world's finest craftsmen have taken up the challenge of creating chessmen worthy of the game's exalted status, making the crafting of chessmen one of the world's most enduring subjects of fine art.

In this book, the reader is invited not only to celebrate chess as a monumental cultural event, but to actually learn to play the various games that have engaged the minds of chess players over the centuries. We think that with a modest investment these games will be found very easy to learn and very rewarding. It is a challenge to learn the language, or even the common customs, of a foreign land. But to open the window onto another culture through its unique form of chess play is simple.

Our journey through the world of chess will begin with the earliest ancestors of our own chess, found in Persia, on through the early Arab world, branching into Central Asia and Mongolia. We also follow chess as it traveled south, from Northern India, following the path of Buddhist monasteries into Burma, Cambodia, Thailand and Sri Lanka. Another major branch of chess takes us across China, through the Korean peninsula. Then, our world tour will show the extraordinary crucible of chess ideas forged in Japan, where the most complex popular form of chess in the world, *shogi*, still thrives (though even with its complications, shogi was originally one of the simpler forms devised by the ancient Japanese monks). Finally, we follow the road of chess as it reached Europe through Italy and Spain, landing in fertile ground to mutate further and spread in its new form, along with other aspects of European civilization.

Beyond history and long-established chess variants, we also peer into the modern world, and consider some of the more insightful innovations that have been offered by modern masters and inventors. The book concludes with an updated look at the birth of chess itself.

The authors hope that readers will find or create their own playing sets and get a real taste of these absorbing games.

## *About This Book*

This book is at once a broad introduction to the chess variants of the world, an updated account of the recent research into chess history, and a practical guide to anyone who would like to play the major chess forms that have arisen over the centuries. We have worked to achieve clarity and accuracy in every aspect, using the standard chess notation and diagrams familiar to chess players, with logical expansions to indicate the new pieces and board configurations for the various games.

### *Diagrams and Annotation*

Most of our diagrams and chess notation will use the familiar "algebraic" system, showing the chessboard as a series of columns, or *files*, lettered left-to-right a, b, c, etc., with the rows, or *ranks*, lettered bottom-to-top 1, 2, 3, etc. The various pieces will be notated in the standard form with King, Queen, Bishop, Knight and Rook indicated by K, Q, B, N and R (note N for Knight because K is King). Pawn moves are indicated with the lack of a letter, so while "Ne3" means, "the Knight moves to the square in column e, row 3," just "e4" means, "the Pawn moves to e4."

When we introduce other pieces, such as Camels, Princes or Elephants, we will give clear instructions explaining their moves and how they are notated in our move descriptions.

Some of the games presented in this book have their own traditional notation systems. These are explained in the text.

### *Chess Terms*

The words "diagonal" and "orthogonal" will often be used in describing the moves of pieces. While the word *diagonal* is commonly understood, we would like to clarify that *orthogonal* simply means the four directions forward, backward, left or right, like the cardinal points of the compass. For instance, the Rook moves any number of spaces *orthogonally*; the King moves one space either *diagonally* or *orthogonally*. In other words, the King moves to any adjacent square.

## Value of the Pieces

In learning chess, it is very useful for players to have a sense of the fighting value of the various pieces. Commonly, players of the modern game learn that a Pawn is worth 1, a Knight or Bishop 3, a Rook 5, and a Queen 9. We are fortunate to have a program, provided by Zillions of Games©, which analyzes our diverse games to give us approximate values of the playing pieces. With this information, beginning players can know at once where their power lies, and how to evaluate possible captures or trades. For uniformity, we use the Rook's well-known value of 5 as our standard, and adjust the other pieces according to that scale. This is convenient because, with the great diversity of chessmen and chess moves in these various games, there is almost always a piece with the exact power of our modern Rook.

## Chess History, Revisited

Each game described here also includes a section on its history. Here, readers will find the most up-to-date information available, based on modern archeology and text investigation. H.J.R. Murray's great book, *A History of Chess*, still stands as one of the foremost resources for chess historians, even 100 years after its publication in 1913, but there has been so much research since then, and there have been so many advances in historic methodology, that we feel compelled to update and expand upon the long-held body of knowledge wherever possible.[1]

As a matter of special interest to historians and theorists, we focus on the often hotly debated question of the actual origin of chess. Much evidence has come to light since the question was first posed, "Where did chess come from?" We hope our review of the most recent evidence and theoretical thinking will leave our readers with a more complete view of what is known of chess's origins—and a more sophisticated understanding of what questions remain unanswered.

## Gender

In order to maintain the greatest simplicity in our presentation, we have relied on the traditional English convention of using the male pronouns, *he*, *him* and *his* to indicate any player of any gender. While this avoids the awkwardness of proclaiming "he or she" and "his or her" at every turn, it is important to note that women and girls, as well as men and boys, carry a substantial role in the propagation of chess in all ages, past, present and future.

## Ancient Texts

Many of the ancient manuscripts mentioned in the text are from international and ancient languages, compelling us to make orthographic choices in spelling and presentation. For the most part, we have taken the most straightforward path, including diacritical marks only on words originally spelled with Roman lettering systems, but dropping that level of complexity in words translated from foreign systems.

Where the titles of ancient texts are concerned, we have chosen the formats most preferred by international historians. Although this leaves some discrepancy with popular spellings and articulations, the reader should have no trouble finding further resources regarding the referenced texts.

The book concludes with some useful resources: a timeline of the major events in chess history and development and a select bibliography of works recommended for further study and of great use in the creation of this book. There is, finally, a comprehensive index.

# ♦ Part I ♦

# Chess of the Arabian Nights

Our exploration begins as a search for the source of the game. The journey leads along the dusty caravan trails of the East, to a time when Iran shone as one of the world's supreme superpowers, centered in the city of Ctesiphon (near modern Baghdad).

It is widely understood that the Arabs brought chess to Europe during the High Middle Ages. The Muslims had learned the game from the Persians, but quickly made it their own, bringing it to every corner of the vast Arab Empire. Art and literature show that the chess of that time was widely practiced and highly esteemed.

Not so often noted are the significant differences between the ancient Arabic game of chess and the chess we commonly play today. In particular, the pieces we know as Queen and Bishop had quite different identities in the ancient game, and had very different moves, giving them much less power on the board. With these differences, the science of expert play was approached in a completely different manner. The development of the game was certainly slower, but no less complex than the chess of today. In fact, checkmate itself—a word we get quite directly from the Persian *shah mat*—was quite rare, and there were other manners of winning the game.

This game, known by its Arabic name *shatranj*, became widely known throughout central Asia. First taken from the Persians, it was carried by the Islamic armies across northern Africa, reaching into the southern tip of Spain. Shatranj spread out in almost every direction, extending southwest to the African coast, reaching back eastward into India, and traveling northward, up into the vast steppes of Turkic tribes and Mongolian horsemen.

All that time, this early form of chess underwent many transformations. Arab manuscripts report numerous variants, often involving expanded playing surfaces and novel chessmen with newly invented powers of movement. It remains a mystery just how widespread these variants were in their day—especially those games reported by very few sources. Certainly, the popularity of many chess variants was experimental and fleeting—but some proved to endure with an astonishing longevity.

# 1. Shatranj

How old is the game of chess? It has long been a matter of speculation, ranging from perhaps a few centuries back to millennia immemorial. But the oldest actual treatise we have, explaining the rules of the game, dates back only to the ninth century. That treatise is credited to the Arabs, in the court of the caliphs of Baghdad, who learned the game from the Persians during the seventh century conquests. The Persians, in turn, had a legendary account of learning the game from an Indian envoy, before the year 600.

"Shatranj"[1] is still the Arabic word for chess in the modern world, but we use it here to indicate the older form of chess, the cultural symbol of the brilliant young Arabic civilization which dominated the world from the banks of the Indus River to the foothills of the Pyrenees Mountains, and continued to expand its influence well beyond those borders. Throughout the Muslim world, kings, scholars, military leaders and intellectuals of all types developed a keen fondness for this tiny, symbolic battleground. It was the Muslims who first celebrated the great chess champions and drafted the first treatises, raising this mere board game to the status of an art to be practiced and a science to be learned.

## *Material*

Shatranj was played over a plain, un-checkered board of 8 × 8 squares. It was usually quite simple, sewn onto a piece of cloth, or even drawn directly on the ground.

Each player had 16 pieces: 1 King, 1 Counselor (or General), 2 Elephants, 2 Horses, 2 "Rukhs"[2] and 8 Pawns.

### *Names of the Shatranj Pieces*

| Classical Arabic name | Neo-Persian name | Meaning | Modern equivalent |
|---|---|---|---|
| *Shah, Nafs* | *Shah* | King | King |
| *Firzan, Firz* | *Dastur, Farzin* | Counselor | Queen |
| *Fil* | *Pil* | Elephant | Bishop |
| *Faras* | *Asp* | Horse | Knight |
| *Rukhkh* | *Rukh* | "Rukh" | Rook |
| *Baidaq* | *Piyada* | Foot Soldier | Pawn |

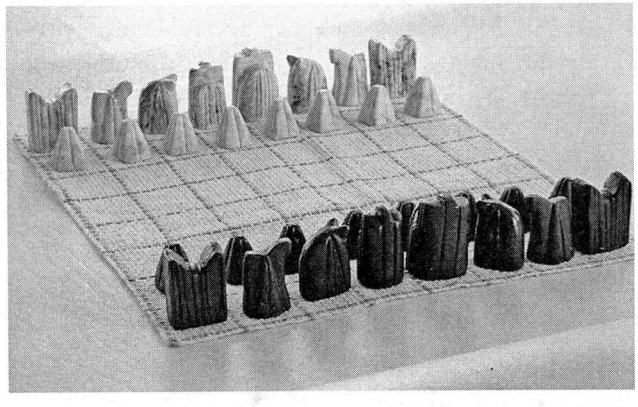

Shatranj board ready to play. KNOWLTON PHOTOGRAPH

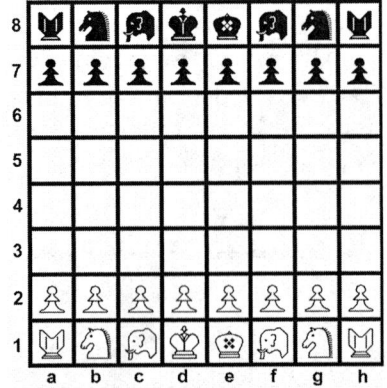

Initial array of shatranj.

The sides were any two colors, most often red versus green, sometimes red versus black. Kings were always aligned face-to-face.[3]

## Rules

MOVES AND CAPTURES. The basic rules of shatranj are similar to those in modern chess. The players take turns choosing to move any one piece, either toward an empty square or toward a square occupied by the opponent, in which case the opponent's piece is taken and removed from the chessboard.

The *King* moves only one step toward one of the eight squares that surround it, provided that this square is not under the threat of an adverse piece. As in the modern game, there is an obligation for the player to move his King out of check. If no possible move will save the King from capture, he has lost the game.

The *Counselor* moves only one square diagonally. This move limits his moves to only half of the squares of a chessboard (the squares that would be of one color on a modern board).

The *Elephant* jumps diagonally over one square to land on the second diagonal square. It does not matter whether the square it leaps over is occupied. With this limited move, the Elephant can only land on eight squares of the entire board!

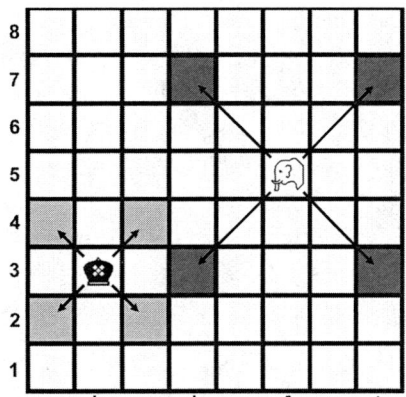

Counselor and Elephant moves.

The *Horse* moves exactly like the modern Knight. It makes an L-shape of two squares in one orthogonal direction (that is, forward, backward or sideways) plus one step at a right angle. The Horse freely leaps over any pieces in its path.

The *"Rukh"* moves just like the modern Rook. It travels any number of squares orthogonally (forward, backward, left or right), but may not jump over any pieces in its way.

The *Pawn* is the only piece which does not capture using its normal move. It normally moves one square forward, but captures by moving one square diagonally forward. This is the same as the Pawn in our modern game, but the ancient Pawn of shatranj is never allowed to move two spaces at once.

SPECIAL RULES. Pawn promotion: a Pawn reaching the last row (or rank) of the board immediately becomes a Counselor, even if one or more Counselors are already on the board. No other promotion is possible.

Castling and *en passant* capture do not exist in shatranj.

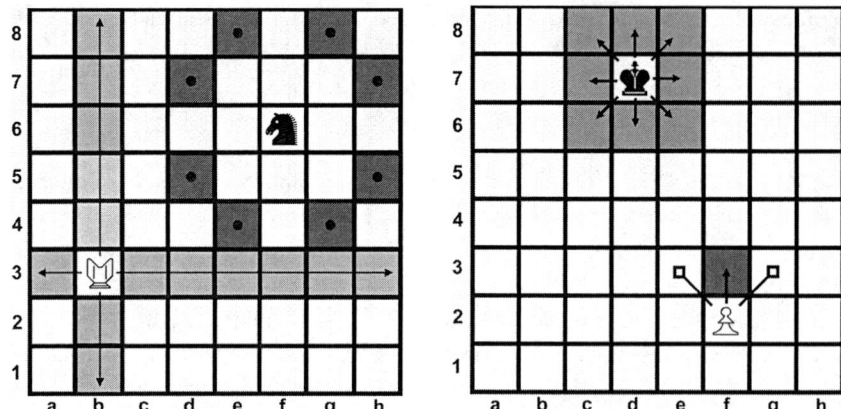

*Left:* Moves of the Rukh and Horse. *Right:* Moves of the Shah (King) and Pawn moves.

END OF THE GAME. The goal of the game is to force surrender of the opposing King, or to leave him stranded with no fighters remaining. There are three ways to win the game:

- Checkmate, in which the opponent cannot remove his King from check. The winner proclaimed *Shah mat*, "the King is lost," the expression that directly led to our modern word, "checkmate."
- Suffocation (*za'id*) in which, the King is not in check, but any possible move will lead to his capture. This is what we call "stalemate" in our modern game, but in shatranj, the suffocated King loses the game.
- Bare King (*Shah munfarid*) is achieved by capturing all of the opponent's men *except* the King. If only the King is left, he has lost the game. There is one exception, however: if the King is left bare and on his very next move he can also capture the opponent's last piece, leaving both Kings bare, then the game is drawn, without a winner.

The game may also be drawn in these familiar ways:

- Perpetual attack. If one player is intent on continually putting the other in check or otherwise attacking endlessly with continual repetition, a draw has been achieved.
- Insufficient force. If it can be demonstrated or agreed that neither player has enough power on the board to force a win, the game must end without a winner.

## Strategy

This game is certainly similar to modern chess but lacks the powerful move of the modern Queen, the long diagonals of the modern Bishop, the double step of the Pawn, the choice to castle, and the decisively powerful promotion of the Pawn. These differences significantly alter one's concept of the game and call for unique approaches to winning strategy.

As the predecessors to our modern chess theorists, the *'aliyat,* great masters, of the ninth and tenth centuries, established their own basis of chess theory. They developed a scale based on their currency, the *dirhem*, to rank the value of the various pieces. We can compare the ancient theorists' assessment to evaluations calculated by a modern computer program which estimates the relative strength of playing pieces. In the table below, we have normalized all values to a familiar scale where the Rook is said to be worth five points.

*Relative values of the shatranj piece given in the manuscripts, converted to the modern point system, and compared to the values calculated with Zillions-of-Games© software.*

| Piece | Arabic manuscripts | Arabic scale in modern terms | Software computation |
|---|---|---|---|
| Rukh | 1 dirhem | 5 | 5 |
| Horse | 2/3 dirhem | 3.33 | 2.9 |
| Counselor | 1/3 dirhem | 1.67 | 1.67 |
| Elephant | 1/4 dirhem | 1.25 | 1.3 |
| Pawns d, e | 1/4 dirhem | 1.25 | 0.7 |
| Pawns b, c, f, g | 1/6 dirhem | 0.85 | 0.7 |
| Pawns a, h | 1/8 dirhem | 0.63 | 0.7 |

Rooks and Knights dominated the ancient chessboard. Rooks were the mightiest, with their grand sweep of the board, while Knights were dreaded for their disastrous forks. In contrast, Elephants and Counselors were essentially defensive pieces, protecting key squares in the midst of battle. Pawns were not underestimated; moreover, their promotion permitted the player to have several Counselors working together. Finally, the King enjoyed a greater relative strength in the old game, allowing him a stronger role in attacking the enemy.

## The Ta'biyat (The Openings)

Just as in modern chess, the ancient theorists divided the game into three stages: opening, middle game and endgame. In the absence of powerful Queens and Bishops, the opening of shatranj developed slowly. Therefore, the players took the time to organize their pieces according to a preconceived arrangement, called a *ta'biya*. The Arabic manuscripts developed several *ta'biyat*, bearing vivid names. The fastest of these openings were reached in a dozen moves and were recommended by such great masters as al-'Adli, as-Suli and al-Lajlaj. Every player had his favorite *ta'biya*.

## Several Ta'biyat

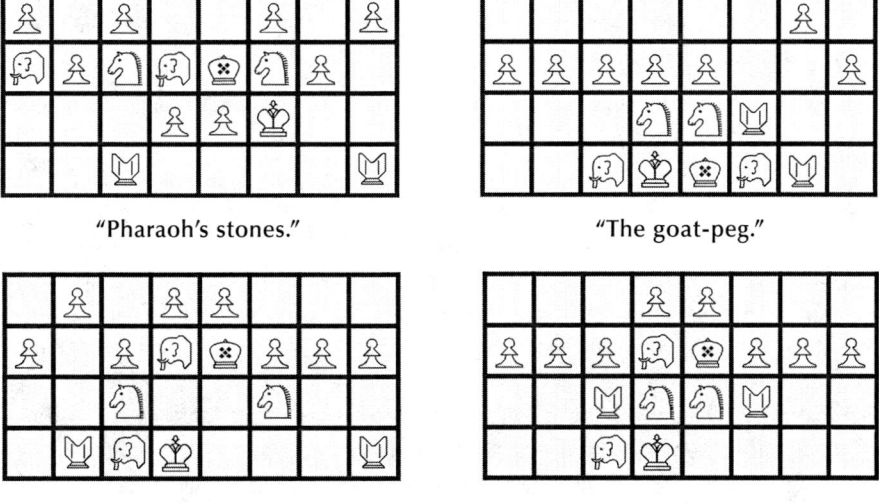

"Pharaoh's stones."         "The goat-peg."

"Moved to and fro."         "The old woman."

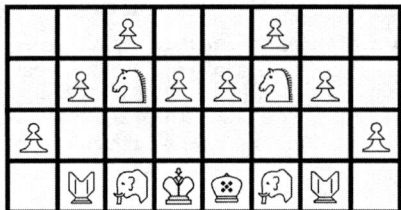
"The flanked."

"The conjoined."

It was always possible, of course, for the opponent to interrupt a player's favorite *ta'biya*. But in general, conflict did not begin between the two sides so rapidly, and each player was allowed to take time arranging things to his liking.

# The Mansubat

The middle game theory is passed over here, since the ancients left only a few general suggestions as to what to watch for. But the great bulk of the shatranj literature was given over to the endgame—finding a win. These endgame puzzles are known as the *mansubat*. Shatranj offers some very different endings from those to which modern players are accustomed. Realization of the mate is difficult—or even impossible—because of the limited moves of several pieces: the Counselors can only reach half of all squares of the board and the two never meet, while each of the four Elephants can only land on eight squares of the entire board—and they also never meet.

Under these conditions, the player who knows how to "read" the accessible and non-accessible squares of this monochrome chessboard tries to place his pieces out of the opponent's reach. Most games end by baring the King, a much more common way of winning than checkmate.

So it was that the endgame became the area most studied by the Arab and Persian masters of the Middle Ages. These *mansubat*, or "chess problems" were recommended to beginners to immerse themselves in the basic mechanisms of the game. More than 500 *mansubat* are known, all preciously collected, recorded and commented upon by Murray.[4]

## The Maiden's Problem

Some *mansubat* are famous, such as the "Legend of Dilaram," which we owe to as-Suli (880–946), a famous champion of the Abbasid caliphs.[5] Although the moral may escape the modern reader, it tells of a chess player's wife, Dilaram, reportedly beautiful and clearly very clever, who saved a game for her husband, a prince, who had foolishly put her up as the stake in a game of shatranj. It wasn't going well, and for all appearances, he was about to lose the game and his lovely wife with it.

With a keen understanding of the game, and more than a little anxiety about the possible outcome, she said to him, "Sacrifice your two Rukhs, but save me!" And, at least this once, he listened to her! The prince saw in a flash his necessary escape from what had seemed certain doom.

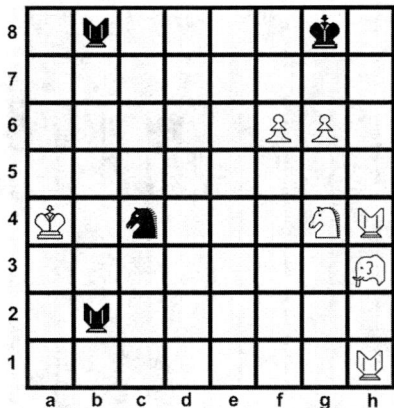

White to play.
The situation looks desperate.

NOTATION
K = King
C = Counselor
E = Elephant
H = Horse
R = Rukh

**1. Rh8+ K×h8 2. Ef5+ Kg8 3. Rh8+ K×h8 4. g7+ Kg8 5. Hh6 mate**

He won and kept his dear Dilaram, perhaps with a little more caution and even a little more respect for his ingenious partner.

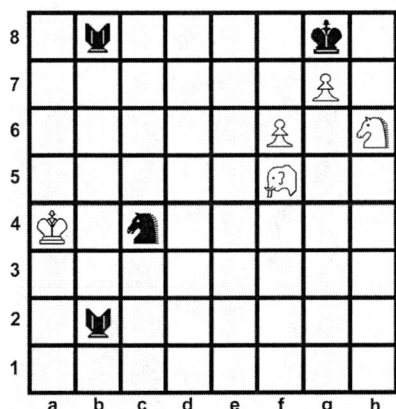

Black is checkmated.

## Dilaram's Legacy

The name of this classic problem tells us that our heroine, Dilaram, has gone on to show her prowess on the chessboard more than once. It is extremely improbable that the following position derived from an actual chess game, so as-Suli explains it in a very different format. He tells us of a legendary tale, unrelated to chess, as a background:

An epidemic has spread through the White army, leaving the remaining White forces almost entirely helpless. Seeing his opportunity for total victory, the Black King sent his Counselor out to accost the White King and bring him back to Black's royal court. But alas, the Counselor was not up to the mission. In his place, he commissioned two Foot Soldiers to advance toward the White King. The Black King found this utterly unacceptable and, in the manner of great despots through the ages, had his cowardly Counselor put to death. (Now we have explained the decimation of the White army, the advance of the two Pawns, and the disappearance of the Black Counselor.)

The story continues: Seeing all this, the desperate White King discerned that surrendering to the Black King would lead to certain death. He was highly motivated (and presumably coached by the brilliant Dilaram) to achieve an upsetting victory at all costs! Here is the position in which White finds himself:

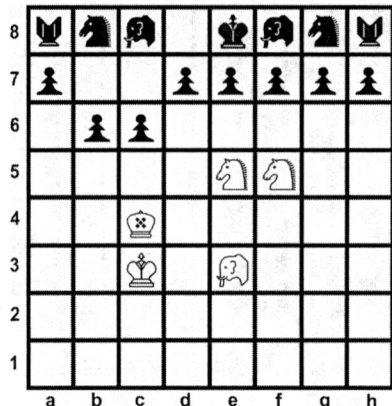

White to move.
He knows that Black is merciless.

With grim determination, White sends his zealous Horsemen out at midnight, charging straightway into the enemy camp.

**1. H×g7+ Kd8 2. H×f7+ Kc7**

A courageous assault—but can it last? The Black King runs to every available square:

**3. He8+ Kb7 4. Hd8+ Ka6 5. Hc7+ Ka5 6. Hb7+ Ka4**

Finally, the White Counselor and Elephant are called upon to do the Black King in:

**7. Cb3+ Ka3 8. Ec1 mate**

# Baring the Shah

The following problem is attributed to another Arab champion, al-'Adli, author of the first known treatise on the game, the *Kitab ash-shatranj*,[6] about 840 C.E. A classic problem, this shows just how clever the Arab masters could be, seeming to pull victories out of thin air.

The problem actually begins with a trap. White is allowing Black to fork his King and Counselor, by moving the Knight to e6. By all appearances, this is a final stroke, leading the game into a hopelessly even draw...

A classical mansuba.
Black plays ... and White wins.

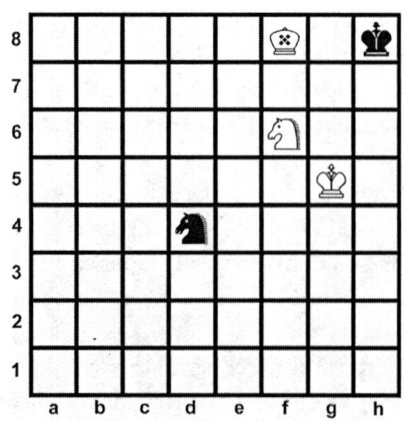

**1. ... He6+ 2. Kg6 H×f8+**

It looks as if Black has succeeded in leveling the playing field, but now he loses perforce:

**3. Kf7 Hh7 4. He4 !**

Notice that if White had played 4. H×h7, Black would have still had one move to recapture with 4. ... K×h7 and the game would have been drawn. But with the final move 4. He4, Black's King cannot move at all, and every square the Black Knight may choose will lead to certain loss. White wins by bare King.

## The "Water Wheel" Problem

Here is another famous *mansuba*, conveyed to us by the great Arab master al-Lajlaj.[7] It is known as the "water wheel" problem, because the Horses actually force the Black King to circle the board twice, making 36 moves, before checkmating him on his home square, d8!

The "water wheel" problem: White plays and wins.

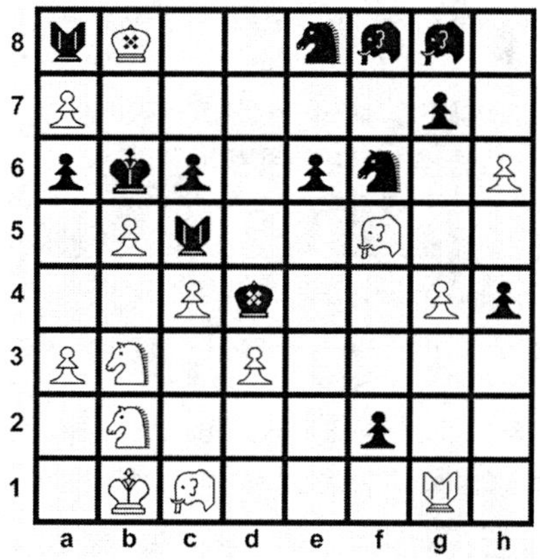

| | | |  |
|---|---|---|---|
| 1. Ha4+ Kb7 | 10. Hg5+ Ke2 | 19. Hb6+ Kd8 | 28. Hf3+ Kc3 |
| 2. Ha5+ Kc8 | 11. Hf4+ Kd2 | 20. Hb7+ Ke7 | 29. He2+ Kb3 |
| 3. Hb6+ Kd8 | 12. Hf3+ Kc3 | 21. Hc8+ Kf7 | 30. Hd2+ Ka4 |
| 4. Hb7+ Ke7 | 13. He2+ Kb3 | 22. Hd8+ Kg6 | 31. Hc3+ Ka5 |
| 5. Hc8+ Kf7 | 14. H(f)×d4+ Ka4 | 23. He7+ Kg5 | 32. Hb3+ Kb6 |
| 6. Hd8+ Kg6 | 15. Hc3+ Ka5 | 24. Hf7+ Kf4 | 33. Ha4+ Kb7 |
| 7. He7+ Kg5 | 16. Hb3+ Kb6 | 25. Hg6+ Kf3 | 34. Ha5+ Kc8 |
| 8. Hf7+ Kf4 | 17. Ha4+ Kb7 | 26. Hg5+ Ke2 | 35. Hb6+ Kd8 |
| 9. Hg6+ Kf3 | 18. H(b)×c5+ Kc8 | 27. Hf4+ Kd2 | 36. H×c6 mate |

The beauty of this extraordinary combination gives a vivid example of the ingenuity and dedication of the very first chess problem composers.

## The History of Shatranj

This direct ancestor to the chess we play today has an impressive history, deeply rooted in legacies and legends. Our earliest record of the game comes to us from the Persian Sassanid Empire, dated toward the end of the sixth century. Known as *chatrang* in ancient Persia, and mentioned in three epic Pahlavi texts, the game was said to be popular among the aristocracy, and stood among the noble arts that all princes of the court were required to master.

FROM CHATRANG TO SHATRANJ. It is the oldest of the Persian texts that is most revealing. The epic poem, *Explanation of Chatrang and the Invention of Nard*,[8] written about 1500 years ago, describes in detail how *chatrang* was delivered to the court of King Khusraw I (531–579) by a royal envoy from Northern India. This classic legend tells us that the Persian court was given the set of chessmen and board, and challenged to determine—just from the playing apparatus—how the game was to be played. The Persians countered this challenge by presenting the Indian envoy with the game of *nard*—an ancestor to our modern backgammon—asking the Indian sages to figure *that* one out. Not too surprisingly, this ancient Persian tale concludes with a Persian victory. The wise men of Khusraw I's court discerned the rules of shatranj, while the Indian envoy was stumped by the counter-challenge.

This famous tale has often been repeated in books of chess lore, and it has been illustrated with beautiful paintings and tapestries. But the modern researcher will regard such tales with caution.

Following the possible Indian origins of the game, the Persian word *chatrang* is borrowed from the Sanskrit *chaturanga*. This word dates back at to the third or fourth century B.C.E. and means "composed of four members." It traditionally referred to the four divisions of the ancient Indian army: infantry, cavalry, elephants and war chariots. But alas, when references to chess are sought in ancient Indian literature, the trail becomes uncertain. These elusive clues are discussed later, when we explore the origins of chess. In any case, it is well established that the Arabs gave the West the first texts detailing how the ancient game was actually played.

Between the years 636 and 651, the Sassanid Persian Empire was attacked and ultimately defeated by invading Arab armies. Persia had risen to become one of the world's great civilizations, boasting unsurpassed resources of wealth, knowledge and cultural refinements. Now these achievements and riches were to be passed to the Arab conquerors and, along with them, the noble martial game of chatrang. The game was adapted quite directly, simply changing the "ch"—which did not exist in Arabic—to "sh," similarly making a small change to the ending, and calling the game "shatranj."

Replica of Islamic chessmen dated to the ninth century. The tall figures on the left, which suggest a sort of throne, are Kings; the same shape, in smaller form, indicates the Counselors. The Horse is indicated by one protuberance (the head), while the Elephant has two points (the tusks). The Rukh is characterized by the V cut, presumably evoking a chariot. And the Pawn is simple, small and unadorned. KNOWLTON PHOTOGRAPH

Shatranj at first assumed a low profile in the Arab society. The earliest Arabic reference to the game appears in a verse by the notoriously satirical poet al-Farazdaq (641–728?). He merely mentions Pawns and alludes to promotion—giving us just enough information to assume that the game was generally familiar to his readers.[9] But could this new Persian game be sanctioned by the leaders and clerics of Muslim law? A serious debate ensued among scholars, and finally Koranic jurists allowed the game to be played under the conditions that it not be used for gambling and that it not interfere with the players' regular religious duties. Players were further advised to use simple, abstract playing pieces, shunning the blasphemous tendency toward idolatry displayed

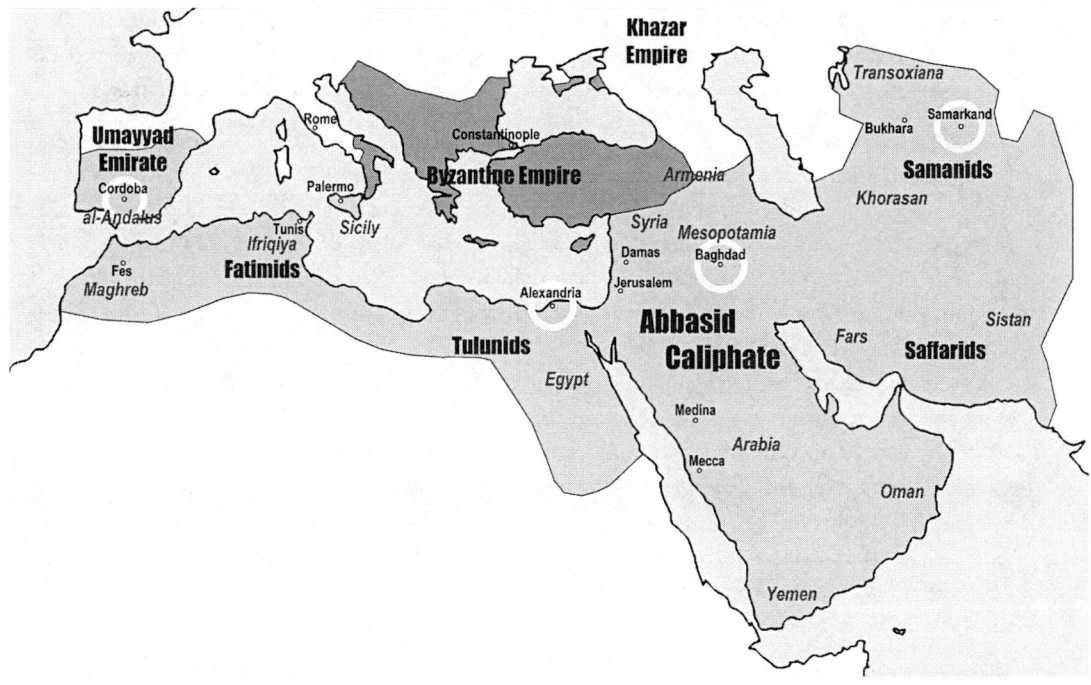

Map of the Islamic and Byzantine worlds around the year 900.

by realistically carved figures.[10] This tendency toward abstraction proved to be a great benefit for the dissemination of the game, since pieces could be made quickly and easily.

As literature and science flourished under the Abbasid Caliphate in Baghdad, shatranj experienced a revolutionary boost in popularity and stature. The best players of the day began traveling to Baghdad in search of fame and royal sponsorship. By the middle of the ninth century, discussions of shatranj could be found throughout Arabic literature. The tenth century saw shatranj immortalized in the writings of the great historians al-Ya'qubi, at-Tabari and al-Mas'udi.

The caliphs of the ninth and tenth centuries surrounded themselves with the greatest of champions. According to traditional accounts, the caliph al-Ma'mun (reign 813–833) enjoyed watching Rabrab Khata'i (a.k.a., Zairab),[11] Jabir al-Kufi and Abu'n-Na'am play against each other. Those three shatranj champions are the first ever recorded, in manuscripts that survive to this day.

Soon after the brightest masters were being recognized, they began composing treatises on the game. These were the first of the great chess writings, mingling histories and legends, conveying the correct rules of play, presenting variants (described later in the present work) and, most notably, developing the theoretical foundations of play. The most famous of these early chess writers were mentioned in ibn an-Nadim's catalog of all known Arabic books, the *Kitab al-Fihrist*, collected in 988. His catalog lists book titles by the ninth century masters al-'Adli and ar-Razi, as well as the great as-Suli and al-Lajlaj of the tenth century. The original works of those masters are now lost, but their contribution was collected and recopied in some 15 manuscripts, between the 12th and 17th centuries. Using those materials, Murray, in the early 20th century, was able to reconstruct the teachings of the great Baghdad Caliphate masters.

As the Arab conquests expanded further, the game of shatranj was carried to the borders of the Islamic Empire and transmitted even further, into Europe to the west, Russia to the north, Africa to the south, and the further reaches of India to the east. In the Middle East, the tradition of theoretical study of shatranj did not survive beyond the Abbasid Caliphate of Baghdad. The last of the great theoreticians was the Persian ash-Shatranji, nicknamed after the game itself in honor of his invincible performance in the court of Timur, at the end of the 14th century.

SHATRANJ IN THE MODERN ERA. While the late 15th and early 16th centuries saw the chess of Europe transformed by the modern moves of the Queen and Bishop, the Muslim authors were slower to adopt the modern changes. Among the last references to the old way of playing was a sermon given by ibn Sukaikir ad-Dimashqa, at the mosque of Aleppo, Syria in 1557. He expounded upon a tale of Sultan Suleiman the Magnificent cheating a skilled blind player at shatranj. This discrepancy did not last for long, however, given the ongoing commerce and exchange along the banks of the Mediterranean Sea.

By the early 18th century, the major cities and trade centers of the Middle East were generally playing chess in accordance with the modern European conventions. But even as the powerful move of the Queen and the long diagonal of the Bishop came into common use, some traces of the shatranj rules persisted. Rules regarding Pawn moves, Pawn promotion, castling and winning of the game still followed the old shatranj traditions.

Thanks to the testimonies of merchants, diplomats and travelers, we can construct a general list of chess rules observed throughout Egypt, Persia, Constantinople and Algiers, through most of the 19th century. Here are the rules of shatranj in the modern era:

- The King of one side faces the Counselor of the other. Most often the Kings are placed to the left on d1 and e8, but in Persia they were usually on e1 and d8.
- The Counselor moves any number of vacant squares, in all directions. Like the modern chess Queen. However, in Turkey, it was not unusual to find players who allowed the Counselor to also move with the Knight's leap.
- The Elephant moves any number of vacant squares diagonally, just like the modern chess Bishop.
- The Pawn's double initial step is forbidden.
- As long as he has not been moved and has never been put in check, the King can, just once in the game, jump like a Horse. In some cases, this move is replaced by a variant of castling: the King moves two or three steps toward the Rukh, and the Rukh jumps over the King, landing on any square up to the King's initial square of departure.
- The Pawn promotes upon reaching the opposite side of the chessboard, but it may only promote to a piece that has already been captured. It is, therefore, impossible to have two Counselors.
- The game may be won by capturing all of the opponent's chessmen except the King, thereby winning by "bare King."

**Brass abstract Muslim style pieces from Rajasthan.**
KNOWLTON PHOTOGRAPH

Curiously, the European visitors were more disoriented by the style of the chess set itself than by the differences in the rules. These travelers found great difficulty in adapting to the monochromatic "un-checkered" chessboard, and especially in differentiating the various pieces from each other. Indeed, the abstract Muslim style, widespread from Maghreb to Northern India, required a discerning eye in distinguishing the Bishop from the Knight, Queen or Rook, as each piece was a subtle variation of the same toadstool-shaped design.

But in the deeper reaches of the old Islamic Empire, the old rules of shatranj persisted into the early 20th century. In areas of Central Asia, including Western Turkestan, among Muslim populations of the East Indies (who played what Murray called "Rumi chess"), and among the inhabitants of Ethiopia and Madagascar, chess was still being played in the ancient form just a century ago. Basically adhering to the rules of the ancient Arab shatranj, these localities did adopt a few minor variations, detailed below.

### Modern Names of Pieces and the Game in the Predominant Middle Eastern Languages

| Arabic | Persian | Turkish | Meaning | Equivalent |
|---|---|---|---|---|
| *Malik* | *Shah* | *Şah* | King, Shah | King |
| *Wazir* | *Vazir* | *Vezir* | Minister | Queen |
| *Fil* | *Fil* | *Fil* | Elephant | Bishop |
| *Hişan, Faras* | *Asb* | *At* | Horse | Knight |
| *Tabia, Qal'a* | *Rokh, Qal'e* | *Kale* | Castle | Rook |
| *'Askari, Bedaq* | *Piyade* | *Piyon* | Soldier | Pawn |
| *Shatranj\** | *Shatranj* | *Satranç* | Chess | |

(*Shatrang in Egyptian).

## Senterej: Ethiopian Chess

Reaching to the southern tip of the Red Sea, shatranj found a home in the land of Abyssinia, known to the modern world as Ethiopia. According to accounts collected by the explorer Alessandro Zorzi, the game known in Amharic as *senterej* was seen played between a Venetian traveler and Lebna Dengel (a.k.a. Dawit II, 1508–1540), the Ethiopian King of Kings *(Negus Negest)*, in the early 16th century. Three centuries later, in 1805, the English artist, antique collector and diplomat Henry Salt brought back the first detailed description of the game. According to Salt, Ras Wolde Selassie (1745–1816), Lord of Tigray, frequently played senterej with his relatives—

Senterej in the Amharic alphabet.

and they always let him win! The most comprehensive review of the Ethiopian game are in the journals of the British consul Walter Plowden (1820–1860), written in 1848 and published twenty years later. The rules of the game and the names of the pieces, given below, show a strong Arabic influence.

## Material and rules

The traditional Ethiopian chessboard was usually red, with squares drawn by fine blue lines. The pieces were of an abstract Muslim style, usually turned in ivory.

To begin the game, the pieces were laid out in the same array as the shatranj pieces, except that the King—the *Negus*—was placed to the right of the Counselor—the *Ferz*. The remaining pieces, the *Fil, Ferese, Der* and *Medeq* had the same placement as the Elephant, Horse, Rukh and Pawn of shatranj, respectively.

All pieces had the same powers of move as those in the Arab game, but the beginning of this game was fascinatingly different. As the game commenced, each player was allowed to move as many pieces as he wished, entirely disregarding the moves and move order of his opponent! This furious opening stage of the game, known as *werera*, essentially corresponding to the Arabic *taʿbiya*, ended at once when a capture was made. From that point onward, moves preceded in turn, one move at a time—what we consider normal play.

In addition to this novel opening, the game had end game rules which set it apart from the shatranj mainstream. It was not considered proper to leave one's opponent with less than two fighting pieces other than Kings and Pawns. When the second-to-last of these pieces was captured, leaving the opponent with only one such piece (only one *Ferz, Fil, Ferese* or *Der*), the attacking player had only seven moves to achieve a checkmate. If he failed to do so, the defender declared the game a draw.

Not all victories in this game were given the same value. A mate delivered by a Pawn *(Medeq)* was considered the most honorable. Mates achieved with the coordinated use of two Elephants *(Fil)* were also considered excellent. However, mates delivered by the powerful Horse *(Ferese)* or Rukh *(Der)* were held in low esteem.

## *Samantsy: Malagasy Chess*

The Malagasy people, on the isolated island of Madagascar, learned of chess from the Arab merchants who came ashore in their traditional *dhow* trading vessels. The earliest apparent trace of *samantsy*, the Malagasy form of chess, was discovered in 1970, by archeologists digging at Rezoky, near Ankazoabo, in the southwest Atsimo Andrefana region of the island. The turned bone artifact, shown below, was found at a site known to be occupied in the 16th and 17th centuries and which had been in contact with the Islamic world.

The first written record of samantsy is credited to Charles Paul Ardant du Picq, an ethnologist and officer in the French colonial army. His article, published in 1912, tells us that this chess variant was practiced by the Tanalas—the "forest people"—of Ikongo, on the southeast part of the great island. Both samantsy and *fanorona*—an original Malagasy form of checkers[12]— were said to be a part of a prince's education.

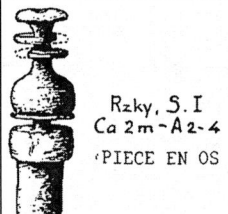

Piece discovered in 1970 by the French anthropologist Pierre Vérin (1934–2010) in Rezoky. He noted: "…seems to us to be a piece of the former chess game samantsy, as described by Ardant du Picq in the Ikongo."

### *Material and rules*

The nomenclature of the pieces is especially inventive. While the Arab King and Counselor here have become a King *(Hova)* and Prince *(Anankova),* the Elephants and Rukhs have become Guns *(Basy)* and Birds *(Vorona).* The Horse maintains its identity as a *Farasy,* but the Pawns in samantsy are mere Children *(Zaza).*

We understand that the moves of the pieces were that of shatranj. However, other moves and piece names have also been reported. According to an article by James Tattersfield published in 1938, the King was called a Chief *(Mpanjaka),* Rukh was a Crab *(Foza)* and Pawns were just

People *(Vakoaka)*. According to this report, the Horse could leap two squares in any direction, and the Bird *(Basy)* moved like a modern Rook but leaped the first square of its move. This report is not entirely clear and has never been corroborated, but it does demonstrate the mutability of shatranj as it traveled to distant lands.

### Names of Pieces at Senterej and Samantsy

| Senterej | Samantsy | Shatranj | Equivalent |
|---|---|---|---|
| *Negus* | *Hova* | King | King |
| *Ferz* | *Anankova* | Counselor | Queen |
| *Fil* or *Saba* | *Basy* | Elephant | Bishop |
| *Ferese* | *Farasy* | Horse | Knight |
| *Der* | *Vorona* | Rukh | Rook |
| *Medeq* | *Zaza* | Foot Soldier | Pawn |

Unfortunately, as has happened to many of the world's chess variants, these two variants are no longer played in their native regions. It seems that the African continent, birthplace of many of the world's greatest board games, no longer maintains its indigenous forms of chess.[13]

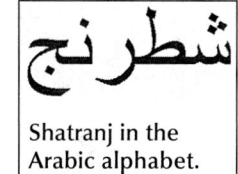
Shatranj in the Arabic alphabet.

Games are invented, thrive and die. Shatranj did not escape this fate. The chess of today owes almost everything to its direct predecessor, but to modern players the game is all but forgotten. Still, we are fortunate to have the contributions of the Arab masters, from their early manuscripts. All of these ancient studies lie dormant, waiting for the day a new generation of shatranj players brings them back out into the light.

# 2. Muslim Chess Variants

Persian and Arabian authors of the Middle Ages showed great interest in shatranj variants. These Eastern adaptations of the game, unlike many variants proposed by European authors, always kept the traditional pieces with their traditional moves. What was changed then, was the shape of the board—and in some cases, new pieces had to be added to fill out the opening array. These variants were respected versions of chess, and were well noted by scholars such as al-Mas'udi in the tenth century, and al-Amuli four centuries later. Conveyed in literature, these variants spread throughout the Muslim world as important aspects of medieval chess.

## Complete Chess

One of the first ideas to capture the imagination of the early Muslim chess innovators was to adopt an enlarged 10 × 10 board. Over several centuries, a number of such attempts were made to "improve" upon shatranj. Finally, a favorite seems to have emerged, known as *shatranj at-tamma*. This translates as "complete chess," perhaps indicating that it had achieved the number 10, the base of the decimal counting system, creating a perfect board of 100 squares. Variants played on such a board are often referred to as "decimal chess."

## Material

The game is played on a plain, uncheckered 10 × 10 square board. Each player has 20 chessmen consisting of the regular shatranj pieces, plus two extra Pawns and two *Dabbabas* (literally, "siege engines").[14] The Arabic and Persian manuscripts explain that this Dabbaba piece is as tall as the Counselor and the Elephant.

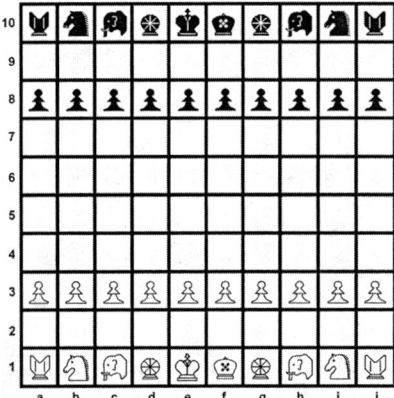

Starting array of shatranj at-tamma.

## Rules

This game follows the rules of shatranj, with these few changes:

*Dabbaba:* moves like a King, one step in any of the eight directions. Unlike the King, the Dabbaba is not limited by "check"; it may be threatened and captured like any other piece.

Three rules differ from standard shatranj:

- *Pawn promotion:* a Pawn reaching the last row promotes to a Counselor, but a player may not have more than one Counselor on the board at any given time. If a Pawn promotes while the Counselor is still on the board, that Counselor must be removed from its present position and placed on the Pawn's promotion square.
- *Half-victory:* if a King succeeds in reaching the original square of the adverse King, his owner wins a victory—but of lower esteem than a normal win. When the game was played for money, the winner took only half of the stake.
- *Bare King:* unlike standard shatranj, the bare King, left with no other chessmen of his own on the board, has not lost the game. The game goes on, just as it would in modern chess. There are only two ways to win the game: checkmate, in which the King is in check and cannot save himself, and stalemate, in which the losing player is not in check, but still cannot make any legal move.

## Tactics

Our computer analysis gives these relative values to the pieces: Rukh (5), Dabbaba (3.1), Horse (2.55), Counselor (1.45), Elephant (1.15), and Pawn (0.5).

The new piece, the Dabbaba, is appreciably stronger than the Horse but remains inferior to the Rukh, which possesses greater power on this enlarged chessboard. The Arab authors agreed with this analysis, assigning a value of 5/6 dirhem to the Dabbaba—equivalent to a scaled value of 4.15.

## Decimal Chess with Camels

In his famous epic of 1011, the *Shahnama*, the Persian poet, Firdawsi, declared that chess had been invented by the legendary Indian prince named Gaw. The poet insisted that in the ancient times, when chess was first conceived, men were superior in quality to those of his day and played a form of chess that was much larger and more complex. He described this game as being played on a board of 100 squares, with two additional Pawns and with two Camels *(Shutur)*, placed between the Horse and the Elephant.

Firdawsi explained, "Like Elephants, the Camels advance three squares." This reflects the older style of counting squares, which includes the square of departure. We would take this to mean that the Camel moved two squares, jumping over the first square whether it was occupied or not, and landing on the second. Unfortunately, this is the only explanation given in the ancient text, but we are able to reconstruct a very sensible game by assuming that the Camel's move was orthogonal (forward, backward, right or left), making it the perfect complement of the moves of the Horse and Elephant.

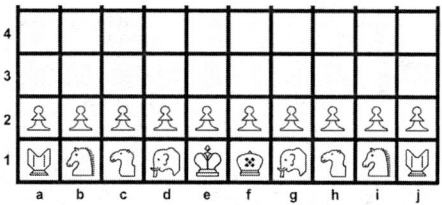

We also know from the original poem that the Pawn was promoted to a Counselor—but instead of placing the new Counselor on the square the Pawn had landed upon, the player was given liberty to place it on any vacant square adjacent to his own King.

Gaw's chess array according to Firdawsi.

The possibility of expanding the chessboard to a 10 × 10 size and adding novel pieces has occurred many times in the history of chess. More examples are found in this book: expanded Indian variants, the Mongolian game *hiashatar*, Carrera's chess and Piacenza's *archi-chess*.

Persian miniature illustrating Firdawsi's Shahnama (Iran, early 14th century).

# Citadel Chess

This later adaptation of the large 10 × 10 chess was quite popular; it was described in several Arabic manuscripts of diverse origins. The game was called *shatranj al-husun,* citadel chess, in reference to the special squares added on to give the King a safe refuge.

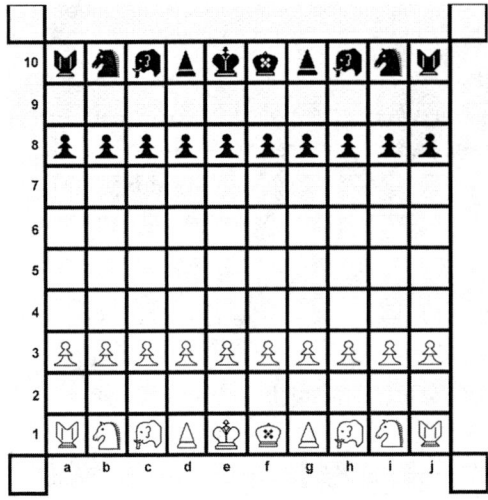

The game is played on a large chessboard of 100 squares, plus four "citadels" *(husun),* squares in the four corners (see illustration). Some sources show these squares placed on the right and left sides of the Rukh squares, or behind the Rukh squares, and some show them attached diagonally, as in our diagram. There are 20 chessmen on each side, much like the arrangement of *shatranj at-tamma* (complete chess). In this game, the Kings usually face each other, as in the diagram, but some sources show them facing the Counselors, for instance, with Kings on f1 and e10. The additional piece is known as a Dabbaba. These pieces may begin between the Elephants and the Kings or Counselors (as shown here), but some sources show them starting on the outside of the Rukhs, in the a and j files, with the normal shatranj array between them in files b through i.

Starting array of shatranj al-husun.

Although the Dabbaba has the same name as the extra piece in complete chess, this one has a very different move.

 *Dabbaba*: moves any number of unoccupied squares in the diagonal directions, exactly like the modern Bishop.

The rules of play are exactly like those of shatranj, with this exception:

- *King Escapes:* if a King succeeds in reaching one of the special citadel squares on the opponent's side of the board,[15] he has escaped persecution and the game is drawn.

On the strength scale, this new piece stood again between Rukh and Horse: Rukh (5), Dabbaba (3.5), Horse (2.15), Counselor (1.4), Elephant (1.15), Pawn (0.5).

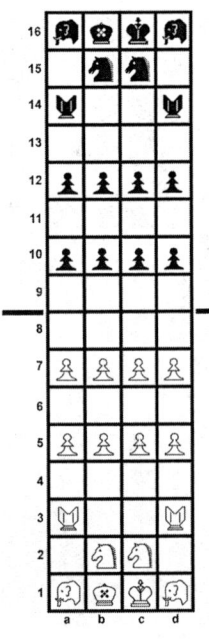

# Oblong chess

*Shatranj al-mustatila*, oblong chess, is mentioned in several Arabic manuscripts. The elongated board fit well on the flip-side of a board used for playing nard—an ancient version of our modern-day backgammon. Also, like nard, this chess variant could be played with dice.

## Material

The chessmen are those of regular shatranj; however, the game is played on a 4 × 16 square board.

Several other starting positions have been reported. Here are six more arrays given by Murray:

**Left:** Starting position at *shatranj al-mustatila*.

## 2. Muslim Chess Variants

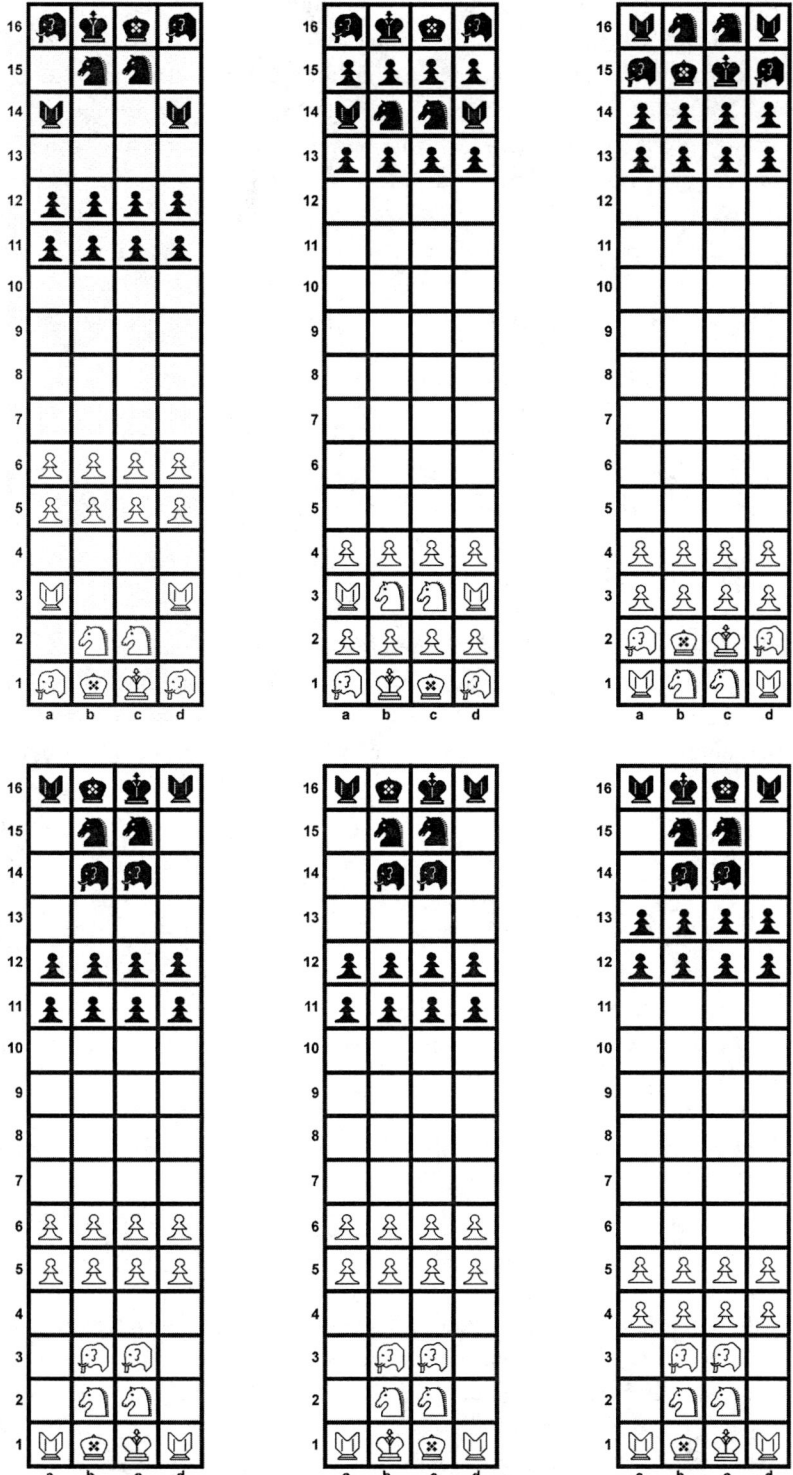

Six starting arrays for *Shatranj al-mustatila*, oblong chess.

From these examples, the initial array has a good bit of variety. But we can also see some consistency: the Pawns are arranged in two complete lines, as far back as the second rank, and as far forward as the seventh rank. All other pieces are arranged between the first and third ranks. The King and Counselor are always beside each other on the b and c files. Rukhs are placed symmetrically on the outer files, a and d; Horses are on the inner files, b and c; and Elephants are sometimes on the inner and sometimes on the outer files. The corners are occupied either by the Rukhs or by the Elephants. The opposing sides reflect each other with the same configuration, sometimes with the Kings facing one another and sometimes with the Kings facing the Counselors.

## *Rules*

The moves of the chessmen are the same as those in the game of shatranj; however, in this variant, a die is often employed to determine which of the pieces is to be moved. Each of the six numbers is associated with a particular sort of piece, as follows: 6 = King, 5 = Counselor, 4 = Elephant, 3 = Horse, 2 = Rukh and 1 = Pawn.

If a player finds that his King is in check, he must roll a number that allows him to get out of check, usually a 6 in order to move the King. If he does not get the necessary roll, his turn must pass without a move. Depending upon the subsequent rolls of the dice, the King will either have the opportunity to escape, or the opponent will succeed in capturing the checked King, thereby winning the game.

Note that oblong chess also makes a fine game without dice, played by the normal rules of shatranj.

## *Tactics*

The use of the die in this game introduces some important strategic considerations. First, the King must avoid being threatened, since even one unlucky check could be fatal. To achieve this, he usually stays in the back ranks, well protected. Second, on the offensive side, the player must mobilize his forces as quickly as possible in an attempt to be the first to threaten and ultimately capture the enemy King.

But when the game is played without a die, a very different approach is prescribed. The King becomes a powerful fighter, often employed as a serious attacking piece, charging headlong into the fray. Pawn promotion on the long board becomes a remote consideration, and these small fellows are quickly sacrificed for positional advantage. Horses and Elephants also lose stature on the long board, since they take several moves to reach the enemy, and lose mobility on the narrow board.

The Rukh, however, gains a significant advantage, dominating the long 16-square files and reaching deep into enemy territory. Counselors hold about the same value as in regular shatranj. With all of these considerations, estimates of the pieces' relative powers become: Rukh (5), Horse (2.45), Counselor (1.5), Elephant (0.95) and Pawn (0.65).

Shatranj, which normally develops more slowly than the modern game, adapts very well to play on the elongated board. Modern chess players will generally prefer the familiar strategic challenges of the game played without a die, but playing with a die still offers a stimulating alternative.

# Byzantine Chess

The spectacle of chess laid out on a circular board has drawn in many thoughtful chess dreamers over the centuries. Even today, clever tinkerers often come up with circular chessboards, as "new" variants on the chess theme. In fact, circular chessboards can be dated back at least a thousand years to Arabic manuscripts.

The Arabs attributed circular shatranj to Byzantium. In their view, chess played on the square board was from the "Indian" East, while chess played in the round was from the "Roman" West. Baghdad players were considered to stand at the center of the world.

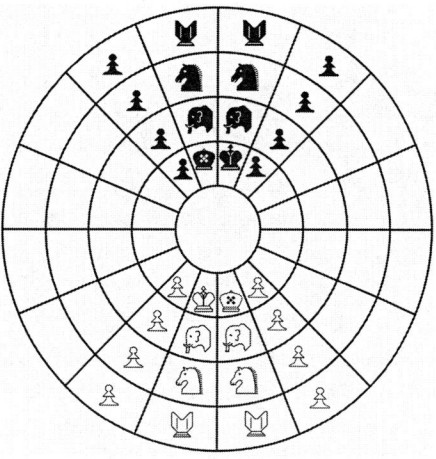

Initial array of Byzantine chess.

## Material

The chessboard is circular, composed of 64 curved "squares" arranged in four concentric rings. Each player has a full shatranj set of 16 chessmen, arranged as shown in the diagram. Note that the King of one side faces the Counselor of the other.

## Rules

This game follows the rules of shatranj, with the Pawn proceeding outward and around the circle, toward the opponent's side. There are special rules, brought about by the "endless" circular board:

- The Pawns do not promote, but continue to go around the circle endlessly.
- If two Pawns from the same side (two Black or two White Pawns) circle around to meet each other face-to-face, their journey is finished and they are immediately removed by the opposing player. The game continues without them.

## Variant with Citadels

There is an interesting variant of this game which utilizes the special refuges found in citadel chess. Note that in this variant, the initial array is reversed, so that the King and Counselor occupy the outer ring, with the Rukhs closest to the center. Also, note that the center circle is divided into four quarters.

This variant follows the same rules of play as the circular game described above, but here—just as in citadel chess—a desperate player may claim a draw if he can get his King into the quarter-circle—the citadel (*husun*)—on the opponent's side of the board.[16]

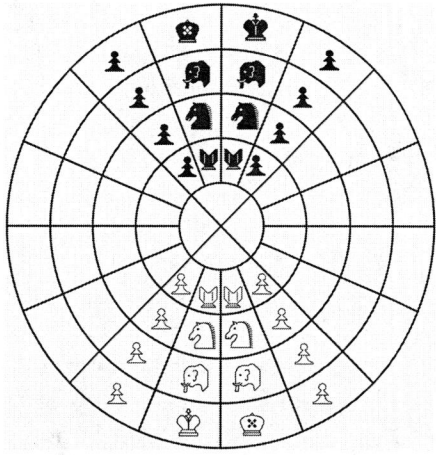

Initial array, with citadels in the center of the board.

## Tactics

Although very different in appearance, the circular board is topologically similar to the elongated 4 × 16 board of oblong chess. Playing on a field of only four squares wide, Pawns can be especially obstructive, Horses and Elephants have limited range, and Rukhs become all the more powerful. In fact, an unobstructed Rukh can circle the entire board, landing on its original square—an elegant way for a player to "pass" without changing the position on the board. The relative value of the pieces has been calculated as follows: Rukh (5), Horse (1.75), Counselor (1), Elephant (0.7) and Pawn (0.45).

Unlike other shatranj variants, the circular game allows the Elephants and the Counselors to confront and possibly capture each other.

When the circular game is played with citadels, the possibility offered by these refuge areas can give the game a very different dynamic. Just as the player in a compromised position enjoys the possibility of drawing the game by reaching the opponent's citadel, the attacking player must use all means possible to block the weakened King and checkmate him before he can escape.

It is likely that modern players will find this game especially intriguing, and more immediately engaging than the oblong variant. In the circular format, the opposing forces encounter each other quickly, and a diversified struggle on the right and left flanks quickly ensues.

## History of the Muslim Chess Variants

Although the fundamental 8 × 8 form of shatranj enjoyed continued popularity, these alternative forms appeared very early in the game's history. In fact, all of the ancient Muslim treatises included such variants, along with *ta'biyat*, *mansubat*, chess origin legends and discussion of chess under Muslim law. Even the famous Arab historian al-Mas'udi named a few shatranj variants in his encyclopedia, *Muruj adh-dhahab (The Meadows of Gold)*. In that text of 947, he mentions *shatranj at-tamma, as-su'diya, al-mustatila, al-muddawara, al-jawarhiya* and *al-falakiya*. Some of these variants are well documented—and some are not!

SOME ENDURING QUESTIONS. A cloud of mystery still obscures those chess variants which are found mentioned but never fully explained. *Shatranj as-su'diya*, meaning "from Upper Egypt," is especially mysterious. It is known that the game was played on an 8 × 8 "Indian" chessboard, and that the Pawns did not promote—but then the manuscript breaks off, leaving us to wonder what form this revered game may have taken.

Another intriguing variant, *shatranj al-jawarhiya*, "anatomic chess," was played on a 7 × 8 squares board with 6 pieces on each side, representing the functional body parts: the mouth to speak, the ear to hear, the eye to see, the hand to catch, the leg to walk and finally, the heart to sustain life. A tantalizing description! But unfortunately, not enough information is available to guess what form this game may have taken.

The sun, moon and constellations of the zodiac play a part in *shatranj al-falakiya*, "celestial chess," but the Arabic texts give no description of the rules, board or pieces. Even so, one may surmise that this refers to the game later known as *escaques*, described in the *Libro de los juegos (Book of games)*, a 13th century codex prepared under the King of Castile, Alfonso X. That game is discussed in a subsequent chapter.

COMPLETE CHESS. Al-Mas'udi mentioned the existence of a game invented by al-Khalil (718–791), an author known for his study of musical harmony. He remains the earliest documented inventor to work at improving the game by adding an extra piece. This novel chessman was a Camel (*Jamal*)—but, alas, its move was not recorded. The historian's lukewarm report tells us that "some of the crowd of chess players played with it, but afterward it was laid aside."[17]

Al-Mas'udi also described *shatranj at-tamma*, "complete chess," which is incidentally mentioned in many Arabic and Persian chess manuscripts. Although the oldest of these treatises is dated 1140, the evidence assures us that the game reaches back to al-'Adli in the middle of the ninth century, before al-Mas'udi's time. The 10 × 10 chessboard inspired many enthusiasts, including the Persian poet Firdawsi, who wrote of this "decimal chess" shortly after the year 1000.

OBLONG CHESS. The 4 × 16 variant, *shatranj al-mustatila*, must also be regarded as one of the oldest on record. Also known as *at-tawila* (long) or *al-mamduda* (lengthened), oblong chess is attributed in Muslim manuscripts to al-'Adli as the original source of the game—a plausible hypothesis. If true, oblong chess holds claim to being the oldest known variant played with dice.

CIRCULAR CHESS. The oldest accounts from Muslim texts tell us that circular chess (*shatranj al-muddawara*) was conveyed from Byzantium by a man named al-Harrani. The game was presented to Tahir ibn Husayn (died 822), governor of Mesopotamia during the Abbasid Caliphate. According to al-Mas'udi's account, circular chess was also known as *shatranj ar-rumiya*,[18] referring to its Byzantine origin. But this tentative trail leaves an open question, since no direct evidence can be found to affirm that the circular game was actually played in Byzantium.

But the Byzantines certainly did play chess, known there by the Greek name of *zatrikion* (ζατρίκιον). Murray asserts that it was received directly from the Persians before the ninth century, since the name of the game derives from the Persian *chatrang*, rather than the later Arabic *shatranj*.

According to the Persian historian at-Tabari (838–923), a chess-based insult was hurled in 802 between the East Roman Emperor Nikephoros I, and the Abbasid Caliph Harun al-Rashid. Nikephoros, successor to the throne of Empress Irene, resented the tribute he was called upon to pay Harun. He declared that Irene had been guilty of a "very feminine weakness" when she cast Harun as a Rukh and herself as a mere Pawn. Nikephoros insisted that now Harun was the Pawn and he, Nikephoros, should be the one receiving tribute. Harun replied with a metaphor and response of his own. Writing to the "dog of the Romans," the caliph proclaimed, "Thou shalt not hear, thou shalt behold my reply!"[19] He marched with his army and heavily defeated the Byzantine in the battle of Krasos at Anatolia.

Evidence of chess from Byzantium itself is scarce.[20] Chess is mentioned in a 10th century treatise on dreams; it appears later as an object of Persian or Assyrian luxury in a biography of Emperor Alexis I, written by his sister, Anna Komnene (1083–1153). Around the same time (1118), the first condemnation of chess by the Greek Church is recorded. Apparently, some otherwise devout fellows had been spending too much time on chess, as well as dice and drink.

There is in fact a lack of evidence for an authentic Byzantine source of circular chess. It seems most likely that chess in Byzantium was much like the shatranj played in other regions, on a square board. The round board may well have been of Arab origin. The Arab Empire, having pushed its borders to the limits of the known world, had acquired a taste for the exotic and mysterious. Various cultural effects, such as chess, found themselves attributed to easily referenced regions of the empire—and it would be hard to untangle the true history based on the popular parlance. Where chess was concerned, there was a literary logic that the circular "Roman" chess stood in opposition to the square "Indian" chess. That from the West was considered modern and fast-paced; that from the East, the older and slower variety.

VARIANTS WITH CITADELS. Another important source of Oriental chess variants is the *Nafa'is al-funun* (*Treasury of the sciences*), an extensive encyclopedia composed by the Persian al-Amuli between the years 1335 and 1342. This great work contains three chapters devoted to chess and describes five historic variants: *shatranj at-tawila, al-muddawara, al-husun, al-kabir* and *al-falakiya*. The list parallels that given by al-Mas'udi in 947, with one addition of special interest. The game of *shatranj al-kabir* (great chess) is a newer variant; it is impressive and has been given its own chapter.

Of particular interest in al-Amuli's encyclopedia is the introduction of variants with citadels—the safe havens which allow a possible draw to the losing player. Both complete chess (then called citadel chess, *shatranj al-husun*) and circular chess included this interesting addition. In accordance with this tendency, great chess (*shatranj al-kabir*) also has a board with citadels.

Notice that citadel chess also introduces a new chess piece, which moves freely along the diagonals—apparently a complement to the Rukh's long range in the orthogonal directions. It is tempting to suppose that this led to the move of the modern Bishop, but it would be a bit of an historical stretch to make that assumption. The long diagonal move of the Persian piece arose quite remotely from the European Bishop move, which can be traced to Spain. In fact, the long diagonal move never did take hold of the chess mainstream in Persia as it did a century later in Europe. Perhaps a deciding factor in the enduring success of the European Bishop's long diagonal move was the fact that European chessboards, unlike those of other lands, were checkered in alternate colors, making the diagonal lines of the board much more apparent.

## *A Long Tradition of Chess Variants*

Several of the variants described above were astonishingly long-lived. The Persian historian ibn 'Arabshah reported that both oblong and circular chess were played at Timur's court in Samarkand around the year 1400. Considering the evidence that oblong chess existed in the mid–ninth century, this is a game that lasted more than 500 years!

Circular chess lasted even longer, and seemed to keep coming back in new contexts. Adapted to modern rules, with the modern European moves of Queens and Bishops, it flourished again in India at the beginning of the 18th century, and then in Europe, where the Englishman Dave Reynolds founded the Circular Chess Society in 1996, which holds world championships to this day.

Decimal chess—those variants played on the 10 × 10 board—also reveals a long legacy of endurance and reinvention. It would be possible to trace a long line of decimal variants, uninterrupted from the earliest reference to the present day. With such a continual history, it is clear that these variants hold much to be admired and enjoyed by game lovers of all epochs.

# 3. Timur's Great Chess

Permanently damaged by a hip injury in childhood, he spent his life with a marked limp. He was descended from a Turco-Mongol tribe in the Sogdian steppes, in the area known today as Uzbekistan. And he considered himself the heir to Genghis Khan.

# 3. Timur's Great Chess

Timur-i Lang ("Timur the Lame," corrupted as "Tamerlane") seized Genghis Khan's legacy of power and domination, and became one of the cruelest and most dreaded conquerors the world has ever seen. In his lifetime, this ruler of Transoxiana conquered all of Central Asia and the Middle East. He ravaged Smyrna, Damascus, Baghdad and Delhi. Finally, at the age of 69, poised to mount an invasion of China, his life was taken by a fever. It is estimated that 5 percent of the world's population perished in the wake of his fury.

In his quiet hours, Timur was a noted patron of the arts, and loved to play chess. As befit a man of his grandeur, he shunned the traditional shatranj, which he derided as *ash-shaghir* ("small chess"), and insisted upon *shatranj al-kabir* ("great chess"). This expanded chess form, often known as Tamerlane chess, is traditionally attributed to the conqueror himself, and stands among the most significant of the historic variants.

## Material

The chessboard has 112 squares, arranged in 10 rows and 11 columns, with one "citadel" square adjoined to camp. Each player has 28 pieces: 1 King, 1 Counselor, 1 Vizier, 2 Giraffes, 2 Scouts, 2 Horses, 2 Rukhs, 2 Dabbabas, 2 Camels, 2 Elephants and 11 Pawns.

Unlike most chess variants, the Pawns of Timur's great chess have individual identities which affect their possible promotion. Originally, each Pawn was a miniature representation of the larger piece with which it was associated. The Pawns, from left to right, are: the Pawn of Pawns (a3), the Pawn of Dabbabas (b3), the Pawn of Camels (c3), the Pawn of Elephants (d3), the Counselor's Pawn (e3), the King's Pawn (f3), the Vizier's Pawn (g3), the Pawn of Giraffes (h3), the Pawn of Scouts (i3), the Pawn of Horses (j3) and the Pawn of Rukhs (k3).

### Names of the Chessmen in Timur's Great Chess

| Arabic name | New Persian name | Meaning |
| --- | --- | --- |
| Wazir | Wazir | Vizier, Governor |
| Dabbaba | Dabbaba | Siege engine |
| Tali'a | Tali'a | Scout[21] |
| Jamal | Shutur | Camel |
| Zurafa | Zurafa | Giraffe |

Several initial arrays have been used. These two arrays were reported in 1851 by the Orientalist Nathaniel Bland. The first is considered "masculine" and the other "feminine." The masculine array was more common:

Starting position of Timur's great chess—the "masculine" array.

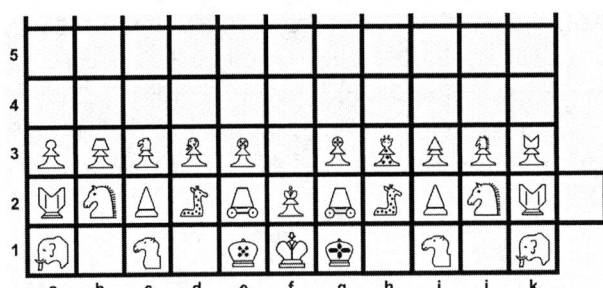

Starting position of Timur's great chess—the "feminine" array.

The Muslim scholar 'Arabshah gives us a third possible arrangement, as witnessed by a manuscript dated 1451, held in the Bibliothèque nationale de France in Paris. Note that this arrangement does not include the citadels.

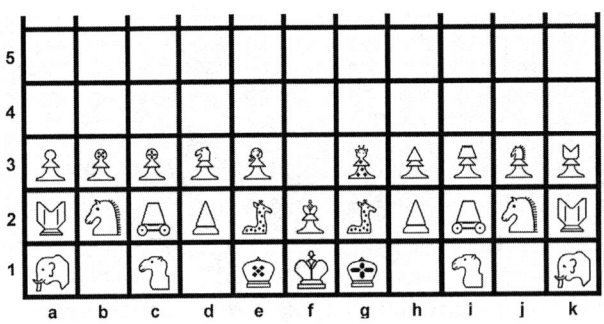

Opening array for Timur's Great Chess, found in the Bibliothèque nationale de France.

In each of these arrays, both players arrange the Pawns in the same order—left to right. Unlike the other pieces, the Pawns do not mirror each other across the board.

# Rules

MOVES AND CAPTURES. • King, Counselor, Horse, Rukh, Elephant and Pawn move and capture as in shatranj.

*Vizier:* moves one square orthogonally—one step forward, backward, left or right.

*Dabbaba:* jumps two squares orthogonally (forward, backward, left or right), regardless whether the intervening square is occupied. The Dabbabas can only reach 30 of the board's 110 playable squares; the Elephant in this game can reach only 15.

*Camel:* can be considered to have an extended Knight's move. It travels 3 squares in an orthogonal direction, plus 1 step at a right angle (see diagram, below). Like a Knight, the Camel may jump over any intervening pieces.

*Giraffe:* has a very peculiar move! It begins by taking one step diagonally, then proceeds orthogonally (moving away from its original square); however, it may not land on the first three squares it comes to—it must complete its move on the fourth square, or further (see the diagram below). Unlike the Horse, Dabbaba and Camel, the Giraffe may *not* jump over any pieces it its path.

*Scout:* moves diagonally like the modern Bishop with a major difference: he cannot move only one square; he must always move two or more squares. He may *not* leap over that first forbidden square if it is occupied.[22]

# 3. Timur's Great Chess

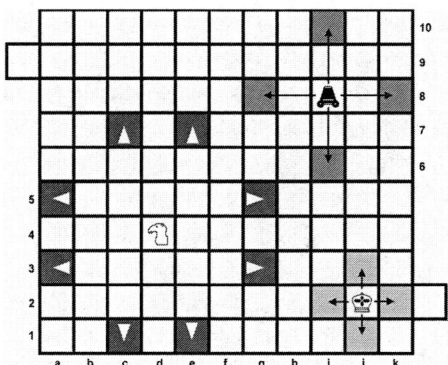

Moves of the Vizier, Dabbaba and Camel.

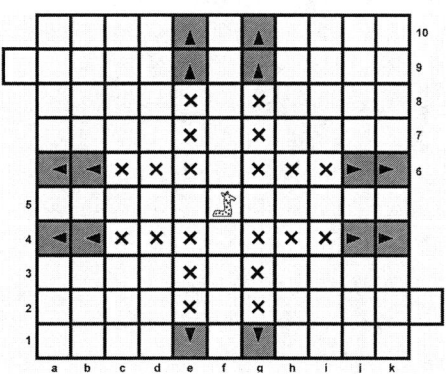

Move of the Giraffe.
(It passes over the squares marked "X" and can be blocked by any piece on those squares.)

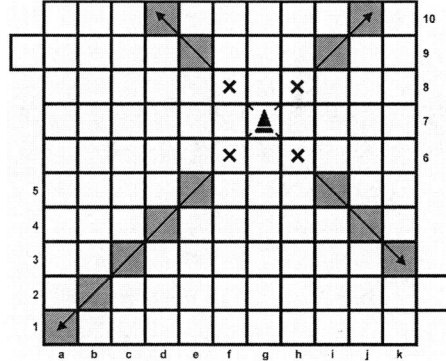

Move of the Scout.
(It can also be blocked by a piece on the squares marked "X.")

Each player's Dabbabas, Camels and Scouts cover the same selected squares on the board. Two Dabbabas, for instance, can stand two squares apart, protecting each other. But these pieces can never meet and capture the same sort of piece from the opponent's side. For instance, a Dabbaba will never have the opportunity to capture an opposing Dabbaba.

PAWN PROMOTION. • *General Rule*: Upon reaching the end of the board, a Pawn promotes to become the piece with which it is originally associated (exceptions follow).
- The King's Pawn is promoted to a Prince (*Shahzada*). It moves like a King but is not limited by threats of check and may be captured like any normal piece.
- The Pawn of Pawns promotes through this rather complex process:
  ◦ (1) Upon arriving at the last row, it remains immobile and cannot be captured. On any subsequent turn, the player may pick that Pawn up, and place it upon any square of the

board, free or occupied, from which it either threatens a piece which cannot escape (has no possible square to move to), or forks two pieces (threatens two pieces at once, thus forcing the capture of one). If that square is occupied by a piece, which may be friend or foe—but not a King—the displaced piece is removed from the board.
- (2) Upon reaching the last row for the second time, it is placed immediately on the starting square of the King's Pawn;
- (3) Finally, when it reaches the last row for the third time, the Pawn becomes an "Adventitious King" (*Shah masnu'a*). This piece moves just like the Prince, that is, like the King but not limited by "check," and is able to be captured like other pieces.

End of the Game. • *Citadels:* only the King may enter the enemy citadel. If he succeeds, the player may declare a draw—or he may switch the position of his King with his own Prince or Adventitious King (if the player possesses at least one of these) and the game continues. No piece can enter its own citadel except the Adventitious King. In this case, he can prevent the enemy King from entering and declaring a draw.
- *Escape of the King:* once during the game, a King who is in check, checkmate or stalemate can switch his position with one of his own pieces. This privilege occurs only once for each player, so it should be used wisely. (It is assumed that the exchange is not permitted with an Adventitious King who is occupying his own citadel.)
- *Winning the Game:* the goal of the game is the forced capture of the adverse King, by checkmate or stalemate, who has exhausted the escape option described above. The bare King (all pieces captured except the King) is not a victory in itself because the King can still try to reach the opposite citadel for a drawn game.

## Tactics

The game consists of nine sorts of pieces, in addition to the King and the Pawns. The Persians sorted them into three movement types, each with three levels of power:

| Power / Class | Straight | Oblique | Mixed |
|---|---|---|---|
| *1st level* | Vizier | Counselor | Horse |
| *2nd level* | Dabbaba | Elephant | Camel |
| *3rd level* | Rukh | Scout | Giraffe |

With the exception of the Horse, the leaping pieces fall into the second level of the table. The third level pieces do not have the leaping privilege; they can be blocked by any piece along their path. Consequently, they are much more useful later in the game, when many pieces have already been captured. With its eight-way attack, the Giraffe can be especially dangerous. Placed across from an undefended King, the Giraffe can lock him into a single file, making him extremely vulnerable.

The value of the chessmen is calculated as follows: Rukh (5), Horse (2.6), Camel (2.3), Giraffe (2.25), Vizier (1.65), Counselor (1.5), Dabbaba (1.45), Scout (1.2), Elephant (1.15), Pawn (0.6).[23]

## History

Because of its extensive documentation by Anglo-Saxon historians and Orientalists, Timur's great chess has become the best-known of all the great chess variants. The English linguist Duncan Forbes granted it a complete and enthusiastic survey in his treatise *History of Chess* (1860).

# 3. Timur's Great Chess

The first known record of this form of chess appears in a sketch found in *Treasury of the Sciences*, compiled before 1342 by Muhammad ibn Mahmud al-Amuli. Not long after that publication, in 1369, Timur seized the throne in Samarkand, ultimately conquering—and destroying—large parts of Asia. His biographer, ibn 'Arabshah (died 1450), bequeathed to us a striking description of Timur's passion for chess. For instance, he baptized his son (who later succeeded him to the throne) with the name Shahrukh, because a messenger had come to announce the child's birth just as Timur was mating an adversary with a Rukh.

We also learn from 'Arabshah that the "small" chess could not satisfy his master's overly excited mind and therefore Timur preferred to play "large" chess, *shatranj al-kabir*. The best players of the empire were invited to take lodging at his court and he liked to challenge the strongest among them, Ali ash-Shatranji of Tabriz, to this giant variant.

The rules of Timur's great chess come to us from a Persian manuscript translated by the Royal Asiatic Society (founded in London, 1823).[24] The document is attributed to Hajji Khalifa (died 1658), but the original author may have been the great champion ash-Shatranji. In addition to instructions on the rules of the great game, the author presented its supposed history—more the stuff of legend to the modern reader. He explained that this "perfect" chess with 56 pieces, *shatranj kamil*, had been invented by the Greek sage Hermes and introduced to India by Alexander the Great and his army. He went on to opine that because the Indians were incapable of mastering such a complex game, the philosopher Sassa reduced the game to 32 pieces on a board of 64 squares and offered it to his king, Kaid. A bit of nationalistic fervor seems to have crept into his account, but these comments do suggest that the game was widespread even in the 14th and 15th centuries.

It is likely that the exact moves of the "extra" pieces—those different from the standard shatranj lineup—had some differences in various times and locations.[25] This view is reinforced by differing reports about the opening array and even by the sheer difficulty of describing some of the moves. The board itself has been recorded with the citadels in different locations and different quantities (4, 2 or none at all), and the number of ranks have been shown as 10, 11 or 12. Only the width of the board, 11 files across, has been consistent. Still, with all of its potential variety, there is enough consistency in literature to consider all of these possible variations of "great chess," which has taken Timur's name.

Timur-i Lang (the Lame) or Tamerlane, the "Iron" Emir of Transoxiana, portrait by Adrianus Canter Visscher, 1700.

## *Variant: Timur's Great Chess, Completed*

Looking further into the variants of Timur's great chess, here is an interesting case of even more pieces being added, actually filling in the spaces left by other arrangements, and adding three novel Pawns to the fourth rank as well.

This comes from a Persian manuscript designated as *Elliot 274*, attributed to al-Amuli. The game includes an Explorer (*Kashshaf*)[26] starting on the square f1, a Lion *(Shir)* on j1 and a Camel *(Shutur)* on i1. Unfortunately, the script which indicates the remaining novel pieces is, according to Murray, illegible. We do however have another source: the Arabic manuscript *7322* in the

British Museum (London) reproduced from a work by 'Arabshah—written during the reign of Timur.

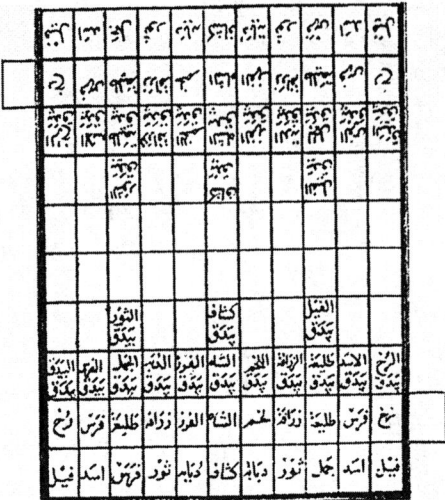

Reproduction of the drawing of Timur's Great Chess, Completed, from the British Museum manuscript MS7322.

This interesting array is reproduced in a simpler standard format, below. On the first rank there is an Explorer (*Kashshaf*) on f1, two Lions (*'Asad*) on b1 and j1 and two Bulls (*Thaur*) on d1 and h1. There is also something rather peculiar: a third Horse has replaced the Camel on c1. This odd placement of an extra Horse almost seems like a mistake—but the same pattern is repeated across the board with a Horse placed on i10. In the second rank is an Aquatic Monster (*Luxm*)[27] in place of the Vizier. Perhaps a small bit of political mockery leveled at this prestigious governmental position?

Transcription of the drawing of Timur's great chess, completed.

Completing the survey of Timur's great chess, we have three extra Pawns, naturally enough associated with the new characters on the board. There is the Pawn of Lions on j3, the Explorer's Pawn on f4 and the Pawn of Bulls on c4.

But the placement of these Pawns raises a new question. Notice that our diagram has the Pawns of the Bulls, Explorers and Elephants facing each other directly across the board on the 4th and 7th ranks. This mirror symmetry is not consistent with all of the other chessmen on the first three rows, which each player has arranged similarly left-to-right. For instance, notice that the Pawns on the 3rd rank do not mirror the Pawns on the 8th rank. Was this discrepancy in symmetry the mere result of an over-tired and inattentive copyist? But the rest of the diagram has been completed with such meticulous care! One really cannot be sure.

A game which received so much attention as to be carefully depicted in a manuscript must have actually been played and must have had a set of rules. In particular, it is thought that the novel pieces must have had their own special moves, and maybe even a higher level of power (a fourth level!) than the pieces already looked at. But what were those moves exactly? Historians do not have any indication, but can give it their best guess.[28]

For those who would like to go ahead and play this interestingly completed variation of Timur's great chess, the present authors propose three long-distance leaping moves, which fill in the move choices left by the already familiar pieces. For the Explorer, there would be a three-square diagonal move—a simple extension of the Elephant's leap. For the Lion, there would be a three-square orthogonal leap—an extension of the Vizier's move. And for the Bull, there would be a leap of three squares orthogonally plus two squares at a right angle—a full extension of a Horse's leap. These three moves neatly fill in the square of possible moves left open by the existing pieces of shatranj and Timur's great chess, as shown by the diagrams below. The relative values would then be: Explorer (1), Lion (1.35) and Bull (1.6).

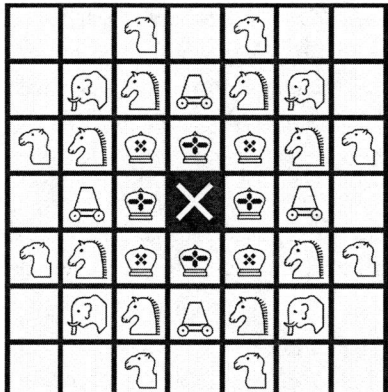 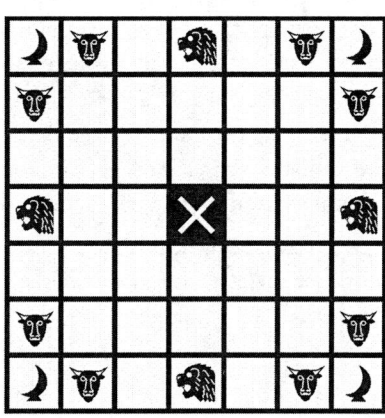

The left diagram shows the compared moves of the known shatranj and great chess pieces. On the right, moves proposed for the three additional pieces: the Explorer, the Lion and the Bull. Each piece symbol shows the particular piece's range, if starting at the square marked "X."

"Completed" or not, the rules of great chess were certainly the subject of discussion, contention and negotiation. Nevertheless, the first rule would probably be stated thus: "Timur is always right." Who would dare defeat him without his consent?

## *Turkish Great Chess*

The spirit of Timur's majesty lives on in this newer chess variant, though separated from the mighty conqueror by some four centuries. This particular *shatranj al-kabir* is presented courtesy of Muhammad Hafid, author of a Turkish encyclopedia published in 1805-06 in Constantinople (Istanbul). The chessboard is even larger here and the list of pieces offers a strange, somewhat disconcerting, hodge-podge of warriors and wild beasts, casting an eerie web of fantasy over this game's metaphoric struggle.

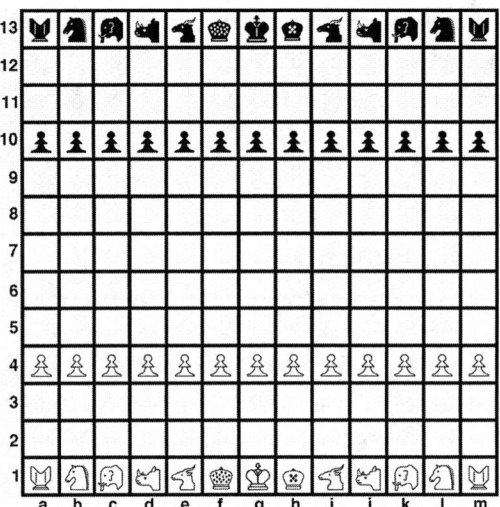

Initial array of Turkish great chess.

It is played on a board of 13 × 13 squares. Each player has 26 pieces: 1 King, 1 Counselor, 1 Grand Ferz, 2 Gazelles (*Ahu*), 2 Rhinoceroses (*Karkaddan*), 2 Elephants, 2 Horses, 2 "Rukhs" and 13 Pawns. Pawns are placed on each player's fourth rank, rows 4 and 10. Counselors, Kings and Grand Ferzes face pieces of their own kind across the board, in mirrored arrangement.[29]

The familiar shatranj pieces have the standard shatranj moves.[30] The move of the Gazelles is the same as that of the Camels in Timur's great chess, and the Grand Ferz takes the very same move as Timur's Giraffe. The new piece is the Rhinoceros.[31]

 *Rhinoceros*: leaps like a Horse or moves any number of squares on the diagonals. In other words, it may move like a modern Knight or Bishop—a powerful combination!

The scale of value is: Rhinoceros (5.4), Rukh (5), Grand Ferz (3), Horse (2.25), Gazelle (2), Counselor (1.2), Elephant (1), Pawn (0.45). In comparison, the modern pieces on this board would rank: Queen (8.1), Bishop (3.25).

All rules of play, including Pawn promotion, would follow the rules of traditional shatranj—with the addition of the extra pieces mentioned.

These great chess variants offer a fascinating glimpse of a distant but widespread chess culture which is all but lost to the world today. Yet, the record is far from exhausted. The Polish historian Jerzy Giżycki, in his book *A History of Chess,* tells us of an Indian variant played on a 12 × 12 square board, sometimes played with dice, and played with Birds, Crocodiles, Giraffes, Lions and even Unicorns as pieces. He goes on to relate that the 15th century Uzbek poet, Alisher Navoï, reported a Central Asian game with Viziers, Elephants, Giraffes, Bears, Camels, "Ruh-birds"[32] and Horses, popular in the 13th and 14th centuries. Large chess variants existed for centuries, varying in details of rules and pieces, but maintaining many of the characteristics we have described here, as the games were passed on down the generations and across the map of Central Asia. The present work describes more large variants, from the further reaches of chess evolution in the following pages. The grand notion of an expanded and greatly diversified game of chess has long held sway over the chess lover's imagination.

Those deeply attached to the orthodoxy of modern chess often look disparagingly at the great variants, as though they were mere distractions from the "real" game, but it can still become a momentous revelation when a chess player is suddenly captivated by the discovery of Timur's great chess, with its marvelous menagerie of characters. Turning the key to discover a few new pieces with surprising moves and intriguing rules, the player may suddenly unlock hidden dimensions of another chess universe.

# 4. Shatar[33]

The vast steppes of Mongolia have given birth to hordes of fierce horsemen who, more than once, surged through the Asian continent, subjugating all others and creating the largest empires the world has ever known. Somehow, chess took hold as a deeply imbedded aspect of the Mongol culture and, curiously, the game relinquished almost all of its allusions to warfare. The symbolic struggle on the Mongolian chessboard resembles not so much a military confrontation as a competition between the ornate icons of two rival nomadic clans.

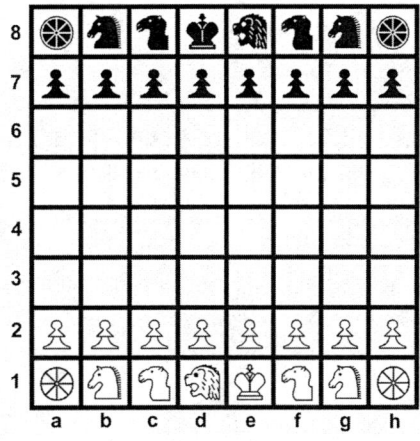

*Above:* Shatar in the Mongolian alphabet. *Right:* Starting array of shatar.

## Material

The traditional chessboard is uniform with 64 squares drawn over a sheet of paper or cloth—although checkered boards and mats now are also common. The traditional pieces are finely carved or cast, and are highly valued by their owners, as they will be passed down from one generation to the next. They are also sought after as coveted collectors' sets.

The figures displayed on the two sides are often very different from each other. And, although the pieces may be very colorful, the color often does not reflect the two sides of the game. Sometimes, the opposing sides will have differently colored bases, but there is no uniformity throughout all sets. More often, the two sides are indicated by the symbolic meaning of the figures. The two sides may represent, for instance, aggressive vs. passive, good vs. evil, Mongolian vs. Russian, Buddhism vs. Shamanism, or they may just be the effects of one clan against another. For instance, one side may have pull-carts while the other side has trucks. There may even be variation among the pieces of one side, such as those sets depicting male figures on one flank and female figures on the other, or those with a variety of unique figures representing the eight Pawns.

All told, the Mongolian tradition of chessmen must be considered the most inherently creative in all of chess. Fine sculpture and diversity among the chess pieces is not a special elaboration; it is the cultural norm. Made of wood, stone (soapstone, marble, steatite), bronze (and other metals), and even mammoth bone and ivory, the possibilities of artistic refinement are virtually without bounds.

Finely carved Mongolian chessmen in the "pastoral" style. KNOWLTON PHOTOGRAPH

Even within this great variety, the forms employed in the Mongolian chessmen do conform to aspects of life in the nomadic culture of the steppes. Here are some of the most common figures found on the Mongolian chessboard:

- The royal piece is the *Noyan*, the Chief of the clan. He is usually represented seated on a throne. Sometimes, one of the players possesses a young bare-faced Chief in opposition to an aged, bearded one. In some games, one Chief is a Soviet officer, kolkhoz director or Chinese warlord. The Noyan is the head of the male flank.
- The "Queen" figure is called the *Bers,* and in this game she is a fierce feline predator. The figure may be a Snow Leopard, or a tiger. It can also be depicted as a mythical "snow lion," with a white body and tufts of green hair, or—especially in neighboring Tuva—a ferocious dog *(yt)*. Not uncommonly, it is depicted as the mythical lion-dog ("*fu* dog"), commonly depicted in Chinese sculptures. The Bers is the head of the female flank.

Typical examples of the shatar *Noyan* (left) and *Bers* (right). KNOWLTON PHOTOGRAPHS

- Bishops are Camels (*Temegen*) here. The Camel is the Bactrian sort with two humps, not to be confused with the dromedary, often depicted in the chess sets of India. An essential animal in the nomadic life, this figure replaces the Elephant of shatranj.
- Next in line is the Horse (*Mori*). It is almost always represented without a rider. The noble stature of this beast in Mongolian society cannot be overstated. Sometimes, these pieces depict a stallion on the male flank and a mare on the female side.

## 4. Shatar

Examples of the *Temegen* (left) and *Mori* (right). KNOWLTON PHOTOGRAPHS

- Carts (*Tergen*) stand at the corners of the board. It is with these pieces that the artists take the most liberty. The piece may be represented simply by a cart, standing alone or drawn by a horse or camel—but this piece can also be a Buddhist wheel of dharma, a bicyclist, a car, a truck or a military tank. Even further afield, it may be an elephant, a yak, Garuda (a Buddhist mythical bird), an endless knot,[34] a lotus flower, a bunch of jumping fish, a peacock's tail, a swastika,[35] a spiral, a triskelion (three interlocking spirals), a diamond shape—and many more.

A variety of shatar *Tergen* (Rooks) and *Küü* (Pawns). KNOWLTON PHOTOGRAPHS

- The word for the Pawns indicates that they are Children (*Küü*). But there is an astonishing diversity here again: these children can be small musicians, couples of small wrestlers (a very popular sport in Mongolia) or diminutive versions of a familiar animal species: puppies, colts, camel calves, cow calves, lambs, ducklings, chicks or rabbits. Not infrequently, the Pawns are depicted as babies of their Bers, cubs or puppies—since each one is a potential Bers in the making.

### Names of the Pieces in Shatar (Mongolia) and Shydyraa (Tuva)

| Mongolian name | Tuvan name | Meaning | Modern Equivalent |
| --- | --- | --- | --- |
| *Noyan* | *Nojan* | Chief | King |
| *Bers (1)* | *Yt (2)* | (1) Snow Leopard, (2) Dog | Queen |
| *Temegen* | *Teve* | Camel | Bishop |
| *Mori* | *A"t* | Horse | Knight |
| *Tergen* | *Terge* | Cart | Rook |
| *Küü* | *Ool* | Child | Pawn |

According to the ethnologist and Orientalist Assia Popova, the traditional initial array always puts the Chief at the player's right. This point, originally important in the symbolic organization of the game, has now given way to the convention of modern international chess; it has become usual to place both Chiefs in the same column.[36]

## Rules

MOVES AND CAPTURES. The gender specifications of the right (male) and left (female) sides have a symbolic character only and do not influence the game. Like most forms of chess brought through the years in smaller communities, there is no established body of official rules—the details vary from place to place. It is possible, however, to give the most generally accepted aspects of the traditional rules. The moves of the chessmen are identical to their equivalents in modern international chess, with one considerable exception:

 The Queen is replaced by a *Bers* (Snow Leopard) that (a) moves or captures any number of squares orthogonally (forward, backward, left or right) or (b) steps only one square diagonally. Thus, it combines the moves of the shatranj Counselor and the Rukh.[37]

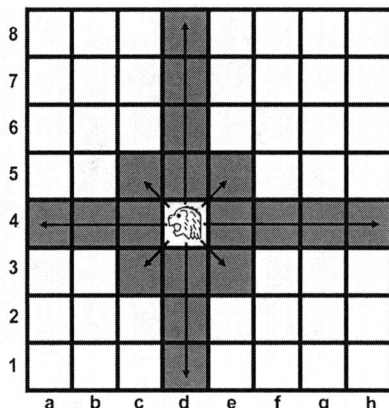

Original Snow Leopard's move.

PARTICULAR RULES. • *The Pawn's initial double step:* in the case where the Chiefs are seated face-to-face in the initial array, the double step is allowed for only one Pawn in the center. It is conventional to start with 1.d2–d4, 1.d7–d5. In the case where the two Chiefs are on the right of their Snow Leopard, the initial double step is not allowed.

- There is no castling and no *en passant* capture in shatar.
- *Pawn promotion:* the Pawn is always promoted to a Snow Leopard when arriving at the last row, without any restrictions.

END OF THE GAME. • There are different forms of check:
  ⊙ *Shak* given by a Snow Leopard, a Cart or a Horse.
  ⊙ *Tuk* given by a Camel.
  ⊙ *Tsod* given by a Pawn.
- Victory is more complex than a mere checkmate. First of all, it is prohibited to checkmate with a Horse.
- To win, it is compulsory to checkmate by a *shak* (check by Snow Leopard or Cart) or by a succession of checks that includes at least one *shak*. For example, if a player checks with a Horse, then with a Pawn and finally mates with a Camel, he wins the game.

- A mate which doesn't fulfill the required conditions is called a "*niol*" and is a draw.
- If there is no Pawn left at the end of the game, it is a draw.
- If a player has his Chief only, and all other pieces have been taken, it is a draw.
- The Chief in stalemate ("*chzhit*") loses the game, because the loss of liberty is considered equal to death by the Mongolian nomadic culture.

SUPPLEMENTARY RULES. Some supplementary rules have been reported by Assia Popova.[38] They are astonishing:

- The Horse can also move like a Bers, starting with its second move and on for the rest of the game. With this move, it becomes the powerful piece.
- The Chief who succeeds in penetrating the eighth and last rank acquires the ability to move like the Horse, in addition to his normal move, thereby becoming very difficult to checkmate.

The Polish ethnologist Iwona Kabzinska-Stawarz has also studied this game and reports different (or complementary) rules in her book *Games of Mongolian Shepherds* (1991)[39]:

- The game always starts by a double step of the Pawn standing in front of the Snow Leopard. The players agree whether this double initial move will be straight, diagonal or a combination of the two.
- A Snow Leopard can only move when all other Pawns or figures have moved.
- A Chief who reaches the eighth row can perform the movements of a Horse (rule similar to Popova).
- A Pawn which reaches the eighth row does not become a Snow Leopard immediately. It must first make one diagonal-step move.

# History

The supplementary rules conveyed by Assia Popova and Iwona Kabzinska-Stawarz (above) are surprising, but not out of place in a land where the horse holds such an important place in culture and history. It is sufficient to recall that from the steppes of Mongolia emerged merciless conquerors: Genghis Khan, Kublai Khan and their line of successors. Thanks to their extraordinary proficiency as horsemen, the Mongolian Empire held domination over Central Asia, Russia, Northern India and China.

Shatar represents the easternmost expansion of Indo-Persian chess, bordering on the other mainstream of chess, the Chinese *xiangqi*. The Italian shatar expert Rodolfo Pozzi made an in-depth study of about 200 sets from three countries that practice this form of chess: Mongolia itself (capital: Ulan Bator), the autonomous region of Inner Mongolia which actually lies in China (capital: Hohhot, with less than 20 percent ethnic Mongolian population today) and the Republic of Tuva, which belongs to the Russian Federation (capital: Kyzyl). The latter is an isolated territory between Siberia and Mongolia, where the inhabitants speak a Turkic language greatly influenced by Mongolian. Further, Murray reported (1913) that the same game spilled over into several other Altaic peoples, from the Kalmyks of the Volga[40] to the Buryats, the Soyots and a number of Siberian tribes, and all the way to Kamtchatka at the eastern tip of the continent. On the southern side, in the Tibetan lands, there were occasional reports in the 18th and 19th centuries of another thread of chess, called *chandaraki*. These reports, endorsed by Murray (1913), seem to depict a chess vaguely similar to the Mongolian chess. The present authors have found no evidence that this has never been confirmed.[41]

In the writings of German zoologist Peter Simon Pallas (1772) can be found the earliest mention of chess among the Kalmyks. However, the origin of shatar may prove to be older. Most probably, the Mongolians brought this game back from their conquests in Central Asia. The word *shatar* appears to be an adaptation of the Arabic *shatranj*, which also came early on to the Turkic peoples as *satranç*.

Brass shatar chessmen with varying pieces on the opposing sides, including horses and camels as Pawns; karmic wheels and bunches of peacock feathers as Rooks. KNOWLTON PHOTOGRAPH

Murray also noted that *Bers* could be a word inspired by a phonetic distortion of the Turkish *Fers*. Shatar's firmly established place in the nomadic Mongolian culture further attests to its antiquity. Assia Popova (1974) reported that chess players always occupy the honorary place in the yurt and that they are allowed to remain seated when a person of superior rank enters the room. There is no family that does not keep a small bag of chessmen, because the artist crafted these miniatures as elements representing the clan itself. This is no handicraft destined to be sold to foreigners (though sometimes they are), but an heirloom to be transmitted from generation to generation, and whose broken or lost pieces will always be repaired or replaced.

## Variant: Hiashatar

As befits a people fascinated by chess, the Mongolians also created an enlarged variant. This traditional game adds a new chessman, the Bodyguard, which has a surprisingly modern-seeming move.

The chessboard possesses 10 × 10 squares and remains monochromatic—not checkered. Each player has twenty chessmen: those of shatar plus a pair of Bodyguards (*Hia*) and the corresponding Pawns.

*Bodyguard:* moves one or two squares diagonally or orthogonally; that is, any direction (but not at an angle like the Knight). However, he is able to capture only by

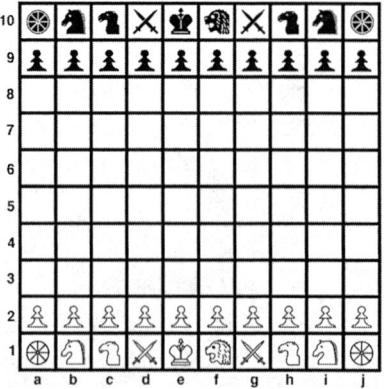

Starting array of Hiashatar.

## 4. Shatar

moving one square diagonally. He does not leap, but may only pass through vacant squares. He also has the special power of arresting the move of any piece which passes through his realm of influence—the eight squares surrounding him. Any piece that aims to pass through one of these squares adjacent to the Bodyguard must stop on that square, until some future move. Nevertheless, this special power does not affect the Horses, which can jump in or out of the Bodyguard's peripheral zone freely.[42]

The diagram below will aid in fully understanding the peculiar features of the Bodyguard's move and his special power:

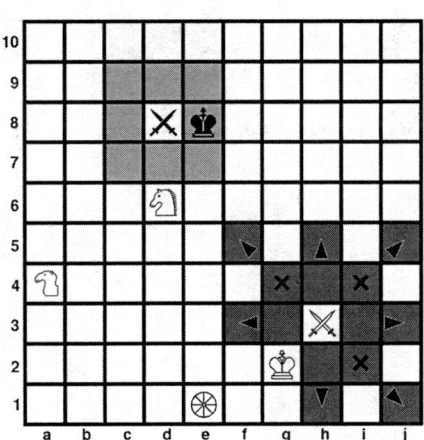

The White Bodyguard can move to any of the dark gray squares. He can only capture pieces on the squares marked "X." Note that he may not jump over a piece, for instance, moving to square f1.

The Black Bodyguard protects his Chief against the attacks of the White Camel, which cannot move beyond d7, and of the Cart, which will be stopped on e7. However, he does not prevent a check by the White Horse.

Other particular rules are:

- The Snow Leopard moves like a modern chess Queen.
- All Pawns can advance one, two or *three* squares on the first move. *En passant* capture is allowed whenever a Pawn advances two or three squares, passing through the capture square of an adverse Pawn.
- There is no castling.
- The Bodyguard cannot capture the opposing Chief, or put him in "check." Therefore, if the players have only their Chiefs and Bodyguard(s) left, the game is a draw.
- The shatar "End of the Game" restrictions do not apply here.

Hiashatar is well documented and several sets are known. Long practiced in Mongolia, its proponents consider it the genuine national game. Tradition holds that it was created 500 years ago, by a great Khan, convinced that the chief's security was always the highest priority.

Mongolian hiashatar in opening array. KNOWLTON PHOTOGRAPH

The particular "End of the Game" rules brought some interest in shatar to the West, where competitions and correspondence tournaments have been organized in recent years. But in Mongolia, Soviet domination has accelerated the adoption of the international chess conventions, notably the checkered chessboard and the modern rules. Still, the manufacture and use of the magnificent Mongolian chessmen persist, to the great pleasure of chess collectors.

*Left:* Mongolian stamps (1981).

## ♦ Part II ♦

# Chess in the Land of Monsoons

The Indian subcontinent yields a diverse and deeply rooted chess history. While many believe India to be the original birthplace of chess, and some will doubt the claim for lack of evidence, the extraordinary history and variety of Indian chess forms is indisputable. From its early traces in Kashmir and the high Ganges Valley, to the Muslim conquerors, to those who fiercely maintained their independence, chess appeared in societies of all types, and in countless permutations.

It should be understood that no two descriptions of chess and its rules prove to be identical. Like other aspects of cultural, the ways of chess varied from place to place and from one age to another. In fact, the modern state of India itself is a relatively recent creation. Within this densely populated country remains a great diversity of peoples, speaking hundreds of languages and practicing countless religious rites. So it has been with the history of chess, parceled out into unknown numbers of variations—only a few of which have been captured and recorded. Though many local chess conventions still survive, they are likely to go the way of minority languages, all being replaced, in this case, by the standard international rules of chess.

Fortunately, for the enduring legacy of chess variants, some of these ancient chess conventions reached beyond the Indian borders, especially in the direction of Southeast Asia, where cultural and economic ties have existed since the first millennium. Through these well-traveled channels came Brahmins who introduced Sanskrit and the Brahmi alphabet. Indian envoys brought their dominant religions, first Hinduism and then Buddhism, which inspired temples and monuments, including the famous sites of Pagan, Angkor and Borobudur. It is most likely that the chess practiced in these countries was also brought through the same cultural flow. These ancient variants evolved further in their new lands to become nationally recognized games, still popular among modern players.

## 5. Chaturanga

According to Arabic tradition, Persians received chess from the Indians. In Kashmir, on the banks of the Indus River or the Ganges, they played *chaturanga*, from a Sanskrit word designating the four-fold army in ancient Indian epics: infantry, cavalry, elephants and chariots.

India is a rich and complex world in which the climate spurs new growth to devour vestiges of the past and where orally transmitted teachings are more common than written language. Under such conditions, it is not surprising that very few written or archeological testimonies on this game remain, and that the rare sources which are found do not agree on the details of the game.

While India has become a powerful force in modern chess, cultivating the massive talent of former World Champion Viswanathan Anand, different sets of rules were common in India at the beginning of the 20th century—at least, in the south of that country. Those were the rules of chess that first spawned the genius of the Mir Sultan Khan (1905–1966), who took the greatest European grandmasters to task from 1930 to 1935. The characteristic rules of Indian chess may well survive in isolated pockets today, but are being quickly overtaken by international standards.

## *Earliest Chaturanga*

Chaturanga was played on the *ashtapada*, the traditional board of India with 8 × 8 squares, formed by embroidered lines on a cloth, or directly drawn on bare ground. Often, several squares were marked with a cross: the four center squares, the two center squares of each side and sometimes at the corners. But the meaning of these markings has been long lost, and they do not affect the play of the game.

In this game, each player has the 16 classic pieces: 1 King (*Raja*), 1 Counselor or Minister (*Mantri*), 2 Elephants (*Gaja* or *Dvipa*), 2 Horses (*Ashva* or *Turaga*), 2 Chariots (*Ratha*) and 8 Pawns (*Padati*). The two sides are colored differently; for instance, one Sanskrit text mentions opposing teams of red and white.

In their initial position, King and Minister are placed at the center of the first row,[1] successively surrounded by the Elephants, the Horses and finally, the Chariots at the corners of the chessboard. Pawns, of course, occupy the second row. Sometimes, players would commence play only after placing their pieces in a configuration known as "*vyuha*." This term referred to the battle arrangement recommended in the *Arthashastra* of Kautilya (around 300 B.C.E.), a famous strategy treatise whose influence extended far beyond the Indian world. Unfortunately, no record remains of how these special configurations were arranged; we only know that one of them was designated as *gomutra*, which means "cow urine." According to Kautilya, *gomutra* indicated a sort of zigzag arrangement of the pieces. Some of these *vyuha* opening positions may have been similar to the Arabic *ta'biyat*.

Initial array of chaturanga according to the *Manasollasa* (1129 C.E. Sanskrit text).

# Rules

MOVES AND CAPTURES. King, Minister, Horse and Pawn follow the same moves of the corresponding pieces in Arabic shatranj. However, the Elephant and the Chariot have exchanged roles.

 *Elephant:* moves like the Rukh of shatranj, i.e., exactly as the modern Rook.

 *Chariot:* this piece, situated at the corners of the board, jumps diagonally over one square to land on the second diagonal square, exactly as the Elephant does in shatranj.

RULES. • *Pawn promotion:* Upon taking its fourth step (arriving on the player's 6th rank, or the opponent's 3rd rank), the Pawn immediately becomes a Minister, even if one or more Ministers are already in play. (It remains a Minister even if it returns to the ranks on which it was formerly a Pawn.)[2]

• *Elephant's jump:* When the Elephant has not yet moved, it has the opportunity to execute its move while leaping over an intervening piece, to arrive on its square. As a manner of quickly getting these powerful pieces into play, this may be done only once with each Elephant, and may not involve a capture. (This is our interpretation of the less specific instruction that "the Elephant may jump to the square of its choice.")

Chariot and Elephant moves.

END OF THE GAME. There are three ways to achieve a victory:

- Checkmate, in which the opponent cannot remove his King from check.
- Suffocation, in which the King is not in check but any possible move will lead to his capture (i.e., stalemated player loses the game).
- Bare King, achieved by capturing all of the opponent's men *except* the King. If only the King is left, the game is lost.

# The History of Chaturanga

The *Manasollasa* (*Joy of the Mind*), is a Sanskrit text composed in 1129 and attributed to the Southwest Indian sovereign, Someshvara III (reigned early 12th century).[3] Therein lies the earliest known Indian description of chess rules. Its historic importance for chess history was revealed only recently by the German historian and Indologist Andreas Bock-Raming, who translated and studied this text in detail. The rules presented here are extracted from his work on the chapter, *Chaturangavinoda* (*Entertainment of Chess*).

The same chapter also mentions chess for four players. Additional chapters of the *Manasollasa* deal extensively with various dice games and race games related to backgammon and finally, a third chess variant, *sarvatobhadra*, which we will describe further. The book is of value not only because of its exposition on contemporary games of the period, but because it presents these games with a genuine Indian character, owing nothing to Persian or Muslim influence.

The history of chess in India, however, is believed to be much older than this rather belated text. Several authors recognize an allusion in the *Harshacharita*, the official history of King Harsha of Kanyakubja (606–648), written in Sanskrit by the court poet, Bana, in about 640. Kanyakubja is the former name of Kannauj, a city at the center of a powerful Indian kingdom in the Gangetic Valley. This historic text associated the words *chaturanga* and *ashtapada* in a context which may indicate chess. Full of puns and double meanings, typical of the style of Sanskrit literature, its interpretation remains difficult. This text is discussed in detail in the last part of this book.

Later, in the middle of the ninth century, two incontestable references to chess appear in the Kashmiri poems, Ratnakara's *Haravijaya* and Rudrata's *Kavyalamkara*. These mentions, however, do not give clues as to the rules of the game. Throughout India's classic and medieval periods, mentions of chess are very few and remain superficial.

More informative are the testimonies of travelers relating the curious details of this foreign land. The first was al-'Adli, in the ninth century, reporting that the Indian Elephant occupied the chessboard corners and moved horizontally or vertically two squares, jumping over the intermediate square. With such a move, it could reach sixteen squares on the entire chessboard, twice the coverage of the Elephant of shatranj, giving it a fighting value approximately equal to that of the Minister. Also of interest, al-'Adli asserts that the player who was put into stalemate won the game instead of losing it. Unfortunately, this Arabic manuscript provides only fragmentary information. It is not known, for instance, whether the Elephants being described begin the game in the corners or beside the Kings and Ministers.

Terracotta elephant found in Northern India, estimated to be from the fourth century C.E.

Its function is unknown but some historians believe that it might have been used to play a predecessor of chaturanga. M.A.J. EDER/FSG PHOTOGRAPH

The second observer was the great Persian scientist and scholar al-Biruni, who visited Punjab, North India, around the year 1030. He reported that the Indian Elephant combined the moves of the Minister and the Pawn, able to move one square diagonally or one square straight forward. These five possibilities were said to correspond to the elephant's five limb: four legs plus the trunk.

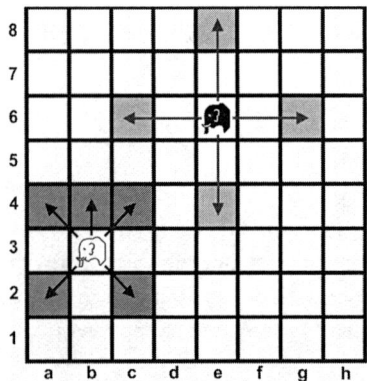

Move of the Elephant in Indian chess according to al-'Adli (on e6) and al-Biruni (on b3).

It can be seen from these accounts that no constant rules governed the moves of the pieces at this stage of chess's development. In fact, an impressive diversity of rules can be found, depending upon the time and place where the game was observed. This diversity seems to have played out most particularly in India, where it appears that the Elephant and Chariot were looking for their definitive moves and placement on the chessboard. The reality of military evolution may have played a part in these changes. While Indian armies were organized around thousands of war elephants up to the 16th century, the war chariot had fallen into obsolescence by the second or third century C.E.

# Traditional Indian Chess

## Chess Goes South

Before the year 1000 or 1100, reports of chess come exclusively from the northern parts of India. But from the 12th century onward, the *Manasollasa* indicates that chaturanga had spread further south into the subcontinent.[4] The *Payyannur Pattu*, written in the 13th or 14th century is the earliest evidence of chess in Southern India. It was written in the Dravidian language of Malayalam, in the southwestern coastal state of Kerala. This horrifying tale revolves around a heroine, Nilakesi, who avenges the death of her brother, at the hands of her husband, by killing her own son. All of the pieces are named: King (*Mannava*), Minister (*Mantri*), Horse (*Kutira*), Elephant (*Varana*), Chariot (*Ther*), and Footmen (*Natakkum chevakan*). Around 1450, the Jain Sanskrit text, the *Pañcha Danda Chattra Prabandha*, (also known as *Tales of King Vikramaditya's Magic Umbrella*), lists all of the pieces needed to play *buddhidyuta*, the "intellectual game." It is doubtlessly a reference to two-handed chess (because a Counselor is included in the set),[5] and is played without dice.

Further evidence of chess in 16th century Southern India has been unearthed in recent years. The *Chaturangastaka*, a work by the celebrated Keralan scholar, Melpathur Narayana Bhattathiri, describes the rules of a game very similar to the Muslim shatranj,[6] but allowing the first-played Foot Soldier to move two squares forward.

THE INDIAN RULES OF THE 17TH CENTURY. From the early 17th century, details of local chess rules appear in the *Bhagavantabhaskara*, an encyclopedia of traditions, laws and political morals composed by Bhatta Nilakantha.[7] In the chapter "Nitimayukha," detailed rules are given of this *krida buddhibalashrita* ("the intellectual game").[8] A few things had changed since the rules appeared in the *Manasollasa*, some 500 years previously:

- The players start with a double movement, advancing the Minister (*Mantri*) and the Pawn (*Patti, Padati*) before him two steps straight ahead.
- Some Pawns can take a double step on their first move (the rules are not clear on which Pawns have this privilege).
- The Pawn is promoted when reaching the last row. If it lands on a square decorated with an "X," it is promoted at once on that square. Otherwise, it is sent back to its original square (from the opening array), and is promoted there. In either case, it becomes a Minister (moving one step diagonally).
- Checkmate and the perpetual check are considered full victories, whereas baring the opponent's King only procures a half victory.

- The player put in stalemate is allowed to remove one of the adverse pieces limiting his King's mobility, and to move the King onto the safe square which has been created.

In this version, the Elephant (*Danti*), like a modern Rook, begins at the corners of the chessboard, while Camels (*Ushtra*) begin alongside the King and Minister and jump two squares diagonally. In the opening array, the Kings face each other.

But differing accounts continue to come from further reports. In the early 18th century, the *Chaturangavinoda* (*The Entertainment of Chess*), a treatise by Vaidyanatha Payagunda from Varanasi, reports that the Chariot (*Ratha*) begins in the corner and jumps diagonally, and that the Elephant (*Dvipa*), begins beside the King and Minister (*Mantri*), and has the long, orthogonal move. Unexpectedly, the Minister is allowed to move on the long diagonals exactly like the modern Bishop. The diversity of chess in ancient India offers surprises at every turn.

## *Traditional Indian Chess in Modern Times*

The great diversity of chess in India did not cease with the arrival of the modern all-powerful Queen and long ranging Bishop.[9] On the contrary, it caused the conventions of chess to multiply further as every community developed or adopted its own rules. Will the international standard ever extinguish these regional variations? One cannot be certain. In spite of the widespread dominance of the international form, Indian society remains extremely complex. In many states and regions, traditional chess forms are very much alive.

INDIAN CHESSMEN. There are basically two types of traditional Indian chessmen. One consists of abstract pieces, basically derived from the old Arab style, except that the V-shaped Rook has been replaced with a flat-topped cylindrical figure. The other line of Indian sets is composed of figurative pieces in which the *Raja* (King) and his Minister (Queen) are perched on howdahs, borne on the backs of elephants. In these sets, an Elephant begins in the corner of the board and has the move of a Rook, a Horse has the starting place and the move of the Knight, and a Camel has the place and move of the Bishop.

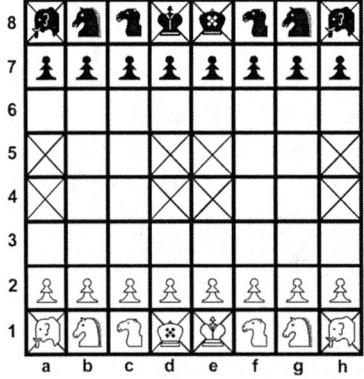

Initial array of traditional Indian chess.

Except for the position of the white King and Minister (which would be on d1 and e1 respectively), it is also the starting position of buddhibala described in the Nitimayukha (17th century).

Although this is the most common traditional Indian array, there are still numerous variations. In Bengal, for instance, two Ships stand in the Rooks' corner squares while a pair of Elephants frame the King and Minister. In Andhra Pradesh, a Southern Dravidian state,[10] the Elephants start in the corners but Chariots stand in the squares we usually hold for Bishops. In any case, the moves of the pieces remain aligned with modern chess: the corner pieces move continually along the horizontal and vertical lines, whereas those situated beside the royalty command the diagonals.

# 5. Chaturanga

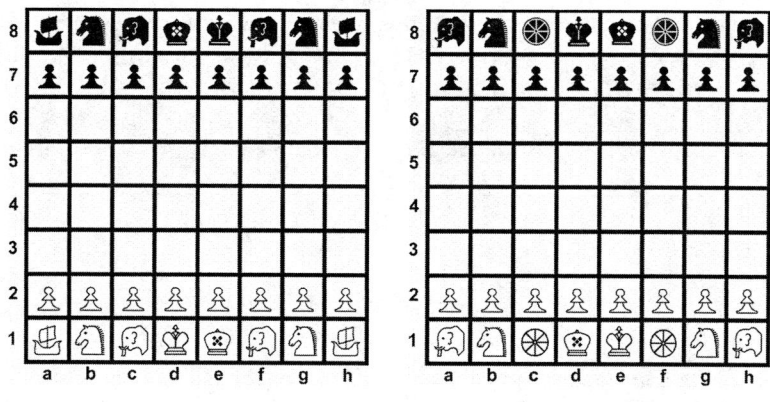

Initial array in Bengal.　　　Initial array in Andhra Pradesh.

Most often, the opposing forces are green against red. The board or playing mat is plain and uncheckered, with certain squares marked by "X's." These "X" markings serve only as a traditional design and do not affect the game.

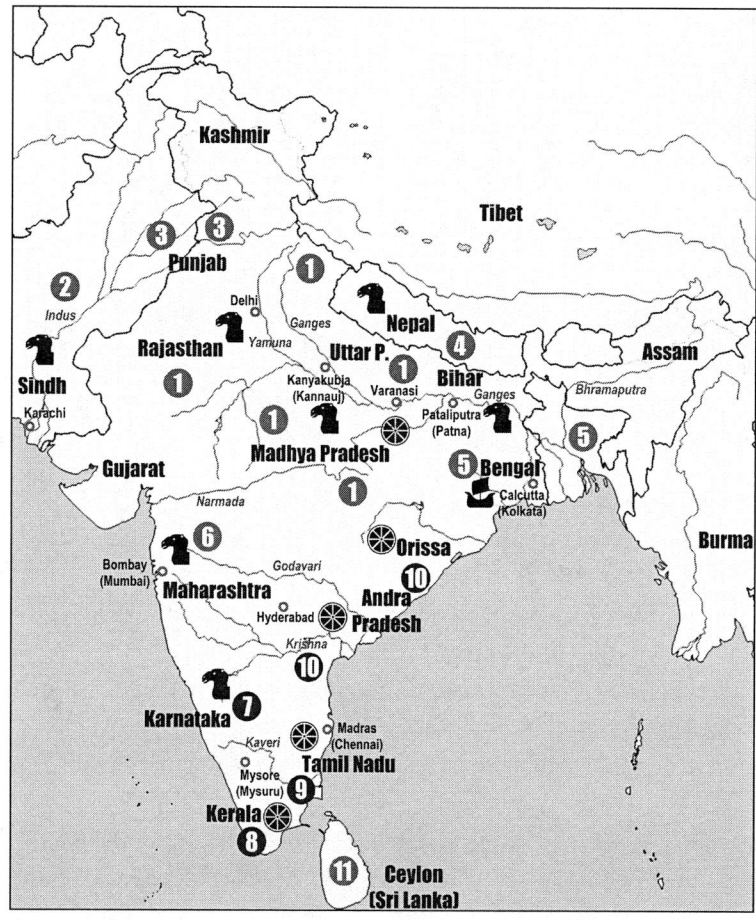

Map of the Indian subcontinent showing where Camel, Chariot or Boat are present in the dominant nomenclature. The circled numbers refer to the languages presented in the tables on page 54.

*Names of the pieces and of the game itself in several Indian languages.*
*In English: (1) Minister, (2) Queen, (3) Camel, (4) Chariot,*
*(5) Horse, (6) Elephant, (7) Ship, (8) Police, (9) Castle*

| Hindi name<br>1 | Urdu name<br>2 | Punjabi name[11]<br>3 | Nepali name<br>4 |
|---|---|---|---|
| Raja | Badshah | Shah, Raje | Raja |
| Vazir (1), Rani (2) | Wazeer (1) | Vazira (1) | Mantri (1) |
| Umt (3) | Oont (3) | Fila[12] | Unta (3) |
| Ghora (5) | Ghoraa (5) | Ghore (5) | Ghoda (5) |
| Hathi (6) | Haathi (6) | Hathi (6), Rukha | Hatti (6) |
| Pyada, Sainik | Sapahi, Piyada | Piada | Prahari (8) |
| **Shatranj** | **Shattrannj** | **Shataranja** | **Buddhical** |

| Bengali name<br>5 | Marathi name<br>6 | Kannada name<br>7 | Malayalam name<br>8 |
|---|---|---|---|
| Raja | Raajaa | Raja | Rajav |
| Mantri (1), Rani (2) | Vjiir (1) | Rani (2) | Rajñi (2), Mantri (1) |
| Hati (6) | Untt (3) | Onte (3) | Ana (6) |
| Ghora (5) | Ghoddaa (5) | Kudure (5) | Kutira (5) |
| Nouka (7), Ruka | Httii (6) | Ane (6) | Ter (4) |
| Bore, Pana | Pyaade | Padaati | Kaalaall |
| **Daba** | **Buddhibll** | **Chaduramga** | **Chaturamgakkali** |

| Tamil name<br>9 | Telugu name<br>10 | Sinhala name[13]<br>11 | Modern equivalent |
|---|---|---|---|
| Araçan | Raju | Raju | King |
| Araci (2) | Mamtri (1) | Rajana (2) | Queen |
| Theer (4), Mandhiri (1) | Shakatu (4) | Dewagathi | Bishop |
| Kudhirai (5) | Gurram (5) | Naytwaraya | Knight |
| Yanai (6), Kottai (9) | Enugu (6) | Maligawa (9) | Rook |
| Cippay, Kalal | Bamtu | Pon | Pawn |
| **Chaturankam** | **Chadarangam** | **Ches** | **Chess** |

RULES. • The pieces move as they do in modern Western chess.

- The two Kings do not face each other. In Bengal, the King is at Minister's left; elsewhere, the King is at Minister's right.[14]
- At the beginning of the game, each player completes three consecutive moves, without capture, before the start of normal play.
- The King can jump like a Horse one time in the game, provided that he has not yet been put in check.[15] He may not capture in this move.
- The Pawn is not allowed a double step; it always moves one square at a time.[16]
- There is no castling, and *en passant* capture does not apply.
- Pawn promotion follows strict guidelines. Upon reaching the end of the board, a Pawn may only promote to the type of piece which starts on that square. The Pawn on the Horse file, for instance, must promote to a Horse. The Pawn promotes to a Minister when it lands on either the King's or Minister's square. Promotion may take place only if one of the promotional pieces has already been captured; otherwise, the Pawn must remain immobile on the

promotional square. A Pawn landing on the "Bishop's" square (a Camel, Elephant or Chariot, depending upon the regional variation) may promote only if the player does not have a "Bishop" piece that could possibly reach that square. In modern parlance, this would be like saying that a player may not have two "black Bishops" or two "white Bishops" (which is legal in modern Western chess).

- The Pawn that promotes to a Horse leaps immediately from that square, as a Horse, without waiting for the next turn.
- A player in a position of stalemate is allowed to remove one of the adverse pieces from the board that prevents his King from moving. He then moves the King, and the game continues.
- If one player loses all of his pieces other than Pawns, the game is a draw. This sort of draw is known as "*burj*."
- Not all checkmates are given the same value. The most highly prized mate is delivered by a Pawn or by the piece equivalent to the Bishop. Other mates are of lower worth.

Although these rules constitute the core of traditional Indian chess, regional variants persist in the details of the game. There is no over-arching body declaring an official set of rules for all players.

Complete Indian set in copper and brass. KNOWLTON PHOTOGRAPH

STRATEGY. The rules of the King's starting position and his Knight's leap, as well as the Pawn's single-stepping limitation, make Indian chess significantly different from its European cousin. But the possibilities of the *burj* draw and the rules of Pawn promotion give the Indian endgame a dynamic all its own. The *burj* rule creates very different endgames than those seen in modern international chess. When one player is down to a single piece (other than King and Pawns), the capture of that piece creates an immediate draw. This last piece is called "immortal" ("*mastu*"), and it can go on a devastating attacking spree, essentially invulnerable to capture. The player striving to win must avoid leaving his opponent with such a terrible rampaging piece, especially taking care that the opponent is not left with an uncapturable Minister (Queen) or Elephant (Rook).

Another interesting aspect of the game is the difference in Pawn promotion. It is often worthwhile to sacrifice a piece, simply to put a threatening Pawn onto a file in which it promotes to one of the less powerful pieces.

The following example, borrowed to Pritchard, shows the *burj* rule in action.

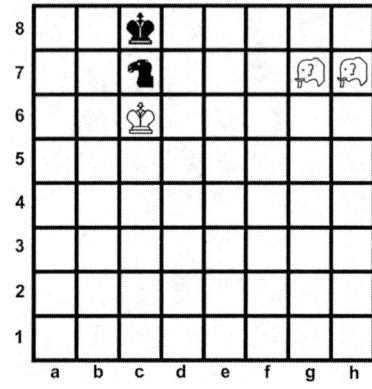

The Elephant and Camel here have the moves of Rook and Bishop, respectively.

The solution to this problem starts with[17]: **1. Eh8+ Cd8 2. Ec7+ Kb8.**

At this moment, capturing Camel on d8 (which would give checkmate at Western chess) would be a *burj*, stripping the black King of his last other-than-Pawn piece—only a draw! This is something White must not allow.

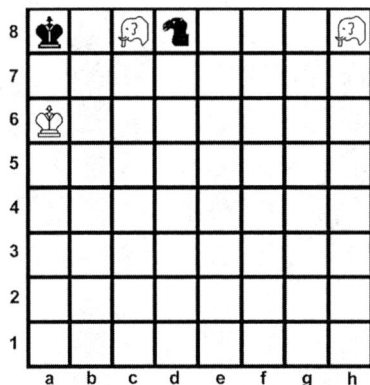

3. Kb6 Ka8
4. Ka6 Kb8
5. Ec6 Ka8
6. Ec8 mate

Finally, White wins!

Traditional Indian chess set, carved sandalwood.
KNOWLTON PHOTOGRAPH

# 5. Chaturanga 57

# Related Games

## Maddat Mari: a Variant

Also known as *joara-joari* and enjoyed by many Indian players, this variant forbids the capture of a protected piece. Moreover, the King can only move when checked. The capture of a protected piece is only allowed if it simultaneously creates a discovered check. Players have reported that the games can last several days!

## Sarvatobhadra or "Maharaja and the Sepoys"

Alternative forms of chess have always had a popular place in the Indian canon of games. As early as the 12th century, the *Manasollasa* mentions a variant for four players (detailed later in this book), as well as this curious asymmetrical game.

This game's name, *sarvatobhadra,* means *"auspicious on all sides,"* indicating the powerful move of the lone Black King, or *Maharaja*. Who has the upper hand in such a contest?

In this 12th century game, White has a full set of pieces, while Black has only the lone King—the all-powerful Maharaja. To begin, the Maharaja is freely placed on any square of the chessboard, while the White pieces are placed in their normal starting array. The Maharaja may move like any of the pieces on the chessboard, while the White pieces have the old moves of the Indian game of the time. Pawns, however, may not promote. White moves first. In the original text, the game is played with dice.[18]

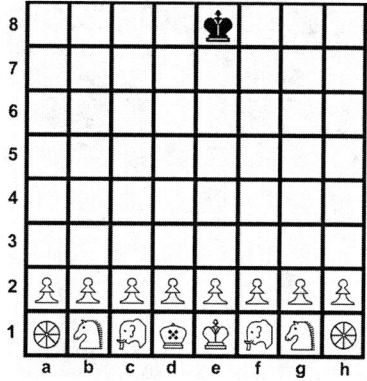

Starting position: the lone Maharaja facing the horde.

This wildly asymmetrical contest proves to be surprisingly balanced. The black Maharaja must be careful not to become blocked within an ever-constricting area. He often wins by forcing the White King into a series of checks, while gradually depleting the White forces. White, on the other hand, will endeavor to keep all of his forces cohesively guarded, while gradually closing in on the Maharaja. Only if White plays with the greatest of care is he likely to triumph over the wild Black King.

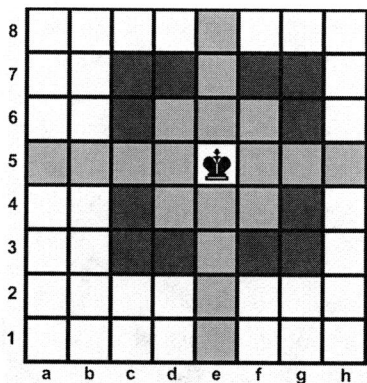

The Maharaja moves without jumping to any of the light gray squares and jumps to the dark gray squares. Note that, in this open position, he attacks 30 of the chessboard's 64 squares.

This game has resurfaced in a modern form in recent centuries. A 19th century Indian encyclopedia of games, the *Kridakaushalya* (1871), by Harikrishna, revives this game with the modern moves of the chessmen. In this version, the Maharaja has the moves of the modern Queen and Knight. This same game appears in the early 20th century treatise, *Mo'allim ul shatranj* (1901) published in Delhi by Lala Raja Babu, under the name of *shatranj diwana shah* (mad king chess). This is the very game that was first described in the West by Edward Falkener as "the Maharaja and the Sepoys," in 1892. It is still popular among chess students of all ages, seeking something different and exciting with a standard set of chessmen.

Indian chessboard and set, painted wood.
KNOWLTON PHOTOGRAPH

## The Modern History of Indian Chess

The long history of the Indian subcontinent attests to an ongoing series of invasions from the west. Turks, Afghans and Persians each left their mark in successive centuries. Beginning in the 12th century, a relatively stable period took hold, with Islam established as Northwest India's dominant religion. The Persian language had become the lingua franca of the Mughal Empire, allowing trade and diplomacy between India's disparate cultural groups, long before English took on that role.

Along with Muslim culture came the Arab form of chess. This type of chess became known in India as *rumi*, an Arabic term indicating Byzantine, pointing to a Western source as its own origin. At the same time, indigenous Indian rules of chess were observed locally, subject to the influence of the Arab and European game, but still following their unique evolutionary paths.

By the 19th century, India was under British rule and was hosting two major chess forms, one more influenced by the Arab game, and one showing a greater European influence. Both forms followed the custom spread during the 19th century into Turkey, Palestine, Persia and India of having the King facing the Minister at the start of the game (usually the Minister was placed on the left by both players); however, they were played quite differently. The Arab-influenced *rumi* chess was played with the limited moves of the old game,[19] while the modernized European-influenced game was played with the long and powerful moves of the new Queen and Bishop.

In the present day, with increased immigration and widespread electronic communication, it is possible to find many accounts of the older Indian forms of chess, which were still prevalent in the mid–20th century. It has been recently reported that chess was known as *chadarangam* in

Telugu, the language of Andhra Pradesh. *Rumi* chess has been reported in the 20th century in Tamil Nadu and in Kerala, two other Dravidian states. Typical pieces were crudely made from plantain stem, very similar to those manufactured in some Indonesian islands.

Chaturanga in Sanskrit.

There is no place on earth more intrinsically diverse and convoluted in its chess traditions than the magical and mysterious subcontinent of India. Even if the original source of chess is forever lost in an endless entanglement of legends and tales, India remains the fertile ground in which games are spontaneously created and reborn, in an endless process of adaptation and renewal.

# 6. Chaturaji

*Chaturaji* means "four kings," as is made clear by the layout of this four-handed chess variant. Early chess historians were often tempted by the simple structure of this game and its use of dice, imagining that it could have been a logical precursor of the later two-player chess of pure strategy. Although it is now understood that the two-handed game preceded all accounts of chaturaji by several centuries, this charming game for four has accumulated about a thousand years of reports attesting to its sustained popularity.

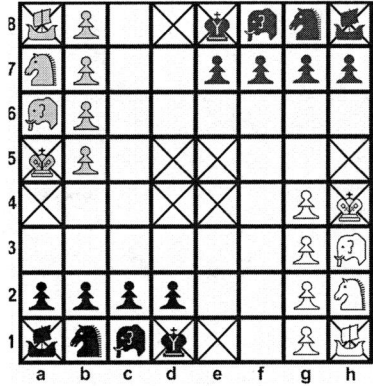

Initial array of chaturaji.

## Material

Chaturaji[20] is played by four players in two teams, on a board of 8 × 8 squares.

Each player has 8 pieces: 1 King (*Raja*), 1 Elephant (*Gaja* or *Hasti*), 1 Horse (*Ashva*), 1 Boat (*Nauka*)[21] and 4 Pawns (*Vati*). The allies are seated facing each other. The colors of the pieces are arranged clockwise in this order: red, green, yellow and black. The players take turns, proceeding clockwise, beginning with a move by Red.

## Rules

We have two sources for the rules of chaturaji. The first is a travel report from al-Biruni; the second is the *Tithitattva*, a Sanskrit poem by Raghunandana (detailed below). Although these two sources are separated by a span of five hundred years, they are very consistent and complement each other in the reconstruction of this ancient game.

In order to make the rules fully practicable, a few details have been added in the following instructions.[22] For clarity, these insertions, not from the original source material, are given in brackets.

THE USE OF DICE. • The choice of the piece to move is determined by the throw of two oblong dice.[23] Each die shows four surfaces marked with the numbers 2, 3, 4 and 5. The 2 and 5 are on opposite faces, as are the 3 and 4. If a standard cubic die is used, the player may simply throw again if a 1 or 6 appears.

- A designated piece indicated by the number thrown must be moved, if such a piece is in play and if it has a legal move. The move must be made even if it is to the player's disadvantage.
- On each turn, the player throws both dice, moving a piece for each die that shows an allowable move. Often, two pieces are moved in a single turn. If only one die indicates a possible move, only that one move is made, or if neither die indicates a possible move, the player must pass.
- If doubles are thrown, the same piece may be required to move twice.

MOVES AND CAPTURES

*King:* moves on the throw of 5 [see also the Pawn, below]. He moves one step in any of the eight directions. The King's starting square is called the *Throne.*

*Elephant:* on the throw of 4, any number of unobstructed squares in the horizontal and vertical directions, just as the modern Rook.

*Horse:* moves on the throw of 3, exactly like a modern Knight, two squares orthogonally plus one at a right angle. The Horse jumps freely over any pieces in its path.

*Boat:* moves on the throw of 2, exactly two squares diagonally. This piece jumps over any piece in its way.

*Pawn:* moves on the throw of 5. It moves one step forward, toward the allied camp. The Pawn captures by moving one square diagonally forward, precisely as in modern Western chess. When the number 5 is thrown, the player actually has a choice between moving the King or a Pawn [if both types of piece are in play].

All pieces, including the King, may be captured; the idea of checkmate does not exist in chaturaji.

## Specific Rules

### PAWN'S PROMOTION: SHATPADA ("THE MOVE OF SIX SQUARES")

- If a Pawn reaches the opposite side of the board on a file corresponding to a Horse or an Elephant[24] (for example, b8, c8, f8 or g8 for Black in the diagram), it is promoted to a Horse (file b or g) or an Elephant (file c or f). However, the promotion is forbidden if the player has three or four Pawns still in play.
- [In that situation, where promotion is forbidden, the Pawn that has reached the 7th rank

- remains on its square, and only when other Pawns of its side are captured may it move to the final square and be promoted.]
- A Pawn reaching the far side of the board in the Boat or King file (for example, a8, d8, e8, or h8), may only promote if the player has only a Boat and the one Pawn at most, in addition to his King, still on the board (so the Player has already lost his Horse, Elephant, and all three additional Pawns). At that moment, the lucky Pawn is called a *Gadhavati* (a "strong" Pawn). It may promote to any piece, including to a Boat, or even to an additional King.

NAVAL BATTLE: VRIHANNAUKA ("THE BOAT'S TRIUMPH")

- Because of their limited two-square diagonal leap, the Boats never meet each other on the chessboard. But if all four Boats converge on adjoining squares, filling in a perfect 2 × 2 square area, the last Boat to arrive captures all three other Boats, removing them from the board.

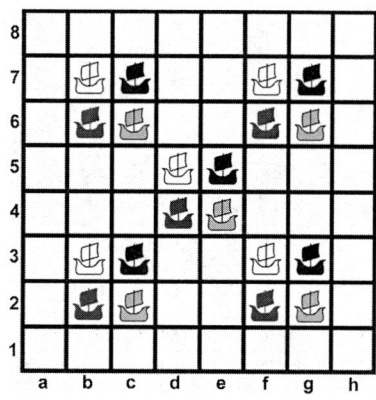

There are only five areas on the chessboard where a naval battle can occur.

SINHASANA ("A THRONE"). • When a King enters the throne of one of the adverse players [i.e., moves the King onto the starting square of an opposing King], his player wins one stake. If he captures the adverse King at the same time, he wins two stakes.
- When a King moves onto the ally's throne, the player wins one stake and takes the control of his partner's troops. [He also takes his ally's turn of play, so that on both his turn and his ally's turn, he may choose to move either his own or his ally's pieces].

CHATURAJI ("THE FOUR KINGS"). • A player who succeeds in taking control of his ally's army and in capturing both adverse Kings achieves *chaturaji*, winning one stake.
- If a player captures both adverse Kings with his own King, then he wins two stakes, and wins 4 stakes if these captures took place on the thrones.
- If *sinhasana* and *chaturaji* are reached at the same time, only *chaturaji* is counted.

NRIPAKRISHTA ("EXCHANGE OF KINGS")[25]. [A captured King is prisoner. His owner's pieces are immobilized but can be captured. His turn of play is lost and his ally fights alone against other two.]
- If a player succeeds in capturing both adverse Kings, but his own allied King has also been captured, he may declare an exchange of Kings. In this case, the allied King and one of the enemy Kings are returned to the board. [They are replaced on original throne squares, or on an adjacent square if the throne square is occupied].

- If a King is made prisoner a second time, he may no longer be exchanged—he is out for the rest of the game.

BARE KING: KAKAKASHTHA ("A DRAW"). • A player having only his King left can retire. For him, the game is a draw, unless an adverse King achieves, on the same turn, a *sinhasana* (meaning that he takes the player's last piece on his throne). *Sinhasana* has priority over *kakakashtha*, which in this case would mean the game is lost for the player left with only a King.

END OF THE GAME. The game ends when one of the teams is completely depleted, either by retiring (*kakakashtha*) or by having the Kings captured. At that point, the stakes are counted to see which side has won the most.

Al-Biruni indicates another manner of calculation: the Pawn is worth 1, the Chariot (equivalent to the Boat) 2, the Horse 3, the Elephant 4 and the King 5. In addition, the player capturing the three other Kings wins 54 points, which represents, by the way, the total of points of the three other armies combined.

## *Tactics*

The game with dice allows limited freedom of choice but a great deal of suspense and surprise. In this way, it brings to mind the great race games of India including *pachisi* (in a cross), *pancha keliya* (along a line) or *thayam* (in a spiral on a 5 × 5 square board), among many others.

Indian sources include some good, sensible advice along with the rules:

- It is necessary to be careful to not to leave Kings, Elephants and Horses subject to capture.
- The King is the most important piece. Immediately following is the Elephant. All other pieces must be sacrificed, if necessary, to save them.
- To obtain a *sinhasana* or a *chaturaji*, all pieces, including the Elephant, may be sacrificed.
- Never let an Elephant be aligned with another Elephant.
- If a player can capture one or the other adverse Elephant, it is preferable to seize the one at his left (since that player has the next move).

The English Orientalist, Duncan Forbes, who showed a passion for this game, proposed an ideal strategic line:

- Bring the two center Pawns to promotion, which will at least double their value.
- Then, bring the King toward the opposite throne in order to take control of the allied pieces. (One might imagine that the allies will appreciate being ejected from the game during this critical moment.)
- Finally, with force and coordination, try to capture the two adverse Kings before they join forces, to achieve *chaturaji*, the supreme victory.

It appears that the English author had not practiced long before giving his sage advice. In fact, chaturaji is a violent scrum in which much of what happens is determined by the fateful turn of the dice. A King or Pawn setting out to reach the other side of the board is embarking on a dubious venture.

Chaturaji without dice is also a historically valid variant, and modern players generally prefer to play without leaving so much to chance. In this case, each player moves one (and only one) piece in each turn. The condition of victory remains the same: winning the most points.

## The History of Chaturaji

Ever since the discovery of chaturaji by European scholars, a simple and pleasingly allegorical story has persisted regarding this game's place in the history of chess. It runs something like this: In the past, feudal warlords vied for power all over India, forming alliances and supplanting each other in endless military campaigns. Borrowing the board and dice from popular race games, chaturaji, the four-player chaturanga, was a natural expression of the unsettled times of multi-lateral military struggles. Later, as sage disciples of Manu and Zoroaster instilled more civil and contemplative ways among the people, dice were abandoned and the four armies were joined into two, competing on a level of pure reason. Chess was born!

THE END OF A MYTH: FOUR-PLAYER CHATURANGA IS NOT THE PROGENITOR OF CHESS. This elegant and seductive theory of chess origins captured the imagination of several British scholars[26] throughout the 19th century, raising the modest variant chaturaji as the forefather of all chess forms. Still today, this fledgling hypothesis of chess genealogy is often repeated, even in the most learned circles.

Entrenched though the theory of chaturaji's primacy has become, it is soundly refuted by further investigation. In particular, H.J.R. Murray clarified the question in his 1913 masterwork *A History of Chess*, and it is discussed at some length in the final part of the present book. All evidence now supports the view that this game is merely an intriguing medieval variant of chaturanga for two players.

The earliest written report of chaturaji remains a travel log: *Tahqiq ma li-l-Hind*, by the Persian al-Biruni, reporting from Punjab in 1030. That was about four hundred years after two-handed chess, with no die, is known to have existed in Persia.

The first Indian writer known to have mentioned the four-handed game was King Someshvara, in the *Manasollasa*, dated about 1129. But in that version, it is a Chariot that stands in the corners of the chessboard. Surprisingly, the pieces are of only two colors, red and white, and the game is played without dice. About this same time, chaturaji is mentioned in Kashmir, in the *Rajatarangini* (*The River of Kings*)[27] by the Brahmin, Kalhana.

There are then no reports for a long interval, until the game appears again in the *Tithitattva* of the Bengalese poet Raghunandana, dating from the end of the 15th or beginning of the 16th century. This text tells the famous story[28] of King Yudhisthira, devoured by the passion for gaming, who had lost both his kingdom and his wife in games of dice—and won them back again. He then wanted to learn (four-handed) chaturanga in order to stake all of his worldly possessions once again. Vyasa, his assistant, taught him the rules and some very valuable strategic advice. Nevertheless, Yudhishthira lost everything at this game dominated by chance. He was exiled far off, into a deep forest, along with his four brothers. It is to this text, which Forbes believed to be much older, that we owe the details of the rules presented here.

From the same period, the *Chaturangadipika* (*The Light of Chess*) by Shulapani presents a version of the game very similar to that given in the *Tithitattva*. It has been suggested by the German Indologist Bock-Raming that Shulapani may have copied Raghunandana's description. This text was unknown to Western scholars until 1936.

At the turn of the 20th century, four-handed versions of chess were still popular in the British Indies, most notably in Bengal. Murray collected the accounts of several witnesses to the game in his time. All of these more recent reports attest to a game played without dice, played in teams with partners facing each other across the board. A typical two-handed set of pieces was used, with the Queens (Ministers) serving as Kings on the partner's side. Victory was attained simply by capturing both adverse Kings, or leaving them bare, with no remaining forces.

The game of chaturaji recently recreated by Front Porch Classics (now out of production).
KNOWLTON PHOTOGRAPH

Though chaturaji may be only one of many later branches in the long evolution of chess, and though it is all but extinct today, it maintains an important association with Indian culture. Like the other great Indian game of *chaupur* or *pachisi*—recreated in recent times as Parcheesi or Ludo—chaturaji shows the potential for popular games made for four players. In a way, this game parallels the development of modern chess, much as the pachisi games parallel the evolution of backgammon.

# 7. Large and Giant Indian Chess

Perhaps the luxurious life of royalty felt a bit too isolated and removed from the dramas of daily life, causing the princes and regional kings of India to seek out distraction in games and novelties. Chess, of course, with its tiny army of dedicated warriors, was the perfect vehicle for grand dreams of perilous ventures and brilliant paths to victory. Throughout the years of British domination, the crowned heads of the great subjugated lands of the exotic Indies dreamed of chess in ever greater forms, creating a land in which the glory of victorious conquest was laid out beneath their own fingertips.

## *History*

While regular chess is played over the classic board of 64 squares, several attempts have been made to enlarge the game to 100 (10 × 10), 144 (12 × 12) or even 196 (14 × 14) square boards.

Such a curiosity is first encountered in the *Harihara Chaturanga*, a Sanskrit text expounding upon science and military strategy. It was written by Godavaramishra, a scientist, poet and minister to Prince Prataparudra who reigned over Odisha, East India, between 1497 and 1540. The eighth chapter, entitled *Kridapariccheda* (*"Games Chapter"*), details a giant chess-like game which could be considered one of the world's first war simulation games. This game used 64 pieces, all with military identities, moving over a 196-square battlefield. Such a trend has appeared often in Indian variants. It departs from the Arabian, Persian or Turkish large chess inventions, which were extended into a fanciful confrontation of wild and exotic animals.

This giant, militaristic chess variant presents very interesting rules that go beyond the variations found in most of the chess forms in this book. Therefore, for the sake of clarity, this special variant is detailed at the end of the chapter, after a few easier and more recent variants have been presented. Indeed, the *Harihara Chaturanga* presents the earliest recorded proposal to increase chess in complexity by adding many chessmen and playing squares. Such explorations were tried many times in subsequent centuries.

The narrative report of a captive English officer, prisoner of Hyder Ali, sovereign of Mysore in the 1780s, mentioned a gigantic chess with a total of 60 pieces. Unfortunately no details were reported.[29] An even larger chess, *shatranj kabir* (great chess), appeared in a diagram placed in the *Sardarnama* ("*Book of Commanders*"), a Persian manuscript published in 1797 or '98 by Shir Muhammad Khan "Iman," servant of Ali Khan Asaf Jah II (1734–1803), Nizam of Hyderabad in Central India.[30] Each player had 32 pieces, but the details of play were not given. Fortunately, a relatively smaller version, with only 22 chessmen per player, was also reported in the same source, along with 12 problems, which allowed the rules of the game to be revealed.

Reports of Indian chess variants were more complete in the following century. The 18th century saw a greater European influence in what became known as the "British Indies." Powerful Maharajas, wielding less political influence over their own territories, were inclined to cultivate their love of arts and games in their own palaces. One such heir to royalty, Krishnaraja Wodeyar III (1794–1868), Maharaja of Mysore, was a tireless creator of new games. He filled his estate with paintings, engravings and realizations of original games, such as unorthodox pachisis for 6, 8 and even 16 players. He also fostered a handwritten treatise on the games in which the Indian historian Mrs. Rangachar Vasantha presented "galactic chess," designed to be "one of the best in the tradition of chess." The sovereign saw an "evocation of nature and its relations with the positions and movements of the zodiac" in this 12 × 12 chessboard.

Near the turn of the 20th century, two treatises of games and pastimes shed a revealing light on some of these large variants. The *Kridakaushalya*, by Harikrishna from Aurangabad in 1871, and the *Mo'allim ul shatranj*, by Lala Raja Babu in 1901,[31] both described games played on boards of 144 and 196 squares. The latter treatise adds one more game, *atranj*, a variant played on a board of 100 squares. An additional variant, played on a 100 square board according to some rather peculiar rules, was also invented by Madhavrao Datey for the enjoyment of Sayajirao Gaikwad, Maharaja of Baroda.[32]

Following are closer looks at these interesting creations.

# Large Chess on 100 Squares

## Hyderabad Decimal Chess

This 10 × 10 version of chess appears in the *Sardarnama*. Among all the enlarged chess variants, medieval and modern, it is this game that John Gollon, specialist of chess variations, considered the most pleasant to play. He stated that one of his associates became so enthralled with this variant that he entirely abandoned orthodox chess![33]

Initial array of Hyderabad decimal chess.

Each player possesses 1 King, 1 Giraffe, 1 Queen, 1 Vizier, 2 *Dabbabas*, 2 Elephants, 2 Horses, 2 Chariots and 10 Pawns.[34] Both sides have the same arrangement with the Giraffe and Vizier at King's left and the Queen on his right.

Kings, Horses and Chariots are equivalent to European Kings, Knights and Rooks.

Queens and Elephants have the modern moves, identical to modern Queens and Bishops. The Pawn always moves one step forward; the initial double step is not allowed.

The other chessmen are:

  *Dabbaba:* may move like a Rook or like a Knight.

  *Vizier:* may move like a Bishop or like a Knight.

  *Giraffe:* may move like a Queen or like a Knight.

Surprisingly, this game makes use of only one chessman combining Bishop and Knight (the Vizier) and two chessmen combining Rook and Knight (the two Dabbabas)!

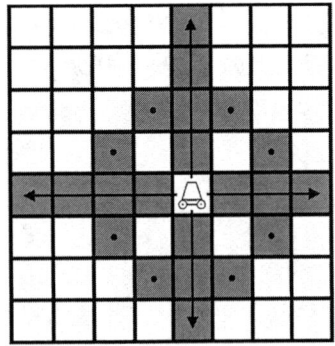 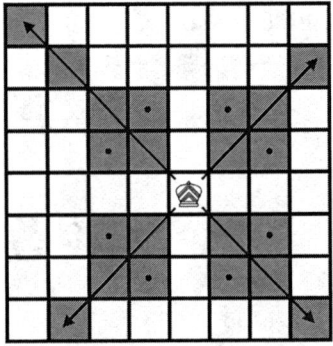 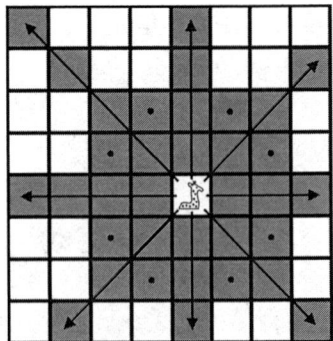

Moves of Dabbaba, Vizier and Giraffe

The relative scale of power is as follows: Giraffe (10.7), Queen (8.2), Dabbaba (7.5), Vizier (6), Chariot (5), Elephant (3.4), Horse (2.6), Pawn (0.6).

PAWN PROMOTION. The actual rule of Pawn promotion has not been recorded for this decimal chess game, nor for the games *atranj* and *shataranja* that follow. In accordance with the general Indian chess tradition (standard as well as variants), it is suggested that a Pawn reaching the opposite edge of the board is promoted to the piece that starts in that file on the player's side, on the condition that this piece has already been captured. For example, a Pawn reaching d10 is promoted to a Vizier. As an additional suggestion, a Pawn reaching f10 (the King's file) is promoted to the piece standing on e2 and f2, in this case, a Dabbaba.

If the piece of the promotion file has not yet been lost, the Pawn must wait on the promotion square until such a piece becomes available.

## *Atranj*

Although a century separates this game from the one just mentioned, the two actually have much in common: 22 chessmen to each player, in a similar arrangement. The main differences are the pieces that occupy the central squares (d1, e1, f1, g1, e2 and f2).

Because this game is relayed to us by Lala Raja Babu, who wrote in Persian, the original names of the pieces bear a Persian nomenclature: King (*Padshah*), Chariot (*Rukh*), Horse (*Ghora*), Elephant (*Fil*), Pawn (*Paidal*). The name of the game is *atranj*, or also *qatranj*, an alteration of the Arabic and Persian word *shatranj*.

A few of the pieces keep the same moves as those of the aforementioned variant, but have different names: Queen, Giraffe and Vizier become, respectively, Vizier (*Wazir*), Prince (*Shahzada*) and Police Chief (*Kotwal*). They are represented by the icons below for sake of consistency with other chess variants found in this chapter.

*Vizier:* stands on d1, g10 and moves like a modern Queen.

*Prince:* stands on e1, f10 and moves like a Queen or like a Knight.

*Police Chief:* stands on g1, d10 and moves like a Bishop or like a Knight.

The difference is the replacement of the two advanced Pawn in e3 and f3 by two additional Horses, and replacement of the two powerful Dabbabas by two "Armed Female Attendants" (*Urdabegini*).

Both sides have the same arrangement with the Prince and Vizier at King's left and the Police Chief on his right.

*Armed Female Attendant*: moves one square toward the enemy King.

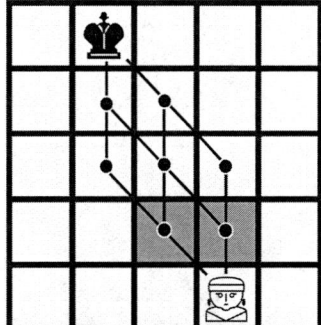

**Right:** The Armed Female Attendant always moves one square toward the opposing King. The different possible paths are illustrated here (providing the King does not move). From each square, the Female Attendant has 1 or 2 possibilities.

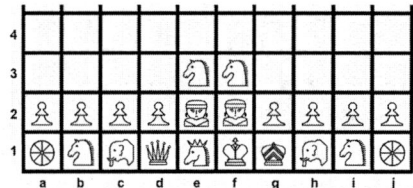
Initial array of atranj.

## Shataranja

The name is simply the literal transcription of the pronunciation of the word *shatranj* in several Indian languages (e.g., Hindi and Punjabi).[35]

This variation is very similar to *atranj*, differing in that the piece on e2 and f2 is a *Begum*, an Indian princess. The piece on d1 remains a Vizier in this variant. The Begum moves one square in any direction, like a King (their relative strength is 3.1). Another small difference with the previous variant: here the King is on e1 and the Prince on f1.

 *Begum*: moves one square in any direction, like a King.

Initial array of shataranja.
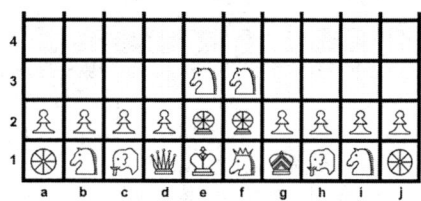

## Atranj, Second Version

Pritchard mentions Goswami, an Indian author who reported this game a little differently: each player has 20 chessmen only, with an extra Minister (moving like a modern Queen) instead of a Police Officer.

Also, in Goswami's game, the *Urdabegs* in e2 and f2 play as extended Pawns which move backward as well as forward. In this case, their relative strength is 1.1).

 *Urdabeg*: moves as a Pawn, but with the additional possibility of moving backward and capturing diagonally backward.

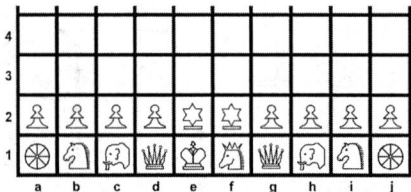
Initial array of atranj, version 2.

## Baroda Chess

As previously mentioned, this variety, invented for the Maharaja of Baroda, deserves to be listed separately. It uses a decimal chessboard (10 × 10 squares) with 30 pieces in each camp.

# 7. Large and Giant Indian Chess

*Right:* Initial array of Baroda chess.

The chessmen employed in this game (other than King and Pawn) are listed here. Some are unique to this game, not found in any other variant.

*Prince:* moves like a Queen or like a Knight.

*Prime Minister:* moves like a modern Queen.

*Chief Army:* moves like a King or like a Camel as in Timur's chess, three squares in an orthogonal direction, plus one step at a right angle, jumping over any intervening pieces.

*Commander:* moves like a Bishop or like a Knight.

*Governor:* moves like a Rook or like a Knight.

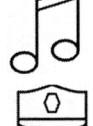
*Bandmaster:* leaps either as a Knight or two squares orthogonally.

*Police:* leaps two squares straight forward or diagonally forward, regardless whether the intermediate square is free or occupied. (This piece becomes immobile when reaching the end of the board. If there existed a continuation of this piece's move, it has been lost.)

*Camel*: moves like a modern Bishop, as in other Indian chess games.

*Horse:* moves like a modern Knight.

*Elephant:* moves like a modern Rook, as in other Indian chess games.

*Citizen:* moves like a King or like a Knight.

The power values are: Prince (10.7), Prime Minister (8.1), Governor (7.6), Commander (6.1), Citizen (6), Chief Army (5.6), Elephant (5), Bandmaster (4.1), Camel (3.4), Horse (2.7), Police (1.1), Pawn (0.6).

PARTICULAR RULES. • The King can move like a Horse but only once in the game.
- Only the a, e, f and j Pawns can move two steps on their first moves.
- Upon reaching the end of the board, a Pawn promotes to become the piece which is originally placed on that file, on the condition that this piece has been already captured. Otherwise, the Pawn must wait on the promotion square until such a piece is available.

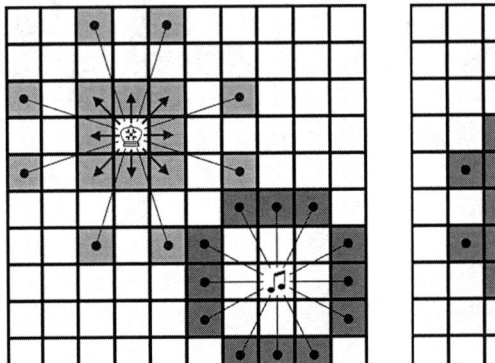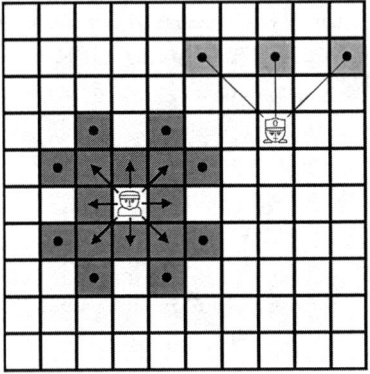

Moves of Chief Army, Bandmaster, Policeman and Citizen.

Having pieces that combine the moves of Queen, Rook and Bishop with that of the Knight, this chess variant seems complete and definitive. The 10 × 10 chessboard is the minimum surface that could practically accommodate such a full assortment of pieces.

# Great Chess on 144 Squares

## Hyderabad Shatranj Kabir

Taking the expansion one logical step further, these great chess variants also place as candidates for the definitive "complete" chess of India. The first which bears mentioning is, unfortunately, incomplete. Murray reports this version from the *Sardarnama* (circa 1798). Three of the chessmen are mentioned only by their abbreviations (*M*, *Shh* and *Wkh*) and the moves remain unknown.[36] The move of the Lion (*Shir*) is also a mystery. The other pieces, which bear the same names as are discussed above in decimal chess, are understood to be identical to those pieces.

(Black is arranged similarly with the King in f12, Lion in i12, M in g11, etc.)

## Galactic Chess

Krishnaraja Wodeyar III (1794–1868), Maharaja of Mysore, has asserted that he was the inventor of this pleasant variant, although his claim cannot be verified. He called it "galactic chess." Harikrishna (1871) and Lala Raja Babu (1901) also described this great 12 × 12 chess, calling it "Mysore chess." The description given here is based on the rendition of Krishnaraja Wodeyar's works as conveyed by the Indian historian, Rangachar Vasantha.

Each player has 24 chessmen: 1 King, 1 Minister, 2 Camels, 2 Chariots, 2 Flags, 2 Horses, 2 Elephants and 12 Soldiers.[37]

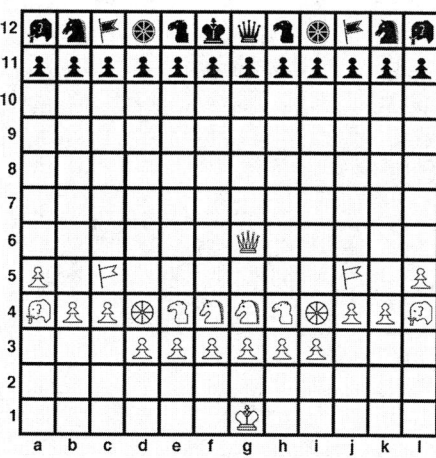

Two different initial arrays of "galactic chess": standard position shown for Black and *garuda vyuha* position shown for White (two different arrays shown here; both players actually start with the same opening position).

RULES. King, Horse and Minister are equivalent to Western King, Knight and Queen, respectively. Considering their position on the board, it is assumed that the Elephant and Camel are equivalent to Western Rook and Bishop, respectively. The Soldier is similar to the Western Pawn except that it never advances two squares in one move. The Chariot and the Flag are original to this variant.

*Minister:* moves as a modern Queen.

*Elephant:* moves as a modern Rook.

*Camel:* moves as a modern Bishop.

*Chariot*: the Indian source says "moves to the fourth square in four directions." It is understood that it leaps three squares orthogonally.

*Flag:* the source says "moves to the third square diagonally." It is understood that it leaps two squares like an Elephant in shatranj.

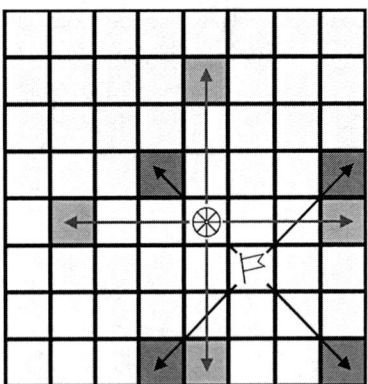

Moves of the Chariot and Flag.

- No rule has been recorded for the Pawn's promotion. It is true that the probability of a Pawn's reaching the opposite side of the board is low. However, it is probably best to adopt the common Indian rule stating that a Pawn promotes to become the piece which is originally placed on that line, on condition that this piece has already been captured; otherwise, the Pawn must wait on the promotion square until such a piece becomes available.

A particular starting array (*vyuha*) was recommended: the one illustrated for White on the initial array diagram. Note that this array corroborates our understanding of the Chariot's and Flag's moves, since they could reach these squares from their standard back rank positions.

The relative values of the chessmen are: Minister (8.3), Elephant (5), Camel (3.4), Horse (2.2), Chariot (1.1), Flag (1), Pawn (0.5).

This game bears a striking resemblance to the *grant acedrex* of Alfonso X, king of Castile, which is described in a later section. A Japanese variant on a 12 × 12 board is also presented.

# *Giant Chess on 196 Squares*

The drive to enlarge the game of chess reached its peak with this extraordinary variant played on a 14 × 14 board of 196 squares. At this pinnacle, even Murray had had enough. He wrote, "*Of the making of these games there need be no end, and I have no doubt that many other varieties have been proposed and perhaps played, of which we have been spared the knowledge.*" The great Murray may have begged for mercy at this point—but perhaps the reader would want to know about it.

The four squares in the center of the board and the two at the center of every side are marked with X's, like the traditional Indian chess mat. Each player has 28 pieces: 1 King, 1 Minister, 1 Queen, 1 Prince, 2 Camels, 2 Chariots, 2 Flags, 2 Horses, 2 Elephants and 14 Pawns. They are arrayed in as shown in the diagram, with the Kings facing Ministers across the board.[38]

Chessmen from the 144-square galactic chess keep the same moves. The two supplementary pieces are the Prince and an Indian Queen that is quite different from the modern Queen and thus is represented here with a different icon. The piece that moves like the modern Western Queen is again a Minister, and is represented here with a Queen icon for sake of consistency with other chess variants.[39]

 *Prince:* moves as Queen or as a Knight

*Minister:* moves as a modern Queen.

*Queen:* moves as the King, one square in any direction.

- Again, no rule has been recorded for the Pawn's promotion, which is even less likely to occur here than in the 12 × 12 variant. In order to complete the game, the following rule may be observed: a Pawn promotes to become the piece which is originally placed on that file (seen from the player's side), on the condition that this piece has already been captured; otherwise, the Pawn must wait on the promotion square until such a piece becomes available.

The power scale of the chessmen is the following: Prince (10.2), Minister (8.3), Elephant (5), Camel (3.4), Queen (2.2), Horse (1.9), Chariot (1), Flag (0.9), Pawn (0.4).

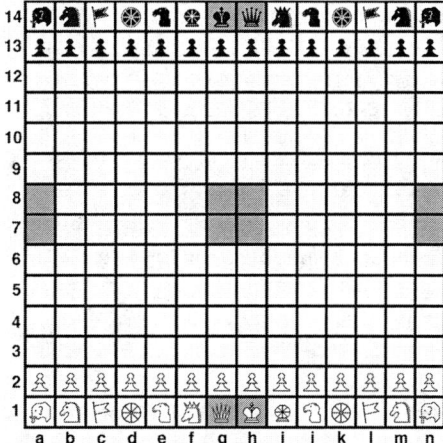

Initial array of Indian giant chess.

This extreme variant was mentioned in the two books already discussed above, by Harikrishna and Lala Raja Babu. Unfortunately, some uncertainty remains as to the exact moves of the pieces. Either the Elephant or Chariot could have the move of the Rook; the Camel or Flag could have the move of the modern Bishop, and the Prince or Minister could have the move of the modern Queen. It runs contrary to the pervading formulation of chess variants to give the same move to pieces of differing identities, so one has to ask which pieces did in fact have the familiar moves, and what moves might have been assigned to the remaining pieces. Unfortunately, the two sources for this game showed a lack of clarity in describing the moves of the Flag and Chariot for the 144 square variant, so we do have some loose ends in fully understanding this game. It does, however, seem logical to follow the rules given by Maharaja Wodeyar for these two pieces. As far as the Prince is concerned, all descriptions on 10 × 10 square boards assign him the move of Queen plus Knight. There is no reason to think that he would lose his power on the larger chessboard.[40]

# *Harihara Chaturanga*

Although also played over a 196-square board, this chess game is quite different in two important ways: It is much older than the other variants presented in this chapter, and it follows very original rules, not found elsewhere. The mere existence of this variant attests to the long survival of the fascination for giant chess boards in the courts of the Maharajas.

The name of this game, *Harihara Chaturanga* ("chess of Harihara"), tells us that it represents the order and chaos of the cosmos. Harihara is a Hindu god of two coexisting identities: that of Vishnu, the supreme god of order and happiness, and that of Shiva, god of destruction and transformation. The opposing sides of this great chess game represent those two forces, in all of their conflict and harmony.

The army strategists of Odisha had another motive for promoting this complicated chess variant. Considering the traditional game of chess too simple, these generals wanted to train their officers at *Harihara Chaturanga*, to give them a more realistic battle simulation.

## *Material*

The chessboard consists of 196 (14 × 14) squares. Several squares are marked with a symbol of a lotus (gray on the diagram).

Each player has 32 pieces: 1 King (*Svamin, Prabhu*), 1 Prince (*Yuvaraja*), 1 General (*Vahinipati, Senanatha*), 1 Minister (*Mantrin, Mantrakovida*), 4 Horses (*Ashva*), 4 Elephants (*Gaja*), 4 Chariots (*Ratha*) and 16 Soldiers of four sorts: 4 Machinists (*Yantrin*), 4 Bowmen (*Dhanvin*), 4 Spearmen (*Shaktika*) and 4 Swordsmen (*Khadgin*).[41]

Before the game begins, the players are free to arrange their pieces in an order of their choosing. The Indian text recommends several different starting formations (*vyuha*) as battle orders, whose names are inspired by Sanskrit martial literature: "fish muzzle," "the chariot," "circular," "half-moon," "invincible," "thunderbolt," "crab shape," "coiled snake," "firm ground" and "strong position." The following table gives the placement of the white pieces in some of the recommended arrays:

| *Vyuha* | Fish muzzle | Chariot | Half moon | Invincible | Thunderbolt |
| --- | --- | --- | --- | --- | --- |
| King | h1 | h2 | h1 | h2 | h2 |
| Prince | g1 | g2 | g1 | g2 | g2 |
| Minister | i1 | i2 | i1 | i2 | i2 |
| General | f1 | f2 | f1 | f2 | f2 |
| Horse | f2,g2,h2,i2 | d2,e2,j2,k2 | e2,e3,j2,j3 | d4,e4,j4,k4 | f3,g3,h3,i3 |
| Chariot | a2,b2,m2,n2 | b2,c2,l2,m2 | f3,g3,h3,i3 | d3,e3,j3,k3 | c3,d3,k3,l3 |
| Elephant | a1,b1,m1,n1 | f4,g4,h4,i4 | f2,g2,h2,i2 | d2,e2,j2,k2 | c2,d2,k2,l2 |
| Machinist | d4,e4,f4,g4 | f6,g6,h6,i6 | b5,d3,k3,m5 | f3,g3,h3,i3 | c4,d4,k4,l4 |
| Bowman | h4,i4,j4,k4 | d4,e4,j4,k4 | a6,c4,l4,n6 | f4,g4,h4,i4 | c5,d5,k5,l5 |
| Spearman | d5,e5,f5,g5 | b3,m3,g7,h7 | b6,d4,k4,m6 | d5,e5,j5,k5 | f4,g4,h4,i4 |
| Swordsman | h5,i5,j5,k5 | d5,e5,j5,k5 | a7,c5,l5,n7 | f5,g5,h5,i5 | f5,g5,h5,i5 |

Black takes the same positions, as reflected symmetrically across the board, but always places the Prince to the left of the King.

## *Rules*

### Moves and Captures.

 *King:* moves an unlimited number of unoccupied squares orthogonally or diagonally, just like the modern Queen. When placed in the center of the chessboard, he can reach a maximum of 51 squares. He cannot be placed on a square in which he is in check.

# 7. Large and Giant Indian Chess

*Prince:* also moves like the modern Queen, but is limited to moving no more than six squares. When placed in the center of the chessboard, he can reach 48 possible squares.

*General:* moves just like the Prince.

*Minister:* also moves like the Prince.

*Chariot:* moves an unlimited number of squares in the four horizontal and vertical directions, only passing over empty squares, just like the modern Rook. When placed in the center of the chessboard, it can reach 26 squares.

**STARTING FORMATIONS**

"Half moon" opening arrangement shown with Black; "fish muzzle" arrangement shown with White.

*Horse:* has the choice between a close move and a remote one. The close move is just like the modern Knight, jumping two squares orthogonally plus one at a right angle. The remote move is a cavalry charge: it first moves six squares like a Rook, provided that this path is completely clear. The Horse may stay on that square or jump from there like a Knight, all in the same move. When placed in the center of the chessboard, it can reach 32 squares.

*Elephant:* may move forward between one and five squares. It may also move backward-diagonally from any of those squares, including the square it starts on (see diagram). It is not allowed to leap over any pieces in its path. When placed in the center of the chessboard, it can reach 17 squares.

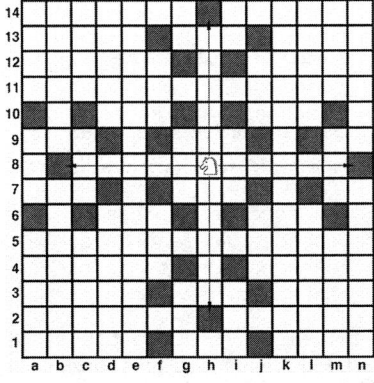
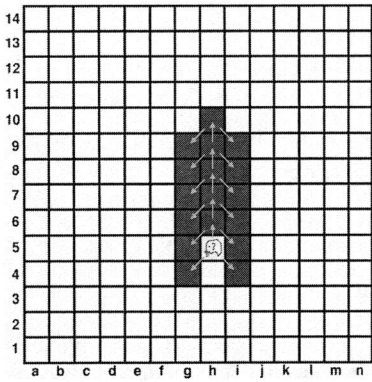

Moves of the Horse (left) and the Elephant (right): all darkened squares.

## The Pawns

*Swordsman:* moves one square forward, forward-diagonally or backward. The Swordsman captures in the same manner as its normal move.

*Spearman:* moves one square forward-diagonally or backward, or one to two squares directly forward. He captures in the same manner, and may not leap over an intervening piece.

*Bowman:* moves one square forward-diagonally or backward, or one, two or three squares directly forward. He captures in the same manner, and may not leap over an intervening piece.

*Machinist:* moves one square forward-diagonally or backward, or up to four squares directly forward. He captures in the same manner, and may not leap over an intervening piece.

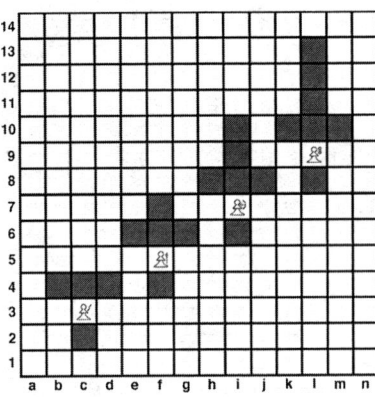

Moves, from left to right: the Swordsman, the Spearman, the Bowman, and the Machinist.

There is no promotion of any of the pieces.

END OF THE GAME. The game ends as soon as a player captures the adverse King or captures all of the opponent's other pieces, leaving a bare King. In the latter case, the points must be tallied. Each piece is worth the number of points corresponding to its maximal mobility:

King (51 points), Prince / General / Minister (48 points), Horse (32 points) Chariot (26 points), Elephant (17 points), Machinist (7 points), Bowman (6 points), Spearman (5 points), Swordsman (4 points).

There are basically three possible endings:

- If a player captures the adverse King, the game is immediately stopped and the winner earns the maximum score, that is, 583 points.
- When the game stops because of a bare King, each player sums up the points corresponding to the pieces he has captured.
- In the same way, if the game is interrupted before a King is captured or left bare, by mutual agreement or any other need to finish playing, each player tallies the points earned by the captures he has made up to this point in the game.

## Tactics

There is no notion of check and mate in the strict sense; the game ends by the King's actual capture. This can happen inadvertently, since check is not declared. Otherwise, with the King's vast power of move, it is almost always possible for the King to scurry away from any threat. Between two heedful players, the course of the game will be a matter of gradually eroding the opponent's army, accumulating as many points as possible in the process.

The relative fighting strength of the pieces is: Prince, General, Minister (6.4); Chariot (5); Knight (4.8); Elephant (2.65); Machinist (1.45); Bowman (1.35); Spearman (1.2); Swordsman (1).

## *A Link with Other Indian Chess Variants?*

The German historian Andreas Bock-Raming, who first revealed this game from its source, the *Harihara Chaturanga*, in 2001, hypothesized that the game's all-powerful King may have been inspired by the Maharaja of the *sarvatobhadra* variation. The point tally system also seems to parallel the point count used in chaturaji. In fact, the uniqueness of this game leaves much room for speculation.

Considering the era of the *Harihara Chaturanga's* composition, in the first half of the 16th century, the existence of pieces with powerful, sweeping moves is especially noteworthy. At that time in history, the powerful moves of the modern Queen and Bishop were only beginning to make the transition through Europe, having begun in Spain toward the end of the 15th century. Were the powerful moves of this game independently invented, or somehow influenced by Portuguese sailors who had made their way to the subcontinent?

# 8. Ouk and Makruk

Cambodians and Thais share a passion for the same chess tradition, known in Cambodia as *ouk* (or *ok*) and in Thailand as *makruk*. This traditional chess form is very popular in both countries, and has also been played in Laos. It is estimated that there are at least two million makruk players in Thailand alone. The game's popularity can be witnessed throughout Cambodia, in the streets, market places and barber shops of Phnom Penh. The attractively stylized chess sets for this game, very similar to those depicted almost a thousand years ago in the bas-reliefs of the Angkor temples, have drawn the interest and curiosity of many Western travelers.

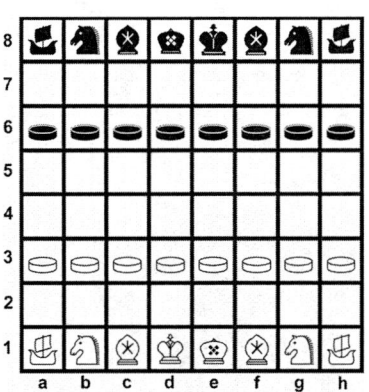

Initial array of ouk or makruk.

## Material

The chessboard is a simple, uncheckered 8 × 8 field. Often, the right and left borders have dishes built into the board, to hold the captured pieces. Each player has 16 chessmen: 1 King, 1 Seed, 2 Noblemen, 2 Horses, 2 Boats and 8 Pawns.

Older, traditional sets often had cowrie shells, which have a natural dark or light coloration, as Pawns. Like many Asian games, this chess form takes advantage of the cowries as pieces which can be flipped over to show either the smooth shell surface or the slotted underside.

Besides the Pawns, the rest of the chessmen are turned figures of very similar design, in different sizes, except for the Horse. It stands out, usually tallest of all the pieces, as a proud and stylish bust of a horse's head.

### Names of Makruk (Thai) and Ouk (Khmer) Pieces

| Thai name | Cambodian name | Meaning | Modern equivalent |
|---|---|---|---|
| Khun[42] | Sdaach, Ang | King | King |
| Met[43] (1) | Neang[44] (2) | 1: Seed, 2: Maiden | Queen |
| Khon (3) | Koul[45] (4) | 3: Nobleman, 4: Guard | Bishop |
| Ma | Seh | Horse | Knight |
| Rua | Tuuk | Boat | Rook |
| Bia (5) | Trey (6) | 5: Cowry, 6: Fish | Pawn |

The Seed is always seated at the King's right.

Traditional game of makruk.
KNOWLTON PHOTOGRAPH

## Rules

MOVES AND CAPTURES. King, Horse and Boat have the same moves as the King, Knight and Rook in Western chess, except that there is no castling.

The Seed has the same move as the Counselor or Minister in ancient Persian or Indian chess.

 *King:* moves only one square in any direction provided that the arrival square is not under the threat of an adverse piece. There is an obligation for the player to move his King out of check. If no possible move will save his King from capture, the player loses the game.

 *Seed:* moves only one square diagonally.

 *Nobleman:* moves one square diagonally or one square forward.

## 8. Ouk and Makruk

*Horse:* moves in the familiar L-shape of two squares in an orthogonal direction plus one step at a right angle. The Horse leaps freely over any pieces in its path.

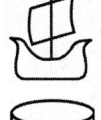
*Boat:* travels any number of squares orthogonally (forward, backward, left or right), but may not jump over any pieces in its way, just like the Western Rook.

*Pawn:* normally moves one square forward, but captures by moving one square diagonally forward. The Pawn of makruk is never allowed to move two spaces at once.

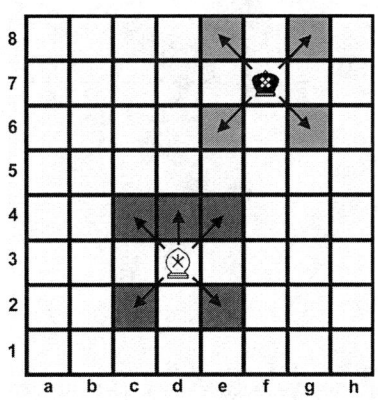

Moves of the Seed (above) and Nobleman (below).

The Pawns of this game begin on the player's third rank, not the second as in most chess variants. These Pawns never have an option of moving two spaces at a time. When the Pawn reaches the opponent's third row (rank number 6 for White, or number 3 for Black), it is flipped over to indicate that it has been promoted to a Seed. It then no longer moves straight forward, but may move one square diagonally, for the remainder of the game. If cowrie shells are used, the promoted Pawn has the slotted side facing up.

CAMBODIAN RULES. The following rules were still in use a hundred years ago in Thailand, but are now ignored by modern players. However, these rules are still commonly practiced in Cambodia.

- *King's leap:* the King may jump like a Knight onto the second row (square b2 or f2 for White, c7 or g7 for Black), providing he has not yet been moved and is not in check.
- *Seed's leap:* the Seed may jump two squares straight forward (to e3 for White, d6 for Black) providing it has not yet moved in the game. Some players allow a capture with this leap; others do not.

END OF THE GAME AND COUNTING RULES. Victory is by checkmate. Stalemate is a draw.

There is no draw by repetition of position in makruk. Instead, there is a special set of rules which involve counting the moves executed before checkmate. These "counting rules" are a significant feature of makruk and play an important role which can affect tactical decisions. Their purpose is twofold: first, they shorten the endgame; second, they create a steep challenge for the player who has already secured a material advantage.

Though the details of these special endgame rules vary slightly from one source to another, they are broadly in agreement. Given here is the description reported by Gary Gifford, who has played Thai chess in official competitions.

Two cases the player should take note of: A. All Pawns have been captured or promoted—

In this case, checkmate should be realized within 64 moves, that is, counting only the moves of the attacking player. If it happens that one side loses his last piece, having only a bare King, then the rules below apply.

B. One side has his King only (bare King)—In this case, the attacking player must achieve checkmate within a limited number of moves, depending upon exactly what pieces he still has on the board. The table below shows the remaining pieces, and how they limit the number of allowable moves.

| Opponent has at least: | Number of moves to checkmate |
|---|---|
| two Rooks | 8 moves |
| one Rook | 16 moves |
| two Noblemen | 22 moves |
| two Horses | 32 moves |
| one Nobleman | 44 moves |
| one Horse | 64 moves |
| four Seeds | 64 moves |

If the attacking player has only Seeds and a King remaining, he must have four Seeds in order to force a checkmate. Any configuration with less material leads to a drawn game.

The attacking player is further constrained by the fact that his opponent will not start counting moves with the number 1, but will first get credit for each of the chessmen standing on the board. This is how it works:

At the moment the player's last piece is captured, leaving a bare King, that player counts each one of the pieces on the board, including both Kings and all of the attacker's additional chessmen. For instance, if there are 1 Nobleman, 1 Horse and 2 promoted Pawns (Seeds), and both Kings on the board, that gives a total of 6 chessmen. According to the table above, the attacker will have 44 moves to checkmate (because his forces include one Nobleman); however, because 6 men are standing on the board, he must begin counting his moves with the number 7. If he reaches the count of 44 and no checkmate has occurred, the game is drawn.

These counting rules are a very important consideration in actual play.

## Tactics

Makruk is a thriving game in Thailand, with its own literature of books and dedicated magazines. Former world chess champion Vladimir Kramnik publicly admitted a fondness for makruk. After playing makruk in 2004, the great Russian champion declared, *"Makruk Thai is more strategic than international chess. You have to plan your operations with total care, since makruk Thai can be compared to an anticipated endgame of international chess."*[46]

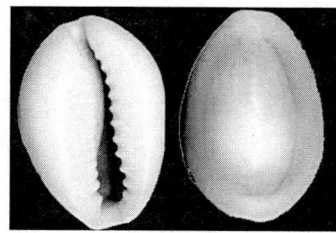

The cowrie shell, traditionally used as a Pawn in makruk.

The theoretical scale of the piece value is: Boat (5), Horse (3), Nobleman (2.35), Seed (1.75), Pawn (0.8).

## Variant: Kar Ouk

In this variant, popular in Cambodia, the first check is fatal. The winner is the first player who succeeds in placing the adverse King in check. All other rules remain the same.

A slightly different variant is practiced by makruk players in Thailand, by the name of *makpong* or "defensive chess." The winner is the first player to force the adverse King to move to get out of check.

Friendly games of ouk, in a Cambodian café. KENNETH LIGHTFOOT PHOTOGRAPH

# *The Curious Case of Shattrong: Is There Another Cambodian Chess?*

Here is a peculiar variant that has caused some confusion—and even controversy—among investigators. Discussion of this game began in a letter, sent in 1975 by John Gollon, American author of *Chess Variations, Ancient, Regional and Modern* (1968). This letter, to the noted chess variant writer Philip Cohen, described a rather odd chess form, relayed to him in 1969 by P.A. Hill, a U.S. serviceman in Saigon. Hill's source was a Cambodian guerrilla officer, there under interrogation.

This game eventually surfaced in D.B. Pritchard's *Encyclopedia of Chess Variants* (1994), listed as "Cambodian chess." Although Pritchard's later (posthumous) edition, the *Classified Encyclopedia of Chess Variants* (2007), clarified that while *ouk*, as described above, properly carries the "Cambodian chess" title, this peculiar variant, described below, continues to arouse some curiosity.

## *Material*

The pieces look like those used for ouk/makruk, but they are placed on the intersections of lines, as in the game of Chinese xiangqi. The board is of 8 × 8 squares, with the long diagonals marked from corner to corner (similar to the traditional Burmese board), making this effectively a board of 9 × 9 intersections.

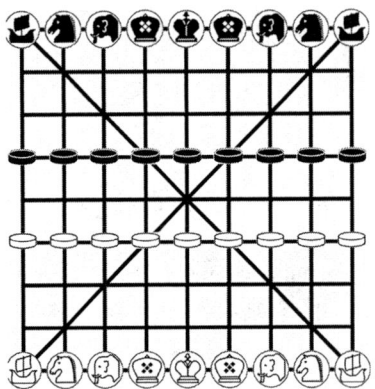

Initial array of shattrong.

There are 18 pieces in each side: one complete row of 9 Fishes (the Pawns of this game) on the fourth rank, and the first rank consisting of 1 King (e1), 2 Officials (d1, f1), 2 Elephants (c1, g1), 2 Horses (b1, h1) and 2 Boats (a1, i1). These pieces are mirrored in the opposing camp, on the sixth and ninth ranks.

### *Name of Pieces at Hill's Cambodian Chess According to Gollon*[47]

| Chessman | Meaning | Equivalent |
|---|---|---|
| *Chhwie* | King (?) | King |
| *Ta Hien* | Official (?) | Queen |
| *Tam Mai* | Elephant (?) | Bishop |
| *Sheh* | Horse | Knight |
| *Tuk* | Boat | Rook |
| *Trei* | Fish | Pawn |

The King, Horse and Boat are identical to their ouk/makruk equivalents. The Official moves one square diagonally, but captures only forward-diagonally. The Elephant moves one square in any direction (like a King) but cannot capture in the three backward directions. The Fish moves and captures one square forward until it enters the opposite side (on its second step) where it is flipped over to indicate promotion, and attains the move of a King, one step in any direction.

## *Did This Game Exist?*

This game looks like a hybrid game, taking its pieces and most of its rules from ouk/makruk, played on the lines of the board, like xiangqi, with some interesting novelties regarding the moves of the Elephant and promoted Pawn. Such a melding of chess forms is almost predictable, since Cambodia lies in the midst of countries in which xiangqi and ouk/makruk are predominant.

However, Gollon himself regretted that the existence of this game had never been confirmed. He admitted in his letter, "*The correspondent later expressed some concern that he may have been mistaken in some details.*" In 2007, the English chess expert, John Beasley, published a revised edition of D.B. Pritchard's book, in which more details from Gollon's letter were given (such as the local names of the chessmen, not included in the first edition). Beasley expressed strong doubt about the authenticity of this chess variant.

In reaction to this publication, Beasley received the information that a set of this chess form had made an appearance at an exhibition in Tokyo in 2002, as well as in several Japanese books that preceded or followed, written by Umebayashi Isao and Okano Shin. They appeared to have rediscovered these rules by translating a book bought in Cambodia. In these reports, the Elephant did not capture sideways. The names given for the chessmen were somewhat different from Gollon (*Kwon, Neamahn, Kwo, Seh, Tuuk, Trey* in the order of the above table). Umebayashi and Okano designated that game under the name of *shattrong*. A photo of a complete set was available showing the 18 pieces over a board with marked diagonals. Then, Beasley published a corrective note in a British chess variants magazine[48] to acknowledge this second "evidence."

But, it seems that this "evidence" has finally vanished. The situation was cleared up in 2012[49] when it was discovered that Umebayashi and Okano's books were simply presenting a reconstruction of the "Cambodian" chess which they had discovered in, yes, Pritchard's first edition! As Pritchard did not name the chessmen in his first edition, the Japanese authors extrapolated the names with the help of a dictionary. No Cambodian books had been consulted or even found. The difference in the Elephant's move was simply a misreading. Finally, looking for an illustration, the authors just set up a set of makruk pieces with additional Fishes and Officials over a facsimile Burmese board that they had on hand and that fitted well with the chessmen.[50]

This story demonstrates the confusing power of rumor and unchecked research—for the time being.

The source for this curious game is reduced to a single informant and moreover a prisoner of war who was under interrogation. Shattrong may then have never existed in any significant cultural context..But an absence of proof is not a proof of absence. There is an active interest in any new sources that may shed light on this, the "other" Cambodian chess.

## *The History of Ouk and Makruk*

In his remarkable capacity as special messenger from the Mongolian Emperor of China, in the Kingdom of Champa, the young Marco Polo made this observation in the year 1285: "*There are elephants in this kingdom, and they have lignaloes in great abundance. They have also planted forests of black wood trees that we called ebony of which they make black chessmen.*"[51]

The traditional chessmen of Chinese xiangqi could well have been made of ebony, as many sets are today. However, the context of Marco Polo's comments—and especially since this is from the pen of an Italian—suggest that this was probably in reference to figurative pieces, particularly since he indicates that it is only the Black chessmen that are made of this material. Considering the location, these figurative 13th century chessmen may have been similar to the modern pieces of ouk and makruk.

Located on the Southern half of modern-day Vietnam, Champa shared a tumultuous history with its neighbor, the Khmer Empire. Both states were directed by an elite class largely dominated by Indian culture, still apparent today in the Khmer and Cham alphabets which are derived from early Brahmi script, and in the predominance of the Buddhist religion. The Khmer Empire, formerly widespread throughout Southeast Asia, culminated with the construction of the monumental temples of Angkor in the 12th century. The walls of these temples, today ensconced in wild rainforest, are decorated with innumerable bas-reliefs illustrating scenes of war and daily life at the Khmer court.

Twelfth century chess in daily life, from the walls of Angkor Wat, Siem Reap, Cambodia.
KENNETH LIGHTFOOT PHOTOGRAPH

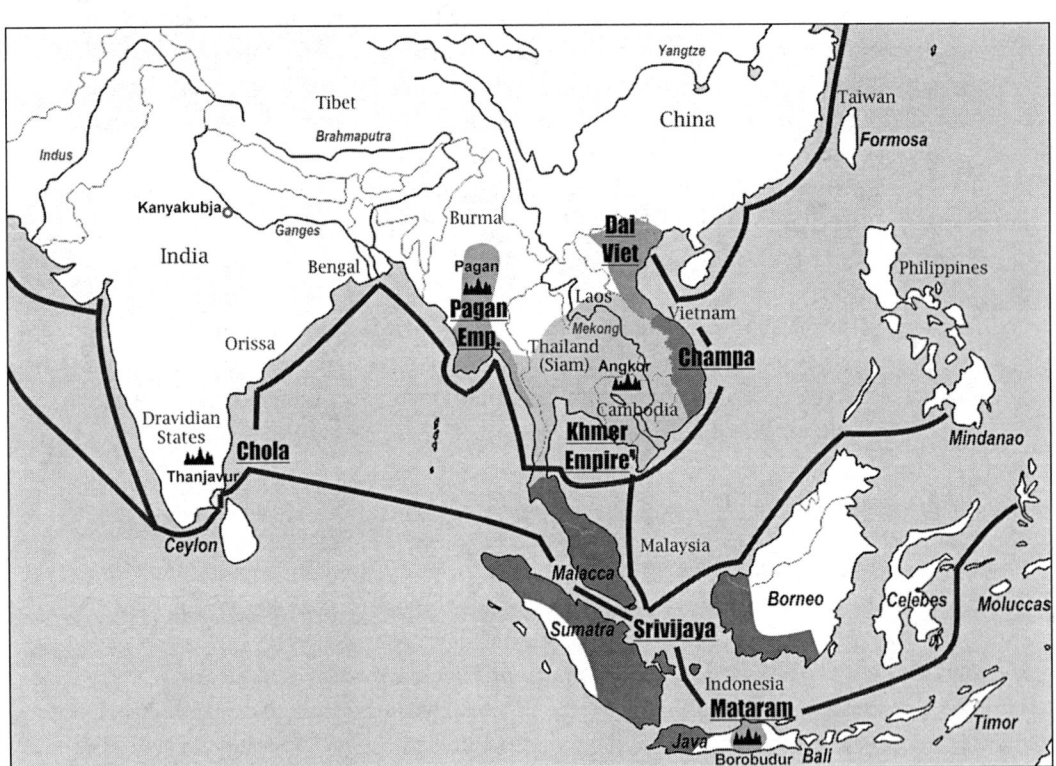

Map of Southeast Asia sea trade routes ca. 1000 C.E.; gray shows areas of imperial influence.

Among these famous depictions of life, some nine hundred years in the past, are clear depictions of players at board games. A close look at the pieces of these games reveals that they are the very same figures—rounded bulbs and elegant spires—that grace the chessboards in the streets of Phnom Penh today. With such rare snapshots into the recreational life of this ancient and remote region, we can have great confidence that the Cambodian style of chess was already alive, in the Khmer Empire of the 12th century as well as the Kingdom of Champa which followed. Although no rules of the game from that period have survived, the complete name of the Cambodian game, *ouk chatrang*, shows a clear line from its Indian source, *chaturanga*.[52]

The Thai people began to settle in the region in the 12th century, immigrating from Southwest China. By the 14th century, the Thais had established the Kingdom of Siam, and began to antagonize the Khmer empire. Angkor was pillaged with increasing frequency, and finally abandoned in 1431. The Khmer Empire was reduced to a small kingdom vassal of Siam. In exchange, the Cambodian culture spread through Siam, probably taking the game of *ouk* into the newly dominant Siamese society.

The earliest literary mention of chess in the region is credited to Simon de La Loubère, extraordinary messenger of King Louis XIV of France, to the Court of Siam in 1687–1688. He observed: "*They play chess to our manner and to the Chinese manner.*" However, he only detailed the latter, with a full description, showing that the Chinese xiangqi had also arrived in Thailand.[53] Western scholars had to wait for the report of Captain James Low, in the first half of the 19th century, to learn how Siamese chess (now considered Thai and Cambodian chess) was played.[54]

Along with Western chess, Chinese xiangqi, Korean janggi and Japanese shogi, makruk is one of the modern world's thriving chess forms. Of all the Asian varieties, this Thai/Cambodian game appears the closest to Western chess, and closest to the ancient game of the Arabs and Persians. Perhaps, in time, makruk will take its long overdue place among the best-known games of the world.

Makruk

*Right:* Children learning the secrets of makruk at the Chiang Mai chess club, Thailand.
KENNETH LIGHTFOOT PHOTOGRAPH

# 9. Sit-Tu-Yin

Despite significant political advances in recent times, Myanmar—the name imposed upon Burma by an autocratic junta since 1962—remains one of the most restricted countries in the world. Within its borders survives one of the most original varieties of chess in the world. This game, *sit-tu-yin*,[55] is uncannily modern and its rules are surprisingly realistic in terms of military strategy. At the same time, the playing pieces of sit-tu-yin convey a centuries-old tradition, often depicting characters from the great Hindu epic *Ramayana*, pitting the black army of the monkeys against the red demons.

## Material

Sit-tu-yin is played on an uncheckered board of 8 × 8 squares, marked corner-to-corner by two long diagonal lines (known as *sit-kei-kyo*) which cross in the center of the board. Each side consists of 16 pieces, usually made of wood, in two colors, often red or black. The pieces are traditionally carved as literal figurative representations of 1 King, 1 General, 2 Elephants, 2 Horses, 2 Chariots and 8 Pawns.

The King and General are commonly depicted crouched down on one knee; the Elephant and Horse usually have riders, and the Pawns sit ready, often with a shield in one hand and sword in the other—but sometimes depicted as monkeys on one side, opposed by a team of little demons. The Chariot shows an interesting mix of identities, sometimes showing characteristics of a *stupa* temple, a cart with two or four wheels, or the bow of a ship. The piece in itself attests to a generous diversity of cultural influences.

### Names of the Sit-Tu-Yin Pieces

| Burmese name | Meaning | Modern equivalent |
|---|---|---|
| *Min-gyi* | Great King | King |
| *Sit-ke* | General | Queen |
| *Hsin* | Elephant | Bishop |
| *Myin* | Horse | Knight |
| *Ya-hta* | Chariot | Rook |
| *Nè* | Foot Soldier | Pawn |

## Rules

Like most of the long-standing chess traditions, sit-tu-yin, played for centuries throughout the valleys of the Burmese mountains, has been practiced with minor differences in rules over the centuries. No set of standards has yet united this game's regional diversity. In particular, rules regarding Pawn promotion and initial setup of the pieces prove to be most mutable. However, in an effort to revitalize this game and to gather players from a wider region, a standard set of tournament rules has been established. The rules presented below were adopted by the Meeting on the Laws of Myanmar Traditional Chess, organized by the Myanmar Traditional Chess Committee of the Myanmar Chess Federation, on 27 February 2011 in Yangon, Myanmar.[56]

MOVES AND CAPTURES. Moves of the King, Horse and Chariot are equivalent to those of the King, Knight and Rook of Western chess, except that there is no castling.

It will be noted that all pieces have the same moves as their counterparts in makruk. The King and General do not have any special first-move leaps or alternative move choices.

*King:* moves one square in any direction, provided the arrival square is not under threat by an adverse piece, just like the King of Western chess. There is an obligation for the player to move his King out of check, and check must be proclaimed by the attacking player. If no possible move will save the King from capture, the game has been lost.

*General:* moves only one square diagonally.

*Elephant:* moves one space diagonally or one space forward. These five directions are said to represent the animal's four feet and trunk.

*Horse:* makes the familiar L-shape of two squares in one orthogonal direction plus one step at a right angle. The Horse freely leaps over any pieces in its path.

*Chariot:* travels any number of squares orthogonally (forward, backward, left or right). It may not jump over any pieces in its way.

*Pawn:* normally moves one square forward, but captures by moving one square diagonally forward. The Pawn of sit-tu-yin is never allowed to move two spaces at once.

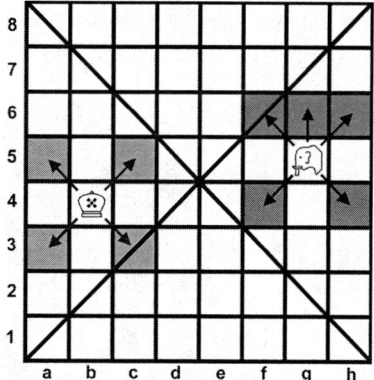

**Moves of the General and Elephant.**

INITIAL POSITION ON THE BOARD. At the beginning, only Pawns are placed on the board. Their position is always the same, as indicated by the following diagram:

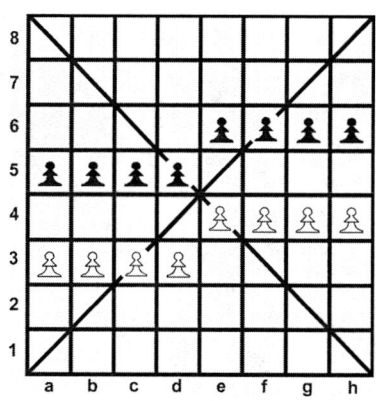

Pawns' initial array in sit-tu-yin.

The Red player will then have to follow some rules to place his main pieces behind his Pawns:

- The Chariot must be placed on the first rank (a1—h1).
- The other pieces are freely arranged on the player's side, behind his Pawns.[57]

Then, the Black player does the same.[58]

The Red player then makes the first move.

PAWN PROMOTION. Pawns may promote to General when they reach a square crossed by one of the long diagonal lines, on the opponent's side of the board; however, promotion is forbidden if the player already owns a General.

Promotion is not immediate, but occurs as a separate move. In this "promotional move," the player may either keep the newly promoted General in place, or may move it one square diagonally.

Placing the opponent's King into check or capturing an adverse piece while making this promotional move is forbidden.

If a Pawn moves on past the marked promotional squares without promoting, it generally forgoes any chance of promoting later in the game.

As a special case, if a player has only one Pawn left on the board, and no other pieces, that Pawn may promote on any square of the board. In this case, the bans on capture and check are lifted, and the new General may capture a piece or give check on the promotional move. Promotion of the last Pawn is not compulsory; it may be declined by the player.

Traditional antique sit-tu-yin chessmen.
KNOWLTON PHOTOGRAPH

END OF THE GAME. The goal of the game is to checkmate the opponent's King.

Stalemate is a draw. If the King is not in check, but the player has no possible legal move, the game ends with no winner. Even if the stalemated player has a Pawn which could possibly promote, he may refuse that option and claim the draw.

Threefold repetition leads to a draw. If the same position occurs on the board three times, with the same player to move, either player may declare a draw.

A player has 50 moves to checkmate. If a player makes 50 consecutive moves without a Pawn advanced or a capture made, the game may be declared a draw.

A special move count may lead to a draw. If one player is left with a bare King, and the other player has at least a Rook, an Elephant plus General, or a Knight plus General, checkmate must be given by the number of moves shown below—or the game is declared a draw.

| Opponent has at least: | Number of moves to checkmate |
|---|---|
| ⊕ | 16 moves |
| 🐘 ♛ | 44 moves |
| ♞ ♛ | 64 moves |

## Strategy

The freedom to create novel arrangements of pieces in the opening adds a profound level of strategy to this game. Such pre-game preparations are more characteristic of modern battle games, like the Chinese luzhanqi or Western Stratego, than they are of an ancient Asian chess tradition. Even Bobby Fischer's *Chess960* (also known as *Fischer Random Chess*), in which pieces are arranged randomly according to a few central rules, carries a similar element of novel arrangement, forcing the players to think strategically from the very first move.

With the Pawns arranged so far forward, already in confrontation with each other, the dynamic interaction—what we usually consider the middle game—starts almost immediately.

FAVORITE OPENINGS. According to Lwin, there are 519,792 possible starting positions. However, fewer than forty are actually found in the written accounts and, according to the traditional chess teacher, U Pe Hsaung, only eight have fundamental importance. These eight preferred positions are provided in the *Burmese Chess Guide*, written in the 1920's which serves as the primary source for both Pritchard and Lwin,[59] They are presented in the table below:

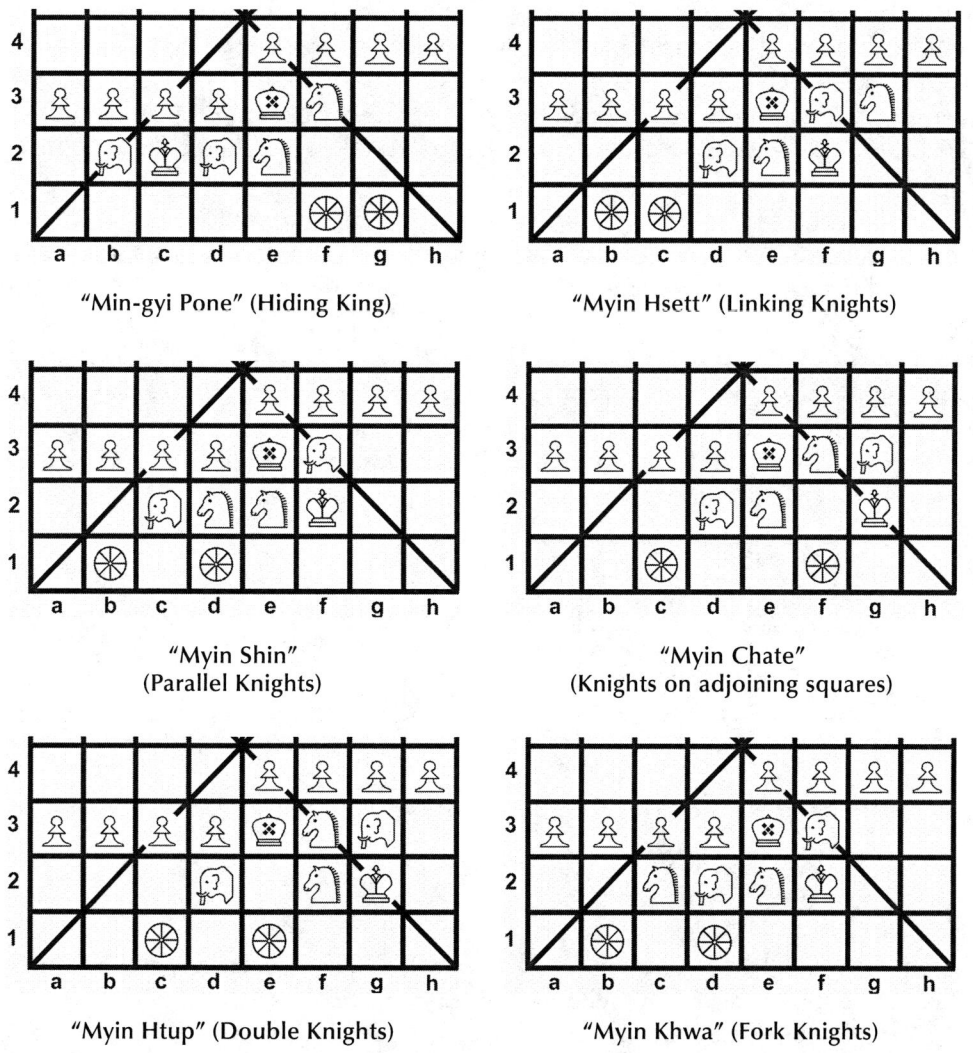

"Min-gyi Pone" (Hiding King)

"Myin Hsett" (Linking Knights)

"Myin Shin" (Parallel Knights)

"Myin Chate" (Knights on adjoining squares)

"Myin Htup" (Double Knights)

"Myin Khwa" (Fork Knights)

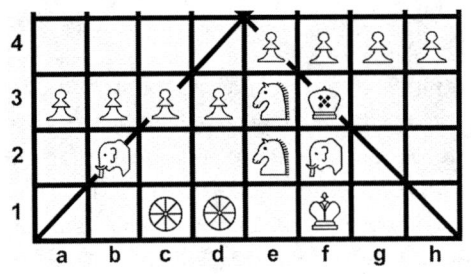

"Ah Twin Sit-ke Pauk"
(Keeping the General inside)

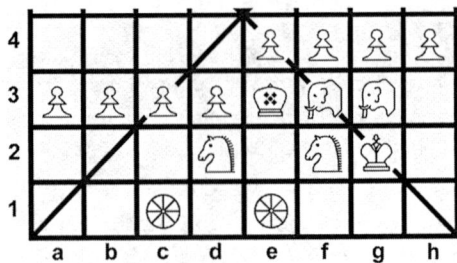

"Hsin Shin Myin Khwa"
(Parallel Elephants and fork Knights)

# Variant: ASEAN Chess

The Association of Southeast Asian Nations (ASEAN) is an international organization founded in 1967, consisting of ten countries: Burma, Thailand, Laos, Cambodia, Vietnam, Malaysia, Indonesia, Singapore, Brunei and the Philippines. To promote competitive sports and games among these countries, two forms of chess have been proposed. One simply follows the international F.I.D.E. rules, while the other follows special rules named *ASEAN chess*. The concept of these special rules is to unify the various Southeast Asian chess forms into a single competitive game.

ASEAN chess is played on a standard, checkered board, with standard, international style pieces. At first, ASEAN chess was devised as a variation of makruk, already common in Thailand, Cambodia and Laos, with some elements borrowed from Western chess, notably, the checkered board and the rules of Pawns promotion. The Pawns in that first version were all placed on the third row. But, for the First ASEAN Chess Competition, which was held in Yangon (Burma) in spring 2011 with 42 players, it was decided that the Pawns of the right wing would start on the 4th rank, as in the initial array of sit-tu-yin. However, some games in subsequent competitions have commenced with all Pawns set on the 3rd rank. Also, the position of the white King is sometimes seen on d1 rather than e1 (the black King being always on e8).

Initial array of ASEAN chess as played in the First ASEAN Chess Competition.

The Queen and the Elephant move exactly like the General and the Elephant in sit-tu-yin, or like the Seed/Maiden and the Nobleman/Guard in makruk/ouk.

Not surprisingly, the four other pieces move and capture as they do both in Southeast Asian varieties and in Western chess. There is no castling, *en passant* capture, or Pawn's initial double step.

The promotion rule is particular: when a Pawn reaches the last rank, it must be exchanged for a new Queen of the same color.[60] This exchange is immediate.

The game is won by the player who has checkmated the opponent's King.

Stalemate is a draw. The game is also drawn when a position has arisen in which neither player can checkmate the opponent's King with any series of legal moves. The game is said to end in a "dead position." This can be decided by agreement between the two players or determined if each player has made at least the last 50 consecutive moves without the movement of any Pawn, and without any capture.

There is also a counting rule. As soon as a player has only a King left on his side, the number of pieces that belong to the opponent must be reviewed and the number of remaining moves is set according to the table below (note, this is the same as the table for sit-tu-yin). The move counting starts with the first move of the bare King. If he succeeds in making the required number of moves without being checkmated, the game is declared a draw.

Here is the table for the final move count. If the opponent has at least

1. 1 Rook, 16 moves
2. 1 Elephant and 1 Queen, 44 moves
3. 1 Knight and 1 Queen, 64 moves

ASEAN chess was played in the 26th and the 27th Southeast Asian Games, held in Palembang, Indonesia (2011) and Naypyidaw, Myanmar (2013), respectively.

## *The History of Sit-Tu-Yin*

Burmese chess went unnoticed by European writers until the end of the 18th century. Michael Symes, British ambassador from Governor-General of India in Burma in 1795, gave a short testimony (published in 1800) in which he named all of the chessmen but did not detail the Burmese rules of play. More information came from Captain Hiram Cox, English officer of the British East India Company, governor of Bengal and familiar to the Burmese court in Amarapura. In a letter to the Asiatic Society in Bengal, written in 1799,[61] Cox revealed Burmese chess in great detail, including names of the pieces, their moves, and a diagram of the board. That letter was published in Calcutta in 1801 after Cox's death, and was then reprinted in London in 1803.

Since that time, several accounts have come into print regarding the game. Unfortunately, the disconcerting rules of the opening and of the Pawns' promotion were not always well understood. Many outright mistakes and omissions have also come into play and, with the lack of oversight unfortunately common in many chess histories, erroneous renderings have often been copied from one book to another without critical review.

Finally, in 1994, D.B. *Pritchard's Encyclopedia of Chess Variants* set the record straight, basing his presentation on an authoritative Burmese book, published by Shwe Kyin U Ba in 1924, with the approval of several sit-tu-yin masters. With the advent of the Internet, and the establishment of wider competitions in Burma, updated information is much more readily available.

While the rules of the game can now be seen more clearly, the history of sit-tu-yin remains obscure and mysterious. The oldest traces of chess in Burma are eight artifacts: glazed earthenware pieces—apparently chessmen—dated from the 14th century by an analysis of thermo-luminescence by the University of Milan (2001). These pieces, belonging now to the Italian collector Rodolfo

Pozzi, bear a striking similarity both to some abstract sets used in India, and particularly to the bulbous, pointed pieces used in Cambodia since the 12th century.

Although there is no known documentation of this game earlier than the European accounts, we can be quite certain that sit-tu-yin is of Indian origin. Burma, like its Southeast Asian neighbors, was extensively influenced by Indian culture, even before the arrival of the ethnic Burmese population in the ninth century. This relationship is so pervasive, including the influx of Hinduism and Buddhism, that it can be seen in all aspects of life, culture and history. Where the game of chess is concerned, the name sit-tu-yin (sounding like "*sit-too-rin*") is similar in sound and related in meaning to *chaturanga,* since *sit* translates as "army." The modern figurative chessmen are identical to many of the ancient Indian pieces which have been found, and the name of the Chariot, *Ya-hta* (sounding more like "*Ratha*"), is essentially the same as the Sanskrit word for the same thing (sometimes transliterated *Rattah*). The five-direction move of the Elephant, typical of Southeast Asian chess variants, can also be traced to India, where it was first reported by the Persian al-Biruni, visiting Punjab in 1030.

Moreover, the traditional sit-tu-yin chessmen replay the mythical battle of the *Ramayana,* the famous Sanskrit mythological epic, symbolizing the struggle of Good against Evil. The Black King is *Yama* (the equivalent of the Hindu *Rama*) and the Black Pawns are monkeys commanded by the faithful *Hanuman,* represented by the Black General. The Red Pawns are little demons, commanded by the demon King, *Da-Tha-Gi-Ri* (the equivalent of *Ravana*), kidnapper of *Yama's* (*Rama's*) wife *Thida* (*Sita*). These clear derivations from the Hindu myth not only point to an Indian origin, but suggest that sit-tu-yin may be very old indeed.[62]

Carved bone Burmese chessmen (20th century). Note that the traditional General is replaced by a Queen. KNOWLTON PHOTOGRAPH

In recent decades, sit-tu-yin has lost ground in Burma, overtaken by Western, international chess. Burmese authorities have responded however, and efforts are afoot to include the traditional Burmese chess in competitions and events which also make room for the modern, international game. National championships are now regularly scheduled, and it can be said that for the present sit-tu-yin has been saved from extinction.

There is no other chess variant like sit-tu-yin. The free placement of the pieces before the action commences is an excellent answer to the inherent problem of slow development as it existed in the early chess of India and Persia. This simple rule completely revolutionized the opening aspect of the game. No evidence has yet been found to help determine the date of that innovation. It is speculated that it may have been inspired by the Indian *vyuhas,* the battle arrangements appearing in Sanskrit military manuals and chess treatises. Among all the thriving chess forms of Eastern Asia, sit-tu-yin remains the least well-known outside its own country—a regrettable injustice! It is a fascinating game with much to offer the modern player.

*Left:* A modern Burmese production of the ancient game of sit-tu-yin. Plastic chessmen on a vinyl board marked for algebraic notation. KNOWLTON PHOTOGRAPH

# 10. Catur

A variety of ancient rules still existed in the early 20th century for indigenous chess forms throughout the Malay Peninsula and the main islands of the archipelago, Sumatra, Java and Borneo. Chess in these regions has now been heavily influenced by modern Western rules, profoundly changing the old *catur*,[63] characterized by complex rules for the King's first move and the Pawn's promotion. Two variants are illustrated here, one played in Malaysia, the other on Java Island. The particular rules obeyed by the Bataks from Sumatra are detailed below.

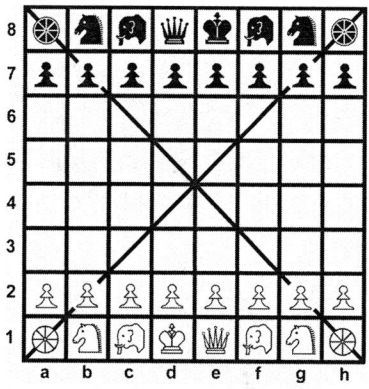
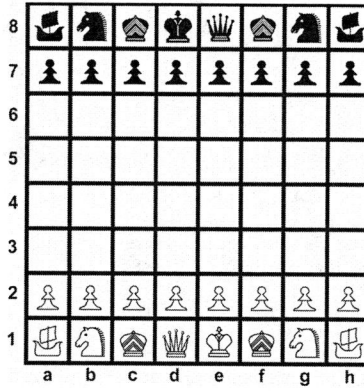

Initial array of Malay chess (left) and Javanese chess (right).

## Material

Once again, the chessboard is uncolored. It may be of wood or merely drawn on the ground. The long diagonals are sometimes marked. The 16 pieces of each side are 1 King, 1 Minister, 2 Elephants, 2 Horses, 2 Chariots and 8 Pawns. In Java, Counselors and Boats replace Elephants and Chariots but this change has no effect on the moves of the chessmen.

## Names of the Catur Pieces

| Malaysian | Javanese | Indonesian | Meaning | Modern equivalent |
|---|---|---|---|---|
| *Raja* | *Ratu* | *Raja* | King | King |
| *Menteri (1)* | *Patih (2)* | *Menteri (1)* | 1: Minister, 2: Lord | Queen |
| *Gajah (1)* | *Menteri (2)* | *Gajah (1)* | 1: Elephant, 2: Counselor | Bishop |
| *Satria (1)* | *Jaran (2)* | *Kuda (2)* | 1: Knight, 2: Horse | Knight |
| *Tir (1)* | *Prahu (2)* | *Benteng (3)* | 1: Chariot, 2: Boat, 3: Fortress (Tower) | Rook |
| *Bidak* | *Bidaq* | *Pion, Bidak* | Pawn | Pawn |

The initial arrangement has the Minister (Queen) always at the King's right, except in Java where he stands always on the left.[64]

H.O. Robinson gave the following description (1904): *"King and Queen are identical in shape, the Queen being about half an inch shorter; the Bishop (Elephant) and Knight are not unlike the above-mentioned pieces in design but with longer necks and diminished in size in proportion to their value. The Rook (Chariot) is always flat like a draughtsman with a little knob on top. The Pawn is a tiny cylindrical piece with a top knot."* Other travelers have reported that the players were able to manufacture their own sets in ten minutes, by a few strokes of a penknife in a stem of bamboo, according to well codified cuts. A similar tradition has also been reported in Tamil India.

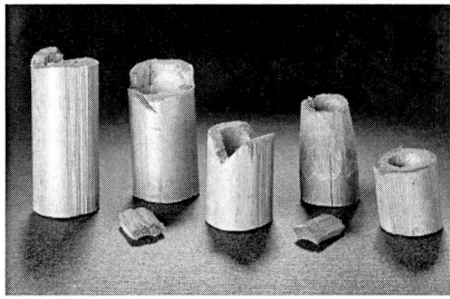

Javanese bamboo Catur chessmen.

# Rules

- All pieces move essentially as their modern European equivalents, with some peculiarities, detailed below. In such a large and variously parceled region, it is not surprising to find some variation.
- *Pawn's double step:* the Pawn can move two squares at its first step.
- *En passant capture:* this move is executed as in Western chess but is allowed only if the Pawn that captures is blocked by an adverse Pawn standing directly in front of it.
- *King's privilege:* on his first move, the King may leap to the second square in any direction (b1, b2, b3, c3, d3, e3, f3, f2, f1 for the King starting on e1). When executing this leap, he may pass over an occupied square. He is permitted to capture an adverse piece on his arrival square. According to most accounts, this jump is not permitted if the King has been in check previously during the game. This jump is allowed to escape a first check, but afterward such an escape is no longer permitted. Players often place the opponent in check early just to deprive the King of his leaping power.

- A sort of two-move castling is often practiced: first, the Chariot is brought close to the King. Then, in the next move, the King leaps to the other side of the Chariot.
- *Pawn promotion:* By a complex process, the Pawn may be promoted to a Minister (in most cases) or to another piece (Chariot, Elephant or Knight).[65] There are two phases in this process. First, the Pawn must arrive at the last row. Then, it must move backward diagonally a certain number of squares: three if it had reached the square of the King or the Minister; two from a square of an Elephant, or one from a square of Horse. Promotion is immediate if it reached a corner square, with no need to move backward.

END OF THE GAME. Victory is obtained by checkmating the opposing King. Stalemate is a draw. According to J.B. Elcum, a bare King must be mated in fewer than seven moves; otherwise, the game is drawn. In addition, mate may not be performed by a discovered check. In Selangor, Robinson stated that the bare King could play as *"he pleased, like a King, Queen, Bishop, Knight, Rook or Pawn."* He is then termed *Raja Lela* and the game is almost always drawn.

## *Bataks' Chess*

The Bataks are a Malay people from North Sumatra, in Indonesia. The presentation that Murray made of them is impressive: *"In appearance they are taller and darker than the true Malay. They still practice cannibalism to some extent. The game is restricted to the male sex entirely. So violent are the passions aroused at times by the game, which is always played for a stake, that the headman of the village has occasionally had to forbid the practice of the game for a season."* This was published in 1913. A few years earlier, in 1904, the games of the Bataks were studied by the German anthropologist Armin von Öfele, who left a very precise description of their chess. The differences from the common Malay game are the following:

- The King's Pawn is allowed to make a double step on its second move if it has not done so on its first move. Consequently, *en passant* capture may occur, in this case capturing the King's Pawn which has just moved to its fifth rank.
- The King's initial leap is not permitted in the two diagonal directions. It is therefore only possible on seven squares (from e1 toward c1, c2, d3, e3, f3, g2, g1). This leap is allowed to escape the first check, but is not permitted after the King has moved, or after the first check has occurred.
- If the King is checkmated by discovered check (called *"aras"*), the game is drawn, without a winner.

The Pawn promotion involves two steps, but they are executed as a single move. The Pawn which reaches the 8th rank is promoted and immediately moves one step diagonally backward. This double move is called *"gelong."*
- The Pawn is allowed to make a capture with this backward-diagonal step.
- However, if the Pawn's backward-diagonal move attacks the opposing King, the Pawn's *gelong* is interrupted. The Pawn is not yet promoted, and the King must move out of check. The Pawn makes its backward-diagonal step as a subsequent move, and promotes at that time.[66]
- If the square the Pawn landed on in the 8th row was under threat, it may be "captured in passing" by the threatening piece. In this case, the piece moves to the 8th row square of promotion, and removes the newly promoted Pawn from its square on the 7th row.

- If the Pawn captures as it reaches the 8th row, the *gelong* is interrupted. The Pawn remains on the square of capture; then, in a subsequent turn, it moves with the power of the promoted piece, but without capturing. Only then, the promotion is complete.

# *The History of Catur*

As the gateway to the eastern spice route, the Malay Peninsula and archipelago occupied an enviable strategic position. Very early, their inhabitants submitted to the Hindu and then Buddhist cultural influences of Southern India. In the seventh century, the maritime empire of the Srivijaya controlled Sumatra, the Straits and the west of Java while, to the east, the Sailendra Dynasty built the Buddhist temple of Borobudur. Other Indianized dynasties followed until the arrival of Islam, which spread extensively from the 13th to the 15th centuries. The following century saw the incursion of the Europeans: first the Portuguese, then the Dutch and, finally, the English.

Catur carries the sediment deposited by these successive passages. Among the many Asian chess varieties, it has been the most receptive to European influence. No one knows precisely when the modern moves of Queen and Bishop were adopted, but it is certain that chess was known in these regions well before the arrival of the first European navigators. Some recent works mention a former older Malay source from around 1370, the *Hikayat Bayan Budiman* (*Seventy Tales of the Parrot*).[67] For the time being, there is no certain indication of chess from the pre–Islamic period. The word *caturanga,* used to indicate a game, is found in the *Wirataparwa*, an old prose rendering of the Sanskrit epic *Mahabharata*, composed in 996 on order of the Javanese king, Dharmawansa. However, whether this term designates chess or another type of board game is still a matter of debate.[68]

The Malay people were also visited by Chinese travelers. In his *Ying-yai Sheng-lan* (*The Overall Survey of the Ocean's Shores*), Ma Houen reported that chess was played in Palembang (Sumatra) for stakes, around 1421.

Investigating local sources, Jiří Jákl has listed several texts that briefly mention chess: the *Undang-undang Melaka*, a Malay law code indicating that chess was played for stakes in the 15th century; the *Sejarah Melayu*, a Malay chronicle also mentioned by Murray, dated 1536 (or possibly 1436); the *Kidung Harsa Wijaya;* and the *Malat*, two Balinese texts composed not earlier than the 16th century. In those times, these regions were already in contact with Europeans. Murray cited the anecdote of Diego Lopez, commander of the first Portuguese expedition in 1509, who was playing chess when a Javanese man was taken on board his ship. The native immediately identified the game of chess which the sailors were playing.

The game retains some technical terms from Arabic, such as *sah mat* (checkmate) and the name given to the Pawn. The abstract form of the pieces also evinces an Arab origin. The Indian layer is more deeply buried. It shows up in some of the rules such as the King's leap and the initial array of chessmen; even more in the nomenclature that is derived from Sanskrit. *Raja*, *Menteri*, and *Gajah*, as well as the name of the game itself, *catur,* leave little doubt of the game's derivation from *chaturanga*. The Tamil language, from South India, also leaves a trace in the words *Tir* and *Kuda*.

Catur was still played in the 19th and in the beginning of the 20th century, as is demonstrated by the descriptions of travelers in the Malay Peninsula (Malacca, Selangor, Johore, and Kalentan) and in the main islands (Sumatra with the Bataks), Borneo in Sarawak and Java. These regions today are essentially divided between Malaysia and Indonesia while traditional chess has widely receded, ousted by the international rules and by xiangqi, dominant in the Chinese Diaspora.

Chess is also popular in the neighboring Philippines.[69] While modern players there favor a particularly stylized Staunton design, a much older form of chessmen is evident in the predominantly Muslim southern region of Mindanao. This exotic design probably predates the Spanish occupation of the 17th century, and may have its roots in the early Arab contact of the 14th century. Today, the modern European rules are observed throughout the Philippine islands.

Traditional chess set of the Maranaos, a Moro Muslim people from Mindanao Island in the Philippines. The Knight is replaced by an okir, a symbol of luck and fortune.
KNOWLTON PHOTOGRAPH

This chess tradition represents the extreme eastward extent of the Indo-Persian game before, of course, the European explorers poured their conventions all over the world. The reports made by Forbes and Murray from the testimonies of anthropologists or colonists of the 19th century appear outdated today. Further studies are now underway to pierce the secrets of chess history and evolution in insular Southeast Asia.

## ◆ PART III ◆

# Gunpowder on the Chinese Board

China too may lay claim to its share of chess origins. Both *weiqi* (known in the West by its Japanese name, *go*) and *liubo* (now extinct) precede any certain evidence of chess by several centuries. Perhaps it was weiqi that influenced Chinese chess, *xiangqi*, to be played on the lines of the board, and perhaps liubo influenced the Chinese chessboard with its distinctive topographical markings of water and palaces. While these aspects of xiangqi, are markedly consistent with their Chinese predecessors, there can be no doubt that the game itself is rooted in the same source as the Western chess forms.

With the inclusion of a piece called a Cannon, xiangqi became truly emblematic of China, the first civilization to devise gunpowder. The game carried its particular Chinese character to neighboring regions, as the game spread to Vietnam and Korea. While many lands accepted xiangqi in its native Chinese form, Korea reconfigured the game with significant differences. The subsequent centuries have seen xiangqi spread throughout Southeast Asia, into the Philippines, Singapore and Malaysia—where many world-class masters have been cultivated. In more recent times, xiangqi has moved into Australia, North America and Europe, where it entices the minds of a fresh population.

Many variants are also derived from xiangqi. There are forms for three or seven players, and games with novel pieces. Some forms have interesting moves, including a few that predate similar developments in European chess that occurred centuries later. More recently conceived games, described at the end of this part of the book, expand the possibilities even further. Though some of these reach the outer limits of what we can rightly call chess variants, they attest to China's deeply rooted and thriving fascination with strategic board games.

# 11. Xiangqi

The hurried tourist who comes upon this game in Beijing or Hanoi may think it some sort of a checkers game. Not at all! It is chess, known as xiangqi.[1] Few people realize, outside of China, that this is the most-played board game in the world—with players numbering about one billion. Older than its distant cousin, European chess, it may appear odd at first, but becomes familiar and engaging very quickly. Each side is organized around a palace and sends its army—soldiers, horses, war chariots and cannons—to assault the enemy position on the other side of the river.

A game of xiangqi begins.
KENNETH LIGHTFOOT PHOTOGRAPH

Xiangqi is played throughout China but is also popular in Vietnam, where it is called *cờ tướng*,[2] It has spread further to the many areas reached by Chinese and Vietnamese immigration. Cheap sets with paper boards and wooden pieces can be found in Asian supermarkets in most Western cities.

## *Material*

Similar to *weiqi* (*go*), xiangqi is played by placing the pieces on the intersections of lines, not inside the squares. The chessboard is not checkered and is slightly oblong, nine lines across and ten lines from front to back. The two sides are separated by a "river" between the 5th and 6th horizontal lines.

楚河　漢界

*Left:* Four characters which are often inscribed inside the river: *Chu he Han jie*, "Chu river, Han's border," in memory of the conflict between the Chu and Han dynasties in 206–202 B.C.E.

Each side has a nine-point "palace" or "fortress" marked by an "X" of diagonal lines. Finally, the initial positions of the Soldiers and Cannons are indicated with small markings around those points. (These markings are covered by the Soldiers and Cannons in the initial array; they can be seen in subsequent diagrams.)

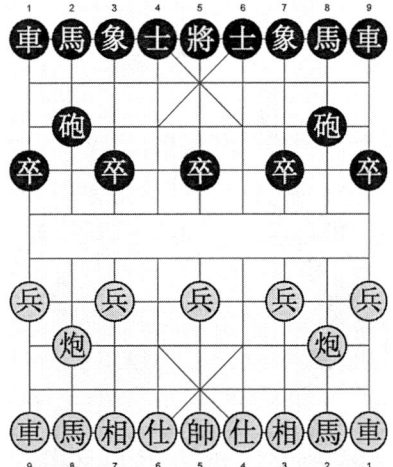

*Right:* Initial array of xiangqi. In the traditional notation, each player numbers the columns from right to left, as viewed from his own side of the board.

- Each player has 16 chessmen which are simple, flat disks, uniform in size, with an engraved Chinese character on each one indicating its identity. One side is usually red and the other usually black or blue. Several of the chessmen bear different characters from their counterparts on the other side of the board.
- The pieces on the first row, arranged symmetrically from the center outward, are: 1 General, 2 Advisors, 2 Elephants, 2 Horses, and 2 Chariots. The 2 Cannons are placed on the 3rd line and the 5 Soldiers are on the 4th, as shown in the diagram.

The red "Elephant" actually bears the character of a Minister. Red Advisors and, sometimes, Horses and Chariots may have the added character (*ren*, 人), indicating a "person" in charge of those units. On the Cannon pieces, the left side of the character may differ between the two sides. These pieces on the Red side include the radical "fire," indicating a Cannon. The same pieces on the Black side may bear the radical for "stone," indicating a Catapult. Contrasting even more, the Red Ministers are opposed by Black Elephants. The two terms are homophonic in Chinese, sounding the same but written differently. The five Soldiers on the two sides are different in appearance, meaning and pronunciation. Though these pieces vary in literal meaning, we generally refer to them as Elephant, Advisor, Horse, Chariot, Cannon and Soldier regardless of the side they play on.

Finally, there is no King in xiangqi but a Governor (or Marshal) on the Red side who faces a General on the Black side. It would be a serious breach of respect to represent the emperor on the chessboard, where he could be symbolically trapped or killed at the leisure of game players.

### Names of the Xiangqi Pieces

| Chinese name | Vietnamese name | Sinogram | Meaning | Equivalent |
|---|---|---|---|---|
| Shuai (Red) Jiang (Black) | Soái Tướng | 帥 將 | Governor General | King |
| Shi | Sĩ | 仕 士 | Advisor (Scholar, Guard) | Ancient Queen |
| Xiang (Red) Xiang (Black) | Tượng | 相 象 | Minister Elephant | Ancient Bishop |
| Ma | Mã | 馬 馬 | Horse | Knight |
| Ju | Xe | 車 車 | Chariot | Rook |
| Pao Pao | Pháo | 炮 砲 | Cannon Catapult | (no equivalent) |
| Bing (Red) Zu (Black) | Binh Tốt | 兵 卒 | Soldier (mercenary) | Pawn |

Although there have been several attempts to "internationalize" the Chinese chessmen, by giving them familiar pictorial symbols or by recreating them as standing 3-D figures (sometimes revised versions of Staunton chessmen), the overwhelming majority of xiangqi enthusiasts continue to prefer the traditional Chinese characters.

*Right:* Ebony xiangqi chessmen on an inlaid wooden board. KNOWLTON PHOTOGRAPH

*Left:* Xiangqi set with Staunton-like chessmen. CAZAUX PHOTOGRAPH

## Rules

While informal games usually allow either side to make the first move, it has become conventional in tournament play for Red to move first.

MOVES AND CAPTURES. Some pieces have movements that are restricted to certain zones of the board. Others can move without such limitations. Pieces move to an empty point or to a point occupied by an enemy piece, which is captured.

*Governor/General:* the central and most important piece of the game, he is confined to the nine points of the palace. He moves one step orthogonally, never diagonally. The Governor (Red) and General (Black) may never face each other on the same file with no intervening pieces. So, if the two pieces are on the same line with a single piece between them, that piece is pinned and cannot move from the line until the situation changes. This becomes important in the endgame, where the Governor and General can limit each other's mobility, and can remotely protect a piece as it invades the enemy palace.

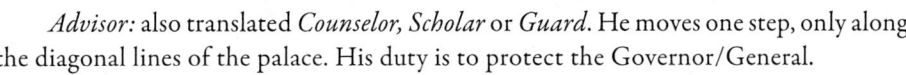

*Advisor:* also translated *Counselor, Scholar* or *Guard*. He moves one step, only along the diagonal lines of the palace. His duty is to protect the Governor/General.

*Minister/Elephant:* moves two points diagonally, but may not jump over an intervening piece. Defending the home front, this piece may not cross the river; it is confined to a range of only seven points on the entire board.

## Part III. Gunpowder on the Chinese Board

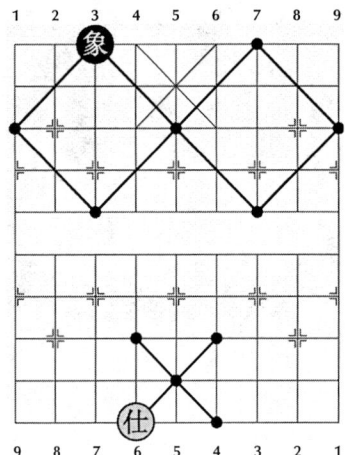

**ADVISOR AND ELEPHANT**

Reachable intersections for the Advisor (5 in total in the palace) and by the Elephant (7 in total on his side of the river).

(Columns here are numbered according to traditional Chinese notation, right-to-left for each player.)

*Horse:* moves one point orthogonally and, continuing away from its point of departure, one point diagonally. This is similar to Horse or Knight moves in other chess forms, but the xiangqi Horse can be blocked by a piece in its path.

*Chariot:* moves any number of unoccupied points forward, backward, left or right, exactly like the Rook of Western chess. In modern use, this character indicates an automobile, so some players call this piece a "Car" (*Che* in Chinese).

*Cannon/Catapult:* has no equivalent in Western chess. When not capturing, it moves just like the Chariot, like a Western Rook. But to capture a piece, there must be one additional piece in its path which the Cannon/Catapult jumps over before landing on the piece being captured. This intervening piece is known as the "screen" and may belong to either player. The Cannon/Catapult may not jump over more than one piece to make its capture, and may not jump over pieces when not capturing.

*Soldier:* at first, is allowed to move only one step forward. After it has crossed the river, it may also move one step left or right. It always captures as it moves, never diagonally. At the end of the board, there is no promotion; the Soldier is limited then to moving side-to-side.

**CANNON**

The red Cannon may move to any of the points marked with the black dots.

It may also capture the Horse or the Elephant (marked with squares) because of the presence of an intervening piece which serves as a screen.

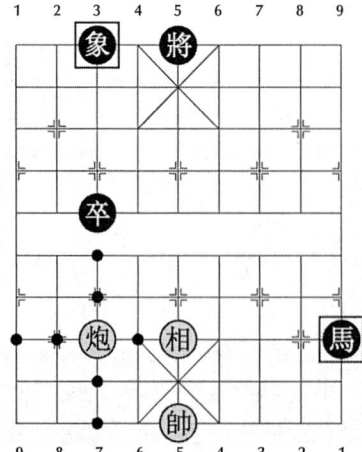

### HORSE AND SOLDIER

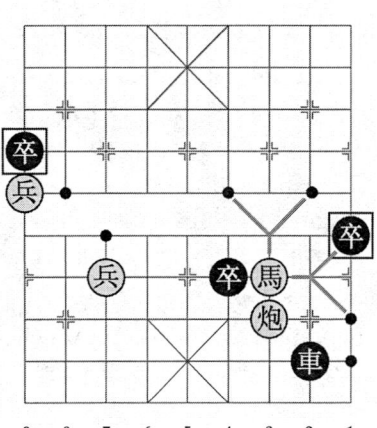

In this diagram, the red Horse may only move in the directions marked with lines, landing on the points marked with dots. It may also capture the black Soldier as shown. It cannot capture the black Chariot because it is blocked by the red Cannon.

The black Soldier that is still in its starting position (left column) can only move one step forward, capturing the red Soldier; however, the red Soldier that has crossed the river may move one step to the side (shown by the black dot) or may capture the black Soldier directly in front of it.

(Columns here are numbered according to traditional Chinese notation.)

The Cannon (or Catapult) introduces unique possibilities to the chess game. It is commonly known that a player in check must escape by blocking the check, capturing the attacker, or moving the King (General). In the case of check from a Cannon, the defender may be able to remove the intervening piece (the screen) which enables the Cannon to capture. Note that capturing the Cannon's screen does not resolve the check, since the capturing piece then becomes the screen for the Cannon.

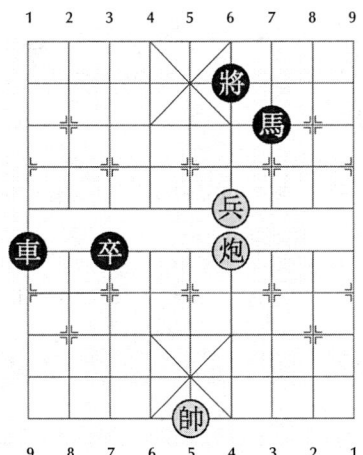

### MATE

The black General is in checkmate.

This diagram shows a mate typical of xiangqi: The red Cannon checks the black General using the red Soldier as a screen. The black General cannot move over to column 5, since he would be facing the Governor on the other side. Checkmate!

END OF THE GAME. The player who forces capture of the adverse General (or Governor) is declared winner. Unlike Western chess, a player who is stalemated in xiangqi, left with no legal moves, has lost the game. Stalemating the General is just as effective as checkmating.

Perpetual check or endless repetition is not permitted; the player forcing the repetition must make a different move. There are rare cases in which the decision as to which side must make a different move may be disputed; these are usually settled by a referee, using technical guidelines beyond the scope of this book.

## Tactics

NOTATION. Xiangqi has its own notation system, officially adopted by the World Xiangqi Federation (WXF). It is widely used in xiangqi literature and throughout the Internet. Only the columns are numbered, and each player numbers them differently, counting 1 through 9 from his own right to left. Each move is described by four figures:

- A letter indicating the piece. English initials have become the predominant international convention: K (King/General), A (Advisor), E (Elephant), H (Horse), R (Rook/Chariot), C (Cannon), P (Pawn/Soldier).
- A number, indicating the column that the piece starts its move from. The columns are counted starting on the right side of the player making the move.
- A "+" if the piece goes forward, a "−" if it moves backward and a "=" if it remains on the same rank.
- A number, the meaning of which depends upon the nature of the piece's movement. If the piece changes columns (as always in the case of a Horse, Elephant or Advisor), it is the number of the column the piece arrives on. If the piece remains on the same column (as in the forward or backward movement of a Chariot, Cannon, Soldier or General), this number will indicate the number of steps taken from the point of departure.

**Examples:**

Case 1 (changing of column): E7+5 means that the Elephant standing on the 7th column goes forward to a point on the 5th column. R2=3 means that the Chariot on the 2nd column moves left to the 3rd column, staying on the same rank.

Case 2 (keeping on same column): C2+7 indicates that the Cannon on the 2nd column moves 7 steps forward, staying on this 2nd column.

Although this system of notation is markedly different from those used in other chess forms, it is extremely efficient. In the rare cases that ambiguities arise, an additional note may be added to this four-figure formula.

RELATIVE VALUE OF THE PIECES. In this game, more than others, the position of the pieces in relation to each other quickly becomes more important than the relative value of the pieces themselves. Beware that merely counting piece values in this game will often not yield a good account of which player has the advantage.

Xiangqi authors show considerable disagreement over the objective values of the pieces. Based on a rigorous survey of the results of many varied games, the following scale has been suggested[3]: Soldier at the beginning (1), Soldier beyond the river (2), Advisor (2), Elephant (3), Horse (4), Cannon (6), and Chariot (10).

ELEMENTS OF STRATEGY. With pieces of relatively limited scope and its landscape of palaces across a river, xiangqi gives the impression of a game of siege, with each team sending out remote forces to seize the enemy commander from the safety of his fortress. This gives the game a different character from that of Western chess.

Not unlike other chess types, the game can be divided into opening, middle game and endgame. The opening generally extends through the first ten moves. It consists of setting the pieces in active confrontation as quickly as possible, seeking out key positions and clearing paths for the Horses and Chariots. One also tries to secure the defense of the palace, and coordinate the positions of the pieces. The most popular opening (practiced in about 50 percent of the games) involves bringing a Cannon to the center by C2=5 (or C8=5), exerting pressure on the enemy central Soldier.

Several principles govern the middle game: build a strong defense before considering an attack on the adverse camp; refrain from attacking without reinforcement; interfere with the opponent's coordination between the left and right wings; capture at least one Advisor or Elephant to undermine the enemy's defense; trade off pieces which support the opponent's defenses, etc.

By definition, the endgame consists of an attack on the adverse palace. There are countless textbook cases illustrating the many basic challenges an attacker may face. Openings also have an abundant share of specialized literature.

Traditional modern xiangqi board and pieces. KNOWLTON PHOTOGRAPH

# Variants

## Yitong[4] (Tongqi) or Manchu Chess

The two sides have unequal armies. Black possesses a complete set of xiangqi pieces whereas Red plays without Horses, Cannons, or the left Chariot. The remaining red Chariot has the combined powers of a Chariot, a Cannon and a Horse. A very lopsided struggle!

## Wuhuqi or "Five Tigers Chess"

In this popular variant, the five tigers are the five red Soldiers who can move two steps on each turn. Alternatively, Red can also choose to move two different Soldiers one step each in the same turn. Once a Soldier crosses the river in the center of the board, it can move two steps sideways or forward, or a combination of step forward and one step sideways, all in the same turn. To compensate Black, who plays with a standard set, Red has no Chariots, Horses or Cannons.

## Minixiangqi

Similar to Western chess and Japanese shogi, xiangqi also has its abridged version. This one was devised by Shigenobu Kusumoto in 1974.

Minixiangqi uses a small 7 × 7 point board, without Advisors or Elephants. The General is the only piece confined to his palace. Here, Soldiers can move forward, left or right immediately from the beginning of the game (like Korean janggi and unlike normal xiangqi).

Soldiers can promote to either Chariot, Cannon or Horse when reaching one of the two last opposite ranks (the 6th or 7th rank for Red). Promotion is optional.[5] All other rules are identical to regular xiangqi.

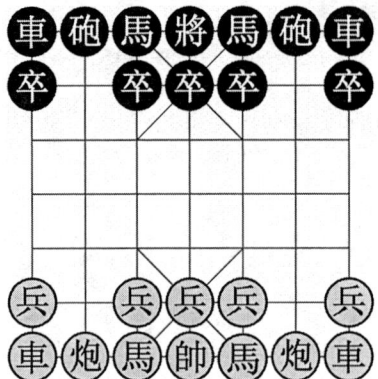

Initial array of minixiangqi.

## Jieqi or Undercover Chess

This interesting variation also appears as *Chaozhou xiangqi* on several Chinese websites, implying that it is popular in the costal Guangdong city of Chaozhou. It is played by placing both Generals in their initial positions and either turning all other chessmen face-down or covering them, and then shuffling the pieces (keeping the two sides separate), then randomly placing them in the starting points on each side of the board. The players begin by each moving one of the face-down pieces, as if it were the piece that normally starts in its starting position. For instance, any piece in the front row would start by moving one step forward like a Soldier. Once a piece has moved, it is flipped over (or uncovered), to reveal its identity. Pieces that have been revealed are subsequently moved in accordance with their shown identities; pieces not yet moved must first move according to their starting positions. Surprising situations may occur as it is possible to meet Advisors outside their palaces. Also, in this game, Elephants are allowed to cross the river and move inside the enemy camp. This variation has been played in official tournaments.[6]

This game is also very popular in Vietnam, known as *cờ úp*.

## Hunheqi or Disordered Chess

This variant also takes advantage of the uniform shape of the Chinese chessmen, which cannot be identified when turned over on their faces. In this game, each player has the General, Advisors and Elephants on their regular starting points. All other chessmen of both sides are flipped over and shuffled together. Each player then draws 11 pieces from the mix, placing them on the normal starting positions on his side of the board. Then, all pieces in the entire board are flipped over, to reveal their identities. There will almost always be pieces already scattered throughout the enemy camp. If one of the players is already in check, his move starts the game.

## The History of Xiangqi

The most widely accepted view sees xiangqi as an offshoot of the Indian chaturanga. Yet, Chinese chess has some characteristics that seem more primitive than their Indo-Persian cousins, and no one has come up with a convincing description as to how this evolution would have occurred. This leaves room for controversy regarding xiangqi's origin, and the origin of chess in general. The characters *xiang* 象 and *qi* 棋 (or *xi* 戲) are found together in texts dating before our era, but it is unlikely that they specifically refer to chess[7]—and clarifying exact meanings in these ancient texts is particularly difficult. Each Chinese character, in itself, can possess a wide range of meanings. For instance, *xiang* (象) can mean, among other things, elephant, portrait, symbol, picture, phenomenon, ivory, or constellation. The second ideogram *qi* (棋), in most cases designates a game piece and has often come to replace the character *xi* (戲), which means *game*. With such broad ambiguities, it would be difficult to assert the certain existence of a particular game.

Later, in the sixth century C.E., two poems make reference to a *xiangxi*,[8] clearly a game inspired by astrology, which may be linked to the present-day xiangqi—but even this is not certain. This xiangxi could have been related to *liubo*, a race game very popular in China at that time, but whose rules are lost today. The first established reference to a chess-type game is in the *Xuanguai Lu* (*Accounts of the Mysterious Marvels*), a collection of fantastic tales completed in the years 827–835 by the Tang minister of state, Niu Sengru. One of the fables clearly evokes a *xiangxi* board which involves several golden pieces: a top General (*Shang Jiang*), heavenly Horses (*Tianma*), Chariots (*Zi Che*) and six Soldiers (*Liu Jia*), described with some clues regarding their movements.[9] If there really were six Soldiers then this xiangxi would be different from present-day xiangqi. As arrows and stones are also mentioned, it is possible that a crossbow or a catapult was intended. The scene is supposed to take place in 762. A contemporary poem (829) of Bai Juyi (772–846), a friend of Niu Sengru, also mentions a xiangxi in which a "*Soldier rushes at a Wagon.*"

Then, anarchy seized China and the history of xiangqi was silenced. With the arrival of the new Song dynasty, which reunified the country (960 C.E.), references appear once again. The river makes its first appearance in the *Xiangxi Shiguang*, a poem by the neo–Confucian philosopher, Cheng Hao (1032–1085), published circa 1055–75. Curiously, a General-in-chief (*Jiang*) is mentioned there which "radiates toward all points," along with Soldiers (*Zu*) which move diagonally once they "cross the river." The other pieces are a Deputy General (*Pian*), an Assistant General (*Bai*),[10] Chariots (*Ju*) and Horses (*Ma*). But there are no Cannons yet. A Catapult first appears as a chessman in Sima Guang's *Qiguo xiangxi ju* (*Description of Seven Realms Xiangxi*), an essay describing the invention of a large variant, published about 1071–85.[11]

In subsequent years, the literary sources lead us to believe that the game in vogue differed from the present xiangqi. This is what the scholar Chao Gongwu stated in a 1249 encyclopedia, citing a lost work from Yin Zhu (1001–1047) in which he described a xiangqi that did not look like the one of his time. Similarly, the scholar, Chao Buzhi (1053–1110), wanted, as Sima Guang before him, to create his own "widened" xiangqi. For that, he announced in the *Guangxiangxi Tu* (*Widened Xiangxi with Illustrations*) (1079), that he wanted to enlarge the "standard game of 11 × 11 lines of his childhood" to a board of 19 × 19 lines and 98 pieces. Alas, only the preface of this work survives and all details of these two games are lost: the large one of 19 × 19 lines, and—even more frustrating—the so-called standard game of 11 × 11 lines. Several historians have tried to reconstruct it but this exercise is highly speculative. Some assert that this 11 × 11 xiangxi employed 34 pieces (6 Soldiers in each side) instead of 32; some contend that a "river" was present; still others suppose that it was played with the pieces standing inside the square, rather than on the intersections.[12] But the accuracy of these reconstructions remains doubtful.

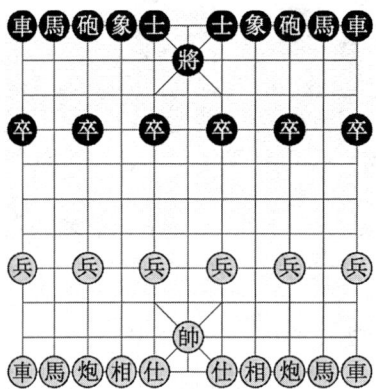

One hypothetical reconstitution of a xiangqi ancestor played on a board of 11 x 11 points with 34 pieces.

Note that if the modern rules were applied, the Generals would be in check in this position.

After the 11th century, the number of references increases, and removes all ambiguity. The earliest extant xiangqi set that has been excavated and identified (dating from about 1100) includes some *Pao* pieces, bearing the drawing of a Catapult, which prefigures the Cannon. In addition, the monk Yuxian explained in his writings (between 1131 and 1162) that the term *boluo sai* designated a game of troops, also called *xiangji*,[13] on the lines of a board separated into two halves by a river, in which each player commanded 16 pieces, including Catapults. About the same period, a drawing of the poet Li Qingzhao (1083–1155), and a picture of the painter Xiao Zhao (in 1162), show a chessboard identical to that of the modern day xiangqi, accompanied by the familiar 32 pieces.[14] Finally, around 1210, a poem by Liu Kezhuang enumerates each of the pieces.[15]

The evidence shows that the xiangqi known today was already established during the 12th century. Several xiangqi manuals appeared during the 13th century, with the frequency of such compositions increasing up to the present day. A famous example is the *Ju Zhongmi* (*The Secret Inside the Tangerines*[16]), a major book published in 1632 which inspired generations of players. In this volume, the author, Zhu Jinzhen, compiled the games and problems of the Ming era. The title comes from a famous legend: "Two enormous tangerines had grown in a tangerine grove. Someone picked them, peeled them and found two old men sitting face-to-face and playing chess inside."

Today, xiangqi is practiced in international competitions throughout Asia, but also outside of Asia, carried by the strength of the communities descended from the Chinese and Vietnamese Diasporas.

Students in Cambodia, enjoying a game of Chinese chess. KENNETH LIGHTFOOT PHOTOGRAPH

Cambodian philatelic block (2001) representing xiangqi.

A rich and brilliant game, spread broadly across Asia and the Pacific, xiangqi still deserves a wider reach into other parts of the world. Perhaps its further popularity is limited most by the use of Chinese characters in the chessmen. But this is a very small obstacle, with only about ten symbols to remember. The game is extremely dynamic with complex, tactical middle games and brilliant mating combinations.

## 12. Janggi

Korea, the "Land of the Morning Calm," also possesses her own chess: *janggi*.[17] Although this native variant is not as popular as *baduk*, the Korean name for the game of go, many enthusiasts find janggi more engaging than its Chinese cousin since several pieces exercise greater mobility across the chessboard.

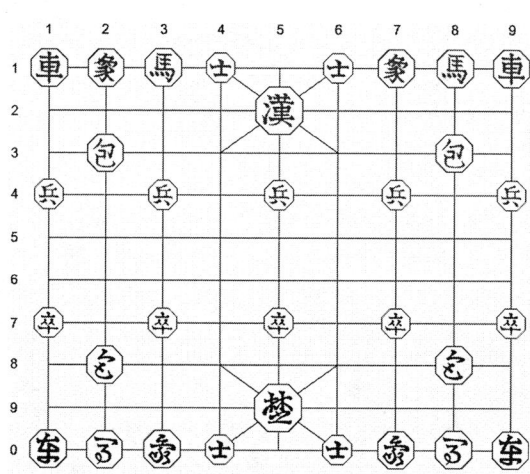

One of the initial arrays of janggi.

## Material

The janggi board is constructed simply, with no special coloration. It is composed of nine vertical and ten horizontal lines, with diagonal lines marking the nine-point fortress on each side. The points along the vertical lines are farther apart than those between the horizontal lines, giving the board a distinctive elongated appearance. Unlike the Chinese chess (xiangqi) board, the Korean janggi board has no specially marked river between the two sides.

The pieces are played on intersections of the lines.

There are 16 pieces on each side, green (or blue) and red. They are: 1 General, 2 Guards, 2 Elephants, 2 Horses, 2 Chariots, 2 Cannons and 5 Soldiers. The pieces are flat, in an octagonal shape, of three different sizes according to their importance: large for the Generals, small for the Guards and Soldiers and medium-size for all others. Each piece is marked with an ideogram indicating its name with a Chinese character (called *hanja* in Korean). Green pieces are written with semi-cursive script, the reds with the traditional script.

### Names of the Janggi Pieces

| Korean name | Hanja R/G | Meaning | Equivalent |
|---|---|---|---|
| Han (red) / Cho (green) | 漢 楚 | General (see below) | King |
| Sa | 士 士 | Guard, Advisor | Ancient Queen |
| Sang | 象 象 | Elephant | Ancient Bishop |
| Ma | 馬 馬 | Horse | Knight |
| Cha | 車 車 | Chariot | Rook |
| Po | 包 包 | Cannon | |
| Byeong (red) / Jol (green) | 兵 卒 | Soldier | Pawn |

Janggi games carry a symbolic significance, representing a confrontation between the States of Han and Chu that disputed China in 206–202 B.C.E. These dynasties are represented by their respective Generals leading their armies. This war, won by the Han, holds a major place in Chinese culture and shows unequivocally that Koreans borrowed their chess from their neighbor. In North Korea, this historic reference is censored, with the central pieces being called *Jang* (General) for Red and *Gwan* (Minister) for the Green.

## Rules

SETUP. The initial setup is appreciably different from that of xiangqi. Each General is placed on the second rank, at the *center* of its palace (the nine points indicated by an "X" on each side). Before the battle begins, each side is allowed to interchange the positions of the Elephant and the Horse on each flank.

Han (the red player) starts by placing his pieces, choosing one of the four possible configurations:

## 12. Janggi

- Horse / Elephant / Elephant / Horse (called "inner Elephant")
- Horse / Elephant / Horse / Elephant (called "right Elephant")
- Elephant / Horse / Elephant / Horse (called "left Elephant")
- Elephant / Horse / Horse / Elephant (called "outer Elephant")

Cho (the Green player) arranges his pieces next, which constitutes a slight advantage. Green also makes the first move.

When the Red player interchanges the Horse and Elephant on one side only, it is advised—though this is not mandatory—that the Green player mirror the change on the same columns as those of his opponent.

MOVES AND CAPTURES. All chessmen capture as they move.

*General:* the most important piece in the game, he remains enclosed within the nine points of his palace (marked by an "X" on each side). He moves one step, orthogonally or diagonally, but only along the lines marked inside the palace. (For instance, he cannot move diagonally from row 9, column 4.)

*Guard (Advisor):* moves like the General. He remains inside the palace and moves along the marked lines.

*Chariot:* moves an unlimited number of unoccupied points along the columns and the rows. When it begins its move inside a palace, it can also move along the marked diagonals.

*Cannon:* moves in the same directions as the Chariot, but must jump over one piece (of either color) each time it moves. This includes the possibility of moving along the diagonals within the palace (only possible from one corner to the other, with a piece standing in the center). It captures just as it moves, jumping over one piece and landing on the piece to be captured. A Cannon can never jump over another Cannon and cannot capture another Cannon. The Cannon has no possible move at the beginning of the game.

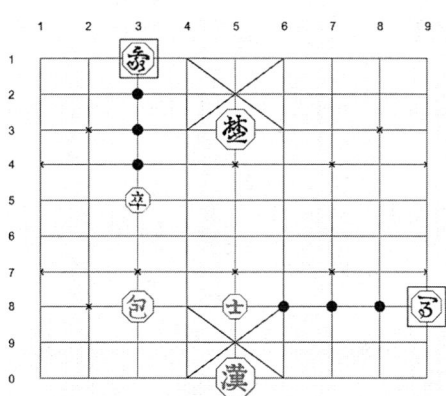

The red Cannon (row 8, column 3) may go to any of the points marked with dots; it must jump over a piece to move.

It may also capture the Horse on row 8 or the Elephant on column 3 (they are marked with boxes).

(Compare this to the equivalent diagram for xiangqi.)

*Elephant:* has a strikingly original move. It moves one step orthogonally (along the rows or columns) and then, continuing away from its point of departure, two steps diagonally. It may cross only empty intersections. Contrary to the xiangqi Elephant, this piece is not confined to one side of the board (which makes sense as there is no river on the janggi board). It can reach all points of the board.

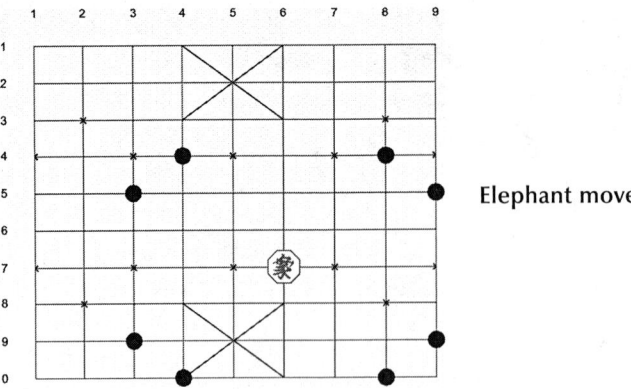

Elephant moves.

*Horse:* moves one step orthogonally then one step diagonally, away from its point of departure. The intermediate intersection must be unoccupied (the same move as the Horse in xiangqi).

*Soldier:* moves and captures one step straight forward or sideways, to the right or left. Inside the opposing palace, it may also move and capture one step diagonally forward, following the marked diagonals. (The green Soldier, below, can move diagonally only on the line printed on the board.) There is no promotion; when it reaches the final row, the Soldier moves only laterally.

Soldier moves.

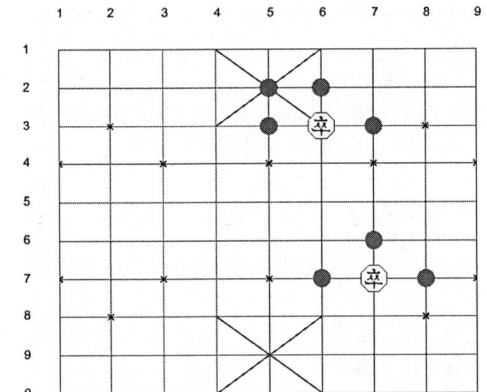

PARTICULAR RULES. • *Generals face-to-face:* Generals should normally not be placed on the same column with no piece in line between them. If a player deliberately makes a move that places his King facing the opponent's King, without any pieces between them, it is called *bikjang*, or "King's check." If the opponent does not do anything to stop the Generals from facing each other in this manner, the game is a draw. This "King's check" is an attempt by the disadvantaged player to create a draw. The opponent may also reject the *bikjang* by either moving the King off that column or by placing a piece between the Kings. The player who has moved into a *bikjang* forfeits his chance of winning the game. Even if he eventually checkmates the opponent, his accomplishment only counts as a draw.

• *Stalemate:* unlike chess, in which a stalemate is a draw, in janggi, when a player has no legal move (his General is not in check but there no move that does not put him in check), he may pass his turn. To indicate this, he simply flips his General over in place. Therefore, a stalemate is not a draw.

END OF THE GAME. Victory is obtained by checkmate of the opponent's General.

In case of perpetual check or repetition of position, the player who repeats the same board position more than three times loses.

POINT SYSTEM FOR COMPETITION. Drawn games can pose a problem in tournaments, where decisive results are needed for each game. To remedy this, the *Korean Janggi Association* recommends that a winner be determined according to the value of pieces remaining on the board. The pieces are given these point values: Soldier 2; Guard 3; Elephant 3; Horse 5; Cannon 7; Chariot 13. To compensate for Green's (or Blue's) advantage of first move, Red is given an additional 1½ points. Note that this increment of a half point makes an even score impossible, so a winner is certain to be declared.

## Technical aspects

The traditional Korean notation, in general use through the 1960s, used a Cartesian coordinate system with Chinese numerals (一, 二, 三, 四, 五, 六, 七, 八, 九, 十) representing the rows and numerals (1, 2, 3...) representing the columns. Later, generally spanning the 1970s–90s, a simple system numbered each point, 1 through 90, from the upper left, descending down each column, ending with 90 in the bottom right corner. Finally, in the early 21st century, the Korean Janngi Association (est. 1956) presented the system that is now official: each point has a two-digit number. The first digit indicates the row, marked from top to bottom, 1 to 9, with 0 as the bottom row. The second digit indicates the column, 1 to 9, left to right. So, the top row consists of numbers 11, 12, 13 ... to 19; the second row consists of 21, 22, 23 ... to 29 and the bottom row has 01, 02, 03 ... to 09.

To note the move of a piece, one must write the coordinates of the point before moving, then the piece name (in Chinese) and finally, the coordinates of the destination point. For example to move a Horse from 03 to 84, one writes 03 馬 84.

*Left:* The janggi board, from green side. *Right:* The janggi board, from red side. KNOWLTON PHOTOGRAPHS

JANGGI IS NOT XIANGQI! The theoretical values of the pieces correspond to those given above, as they are counted at the end of a game. The absence of a river makes a considerable difference between janggi and xiangqi both in the moves and the values of several chessmen. Thus, the Soldiers (Pawns) have a more important role in the Korean game, thanks to the lateral movement which they have from the beginning. On the other hand, the Cannon is weaker because it requires a screen for every move—especially at the end of game when the chessboard is becoming depleted. Also, as the Cannon cannot jump over another Cannon, a player may counter the check given by an opposing Cannon by seizing the screening piece with a Cannon of his own, an option that does not exist in Chinese chess.

The Elephant is a completely different piece: mobile on the full playing field, not constrained to its own side as in the Chinese game. Its range is very long with a wide, far-reaching step. However, it is easily blocked by the other pieces, since it must pass over two free points to reach its target.

In the palace, the Korean General and Guards have greater mobility, moving equally on the diagonal, horizontal and vertical lines, making them less constrained by topological markings than their Chinese cousins.

# *Variants*

## *Gidongcha Janggi*

There have been reports from various sources that one additional opening arrangement is used in North Korea.[18] This setup is called *gidongcha*, which means "starting Chariots." It involves interchanging the positions of Chariots and Elephants on both sides.

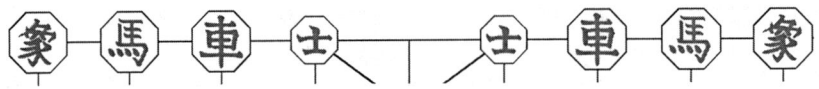

The *gidongcha* janggi set-up.

## *Gwangsanghui*

The Korean name of this game, 광상희, seems to be a phonetic rendition of the Chinese 廣象戲 (*guang xiangxi*), meaning "large xiangqi." That giant chess variant was invented in the 18th century under the Joseon Dynasty. It is described in the *Noeyonjip* (*Collected works*), a collection of texts written in Chinese script (*hanja*) by Nam Yu-yong, a royal instructor.[19]

A short passage gives some clues of the rules, though it is alas, incomplete. The description of the starting array allows a partial reconstruction; the moves of the pieces are not, however, given with sufficient precision.[20] Each of the two players commands 43 pieces, which are placed on the points of a riverless board of 15 columns and 14 rows. There are three palaces on each player's side of the board, the central one with a Marshal (帥) standing in its center, and two lateral palaces hosting a General (將). Each player's army comprises four of the following regular janggi pieces: Elephant (象), Horse (馬), Guard (士), Chariot (車) and Cannon (actually, Catapult, 砲), which have the names and moves found in standard janggi. The front line on the 6th row is made up of four blocks of three units each, which are for half Infantry units (步), playing as the janggi Soldier, and half Cavalry units (騎). However, the respective positions of these blocks cannot be reconstituted with certainty. Finally, additional military units, specific to this game; one Vanguard (前), one Rearguard (後將), two Mobile units (游), two Elite units (奇) and two Ambush units (伏), complete each player's army.

The capture of the Marshal is the goal of the game.

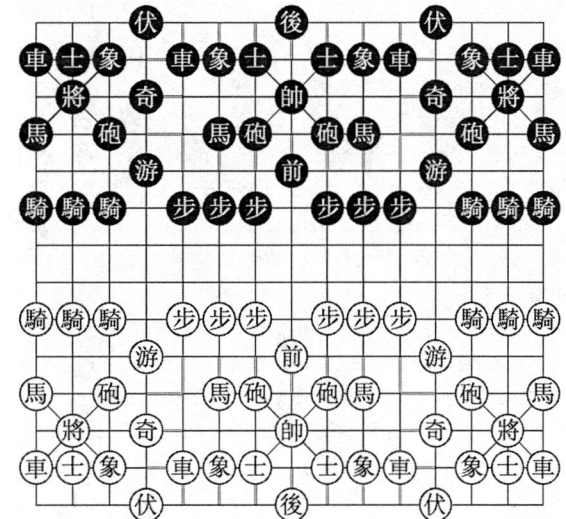

Reconstructed initial array of gwangsanghui.

Nothing is known about the popularity of this game, but it serves as a testament that Korea, too, has been tempted by giant chess variants, along with its Chinese and Japanese neighbors.

## Tokyo Janggi

The Korean Janggi Association Tokyo Branch in Japan has proposed a new experimental rule revision in 2005: on reaching the opposite side of the board (10th rank), a Soldier can promote to a friendly piece (other than a Guard) that has already been captured. This variant strongly affects the endgame, and deserves to be tried.

## The History of Janggi

Unlike its neighbor China, the Korean peninsula is not rocked by the capricious rhythm of great rivers. Is this the reason no "river" survives on the Korean chessboard? It may be, but no evidence has been discovered to support this hypothesis. Perhaps the river was added to the Chinese game later, after an earlier form had passed into Korea. Janggi is remarkable in the sense that it preserves a rigorous regularity: all pieces, Cannon included, capture as they move; the Soldiers (Pawns) never change their moves; and all chessmen follow the marked lines, including the diagonals in the palaces, within the limits of their respective powers. Are those characteristics primitive or derivative?

Although zealously maintaining its independence, Korea has discerningly absorbed large parts of the Chinese culture. There can be no question that janggi is among the many things borrowed from China, for it is essentially a variant of the Chinese game. But it cannot be certain to what extent it evolved within Korea and what aspects of the game were imported "as is" from a Chinese region. The Neo-Confucian scholar Seongho Yi Ik (1681–1763) attested that janggi was already popular during the Goryeo period (918–1392). There is a story that tells of a Chinese Song merchant who fooled a man and took his beautiful wife away as a stake in a janggi game. This happened in a place near the mouth of the Yeseong River. It is known that the Goryeo and Song dynasties had close relationships up until 993 when the alliance was broken.

The history of janggi is poorly documented. The first mention of a chess game in a Korean text dates back to the late 16th century with the notes of a Confucian scholar, Yu Hui-Chun (1513–1577), who played against a certain Kim Yo, but it is not known if they played janggi or another chess form. Shortly thereafter, another author, Sim Su-Gyeong (1516–1599), made a first brief description of janggi chessmen of lacquered wood. Finally, a description appeared in the "*Gyegokjip*," an essay by Jang Yu (1587–1638),[21] indicating a game already identical to modern janggi (with the General in the middle of the palace and a riverless board). Unfortunately, these texts are silent about the shape of the chessmen, not indicating whether they were circular or octagonal.

The oldest known janggi pieces were found in a sunken ship in the waters of Taean County dated between 1265 and 1268 (end of the Goryeo period), having probably been en route to Ganghwado, the temporary capital at the time. The pieces consist simply of smooth, small stones with rounded edges and Chinese characters painted with ink on one side.[22] Two ancient sets (date unknown), conserved in Korean museums, show vaguely octagonal pieces and vary in size as janggi pieces do today.[23] Perhaps historians and archeologists will one day improve upon these scant traces of historic information.

In Korea, janggi rivals the popularity of other board games such as *yut* (or *nyout*, a race game played mostly by children) and *baduk* (the game of go). The first janggi association was formed in 1956, and now, formal tournaments are held on a regular basis. In Korea, professional players have emerged. Janggi is also played outside Korea by Korean minorities in Japan and in neighboring China, especially in the Yanbian Korean Autonomous Prefecture. In 2009, the first World Janggi Tournament was held in Harbin, Northeast China. Now, the Internet contributes to its increasing popularity in the Western world.

Janggi in Korean characters.

Janggi allows a diversion, a bit of intriguing variety, for the more numerous lovers of Chinese chess. A xiangqi set can easily serve for the game of janggi if one simply ignores the river. Beyond obvious similarities, the differences are surprising: an Elephant that's flying all over the chessboard, a Cannon immobile without a piece to jump over, Pawns very mobile from the start, and the increased mobility of most pieces within the fortress. In addition, the game is renewed almost endlessly, owing to the choice of the initial setup. All these peculiar features culminate in an impressively unique chess variant.

# 13. Qiguo Xiangxi

And now, a game for seven players! With more than a hundred pieces scattered on an enormous chessboard, this is a curious, possibly disconcerting chess variant, whose name means "game of the Seven States." More surprisingly, the rules of this seven-player Chinese chess come to us from an earlier source than any known report of the rules of two-player xiangqi.

With a good sense of humor, the Chinese sources present *qiguo xiangxi* as a "drinking game." Get your friends together and let's play!

# 13. Qiguo Xiangxi

## Material

This is played on a *weiqi qipan* (go board) of 19 × 19 points. The setup is not symmetrical (otherwise it would have been a game for eight players!).

There are 120 pieces in total. The names of the different states and their associated colors are summarized on this table:

| State | Ideogram | Position | Color |
|---|---|---|---|
| **Qin** | 秦 | West | White |
| **Chu** | 楚 | South-West | Red |
| **Han** | 韓 | South-East | Cinnabar |
| **Qi** | 齊 | East-South | Indigo |
| **Wei** | 魏 | East-North | Green |
| **Zhao** | 趙 | North-East | Purple |
| **Yan** | 燕 | North-West | Black |
| *Zhou* | 周 | *Center* | *Yellow* |

Each player commands an army of 17 pieces: 1 General (*Jiang*), 1 Deputy General (*Pian*), 1 Assistant General (*Bai*), 1 Emissary (*Xingren*), 1 Catapult (*Pao*), 1 Bow (*Gong*), 1 Crossbow (*Nu*), 2 Knives (*Dao*), 4 Swords (*Jian*) and 4 Cavalry (*Qi*).

In the center of the board lies a neutral yellow piece, the powerless King of the Zhou Dynasty, who can neither move nor be captured.

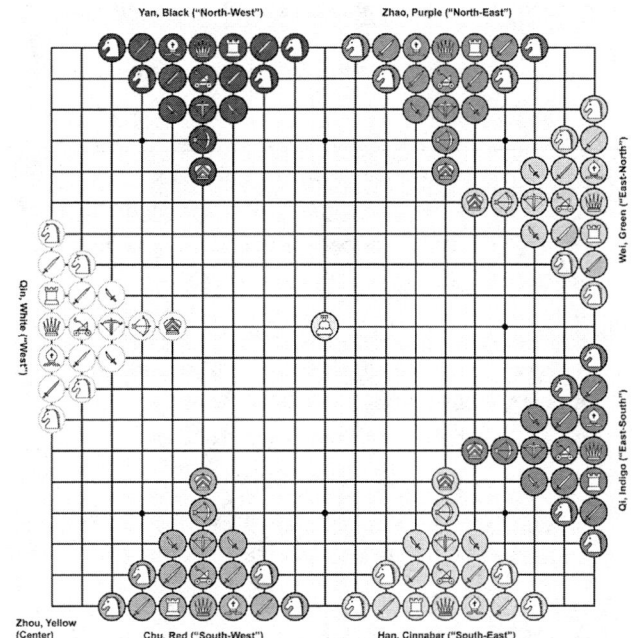

Initial array of qiguo xiangxi.

## Rules

SETUP. With seven players, each takes one Kingdom. With six players, one player takes Qin plus another Kingdom. With five players, Chu also takes an additional Kingdom. With four players, it is Qi that adds an alliance. With three players, the Qin player adds one more ally, commanding a total of three kingdoms.

The order of play is counterclockwise: Qin, Chu, Han, Qi, Wei, Zhao and Yan. In a traditional Chinese set, the general of each army bears the character that represents its own kingdom.

MOVES AND CAPTURES

*General:* travels an unlimited number of free intersections in any direction in a straight line, just like the Queen of Western chess. In the original Chinese form, each General is represented by the Chinese character of its state.

*Deputy General:* travels an unlimited number of free intersections orthogonally (in rows and columns), exactly like the Chariot in regular xiangqi or the Rook of Western chess.

*Assistant General:* travels an unlimited number of free intersections diagonally, like the Bishop of Western chess.

*Emissary:* moves like the General (or the Western Queen) but cannot capture or be captured.

*Catapult:* moves an unlimited number of free intersections in orthogonal directions (rows and columns) but it needs to jump over an intervening piece to capture an enemy piece. This is exactly the same as the Cannon of xiangqi.

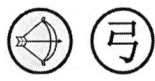
*Bow:* moves four spaces (never less) in a straight line vertically, horizontally, or diagonally. It cannot jump over an intervening piece.

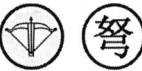
*Crossbow:* moves five steps (never less) on each move in a straight line vertically, horizontally, or diagonally. It cannot jump over an intervening piece.

*Knife:* moves only one step in any of the four diagonal directions.

*Sword:* moves only one step in one of the four orthogonal directions, forward, backward, left or right.

*Cavalry:* moves one step orthogonally plus three steps in a diagonal direction, continuing away from its point of departure. It cannot jump and may only cross unoccupied points.[24]

PROGRESS OF THE GAME. • Each player may choose an alliance with another player with whom he will not fight. If a player attacks an allied piece by mistake, then the entire army of that ally is withdrawn from the board.

- Except for established allies, each player promises that he will not solicit the help of another player to defeat a third one. A player who transgresses this rule must drink a glass of liquor.
- A player cannot play the reverse move of the move he played on the previous turn (moving a piece back to its previous spot). The one who forgets this ... empties his glass.

END OF THE GAME. A player beats an opponent by taking his General or a total of any ten pieces. The remaining pieces of the defeated player are withdrawn from the board, captives of the winning player. The defeated player drinks a glass. At the end of the game, the player who has captured the most pieces is the ultimate winner.

The player who succeeds in capturing two Generals or thirty hostile pieces becomes a "hegemon" (*ba*). All others players must then submit to him and must drink their glass. They celebrate the winner who then drinks the glass of victory.

VALUE OF THE PIECES. Chinese sources suggest relative values for the chessmen as follows:

Bow, Crossbow, Knife or Sword 1; Cavalry 2; Catapult 3; Assistant General 4; Deputy General 5.

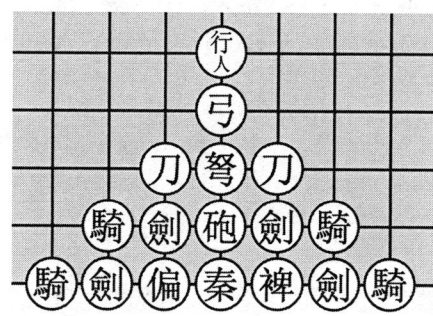

Detail showing the arrangement of one side (here Qin) with traditional pieces.

## The History of Qiguo Xiangxi

This curious chess game appears to originate toward the end of the 11th century and is attributed to the famous historian and imperial minister Sima Guang (1019–1086) who reported the rules in an essay entitled *Qiguo Xiangxi Ju (A Sketch of an Old Form of Xiangxi)*, composed circa 1071–1085.[25] Chinese sources[26] indicate that the scholar, Pei Zixi, from Yizheng, engraved the rules of the game on blocks of wood allowing them to be transmitted to the generations to come. This took place on the day of the Lantern Festival, very precisely, in the second year of the Kaixi era, under the reign of the Emperor Ningzong of the Southern Song Dynasty, on 24 February 1206.

The game evokes the Warring States period (475–221 B.C.E.), a turbulent time in Chinese history, chaotic and anarchical, but culturally very rich. The Zhou dynasty, founded in 1046 B.C.E., had declined but was still represented by a powerless king, unable to prevent the independence of seven rival Kingdoms. In the third century B.C.E., the state of Qin became the most powerful and, after bloody wars, defeated and absorbed all of the other Kingdoms. In 221 B.C.E., Ying Zheng, ruler of Qin, succeeded in unifying China[27] and was proclaimed Emperor under the name of Qin Shi Huangdi. This epic forms the heart of the *Zhanguoce*, a classic book of Chinese history.

Qiguo xiangxi has a particular importance in history because it is the first Chinese chess of any sort for which the complete rules have been conserved, preceding the earliest description of two-handed xiangqi rules. Also, among the chessmen, the Catapult, predecessor of the Cannon, makes its first appearance. This probably indicates that the Catapult was also in use in 11th century regular xiangqi.

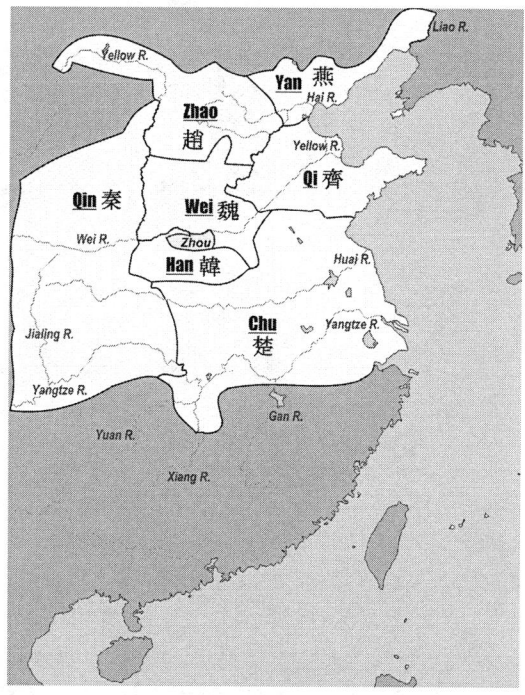

Map of the Warring States toward 260 B.C.E. The respective position of the players around the qiguo xiangxi board recalls the location of the different states.[28]

Moreover, it seems that Sima Guang deliberately tried to eliminate all foreign influence. For example, he specifically refused to incorporate Elephants. According to him, these pachyderms had no business on a Chinese battlefield.[29]

Qiguo Xiangxi in Chinese characters.

What a surprise! This game demonstrates that the Chinese advanced the idea of chessmen having the moves of the modern Queen and Bishop about four centuries before their introduction into the chess of Europe. The play on points of a monochromatic board made it difficult to visualize the diagonal directions; perhaps this is why these innovative pieces were not carried on in Chinese chess.

# 14. Sanguo Qi

Its name means "game of the Three Kingdoms" and, indeed, it comprises three opponents. This xiangqi adaptation is supposed to evoke the war of the Three Kingdoms, another famous episode in Chinese history. This period saw three dynasties, Wei, Shu and Wu, fighting for empire domination in the third century of the present era.

## *Material*

The chessboard is a hexagon with three groups of 9 × 5 intersections; there are 135 intersections in total. Each camp is separated from the others by a "river," and each has a nine-point "palace" in its center.

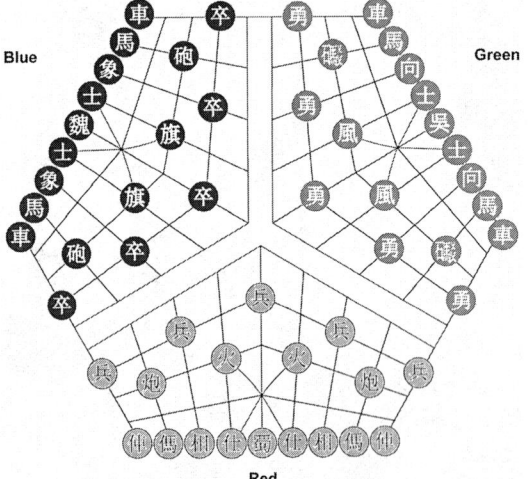

Initial array of sanguo qi.

The colors of the pieces are blue, red and green. Each player has 18 pieces: the classical 16 of regular xiangqi and two new ones which stand on the same rank as the Cannons. The new pieces have different names depending on their side: Fire (*Huo*), for red, Flag (*Qi*) for blue, Wind (*Feng*) for green. The Generals bear the names of the historic Chinese realms: *Shu* for red, *Wei* for blue, *Wu* for green. Several other green pieces also have different names. The Soldier is a Brave (*Yong*), the Cannon is a more powerful *Pao,* and the Minister is another "*Xiang*" ("Protector").

Here is the complete table:

| Red | Blue | Green |
|---|---|---|
| 蜀 General (*Shu*) | 魏 General (*Wei*) | 吳 General (*Wu*) |
| 仕 Advisor (*Shi*) | 士 Advisor (*Shi*) | 士 Advisor (*Shi*) |
| 相 Minister (*Xiang*) | 象 Elephant (*Xiang*) | 向 Protector (*Xiang*) |
| 傌 Horse (*Ma*) | 馬 Horse (*Ma*) | 馬 Horse (*Ma*) |
| 俥 Chariot (*Ju*) | 車 Chariot (*Ju*) | 車 Chariot (*Ju*) |
| 炮 Cannon (*Pao*) | 砲 Catapult (*Pao*) | 礮 Ballista (*Pao*) |
| 火 Fire (*Huo*) | 旗 Flag (*Qi*) | 風 Wind (*Feng*) |
| 兵 Soldier (*Bing*) | 卒 Soldier (*Zu*) | 勇 Brave (*Yong*) |

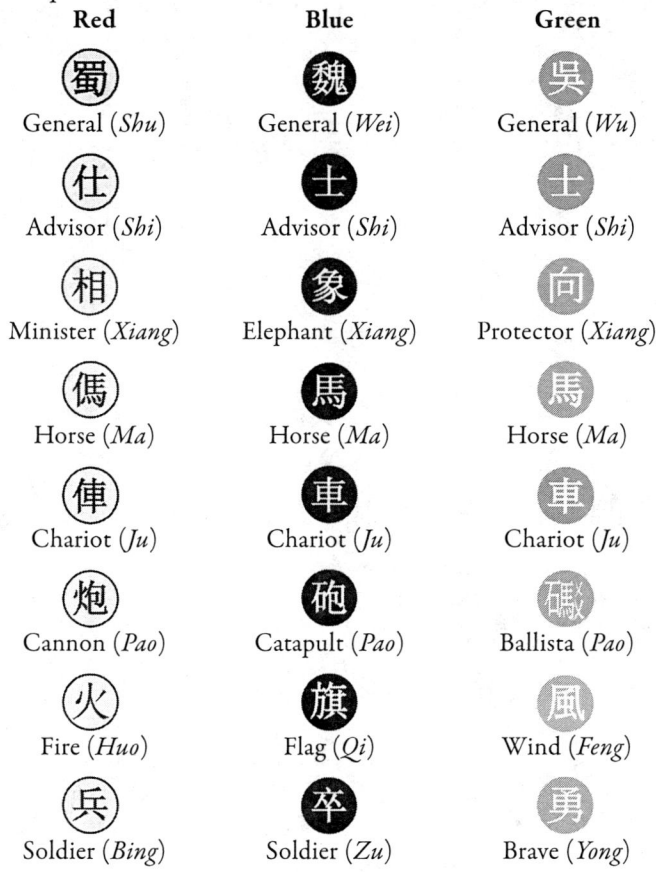

## *Rules*

MOVES AND CAPTURES. Chessmen that are included in regular xiangqi maintain their familiar moves.

火 旗 風 *Fire, Flag, Wind:* move two steps orthogonally followed by one step outward diagonally. They cannot jump over any intermediate points that are occupied. This movement resembles, without the jump, the Camel of Timur's chess.

PARTICULAR RULES. • A piece that crosses the river at the center of the board may choose to cross over into either of the opposing camps.

END OF THE GAME. Each player plays against the other two. Victory is obtained by mating or stalemating both opponents. When a player mates an adversary, he withdraws the vanquished General from the board and assumes control of the defeated player's remaining pieces. In case of stalemate, the player who made the most recent move in blocking the General inherits any remaining pieces from the defeated camp.

三國棋

**Sanguo Qi**

# Variant: Sanyou Qi

*Sanyou qi*, the "game of three friends," is another three-handed xiangqi variant. Two of the Soldiers are replaced by pieces called "Fires" which move one step forward diagonally. They cannot move backward.[30] There are also two "Flag" pieces on each side, at the front of each palace. Their movement is different from that in the previous game: they advance two steps straight ahead as long as they remain in their territory; then, in an opponent's territory, they move one step in any of the eight directions.[31]

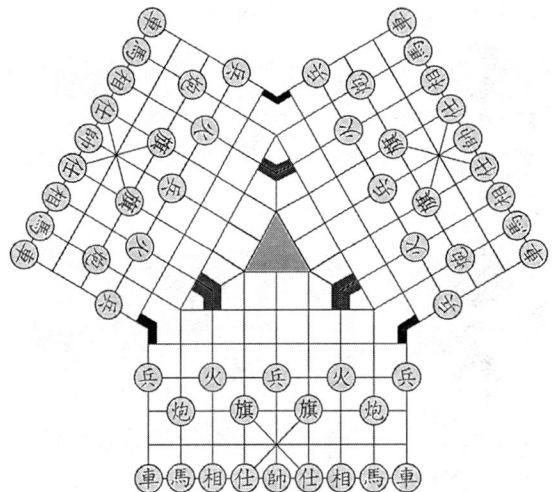

The sanyou qi board.

From the edges toward the center, the gray zones show the defensive walls, the mountains and the sea.

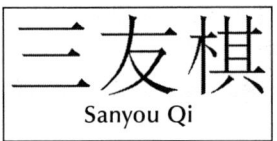

At the center of the board, an empty space represents the sea. Horses and Chariots cannot cross it. At the junctions of sides are defensive walls and mountains that cannot be crossed by Horses, Chariots or Cannons.

## The History of Sanguo Qi and Sanyou Qi

It would be wrong to think that Sanguo Qi is as old as the epic that it represents. At the fall of the Han dynasty in 220 C.E., the three Kingdoms of Shu, Wu and Wei struggled for domination of China. Wei finally submitted to Shu but, shortly thereafter, power was seized by Sima Yan who founded the Jin dynasty in 265 and finally defeated Wu in 280. This episode, one of the bloodiest in Chinese history, made a lasting impression in popular culture. It is not surprising that it provided the framework for a three-way chess game.

*Sanguo qi* has been attributed to the Southern Song Dynasty (1127–1279), but this is controversial because the two books reported to have made that assertion (the *Sanguo Tuge* and the *San Xiangxi tu*) are now lost. According to Leventhal, both three-handed games were invented under the Qing Dynasty (1644–1911) and the addition of Flags betrays the distinctive placement of banners in the military organization of the Manchurian rulers (the Qing kings were of Manchurian origin).[32]

In particular, *sanyou qi* would have been created by Zheng Jinde of Shexian, in the Anhui province, during the reign of the Kangxi Emperor (reigning 1661–1722). Zheng Jinde was a friend of Zhang Chao, one of the greatest of the Chinese essay writers. His book, entitled *Zhao dai cong shu* (*Collection of Volumes in the Present Age*), published in 1697, gives the rules of Zheng's game. The Chinese scholar Zhu Nanxian believed that Zheng Jinde may have seen the now-lost book *Sanguo Tuge,* and copied or amended *sanguo qi* to design his *sanyou qi*.

During the reign of the Qianlong Emperor (reigning 1735–1796), another book of games, *Muzhu xianhua* (*Swineherd's Chat*), by Jin Xueshi, also cited this game. The rules are also found in Liang Shaoren's essay "Liang Ban Qiuyuan Suibi" ("Dissimilar Essays in Autumnal Rain-Thatched Hut"). Liang Shaoren lived during the reign of the Daoguang Emperor (1820–1850).[33]

In modern times, many three-handed and also four-handed xiangqi (*siguo xiangqi*)[34] games have been invented in China, sometimes being commercialized with limited success.

Three-handed xiangqi, like three-handed chess, is a curiosity that has been reinvented several times, notably in modern times, always with novel peculiarities which lead one to suppose that each new inventor imagines himself to be the first....

# 15. Banqi

*Banqi* means "half chess" but this game is also known as *anqi*, "dark chess" or *mangqi*, "blind chess." This is a very enjoyable game, particularly popular throughout China. The pieces are first placed upside down and then flipped over one by one to discover their values. From there, captures are made in respect to a specific hierarchy.

## Material

In order to play *banqi*, a complete traditional xiangqi set is necessary. The chessmen have a disk shape and possess a uniform back side, with no distinctive markings. The board is an arrangement of 8 × 4 squares, often utilizing one half of a standard xiangqi board. Unlike xiangqi, banqi proceeds with the pieces placed in the squares of the board, not on the intersections.

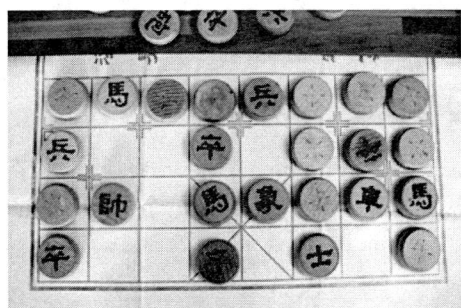

A banqi game.
CAZAUX PHOTOGRAPH

## Rules

- The 32 pieces are turned upside down, mixed, and then deployed at random on the 32 squares of a half xiangqi board.

- The first player picks up a piece and flips it, discovering its identity. Its color assigns him the side he will play for the rest of the game. His opponent, who gets the other color, flips another piece over, and the game continues with the two players taking turns.
- There are three kinds of move: flipping an undiscovered piece, moving a piece to another square, or capturing an adverse piece.
- One can only move pieces of one's own color. All pieces move one step, forward, backward or sideways, but never diagonally. The move must always be toward an empty square, unless it is a capture.
- All pieces capture as they move. Only discovered adverse pieces may be captured. Capture is by displacement; the attacking piece takes the place of the captured piece, which is removed from the board.
- The captures must respect the hierarchical order. It is only permitted to capture a piece of equal or lower rank. The order is as follows: General ⇒ Chariot ⇒ Horse ⇒ Cannon ⇒ Advisor ⇒ Elephant ⇒ Soldier.[35] As an exception, a Soldier can seize the General and the General cannot capture a Soldier.
- The game ends when one of the players cannot play anymore, either because he does not have any pieces left, or his pieces have no possible moves. The opponent is then declared the winner.
- In the case of repetitive movements, the players may agree that the game is a draw.

TAIWANESE RULES. The rules are somewhat different in Taiwan:

- The hierarchy there is: General ⇒ Advisor ⇒ Elephant ⇒ Chariot ⇒ Horse ⇒ Soldier.
- The Cannon can capture any piece and be captured by any piece except the Soldier. It does not capture as it moves, but captures as in xiangqi, which means that it must jump over another "screening" piece (friend or enemy) to seize a piece placed on the same file or column. All squares between the Cannon and the screening piece, as well as between the screening piece and the target, must be empty.

Note: thus, a Cannon cannot seize a piece on an adjacent square.

OTHER VARIANTS. In the absence of official regulation, variants are numerous. Every region has its conventions; every community has its preferences. Among the most remarkable are these:

- The possibility of a General capturing a Soldier if the General moves first (played in Mainland China).
- The possibility of capturing an undiscovered piece with the Cannon. If the attacked piece proves to be superior to it, or to be of the same color, it is left in place, discovered, and the turn stops there. The attacking piece remains in its original place.
- The possibility of making multiple Cannon captures in a single turn, of both discovered and undiscovered pieces, in succession, until no more capture moves are possible.

# Strategy

Because there are five Soldiers, the Generals are not the strongest pieces. This honor goes to the second piece on the list.

It bears mentioning that playing first constitutes a slight disadvantage in the Taiwanese variant.

## The History of Banqi

The history of banqi is unknown, but is not an isolated example. Chinese players do not hesitate to repurpose xiangqi sets for other games which are sometimes quite different. For example, *giog,* which uses xiangqi chessmen in a game more akin to cards or dominoes. Banqi, however, is a true board game—but only its playing material makes it directly related to chess. This game is greatly enjoyed throughout the Far East; in China of course, but also in all countries populated by the Chinese diaspora.

China's contribution to the history of games is considerable. The Chinese invented *weiqi* (the game of go), playing cards, dominoes, mahjong, liubo (now extinct) ... and new inventions are always on the horizon. Banqi offers a stimulating diversion for xiangqi players, allowing a very different game with the same playing material. Two great games for the price of one!

Banqi in Chinese characters.

---

# 16. Doushouqi

This delightful little game, pronounced "doe show chee" and meaning "fighting animal game," possesses other nicknames such as "the jungle game," "animal battle chess" and even, in Asia, "children's chess." But, is it a chess game? Maybe not *sensu stricto,* but a certain close kinship cannot be denied. The presence of differentiated pieces and the captures by displacement are obviously chess-like elements. Moreover, it is likely that it was originally derived from xiangqi.

## Material

*Doushouqi* is played over a board of 7 × 9 squares. Several squares are marked with drawings or symbols. The central squares of the 1st and the 9th rows are the "dens." Each den is surrounded by three "traps." Two lakes of six squares each stand in the center of the board.

Each player has eight pieces, each representing a different animal. As in xiangqi, they are uniformly sized discs, red for one side, blue, green or yellow for the other. Before the game starts, the pieces are placed on their squares, which show images to indicate the starting position of each animal.

## Rules

MOVES AND CAPTURES. Blue starts the game.

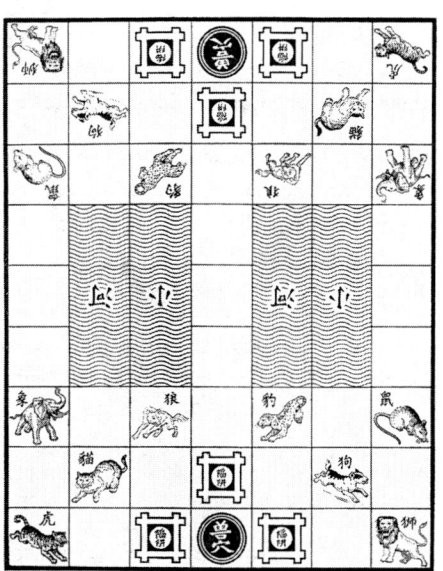

The doushouqi board.

All pieces move by taking one step horizontally or vertically, never diagonally. Captures are made by one piece moving in and taking the place of the other (as in chess). Capturing is not compulsory.

The pieces can only capture adversaries which are of lower or equal power. This is the hierarchy, from strongest to weakest:

**Elephant ⇒ Lion ⇒ Tiger ⇒ Leopard ⇒ Dog ⇒ Wolf ⇒ Cat ⇒ Rat**[36]

The doushouqi set.

### Names of the Doushouqi Pieces

| Force | Piece | Name | Meaning |
|---|---|---|---|
| 8 | 象 | *Xiang* | Elephant |
| 7 | 獅 | *Shi* | Lion |
| 6 | 虎 | *Hu* | Tiger |
| 5 | 豹 | *Bao* | Leopard |
| 4 | 狗 | *Gou* | Dog |
| 3 | 狼 | *Lang* | Wolf |
| 2 | 貓 | *Mao* | Cat |
| 1 | 鼠 | *Shu* | Rat |

In addition, the Rat can take the Elephant. To explain this, it is said that the Rat crawls into the Elephant's ear and eats its brain!

Any animal can capture the same type of animal, which is of equal power. In this case, whichever animal strikes the other becomes the one making the capture.

PARTICULAR RULES. • *The Traps*: all pieces move freely on and off the trap squares, but an animal which has moved onto the opponent's trap square loses all of its power and may be captured by any other animal, no matter how low in rank.

- *The Rat and the Lakes:* only the Rat may move on the squares of the lakes. While there, it is safe from capture from any other piece, except for another rat which may also swim in the lake. The Rat is not allowed to capture on the move of entering the lake or stepping back onto dry land. Therefore, it may not attack the Elephant from the water, and may not attack another rat while crossing to or from the water.[37]

- *The jumps of the Lion and the Tiger*: these two animals can jump over the lakes, from one bank to the other, straight forward, backward, or side-to-side. They are allowed to capture in this move, pouncing on an animal across the water. Jumping over the lake is not allowed, however, if a Rat is in the water, blocking the path of the Lion or Tiger.

- No animal is allowed to enter its own den.

- It is not permitted to repeat the same position twice.

END OF THE GAME. The goal is to move one piece—any animal—into the opponent's den.

## Variants

This game is sometimes played with minor variations in the rules, which lead to a different game. Some of them deserve to be tried:

- The Elephant cannot eat the Rat. In this case, the Rat takes on a greater importance, and the game invites a higher degree of tactical maneuvering.
- The Leopard can jump over the lake, but only side-to-side (horizontally), providing it does not leap over the Rat in the water.
- The Lion is not allowed to jump over the lake horizontally.
- The Lion and the Tiger are equally strong; either one may capture the other.
- The Dog (because it is a good swimmer) can also move in the lake. In this case, it is subject to the same limitations as the Rat.
- The traps weaken all pieces, whatever their side. A piece standing on a trap may be captured by any piece, regardless of power ranking, even if it is on its own side of the board.

## Strategy

Doushouqi is a very pleasing game, of great interest to young players but quite engaging to older players as well.

The strategy is simple, the game being articulated around the four major pieces: the Elephant, Lion, Tiger and Rat. The four other pieces serve as defense, seldom penetrating the opposing camp. On the other hand, the game requires some tactical subtlety. A Cat is sufficient to block a Lion approaching a trap, and it is generally necessary to lead the attack with at least two pieces to win. The first error is often fatal and the greatest vigilance is required to hold out to the very end.

# Dongwuqi

This name means "animal game," often translated as "animal chess"—a term sometimes used in referring to doushouqi. There are, in fact, several games designated by that same term.

One is particularly interesting. It has circular pieces (similar in shape to doushouqi pieces) with iconic images of animals, along with their Chinese characters, engraved on the upper surfaces. Two players have 16 different animals each, blue on one side, red on the other.

The animals are divided into four categories and ranked according to power in descending order:

- Wild beasts (猛獸): Lion ⇒ Elephant ⇒ Tiger ⇒ Leopard ⇒ Bear. They move exactly three steps, but not diagonally. The exception is the Lion, the king of all animals. More powerful than the others, it can move one, two or three steps in all directions, including diagonally.
- Domestic animals (家畜): Horse ⇒ Cow ⇒ Sheep ⇒ Dog ⇒ Cat. They move exactly two steps, but not diagonally.
- Insects and bugs (蟲類): Bee ⇒ Spider ⇒ Butterfly. They move one step in any direction.
- Birds (飛禽): Eagle, Sparrow, Swallow. They fly, which means they move one, two or three steps but diagonally only.

The pieces move along the marked lines on the board and those moving two or more steps may change direction during a move.

The game is played over the intersections of a 9 × 13 board, which is simply printed on rough paper. The intersections are indicated by horizontal and vertical lines. In addition, every other point is connected by diagonal lines. The starting points of the pieces are marked by circles inscribed with characters which indicate the categories of pieces that may begin on those spots. The players are free to start their pieces on any of the marked points, as long as each one is assigned to the correct category. The Lion starts in the middle of the first row.

Heavy lines define a 7 × 4 "mountain" area on each side. The Lion in each camp must stay in this area. A piece captures by taking the place of the enemy piece, which is removed from the game. A piece may capture any piece that belongs to a different category. But within each category, an animal may only capture those that are of lesser power. Therefore, the players should carefully plan their initial setup.

The player who captures the opposing Lion is the winner.

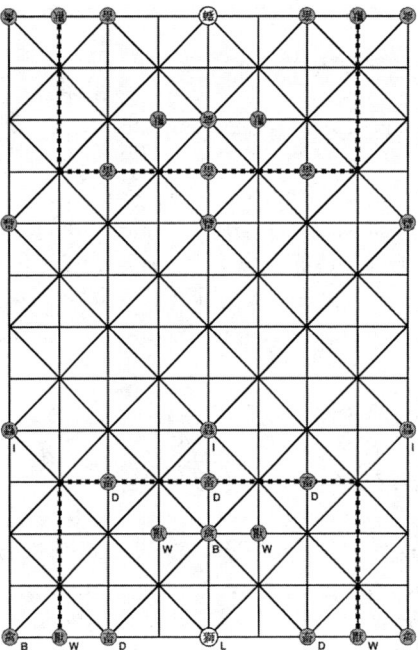

*Left:* The dongwuqi board (L: Lion; W: Wild animal; D: Domestic animal; I: Insect; B: Bird).

*Above:* The dongwuqi pieces.

This dongwuqi set appeared in an online auction in China. The pieces have been dated from the early 1950s, according to the style of Chinese characters used at that time. The characters used on the pieces, the box, and the rules page are "traditional" Chinese script, which underwent a change when the Communist government of Mainland China began a campaign promoting "simplified" Chinese script, in an attempt to increase literacy.[38]

動物棋
Dongwuqi

# *Taï-Hou*

Online auctions have become a valued resource for the game historian. The game of Taï-Hou, quite possibly a predecessor to doushouqi, appeared online in France in 2016. This game, produced in 1925, claimed to be a Chinese game that "combines chess and checkers," with the "advantage of being played like mahjong." It comprises four sets (red, yellow, blue and green), each of 11 Bakelite pieces, in the shape of dominos or mahjong tiles. Each piece displays an animal or a weapon, and a value (both in Chinese and Western numerals). The monochromatic board has 12 columns with 11 ranks, with six squares in the center marked by dots to form a "lake" (e5, e7, f6, g6, h5, h7).

The rule booklet accompanying Taï-Hou is complex and somewhat ambiguous; perhaps this lack of precision limited the game's appeal. It is played by two to four players, and three game variations are presented. The pieces fall into three categories with the Emperor's Weapons being most powerful (Arrow 10 and Saber 9), followed by the Buddha's Large Animals (Elephant 8, Snake 7 and Tiger 6), and finally the Small Animals (Bat 5, Pheasant 4, Turtle 3, Toad 2 and Nightingale 1). There is also an unnumbered Lotus Flower which replaces a player's first-captured Arrow or Saber. Captures are made according to numerical hierarchy. In addition, the Weapons and Large Animals able to capture anyone within their own categories—but following specified restrictions.

With three or four participants, the pieces are shuffled and randomly placed on each player's first two rows. But when played by only two, a screen is placed between the two sides, and each player strategically arranges his pieces, before the game commences. All pieces move one square straight ahead. They can be rotated to change direction, and this counts as one move.

In one variation, the six "lake" squares are impassable by most pieces. Only the Toad may enter the lake and only the Bat, Pheasant and Nightingale are able to "fly" over the lake and land on the opposed square, if it is free.

Although the booklet is subtitled *"Nouveau jeu chinois"* (New Chinese game), it gives no further indications of its origin. Rather, it expounds upon the Chinese people's great interest in games, with the popular mahjong as an example—which probably served as inspiration for this game as well.

The booklet indicates that the game was patented, and was sold by a company named E.M.F. (Éditions Musicales Perforées, *Perforated Music Editions*) located at 16 rue de Hanovre, Paris. E.M.F. was stationed there from 1919 until 1928, and ceased operations altogether by 1930. The game's patent, in a simplified version, was submitted February 9, 1925 (French patent number 593094), by the painter and interior designer Samuel-Alexandre Gontier (1877–1944). Interestingly, Gontier's address on the patent is *rue de la Chine, Paris*, giving the game a curious Chinese connection.[39]

An advertisement for Taï-Hou from the French magazine *L'Illustration*, 1925.

## History

Doushouqi and the related Chinese animal games are probably a relatively recent development, though no precise date or original inventor is known. The first publication of such a game in the West was given in English by R.C. Bell, in 1960, describing a game he had received from Hong Kong. Shortly thereafter (ca. 1963), a version named *Jungle King* was published by Waddingtons in the United Kingdom.

It is possible that doushouqi was derived from xiangqi, considering the similarities between doushouqi's lakes and dens, and xiangqi's river and palaces. On the other hand, the manner of moving the pieces and capturing according to a set hierarchy suggests a relationship with banqi—which is normally played on one half of a xiangqi board.

Animal chess with 16 different pieces could be the missing link. Played with disks engraved on one side, dongwuqi appears to be an adaptation of xiangqi set to an animal theme. The next step would have been to further refine the board with the additions of traps, dens and lakes; and to reduce the number of pieces, to better fit the taste and abilities of young children.

Similarities to the newly rediscovered Taï-Hou are striking. Like doushouqi, this Chinese-inspired Parisian game has animal pieces, hierarchical ranks, a lake that protects a weak piece and is jumped over by specified others. Like dongwuqi, Taï-Hou categorizes the pieces into larger families. Dated with certainty to 1925, it predates the earliest record of Chinese animal-fighting games by at least 25 years. It would be ironic indeed if this Chinese-inspired game traveled from Paris to the Orient, and there became an authentic Chinese game.

The principle of captures being made according to a set hierarchy also relates this to another family of games, that of luzhanqi and Stratego—which are presented in the following chapter. But no specific evidence has yet been found to indicate which one came from the other. In the games to be discussed, the flat pieces stand up, so that each player can see only the identities and values of his own pieces. But doushouqi, like chess, is a strategy game of "full disclosure." Every aspect of the game is shown at all times, with nothing hidden from either player.

Doushouqi has further similarities to the Western game Stratego, in that it shows two lakes in the center, and has pieces moving on the squares of the board. Dongwuqi and luzhanqi maintain the xiangqi-like convention of moving the pieces on the intersections of lines. The one has mountains serving as palaces of the Lion kings; the other has mountains as obstacles to be circumnavigated between the two camps.

The list of animals in doushouqi does not suggest a very old history. Some animals, such as wolves and lions, do not belong to the traditional Chinese bestiary—not appearing, for instance, in the Chinese zodiac. And the inclusion of domestic animals, such as dogs and cats, gives the distinct impression that the game was designed with 20th century children in mind. Doushouqi appears to be the most recent in the rich lineage of Chinese games. The history of these games leaves much still to be discovered.[40]

A doushouqi set with 3-D figurative chessmen.
KNOWLTON PHOTOGRAPH

Today, this game is relatively well known in the Western world. Children feel particularly drawn to this *petite menagerie* with its instinctively understood pecking order. Doushouqi owes its international success to pieces that do not require knowledge of international characters, to inexpensive availability in Chinese shops and to simple rules of play. A wonderful little game whose popularity is well deserved.

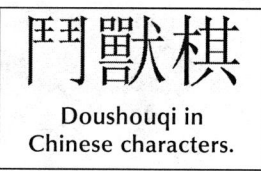

Doushouqi in Chinese characters.

# 17. Luzhanqi

This game, whose name means "land battle game," is very popular throughout Asia. Luzhanqi[41] is also known as *luzhanjunqi* ("land battle army game") or simply *junqi* ("army game"). Its board includes a complex network of railroad tracks, roads, mountains and camps. This game shares many characteristics with other Chinese board games such as *xiangqi* and *doushouqi*, and similarities to several Western war games are especially intriguing.

## *Material*

THE BOARD. The playing "board" is usually simple folded paper or thin vinyl, printed with the markings of the playing surface.

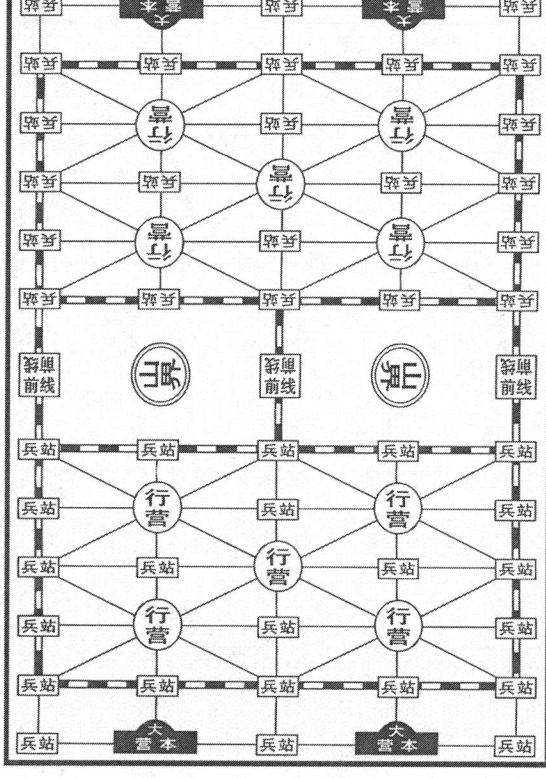

The luzhanqi board.

| Marking | Signification | Corresponding rule |
|---|---|---|
| 兵站 | Soldier station | An ordinary playing space. Pieces are moved on and off these spots, and can be attacked while standing on them. |
| 行營 | Camp | A safety circle. A piece on this spot cannot be attacked. |
| 大本營 | Headquarters | There are two of these on each side. The Flag is stationed on one of these two spots. |
| 前线 | Front line | These markings stand between the two sides of the board. Pieces do not land on these squares; they pass over them. |
| 山界 | Mountain border | Two obstacles that stand in the dividing line of the board. Pieces do not move onto or over these spaces; they are forced to pass over the front Line. |
| / | Lines | Pieces move from one playing space to the very next one, following these lines. |
| ▬ | Railroad | Any moving piece is allowed to go any number of playing spaces on these tracks, as long as it stays on one straight railroad line. The Sapper has the special ability to travel around Railroad corners as well. |

THE PIECES. The pieces are rectangular flat tiles with inscribed characters indicating their values, in red or black depending on the side. Modern sets are commonly made of plastic but older wooden sets may also be found.

Each player has 25 pieces: 1 Field Marshal, 1 General, 2 Lieutenants Generals, 2 Brigadiers, 2 Colonels, 2 Majors, 3 Captains, 3 Platoon Commanders, 3 Sappers, 2 Bombs, 3 Landmines and 1 Flag.

### Names of the Luzhanqi Pieces

| Rank | Piece | Name | Meaning |
|---|---|---|---|
| 1 | 司令 | Siling | Field Marshal |
| 2 | 軍長 | Junzhang | General |
| 3 | 師長 | Shizhang | Lieutenant General |
| 4 | 旅長 | Luzhang | Brigadier |
| 5 | 團長 | Tuanzhang | Colonel |
| 6 | 營長 | Yingzhang | Major |
| 7 | 連長 | Lianzhang | Captain |
| 8 | 排長 | Paizhang | Platoon Commander |
| 9 | 工兵 | Gongbin | Sapper (Engineer Scout) |
|  | 炸彈 | Zhadan | Bomb (Hand Grenade) |
|  | 地雷 | Dilei | Landmine |
|  | 軍旗 | Junqi | Flag (Army Banner) |

## Rules

SETTING UP. To begin the game, each player places his 25 pieces on the Soldier Stations and Headquarters spaces on his side of the board. Pieces do not begin on the Camp circles. They are placed so that each player can see the identities of his own pieces, but not those of his opponent.

Arranging the pieces is the first strategic consideration of the game.

- The Flag must be placed on one of the two Headquarters squares.
- The Landmines must be placed somewhere in the two rows closest to the player (i.e., the Headquarters row, or the one next to that).
- The Bombs may not be placed on the front row (but the players probably would not want them there anyway).

MOVES. Either player begins by making a move, and then the two opponents take turns, as in most strategy board games.

- Soldiers (all ranks, 1 through 9) and Bombs move along a line a single step to the very next playing space (to any Soldier Station, Camp or Headquarters).
- On the Railroad, all mobile pieces may move as many spaces as desired, staying in one straight line, and not passing over any other pieces.
- The Sapper (rank 9) has the special power of continuing around corners on the Railroad. As long as his path is unobstructed, his move may cover any number of Railroad-linked spaces, turning as many corners as he likes.
- The Landmines and Flag do not move. They remain in place until attacked by an enemy piece.

CAPTURE. Among soldiers, it is the pieces of higher rank that capture the pieces of lower rank (as if they went out onto the battlefield and "out-ranked" each other).

- When a piece attacks by moving onto a space occupied by an opposing piece, the piece of lower rank is removed, and the one of higher rank remains. (Note "1" is the highest rank; "9" is the lowest.) If a piece attacks another of equal rank, both pieces are removed.
- If a Bomb attacks or is attacked by any piece, both pieces are removed.
- If any piece other than a Sapper attacks a Landmine, both pieces are removed, but if a Sapper attacks a Landmine, the Landmine is removed and the Sapper remains.[42]

All pieces are safe and may not be attacked while on a Camp space.

END OF THE GAME. When a piece attacks and seizes the opponent's Flag, that player has won the game.

THE REFEREE. It is preferred that this game be played in the presence of a third person who acts as a referee. Whenever a piece is attacked, the referee determines which piece (or pieces) must be removed. The players never see the opposing pieces and are never told their identities, even when attacks are made and pieces are removed. This mystery is the fun and intrigue of the game.

If no referee is available, the game proceeds in the same way, but every time there is an attack the players must temporarily show the identities of the two pieces, to determine the outcome of the attack. A little less mystery.

# Asian Variants

In recent decades, many similar games have been invented in Asia, which exploit the same military theme. The goal is always the same: capture the opponent's Flag (or occupy his headquarters). The presence of a referee in addition to the players is usually the most suitable way of playing the game.

## Siguodazhan

This game, which means "four countries great battle," is the four-player version of luzhanqi. The complete form, *siguodazhanqi,* is also found, as well as *siguojunqi,* "four countries army game." Each of the players has a complete set of 25 pieces of one color, red, yellow, blue or green, which are set up on a cross-shaped board. Each side has a grid of 5 × 6 stations, as in luzhanqi.

The center of the board indicates mountain ranges with various railroads passing through. There are only a few adaptations needed to play this version of luzhanqi made for four players:

- The four players are divided into two teams. The teams command the armies next to each other (not across the table, as in bridge).
- The pieces move on the *curved* railroad tracks, just as they would move on straight railroad tracks in the two-person game. The Sappers (Engineers) are still the only ones allowed to continue their moves at railroad corners.
- When one of the players has his Flag captured, all of his pieces are removed from the board. His partner fights on until one team is entirely vanquished.

In order to keep the game moving along, each person is generally allowed 90 seconds to make his move.

Versions with specially designed boards for play by six or eight players have also been marketed in China.

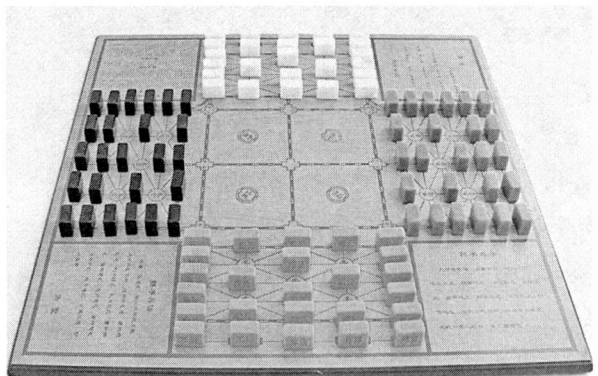

**The siquodazhan board, set to play.**
KNOWLTON PHOTOGRAPH

## Haijunqi

This one is a "navy game," a maritime counterpart of luzhanqi. First produced in the late 1970s, the board presents two seas consisting of 4 lines of 7 points each, separated by a land area of 3 lines.

Each player has 20 pieces, which represent different ships of different values, plus 3 Missiles, 3 Mines and 1 Flag. The principles of play are identical to those of luzhanqi.

# Luhaikong Zhanqi / Luhaikong Sanjunqi / Hailukong Junqi

The name, found in several variations, means "land-sea-air three army game." It can be seen as a modernized luzhanqi with most modern units of 20th century warfare: tanks, ships and planes, in addition to several troops. All the basic weapons are there: cruisers, gunboats, destroyers and submarines form the Navy; fighters and reconnaissance aircraft constitute the air force; and tanks, anti-aircraft guns, bombs, mines, poison gas, and even atomic missiles complete this dreadful arsenal.

The board is large and divided into three distinct parts of similar area: a sea in the center and a land area in front of each player. The game opens with a naval battle to control the sea, with ships assisted by the air force, before the invasion of the opposite land can be achieved.

This "three-armed" board game is by far the most complex game of the family. It is popular in Taiwan, which is not surprising since that country has lived under threat of invasion from the mainland since 1949.

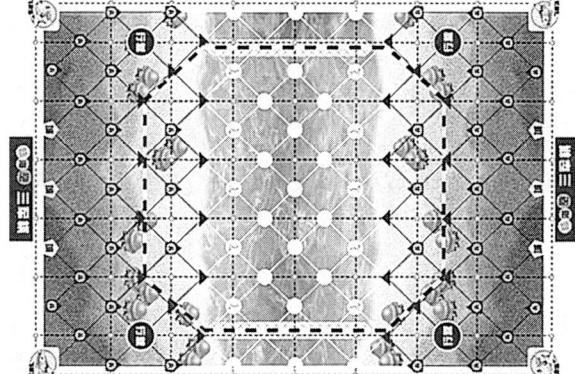

The luhaikong zhanqi board.

# Dongwuqi (Modern Version)

This is another "animal game," also known as *dongwuqi*, still played by children in China and Taiwan. The board has only 59 points, all connected by vertical and horizontal lines, with every point also connected by diagonals. Each player has 16 tile-shaped pieces, two each of eight different animals. Surprisingly, they are exactly the same animals found in doushouqi!

The pieces are placed upside down, hiding their values. Penetrating the opponent's den wins the game.

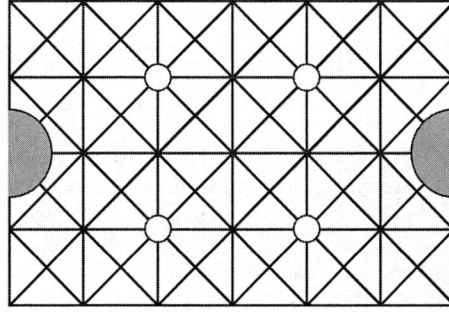

The small dongwuqi board designed for children. There is a den for each side and four safety spots on the board.

## Gunjin Shogi

*Gunjin* or *kogun shogi* means "military shogi" (*shogi*, Japanese chess, is presented later in this book). This Japanese game has much in common with the other games described in this chapter. Two armies of pieces with values hidden from their opponents attempt to seize the opponent's headquarters, represented by one or two squares at the players's side. A referee may be used to resolve captures.

There are several variations of this game, with various board sizes. A common version uses two camps of 6 × 4 squares each, separated by a no-man's-land with two bridges that create contact points between the armies. Each of the two players has 23 pieces: 1 Ensign, 12 Officers of various ranks, 2 Planes, 2 Tanks, 1 Cavalry Unit, 2 Sappers, 1 Spy and 2 Landmines. Pieces of higher rank can capture pieces of lower rank, and there are additional rules for the Spy, Landmines, etc., which are similar to the rules of luzhanqi.

A larger version, 8 squares wide, has a sea crossed by four bridges. In this game, each player commands 31 pieces (four additional Officers of various ranks, and one additional Tank, Cavalry, Sapper and Landmine).

Today, there is a Japanese Gunjin Shogi Federation, founded in 1998, which organizes championship matches played on a 9 × 9 square board with 25 pieces per player—including an atomic bomb![43]

## Salpakan or the Game of the Generals

This game was invented in the Philippines by Sofronio H. Pasola toward the end of the 1960s and commercialized in 1973. The goal of the game is to capture the opponent's Flag, or to maneuver one's own Flag safely to the other end of the board.

Each player commands 21 pieces, either red or blue, of various ranks which are hidden from the opponent. Like the other games of this family, a piece of higher rank seizes a piece of lower rank. There are two Spies who can take any piece except a Private. The six Privates can be taken by any officer and can only defeat a Spy.

All pieces, including the Flag, can move one space forward, backward, or sideways on the squares of a plain 9 × 8 board. Each player arranges his army secretly, deploying the pieces on his choice of squares in the first three rows.

This game has achieved a certain degree of success, claiming 2,500 clubs in 34 countries. It is available in electronic form.

This version, marketed in 1980 as "The Generals" uses an electronic arbiter on the side of the board, allowing pieces to be compared without revealing their values.
KNOWLTON PHOTOGRAPH

# L'Attaque and Stratego, Two Related Games

Games designed on the same "capture-the-flag" principle have also been invented outside of Asia. We offer a brief review of these games, before considering how they may be related.

## L'Attaque

*L'Attaque* is the European predecessor of Stratego. It is a capture-the-flag game, with pieces of various values, hidden from the opponent. Two identical armies are set in opposition to each other, secretly arranged in the starting array.

The two camps, often Red against Blue, have 36 pieces each, usually rectangular cards held upright on small platforms made of metal or plastic. The board consists of 10 rows of 9 columns. In the middle of the board lie three "rivers" of 2 squares each, obstacles which cannot be passed over by any piece.

The pieces are ranked according to strength, from weakest to strongest: 1 Flag (rank 1); 8 Scouts (2), 4 Sappers (3), 4 Sergeants (4), 4 Lieutenants (5), 4 Captains (6), 2 Majors (7), 2 Colonels (8), 1 Brigadier General (9) and 1 Army Chief (10). In addition, there are 4 Mines and 1 Spy on each side. Mines and Flags are immobile. The other pieces, except the Scout, move one step forward, backward or sideways (never diagonally). The Scout may move several squares (like a chess Rook). When a piece enters a square occupied by one off the opponent's,[44] the players show the pieces to each other. The piece of higher rank wins and the defeated piece is removed from play. If the two pieces are of equal value, they are both removed.

Any piece that attacks a Mine, except the Sapper, is lost and removed from play. If the Sapper attacks a Mine, he removes it successfully, and the Sapper remains in play. Any piece may capture the Spy, except the Army Chief; the Army Chief may be captured by the Spy. Any piece may capture the Flag, thereby winning the game.

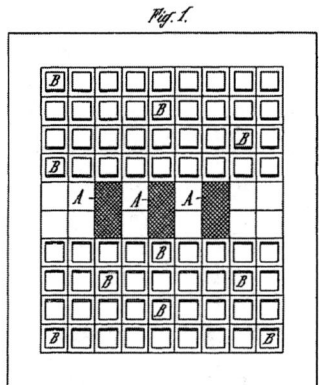

Figure from *L'Attaque*'s patent (1909) showing the game board.

## Stratego

Stratego is a commercially trademarked game that has enjoying immense popularity for several decades. Some readers may be surprised to find it in a book dedicated to chess of the world, but it is a clear descendent of the chess family of games.

The main difference between Stratego and *L'Attaque* lies on the board layout. The Stratego board has a more regular 10 × 10 board, instead of the 9 × 10 arrangement of its predecessor. Increasing the width to ten columns, it was wise to extend the three two-square lakes of impenetrable water to two four-square lakes in the center (c5–c6–d5–d6 and g5–g6–h5–h6). As one might expect, the lakes cannot be played upon or passed over by any of the pieces.

Each of the two players commands an army, logically extended to 40 pieces, Red against Blue, which stand upright, displaying their values only to their own player. They are (with values in parentheses): 1 Spy (1); 8 Scouts (2), 5 Miners (3), 4 Sergeants (4), 4 Lieutenants (5), 4 Captains (6), 3 Majors (7), 2 Colonels (8), 1 General (9), 1 Marshal (10). In addition, each player has 6 Bombs and 1 Flag, whose capture is the goal of the game. Bombs and Flag remain immobile. All other pieces move one square horizontally or vertically, except the Scout who can move any distance horizontally or vertically, like a Rook.

Initially, the pieces are deployed by each player filling his first four rows. As in *L'Attaque,* the Bomb destroys any piece that attacks it, except the Miner who can defuse the Bomb and remove it. A piece can capture any other piece of an inferior rank. The exception is the Spy, who can capture the Marshal. Pieces confronting each other of equal rank are both removed from play.

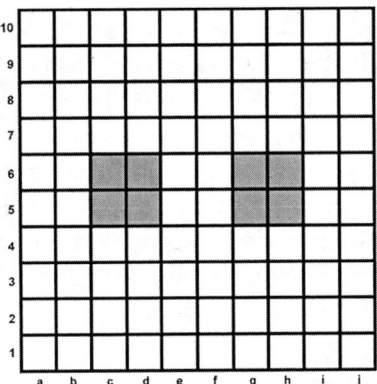

The Stratego board.

## Unraveling a Kinship

All of these games have two principles in common: they are games with concealed information, similar to card games and unlike chess or checkers; and they have hierarchical and cyclic captures, a pecking order with specific exceptions. It is necessary to dive into their history to understand if those similarities are the result of coincidence or if they all derive from a common ancestor.

## The History of L'Attaque

*L'Attaque* was invented by the French woman Hermance Edan, who filed a patent application on November 26, 1908, naming it, "*Jeu de bataille avec pièces mobiles sur damier*" (Battle Game with Movable Pieces over a Game Board). The patent was delivered on February 5, 1909, by the French National Industrial Property Office (N°396.795). Edan also obtained a U.K. patent for her game on November 25, 1909.

The French game historian, Michel Boutin, has suggested that Edan could have been inspired by a previous French patent for a game established by Julie Berg, born Moller, on June 24, 1907, with a similar board and pieces hiding their values from the opponent.[45] However, Edan was the first to describe a fully playable game. Her complete rules introduced the principle of hierarchical and cyclic capture whereby a piece captures those of lower (or equal) rank only; with the exception of the weakest able to capture the strongest one.

The game *L'Attaque* was not very successful in France, its country of birth, where it was sold until the early 1930s. Instead, it was an English publisher, H.P. Gibson, who broadly marketed the game in Great Britain and in the British Empire under the name *Attack,* with several editions beginning in the 1920s. The term of the contract between Gibson and Edan are not known because these documents were destroyed during the Blitz of 1940-1941. L'Attaque was reissued in the 1970s, long after its competitor, Stratego, had achieved substantial success.

## The History of Stratego

Stratego's paternity is sometimes attributed to a Dutchman, Jacques Johan Mogendorff (1898–1962), who is reported to have conceived this game while in hiding from the Nazi persecution of Jews with his family in The Hague during World War II. The name *Stratego* was registered in 1942 and the first edition of this game appeared in Amsterdam at the end of 1944, commercialized by Smeets & Schippers. The Dutch historian Fred Horn has established that Mogendorff had played a game named *Tek*, fabricated in three copies by a certain Michel Voorn, according to reports, a shot-down Canadian pilot also seeking refuge in The Hague. Horn has discovered a surviving copy of Tek which is very similar to *L'Attaque*. It proves to be a recreation from memory of the British version, Attack, that the Canadian would have played back home. From this evidence, there is little doubt that *L'Attaque* is a forerunner of Stratego.

The license of Smeets & Schippers expired in 1949 and Mogendorff sold his game to Jumbo, a brand name under Hausemann & Hötte, in 1958. Jumbo started marketing it in Europe at the end of the year. Jumbo still holds the rights to Stratego today. In 1962 the game was licensed to the Milton Bradley Company for American distribution, which further propagated it throughout the world. Stratego has been produced in many variants, including sets for four players.

## The History of Luzhanqi

The history of luzhanqi is not known because this game has been documented only in recent times. Murray (1951) and Bell (1960), among the most prominent games historians in the modern era, do not mention it. This could be because it was perceived as a commercial game rather than a traditional pastime, a status which has changed today. Those authors did not comment on *L'Attaque* or Stratego either. So, the question of luzhanqi's origin remains unanswered.

Played with domino-like pieces, luzhanqi seems to be a cross-over between xiangqi and mahjong. From the former, it retains the idea of a military capture game on a board defined by specific markings. There is a river in xiangqi; there are two mountains separating the camps in luzhanqi. As in xiangqi, the pieces play on points (or stations) at the intersections of lines, rather than inside the squares. Mahjong, which first appeared in the second half of the 19th century, is structured much like a card game. It is played with domino-shaped pieces, similar to the pieces of luzhanqi. Note also that the hierarchical order of capture is also present in banqi, a game played with xiangqi chessmen.[46]

The symbols appearing on luzhanqi's material may give some clues. Both the pieces and the board recall the predominant means of transport and military technologies that characterize their epoch. There are railroads, mines and bombs (shown as hand grenades on the oldest editions). In its seminal and most widespread form, this game does not involve planes, paratroopers, or any weapons that would bespeak the prevalent technologies of World War II. Considering the earliest likely date, railroads just started being built in China in the 1910s and did not play any role in military tactics until a few years later. This gives good reason, although no definitive proof, to suppose that luzhanqi was probably invented in the second or third decade of the 20th century.

This would satisfactorily depict the invention of this family of games, except that the existence of comparable, quite similar, games in the Western world must also be addressed. Is there any direct relationship between luzhanqi and *L'Attaque*? At this point, that question remains unanswered. Separate invention with such a remarkable convergence between the European and the Chinese games seems improbable. The idea of luzhanqi inspiring *L'Attaque* could be considered, but this hypothesis is weakened by the fact that luzhanqi is unlikely to be older than the 1908 patent of *L'Attaque*. It is also possible to consider that the European game may have been sold by its English publisher in Hong Kong in the 1920s, and could have inspired a Chinese version, influenced by the practice of xiangqi, which would have led to luzhanqi. Perhaps railroads and stations were introduced to make the game more current, since those means of transportation had been instrumental in the modern wars that tormented China throughout the 20th century. Being modeled as a conflict on the scale of a country, rather than a Napoleonic-era battlefield, mountains have replaced the lakes of the European game. This interpretation gives a realistic scenario but does not constitute a definitive theory for the birth of these intriguing games.

## *The History of Gunjin Shogi*

Recently, the attention of Western historians has been drawn to Japan, where gunjin shogi appears to be older than Julie Berg Moller's game, predating all known games of this type.

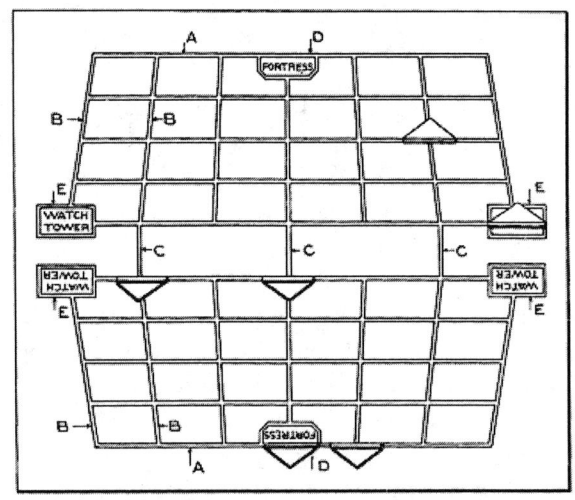

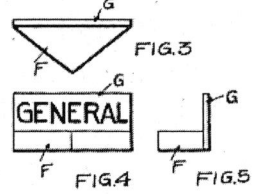

Tilden's U.S. patent, filed 1908 and granted 1915, apparently designed after the Japanese game gunjin shogi.
U.S. PATENT OFFICE

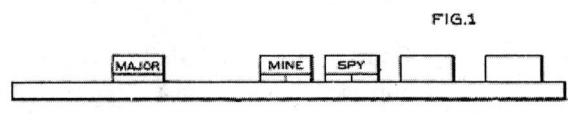

According to Michel Boutin, Japanese sources testify that gunjin shogi was invented toward the end of the First Sino-Japanese war (1894–1895). The oldest known box for this game is dated 1895 and the earliest published Japanese description is dated 1907,[47] establishing gunjin shogi as the eldest of this entire family of games.

It is now understood that the idea of gunjin shogi had sprung quickly from the Empire of the Rising Sun. Exploring the vaults of Western Patent Offices, Michel Boutin has exhumed a U.S. patent filed 1908 by Josephine E. Tilden, a botanist who had travelled to Japan, to protect a game named *Togo* or *The Game of Strategy*, which had the same structure as gunjin shogi. Even more interesting is a paper written in 1905 in a German journal, *Velhagen & Klassings Monatshefte*, by a certain Dr. Junghans, titled "Ostasiatische Brettspiele" (*Gameboard from Far East Asia*). This article simply presented gunjin shogi as a new game invented in Japan at the beginning of the Russo-Japanese war (1904–1905).

It is possible that either Julie Berg-Moller, who was living in Russia, or Hermance Edan, who had connections with artists, diplomats and officiers, was aware of this new military game that had appeared in Japan. Today, the strongest hypothesis is that the first game of this prolific family was invented in Japan, then discretely transplanted in France and England from where it conquered the rest of the world, finally returning to Asia and successfully popularized in the Chinese sphere. Of course, another hypothesis considers a possible direct link between the Japanese and the Chinese versions of the game with no intermediary link with the Western Attack or Stratego. Perhaps new research will improve our knowledge in years to come.

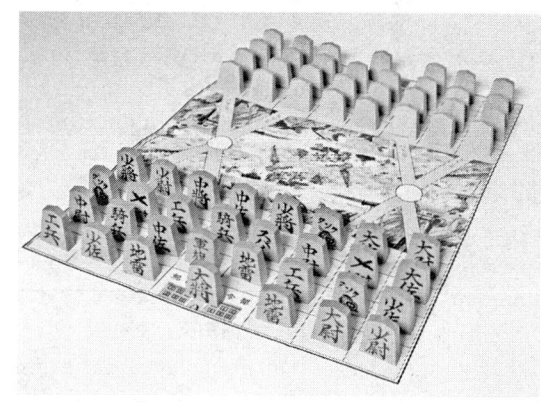

A modern edition of gunjin shogi. Wooden pieces painted yellow and orange are kept secret from the opponent, deployed standing (as shown) or face down.
KNOWLTON PHOTOGRAPH

陆战棋
Luzhanqi in Chinese characters.

Not only did chess propagate an unsurpassed family of games, but it generated other game families as well. Luzhanqi is now the prominent member of a "capture the flag" group of games, with many related games in the Orient, as well as the Occident.

◆ Part IV ◆

# Generals and Mercenaries of the Rising Sun

Isolated on the archipelagos of the Rising Sun, the Japanese branch of chess games exploded into so many sizes and mutations that even Charles Darwin would have been impressed! In this singularly remote and culturally rich land, where poetic fantasy may mingle with military struggle, the game of chess has been elaborated with warriors, demons and beasts, and has ranged from miniature vignettes to epic clashes with hundreds of warriors.

After a long, turbulent period of development, the small, compact form became the standard of Japanese chess, *shogi*, edging out the many more elaborate variations. But even this simplified game, having much in common with the other dominant world chess forms, carries unique features that set it apart. For one, directional asymmetry is the rule for most of the Japanese chessmen. These pieces with asymmetrical moves follow different patterns depending upon whether they are moving forward, backward or sideways. Some variants even have pieces which move differently to the left or right side. Promotion of pieces is another surprising characteristic. While most types of chess allow only Pawns to promote, the Japanese games allow most of the pieces to promote upon reaching the opponent's side of the board. Finally, and most exceptionally, modern Japanese chess allows captured pieces to be dropped back into play, on the side of the player who took them prisoner. This is an enormous change, effectively causing all pieces to remain in play for the entire game. These startling alterations result in a profound transformation, placing shogi, along with the game of go, at the summit of Japanese art and culture.

Traditional shogi. KNOWLTON PHOTOGRAPH

Today, many variants still exist in the shadow of the standard game of shogi. Each one claims a constituency of dedicated followers within Japan and now throughout the world. With the advent of the Internet, fans of these games find each other, share their passions and discoveries, and even organize competitions. In this way, the modern community follows in the footsteps of ancient Buddhist monks who challenged their imaginations to uncover ever more exotic chess variants.

# 18. Shogi

This is the "game of generals." Almost every piece promotes to a new value when reaching the opponent's side, and captured pieces switch allegiance to join the army of their captor—creating a double sting to a player who loses a piece. Amid this complexity, the board and pieces themselves are laid out with a pure Zen elegance.

Here is the modern game of shogi![1]

Initial array of shogi.

## *Material*

Shogi is played over a monochromatic board, the *shogiban*, with 9 × 9 rectangles slightly elongated vertically. Four points mark out the four corners of the promotion zone. The traditional *shogiban* are carved into massive wooden blocks, set up as tables about fourteen inches high. Players kneel on each side, in Japanese style.

The crafting of these boards has been elevated to a high art, with the most prized works cut from a single piece of wood such as *katsura* or the precious *kaya*. Such boards are made by renowned artists, with the greatest care to every aspect of the grain and quality of the wood. Wooden stands, *komadai*, accommodate these playing tables, to hold the captured pieces in plain view—very important, since captives in this game will be coming back into play at any moment. The board and *komadai* together create a stunning piece of Japanese furniture.

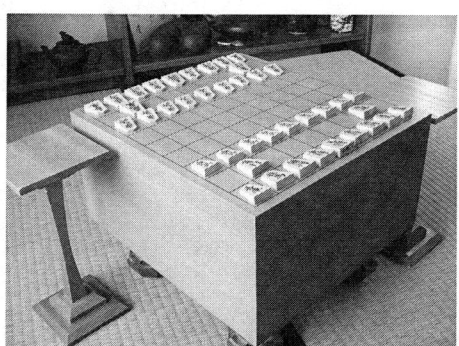

Traditional Japanese shogi table with *komadai* stands for captured pieces. FABIEN OSMONT PHOTOGRAPH

The pieces (*koma*) are flat, slightly beveled, in a pentagonal wedge shape with their names handwritten or engraved with black ink in two *kanji* (Chinese characters which are also used in the Japanese language). All pieces are of the same color; the opposing sides are indicated by the orientation of the tips which point toward the adversary. On the reverse side of most pieces, another character indicates the value of the piece after promotion. This promoted value is sometimes printed in red ink, though the older tradition uses only black. The playing set, as a whole, evinces a refined aesthetic of tasteful restraint.

Shogi pieces playing on an early 20th century shogiban.
KNOWLTON PHOTOGRAPH

*Names of the shogi pieces and their promoted forms.*
*Abbreviated names are in bold print.*

| Chessman | Japanese name | Western name [*meaning*] | Promoted piece | Japanese name | Western name [*meaning*] |
|---|---|---|---|---|---|
| | **O**sho **Gyoku**sho | King [*King General, Jeweled General*] | | | |
| | **Kin**sho | Gold [*Gold General*] | | | |
| | **Gin**sho | Silver [*Silver General*] | | Narigin | Promoted Silver |
| | **Kei**ma | Knight [*Katsura Horse*] | | Narikei | Promoted Knight |
| | **Kyo**sha | Lance [*Incense Chariot*] | | Narikyo | Promoted Lance |
| | **Hi**sha | Rook [*Flying Chariot*] | | Ryuo | Dragon [*Dragon King*] |
| | **Kaku**gyo | Bishop [*Angle Mover*] | | Ryuma | Horse [*Dragon Horse*] |
| | **Fu**hyo | Pawn [*Soldier*] | | Tokin | Promoted Pawn [*Gold Attained*] |

Although the pieces are all of one color, the two sides are known as Black (*Sente*) and White (*Gote*).[2] As in the game of go, Black has the first move. In diagrams (not shown here), Black begins on the bottom and White at the top. Each piece is indicated by only one character, with White's pieces written upside-down, as they would appear on the board from Black's perspective.

The first row of pieces is laid out symmetrically, with 1 King in the center, flanked by 2 Gold Generals, then 2 Silver Generals, 2 Knights, and 2 Lances. On the second row there is only 1 Bishop at the player's left, and 1 Rook at the player's right. These are placed on the 2nd and 8th columns. In this way, the Rook on one side is in the same file as the opponent's Bishop. 9 Pawns fill the 3rd row.

There is a subtle difference between the opposing Kings. On one side, the two Chinese characters indicate *Osho*, "King General," while the other side has a small additional mark which forms the words *Gyokusho*, "Jeweled General." This difference does not affect the play of the game; for all practical purposes the two sides are perfectly equal.

## Rules

*Sente* plays first; in fact, *Sente* means "initiative."

Although each piece shows two *kanji* on its upper face, diagrams are simplified by displaying only the first of the two characters, as shown below.

MOVES AND CAPTURES. All pieces capture as they move, displacing any enemy piece they land upon.

| *Abbreviation* | *Piece* |
|---|---|
| 王玉 | *King:* the central piece of the game. He moves one step in any of the eight directions. |
| 飛 | *Rook:* seated at the right hand of each player, this "Flying Chariot" moves like the Western Rook, any number of squares orthogonally (forward, backward, left or right), but may not jump over any pieces in its way. |
| 龍 or 竜 | The Rook promotes to a *Dragon King*, abbreviated as *Dragon*, which augments its choice of move with one step in any direction. The Dragon King moves like a Rook or a King. |
| 角 | *Bishop:* seated at each player's left hand, the lost sense of its original name indicated a "Horned Chariot," but it is now considered an "Angle Mover." It moves exactly like the Western Bishop, traveling any number of squares diagonally, not allowed to jump over any pieces in its way. |
| 馬 | The Bishop promotes to a *Dragon Horse*, abbreviated as *Horse*, which adds the possibility of moving one step in any direction. The Dragon Horse moves like a Bishop or like a King. |
| 金 | *Gold General:* abbreviated as *Gold*, this piece moves one square in six possible directions: forward, backward, sideways or diagonally forward. The direction he may *not* move is diagonally backward. He does not promote. |
| 銀 | *Silver General:* abbreviated as *Silver*, this piece moves one square in 5 directions: diagonally or straight forward. He cannot go backward or sideways. |
| 全 | The Silver promotes to a *Narigin* which has the same move as Gold. |
| 桂 | *Knight:* literally "Katsura Horse,"[3] leaps one step forward plus one step diagonally forward. It cannot be blocked by an intervening piece. In other words, it moves like a Western Knight, but only to the two foremost squares. It is the only shogi piece allowed to jump over intervening pieces. |
| 圭 or 今 | The Knight promotes to a *Narikei* which has the same move as Gold. |

| Abbreviation | Piece (continued) |
|---|---|
| 香 | *Lance:* literally "Incense Chariot,"[4] travels any number of squares directly forward, remaining in only one column. It may not jump over any pieces in its way. |
| 杏 or 全 | The Lance promotes to a *Narikyo* which has the same move as Gold. |
| 歩 | *Pawn:* always moves one step straight forward. It captures the same way. It never moves diagonally. |
| と or 个 | The Pawn promotes to a *Tokin* which has the same move as Gold. |

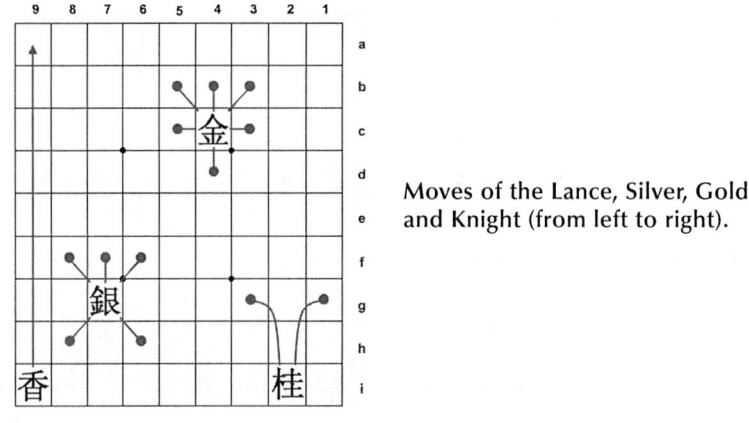

Moves of the Lance, Silver, Gold and Knight (from left to right).

Shogi presents two important novelties: promotions and drops.

PROMOTIONS. • The 7th, 8th and 9th ranks on the board are the promotion zone. These are the three ranks on the far side of the board, the area in which the opponent's pieces are originally set up. Each zone is marked by two dots on the shogiban.

- Most pieces have the option of promoting when they reach the promotion zone. When a piece is promoted, it is flipped over, to show its promoted value (written in red in some sets).
- A piece has the option of promoting upon the completion of any move in which it travels *into*, *out of*, or *within* the promotion zone.
- Promotion is compulsory only for a Lance or Pawn arriving on the last row, or for a Knight arriving on one of the two last rows. This is because those pieces would have no possible future move if they did not promote. In all other cases, promotion is optional.
- Once promoted, the piece maintains its promotional value until it is captured, or until the end of the game.

DROPS. • The captured pieces are removed from the board, but they are still in the game: they become subjects of their captor and sit ready, "in hand," to play for the side of the captor! The new owner places them on his *komadai*, the special platform for holding these captives, or on the side of the board at his right hand if no *komadai* is present. Then, on any subsequent turn, he may choose to either move a piece on the board or to drop one of his reserve pieces onto a free square. The dropped piece is placed with its point directed toward the opponent, its previous owner. Dropping a piece into play completes the player's turn.

- Captured pieces are always kept with their original, unpromoted values showing, and they are always dropped into play as unpromoted pieces, even if they are placed in the promotion zone.

There are some restrictions to the drops:

- A dropped piece in the promotion zone must enter as its unpromoted value. It will have the option of promoting on a subsequent turn, whenever it moves into, out of, or within the promotion zone.

- A player may not drop a Pawn onto a file (a column of squares running front to back) which already contains one of his own Pawns. Only one Pawn per file! This rule does not apply to files occupied by promoted Pawns. This is known as *nifu*, the "two Pawns" rule.

- A Pawn may not be dropped to give checkmate (winning the game) on that move. On the other hand, checkmate by dropping of any piece other than a Pawn is permitted. Also, a Pawn, like any other piece, may be dropped giving *check* to the King; only *checkmating* by dropping a Pawn is forbidden. This is the *uchifuzume* rule.[5]

- No piece may be moved or dropped onto a square from which it will have no possible future move. For instance, a Pawn or Lance may not be dropped onto the 9th row. A Knight, for the same reason, may not be dropped onto the 8th or 9th row. If a Pawn, Knight or Lance moves onto one of these rows, it must promote, so that it will have a possible future move from that square.

Note that a piece *may* be dropped onto a square that it could not have reached just by moving on the board: for instance, a Lance may be dropped into any of the 9 columns; a Knight may be dropped into the 2nd, 4th or 6th row; a Bishop may be dropped onto a diagonal that it could not have reached by its move on the board.

END OF THE GAME. The goal of the game is to put the adverse King in a situation in which it cannot avoid being taken at the next move: a checkmate. The game is then won.

In tournament play, any illegal move immediately loses the game for the offending player. This includes any irregularity: capturing one's own piece, dropping a piece in a place where it is not allowed, making two moves in a row without an opponent's move in between, promoting where one is not allowed to do so, demoting a piece during play, playing a piece to a square it cannot move to, dropping a Pawn onto a file on which one already has an unpromoted Pawn, mating with a dropped Pawn, or moving while remaining in check (which is usually not announced). In the latter case, the King may actually be captured; however, this is an academic point, since the game ends at the moment the illegal move is made.

Drawn games are rare, but not impossible. If a position is repeated (*sennichite*) four times with the same player to move and with the same pieces *in hand* (off the board), the game is declared a draw. Another case of draw, known as *jishogi*, exists in which all pieces, particularly the Kings, have reached the promotion zone and no player has the hope to mate or win material. In that case, the players may agree to make a computation: 5 points for each Rook and Bishop, and 1 point for each of the other pieces (including Pawns), both on the board and in hand (Kings are not counted). If each player gets at least 24 points, the game is declared a draw. If one player gets less than 24 points, he loses the game. Some particular cases can make this situation even more complex, but they are very rare.

Perpetual check is forbidden. A player may not force repetition by giving an endless series of checks. In this case, the player giving the checks must make a different move.

Because of the possibility of dropping captured pieces on the board, stalemate, for all practical purposes, is virtually impossible.

## Traditions

Tradition is a central constituent of Japanese cultural expression, and the playing of shogi is no exception. Professional players, and many amateurs as well, respect a strict protocol. Several additional rules, etiquette or conventions are followed in actual play. Here are the most widely practiced.

SETTING UP THE PIECES. Placing the pieces on the board traditionally follows a certain order. This is commonly done in one of two ways:

- The *Ohashi* method: King is placed first; then the pieces around him, one left, one right, Golds, Silvers, Knights, Lance; then the Bishop, the Rook; then the Pawns starting from the center again, then one left one right until the outer files are reached.
- The *Ito* method: starting the same way until the Knights are placed; then the Pawns from the left side to right side of the board; then the Lances; then the Bishop and, finally, the Rook.

DESIGNATION OF THE FIRST PLAYER. The *sente* player, is determined by *furigoma* (lit.: tossing of pieces—in this case, Pawns): the stronger player or, if the players are of equal strength, the elder, takes the five middle Pawns in his hand and throws them like dice. Everything that does not lie completely flat is removed from the throw. If more unpromoted Pawns than promoted ones show, the thrower is Black (*Sente*) and moves first. If more promoted Pawns show, he is White (*Gote*). In the case of a tie (2–2 or 1–1) there is another throw.

TOUCHING AND PLAYING A PIECE. There is no touch-move rule in shogi. A piece may be freely touched (typically, in order to adjust its placement on the square). When a player makes a move and no longer touches the piece, the move is final. However, it is considered annoying to the opponent and unfair practice to make a move and continue touching the piece while thinking, with the piece in the new position.

## Handicapped Games

As with many Asiatic games, shogi is widely played with handicaps (*komaochi*), when the players are of disparate strengths. In this case, White permanently removes one or more pieces.

In a handicapped game, it is White who plays first. Handicaps are ranked in order of severity and agreed upon according to the difference of grade between the players. The most common systems are these:

- Lance handicap (*kyoochi*): White removes his Lance on 1a.
- Bishop handicap (*kakuochi*): Only the Bishop on 2b is removed.
- Rook handicap (*hiochi*): Only the Rook on 8b is removed.
- Rook + Lance handicap (*hikyoochi*): The Rook on 8b and the Lance on 1a are removed.
- Two Piece handcap (*nimaiochi*): The Rook on 8b and the Bishop on 2b are removed.
- Four Piece handicap (*yonmaiochi*): The Rook on 8b, the Bishop on 2b, and both Lances are removed.
- Six Piece handicap (*rokumaiochi*): The Rook on 8b, the Bishop on 2b, both Lances, and both Knights are removed.
- Eight Piece handicap (*hachimaiochi*): The Rook on 8b, the Bishop on 2b, both Lances, both Knights, and both Silvers are removed.

- Ten Piece handicap (*jumaiochi*): The Rook on 8b, the Bishop on 2b, both Lances, both Knights, both Silvers, and both Golds are removed.

The relationship between handicap and difference in grade is a complicated matter subject to several different systems and is beyond the scope of this book.

## Tactics

NOTATION. Shogi uses a specific system of notation. Files are numbered from right to left with Arabic numerals (1 through 9). The ranks are noted by traditional Japanese kanji numerals (一, 二, 三, 四, 五, 六, 七, 八, 九), which are replaced in international notation by lower-case letters (*a* through *i*), starting from the top of the board. So the square "1a" stands on the top right of the *shogiban,* and the square at the bottom left corner is "9i."

A move is written in this way:

- the initial of the piece (even if it is a Pawn): K (King), P (Pawn), L (Lance), N (kNight), S (Silver), G (Gold), B (Bishop), R (Rook), preceded by a "+" if it is a promoted piece; then
- the kind of move: "–" or nothing in the case of a regular move, "x" for a capture, and "*" for a drop; then,
- the coordinates of the destination square; then,
- if the piece is promoted, a "+" is added at the end of the move.
- if the piece is not promoted when a promotion is permitted, an "=" is added at the end of the move.

As in other notation systems, if several pieces of the same kind can reach the same destination square, the coordinates of the departure square are added to avoid any confusion.

Checks are not noted.

**Example:** a Lance moving from 5g to 5c, where it captures an enemy piece and gets promoted, is notated: Lx5c+.

ELEMENTS OF STRATEGY. Shogi is a very aggressive game: many pieces have limited backward mobility—or none at all. Those which are captured are reintroduced against their former owner, exacerbating the loss. The happy consequence of this is that draws are very rare, a significant advantage of shogi over Western chess.

A game of shogi generally follows a trajectory of escalating intensity. The opening is relatively quiet, the middle game is an active fight, and the end game is a mad race to checkmate the opponent.

The Rook and the Bishop occupy privileged positions which play a decisive role opening the game. The opening is denoted as "static" (*ibisha*) when the Rook is kept on its starting column, or "ranging" (*furibisha*) when the Rook is moved toward the center or left of the board. The first moves follow a methodical rhythm, as each player tries to shelter his King in a "castle" (*kakoi*) constructed of defensive pieces. This usually consists of three Generals (Gold and Silver). Popular configurations, such as the *Yagura,* are abundantly documented in the specialized literature.

A castle called *Yagura.*

The impossibility of forming a protective chain of Pawns is often disconcerting to the Western player. But, far from being an inconvenience, this characteristic gives shogi much of its rich variability. The protective function often falls to the Gold and Silver Generals, which create strong and dynamic formations.

Watching vacant squares is crucial to shogi strategy. It is necessary to always consider and prepare for a drop into any unoccupied spot. A typical defensive move sometimes involves dropping one's own piece into a space where an enemy drop is feared. The well-timed skill of acquiring, holding and dropping pieces into play constitutes a significant aspect of shogi tactics.

The endings can often be summarized as an assault on the enemy King by a well-planned succession of drops. It is necessary to attack the King on all sides and to deprive him of flight squares. The mistake to be avoided is checking the King at every turn without sealing off all possible exits. The player who invests all of his pieces in a futile attack has wasted his valuable dropping potential. Furthermore, a King who reaches the adverse camp becomes very difficult to capture since his pursuers have more power moving forward, and achieve promotion on the other side of the board. Meanwhile, this refugee King fortifies his sanctuary with promoted pieces of his own.

Ideally, an attack proceeds by tightening the grip on the enemy King from all directions. One of the many mottoes learned by shogi students is "Keep one Gold for the end." Indeed, one Gold can mate a King stuck on his back rank with the support of only one other piece. And while most pieces promote to Gold after moving in the promotion area, the Gold itself has its full power the moment it is dropped into play. Checkmate!

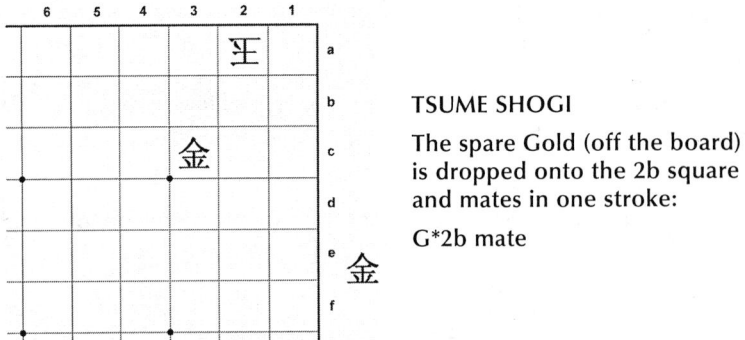

**TSUME SHOGI**

The spare Gold (off the board) is dropped onto the 2b square and mates in one stroke:

G*2b mate

Students of shogi can benefit greatly from studying *tsume shogi*, "checkmate compositions" which are very popular in Japan, often appearing in newspaper columns. These studies follow strict guidelines. Black must give checkmate, using the material shown on the board (often only a section of the board is presented), and utilizing all of the pieces shown at the side of the board to be dropped in. White, on the other hand, is considered to have all possible pieces in reserve to be dropped in, in his defense. Black makes the first move and all of his moves have to be checks. He must finish with a forced checkmate, with no pieces left in reserve.

RELATIVE VALUE OF THE PIECES. The relative value of chessmen has limited importance in shogi—some would say it is virtually useless. Promotions and drops continually affect the value of the material in the game. One may simply remember that the bigger the actual piece, the stronger or more important it is. The sizes come in groups: Pawn; Lance and Knight; Gold and Silver; Rook and Bishop; and of course, King.

A temporal advantage often prevails over material superiority, especially at the end of the game in which victory is granted to the player who finds checkmate most quickly.

Shogi, set to play.
KNOWLTON PHOTOGRAPH

## Variant: Annan Shogi

Misleadingly nicknamed "Korean chess" in Japan, this variant is practiced with the standard material, but has a change in move power. Any piece standing on a square immediately in front of another piece from its own camp has its move temporarily changed to that of the piece standing behind it. Pieces in front of empty squares or squares occupied by enemy pieces maintain their standard move. The starting array has a sensible modification: Pawns placed before the Bishop and the Rook are set one square forward, on the 4th rank.

## History

The flat calligraphed pieces, the board with nine columns, the King's central position, and the Pawn that captures straight forward are characteristics that could lead one to believe the Japanese first borrowed their chess from China. But today, that immediate association is contested, since other elements recall the chess forms of Southeast Asia: the play on the squares rather than the intersections, the complete row of Pawns on the third rank, their promotion to first counselor,[6] promotion being attained by penetrating the opposing camp and marked by flipping the piece, the Knight that leaps over intervening pieces and finally, the Silver General which is identical to its Burmese/Thai/Cambodian counterpart. In the first millennium of the present era, Japan was broadly absorbing Chinese culture, but Japanese sailors were also traveling south to the Malay coasts and straits, controlling the maritime routes.[7] Could shogi be a composite of the two diverse strains?

The arrival date of chess in Japan is not known.[8] No chess form other than shogi has ever been found in the islands predating modern times. The most complete evidence of ancient shogi is the *Kirinsho (Notes about the Kirin)*, a seven-volume work composed around the year 1000, which explained how the calligrapher was to inscribe the pieces with two characters.[9] It is a distinctive detail because the Chinese write only one character on their chessmen. However, this text is controversial since it has been suggested that the section about shogi may have been added by a writer from a later generation. The next available testimony is from the *Shinsarugakuki (An Account of the New Comic Entertainment)*, a diary composed before 1064, in which shogi is quickly mentioned among other games and pastimes.[10]

Sixteen wooden pieces were excavated in 1993 during a renovation on the grounds of the Nara Prefecture Culture Center, the feudal capital of the archipelago.[11] The pieces already bear two kanji each, and show the characteristic pentagonal shape still observed in modern sets. The set includes three Jewel Generals (Kings), four Gold Generals, one Silver General, one Katsura Horse (a Knight) and five Soldiers. The pieces were found with three *mokkan*s, strips of wood used as an inexpensive medium for calligraphy training. On one of these mokkans is written, "the sixth year of the Tengi era." Because of this, the set is dated to that year, 1058. Another mokkan from the 11th century, found in Dazaifu on Kyushu Island (West Japan), indicates an Incense Chariot (Lance), Knights and Soldiers, showing that shogi was already well spread throughout the Islands, strikingly similar to its modern form.

The earliest known shogi pieces, dated 1058, are conserved in the Kofuku-ji, an important Buddhist temple in Nara, Japan.

Four additional pieces were unearthed in 2013; buried just a few feet away from the original find at Nara, they have been dated to the same period.[12] This new find includes one Knight, one Pawn, one not readable, and one last piece which is quite interesting: a Drunk Elephant (*suizo*), blank on the reverse side, which probably indicates that it did not promote. The Drunk Elephant was to play an important role in the development of shogi in the following centuries, but such an early apparition is intriguing.[13] This has led to the hypothesis that early shogi may have been played with a Drunk Elephant—a tantalizing theory which awaits further confirmation.

Apart from few other short mentions of shogi in personal diaries of noblemen in the 12th century, one must look forward another generation or two to find a more precise description: the *Nichureki (From the Two Chureki)*, a 13-volume encyclopedia whose author is not known, estimated to have been published under the reign of Emperor Juntoku Tenno (1210–1221). It compiled two previous works, the *Shochureki*, and the *Kaichureki*, both written by Miyoshi no Tameyasu, a noble mathematician of the Heian Court (*Heian* means "peace and tranquility" and gives the name of the historic period spanning 794 to 1185). Only a part of the original *Shochureki* is extant today; the remainder of both works is only known from the *Nichureki*.

The *Nichureki* details two different forms of shogi.[14] First, a small one is presented with the moves of the Jewelled General (King), the Gold General, the Silver General, the Katsura Horse (Knight), the Incense Chariot (Lance) and the Soldier exactly as we know them today. The text then says, "*All become Gold Generals when penetrating in the opponent's three lines. If the only adverse piece is the King, it is a victory.*" Neither the board size nor the piece count is indicated, which allows several possible reconstitutions: an 8 × 8, 9 × 8 or 9 × 9 square board, and 32 or 36 pieces.[15] Theories have been put forth to explain which was the seminal board configuration and, if it differed from the modern 9 × 9 board, how it evolved. These theories, however interesting, remain speculations, unsupported by any historical evidence. It must honestly be admitted that the original form of the *shogiban* and the reason for its 81 squares today remain unknown.

It seems that victory in this first game was obtained by baring the opposing Kings, a rule shared with other forms of medieval chess. In the absence of Bishops and Rooks, reconstructions of the game show that it was indeed the most probable ending. Historians call this historic version *Heian shogi*.

The second shogi presented in the *Nichureki* was a large version on a 13 × 13 square board, which will be described further in a following chapter. A "Flying Dragon," precursor of the Bishop with a diagonal move, and "Free Chariot," sort of "half a Rook" moving only vertically, appear in this widened variant. This duality of small and large shogis persisted into the 14th century. The *Futsu Shodoshu (Collection of Sermons for Everyday Use)*, a compilation attributed to the monk Ryoki, contrasts a *sho shogi* ("small shogi") to a *dai shogi* ("large shogi"), which is presented further in this book. The *Futsu Shodoshu* only mentions a few pieces, and indicates that *sho shogi* had Pawns and Knights (Katsura Horse) that promoted to Gold and Silver, respectively.[16] Interestingly, the Flying Chariot (*Hisha*), which we refer to as the Rook today, is mentioned in dai shogi only, and this is its earliest mention in shogi of any sort.

Toward 1350, an intermediate version appeared on 12 × 12 squares, derived from dai shogi: *chu shogi* (middle shogi). For two centuries, chu shogi was the most popular chess in Japan. At that time, 15 × 15 dai shogi was apparently considered too complex, and 9 × 9 sho shogi was viewed as a trivial game. But, at a particular moment of the 15th century, which is difficult to pinpoint, three new chessmen taken from chu shogi were added to sho shogi, giving it a total of 21 pieces per player. Those pieces were a Rook, a Bishop and a Drunk Elephant (*Suizo*). The latter piece, seated just in front of the King, moved one step in all directions except straight backward. It was promoted to a Crown Prince (*Taishi*) which could replace the King if the King himself was captured.

In the 16th century, drops were introduced in sho shogi. This idea may have been inspired by warlords and mercenaries who allied with the most promising side of every conflict, not hesitating to switch their allegiance. The particular form of shogi chessmen, always pointing toward the opponent, seems to make the innovation of returning captured pieces as fighters against their former owner a natural development.

The Drunk Elephant (still present in a sho shogi set dated to 1567, found in the Asakura family ruins near Fukui) was then removed from the game,[17] probably because its overpowering promotion did not fit with the new rules of dropping pieces. A picture in the diary of the samurai Matsudaira Ietada, dated 1587, shows a game identical to the one of today. Modern shogi was born!

The new shogi spread quickly. Many shogi pieces have been excavated by archeologists, dated to the end of the 16th century from diverse Japanese provinces. The earliest recorded game of shogi was between Honinbo Sansa, the best Go and shogi player of his time, and Ohashi Sokei, in 1607.[18] In 1612, the Tokugawa shogun asked Honinbo Sansa to found the first professional academy for these two games. Honinbo Sansa created the academy with Ohashi Sokei, who became the First *Meijin* (grandmaster, literally, "excellent man"). In 1636, the grandmaster's son, Ohashi Soko, himself Second Meijin, published the first treatise—the *Shogi Zushiki* (*Illustrated Explanations of Shogi*)—containing the codified rules of shogi as they exist to the present day.

Nowadays, shogi is the most popular board game in Japan with about ten million regular players and twice as many occasional players. A system of *kyu* and *dan* permits players to increase their rankings as they improve. About two hundred professional players meet regularly in famous tournaments which are covered in newspapers and television broadcasts. The tournament that awards the title of Meijin is the most prestigious. Outside of Japan, the West offers dynamic clubs for amateurs. Westernized pieces, inscribed with stylized symbols or bearing small diagrams indicating their moves, have been produced in order to ease the diffusion of the game outside Japan.

These attempts, sometimes endorsed by famous champions, have not met with great success among amateurs who remain attached to the delicate wooden engraving and the noble heritage of the Japanese *koma*.

Shogi in Japanese characters.

For a long time, Japanese culture has fascinated, attracted and seduced the Western public. After the martial arts, the floral art of *ikebana*, the *anime* and *manga* productions, the culinary pleasures of *sushi* and *sashimi*, Japanese games are also coming out of their isolation. The game of go (which is of Chinese origin) has already achieved widespread recognition and, while *renju* (a five-in-a-row variant) and *hanafuda* (a brilliant flower-based card game) still wait in the wings, shogi moves ahead quickly, determined to conquer the West.

# 19. Chu Shogi and Dai Shogi

## *Chu Shogi*

The history of shogi is rich with variants in many sizes. In fact, at one time, during Japan's feudal era, the 12 × 12 *chu shogi* was considered the most common form. The game remains popular even today, with a strong following in Japan, naturally, but also with many enthusiasts in Europe and North America. Some are even willing to call this game "the best large chess variant in the world."

Chu shogi board as the game begins.
WOUT BLOMMERS PHOTOGRAPH

## *Material*

The board is plain, with clear, narrow lines defining a 12 × 12 playing surface. Each player has 46 pieces, 12 of which are Pawns. The setup is identical for each side. Pieces have the same shape as regular shogi pieces, each one identified by a pair of kanji on the upper face for its initial value, and two characters on the bottom surface for the promoted value. Except for the King, the Lion and the Free King, all pieces may be promoted.

## 19. Chu Shogi and Dai Shogi

Initial array of chu shogi.

Initial array of chu shogi showing the abbreviated kanji.

## Rules

MOVES, CAPTURES AND PROMOTIONS. All chessmen capture as they move. The pieces which are familiar from standard shogi have the same moves, but note that chu shogi does not have Knights. There are a total of 29 types of pieces, 8 of which are obtained only by promotion.

Pieces on the first rank:

| Kanji | Abbr. | Piece |
|---|---|---|
| 王将 / 玉将 | 王 | *King (Osho, Gyokusho):* same move as in shogi, one step in any direction. |
| 酔象 | 象 | *Drunk Elephant (Suizo):* moves one step in any direction *except* directly backward (seven directions). |
| 太子 | 太 | The Drunk Elephant promotes to *Crown Prince (Taishi)* which moves like a King and may indeed become a second King. |
| 金将 | 金 | *Gold General (Kinsho):* same move as in shogi, one step orthogonally or diagonally forward, but promotes to *Rook (Hisha)*. |
| 銀将 | 銀 | *Silver General (Ginsho):* same move as in shogi, one step diagonally or one step directly forward, but promotes to *Vertical Mover (Shugyo)* (see description below). |

| Kanji | Abbr. | Piece (continued) |
|---|---|---|
| 銅将 | 銅 | *Copper General (Dosho):* moves one step forward, backward, or to the two forward-diagonal directions (four possible directions) but promotes to *Side Mover (Ogyo)* (see description below). |
| 猛豹 | 豹 | *Ferocious Leopard (Mohyo):* moves one step forward, backward or diagonally (six possible directions). It can promote to *Bishop (Kakugyo)*. |
| 香車 | 香 | *Lance (Kyosha):* same move as in shogi, any number of unoccupied squares directly forward. |
| 白駒 | 駒 | The Lance promotes to *White Horse (Hakku),* which moves any number of free squares directly backward, forward, or along either of the forward diagonals (four directions). |

On the second rank:

| | | |
|---|---|---|
| 麒麟 | 麒 | *Kirin*[19]*:* jumps to the second square in one of the four orthogonal directions (leaping over any piece on the intervening square), or moves one step diagonally. Note that an unpromoted Kirin can only reach half of the squares on the board. It promotes to *Lion (Shishi)* (see description below). |
| 鳳凰 | 鳳 | *Phoenix (Hoo):* jumps to the second square in one of the four diagonal directions (leaping over any piece on the intervening square), or moves one step orthogonally. It promotes to *Free King (Honno)* (see description below). |
| 盲虎 | 虎 | *Blind Tiger (Moko):* moves one step in any direction *except* directly forward (seven directions). It promotes to *Flying Stag (Hiroku)* which moves any number of free squares directly forward or backward, or one step in any direction. |
| 飛鹿 | 鹿 | |
| 角行 | 角 | *Bishop (Kakugyo):* same move as in shogi, the move of the Bishop in Western chess. It promotes to *Dragon Horse (Ryuma)*. |
| 反車 | 反 | *Reverse Chariot (Hensha):* moves any number of free squares directly forward or backward. |
| 鯨鯢 | 鯨 | The Reverse Chariot promotes to *Whale (Keigei)* which moves any number of free squares directly forward, backward, or diagonally backward (four directions). |

On the third rank:

| | | |
|---|---|---|
| 獅子 | 獅 | *Lion (Shishi):* moves one or two steps in any direction. When moving two steps, it can jump over an occupied square. The two steps are completely independent: it can change direction after the first step; it can continue after a capture on the first step, potentially capturing two pieces per turn. It can step to an adjacent empty square and back without capturing anything, leaving the board unchanged and effectively passing a turn (*jitto*). Or it can capture with the first step, then return to its starting square with the second step, effectively capturing a piece on an adjacent square without moving. This is called *igui*, "stationary feeding." The Lion does not promote. |
| 奔王 | 奔 | *Free King (Honno)*[20]*:* moves any number of free squares along any of the eight orthogonal or diagonal directions, just like the Queen of Western chess. The Free King does not promote. |

| | | |
|---|---|---|
| 龍王 | 龍 or 竜 | *Dragon King (Ryuo):* same move as in shogi, any number of squares like a Western Rook, or one square diagonally. |
| 飛鷲 | 鷲 | The Dragon King promotes to *Soaring Eagle (Hiju)* which moves any number of free squares along a straight line in any direction *except* the forward diagonals (six directions). On the forward diagonals, it moves like a Lion, including *jitto* and *igui* (described above), but does not move off of the diagonal. |
| 龍馬 | 馬 | *Dragon Horse (Ryuma):* same move as in shogi, moving like the Western Bishop or one step orthogonally. |
| 角鷹 | 鷹 | The Dragon Horse promotes to *Horned Falcon (Kakuo),* which moves any number of free squares along a straight line in any direction *except* directly forward (seven directions). When moving straight forward, it moves like the Lion, including *jitto* and *igui,* but not deviating from the forward line. |
| 飛車 | 飛 | *Rook (Hisha):* same move as in shogi, just like the Western Rook. It promotes to *Dragon King (Ryuo).* |
| 竪行 | 竪 | *Vertical Mover (Shugyo):* moves any number of free squares orthogonally, either forward or backward, or steps just one square directly sideways. |
| 飛牛 | 牛 | The Vertical Mover promotes to *Flying Ox (Higyu)* which moves any number of free squares forward, backward, or diagonally, but not to the sides (six directions). |
| 横行 | 横 | *Side Mover (Ogyo):* moves any number of free squares orthogonally sideways; or, one step directly forward or backward. |
| 奔猪 | 猪 | The Side Mover promotes to *Free Boar (Honcho),* which moves any number of free squares diagonally or sideways, but not directly forward or backward (six directions). |

On the fourth and fifth ranks:

| | | |
|---|---|---|
| 歩兵 | 歩 | *Pawn (Fuhyo):* same move as in shogi, just one step forward. |
| と金 | と | The Pawn also promotes to *Tokin* which has the move of a Gold General (*Kinsho*). |
| 仲人 | 仲 | *Go-Between (Chunin):* steps one square directly forward or backward. Promotes to *Drunk Elephant (Suizo).* |

PARTICULAR RULES. *Lion capturing Lion:* a Lion cannot capture an adverse Lion unless certain criteria are met. These rules are designed to avoid the careless loss of this valuable piece.

- A Lion can always capture an adjacent Lion (i.e., on one of the eight surrounding squares).
- A Lion can always capture a non-adjacent Lion (two squares away) that is unprotected (i.e., has no piece ready to capture the attacker in return).
- A Lion may only capture a non-adjacent, protected Lion if it first captures another piece so that it is then adjacent (double capture), and only if the other piece being captured is something other than a Pawn or a Go-Between.
- Finally, if one player captures a Lion with a piece other than a Lion, the opponent cannot then capture a Lion on the next move with anything other than another Lion (as is possible since Kirin promotes to Lion), and this may only be done if the rules listed above are met.

These restrictions do not apply to the two other pieces that have special capturing abilities similar to the Lion's: the Soaring Eagle and the Horned Falcon.

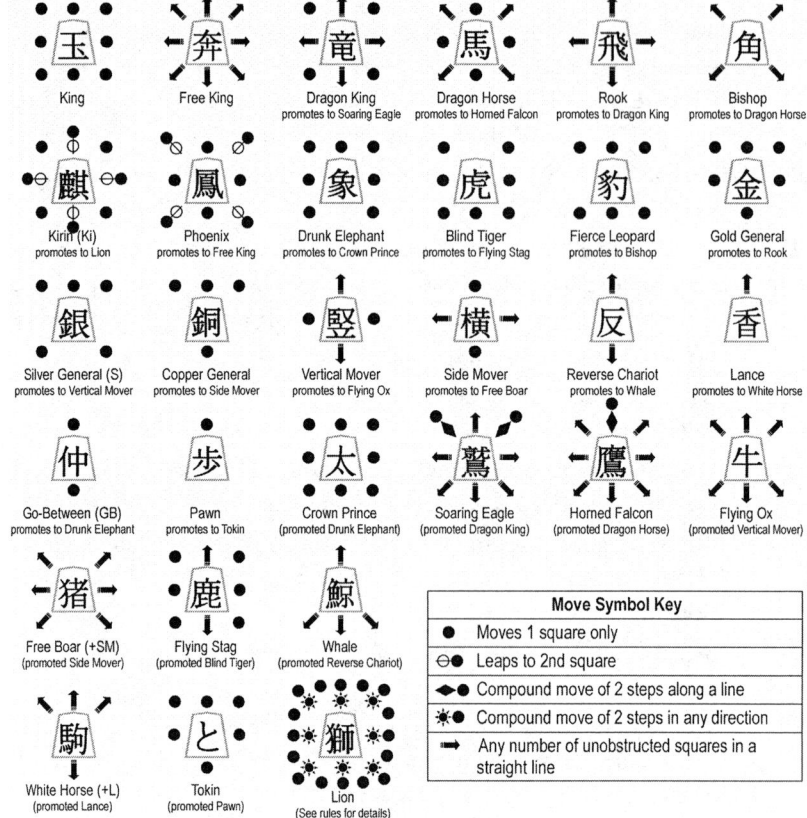

Moves of the chu shogi pieces.

PROMOTION. The promotion zone for each player is the four first ranks of the opponent.
- As in shogi, promotion may in principle take place while entering, moving within, or leaving the promotion zone.
- Promotion is optional, unless a piece moves onto a square from which its unpromoted form would have no possible future move (for instance, a Pawn on the final rank).
- If a piece other than a Pawn enters the promotion zone and does not promote on that move, it will not be allowed to promote until it leaves the zone and reenters it, unless its move from or within the promotion zone involved making a capture. In other words, a non–Pawn piece can only promote by a non-capture move when it enters the zone. Once in the zone, pieces can only promote by making a capture.[21]
- If a Pawn does not promote immediately upon entering the promotion zone, it remains unpromoted until it reaches the last rank, where its promotion becomes compulsory.
- Promotion is permanent and a promoted piece cannot promote a second time (after all, a piece has only two sides).

NO DROPS. There is no dropping of pieces into play in chu shogi. Captured pieces are simply removed for the remainder of the game.

END OF THE GAME. Victory is obtained either by capturing the opposing King (if the opponent has gotten a Crown Prince, this one must be captured as well) or by capturing all adverse pieces, baring the King (or Crown Prince). However, if the opponent can make a final capture on the following move, leaving each player with bare King (or Crown Prince), the game is a draw.

Unlike the conventions of Western chess, the rules of chu shogi allow a player to leave the King in check, subject to capture. This may even be done deliberately in cases where one side has attained a Crown Prince, affording him one King to lose.

Perpetual check is forbidden. The player making repeated checks must choose a different move. Otherwise, if a position is repeated four times, with the same player to move, the game is a draw.

## Tactics

The scale of relative strengths indicated by *Zillions-of-Games©* software is as follows: Lion (7.7), *Soaring Eagle* (6.8), Free King (6.7), Dragon King (6.4), *Horned Falcon* (6.4), Dragon Horse (5.2), Rook (5), *Free Boar* (4.6), *Flying Ox* (4.5), Bishop (3.7), *Flying Stag* (3.6), Vertical Mover (3.5), *White Horse* (3.3), Side Mover (3.2), *Whale* (3.2), Kirin (3), Phoenix (2.9), Drunk Elephant (2.8), Blind Tiger (2.7), Reverse Chariot (2.7), Gold (2.4), Ferocious Leopard (2.3), Silver (1.9), Copper (1.6), Lance (1.4), Go-Between (0.8), Pawn (0.4).

Pieces written above in *italics* are obtained by promotion only.

## Variant: Heisei Chu Shogi

This is a lively game in which several pieces are absent from the original board setup, but begin in the player's reserve, ready to be dropped into play. Once the game is underway, a player may use any turn to drop a piece of his choice onto any square adjacent to one of his own pieces. Lances, Coppers, Silvers, Side Movers, Vertical Movers, Reversed Chariots, Kirin and Phoenix form the reserve. The Lance must not be dropped on the last rank (from which it would have no future move). If the drop is done within the promotion zone, the piece is either promoted immediately or promoted on its next move, at the discretion of the player.

All other rules are kept; in particular, captured pieces are *not* dropped back into the game.

# Dai Shogi

Along with "small" shogi and "intermediate" shogi, it follows that the next step up is a "large" version, *dai shogi,* to complete this historic Japanese chess triptych.

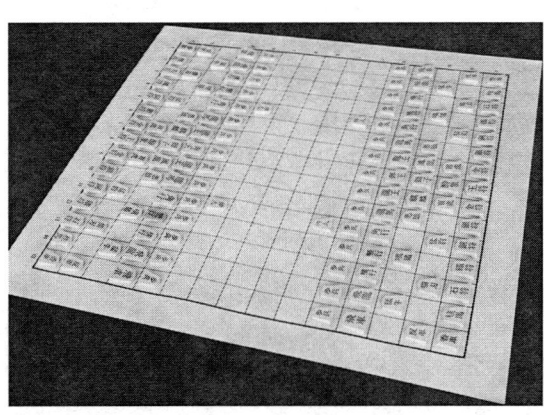

Pieces set for a game of dai shogi.
WOUT BLOMMERS PHOTOGRAPH

## Material

The board is composed of 15 × 15 squares. Each player commands 65 pieces of 29 different types. The pieces are the same pointed wedge shapes as found in the other shogis, and each one bears a pair of kanji characters on the top side indicating its initial value, with a promoted value painted on the underside.

For clarity, the illustrations below show a preference for the abbreviated, single-kanji characters, which are generally used for study and easy reference.

Initial array of dai shogi, laid out in the same order, left-to-right, for each player.

## Rules

Play proceeds as in chu shogi, with no drops.

MOVES, CAPTURES AND PROMOTIONS. All pieces from chu shogi are carried over to dai shogi, including those obtained by promotion. However, there are eight additional chessmen, all of which promote to Gold:

| Kanji | Abbr. | Piece |
|---|---|---|
| 鉄将 | 鉄 | *Iron General (Tessho):* moves one square forward, either orthogonally or diagonally (three directions). |
| 石将 | 石 | *Stone General (Sekisho):* moves one square diagonally forward (two directions). |
| 桂馬 | 桂 | *Knight (Keima):* the Katsura Horse, absent in chu shogi, moves as in shogi: one step straight forward plus one step diagonally forward, with the ability to leap over any intervening piece at most (two possible choices of move from its starting square). |
| 猫刃 | 猫 | *Cat Sword (Myojin):* moves one square in one of the four diagonal directions. |
| 悪狼 | 狼 | *Evil Wolf (Akuro):* steps one square sideways, forward or diagonally forward (five directions). |
| 嗔猪 | 嗔猪 | *Angry Boar (Shincho):* steps one square orthogonally (vertically or horizontally) (four directions). |
| 猛牛 | 猛牛 | *Violent Ox (Mogyu):* moves one or two empty squares orthogonally. It does not jump over intervening pieces (four directions; eight possible moves). |
| 飛龍 | 龍 | *Flying Dragon (Hiryu):* moves one or two empty squares along one of the four diagonal directions. It does not jump. |

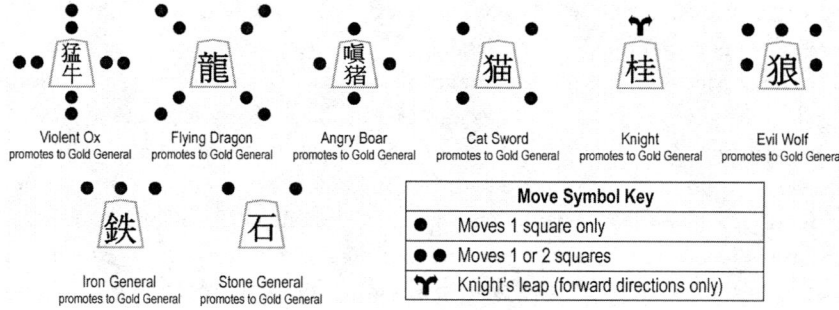

Moves of specific dai shogi's pieces.

## Particular Rules

- Unlike chu shogi, dai shogi has no restriction against a Lion capturing another Lion.
- Each player's promotion zone consists of the five ranks farthest from his starting position. These zones are indicated by the dots on the board. The rules of promotion are the same as those in chu shogi. Upon reaching the far end of the board, the Iron General, Stone General, Knight and Pawn are required to promote, since they would have no possible further move if not promoted.

## History

The Heian period was drawing to a close when Fujiwara no Yorinaga, the high ranking tutor to the crown prince and general of the *Bodyguard of the Left Section*, mentioned playing dai shogi in the *Taiki*, his diary written between 1135 and 1155, establishing that a large version of shogi existed at these early times. When the rules of Japanese chess were articulated for the first time, in the *Nichureki*, this 12th or 13th century encyclopedia did not describe one but two shogis. One is the direct ancestor of standard shogi but, in the *Nichureki*, that game only serves as an introduction to the second game which is described in more detail. This second game is played on a large board of 13 × 13 squares.[22] Each player has 34 pieces (as we understand from the description) of 13 different types: King, Gold, Silver, Copper, Iron, Knight, Lance, Side Mover, Ferocious Tiger, Flying Dragon which "flies on the diagonals," Free Chariot which "goes before and behind," Pawn, Armed Workman (same as the aforementioned Go-Between but with a different ideogram). Apparently, the modern Bishop's move is already present as the Flying Dragon; the Free Chariot has part of the move of the modern Rook.

Reconstructed initial array for Heian dai shogi.

Historians who have tried to reconstruct this game generally find that it does not play very well. Indeed, when the *Futsu shodoshu (Collection of Sermons for Everyday Use)*, a prayer anthology by the monk Ryoki, also evokes a sho shogi and a dai shogi around year 1300,[23] it seems that some pieces were modified for the large version. For the first time in the history of all types of shogi, a Flying Chariot—i.e., a Rook—is mentioned.

Several testimonies from the 14th century reveal that dai shogi was an enjoyable pastime. It was probably during that period that it reached the form that has been passed along to us with 65 pieces over a spacious 15 × 15 square board.[24] But soon, dai shogi faced competition with a simpler shogi that left out some of the less appealing chessmen: chu shogi, known as "middle shogi" because of its intermediate size. The earliest reference to chu shogi appears in the *Yugaku Orai*, a text from the mid–14th century, which also mentions dai shogi.[25]

This shogi trio continued into the 15th century. In 1424, the diary *Hanasakai Sandaikai* commented on a shogi game in which a player had a Free King handicap. That piece is only present in the middle and large forms of shogi. The comment is also interesting because the Free King, which moves at will in all directions, is the exact equivalent of the modern Queen of Western chess, which would soon be invented on the other side of the world.

In 1444, the courtier Nakahara Yasutomi noted in his diary that he had played chu shogi. In 1476, another text, the *Aro Kassen, Monogatari*, written by the scholar and emperor's regent, Ichijo Kaneyoshi, enumerated some of the chu shogi pieces without giving details. Many diary references of the time seem to maintain the distinction between large shogi, middle shogi and little shogi, and indeed many of them imply that middle shogi was held in highest esteem while little shogi was considered a trivial game.[26] In the 16th century, several testimonies from influential noblemen, *daimyo* (feudal rulers) and Buddhist monks proclaim that chu shogi continued with an appreciative following.[27]

The introduction of drops into small shogi drastically altered that situation. In 1602, the *Shogi Koma no Nikki*, an inventory of a game piece maker, Minase Kanenari, gave a list of the 735 games he had manufactured, counting 618 sho shogi, 106 chu shogi and only 2 dai shogi. At this point, chu shogi had been surpassed in popularity and dai shogi was beginning to vanish, even as new variants, some still larger, were being invented. Those will be described in the following chapters of this book.

In 1663, Ito Sokan (1618–1694), the Third Meijin, published his *Chu Shogi Zushiki (Illustrated Explanations of Middle Shogi)*, which gives a full description of chu shogi. A few years later, he published a collection of 50 chu shogi problems.

But in the years that followed, chu shogi all but faded away, maintained only by a few passionate Japanese players. For example, the great professional champion of shogi, Oyama Yasuharu (1923–1992), Fifteenth Meijin, held chu shogi in high regard. In 1970, he declared that its practice had influenced his prudent and tenacious style of playing standard shogi, improving the cohesion of his pieces.

In subsequent years, the Englishman George Hodges disseminated shogi throughout the Western world. It was a real rebirth and, with the help of the Internet, it is now possible to join chu shogi associations and to participate in international tournaments.

With the absence of drops, chu shogi is less disconcerting to the uninitiated than standard shogi. With unique chessmen, such as the Lion, which have no equivalent in any other chess variant, or with the Crown Prince, a genuine substitute for the King, the smallest of the "large" shogis draws in fans of "exotic" chess from all over the world. Dai shogi remains relatively remote, but still generates a strong historic interest.

# 20. Tenjiku Shogi

Tenjiku shogi is without doubt one of the most interesting among the large shogis. Derived from chu shogi, it deserves the name *tenjiku*, meaning "exotic," with the introduction of a unique collection of chessmen including a mighty *Fire Demon* which burns everything around it.

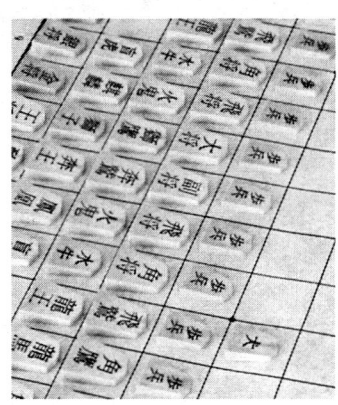

Close-up of the tenjiku shogi pieces, before the game begins.
WOUT BLOMMERS PHOTOGRAPH

This game requires a large, unchecked, 16 × 16 square board and 78 chessmen of 36 different types for each side. Typical of shogis in general, the pieces are the shape of pointed wedges. Each piece bears a pair of black kanji indicating its value on the top and, sometimes appearing much later, the promoted value on the bottom written in red ink.

Initial array of tenjiku shogi, laid out left-to-right as shown, for each player.

## Rules

The rules are similar to those of chu shogi. There are no drops; captured pieces are withdrawn from the board for the remainder of the game.

MOVES, CAPTURES AND PROMOTIONS. Tenjiku shogi includes all of the pieces from chu shogi except the Go-Between. The Soaring Eagle (*Hiju*) and the Horned Falcon (*Kakuo*) are present from the beginning of the game. Also included are the Knight (*Keima*) and the Iron General (*Tessho*), familiar from dai shogi, and 12 entirely new pieces:

| Kanji | Abbr. | Piece |
|---|---|---|
| 車兵 | 車 | *Chariot Soldier (Shahei)*: can move any number of free squares in the four diagonal directions, or directly forward or backward (six directions). It can also move just one or two squares sideways. |

| Kanji | Abbr. | Piece (continued) |
|---|---|---|
| 四天王 | 天 | The Chariot Soldier promotes to *Heavenly Tetrarchs (Shitenno)*,[28] which cannot move to any adjacent square, and is not blocked from moving by pieces on the adjacent squares; it can, however, capture adjacent pieces without moving (*igui*). It can also move any two or more free squares along any of the four diagonals or along the vertical file (forward and backward), skipping over any intervening piece on the adjacent square.[29] This promoted piece can also move two or three squares orthogonally sideways, with the possibility of skipping over a piece on the first square but not on the second square. If it captures a piece that is not on one of the adjacent squares, it must land on the square of capture. |
| 獅鷹 | 獅鷹 | *Lion Hawk (Shio or Shitaka)*: moves any number of free squares diagonally (like a chess Bishop) or moves like a Lion (including *jitto*, *igui* and double captures abilities detailed in the description of the chu shogi Lion). It is not limited by the special Lion capture rules of chu shogi. The Lion Hawk does not promote. |
| 奔鷲 | 奔鷲 | *Free Eagle (Honju)*: moves any number of free squares in any direction (like a chess Queen) or moves diagonally like a Lion (so it may take two diagonal steps, regardless of any intervening piece, possibly changing direction (thereby landing on the second square vertically or horizontally). It has the abilities of *jitto*, *igui* and double captures.)[30] It does not promote. |
| 火鬼 | 火 | *Fire Demon (Kaki)*: moves any number of free squares diagonally (like a chess Bishop) or any number directly vertically (six directions).[31] It can also execute an "*area move*" (described below) of three squares. Finally, it possesses the power of "*burning*" all enemy pieces which are adjacent to it. These pieces are instantly burned when the Fire Demon arrives on a new square, or when an enemy piece (except another Fire Demon) lands adjacent to it. See details below. It does not promote. |
| 水牛 | 水 | *Water Buffalo (Suigyu)*: moves any number of free squares diagonally or horizontally (six directions). It also has the power to move just one or two unobstructed squares directly forward or backward. Promotes to *Fire Demon*. |
| 竪兵 | 竪兵 | *Vertical Soldier (Shuhei)*: moves any number of free squares vertically forward, or one or two squares horizontally (without jumping over other pieces), or a single square directly backward. It promotes to *Chariot Soldier*. |
| 横兵 | 横兵 | *Side Soldier (Ohei)*: moves any number of free squares horizontally (sideways), or one or two squares directly forward (without jumping), or a single square directly backward. It promotes to *Water Buffalo*. |
| 大将 | 大 | *Great General (Taisho)*: when not capturing, moves any number of free squares in the eight directions (like a chess Queen). It captures by moving in the same direction but may jump over any number of lower-ranking pieces in its path (all but the King, Crown Prince or another Great General) (This is known as "*range jumping*"). It does not promote. |
| 副将 | 副 | *Vice General (Fukusho)*: When making a capture, this piece may jump over any number of lower-ranking pieces (any except King, Crown Prince, Great General or another Vice General) in any one of the four diagonal directions ("*range* |

*jumping"*). Otherwise, when not capturing, it moves without jumping (like a chess Bishop). It can also make an *"area move"* (see below) of three squares. It does not promote.

飛将　升　*Flying General (Hisho)*: may jump over any number of lower-ranking pieces in any one of the four orthogonal directions when making a capture (*"range jumping"*). Otherwise, it moves orthogonally without jumping (like a chess Rook). (It may not jump over a King, Crown Prince, or Vice, Flying or Horned General.) It promotes to *Great General*.

角将　用　*Horned General (Kakusho)*: jumps over any number of lower-ranking pieces in any one of the four diagonal directions when making a capture (*"range jumping"*). Otherwise, it moves diagonally without jumping (like a chess Bishop). (It may not jump over a King, Crown Prince, or Vice, Flying or Horned General.) It promotes to *Vice General*.

犬　犬　*Dog (Inu)*: moves one square directly forward, or diagonally backward (a total of three directions).

雑将　雑　The Dog promotes to *Multi General (Suisho)* which moves any number of free squares directly forward or diagonally backward (a total of three directions).

## Particular Rules

AREA MOVE. A piece making an "area move" may take two or three steps in a single turn, in a straight line or changing direction, but only passing through unoccupied squares. The piece can even come back to its starting square, allowing its player to effectively pass his turn (*jitto*). An area move must stop on the spot where any capture is made; therefore, it is not possible to make several captures in the same turn.

RANGE JUMPING. This consists of moving freely in a given direction, jumping over any number of intermediate squares if they are occupied by pieces of strictly lower rank, friend or foe. This move must finish with a capture, and is not allowed when not capturing.[32] The rank of the captured piece does not matter. Ranks are defined as follows, from highest to lowest: (1) King and Crown Prince; (2) Great General; (3) Vice General; (4) Flying General and Horned General; (5) all other pieces.

THE BURNING POWER OF THE FIRE DEMON. • The Fire Demon burns all opposing pieces (except other Fire Demons) adjacent to the square it arrives on.

- It passively burns and withdraws from the board any opposing piece that finishes its move on an adjacent square (after that piece makes its capture, if any). This passive burning does not count as the Fire Demon's move, and the player still proceeds with a move of his choice.

- When a Fire Demon lands on a square adjacent to another opposing Fire Demon, only the piece just arriving is burned. The stationary Fire Demon survives, as well as all other adjacent pieces.[33]

- When a Water Buffalo is promoted to Fire Demon, its power to burn adjacent pieces is only applied on its subsequent moves.

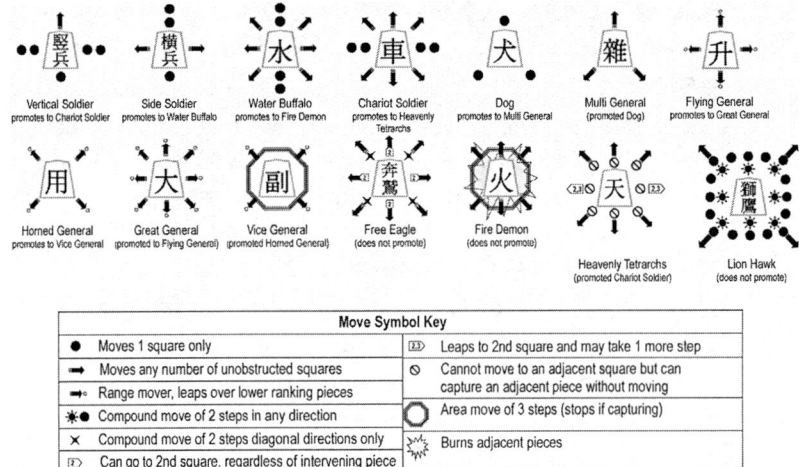

Moves of specific tenjiku shogi's pieces.

PROMOTION. The five ranks closest to the opponent constitute the promotion zone.
- Promotion takes place while entering, moving within or leaving the promotion zone. A piece that enters and leaves the zone all in one move can be promoted.
- Promotion is optional, unless the unpromoted piece would have no possible future move; in that case, promotion is compulsory.
- If a piece does not immediately promote while entering the promotion zone, it will be allowed to promote on its next move *only if it makes a capture*. On subsequent moves, it may promote without restriction.
- Promotion is permanent, and a promoted piece may not promote a second time.

END OF THE GAME. Victory is attained by capturing the opposing King. If the opponent has acquired a Crown Prince, this one must be captured as well.

Victory can also be attained by "bare King," capturing all of the adverse pieces except the lone King or Crown Prince. However, if the opponent can bare the other's King or Crown Prince, capturing the last defending piece, on the immediately following move, the game is drawn.

It is allowed to leave or even place one's own King or Crown Prince in check, subject to capture. Perpetual check is forbidden.

It is forbidden to repeat a position on the board with the same player to move (*sennichite*). This rule avoids draws by repetition.

DIFFERENCES WITH CHU SHOGI. • Two pieces here have different promotional values: the Iron General (promotes to Vertical Soldier) and the Knight (promotes to Side Soldier). Four additional pieces that cannot be promoted in chu shogi do promote in tenjiku shogi: the Lion (promotes to Lion Hawk), the Free King (promotes to Free Eagle), the Soaring Eagle (promotes to Flying General), and the Horned Falcon (promotes to Horned General).
- There are no restrictions on *Lion capturing Lion* in tenjiku shogi.

# History

Tenjiku shogi is first mentioned at the end of the 17th century in a work entitled *Shogi Zushiki*, which is discussed in the following chapter. Given this date, the game is more recent than most of the large shogis. This game may have been designed by a Buddhist monk trying to revive a moribund form of dai shogi.

With the original features of area moves, range jumping and burning powers, it is easy to see why this game was designated *tenjiku*, a term literally meaning "celestial bamboo," referring to India and, by extension, all things exotic. Exotic it is indeed, standing alone as a unique creation in the broad family of shogi games.

Re-discovered by some enthusiastic amateurs, tenjiku shogi is indebted to the Internet for its new surge of surprisingly strong interest. The Englishman Colin Adams, for instance, has published a large e-book surveying the game's openings. The game has now been tested in actual play on a very wide scale—a unique moment in historic game re-creation. As a result, players have expressed the need to define the movements of certain pieces and other specific rules to assure the game's playability. We have honored their achievement by presenting the rules here as they are now established for modern players.

# 21. Giant Shogis

## *Dai Dai Shogi*

We now enter the abyss of complexity. Following an inflationary trend, the Japanese monks propel us onto gigantic chessboards teeming with barbarians and demons in mortal combat. Dai dai shogi stands in contrast to the previous games with piece promotions obtained merely by making captures and by the inclusion of overpowering pieces, such as the dangerous Hook Mover, that terrorize the chessboard.

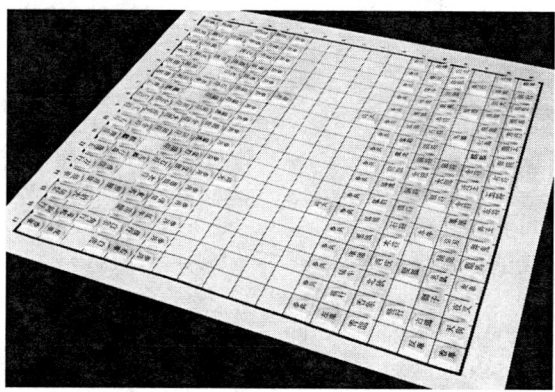

The array of dai dai shogi.
WOUT BLOMMERS PHOTOGRAPH

## *Material*

The board is composed of 17 × 17 squares. Each player commands an army of 96 pieces, shaped the same as those in the other shogi variants. There are 64 different pieces on the initial array—as many types of pieces as there are squares on the Western chessboard!

Initial array of dai dai shogi, identical for both players.

The starting setup is highly asymmetrical. The following list names every piece, from left to right, beginning with the first rank. The central piece is written in bold print, to help in the identification process.

- First rank, from left to right: Lance, Long-Nosed Goblin, She-Devil, Racing Chariot, Dragon Horse, Free Demon, Free King, Left General, **King**, Right General, Free Dream-Eater, Dragon King, Square Mover, Rook, Dove, Hook Mover, Lance.
- Second rank: Reverse Chariot, Old Kite, Lion, Old Rat, Prancing Stag, Cat Sword, Phoenix, Gold General, **Neighboring King**, Gold General, Kirin, Rushing Bird, Flying Dragon, Blind Monkey, Lion Dog, Poisonous Snake, Reverse Chariot.
- Third rank: Vertical Mover, Enchanted Fox, Water Buffalo, Silver General, **Great Dragon**, Silver General, Flying Horse, Enchanted Badger, Bishop.
- Fourth rank: Blue Dragon, Fragrant Elephant, Northern Barbarian, Western Barbarian, Wood General, Stone General, Iron General, Copper General, **Golden Bird**, Copper General, Iron General, Stone General, Wood General, Eastern Barbarian, Southern Barbarian, White Elephant, White Tiger.
- Fifth rank: Left Chariot, Side Mover, Violent Ox, Angry Boar, Evil Wolf, Violent Bear, Ferocious Leopard, Savage Tiger, **Standard Bearer**, Savage Tiger, Ferocious Leopard, Violent Bear, Evil Wolf, Angry Boar, Violent Ox, Side Mover, Right Chariot.
- Sixth rank: 17 Pawns, and on the Seventh Rank: two Howling Dogs.

# Rules

Dai dai shogi is a contemporary of dai shogi and predecessor of tenjiku shogi (with which it shares the Water Buffalo), but its complexity is greatly increased. Compared to dai shogi, this variant has 38 new pieces, or 42 if one includes the pieces made by promotion. The following diagram gives an efficient reference for the moves of the various pieces. A more detailed review of this game, beyond the scope of this book, can be found in the pages of Wikipedia.

The strangest pieces are the Hook Mover (鉤行 *Kogyo*) and the Long-Nosed Goblin (天狗 *Tengu*), equivalent to a double Rook and a double Bishop, respectively (the Long-Nosed Goblin has, in addition, the power to move one square orthogonally). These pieces move an unlimited number of empty squares in a given direction, but with the possibility of performing a 90° turn at any moment, continuing along in this new direction. They can only change direction once per move, and may also move without the 90° turn. When capturing, they must remain on the spot where the capture was made. The most dangerous is the Hook Mover which, unobstructed, could reach any square on the chessboard!

Also curious are the Enchanted Fox (変狐 *Henko*) and the Old Rat (老鼠 *Roso*). These two pieces have the exact same move (one or two squares along three directions: forward diagonally or straight backward orthogonally). They promote differently, however, to a She-Devil (夜叉 *Yasha*) and to a Wizard Stork (仙鶴 *Senkaku*), respectively.

The Lion Dog (狛犬 *Komainu*) is another piece whose move has been misunderstood by Western players. It can move one, two or three steps in eight directions (orthogonal and diagonal). These are special "Lion-like" steps, in which the Lion Dog can capture an opposing piece on each of its three steps; or capture twice on the first and on the second square and then come back to the first square of capture (a total of three steps); or it may capture on the first square and then come back to where it started (*igui*)—but it cannot take a third step in the opposite direction. In addition, the Lion Dog can jump to the third square, or jump to the second and continue on to the third, leaping over pieces in its way. It can also pass its turn and remain immobile. It is not required to take all three steps. But as soon as it completes its capturing move (which could include one, two or three captures) it is "promoted" to a Great Elephant—much less powerful.

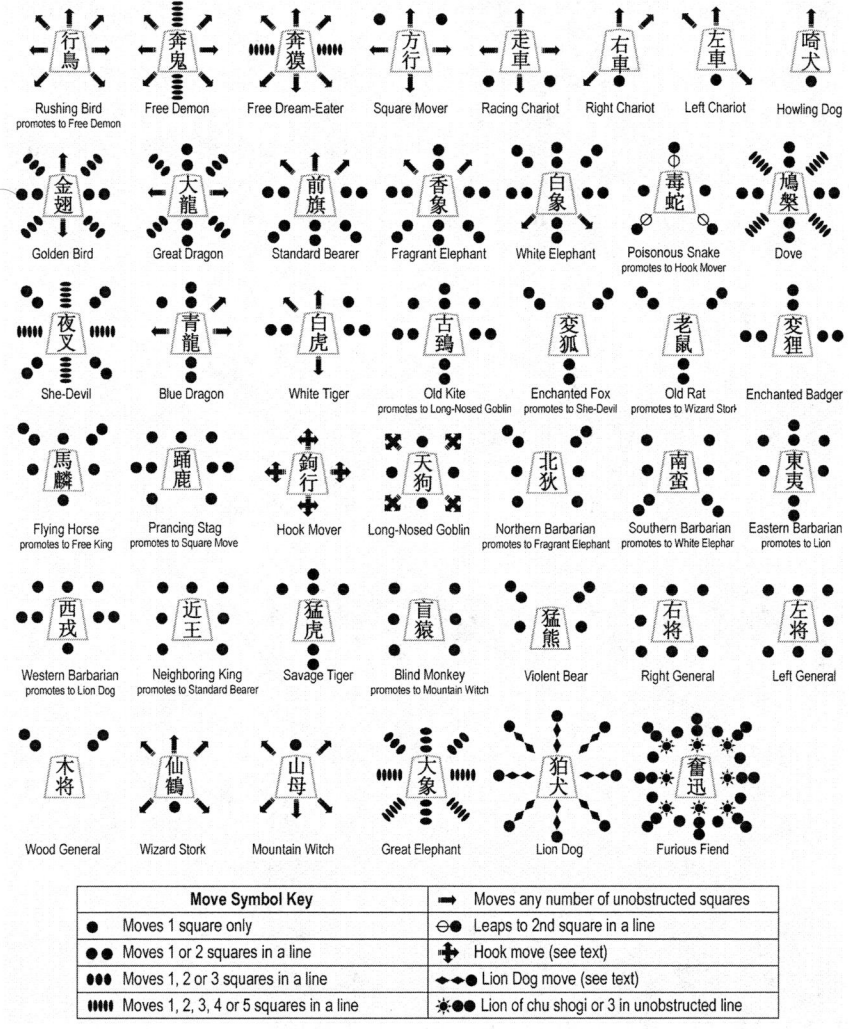

Moves of specific dai dai shogi's pieces.

Note: There are no drops. Captured pieces are withdrawn from the board for the remainder of the game.

PROMOTIONS. Unlike smaller shogis in which promotion is obtained by reaching the opponent's starting zone, in dai dai shogi a piece simply promotes when it makes its first capture. The same rule also applies to shogis larger than dai dai shogi.

When an unpromoted piece captures an enemy, it is flipped over and shows its new value. Promotion is compulsory and permanent.

Of the 64 types of pieces in dai dai shogi, only 21 are able to promote. Pawns do not promote, but remain immobile if they reach the last rank.

Four types of pieces are obtained only by promotion: the Mountain Witch (from the Blind Monkey), the Great Elephant (from the Lion Dog), the Wizard Stork (from the Old Rat) and the Furious Fiend (from the Lion).

The other promotions are: Hook Mover (from Poisonous Snake), Long-Nosed Goblin (from Old Kite), Dragon King (from Flying Dragon), Square Mover (from Prancing Stag), Free Demon (from Rushing Bird), Dragon Horse (from Cat Sword), Great Dragon (from Kirin), Golden Bird (from Phoenix), Standard Bearer (from Neighboring King), Dove (from Enchanted Badger), She-Devil (from Enchanted Fox), Free King (from Flying Horse), Free Dream-Eater (from Water Buffalo), White Elephant (from Southern Barbarian), Fragrant Elephant (from Northern Barbarian), Lion (from Eastern Barbarian), Lion Dog (from Western Barbarian).

When a piece which can only step forward (such as the Pawn, the Lance, the Stone General, the Wood General, the Iron General, etc.) reaches the opposite side of the chessboard, it stays there, immobile, until it is captured.

## *Maka Dai Dai Shogi*

Still bigger! This is the "ultra large large shogi"[34] in which almost every piece can be promoted, even the King who aims to become Emperor! Beyond the huge inflation of size and numbers, several of the new pieces here are strikingly original. Maka dai dai shogi is one of the most fascinating of the Japanese chess variants.

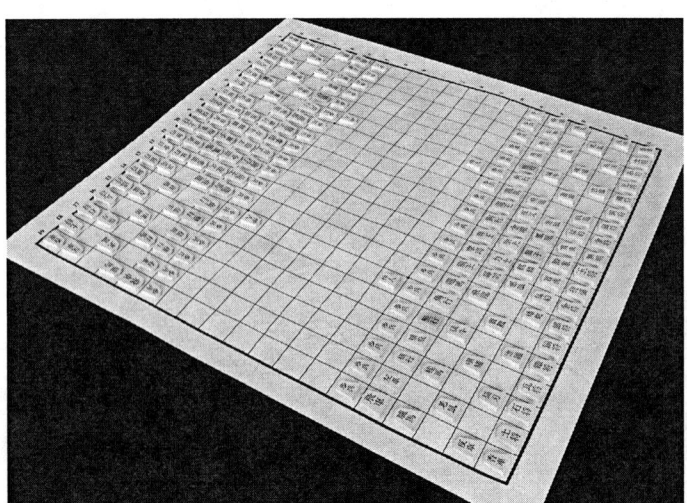

The great 19 x 19 array of maka dai dai shogi.
WOUT BLOMMERS PHOTOGRAPH

## 21. Giant Shogis

## Material

The unchecheckered board has 19 × 19 squares. Although this board is bigger than that of the dai dai shogi board, there are still 96 pieces allotted to each player. There is less diversity here with "only" 50 different kinds of pieces.

Initial array of maka dai dai shogi laid out in the same order, left-to-right, for each player.

The pieces are arranged as follows, with the center pieces in **bold** type. "G" is for "General":

- First rank, from left to right: Lance, Earth G., Stone G., Tile G., Iron G., Copper G., Silver G., Gold G., Deva,[35] **King**, Dark Spirit, Gold G., Silver G., Copper G., Iron G., Tile G., Stone G., Earth G., Lance.
- Second rank: Reversed Chariot, Cat Sword, Chinese Cock, Coiled Snake, Ferocious Leopard, Blind Tiger, **Drunk Elephant**, Blind Tiger, Ferocious Leopard, Reclining Dragon, Old Monkey, Cat Sword, Reverse Chariot.
- Third rank: Old Rat, Angry Boar, Blind Bear, Evil Wolf, Kirin, **Lion**, Phoenix, Evil Wolf, Blind Bear, Angry Boar, Old Rat.
- Fourth rank: Donkey, Knight, Violent Ox, Flying Dragon, Buddhist Devil, Wrestler, **Lion Dog**, Guardian of the Gods, She-Devil, Flying Dragon, Violent Ox, Knight, Donkey.
- Fifth rank: Rook, Left Chariot, Side Mover, Side Flyer, Vertical Mover, Bishop, Dragon Horse, Dragon King, Capricorn, **Free King**, Hook Mover, Dragon King, Dragon Horse, Bishop, Vertical Mover, Side Flyer, Side Mover, Right Chariot, Rook.
- Sixth rank: 19 Pawns and on the Seventh Rank: two Go-Betweens.

## Rules

The rules are similar to those of the other giant shogis. There are no drops, and promotion is obtained by capturing an enemy piece. Promotion is optional when capturing an unpromoted enemy piece; it is, however, compulsory, if possible, when capturing a promoted piece. One could say that promotion is "contagious."

Only three pieces are never promoted: the Dragon Horse, the Dragon King and the Free King. Twenty-six types of pieces promote to new pieces that are not present in the initial array, including an Emperor (自在天王 *Jizai Tenno*), obtained when the King promotes.

The Emperor can jump to any unprotected square on the board. If that square is occupied by an enemy, the enemy is captured. The Emperor cannot capture an enemy that is protected by another piece (where he could be captured in return), even if this move would win the game (for instance, capturing the opposing Emperor). Although it is not recommended, an Emperor can move to an empty square controlled by the opponent (moving into check) if his side also has a Prince (from the promotion of a Drunk Elephant). If both players have an Emperor, and no Prince is in play, then the Emperor cannot move to a square that is not guarded by one of his own pieces. If he did, the other Emperor could capture him immediately; therefore, he would have moved into check.

Several of the promoted values have "Free," in the sense of *unfettered*, in their titles: Free Gold, Free Silver, Free Copper, Free Iron, Free Tile, Free Cat, Free Snake, Free Leopard, Free Tiger, and Free Goer. They are promotions of their respective similarly-named pieces named as the "Generals" (e.g., Gold General becomes Free Gold, etc.), or other descriptors (e.g., the Cat Sword becomes the Free Cat, etc.). In such cases, the "Free" promoted piece ranges any number of squares in the same directions which were allowed to the unpromoted piece. For example, the Tile General (瓦将 *Gasho*) moves one step diagonally forward or straight backward. It is promoted to a Free Tile (奔瓦 *Honga*) which moves any number of squares in the same three directions.

The other promotions are as follows: Buddhist Spirit (from Dark Spirit), Teaching King (from Deva), Mountain Witch (from Old Monkey), Wizard Stork (from Chinese Cock), Prince (from Drunk Elephant), Bat (from Old Rat), Golden Bird (from Phoenix), Great Dragon (from Kirin), Furious Fiend (from Lion), Free Dragon (from Reclining Dragon), Free Boar (from Angry Boar), Free Bear (from Blind Bear), and Free Wolf (from Evil Wolf).

Two of these promoted pieces have very mighty and mobile powers. The Buddhist Spirit (法性 *Hosei*) combines the powers of the Lion, which can link two steps in the same turn, with the Free King, which moves like the chess Queen. Even more powerful is the Teaching King (教王 *Kyoo*) which combines the powers of the Lion Dog (see dai dai shogi) and the Free King.

Twenty-one pieces get promoted to Gold General: Lance, Reverse Chariot, Donkey, Knight, Violent Ox, Flying Dragon, She-Devil, Buddhist Devil, Guardian of the Gods, Wrestler, Lion Dog, Rook, Right Chariot, Left Chariot, Side Mover, Side Flier, Vertical Mover, Bishop, Hook Mover, Capricorn, and Pawn. For several of them, this "promotion" is actually a demotion, since the change does not constitute an advantage in power. The objective of this rule is to reduce these very powerful pieces to something more moderate after they have begun capturing the opposing pieces.

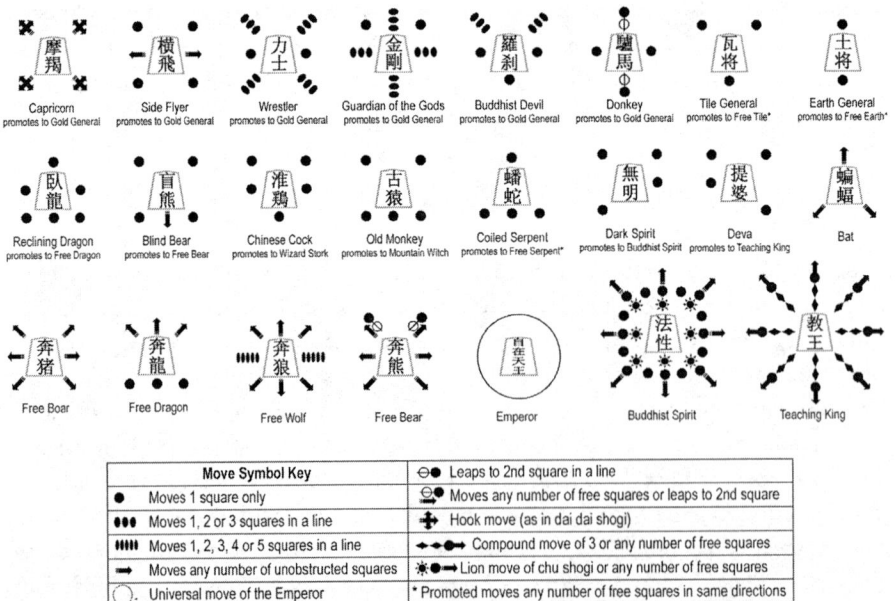

Moves of specific maka dai dai shogi's pieces.[36]

## 21. Giant Shogis

Any non-royal piece (i.e., not the Emperor, King, Prince, or Drunk Elephant), unpromoted or promoted, that captures a Deva or a Teaching King immediately becomes a Teaching King itself. In the same way, any piece that captures a Dark Spirit or a Buddhist Spirit becomes a Buddhist Spirit. This rule is accomplished on the board by replacing the attacking piece with the captured piece, with its promoted side up, pointing in the direction of its former owner.

The victory goes to the player who captures the opponent's last remaining King (or Emperor) or Prince. As long as both players have at least one of these royal pieces, the game must go on.

## Tai Shogi

For a long period, this game was considered the height of excess. It was said to be the largest traditional chess variant in the world. *Tai shogi* ("giant shogi"), also known as *mujo dai shogi* ("supreme large shogi"), is enormous indeed with 354 pieces in play over a board of 625 squares. A game of tai shogi can easily exceed 1000 moves per player!

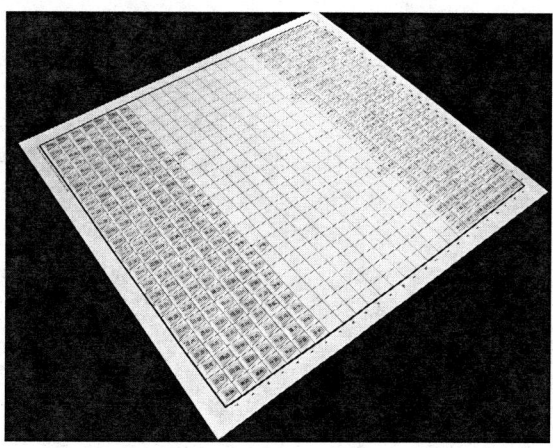

Approaching the upper limit of a game that can actually be played, tai shogi has 93 different types of chessmen, played on a board of 625 squares.
WOUT BLOMMERS PHOTOGRAPH

## Material

The board is an immense table of 25 × 25 squares. Each player starts with 177 pieces, including 25 Pawns. There are 93 different types of chessmen in the opening array.

Initial array of tai shogi, identical for both players.

Following is a list of the pieces as they are arranged on the board. The promoted values are indicated in parentheses. Sources vary regarding the promotion of some pieces; in those cases, both possibilities are mentioned. The central piece of each rank is in **bold** print. Many pieces promote to Gold General, which is noted here simply as "Gold."

- First rank, from left to right: Lance (Gold), White Tiger (Gold), Whale (Gold), Flying Dragon, Long-Nosed Goblin (Gold), Dove (Gold), Rook (Gold), Dragon Horse, Dragon King, Free King, Gold General (Free Gold), Deva (Teaching King), **Emperor**, Dark Spirit (Buddhist Spirit), Gold General, Free King, Dragon King, Dragon Horse, Rook, Dove, Long-Nosed Goblin, Flying Dragon, Whale, Turtle-Snake (Gold), Lance.
- Second Rank: Reverse Chariot (Gold), Side Dragon (Gold), Soaring Eagle (Gold), Knight (Gold), Poisonous Snake (Hook Mover), Free Dream-Eater (Gold), Bishop (Gold), Fierce Eagle (Gold), White Elephant (Gold), Free Demon (Gold), Silver General (Free Silver), Left General (Gold), **Crown Prince**, Right General (Gold), Silver General, Free Demon, White Elephant, Fierce Eagle, Bishop, Free Dream-Eater, Poisonous Snake, Knight, Soaring Eagle, Side Dragon, Reverse Chariot.
- Third rank: Side Chariot (Gold), White Horse (Gold), Ram's head Soldier (Gold), Violent Ox (Gold), Cat Sword (Free Cat), Blind Bear (Free Bear), Silver Hare (Gold), Gold Deer (Gold), Blind Monkey (Mountain Witch or Gold), Blind Tiger (Free Tiger), Buddhist Devil (Gold), Wrestler (Gold), **Neighboring King** (Standard Bearer), Guardian of the Gods (Gold), She-Devil (Gold), Blind Tiger, Blind Monkey, Gold Deer, Silver Hare, Blind Bear, Cat Sword, Violent Ox, Ram's head Soldier, White Horse, Side Chariot.
- Fourth rank: Soldier (Gold), Water Buffalo (Free Dream-Eater), Ferocious Leopard (Free Leopard), Western Barbarian (Lion Dog), Eastern Barbarian (Lion), Chinese Cock (Wizard Stork), Horned Falcon (Gold), Old Monkey (Gold or Mountain Witch), Old Kite (Long-Nosed Goblin), Peacock (Gold), Great Dragon (Gold), Kirin (Great Dragon), **Lion** (Furious Fiend), Phoenix (Golden Bird), Golden Bird (Gold), Peacock (Gold), Rushing Bird (Free Demon or Gold), Old Monkey, Horned Falcon, Chinese Cock, Southern Barbarian (White Elephant or Gold), Northern Barbarian (Fragrant Elephant or Gold), Ferocious Leopard, Water Buffalo, Soldier.

The Kirin, a hybrid creature inspired by the Chinese mythology, carrier of good omens (18th century Japan, Edo period).

- Fifth rank: Left Chariot (Gold), Blue Dragon (Gold), Wood General (Gold), Earth General (Free Earth), Stone General (Free Stone), Tile General (Free Tile), Iron General (Free Iron), Copper General (Free Copper), Old Rat (Bat), Coiled Snake (Free Snake), Reclining Dragon (Free Dragon), Capricorn (Gold), **Drunk Elephant** (Crown Prince), Hook Mover (Gold),

# 21. Giant Shogis

Reclining Dragon, Coiled Snake, Old Rat, Copper General, Iron General, Tile General, Stone General, Earth General, Wood General, Vermillion Sparrow (Gold), Right Chariot (Gold).
- Sixth rank: Howling Dog (Gold), Flying Horse (Free King), Enchanted Badger (Dove), Donkey (Gold), Flying Ox (Gold), Side Mover (Gold), Vertical Mover (Gold), Violent Bear (Gold), Standard Bearer (Gold), Prancing Stag (Square Mover), Angry Boar (Free Boar), Evil Wolf (Free Wolf), **Lion Dog** (Gold), Evil Wolf, Angry Boar, Prancing Stag, Standard Bearer, Violent Bear, Vertical Mover, Side Mover, Flying Ox, Donkey, Enchanted Badger, Flying Horse, Howling Dog.
- Seventh rank: 25 Pawns (Gold) and on the eighth rank: two Go-Betweens (Free Go-Between).

## Rules

The rules are similar to those of other very large shogis: no drops; pieces are promoted as soon as they make their first capture. Many of the pieces—nearly all—are identical to those of the other shogi variants.

Most remarkable in this game is certainly the Emperor, which is in play from the starting array. Placed in the center of the first rank, he is both the most important and the most powerful chessman of tai shogi.

The Emperor can jump to any square on the chessboard, regardless of the number of pieces he may be leaping over. There is only one restriction: he cannot capture a piece protected by another piece; hence, moving into check. This rule prevents the Emperor from capturing the adverse Emperor in the very first stroke of the game. Knowing that the adverse Emperor protects all pieces of his own side by the same rule, an Emperor cannot capture as long as the opposing Emperor remains on the chessboard.

**The almighty Emperor (*Tenno*).**

In addition to the Emperor, there are only four other pieces that never promote: Crown Prince, Dragon Horse, Dragon King and Free King. For those that promote, "promotion" is not always an advantage. This is especially true of the many pieces that promote to Gold General. The promotion is actually a *demotion*, so those pieces may use their original powers to capture only once. It is essential to make good use of them!

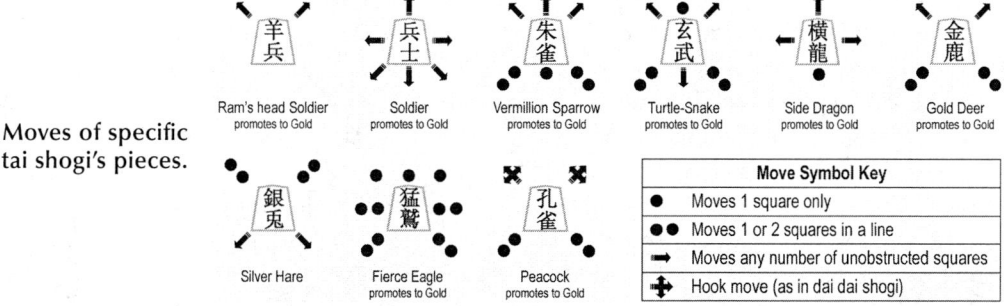

Moves of specific tai shogi's pieces.

Apart from the Gold General, eight promotions uncover entirely new pieces not present at the start of the game.[37] Players will need to be acquainted with these pieces and moves. as well as the original array.

The winner is the first player to succeed in capturing both the Emperor and the Crown Prince of his opponent. There is a somewhat facetious rule passed along indicating that it is forbidden to collude with the enemy and agree to a draw. Every game started must be played out to the bitter end!

## History

As one might expect, the earliest evidence of these giant games lies in very murky historic waters. The earliest citation, small, obscure and incomplete, is found in the anonymous *Isei Teikin'orai (Correspondence Manual for Family Teaching)*, a text from the mid–14th century,[38] which says, "Shogi is the representation of a battle. The one that is not dense reproduces the alignment of 36 beasts. The one that is dense is in agreement with the 360 days of the lunar calendar." It may be that Heian shogi has 36 pieces, but no variation is known with 360 pieces. The closest is tai shogi which has 354 pieces. Or could that mean a game on a 19 × 19 board (361 squares) such as maka dai dai shogi? Is this actually a first evocation of a giant shogi? The obscurity of this isolated passage yields no further clues.

The original sources of the large and giant shogis are found in chronicles from Japan's Edo period (1603–1868), beginning with the *Shogi Rokushu no Zushiki (Illustrated Explanations of Six Sorts of Shogi)*. This book has an obscure and tantalizing history. It first appeared in 1811 under the authorship of Tsurumine Shigenobu (1788–1859), but is known today because of its inclusion in the *Zatsugei Sosho*, a book published in 1915. Modern research has established that the *Shogi Rokushu no Zushiki* is a copy of the *Shogi Zu (Illustrations of Shogi)*, authored by Minase Kanenari in 1591. The *Shogi Zu*, now conserved at Shimamoto, presents sho shogi (played over a 9 × 9 board), chu shogi, dai shogi, dai dai shogi, maka dai dai shogi and tai shogi. Minase explains that he had copied another book entitled *Shogi Shushu no Zu (Illustrations of Shogi Varieties)*, now lost, which he had borrowed from the Manshu-in temple in Kyoto. The author of that book is unknown, but its date is 1443. Minase also indicates that this *Shogi Shushu no Zu* was itself the copy of a more ancient text of which we, unfortunately, have no further information.

Both the *Shogi Rokushu no Zushiki* and the *Shogi zu* mention that they have been modified once. Three presentations of games (among the six) are signed by Minase and three are unsigned. It is assumed therefore, that the three signed games were the modified ones. If this is correct, it is quite probable that the three signed games were invented between 1443 and 1591. These three newer games are dai dai shogi, maka dai dai shogi and tai shogi.[39]

Later, in 1694, the *Sho Shogi Zushiki (Illustrated Explanations of Small Shogi)* appeared, a four-volume work compiled by Nishizawa Teichin. The first volume describes the different sorts of shogi: sho shogi (with and without the Drunk Elephant), wa shogi (which is described below), chu shogi, dai shogi, tenjiku shogi, dai dai shogi, maka dai dai shogi and tai shogi.

Also before the end of the 17th century, a treatise entitled *Shogi Zushiki (Illustrated Explanations of Shogi)* covered standard shogi, chu shogi, dai shogi, tenjiku shogi, dai dai shogi, maka dai dai shogi and tai shogi. It also mentions wa shogi, tang shogi (which is merely the Chinese seven-player qiguo xiangxi), ko shogi and taikyoku shogi (these two variants are described further in this book). However, this *Shogi Zushiki* seems a different work than Ohashi Soko's *Shogi Zushiki*, quoted previously regarding the history of standard shogi.

These historical texts are not entirely consistent in their descriptions of the largest variants, but Japanese researchers have studied the available evidence and recommended cohesive sets of rules. The results of their work shape the basis for the rules transmitted to Western amateurs by George Hodges (1934–2010) who marketed many large and giant shogi sets to the Western world in the 1970s. The advent of the Internet has augmented the available information with contributions by modern Japanese shogi variant experts.

The enormousness of these chessboards has brought the authenticity of some of the games into question, especially the monstrous tai shogi. For a long time, it was difficult to believe that this game had ever been played. However the inventory of craftsman Minase Kanenari, dated from 1602 (previously cited regarding chu shogi), mentioned the manufacture of two sets of dai dai shogi, three sets of maka dai dai shogi and four complete sets of tai shogi, which leads one to believe these games were actually implemented.

Before the dawn of the 21st century, tai shogi was considered to be the largest chess game in the world, if not in fact the largest board game ever played. But then, new evidence has crept out of Japan that something even bigger than tai shogi once existed....

# 22. Wa Shogi

And now, *wa shogi*, the "peaceful shogi." It is one of the most recent among the ancient shogi variants, first appearing in the 17th century. This shogi is considerably different from the others, abandoning any reference to warfare, offering instead a fabulous menagerie. Poetically conceived and inspired by nature, wa shogi presents a universe of animals and birds endowed with original moves, lending a certain elegance to this refined game.

Initial array of wa shogi.

## Material

The chessboard is uncheckered with 11 × 11 squares. Like other shogis, the pieces are wedge-shaped, their tips directed toward the adverse camp, with their names written on the upper faces and the promotion values on the bottom faces. Each player has 27 pieces, sized according to rank.

There are 11 Sparrow Pawns and 16 additional pieces that do not repeat, making the left flank totally different from the right.

## Rules

While this game has a very original appearance, several of the pieces have moves similiar to the other shogi variants. As in other shogis, the pieces capture as they move.

牛車    *Oxcart (Gissha):* moves any number of free squares straight forward like the Lance in regular shogi.

耷牛    The Oxcart promotes to *Plodding Ox (Sengyu)*, which moves like a shogi King.

盲犬    *Blind Dog (Moken):* steps one square diagonally forward, orthogonally sideways or directly backward (five directions). This is the move of the Chinese Cock at maka dai dai shogi. It promotes to *Violent Wolf*.

烏行    *Strutting Crow (Uko):* steps one square directly forward or diagonally backward (three directions). This is the move of the Dog at tenjiku shogi. It promotes to *Flying Falcon*.

鳫飛    *Flying Goose (Ganhi):* steps one square directly forward or backward or one square diagonally forward (four directions), like the Copper General of chu shogi. It promotes to *Swallow's Wings*.

猛狼    *Violent Wolf (Moro):* steps one square in any of the four orthogonal directions or diagonally forward (six directions), like the Gold General of shogi.

熊眼    The Violent Wolf promotes to *Bear's Eyes (Yugan)*, which moves like a shogi King.

霸玉    *Crane King (Kakugyoku):* central piece of the game, it steps one square in any direction like the shogi King. The capture of the adverse Crane King is the goal of the game.

猛鹿    *Violent Stag (Moroku):* steps one square in any of the four diagonal directions or straight forward (five directions), like a shogi Silver General.

行猪    The Violent Stag promotes to *Roaming Boar (Gyocho)*, which steps one square in any direction, orthogonal or diagonal, except directly backward (seven directions). This is the move of the Drunk Elephant in chu shogi.

鶏飛    *Flying Cock (Keihi):* steps one square orthogonally sideways or diagonally forward (four directions).

延鷹    The Flying Cock promotes to *Raiding Falcon (En'yo)*, which moves any number of free squares orthogonally forward or backward. It can also step one square sideways or diagonally forward.

鴎行    *Swooping Owl (Shigyo):* moves exactly like the *Strutting Crow*. It promotes to *Cloud Eagle*.

登猿    *Climbing Monkey (Toen):* moves exactly like the *Flying Goose*. It promotes to *Violent Stag*.

風馬    *Liberated Horse (Fuma):* moves any number of free squares orthogonally forward or steps one or two squares directly backward.

天馬　The Liberated Horse promotes to *Heavenly Horse (Temma)* which jumps one square forward plus one square diagonally forward; or, one square backward plus one square diagonally backward in a single motion, ignoring any intervening piece. This is similar to a Knight's leap, but the Heavenly Horse can reach a maximum of four squares—twice the number reached by a shogi Knight, but only the half as many as a Western chess Knight.

飛鷹　*Flying Falcon (Hiyo):* moves any number of free squares along any of the four diagonal directions, or steps one square forward.

鶏鷹　The Flying Falcon promotes to *Tenacious Falcon (Keiyo)* which moves any number of free squares forward, backward or diagonally (six long directions). It can also step one square sideways.

燕羽　*Swallow's Wings (En'u):* moves any number of free squares sideways or steps one square orthogonally forward or backward. This is the move of the Side Mover of chu shogi.

燕行　The Swallow's Wings promotes to *Gliding Swallow (Engyo),* which moves like a Rook.

雲鷲　*Cloud Eagle (Unju):* moves any number of free squares directly forward or backward or steps one, two or three squares diagonally forward (not jumping over pieces in its way, and stopping on the square if it makes a capture). It can also step one square sideways or diagonally backward. It does not promote.

隠狐　*Treacherous Fox (Inko):* steps one square in the four diagonal directions, or directly forward or backward (six directions). It can also jump to the second square in any of those directions, passing over any intervening piece. It does not promote.

走兎　*Running Rabbit (Soto):* moves any number of free squares directly forward or steps one square in the four diagonal directions or straight backward. It promotes to *Treacherous Fox*.

雀歩　*Sparrow Pawn (Jakufu):* steps one square forward like a shogi Pawn.

金鳥　The Sparrow Pawn promotes to *Golden Bird (Kincho)* which moves like the Gold General in shogi.

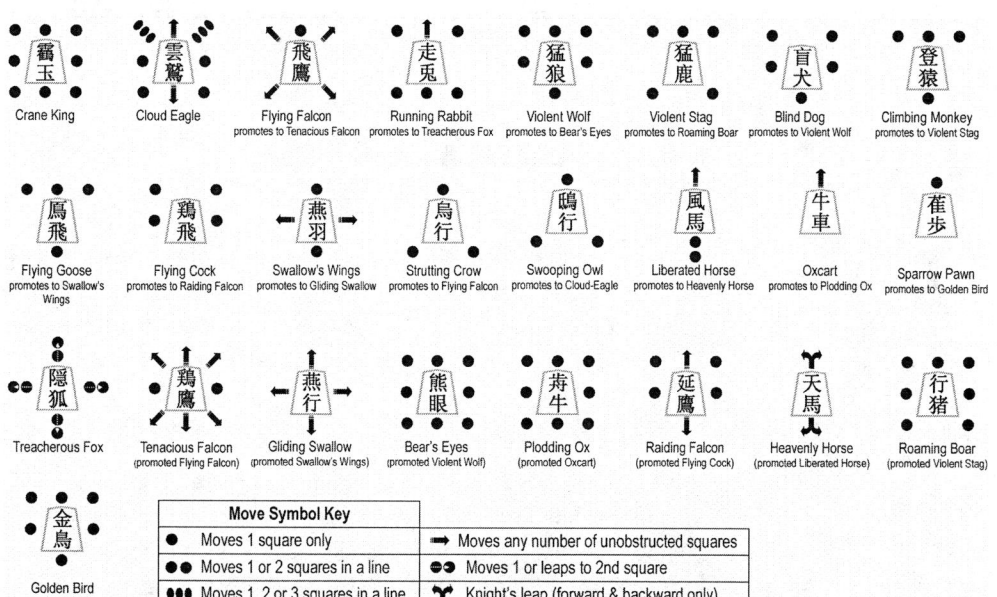

Moves of wa shogi's pieces.

DROPS. Beyond the initial setup and the moves of the pieces, little is known about this historical game. It is assumed that the rules of play were identical to standard shogi, but it is unclear whether the game was played with or without drops.

According to R. Wayne Schmittberger, American author and game expert, the majority of modern players have chosen to play wa shogi with drops. In this case, all of the rules of standard shogi apply.

PROMOTIONS. As in standard shogi, pieces may be promoted at the end of any move that starts, ends or travels within the promotion zone; that is, the farthest three rows of the board.

Also, similar to standard shogi, promotion is mandatory for the pieces that would be stuck with no possible future move if they did not promote. This is the case for the Sparrow Pawn or the Oxcart if they arrive at the last rank. If the game is played with drops, pieces dropped in also must have a possible future move.

## History

Three sources from the end of the 17th century mention this game, also known as *Yamato shogi*,[40] but with important differences. The *Kokon Shogi Zui* (*Illustrations of Past and Present Shogi Styles*), published in 1697,[41] and the *Shogi Zushiki*, already cited for other shogi variants, give moves with limited range to the pieces. According to John Fairbairn, that could suggest the possibility of drops. The *Sho Shogi Zushiki*, also previously mentioned regarding other variants, gives more powerful moves to the pieces which are therefore less compatible with drops. Exactly how and when these various rules were implemented remains an open question.

Amateurs who take up this game to give it new life generally play with drops according to modern shogi rules. If this was not the intention of the original players centuries ago, it offers a worthy further evolution of this delightful game.

# 23. Tori Shogi

Initial array of tori shogi.

*Tori shogi* or "bird shogi" is the smallest of the historic shogi variants. This game has achieved some success, as recently reported by some modern shogi associations. The moves are gracious and in agreement with the sense of an ornithological battle.

## Material

The board is composed of 49 squares in a 7 × 7 array. Each player has 16 pieces representing various birds. The pieces are wedge-shaped and pointed, like regular shogi pieces, pointing toward the opponent. These are the pieces in each side: 1 Phoenix, 2 Cranes, 2 Pheasants, 1 Left Quail, 1 Right Quail, 1 Falcon and 8 Swallows.

# 23. Tori Shogi

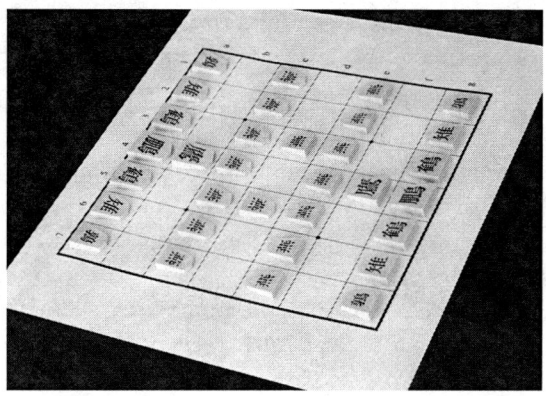

In tori shogi, birds compete across a simple 7 × 7 square board.
WOUT BLOMMERS PHOTOGRAPH

## Rules

MOVES, CAPTURES AND PROMOTIONS. All pieces use their normal moves to capture, landing on an enemy piece and removing it from the board. Some pieces are familiar from other shogi variants.

鵬　*Phoenix (Otori):* main piece of the game. It steps one square in any direction, orthogonally or diagonally, like a King. As expected, the capture of the opposite Phoenix is the goal of the game.

鶴　*Crane (Tsuru):* moves one square diagonally or straight forward or backward (a total of six directions). This is the move of the Ferocious Leopard in chu shogi.

鷹　*Falcon (Taka):* moves one square in any direction except straight backward (thus seven directions total). This is the move of the Drunk Elephant in chu shogi.

鵰　Promotes to *Mountain Eagle (Washi, Kumataka)* which ranges any number of free squares either diagonally forward or straight backward (a total of three long directions). It can also step one square straight forward or sideways (three short directions) or step one or two squares diagonally backward (two mid-range directions). It does not jump.

雉　*Pheasant (Kiji):* jumps to the second square straight ahead or steps one square diagonally backward. Therefore, the Pheasant can reach only half the squares of the board.

鶉　*Quail (Uzura):* there are two types: Left 左 and Right 右. They step only one square toward the rear diagonal on their name (back diagonally left or back diagonally right, respectively), or range any number of free squares straight ahead or along the other rear diagonal. They do not jump over pieces in their paths.

燕　*Swallow (Tsubame):* moves one step straight forward and captures the same way, similar to the Pawn in shogi.

鴈　Promotes to *Wild Goose (Kari)* which jumps to the second square diagonally forward or orthogonally backward (three directions).

PARTICULAR RULES. • *Promotion:* only the Falcon and the Swallow promote, and their promoted moves are quite novel. Promotion is compulsory and must be effected immediately upon reaching either of the first two ranks of the opponent's camp.

• *Drops:* Captured pieces may be dropped into play, as they are in modern shogi. When a capture is made, the player keeps it off the board at his right-hand side. On any turn, that piece may be dropped into play on a vacant square. It is always dropped in as its unpromoted value. If it is dropped into the promotions zone, it starts as an unpromoted piece but must be promoted (if it can promote) on its first move from that point.

There are restrictions when dropping Swallows. It is not permitted to drop a Swallow into a file (vertical column) which already contains *two* other unpromoted Swallows from the same side. A Swallow may not be dropped to give immediate checkmate on that move. A Swallow may not be dropped on the furthest rank, since it would have no possible future move. These restrictions are consistent with the Pawn-dropping restrictions of standard modern shogi, except that here two (but not three) Swallows may be placed in the same file.

A same position (with the same pieces in hand) may not be repeated more than three times. The player about to create such a repetition must select a different move.

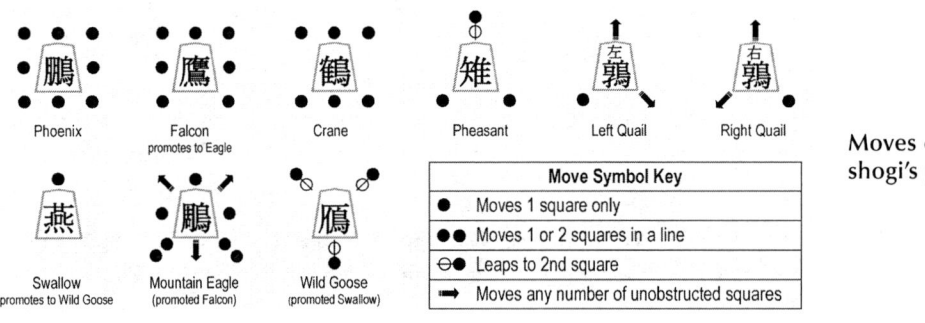

Moves of tori shogi's pieces.

## Variant: Whale Shogi

Following the shogi of the skies, we now dive down into a shogi of the oceans. This variant is also a "small" shogi involving different species of Cetaceans. Whale shogi fosters several novelties. The most interesting is the Porpoise's transformation into a Killer Whale, which strongly increases the power of drops.

The board is a plain surface of 6 × 6 square. Each player has 12 pieces. Similar to other shogis, the pieces, identical for both players, are pointed toward the opponent. They are: 1 White Whale, 1 Blue Whale, 1 Gray Whale, 1 Humpback Whale, 1 Narwhal, 1 Porpoise and 6 Dolphins.

**W** *White Whale (Hakugei):* main piece whose capture is the goal of the game. It steps one square in any direction, like a King.

**P** *Porpoise (Nezumi Iruka):* steps one square sideways only.

**K** The Porpoise promotes to a *Killer Whale (Shachi)* which ranges any number of free squares orthogonally or steps one square diagonally. This is the move of the Dragon King in shogi.

**G** *Gray Whale (Koku Kujira):* ranges any number of free squares straight ahead or toward the rear diagonals (a total of three directions). This is the move of the Bat in maka dai dai shogi.

**N** *Narwhal (Ikaku):* steps one square sideways or straight backward (thus three directions) or jumps to the second square straight forward, leaping over any intervening piece.

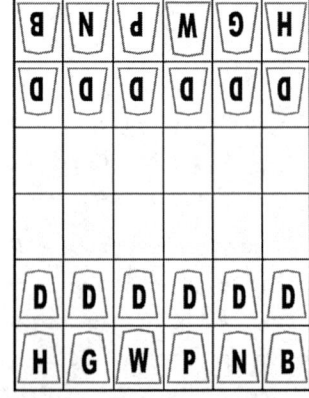

Initial array of whale shogi.

H   *Humpback Whale (Zato Kujira):* steps one square diagonally or straight backward (a total of five directions). This is the move of the Old Monkey at maka dai dai shogi.

B   *Blue Whale (Shironagaze Kujira):* steps one square diagonally forward or directly forward and backward (thus four directions). This is the move of the Copper General in chu shogi.

D   *Dolphin (Iruka):* steps one square straight forward. When it reaches the last rank, it can move one time any distance diagonally backward. Then, on the next move, it resumes stepping one square forward until it reaches the last rank again.

Regular drop rules apply, and the Dolphin follows the same restrictions as the shogi Pawn. It may not be dropped into a file that contains a Dolphin of its own camp; it may not give checkmate; and it may not be dropped on the final promotion rank, from which otherwise it has its special long diagonal move.

The Porpoise is the only piece that promotes. If the Porpoise is captured, it must be promoted to a Killer Whale when it is dropped back on the board. Unlike standard shogi, this piece is dropped into play already promoted—a very powerful move!

Perpetual check is forbidden. The attacker must make a different choice.

## *History*

The invention of tori shogi is traditionally attributed to Ohashi Soei (1756–1809), Ninth Meijin of shogi, in 1799, though the English shogi and go historian John Fairbairn asserts that the actual creator was Soei's pupil, Toyota Genryu, who published it for the first time in 1828. However it first came about, tori shogi has an enthusiastic following among amateur players, though it remains in the shadow of its big brother, standard shogi. For two years, competitive tori shogi matches were held in the early 1980s, in Utrecht, the Netherlands. Game sets are sold in Japan and on the Japanese version of Amazon.com.

Whale shogi is neither Japanese nor a historic game. It was invented in 1981 by the American expert of chu shogi, R. Wayne Schmittberger, already cited regarding wa shogi. His shogi invention falls very well in line with the spirit of the Japanese historic variants. Perhaps this game will help draw attention to the plight of the large sea mammals, now facing multiple dangers from fishing and environmental calamity.

Tori shogi now contends with chu shogi and some modern minishogis for the title of the second-most practiced form of shogi. A very elegant game, probably influenced by, if not directly derived from, wa shogi.

# 24. Dobutsu Shogi (Let's Catch the Lion!)

Shogi variants are not necessarily large or oversized. Tori shogi showed that it was possible to play on a smaller board. Several modern creations have pushed this concept even further, with the record held by dobutsu shogi, which means "animal shogi," on a field of only 12 squares. Fortunately, this tiny game is indeed very pleasant and enthusiastically embraced by the youngest of players. This simple little shogi gem, created to help children learn standard shogi, was invented by Madoka Kitao, with charming drawings by Maiko Fujita. Both creators are officially recognized as professional women shogi players.

Dobutsu Shogi is marketed worldwide under the name, "Let's Catch the Lion!"[42]

## *Material*

The board size is minimal, with only 3 × 4 squares. The first rank of three squares of each camp is colored, green for the "Land" side and blue for the "Sky" side. Each player has four wooden pieces representing animals: 1 Lion, 1 Giraffe, 1 Elephant and 1 Chick.

Initial array of dobutsu shogi (courtesy Maiko Fujita).

The pieces are square wooden blocks, ½ inch high and 1½ inches across. Instead of the traditional kanji script used in other shogi variants, they bear cartoon-like drawings of animals, oriented to face the player they belong to. The pieces also bear red dots which show the allowed move directions. The bottoms of the pieces are plain wood except for the Chick, which promotes to a Hen, illustrated with blue dots on the reverse side.

## *Rules*

MOVES, CAPTURES AND PROMOTIONS. All captures are made by moving onto a square occupied by an opposing piece, and removing it from the board.

 *Lion:* steps one square diagonally or orthogonally. It can reach all squares around it.

 *Giraffe:* steps one square orthogonally.

 *Elephant:* steps one square diagonally.

## 24. Dobutsu Shogi

*Chick:* steps one square straight forward.

Promotes to a *Hen,* which moves one step in any direction except the rear diagonals (thus, six directions).

PARTICULAR RULES. • *Promotion:* only the Chick promotes. Promotion is obtained upon reaching the last rank. The Chick is then flipped over and becomes a Hen.

• *Drops:* A player who captures one of the opponent's pieces keeps it on the side of the board and may drop it into play on any future move. When a piece is dropped into play, that constitutes the player's move, passing the turn on to the other player. Pieces can be dropped onto any vacant square of the board.

A Chick directly dropped on the last rank remains a Chick. (From there, it cannot move and simply waits to be captured).[43]

END OF THE GAME. There are two ways to win at dobutsu shogi:

• "*Catch the Lion*": capturing the opponent's Lion is a victory.
• "*Reach the other area*": bringing the Lion *safely* to the opponent's first rank (Land or Sky) is also a victory. "Safely" means that if the Lion is captured on the next move, the game is lost!

If the same position is repeated three times, the game is a draw.

## *Theoretical Issues*

According to mathematical analysis, there are 1,567,925,964 reachable positions in the game. The game has been *solved*, meaning that it has been analyzed to the point of proving what the result will be if both players make the best possible moves. Theoretically, the player who starts cannot win if his opponent plays well. If the second player plays correctly, he can always force a win, though it may take as many as 39 "perfect" moves. There are four possible opening moves and the strongest one, giving the best chance to avoid defeat, is to use the Chick to capture the opposing Chick.[44]

But only experienced shogi players will be able to view this game at such a sophisticated level. The game is very successful in meeting its goals of amusing the children (and often adults as well), and teaching the basics of shogi.

# *Other Miniature Shogis*

There are several miniature shogi variants that have been invented, most often with the idea of teaching the shogi basics. All of them use a *shogiban* of reduced size and a limited selection of regular shogi pieces.

## *Goro-Goro Shogi*

This game is widely used in Japan to teach the most important shogi concepts such as the handling of the Generals, the importance of Pawn promotion and the effective use of successive drops. Goro-goro can be translated as "rumbling" or "purring."

The board has 5 × 6 squares. Each player has 1 King, 2 Golds, 2 Silvers and 3 Pawns.

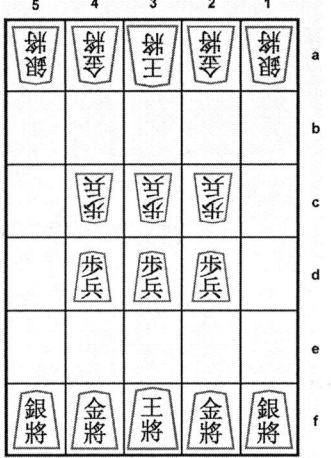

Initial array of goro-goro shogi.

Silvers and Pawns promote to Tokin (playing as Gold) upon reaching, moving within, or leaving the two farthest ranks of the board. All shogi's rules apply, notably the restrictions on dropping Pawns.

There is a variant in which each player has a Lance and a Knight in hand. Another game is *sho-chan shogi*, which uses the same material as goro-goro shogi with two differences: the Silvers do not promote, and the promotion zone (for the Pawns) is limited to the farthest rank of the board.

Goro-goro shogi has been newly marketed, with child-friendly animal faces, by the makers of Dobutsu Shogi.

# Gogo Shogi (Minishogi)

Gogo shogi uses a small board of 5 × 5 squares. Each player has only six pieces: 1 King, 1 Gold, 1 Silver, 1 Bishop, 1 Rook and 1 Pawn.

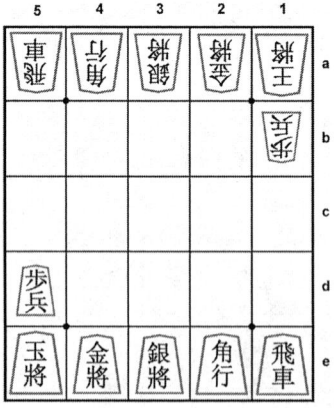

Initial array of gogo shogi.

Pieces promote upon reaching the end of the board, achieving their standard shogi promotional values. All of shogi's rules apply, notably for drops.

It is the smallest board to include the long-range pieces Bishop and Rook.

## Kyoto Shogi

Kyoto shogi also uses the small 5 × 5 board. Here, each player has only five pieces.

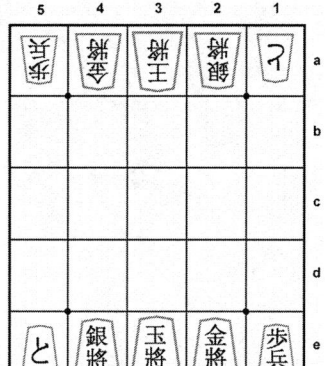

Initial array of Kyoto shogi.

The unique feature of Kyoto shogi is that pieces alternately promote and demote. There is no promotion zone, and the promotions differ from standard shogi. Except for the King (which does not promote), each piece has a dual identity: every time a piece makes a move, it changes its state. These double-identity pieces are: 1 Rook/Pawn (*Hifu*), 1 Gold/Knight (*Kinkei*), 1 Silver/Bishop (*Ginkaku*), and 1 Lance/Tokin (*Kyoto*). Some special sets have been manufactured with both names written on the upside and bottom faces.

The names of the pieces are plays on words; for instance, "Kyoto" combines the words for Lance (Kyo) and Tokin (shortened to To), which happens to create the name of one of Japan's most famous cities.

A captured piece may be dropped with either side facing up. Contrary to standard shogi, it is permitted to move or drop a piece in such a position that it will not be able to move on a future turn. For example, a Tokin can move onto the farthest row, becoming a Lance, which is then unable to move.

## Gofun Maka Shogi (Five Minute Poppy Shogi)

Also known as "micro-shogi," this game uses a very small 4 × 5 square board. Initially, each player has 1 King, 1 Bishop, 1 Gold, 1 Silver and 1 Pawn.

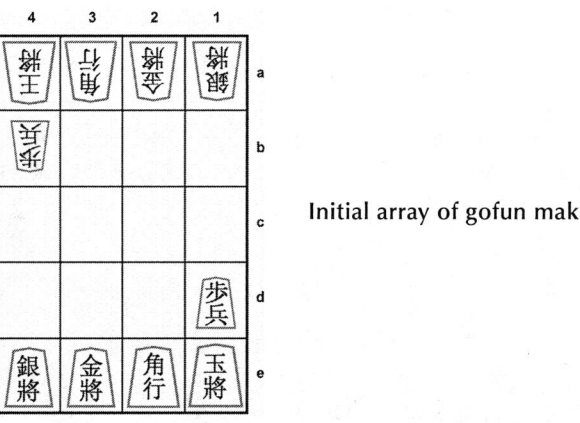

Initial array of gofun maka shogi.

There is no promotion zone, but the pieces promote every time they make a capture. When a promoted piece makes a capture, it reverts back to its initial value. Thus, each piece has a double identity. They are: Bishop/Tokin, Gold/Rook, Silver/Lance and Pawn/Knight. The King does not promote.

Several of the restrictions of standard shogi do not apply. It is permitted to have two Pawns on the same file, a piece can be dropped or moved to a spot where it has no future move, and a Pawn can be dropped to give immediate checkmate. The players can choose which face is up when they drop a piece into play.

## History

Miniature shogis have generated an increasing interest, toward the turn of the 21st century, as convenient tools in the teaching of standard shogi.

Shigenobu Kusumoto, of Osaka, Japan, invented or rediscovered gogo shogi in 1970. A few years later, Kyoto shogi was invented by the Japanese game creator Tamiya Katsuya (1976); and the great shogi champion Oyama Yasuharu (1923–1992), Fifteenth Meijin, invented gofun maka shogi in 1982. Goro-goro shogi is the most recent addition to the family, invented by the Japan Shogi Association in 1994.

In 2008, Madoka Kitao created dobutsu shogi, assisted by Maiko Fujita who had the idea of the Chick promoting to a Hen and who designed the pieces and the board. Lately, this game has met with great success. It has been introduced and played in many shogi tournaments in different countries around the world.

Madoka Kitao created Nekomado Co, Ltd., in 2010, to merchandize shogi related material. For example, their catalog includes versions of goro-goro shogi and standard shogi fully designed with "dobutsu" shogi pieces.

According to its creator, the dream of Dobutsu Shogi is that it be embraced by children around the world.

# 25. Ko Shogi

*Ko shogi*, which means "wide shogi," sprung from the audacious idea of playing chess with the stones of a go game. This process takes extraordinary patience, first writing all of the tiny *kanji* characters on the stones, then placing them correctly on the *goban* and finally, learning all the complex moves before commencing the game. The present authors invite readers to rise to the challenge.

## Material

A standard *goban* with 19 × 19 points serves as the board. Like the games of go and xiangqi, ko shogi is played on the intersections of lines, not on the squares. Each side has 90 pieces of 34 different types. The pieces are round since these are indeed go stones with the names of pieces written in fine calligraphy, white ink on the black stones and black ink on the white stones. In both cases, the pieces bear the names of their promotional values on the bottom sides in red ink.

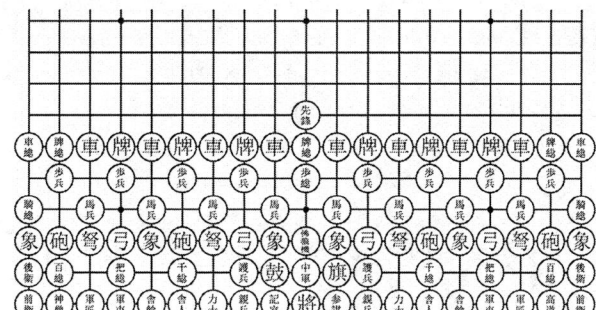

Initial array of ko shogi, identical for both players.

Here are the chessmen, listed from the back rank to the front, with the central piece of each rank in **bold** type:

- First rank, from left to right: Advance Guard, Spiritual Monk, Engineer, Chief of Staff, Staff, Aide, Sumo Wrestler, Aide de Camp, Clerk, **General**, Staff Officer, Aide de Camp, Sumo Wrestler, Aide, Staff, Chief of Staff, Engineer, Taoist Priest, Advance Guard.
- Second rank: Rear Guard, Centuria, *void*, Quartermaster, *void*, Millenary, *void*, Sentry, Drum, **Middle Troup**, Banner, Sentry, *void*, Millenary, *void*, Quartermaster, *void*, Centuria, Rear Guard.
- Third rank: Elephant, Cannon, Crossbow, Long Bow, Elephant, Canon, Crossbow, Long Bow, Elephant, **Machine Cannon**, Elephant, Long Bow, Crossbow, Cannon, Elephant, Long Bow, Crossbow, Canon, Elephant.
- Fourth rank: Cavalry, *void*, Cavalryman, *void*, Cavalryman, *void*, Cavalryman, *void*, Cavalryman, ***void***, Cavalryman, *void*, Cavalryman, *void*, Cavalryman, *void*, Cavalryman, *void*, Cavalry.
- Fifth rank: *void*, Pawn (Soldier), *void*, Pawn, *void*, Pawn, *void*, Pawn, *void*, **Patrol Unit**, *void*, Pawn, *void*, Pawn, *void*, Pawn, *void*, Patrol Unit, *void*.
- Sixth rank: Chariot Unit, Shield Unit, Chariot, Shield, Chariot, Shield, Chariot, Shield, Chariot, **Shield Unit**, Chariot, Shield, Chariot, Shield, Chariot, Shield, Chariot, Shield Unit, Chariot Unit.
- Seventh rank: **Vanguard**.

# Rules

MOVES, CAPTURES AND PROMOTIONS. Because of the great number of pieces, the following move descriptions are relatively brief.

- *General*: One step in any of the eight directions (like a King). It does not promote.
- *Middle Troup*: One step in any of the eight directions. It promotes to *Governor*: same move but acts as a second General.
- *Clerk*: One step diagonally or leaps to second point orthogonally (like Kirin in chu shogi). It promotes to *Master of Arms*: same move but moves twice in each turn, which may include capture(s) and may return to original point (*jitto* or *igui*).

- *Officer*: One step orthogonally or leaps to second point diagonally (like Phoenix in chu shogi). It promotes to *Banner and Drum*: same move but twice in each turn, which may include capture(s), and may return to the original point (*jitto* or *igui*).
- *Aide de Camp*: One step in any direction *except* straight backward (like Drunk Elephant in chu shogi). It promotes to *Quartermaster*, described below.
- *Sumo Wrestler*: Two consecutive steps in any directions, like two General's moves. It may change direction. Its moves may include capture(s) and may return to the original point (*igui*). (Unlike Lion in chu shogi, it cannot jump.) It does not promote.
- *Aide*: One step orthogonally or diagonally forward (like Gold General in shogi). It promotes to *Town Brigade*: any number of free points vertically or one step in any direction (like Flying Stag in chu shogi).
- *Staff*: One step diagonally or straight forward (like Silver General in shogi). It promotes to *Village Brigade*: any number of free points sideways or one step in any direction.
- *Chief of Staff*: One step diagonally, straight forward or backward (like Ferocious Leopard in chu shogi). It promotes to *Vice Commander*: any number of free points straight forward or diagonally (five directions).
- *Engineer*: One step forward, backward or diagonally forward (like the Copper General in chu shogi). It promotes to *Poison Flame*, which moves like *Engineer* but "burns" (captures) all enemy pieces adjacent to its point of arrival (similarly to the Fire Demon at tenjiku shogi).
- *Taoist Priest / Spiritual Monk*: captures by jump or "shooting" (explained below). It leaps to the second point in any of the eight directions to move or to capture a *Taoist Priest* or a *Spiritual Monk*. It does not capture other pieces with this leap but captures any other piece by landing on a point and "shooting" (capturing) an enemy piece adjacent to its point of arrival. If a player loses the *Taoist Priest*, his *Drum* and *Banner* may not promote, or must revert back to *Drum* and *Banner* if they have promoted (the loss of the Spiritual Monk has no particular effect). Piece promote to *Twelve-Mile Fog*[45] and *Immaculate Light*, respectively: two moves of *Taoist Priest* or *Spiritual Monk* in one turn, with the possibility of shooting an adjacent piece each time. The *Twelve-Mile Fog* cannot be shot, except by the *Machine Cannon*, and only at a distance of six or seven points.
- *Advance Guard*: any number of vacant points forward or one step backward. It promotes (only if the *Clerk* has already promoted) to *Heaven's Vengeance*: any number of vacant points diagonally forward or sideways (four long directions in all) or one step backward.
- *Drum*: One step diagonally or sideways (a total of six directions). If the Drum has been captured, Pawns may no longer go forward. It promotes (only if the Taoist Priest is not captured) to *Thunderclap*: five orthogonal steps with the possibility of changing direction and capturing at every step! Never fewer than five steps. If player's *Taoist Priest* is captured, the *Thunderclap* reverts to a *Drum*.
- *Banner*: One step diagonal or sideways (*same as the Drum*). Promotes to *Roaming Assault*: One to five orthogonal steps (without changing direction), with the possibility of capture at every step. If the *Taoist Priest* is captured, the *Roaming Assault* reverts to a *Banner*.
- *Sentry*: One step in any direction *except* straight forward (like the Blind Tiger in chu shogi). It promotes to *Centuria*, described below.
- *Millenary*: ranges in any of the eight directions (like the Free King in chu shogi or the chess Queen). It promotes to *Dragon Ascending*, which adds the moves of the Sumo Wrestler to those of the Millenary.

- **Quartermaster**: any number of points orthogonally or one diagonal step (like the Dragon King in shogi). It promotes to **Tiger Wing**: one or two diagonal steps, which can change direction and possibly capture twice; may finish its move on its point of origin (*jitto* or *igui*).
- **Centuria**: any number of steps diagonally or one orthogonal step (like the Dragon Horse in shogi). It promotes to **War Hawk**: one or two orthogonal steps which can change direction and possibly capture twice; may finish its move at its point of origin (*jitto* or *igui*).
- **Rear Guard**: any number of points straight backward or one step forward. May promote (only if the Clerk is promoted already) to **Earth's Vengeance**: any number of free points diagonally backward or sideways (four long directions in all) or one step forward.
- **Machine Cannon**: One diagonal step, not capturing on that spot. Upon arriving on its new point, it may "shoot" one or two times in any of the eight directions, hitting (capturing) one or two enemy pieces. The captured pieces must be no more than seven points away from the *Machine Cannon*, and the shots must be unobstructed by intervening pieces. It may shoot two pieces in one line by shooting the first and then the second after the first is removed. Otherwise, the two shot pieces may be in different directions. Restrictions: The *Machine Cannon* may not shoot a *Shield Unit* or an *Imperial Base*. It may only shoot a *Twelve-Mile Fog* if it is at least six points away.[46] It promotes to **Chariot of the Gods**: moves orthogonally in a straight line, one to five steps, not capturing on its spot of arrival; it then shoots with the same powers and limitations of the *Machine Cannon*.
- **Elephant**: any number of free points diagonally, like a Bishop. No promotion.
- **Long Bow**: One diagonal step, not capturing on that spot. Upon arriving on its new point, it may "shoot" once in any of the eight directions, hitting (capturing) an enemy piece. The shot piece must be no more than three points away, with no obstructions. It cannot shoot an *Imperial Base*, a *Shield*, a *Shield Unit*, a *Chariot*, a *Chariot Unit*, a *Gun Carriage* or a *Twelve-Mile Fog*. It promotes to **Long Bow Cavalryman**: moves like the Cavalryman, not capturing on its arrival point, and shoots like the *Long Bow*, with the same limitations.
- **Crossbow**: just like the Long Bow, but with a longer shooting range, able to shoot an enemy up to five points away. It cannot shoot an *Imperial Base*, a *Shield*, a *Shield Unit*, a *Chariot*, a *Chariot Unit*, a *Gun Carriage* or a *Twelve-Mile Fog*. It promotes to **Crossbow Cavalryman**, which moves like the *Cavalryman*, not capturing on its arrival point, and shoots like the *Crossbow*, with the same limitations.
- **Cannon** (similar to the *Crossbow* but able to shoot through (over) intervening pieces): One diagonal step, not capturing on that spot. It may then shoot once in any of the eight directions, capturing an enemy piece. The shot piece must be no more than five points away, and may be shot despite any pieces in the way. It cannot shoot an *Imperial Base*, a *Shield Unit* or a *Twelve-Mile Fog*. It promotes to **Gun Carriage**: orthogonally in a straight line, one to five steps, not capturing on its spot of arrival; it captures like the *Cannon*, under the same constraints. It cannot shoot an *Imperial Base* and cannot be shot by a *Long Bow* or a *Crossbow*.
- **Cavalryman**: exactly like the chess Knight, leaping over any piece in its path. Promotes to **Cavalry** when it captures the *Machine Cannon*.
- **Cavalry**: moves like the Cavalryman twice in one turn. The first jump establishes the direction of motion: either forward, backward, right or left. The second jump continues that same direction, with the choice of only two possible landing spots. May capture pieces in both leaps. As another option, may make its second leap back to its starting point (*jitto* or

*igui*). It promotes to ***Winged Horse***: moves like the Cavalryman but without any restriction on the direction of its second jump.

- ***Pawn***: One orthogonal step. If the *Drum* is captured, the *Pawn* can no longer move. It promotes to ***Patrol Unit***.
- ***Patrol Unit***: any number of vacant points straight forward or backward, or one step left or right (like the Vertical Mover in chu shogi). It promotes to ***Commissar***: any number of vacant points straight forward, backward or along the four diagonals (like the Flying Ox in chu shogi).
- ***Shield***: One diagonal step. Cannot be shot (captured) by the *Long Bow* or *Crossbow*. It promotes to ***Shield Unit***.
- ***Shield Unit***: One diagonal step or any number of free points straight left or right. Cannot be captured by the *Long Bow*, *Crossbow*, *Cannon* or *Machine Cannon*. It promotes to ***Imperial Base***: any number of free points straight left, right or along the four diagonals (like the Free Boar at chu shogi). Cannot be captured by the *Long Bow*, *Crossbow*, *Cannon*, *Gun Carriage*, *Machine Cannon*, *Chariot of the Gods*, *Chariot* or *Chariot Unit*.
- ***Chariot***: One to five free intersections in any of the four orthogonal directions. It cannot capture the *Imperial Base* and cannot be captured by the *Long Bow* or the *Crossbow*. It promotes to ***Chariot Unit***.
- ***Chariot Unit***: ranges orthogonally like a chess Rook. Cannot capture the *Imperial Base* and cannot be captured by the *Long Bow* and the *Crossbow*. It promotes to ***Millenary***.
- ***Vanguard***: One to five steps straight forward. It promotes to ***Commissar***.

No fewer than 23 new pieces appear by means of promotion!

SPECIAL RULES. The promotion rules are very complex. Generally, promotion is attained by moving a piece into, out of or within the promotion zone, that is, the six ranks closest to the opponent (this is similar to the promotion rules of standard shogi).

But there are other manners of promotion as well:

- A piece that captures an adverse commanding piece (General, Governor, Middle Troop or Banner) is immediately promoted.
- A piece that can move only one step and captures the Sumo Wrestler, the Dragon Ascending, the Roaming Assault or the Thunderclap is immediately promoted. (The sources of these rules are not clear as to whether this special promotion applies to pieces that move one step to a vacant square and then shoot from there to make their captures. Players may decide on the interpretation of this point.)
- The Cavalryman is promoted if it captures a Machine Cannon.
- When the Clerk gets promoted to Master at Arms, the Advance Guard and the Rear Guard promote as well; at the same time, the opposing Flame Poison is eliminated. However, the Clerk can be promoted by reaching the promotion zone only if both the Advance Guard and the Rear Guard are already standing in that zone.

Several pieces have their fates intertwined; hence, more rules must be applied:

- If the Taoist Priest is captured, the Drum and the Banner lose the possibility of promoting. If they have already promoted (to Thunderclap and Roaming Assault, respectively), they revert to their initial values of Drum and Banner.

- When an enemy Immaculate Light comes within a distance of five points in a straight line, orthogonally or diagonally, from the enemy Twelve-Mile Fog, that Twelve-Mile Fog reverts to a Taoist Priest.

Finally, there are no drops in ko shogi. (What madness would ensue if there were!)

END OF THE GAME. The winner is the player who succeeds in capturing two opposing pieces: the General, and either the Middle Troop or the Banner. However, if the Middle Troop has been promoted to Governor, that Governor must be captured as well as the General. In other words, having either a General, a Governor or both Middle Troop and Banner on the board provides the authority to fight on!

When capture of one final piece will lead to victory, it is forbidden to put that piece in perpetual check. Otherwise, if the same position occurs four times with the same player at move, the game is declared a draw.

## History

Ko shogi is the most recent of all large shogis but it is also the most poorly documented. But is this game a real shogi? Invention of this game is attributed to the Japanese Confucian philosopher Ogyu Sorai (1666–1728), who wanted to create a large version of *xiangqi*. Indeed, this game is also known as *yan xiangqi*, traditionally credited to a certain Chao Wuchiu. Chao Wuchiu here may possibly be the Chinese philosopher, Chao Buzhi, who lived in China in the 11th century.

So, is it Japanese or Chinese? It is incontestable that this game has a Chinese flavor. The pieces are round, some of them shoot, and even a Cannon is present on the board. The Long Bow and the Crossbow have similarities to those found in qiguo xiangxi (described in this book), which also uses a goban. However, in ko shogi, Japanese features are dominant. Some pieces have double moves or can "burn" enemies, as in tenjiku shogi. The main piece is a General, as in other shogis, and there is a piece that becomes a second General which must also be captured to win. This principle is precisely similar to the Drunk Elephant becoming a Prince, a theme found in several of the large shogis. The starting array does not respect the left-right symmetry consistently found in Chinese chess, whereas several Japanese chess variants display this asymmetry. Finally, the concept of promotion is mostly ignored in Chinese chess variants, while it is fundamental to the Japanese games. In the balance, ko shogi falls more on the Japanese side.

It must be recognized that, though it is not the largest, this shogi proves to be by far the most complex and the most peculiar. Ko shogi has lately been rediscovered by shogi variant enthusiasts. Its exact rules are not strictly defined, with the moves and names of several pieces open to interpretation.

Creating a game can be as enjoyable as playing a game. Chess variants, always employing several—sometimes many—kinds of pieces, represent a rich opportunity for inventive minds to latch onto. In this respect, ko shogi is an impressive and remarkable model. Ko shogi is playable only with a great deal of effort, and probably has not been played very much. Still, it shows an admirable precision in concept and construction. The rules, though delightfully complex, are not excessive; they are unified by a consistent logic that gives this game a clear integrity.

# 26. Taikyoku Shogi

This part concludes with a chess form that holds the absolute record: 804 pieces on a board of 1296 squares! For a long time, this game was believed to be a legend or a hoax. Tai shogi was then considered the world's largest chess. But today, it is certain that *taikyoku shogi* indeed existed. Some Japanese experts have begun to reconstruct the rules, but their work is not yet finished.

If the board is kept to a practicable size, the first difficulty lies in deciphering the minuscule characters identifying a nearly endless crowd of pieces. The players must have long arms, tiny fingers, microscopic vision and a huge memory. Any dedicated student of chess variants, who does not find the task daunting, may be ready to meet the challenge of taikyoku shogi, the "supreme shogi."

Initial array of taikyoku shogi, laid out in the same order, left-to-right, for each player. The game is played on a board of 36 x 36 squares with 402 pieces on each side.

## *Material*

The board is a uniform field of 36 × 36 squares. The pieces are pointed wedge shapes, like almost all shogi variants, their names written in kanji characters on the upper faces and the promoted values on the downsides. Each player commands a troop of 402 pieces of 209 different types.

To describe each piece would exceed the desired scope of the present volume. We will go so far as to mention each piece by name, many of which are familiar to us from the other large shogis. Here is the list of all these pieces, beginning with the first rank. To simplify the task of locating the pieces on the board, the two central pieces of each rank are in **bold** type.

- First rank, from left to right: Lance, Turtle-Snake, Running Rabbit, Whale, Fire Demon, Mountain Eagle, Long-Nosed Goblin, Beast Cadet, Running Horse, Free Demon, Earth

Dragon, Ceramic Dove, Free-Dream Eater, Free King, Rear Standard, Left General, Gold General, **King, Crown Prince**, Gold General, Right General, Rear Standard, Free King, Free-Dream Eater, Wooden Dove, Earth Dragon, Free Demon, Running Horse, Beast Cadet, Long-Nosed Goblin, Mountain Eagle, Fire Demon, Whale, Running Rabbit, White Tiger, Lance.

- Second rank: Reverse Chariot, White Elephant, Mountain Dove, Flying Swallow, Captive Officer, Rain Dragon, Forest Demon, Mountain Stag, Running Pup, Running Snake, Side Snake, Great Dove, Running Tiger, Running Bear, Buddhist Devil, Wrestler, Silver General, **Neighboring King, Drunk Elephant**, Silver General, Guardian of the Gods, Yaksha,[47] Running Bear, Running Tiger, Great Dove, Side Snake, Running Snake, Running Pup, Mountain Stag, Forest Demon, Rain Dragon, Captive Officer, Flying Swallow, Mountain Dove, Fragrant Elephant, Reverse Chariot.

- Third rank: Gold Chariot, Side Dragon, Running Stag, Running Wolf, Horned General, Flying General, Left Tiger, Left Dragon, Beast Officer, Wind Dragon, Free Pup, Rushing Bird, Old Kite, Peacock, Water Dragon, Fire Dragon, Copper General, **Kirin Master, Phoenix Master**, Copper General, Fire Dragon, Water Dragon, Peacock, Old Kite, Rushing Bird, Free Pup, Wind Dragon, Beast Officer, Right Dragon, Right Tiger, Flying General, Horned General, Running Wolf, Running Stag, Side Dragon, Gold Chariot.

- Fourth rank: Silver Chariot, Vertical Bear, Knight, Pig General, Chicken General, Pup General, Horse General, Ox General, Center Standard, Side Boar, Side Rabbit, Golden Deer, Lion, Captive Cadet, Great Stag, Violent Dragon, Woodland Demon, **Great General, Vice General** (the rest of the right flank is symmetrical to the left, with Silver Chariot the last piece on the right).

- Fifth rank: Stone Chariot, Cloud Eagle, Bishop, Rook, Side Wolf, Flying Cat, Mountain Falcon, Vertical Tiger, Soldier, Little Standard, Cloud Dragon, Copper Chariot, Running Chariot, Ram's Head Soldier, Violent Ox, Great Dragon, Golden Bird, **Deva, Dark Esprit** (symmetrical on both flanks, with Stone Chariot the last piece on the right).

- Sixth rank: Wooden Chariot, White Horse, Howling Dog, Side Mover, Prancing Stag, Water Buffalo, Ferocious Leopard, Fierce Eagle, Flying Dragon, Poisonous Snake, Flying Goose, Strutting Crow, Blind Dog, Water General, Fire General, Kirin, Capricorn, **Great Turtle, Little Turtle**, Hook Mover, Phoenix (the rest of the line is symmetrical to the left flank, with Wooden Chariot the last piece on the right).

- Seventh rank: Tile Chariot, Vertical Wolf, Side Ox, Donkey, Flying Horse, Violent Bear, Angry Boar, Evil Wolf, Liberated Horse, Flying Cock, Old Monkey, Chinese Cock, Western Barbarian, Eastern Barbarian, Violent Stag, Violent Wolf, Treacherous Fox, **Roc Master, Center Master**, Treacherous Fox, Violent Wolf, Violent Stag, Southern Barbarian, Northern Barbarian ... (the rest of the line is symmetrical to the left flank, with Treacherous Fox the last piece on the right).

- Eighth rank: Earth Chariot, Blue Dragon, Enchanted Badger, Horseman, Swooping Owl, Climbing Monkey, Cat Sword, Swallow's Wing, Blind Monkey, Blind Tiger, Oxcart, Side Flyer, Blind Bear, Old Rat, Square Mover, Coiled Snake, Reclining Dragon, **Lion Hawk, Free Eagle**, Reclining Dragon, Coiled Snake, Square Mover, Old Rat, Blind Bear, Side Flyer, Oxcart, Blind Tiger, Blind Monkey, Swallow's Wing, Cat Sword, Climbing Monkey, Swooping Owl, Horseman, Enchanted Badger, Vermillion Sparrow, Earth Chariot.

- Ninth rank: Chariot Soldier, Side Soldier, Vertical Soldier, Wind General, River General, Mountain General, Front Standard, Horse Soldier, Wood General, Ox Soldier, Earth General, Boar Soldier, Stone General, Leopard Soldier, Tile General, Bear Soldier, Iron General, **Great Master, Great Standard** (symmetrical as before).
- Tenth rank: Left Chariot, Side Monkey, Vertical Mover, Flying Ox, Longbow Soldier, Vertical Pup, Vertical Horse, Burning Soldier, Dragon Horse, Dragon King, Sword Soldier, Horned Falcon, Soaring Eagle, Spear Soldier, Vertical Leopard, Savage Tiger, Crossbow Soldier, **Lion Dog, Roaring Dog** (symmetrical to the left flank, ending with Right Chariot).
- Eleventh rank: 36 Pawns.
- Twelfth rank: 5 *voids*, Dog, 4 *voids*, Go-Between, 3 *voids*, Dog, 6 *voids*, Dog, 3 *voids*, Go-Between, 4 *voids*, Dog, 5 *voids*.

## Rules

Obviously, a game of taikyoku shogi lasts a long, long time. The goal is to capture both the opposing King and Crown Prince. The game ends when the last of these is captured. It is estimated that more than 2,000 moves may be necessary to reach such a conclusion.

As with the other large shogis, there are no drops. Pieces achieve promotion when they make their first captures; sometimes they become new pieces that are not present on the initial array.[48] So, it is necessary to remember 253 different moves of pieces. Several of the exact moves are still subject to speculation and debate among experts. The interested reader will follow the details of this quest on the Internet, notably on the Wikipedia page dedicated to taikyoku shogi.

## History

Taikyoku shogi was mentioned as early as the 17th century in the *Shogi Zushiki*. Truly monstrous, this game can best be seen as a part of an artistic movement, an exploration of perfectly excessive logical creativity, rather than a game intended for ordinary use. It was probably never played much, and became such an extraordinary oddity that many scholars doubted it had ever existed.

But, in Japan, the large shogis are a subject of serious research. In 1997, the game researcher, Isao Umebayashi, published a *Sekai no Shogi* with more than 30 pages dedicated to this game including the names and moves of each piece. Three years later, the content was distributed on the Internet, immediately capturing the attention of several Western enthusiasts of shogi variants.

According to the English shogi promoter George Hodges, dedicated advocate of shogi and its many historic variants, at least three sources for this game can be identified. Unfortunately, they are not in agreement regarding the details of the game. Moreover, several pieces that are also found in other large shogis have different moves in taikyoku shogi. Given the huge number of rules and the very limited historic resources, many aspects of the game remain speculative.

If the best sources prove to be manuscripts recopied from generations of Buddhist monks, the reports of this game may have accumulated many errors over the centuries. Researchers, linguists and historians are at work, and it is likely that a consensus will emerge in the coming years, establishing this game with the conformity and consistency found among other members of the large-shogi family.

## 26. Taikyoku Shogi

**Large shogi King, eight inches high, made to stand upright as a decorative object.**
WOUT BLOMMERS PHOTOGRAPH

Played on a field more than twenty times the size of the classical chessboard, the opposing armies of taikyoku shogi are 25 times the size of the familiar chess lineup. This game holds the record. It could be possible to create an even larger game, racing further toward a creation of infinite size—but to what end? This game probably does reach the very limits of a game that can actually be manufactured and played.

# ◆ Part V ◆

# Evolution and Revolution in Europe

The seed of chess, planted in the predominantly Christian world, found fertile soil for rapid growth and unprecedented development. Not fully understanding the characters indicated by the abstract Arab style chessmen, the Europeans attributed new identities to the pieces based on the esteemed figures of the day. Chess was re-envisioned, transformed from an openly warring battlefield into a confrontation between two royal courts, with political forces preceding military might. Most conspicuous in this transformation was the Queen, closest advisor to the King and central to the royal mystique of the kingdom. She became, in fact, the most powerful piece on the chessboard. This extraordinary shift of power not only presaged a strikingly modern cultural norm, but recast chess as something entirely new. The old chess was soon all but forgotten, as it was quickly supplanted by this revolutionary new game.

Chess players in the Szechenyi baths of Budapest. Wiki-media Commons photograph

But viewing the European evolution of chess as an easy blend of Christendom, civic order and budding feminism would be more simplistic than the convolutions of history honestly reveal. The following pages will elucidate a more complex metamorphosis, including several false starts, alternate paths and extreme divergences, as chess wended its way toward modernity.

Though these branches and blossoms of the chess tradition did not all meet with widespread success, they are well worth another look. Bear in mind that our modern standard chess started in this same way, as a variant idea beginning in Valencia, Spain—an idea which caught on particularly well.

# 27. Medieval Chess

First transmitted by the Moors to the Christians of Spain, chess underwent two immediate changes upon crossing the European threshold: the board became checkered with two alternating colors, and the army was given a feminine element by identifying the King's companion as his Queen. This new game proved to be the perfect pastime to fill long evenings within the confines of castle walls. While it captivated the martial instincts of the knights, the game was equally accessible to the ladies of the court. Soon, minstrels extended their dramas of the heart to include jousts around the chessboard in the quest of *amour courtois*. Then, as chess spread into all echelons of society, members of the various castes and professions saw their own social roles mirrored on the chessboard, replete with the moral teachings of the day.

The chess of the Middle Ages was quite different from the game played today. Modern players might find it tedious to revert to the old rules, which were essentially the same as those brought in from the Arab chess tradition. It was not until the late 15th century that the Bishop and Queen received their powerful, wide-ranging moves. But these were other days, with other ways. The old game, with its slow start and gradual buildup, was marvelously successful throughout Medieval Europe.

## *Material*

Each player has 16 pieces: 1 King (Latin: *Rex*), 1 Fers or Queen (*Regina*), 2 Aufins or Bishops (*Alphicus*), 2 Knights (*Eques*), 2 Rooks (*Rochus*) and 8 Pawns (*Pedes*).

The names and identities of chessmen varied widely throughout medieval Latin treatises. Also common were *Femina* for the Queen, *Marchio* (margrave) for the Rook, *Miles*, *Caballarius* or *Equester* for the Knight, and *Pedester* or *Pedinus* for the Pawn. The greatest diversity appeared in identifying the Aufin/Bishop. Its name included, among others, *Alphiles*, *Alfinus*, *Alficus* (all loanwords from Arabic *[al-] Fil*), *Comes* (count), *Senex* (old man), *Curvus* ("curved," i.e., old man), *Calvus* (baldhead), *Stolidus* or *Stultus* (fool), and even *Episcopus* (Bishop) or *Cornutus* (horned, also referring to a Bishop)!

The chessboard is the standard board of 8 × 8 checkered squares. In the Middle Ages, no convention fixed its orientation, so the corner square at each player's right could be either black or white. Nevertheless, the Kings always started by facing each other across the board. The rule of the King starting on the opposite color (dark King on light square; light King on dark square) was first recorded by the Lombard Jacobus de Cessolis in the 13th century.

Initial array of medieval chess.

Replica of the so-called "Charlemagne" set: Pawn, Rook, Knight, Bishop, Queen, King (set reproduction by Ivan Simberg).
KNOWLTON PHOTOGRAPH

# Rules

Beginning around the year 1000, European chess followed the rules of shatranj, borrowed from the Arabs. However, modifications arose quickly. Although the Latin language helped to unify the continent, and leant some consistency to the game, many small variations occurred between various countries and particular localities. The rules given here were known as the Anglo-French "long assize" of chess, predominantly observed on both sides of the Channel, from the 12th to the 15th century.

## Moves and Captures

Kings and Pawns are similar to the modern pieces. There are minor differences which are detailed below.

Knights and Rooks are similar to the modern pieces.

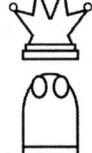

Queens and Bishops are different from their modern counterparts. They have conserved the moves of Arab shatranj. Consequently, the Queen steps only one square diagonally, therefore able to reach only half the squares of the board. The Bishop jumps to the second square diagonally, and is therefore limited to eight squares on the entire board, none of which can be accessed by any of the other three Bishops.

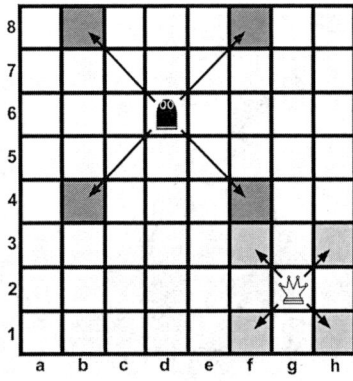

*Left:* Queen and Bishop moves.

*Right:* Squares that can be reached by each of the four Bishops.

PAWN PROMOTION. • A Pawn reaching the last square of a column is replaced by a "Fers" (Lat: *Ferzia*) which plays precisely like a Queen, even though the initial Queen or other "Ferses" are already present on the chessboard.[1]

RULES OF FIRST MOVE. • *The Queen's jump:* for her first move, the Queen has the possibility of leaping two squares either orthogonally or diagonally. From d1 she can jump on b1, b3, d3, f3 or f1. She may leap over any intervening piece. She is not permitted to capture an adverse piece or check the adverse King with this jump. The same privilege also applies to the Fers obtained by promotion of a Pawn, taking its first move from its square of promotion.[2]

- *The Pawn's double step:* for its first move, the Pawn has the possibility of stepping two squares straight ahead. Unlike modern chess, Pawns lose the privilege of taking the double step after the first capture of the game has been made.[3]
- En passant *capture:* corollary of the previous rule, a Pawn that uses its double step to pass over a square under the threat of an adverse Pawn can then be captured by that enemy Pawn. The capturing Pawn moves diagonally forward, to its square of capture, and removes the captured Pawn from the board. This rule of *en passant* (French: "in passing") capture is still in use today.[4]
- *The King's jump:* for his first move, the King may leap to the second square orthogonally, diagonally or like a Knight. From e1, he can jump to c1, c2, c3, d3, e3, f3, g3, g2 or g1.[5] He may not pass over a square threatened by an adverse piece. He may not capture an adverse piece with this jump, and he may not make this jump to escape a check. However, it does not matter whether the King has previously been placed in check. This move is the ancestor of modern castling, with many of the same limitations.

END OF THE GAME. There are two ways to win the game:

- Checkmate: when a player cannot remove his King from a check. The winner proclaims "checkmate."
- Bare King: the King has lost all his pieces, including Pawns, thereby losing the game.[6]

Stalemate, in which the opponent is not in check but any possible move would put him in check, is considered a draw.

## Variants: The "Assizes"

Every region in every land had its own customs of play, called "assizes." Here are a few examples of rules diverging from the Anglo-French standards described above:

SPANISH ASSIZE. • The Pawn reaching the last row can be promoted only if the player has already lost his Queen.
- The King cannot make the initial jump if he has already been placed in check.
- Stalemate is a victory for the player who traps the adverse King, but a victory of lesser value than checkmate, winning only half the stake.
- Baring the adverse King also accounts as only a half victory. However, if a player delivers checkmate while taking the last adverse piece, it is a full victory.

LOMBARD ASSIZE. • The King can perform an even longer jump on his first move. From e1 he can choose a jump to c1, c2, c3, d3, e3, f3, g3, g2 or g1, but also to b1 or b2.

- A King and Queen who have not yet moved may make their first move at the same time. This counts as a single turn.
- *En passant* capture is forbidden. A Pawn that escapes the threat of an enemy Pawn by making a double step is said to *passar battaglia* (Italian: "pass the battle").[7]
- A bare King has not lost. The game goes on and can be won only by checkmate.

GERMAN ASSIZE. • A King and Queen who have not yet moved can make a joint move. If necessary, a Pawn may also be moved in order to free a square to his King. This double or triple play counts as only one single turn.

- An unmoved King is allowed to jump (same leap as in the Lombard assize) to escape a check.
- The initial Pawn's double step is allowed only for the Pawns standing before the King, the Queen and the Rooks. It is forbidden for the others.

## *Les Eschez amoureux*

The Medieval European contribution to the science of play is so limited that it is generally ignored. Essentially, the writers of technical treatises were merely copying from Muslim studies, not necessarily aware of the source of their material. But what the European writers lacked in technical finesse, they made up for in rich allegory and creative variation.

One concern the Europeans addressed was the lengthy game opening. The rules of the medieval game required many moves of adjustment and positioning before the two sides engaged in an interesting confrontation. To reduce the tedium of the opening phase, the pieces were set up in an alternate array, known as the "short assize." In this arrangement, the Pawns started on the third row, with the Rooks and Knights (the most powerful pieces) right behind on the second row. Curiously—and very unusual—the Queen also began on the third row *sharing her square with a Pawn*. Perhaps this symbolized motherhood or the Queen's support of the troops. In any case, it was an exception, with no further double-occupancy of squares allowed in the rest of the game. The two would depart from that square independently, in separate moves. There was a danger, however, of them staying together. If an enemy piece happened to capture on that square occupied by the two, they were taken together in a single stroke. This is exactly what occurred in the game which frames the famous romance, *Les Eschez amoureux*.[8]

This 13th century French tale was inspired by the *Roman de la Rose* and has been preserved both in poetic and prosaic form. In the story, a knight by the name of the Actor meets a beautiful Lady in the Garden of Pleasure, who happens to be a skillful chess player. The chessboard is richly decorated with amber and adamant, and the Lady's pieces are made of ruby, sapphire, heliotrope and topaz. Her King is made of diamond. Her emerald Pawns each represent a different quality: Youth, Beauty, Simplicity, Sweet Look, Kindness, Providence, Goodness and Nobility. Her lover faces her with pieces modeled in pure gold, whose Pawns represent other notions: Irrelevance, Look, Sweet Thought, Offense, Doubt to Fail, Souvenir, Beautiful Bearing and Well Concealed. The other pieces also have their own nicknames.

This opens all allegories to the poet, thus beginning a very lovely interplay: "the Lady plays her Beauty and He answers by his Look. Then, she defends her Beauty with her Simplicity and He retorts with his Sweet Thought." The dance of love has begun!

Here is a reconstruction of this game of great courtesy and poignant suggestion. The Lady begins, playing Black:

## 27. Medieval Chess

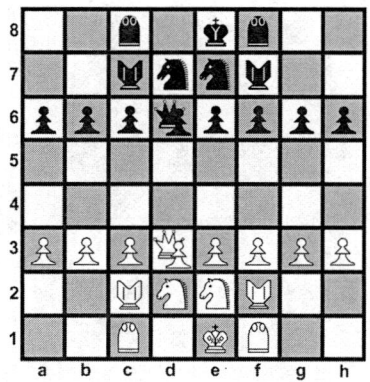

Starting position in *Les Eschez amoureux*, following the short assize.

**1. b5 b4 2. c5 c4 3. b×c4 b×c5 4. c×d3**

White loses his Queen and her accompanying Pawn in one swoop!

**4. ... B×d3 5. N×c5 g4 6. N×d3+ Kf1 7. R×c2 Ne4 8. N×f2**

The situation is dire for White. He has lost his second Rook.

**8. ... N×f2 9. Nd5 e4**

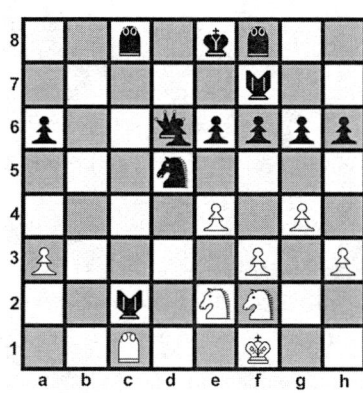

The Actor in a desperate position, but perhaps this is what he was after! The Lady has him cornered— which he rather enjoys. Still, he fights on.

Unfortunately, the poet did not give us the continuation of the moves. The game resumes at a much later point, after 12 pieces have disappeared.[9]

The end is near but the Lady wishes to win specifically with the Queen:

The final assault

1. a4 Kb1
2. a3 Ka1
3. Qc3 Kb1
4. a2+ Ka1
5. Qb2 mate

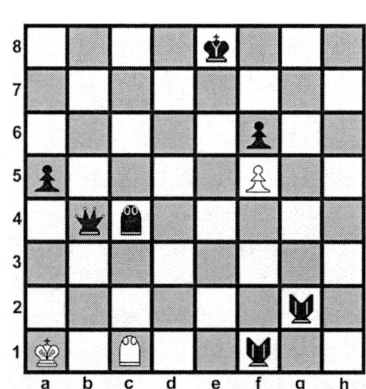

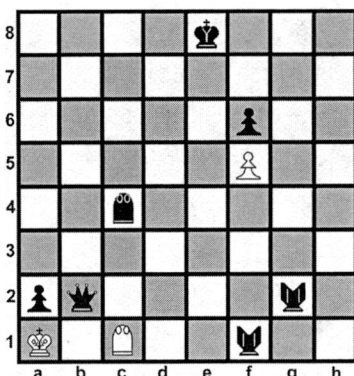

"Et lors sauldra la Fierge qui traira de c3 en b2, en lui disant eschec et mat en l'angle." (And then the Queen will spring, stepping from c3 to b2, saying checkmate in the corner.)

Thus this game ends with the merciless victory for the Lady, who subdues the King with her Queen, just as it should be.[10]

# History

THE ARRIVAL OF SHATRANJ IN ANDALUSIA. Naturally, the Arab game of shatranj spread with the Muslim conquests, expanding the realm of chess into a vast empire. After seizing Egypt from the Byzantine Empire and *Ifriqiya* (North Africa) from the Berbers, Mohammed's soldiers crossed the Strait of Gibraltar in 711. Proceeding northward, they conquered *Hispania*, the Iberian Peninsula, with the exception of some isolated Cantabrian and Pyrenean valleys. A few years later, far from the Western reaches of the empire, a bloody revolution dethroned the Umayyad caliph in Damascus in favor of a new dynasty, the Abbasids, who moved the Empire's capital to Baghdad. Though many Umayyads were slaughtered, the prince, 'Abd ar-Rahman, successfully escaped to Spain where he established an independent emirate in Córdoba in 756, breaking the unity of the Muslim world.

'Abd ar-Rahman's grandson, 'Abd ar-Rahman II, inherited a powerful, stable and influential state which drew in many artists and scientists including the Kurdish Ziryab, already famous as a poet and musician to the Abbasid court in Baghdad. Safe in Córdoba, Ziryab became the emir's primary counselor and confidant. A skilled geographer and astronomer, he left an impressive cultural footprint. He introduced new sartorial fashions, formulated delectable recipes, and compiled a vast catalog of songs, astrology and magic. In the middle of all these refinements, he also brought new diversions: polo and shatranj. In this year, 822, chess had penetrated Europe.[11]

THE IBERIAN PENINSULA: FRICTION AND FRUITION BETWEEN TWO WORLDS. 'Abd ar-Rahman III went one step beyond his predecessors: he proclaimed a caliphate in Córdoba in 929. Al-Andalus was then at its zenith, dominating and radiating over the Iberian Peninsula and beyond, from Maghreb to Provence.

During this period, Spain was divided into two very different worlds: Christendom in the north and Islam in the south. Several small mountain kingdoms and counties (Galicia, León, Castile, Navarre, Aragón, Sobrarbe, Ribagorza, Urgell, and Barcelona) resisted the Muslim conquest, often with the help of southern French knights. But in spite of the ongoing tensions, repeated raids and *razzias*, the border between these regions was permeable to trade, travel and transmission of knowledge. New ideas were spread by scholars and physicians, moving between schools and universities. A flourishing Jewish community strengthened ties between cities, its

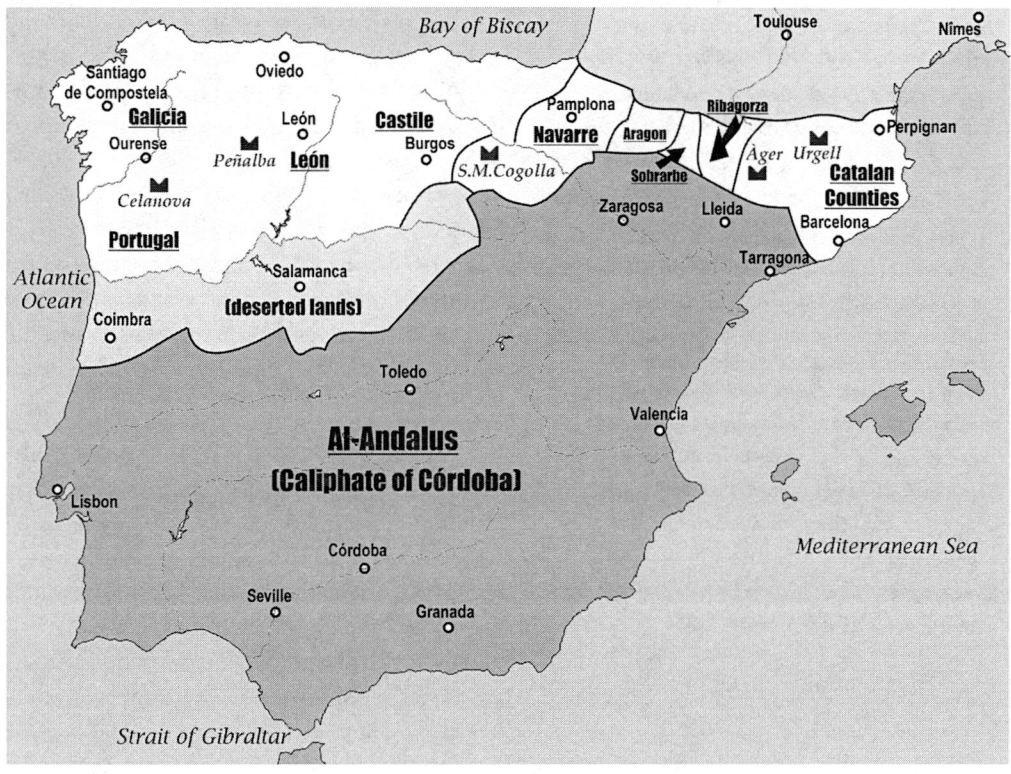

Map of Spain under 'Abd ar-Rahman III (912–961).

members sometimes active in high administrative positions. Religious conversions were not uncommon, and rituals sometimes blended elements of varied traditions.

Alliances, allegiances, often even marriages bound one Christian count and Moorish prince to another count or prince. Not surprisingly, chess was a part of the cultural intermingling. By about the year 900, chess had penetrated into Christendom. This early spread of chess into the Christian parts of Europe is confirmed by the oldest known European chessmen, all of which were found in Spain:

- Four ivory Mozarab[12] pieces from the monastery of Peñalba de Santiago, along the Santiago de Compostela trail, in the Spanish province of León. Traditionally assigned to San Genadio, bishop of Astorga, found buried in the church of Peñalba, built in 936.
- Another contemporary set from the monastery of Celanova, close to Ourense in Galicia. It consists of eight rock crystal pieces in the Fatimid style[13] which are mentioned in the record of a donation made to the monastery in 938.
- Three more pieces made of the same type of crystal decorated the lid of a reliquary in the Yuso monastery of San Millán of the Cogolla, in the Rioja province. It is known that they were given by Sancho III, king of Navarre, in 1033.
- A fourth group, constituted of several sets, was a part of the treasure bequeathed by the knight of Urgell, Arnau Mir of Tost (1000–1072), to the monastery fortress that he built in Àger, close to Lleida in Catalonia.

All of these pieces are finely sculpted in rock crystal and are believed to come from a Fatimid

Fragment of Ermengol I's will.

Egyptian crafter. Nineteen are kept in Lleida and 14 have been acquired by the emir of Kuwait. Several wills from the noble relations of the Barcelona counts demonstrate that chess was familiar to the Christian castles of Catalonia. In 1008 or 1010, Ermengol I, count of Urgell, bequeathed his chessmen, with other jewels, to the monastery of Saint-Gilles near Nîmes, France. Ermessenda, daughter of the count of Carcassonne and spouse of Ramon Borell, brother of Ermengol and the count of Barcelona, did the same upon her death in 1058.

A BRIDGE OVER THE MEDITERRANEAN: SICILY. The prized island of Sicily, set imposingly in the Mediterranean Sea, was highly valued by civilizations through the ages. Firmly held by the Byzantines, it fended off several Saracen invasions throughout the eighth century. After a tumultuous struggle, between 827 and 878, it finally succumbed to Muslim rule. With the proclamation of the Fatimid caliphate, the island became an emirate of this powerful state, ruled from Cairo, in the second half of the tenth century. It was the pinnacle of Islamic Sicily.

Maintaining commercial relations with Africa, the Orient, and the Italian mercantile republics, Sicily developed a refined and tolerant society in which Christians remained in the majority and escaped forced conversion, even while Islam dominated and broadly imposed its cultural norms. It was only in the second half of the 11th century that the Cross overtook the Crescent, following campaigns of the Norman knights under the leadership of Robert Guiscard and Roger of Hauteville, rulers of Southern Italy. Still, the influence of Islamic culture persisted in many spheres, exemplified by the Andalusian geographer al-Idrisi who, under the command of King Roger II of Sicily, drew a famous map detailing all the lands known in 1157.

Not surprisingly, carved chessmen of the abstract Muslim style have been exhumed in Italy. Discovered in 1932, in Venafro (Molise region); now housed in the National Museum San Chiaro of Venafro, they became a longstanding point of controversy. Hailing as they did from the land of a Roman necropolis, their seniority was first estimated at the second century C.E., under the Roman Empire—making these Venafro chessmen the oldest in the world![14] It was not until 1993 that a mass spectrometry examination was applied to determine a scientific and more plausible dating for these bone and ivory pieces. Their date of manufacture is now estimated toward the end of the tenth century. So, chess seems to have penetrated the Italian peninsula at the very moment it was crossing the Pyrenees from Spain.

The typical form of chessmen when chess first entered Europe, 20th century reproduction. KNOWLTON PHOTOGRAPH

A Queen on a Checkered Board. The first known European treatise of chess rules is the *Versus de Scachis*, a Latin poem dated 997, found in two manuscripts kept at the monastery of Einsiedeln, Switzerland.[15] Immediately, at this early date, two remarkable changes in chess conventions had taken place. The board was established as a field of alternating colored squares and the piece seated beside the King was identified as the Queen. These two features, still familiar in the modern game, had never been suggested in the long history of chess before entering Europe—and here they were, together in the very first European book of chess instruction.

Indeed, the Europeans made chess their own from the very beginning, considering the Queen to be the natural companion of the King, and adorning the board in the "checkered" style which became the recognized symbol of the game for posterity. The rules of play however, remained identical to the Muslim game of shatranj.

From that moment, chess quickly invaded Europe, as evinced by numerous traces found along many routes. France was quickly seduced by the game, judging by the many pieces uncovered in archeological excavations dated to the 10th and 11th centuries.[16]

Around the years 1050 to 1070, a monk from the Tegernsee Abbey in the Bavarian Alps composed the *Ruodlieb*, a Latin poem which describes a series of chess games played in 1023 between King Robert II the Pious of France and the knight Ruodlieb, ambassador of the Germanic Emperor Henry II, at their summit in Yvois.[17]

In Italy, chess was so popular that, in 1061, Petrus Damiani, cardinal-bishop of Ostia, wrote to the newly elected Pope Alexander II, condemning the bishop of Florence for spending too much time on chess instead of dedicating his attention to his mission. The zealous informer was later regarded as a saint, with his feast day celebrated on 23 February.

The arrival date of chess in England is a matter of debate. There are sources that report that Cnut the Great (c. 990–1035), king of Denmark, Norway and England, was a chess player, but these accounts were all written one to two centuries after the king's death and are not accepted as strong evidence. Chess had, however, crossed the English Channel at the time of the Norman conquest of 1066. For instance, the Norman term *escheker* came to designate an abacus used in the calculation of tax liabilities and became associated with the banking administration.[18] The *Winchester Poem*, composed before 1150, reiterates the familiar Arab rules of chess, and Arab style chessmen from that period have been discovered on the banks of the River Thames. Also, around 1150, chess was evident in Scotland and in Norway, where it competed with and gradually replaced *hnefatafl* and other boardgames of the same family.[19] About 1230, the game is mentioned in Scandinavian chilvaric sagas.[20]

In 1270, a merchant of Riga, Latvia, was mentioned by the nickname *Shakhmat*, demonstrating that chess had reached this Baltic region ruled by the Teutonic Knights. But the presence of chess in the Baltic is probably more ancient and could also be due to the contact of the Varangians, the Eastern Vikings, with Byzantium or the Muslim world through neighboring Russia. By that time, the Russians had already acquired chess many years earlier, probably receiving it from the Persians via trade routes that bordered the Caspian Sea, continuing through the Volga and Don rivers.[21] That same route, taken the other direction, brought slaves to Baghdad. The powerful state founded by the Khazars,[22] north of Caucasus, may have played a role in this transmission. The Russian historian, Isaac Linder, has underlined the accumulation of Islamic abstract style pieces dated from the eighth to the 12th centuries excavated by archeologists along that famous trade route. Finally, a religious interdiction, dated around 1150, constitutes the first textual proof of chess in Russia.

THE NAME OF THE GAME: A MISUNDERSTANDING. The earliest manuscripts mentioning chess from Italy, France, England, Flanders and Germany, all written in Latin, inform us about the game's etymology. Westerners first retained the term *scac*, adapted from the Persian and Arabic *shah* (chess King). *Scac* at first became the interjection used upon putting the opposing King in check. Eventually, this word evolved, in its pluralized form, to refer to the set of chessmen. From this word, *scachi*, come most of the names adopted by Western and Central Europe: *escacs* in Catalonian, *scacchi* in Italian, *escacs* in Occitan ("*Langue d'oc*"), *esches* then *échecs* in French, *chess* in English, *skake* in Frisian, *schaak* in Dutch, *Schach* in German, *skak* in Danish, *skák* in Icelandic, *sjakk* in Norwegian, *schack* in Swedish, *szachy* in Polish, *šachy* in Czech, *šach* in Slovak, *sakk* in Hungarian, *şah* in Rumanian, *šahs* in Latvian, *shakki* in Finnish, *šah* in Slovenian, Croatian and Serbian, etc.[23]

In all these countries, chess is therefore, literally, the "game of Kings." Two languages are missing in this long list: Spanish and Portuguese. The long Muslim presence in the Iberian Peninsula explains these exceptions: their names derive from the Arabian *al-shatranj*, via the Castilian *acedrex*, which became *ajedrez* in modern Spanish and *xadrez* in Portuguese.

The nomenclature of the chessmen is also revealing. Identifying the Shah as King and the Baidaq, a foot soldier, as a Pawn never created any confusion.[24] Also naturally, the Arabian Horse (*Faras*) has been associated with a Knight. To the European ear, the word *Rukh* has been taken for a "rock" but its origin is the Old French *Roc* from which comes the English *Rook*.[25]

As previously mentioned, the Arab *Firzan* underwent a rapid transformation in Christian Europe. A popular but incorrect etymology has asserted that the Arab word transcribed *Ferzia* in Latin (or *Fierce* in medieval French) led to *Vierge* (virgin), which in turn was transposed to *Queen*. Murray demonstrated that this was a false lead. As often happens, the reality is more prosaic: In the medieval European mind, the natural companion beside the King would be the Queen. Thus, did chess receive its feminine touch. Nevertheless, the Latin word *Ferzia* continued to be used to designate the promoted Pawn, distinguishing it from the original Queen, though the two were functionally identical.

The Arabic *al-fil*, Elephant, was then a weak piece, and only Russians understood its original identity. Spanish players, who learned it from the Arabs, kept the word as *Alfil*, forgetting its meaning as "the elephant." In Italian, a phonetic alteration made it an *Alfiere*, which means "standard bearer." In medieval French, the word evolved to *Alphin*, *Aufin* and other phonetically related variants. In Provence (Southern France), it was a *Fol*, which means "fool,"[26] whereas, on the contrary, Northern Europeans saw this piece as a Sage. The Germans called the Bishop *Alte* or *Alde* ("old") before this term was replaced at the end of the

Diffusion of chess in Europe.

16th century by *Schütze* ("archer"). Finally, the two-horn protuberances that identified the abstract style Arab piece, symbolizing animal's tusks, were assimilated into the cleft miter borne by the bishops, giving it its English identity.[27]

Chess had a widespread impact on European culture. Fascination for the game appears in countless paintings, illuminated manuscripts, engravings and works of stained glass. Some sets are true masterpieces: first, the famous set mistakenly named the "Charlemagne Chessmen," now includes 16 ivory miniatures housed in the Bibliothèque nationale de France, in Paris.[28] These magnificent pieces were sculpted toward the end of the 11th century in Salerno, Southern Italy, under the Norman tutelage.[29] The presence of Queens next to the Kings affirms their European character; however, the presence of Elephants and Chariots shows a nearby Arab influence. Perhaps even more famous are the walrus ivory pieces from the Isle of Lewis, discovered in rather large quantity (almost four complete sets of figurative pieces, with a smaller quantity of Pawns) in the Hebrides, in the north of Scotland. In all probability, they were made in Trondheim, Norway, in the second half of the 12th century. In these sets, Bishops already replace Aufins, and the Rooks are presented as armed warriors carrying heavy shields.[30]

Replicas of the Lewis chessmen, 12th century. KNOWLTON PHOTOGRAPH

CHESS IN MEDIEVAL LITERATURE. From the beginning of the 12th century, chess permeated the writings of the Middle Ages. Many passing allusions and several dedicated chess scenes illustrate the *chansons de geste*. The English chess historian H.J.R. Murray, has collected all of these medieval epics from the Arthurian cycle, the Alexander romance, the Charlemagne legend and many others. Later, the literary ground shifted with the *Moralities*. In this very popular medieval mode, these texts endeavored to explain and to justify all aspects of society to their contemporaries.

Here are some of the main ideas: Before or after death, all beings are equal, like chessmen stored in a bag. But in life, each person takes his or her designated role, like the various functions of pieces on the board. The King moves and captures equally in all directions, because he is the Law. The Queen's move *"is aslant only, because women are so greedy that they will take nothing except by rapine and injustice."*[31] The Bishops are judges, seated beside the King, administering justice which can be surprising but men must bow to it. The Knights walk into battle with a vivid courage, and the Rooks are legates of the King spreading his reign across the entire kingdom. In this great allegory, each Pawn represents a particular profession: farmer, blacksmith, scribe, merchant, physician, innkeeper, gatekeeper and gambler. Each one stands in his place and there is a place for everyone, completing the fully functioning society, perfectly fulfilling to those in power.

These accounts of chess as the ideal representation of society attained an unprecedented success. Such a doctrine was composed by John of Wales, a Franciscan theologian, in a brief passage around 1250 to 1260 (it was rumored that the author may have been Pope Innocent III himself).

The most famous version of the *Moralities*, serving as the basis for countless copies and translations to come, was written between 1259 and 1273.[32] The work is ascribed to Jacobus de Cessolis, a Lombard Dominican monk, and entitled, *Liber de Moribus Hominum et Officiis Nobilium Super Ludo Scacchorum* (the Book of the Customs of Men and the Duties of Nobles on the Game of Chess). Throughout the Middle Ages, this work was translated into nine languages, and became the most-copied book second only to the Bible.

More technical works on the game also appeared in the 13th century. In 1283, the King of Castile, Alfonso X the Wise, commissioned a richly illustrated codex, to be discussed further in a later chapter, regarding its renditions of chess variants. The book described about a hundred chess problems, a majority of which were copied from Muslim sources. Composed about the same time, the *Bonus Socius*,[33] drew on the entire base of contemporary chess knowledge with 194 problems (*partiti*), along with additional problems for the games of *tables* (games of the backgammon family) and merels. Probably written in Lombardy, this book met with great success in France. It inspired an even larger work, also presumably from Lombardy, with 288 chess problems: the *Civis Bononiæ* ("*Citizen of Bologna*"), a title meant to honor its anonymous author. It appeared about 1450 and became very popular in Italy.

As far as technical advances in playing the game skillfully however, Medieval Europe had very little to show. Virtually all texts on the mastery of the game originated in Eastern societies. The only European innovation consisted of allowing longer initial moves. Times were changing and chess was losing ground to the innovation of playing cards, which appeared toward the end of the 14th century. Simpler, easily portable, more varied and adaptable, cards made steady gains, broadly replacing chess as the game of choice. Chess, as a mirror of medieval society, might have declined and fallen by the wayside if not for a far more radical change. Almost at once, the game was given a quicker development and new level of dynamic interaction with long-ranging Bishops and, most of all, an almighty, powerful Queen.

The arms of Rocamadour (France) displaying three "*Rocs*" (Rooks). This "charge," very common in European heraldry, is one of many examples of how chess permeated medieval culture.

For five hundred years, the chess of Europe maintained the form borrowed from the Middle East. The European pilgrim, crusader or merchant would have engaged an opponent from Damascus or Cairo without any difficulty, though today's Western players would barely recognize their favorite game from that period. Yet, medieval chess represents much more than a prelude to the modern game. Chess has never seen a greater era of pure devotion.

Princesses playing chess (miniature from the codex of Alfonso X, 1283).

# 28. Rithmomachy

The Middle Ages provide an endless wellspring of surprises. While often depicted as a dark depression between the rich sources of Antiquity and the light of the Renaissance, the era cultivated an active intellectual life. Among the creative offerings of the day, the pious medieval thinkers have conveyed to us an abstract game which is indeed very complex, shaped by arithmetic and the detailed study of numbers. Beside this exalted game, chess would have appeared a futile distraction, reserved to fill the bored hours of lords and princesses. References and discussions of rithmomachy are strewn throughout six centuries of literature. Sources agree in referring to it as *ludus philosophorum*, the "philosophers' game"; on the other hand, its more formal name has undergone many local and cultural variations: *rithmomachy, rithmomachia, rithmimachy, rythmomachy, rhythmomachy, arithmachy*, etc. Whatever it is called, its intention is clear; this is indeed the "battle of the numbers."

## *Material*

Rithmomachy is played over a board of 8 × 16 squares, which corresponds to two standard chessboards joined on one side of each board.[34]

Each player has 23 flat pieces of circular, square and triangular shapes. Each piece is reversible, black on one side and white on the other, with the same number showing on top and on bottom.

In addition to the 23 flat pieces, each side has a Pyramid, sometimes called a King, made up of smaller numbered pieces stacked on top of each other. These pieces are not reversible.

Rithmomachy is an asymmetrical game, as both players have different values. It is common practice to designate the two camps as "Odd" and "Even."

The Even player starts with certain quantities of geometrically shaped pieces, each piece bearing a different number, as follows:

- 8 Circles: 2–4–6–8–4–16–36–64
- 8 Triangles: 6–9–20–25–42–49–72–81
- 7 Squares: 15–25–45–81–153–169–289
- 1 Pyramid with a total value of 91, made by stacking 2 Circles (1, 4), 2 Triangles (9, 16) and 2 Squares (25, 36).

The Odd player begins with these shapes, bearing these numbers:

- 8 Circles: 3–5–7–9–9–25–49–81
- 8 Triangles: 12–16–30–36–56–64–90–100
- 7 Squares: 28–49–66–120–121–225–361
- 1 Pyramid with a total value of 190, made by stacking 1 Circle (16), 2 Triangles (25, 36) and 2 Squares (49, 64).

The initial setup of the pieces on the board follows a very precise order in accordance with the relationships between the numbers. The actual colors attributed to each side vary among the historic texts.

Initial setup at rithmomachy.

Most often, the rules state that the Odd side plays first.

A modern reconstitution of rithmomachy.
WIKIMEDIA COMMONS PHOTOGRAPH

The initial array has several variations. The English Puritan William Fulke (1538–89), for example, indicated two other opening arrangements (with some mistakes) in a manual of the 16th century.

## 28. Rithmomachy

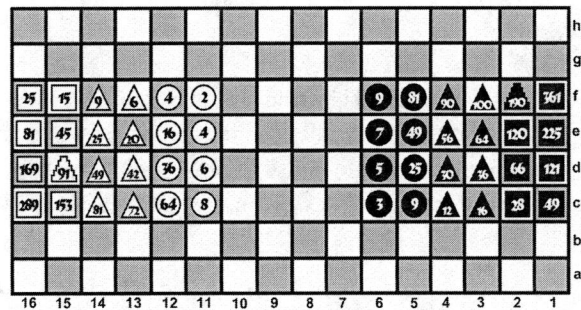

One array, according to William Fulke, 16th century.

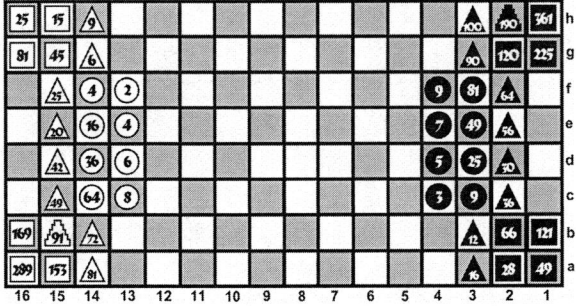

Another array, according to William Fulke (these diagrams have Fulke's mistakes corrected).

WHY THESE NUMBERS? Rithmomachy symbolizes a battle of numbers. The front row of each side is composed of Circles showing odd values on one side and even on the other. Those values are mathematically manipulated to produce the values of the remaining pieces, according to the following table:

|            | Evens |    |    |    | Odds |    |     |     |
|------------|-------|----|----|----|------|----|-----|-----|
| $n$        | 2     | 4  | 6  | 8  | 3    | 5  | 7   | 9   |
| $n^2$      | 4     | 16 | 36 | 64 | 9    | 25 | 49  | 81  |
| $n(n+1)$   | 6     | 20 | 42 | 72 | 12   | 30 | 56  | 90  |
| $(n+1)^2$  | 9     | 25 | 49 | 81 | 16   | 36 | 64  | 100 |
| $(n+1)(2n+1)$ | 15 | 45 | **91** | 153 | 28 | 66 | 120 | **190** |
| $(2n+1)^2$ | 25    | 81 | 169| 289| 49   | 121| 225 | 361 |

Note that each of the Pyramids (as described in the original list of even and odd pieces) is the sum of squared integers: $91 = 1^2+2^2+3^2+4^2+5^2+6^2$; $190 = 4^2+5^2+6^2+7^2+8.^2$

The pyramid on the Even side was known as *perfecta* ("perfect" because it totaled the full series of squared digits from $1^2$ through $6^2$), while the one on the Odd side was called *tricurta* ("three short" because it "lacked" the first three squared digits, $1^2+2^2+3,^2$ beginning its series with $4^2$).

The stacking of the Pyramids (Kings) according to William Fulke: tricurta (left) and perfecta (right).

## Rules

Various sources give significantly different rules of play for rithmomachy, and some sources give more than one variation. Fulke, for example, offered three options. A universal set of standard rules never took hold, so players would necessarily have to agree on the variant being played before starting a game. Following are the rules given by Fulke in the first variation he presents.[35]

MOVES. While there is some variety in the rules of play, there are also a few principles which hold regardless of the particular variation. In order to understand the principles of moves, it is necessary to consider the medieval way of counting spaces on the board.

When considering the move of a piece, the space of departure was always included in the counting. For instance, the Circle pieces moved "two," from one square to the second square; in the modern manner of counting, we would call this moving one step. Logic had it that the Triangles moved three (including the square of departure; therefore, two steps), and the Square moved four (what we would call moving three steps).

For several centuries, the Circles, Triangles, Squares and Pyramids had "regular" moves associated with each sort of piece. Beginning in the 16th century, these move choices were augmented with "irregular" moves—angular movements pieces could choose but could not use for capturing.

- *Circle:* moves diagonally 2 spaces (1 step in the modern way of counting). The Circle does not have a special irregular move.
- *Triangle:* regularly moves orthogonally 3 squares (2 steps by modern count), not passing through any occupied spaces. For the irregular move, it can also move as a Knight, and is allowed to leap over any pieces in its path.
- *Square:* regularly moves orthogonally 4 fields (3 steps by modern count), not passing through any occupied spaces. For the irregular move, it has a sort of extended Knight's leap, proceeding 1 square further than a Knight (as if going 3 steps orthogonally and 1 at a right angle, by modern count). This irregular move cannot be blocked. See the diagram below.

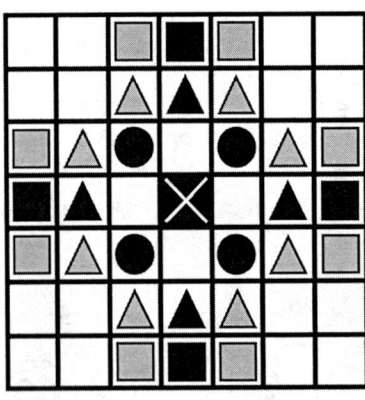

Moves of the various pieces from the central field. Black symbols show the regular moves and gray symbols show the irregular moves.

- *Pyramid:* may make the *regular* moves of any of the pieces in its stack. If it loses a certain type of piece, it may no longer make that type of move.

VARIANTS. Although various sources give the moves of two, three and four spaces consistently for the Circle, Triangle and Square, respectively, it is difficult to find two classic texts describing the same manner of play. The diversity is staggering. The diagrams below summarize some of various ways of moving the pieces, marked in **bold** type **1, 2, 3** or **4** according to their sources. In addition, according to Barozzi and Selenus [4], the Pyramid could execute a Knight's leap once in the game.

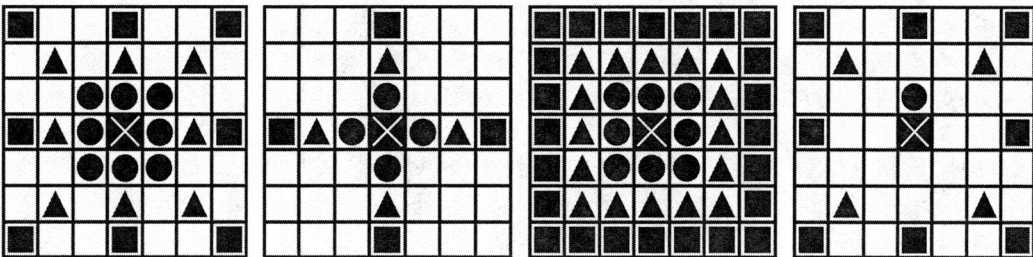

Moves of pieces from the central field according to (from left) 1, 2, 3, 4: 1 Sherwood (1482) and Fulke (second version, 1563); 2 Faber (1496) and Fulke (third version); 3 a manuscript from Florence attributed to Varchi (ca. 1539); 4 Barozzi (1572) and Selenus (1616). (The second version from Fulke also included the irregular moves and allowed the jumps over occupied fields.)

SOME ARITHMETIC. Mathematical progressions, creating particular numerical sequences, play a fundamental role in the workings of the game. There are three basic categories:

- *Arithmetic Progression:*

   A series of numbers that increases or decreases in accordance with a given constant. For instance, the natural integers 1, 2, 3, 4 form an arithmetic progression with the difference of 1. In algebra an arithmetic progression of difference d is written: x; x+d; x+2d; x+3d...

- *Geometric Progression:*

   A sequence of numbers in which each term after the first is found by multiplying the previous one by a fixed number called the common ratio. For example, the series 2, 4, 8, 16, 32, 64, 128 is a geometric progression of the common ratio 2. The terms of a geometric progression of ratio r can be written: $x; xr; xr^2; xr^3;...$

- *Harmonic Progression:*

   A series of three numbers (call them *a*, *b* and *c*, in order from lowest to highest value), which have the following relationship: The highest number (*c*) divided by the lowest number (*a*), is equal to the highest number (*c*) minus the middle number (*b*), divided by the middle number (*b*) minus the lowest number (*a*). This can be written **c/a = (c−b) / (b−a)**

   For example, 2, 3, 6 is a harmonic progression because 6/2 = (6−3) / (3−2); that is, 6/2 = 3/1. And 5, 9, 45 is a harmonic progression because 45/5 = (45−9) / (9−5); that is, 9 = 36/4. This logic may not come intuitively to the average modern mind—the chart below can offer a little help.

   The study of all available numbers shows that there are 62 arithmetic, 30 geometric and 18 harmonic progressions possible at rithmomachy.[36]

| Arithmetic | | |
|---|---|---|
| 2 | 3 | 4 |
| 2 | 4 | 6 |
| 2 | 5 | 8 |
| 2 | 7 | 12 |
| 2 | 9 | 16 |
| 2 | 15 | 28 |
| 2 | 16 | 30 |
| 3 | 4 | 5 |
| 3 | 5 | 7 |
| 3 | 6 | 9 |
| 3 | 9 | 15 |
| 3 | 42 | 81 |
| 4 | 5 | 6 |
| 4 | 6 | 8 |
| 4 | 8 | 12 |
| 4 | 12 | 20 |
| 4 | 16 | 28 |
| 4 | 20 | 36 |
| 4 | 30 | 56 |
| 5 | 6 | 7 |
| 5 | 7 | 9 |
| 5 | 15 | 25 |
| 5 | 25 | 45 |
| 6 | 7 | 8 |
| 6 | 9 | 12 |
| 6 | 36 | 66 |
| 7 | 8 | 9 |
| 7 | 16 | 25 |
| 7 | 28 | 49 |
| 7 | 49 | 91 |
| 7 | 64 | 121 |

| Arithmetic | | |
|---|---|---|
| 8 | 12 | 16 |
| 8 | 25 | 42 |
| 8 | 36 | 64 |
| 8 | 49 | 90 |
| 8 | 64 | 120 |
| 9 | 12 | 15 |
| 9 | 45 | 81 |
| 9 | 81 | 153 |
| 12 | 16 | 20 |
| 12 | 20 | 28 |
| 12 | 42 | 72 |
| 12 | 56 | 100 |
| 12 | 66 | 120 |
| 15 | 20 | 25 |
| 15 | 30 | 45 |
| 15 | 120 | 225 |
| 16 | 36 | 56 |
| 20 | 25 | 30 |
| 20 | 28 | 36 |
| 20 | 42 | 64 |
| 28 | 42 | 56 |
| 28 | 64 | 100 |
| 30 | 36 | 42 |
| 42 | 49 | 56 |
| 42 | 66 | 90 |
| 42 | 81 | 120 |
| 49 | 169 | 289 |
| 56 | 64 | 72 |
| 72 | 81 | 90 |
| 81 | 153 | 225 |
| 91 | 190 | 289 |

| Geometric | | |
|---|---|---|
| 2 | 4 | 8 |
| 2 | 12 | 72 |
| 3 | 6 | 12 |
| 4 | 6 | 9 |
| 4 | 8 | 16 |
| 4 | 12 | 36 |
| 4 | 16 | 64 |
| 4 | 20 | 100 |
| 4 | 30 | 225 |
| 5 | 15 | 45 |
| 9 | 12 | 16 |
| 9 | 15 | 25 |
| 9 | 30 | 100 |
| 9 | 45 | 225 |
| 16 | 20 | 25 |
| 16 | 28 | 49 |
| 16 | 36 | 81 |
| 20 | 30 | 45 |
| 25 | 30 | 36 |
| 25 | 45 | 81 |
| 36 | 42 | 49 |
| 36 | 66 | 121 |
| 36 | 90 | 225 |
| 49 | 56 | 64 |
| 49 | 91 | 169 |
| 64 | 72 | 81 |
| 64 | 120 | 225 |
| 81 | 90 | 100 |
| 81 | 153 | 289 |
| 100 | 190 | 361 |

| Harmonic | | |
|---|---|---|
| 2 | 3 | 6 |
| 3 | 4 | 6 |
| 3 | 5 | 15 |
| 4 | 6 | 12 |
| 4 | 7 | 28 |
| 5 | 8 | 20 |
| 5 | 9 | 45 |
| 6 | 8 | 12 |
| 7 | 12 | 42 |
| 8 | 15 | 120 |
| 9 | 15 | 45 |
| 9 | 16 | 72 |
| 12 | 15 | 20 |
| 15 | 20 | 30 |
| 25 | 45 | 225 |
| 30 | 36 | 45 |
| 30 | 45 | 90 |
| 72 | 90 | 120 |

Tables of progressions achievable by the player of the Even side (in light gray) and those achievable by the player of the Odd side (in dark gray). The progressions attainable by either side, Even or Odd, are shown in white.

CAPTURES. Several rules for capture exist, not all of which are recognized by the various authors. Players must decide at the start which rules of capture they mean to employ.

- *Encounter* If the player's piece can use its move to land on a square occupied by the opponent, and the two pieces show the same value, the opponent's piece may be captured.

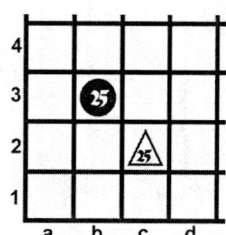

Encounter

In this position, the black Circle 25 may capture the white Triangle 25 but the Triangle may not capture the Circle because a Triangle is not allowed to move only one square (that is, to "the second square" in the medieval way of counting).

- *Ambush:* If the player has two pieces both able to use their moves to attack an opposing piece, and if all three pieces together complete an arithmetical operation (sum, difference, product or quotient), the opposing piece may be captured.

Ambush

The white Square 15 is captured by the black Circles 8 and 15 because it stands where each Circle would be able to make its move and because 3 × 5 = 15. The "ambushed" Square is removed from the board. This is called a "capture by product."

- *Power:* If the player's piece is positioned to move onto the square of an opposing piece, and one is a power or root of the other, the opponent's piece may be captured.

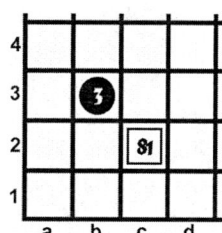

Power

Black Circle 3 captures the white Square 81 because $3^4 = 81$.

- *Progression:* If the player has two pieces both able to use their moves to attack an opposing piece, and if all three pieces together complete an arithmetic, geometric or harmonic sequence, the opponent's piece may be captured.

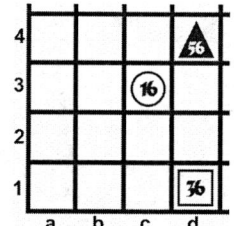

Progression

Black Triangle 56 is captured because it completes the arithmetic progression 16 / 36 / 56.

- *Assault:* If the player's piece and opponent's piece both stand on one horizontal, vertical or diagonal line, and the *number of squares separating the pieces* is the product or the quotient of the numbers of the two pieces, the opponent's piece may be captured. The captured piece here does not necessarily stand on a square that the attacking player could normally move to.

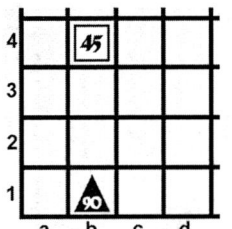

**Assault**

The black Triangle 90 may take the white Square 45 (and vice-versa) because they are separated by two spaces and 90/2=45.

- *Siege:* consists in seizing a piece by surrounding it and blocking all of its possibilities of move. This method of capture does not involve any mathematical operation; however, the opponent's piece is not blocked if it can seize one of the attacking pieces or if one of the pieces blocking its movement is on its own side.

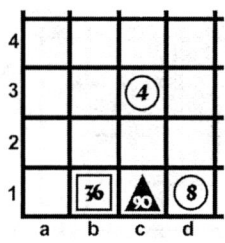

**Siege**

The black Triangle 90 is blocked from every direction by white pieces. It cannot capture any of its blockers; therefore, it is lost.

    A capture may precede or follow the player's move on the board. The attacking piece may move into the opponent's square and remove the captured piece from the board. Usually, however, the attacked piece remains on the board but changes allegiance. In this case, it is merely flipped over in place, showing the same number and shape, but changing color.

    A piece that has switched sides cannot be moved or captured a second time. It remains on its square, immobile and invulnerable, but it may participate in numerical combinations for the benefit of its new owner.

    Multiple captures in a single turn are permitted. Capture is not compulsory; however, if a player points out that his opponent has passed up a capturing opportunity, he may remove the opponent's piece or pieces which failed to complete the capture from the board (known as "huffing" or "blowing" a piece).[37] After capturing in this way, the player proceeds with a move of his own.

SPECIFIC RULES FOR THE PYRAMIDS. • A Pyramid may be taken by a siege—i.e., by blocking all of its possible moves.

- A Pyramid may also be taken by an arithmetical relationship, either at once based on its total numerical value (sum of all of numbers in its stack), or one piece at a time based on the number of the individual piece. When an individual piece is taken from the Pyramid, that piece is simply removed from the board.
- The same principle also holds for attack: one can either consider the overall value of the Pyramid or the value and moving ability of an individual piece that participates in a capture.
- A Pyramid moves as a single unit; it does not separate into individual pieces or partial stacks.

END OF THE GAME. Victory is obtained after two distinct steps:

- First, the opponent's Pyramid (King) must be *captured*. When this is done, only the largest piece of the Pyramid, stays on the board, flipped over to show its new allegiance and remaining on its spot of capture. The other pieces in the stack are removed from the board.
- Second, a *triumph* must be obtained.

A triumph consists of placing three or four pieces in a straight line (horizontal, vertical, diagonal) or in a pattern defining the points of a square, forming a specific sequence. The order of the pieces must respect the numerical progression. Three kinds of triumph are recognized:

- **Great Victory** (*victoria magna*): one of these three sequences must be established: arithmetic, geometric or harmonic. The three pieces must be aligned equally spaced, in a line, column or diagonal, with only empty squares between them. Some rules also accepted arrangements in a right angle or a non-equidistant alignment.

Great Victory

The Even side (White) wins by Great Victory with a harmonic sequence (9, 16, 72). The pieces are arranged in a "right angle" and equal spacing between 9 and 16, and 16 and 72.

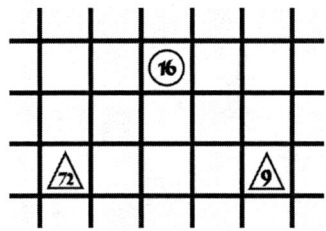

- **Greater Victory** (*victoria major*): if two different progressions are simultaneously realized with four pieces.

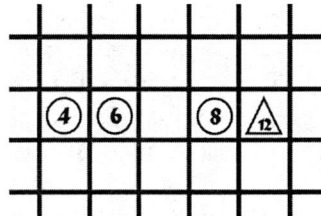

Greater Victory

The Even side (White) wins by Greater Victory with both an arithmetic sequence (4, 8, 12) and a harmonic sequence (6, 8, 12). The white Triangle 12 is a captured piece that has been flipped over. The pieces are arranged in line with a nonequidistant alignment.

- **Most Excellent Victory** (*victoria excellentissima*): the most difficult and most sought after victory. To obtain it, one must simultaneously achieve the three sorts of sequence.

Victoria Excellentissima

The Even side wins by Most Excellent Victory with an arithmetic sequence (6, 9, 12), a geometrical sequence (4, 6, 9) and a harmonic sequence (4, 6, 12). The pieces are arranged in a square.

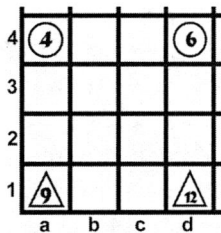

While one player has captured the other's Pyramid (King), and is endeavoring to create the winning triumph, the player who has lost his Pyramid plays on normally.

A QUICKER GAME: THE COMMON VICTORIES. For a shorter game, the players may agree on alternative objectives for winning the game. Five types of "common victories" are recognized:

- **Victory by body** (*de corpore*): at the start of the game, the players agree on a number of pieces to be captured. For example, the winner will be the first to capture seven opposing pieces.
- **Victory by assets** (*de bonis*): the winner is the first player to reach or exceed a certain sum with his captures. For example, the winner is the first who will get at least 100 points, totaling the numbers inscribed on his captured pieces.
- **Victory by proceeds** (*de lite*): for this kind of victory it is necessary to count the number of digits written on the captured pieces. The winner is the first who reaches both a sum and a quantity of digits. For example, for a victory by proceeds of 100 at 8 digits, it is possible to win by capturing the 2, 4, 6, 8, 25, and 64: the sum makes 109 and is reached within 8 digits (2, 4, 6, 8, 2, 5, 6 and 4).
- **Victory by honor** (*de honore*): any combination of the first two cases above. In this case, the winner must capture a certain number of pieces, and the sum of the inscribed numbers must reach a certain total.
- **Victory by proceeds and honor** (*de honore liteque*): combination of all three criteria for winning: a certain number of captures must be made, the sum of the inscribed numbers must reach a certain total, and the captured pieces must show a certain quantity of digits.

## History

Rithmomachy was born in Germany around 1030, first mentioned by Asilo, a clerk from Franconia.[38] The American historian, Ann Moyer, identifies this mysterious Asilo as Adalbero (c. 1010–1090), son of the Carinthian count Arnold II, and future bishop of Würzburg, later canonized. Further writings on rithmomachy quickly followed throughout the German lands of the Holy Roman Empire. It then appears in 1040 in the writings of the famous monk of Reichenau, Hermannus Contractus (Hermann the Cripple). Paralyzed since childhood, he dedicated his life to the study of music, astronomy and mathematics. In 1070, the anonymous *Manuscript of Liège* reveals for the first time the size of the board (12 × 8 squares), and suggests that adept players were developing the game at a masterful level. Could this be an indication that rithmomachy was even more ancient than is confirmed in the written record?

The term rithmomachy derives from the Greek words *rhythmos* and *machia* meaning "battle of the numbers." The monks of the High Middle Ages considered numerology to be of the greatest importance, following the lead of Gerbert of Aurillac (c. 945–1003), philosopher and keen mathematician. Gerbert mined the richest intellectual resources of his day, notably in Catalonia where he began using the nine Arabic numerals that he introduced to Western Europe for the first time upon his return. He served as tutor to many princes and emperors including Otto III, who promoted his ascension to Pope under the name of Sylvester II. Gerbert was among the most brilliant personalities of his time. He boosted the study of the *quadrivium*, the four mathematical disciplines: arithmetic, geometry, astronomy and music, in the monastic schools. The *quadrivium*, together with the *trivium* (grammar, rhetoric, dialectic) constituted the "seven liberal arts," as first advanced by the Roman philosopher Boethius (c. 480–525), heir to the Pythagorean school for the study of numbers and their properties.

The influence of Gerbert and the *quadrivium* undoubtedly laid the groundwork for the creation of rithmomachy. This "philosophical" game was often presented in manuscripts of music, abacuses and computation.

In these times of religion and morality, tutors and abbots challenged their imaginations and creativity to establish noble and instructive games for pupils of the monastic schools. Rithmomachy was not an isolated example in this playful intrigue at the turn of the 11th century. In this spirit, circa 960, Bishop Wibold of Cambrai (Northern France) invented a game of dice called *ludus regularis seu clericalis* ("game suitable for monks and priests") of an edifying complexity but exalting the most reputed Christian virtues.[39]

About that same time, the game of chess crossed the Pyrenees, via Catalonia, reaching the Alpine monasteries. Could we reasonably assess that the parallel diffusion of chess and rithmomachy is coincidental? The beginnings of these two games in Europe seem intimately intertwined.

Boethius with Indian numbers surpasses Pythagoras and his abacus (reproduction of a wood engraving of 1508).

David Parlett has noted that this game of numbers paralleled the current military organization as well. Just as Chariots, Elephants, Cavalry and Infantry represented the four arms of the ancient Indian army, the three types of pieces—Circles, Triangles and Squares—well represented the Roman legions with a relatively static central phalanx (the Circles), followed by the more mobile archers and lancers (the Triangles), flanked by the cavalry (the Squares).

But the game of the knights, princes and noblemen, was chess. Rithmomachy was a game of applied arithmetic education and its public remained limited to the male clerical elites. Unlike chess, which was sometimes played with dice, rithmomachy was never condemned by the church.

From Germany, rithmomachy spread into France and England, and later into Italy. It was noticeably absent from other European countries such as Spain. New reports of rithmomachy from the 12th to the 15th centuries attest to its ongoing vitality. One mention is found in the *De Vetula*, a poem composed toward 1240[40]; another is found in the recommendations of the English monk and philosopher Roger Bacon (1214–1294) to his students. The use of rithmomachy spread out from the monasteries to the earliest universities, where its practice was associated with the teaching of Boethian arithmetic.

Like most things, rithmomachy was subjected to a jolt of new ideas during the Renaissance. One text followed another, with each author promoting his own novel contributions. In 1482, a text from John Sherwood (future bishop of Durham, England) was printed in which the power of the Pyramids was explained. But in a Latin treatise by the French theologian Jacques Lefèvre d'Étaples (Jacobus Faber Stapulensis, c. 1455–1536),[41] the Pyramids included only Squares. This latest work, published in 1496, presented a short board of 9 × 8 squares with only one row separating the two camps.

Shortly afterward, the English philosopher Thomas More (1478–1535), also a scholar, theologian and humanist, made rithmomachy the favorite diversion of the inhabitants of his fairy Utopia (1516). While the placement of rithmomachy in this ideal society shows it was held in the greatest esteem, it also reveals a less flattering truth: the game was so limited in popularity as to be considered a fitting pastime for foreigners. In less than a century, the chess reform that freed the moves of Queen and Bishop had conquered every corner of the European continent. Rithmomachy lost out in the transition, dropping in widespread appeal, and was eventually relegated to isolated circles of scientists and academics.

The 16th century saw a resurgence of interest on behalf of some cultivated minds striving against the sharp decline of the preceding century. A manuscript kept in the Laurentian library of Florence shows that the Italian intellectuals of that day tried to improve upon Faber's rules. This codex, roughly dated 1539, compiled a treatise on "the proportions and proportionality" (*Trattato delle proportioni et proportionalita*) attributed to Benedetto Varchi (c. 1502–1565), a Florentine historian and humanist poet. It included a presentation of the rules of "Pythagoras's game," written by Varchis's disciples. The first French treatise on "the very excellent and ancient Pythagorean game, called Rithmomachy" (*Le tres excellent et ancien ieu Pythagorique, dict Rithmomachie*), published by Claude de Boissière (Buxerius) in 1554, attempted to reinvigorate the game. It includes the Circles and Triangles in the composition of the Pyramids, and returns to the 16 × 8 square board, also introducing so-called "irregular" moves (without capture) in order to accelerate the pace of the game. In 1563, William Fulke and Ralf Rising, professors at the Saint-John College of Cambridge, published *The Most Noble, Aunciet, and Learned Playe*, presenting three different variants of the game. Their treatise, which was strongly influenced by Boissière's work, became the basis of most modern descriptions. Fulke had a great love of mathematics and published two additional treatises of his own, even more complex, inventions.[42] These games made a certain contribution to the math teaching in English universities in the second half of the 16th century.

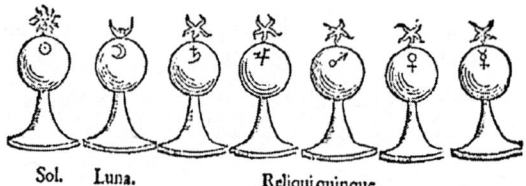

The pieces for playing ouranomachy according to William Fulke.

Along with other works appearing in Germany and Italy, these treatises contained long lists of winning numerical sequences. Indeed, few people possessed the necessary arithmetic knowledge to find or to verify these combinations; and these charts proved to be very useful.

In spite of all this, the interest in rithmomachy continued a rapid decline, unable to compete with the wildly successful reformed chess, which had become the intellectual game *par excellence* and the object of intense theoretical study. In its final moment, the old "philosophers' game" was granted a dedicated section in a 1616 treatise by the Duke of Braunschweig-Lüneburg, better known under his pen name Gustavus Selenus. The fame of this book, *Das Schach- oder König-Spiel*, saved the *Zahl-Damenspiel*, literally the "game of checkers of the numbers," from total oblivion. Finally, although the English writer Robert Burton did mention the game in his *Anatomy Melancholy* (1621) amidst a list of winter diversions, the hour of rithmomachy had passed. The Pythagorean theory of numbers that supported it had moved on as well; the advent of algebra had begun. Mathematicians also developed a newfound interest in games of luck, with the rise of theories of probability. Blaise Pascal (1623–1662), the brilliant mathematician, intent on optimizing his winnings in games of chance, took mathematics into an entirely new direction, along with Pierre de Fermat (c. 1605–1665) and Christian Huygens (1629–1695), throughout the mid–17th century.

Rithmomachy, though exceptionally complicated, is still quite playable. The variations in the rules prove to be rather small and the number of possible combinations is not very high. With some familiarity and practice, recognizing the possible combinations of numbers is quite manageable.

The game has surprising similarities to distant games, such as the captured pieces switching sides as they do in Japanese shogi—a characteristic shared with the Reversi/Othello family of games. And the captures by enclosure are reminiscent of *ludus latrunculorum,* played under the Roman Empire, and of some medieval Scandinavian games such as *hnefatafl.*

Recently, several professors of mathematics have attempted to resurrect rithmomachy as an appealing introduction to mathematical concepts. A few game-playing programs have been developed, with rithmomachy slightly simplified, and some have been marketed.

Because numbers are a source of deep mysteries, this battle between them still exerts a seductive force on many players.

# 29. King Alfonso's Games

Perhaps the greatest source of information on board games ever compiled during the Middle Ages is the *Libro de los Juegos* (*Book of Games*). This famous work was commissioned by Alfonso X, King of Castile and León (1251–1284), completed in Seville in 1283.

The codex contains 98 leaves and is organized into seven "books." Already mentioned is the *Libro del Acedrex* that contains 103 chess problems. There is also the *Libro de los Dados,* with 12 games of dice; the *Libro de las Tablas,* describing 15 games of "tables" including the *todas tablas,* which is very similar to modern backgammon; the *Book of Large Games* which includes the *grant acedrex*; the *Book of Four-Player Games,* chess and tables; the *Libro del Alquerque,* dealing with merels, morris and *alquerque,* an ancestor of checkers; and the *Book of the Astrological Games.*[43]

The full text, written in ancient Castilian, can be found on the Internet. Its pages are illustrated with over 150 colorful, richly embellished miniatures. Several resources on the web give detailed images and information from this exceptional text.[44]

Illustration showing a game of grant acedrex (*Libro de los Juegos,* f82v).

# Large Chess (Grant Acedrex)

It is not only in the East that chess has been taken to excessive extremes. One of the "books" of the *Libro de los Juegos* is dedicated almost entirely to a *grant acedrex*, "large chess," reportedly derived from India, illustrated as a game between two bearded noblemen.

Of all the historic variants, this one lies farthest from the spirit of military conflict. The troops are a fabulous menagerie, also of eastern origin, and a closer look reveals many surprises.

## *Material*

This game uses a large, checkered, 12 × 12 square board. Each player has 24 pieces: 1 King (*Rey*), 1 Giant Bird (*Aanca*), 2 Crocodiles (*Cocatriz*),[45] 2 Giraffes (*Zaraffa*), 2 Rhinoceros (*Unicornio*), 2 Lions (*Leon*), 2 Rooks (*Roque*) and 12 Pawns (*Peon*). Kings are placed face-to-face.

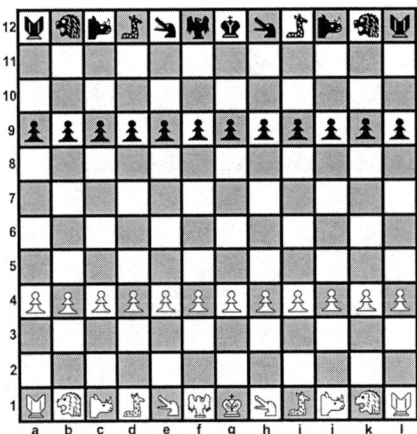

Initial array of grant acedrex.

## *Rules*

Written in medieval Castilian, without punctuation, the rules are not entirely easy to decipher. It appears that H.J.R. Murray's interpretation, adopted without question in all subsequent works, is not entirely accurate. Recent works have re-examined the original Spanish text, and the rules presented below result from this careful study.[46]

### MOVES AND CAPTURES

*King, Rook and Pawn:* move and capture like their counterparts at standard chess, medieval or modern.

*Crocodile:* moves exactly as the modern Bishop. It travels any number of squares diagonally, but may not jump over any pieces in its way.

*Giant Bird:* steps one square diagonally, then moves any number of squares orthogonally, continuing away from its point of departure. It may not jump over any pieces in its way, and must always start with the diagonal step.

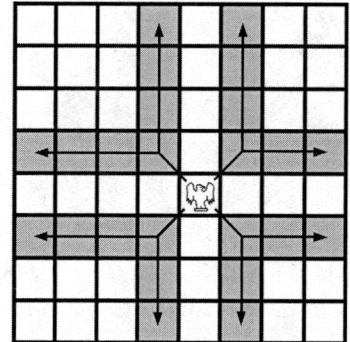

Giant Bird moves.

 *Giraffe*: moves one step orthogonally followed by two steps diagonally, essentially like a Knight's leap extended by one more diagonal square. The Giraffe is not blocked by any piece in its path.[47]

 *Lion*: jumps three squares orthogonally, or two squares orthogonally followed by one diagonally. It may leap over occupied squares.[48]

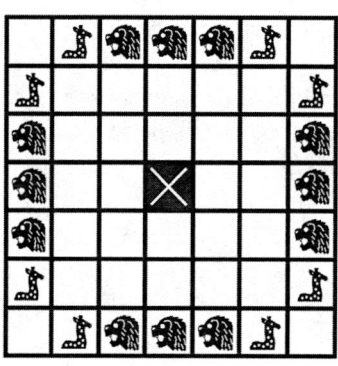

Moves of the Giraffe and the Lion, showing their complementary nature. The symbols indicate the squares that can be reached by each piece from the central black square.

The Rhinoceros follows a complex move whose description in the Spanish codex remains ambiguous.[49] Two interpretations are plausible. The players may choose the one they prefer.

 *Rhinoceros: Interpretation 1:* leaps like a Knight then, proceeds diagonally away from its starting square any number of vacant squares. *Interpretation 2:* leaps like a Knight, then proceeds diagonally forward in the direction of the opponent's camp any number of vacant squares. It may not move diagonally backward, which means that only a Knight's jump allows it to retreat.

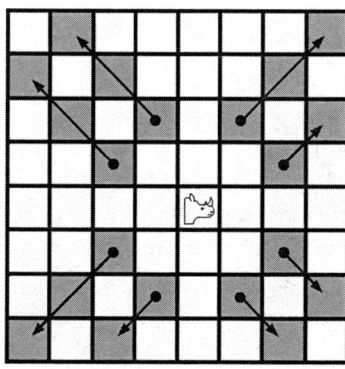

Rhinoceros moves: Interpretation 1 (left) and Interpretation 2 (right).

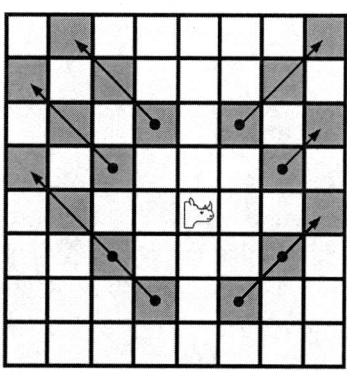

PARTICULAR RULES. • *The Pawn's double step:* all Pawns may move one or two squares forward on their first move, until a capture occurs in the game. After the first capture, Pawns may no longer take a double step.

- *Pawn's promotion:* when a Pawn reaches the opposite side of the board it is replaced by the piece corresponding to the file on which it lands. On the g file (the Kings' file), the Pawn is promoted to a Giant Bird.
- *The King's privilege:* for his first move, the King may jump to the second square in a straight line: straight ahead, diagonally or sideways. He may pass over an occupied square. The codex insists that this jump is similar to the Queen's (*Alfferza*) move that is found in the standard chess of the time. Therefore, the King cannot capture when jumping.[50]
- Nothing is said about the game's conclusion in the codex. The rules for the end of the game were probably similar to those of the Spanish assize of medieval chess.

## *Tactics*

Because he found the game "slow and long to finish," King Alfonso X recommended this game be played with the help of an octahedral die (eight triangular sides) to designate the piece to be moved. The corresponding pieces are 8 (King), 7 (Giant Bird), 6 (Rhinoceros), 5 (Rook), 4 (Lion), 3 (Crocodile), 2 (Giraffe), 1 (Pawn). This order corresponded to the values that the Spanish king assigned to the pieces, the codex being very clear on this point. This is an important clue to help in understanding the intended moves of the pieces whose explanations are often somewhat mystifying.

Nowadays, the relative values calculated by software according to the present authors' interpretation of the text are the following: Giant Bird (7.9), Rhinoceros (interpretation 1: 5.6 or interpretation 2: 6), Rook (5), Lion (3.3), Crocodile (3.3), Giraffe (1.9), Pawn (0.5).

## *Alternative Moves According to Murray*

A hundred years after the publication of his great book, *A History of Chess* (1913), the English historian remains a recognized authority. Even though it seems likely that he misinterpreted some details on the Spanish text, it is interesting to observe the rules of moves that he reported:

- *Giraffe:* jumps to the opposite corner of a 5 × 2 squares rectangle, which is a different kind of elongated Knight's jump. It changes its color of square in each move.
- *Rhinoceros:* on its first move, it jumps like an orthodox Knight, but it may not capture. For the subsequent moves, it ranges diagonally, like a modern Bishop.
- *Lion:* jumps three squares horizontally or vertically.

The relatives values calculated for these pieces with Murray's moves are: Rhinoceros (3), Giraffe (1.9), Lion (1.1). While the Giraffe retains the same strength as in the present authors' analysis above, the Rhinoceros and Lion of Murray's interpretation are abnormally weak.[51] Murray implied that the Castilian King badly misunderstood the relative strength of the pieces. It is more likely that Murray had not interpreted the moves correctly, perhaps because of a lack of interest in this particular variant.[52] It is fair to assume that Alfonso had a good understanding of the workings of his most exceptional chess variant.

## Discussion

In his introduction to this game, Alfonso X establishes that the ancient Indian kings who invented it had placed exotic beasts in the ranks to impress the troops with their nobility, making them more obedient.

It appears that an effort was made to accelerate the game by adding extremely mobile pieces and giving the Pawn its initial double step, foreshadowing the great changes to come two centuries later with the advent of modern chess with its long-ranging Queens and Bishops.

Is that a mere coincidence? One may note the presence of a Crocodile having exactly the move prefiguring the Bishop. There is perhaps a fragile link, but would place the *grant acedrex* among the forerunners of modern chess, a valid possibility since Spain is precisely the place where the new game first appeared.

There are a few other animals here of special interest. What the codex calls "*Unicornio*" is not at all the picture of the mythical, gracile unicorn. The description is quite clear: "a very big and very strong beast, which has two horns, one on the forehead and another on the nose, big like an elephant and with ears of a pig, etc.," leaving no doubt that this is indeed a Rhinoceros. This is confirmed by the illustrated diagram on the codex depicting that piece as a massive short-legged silhouette.

The Giraffe may seem out of place to us as a bold fighter; however, the medieval writers were not acquainted with the docile creature we see nibbling leaves on the savanna. The few who had reported back to Europe on their impressions of this animal found it an awesome, powerful beast.

Most curious of all members of this strange bestiary is the one named *aanca* in the Spanish text. It is described as a magnificent and terrifying bird (also denoted as "*anka*") in the Arabian legends. Murray translated this as "griffin"—but the griffin is a mythological bird, half-eagle, half-lion. Sonja Musser rightly observes that this does not match the illustration or the text of the manuscript. In fact, the *aanca* is another gigantic mythical bird which was said to populate India, and is described in the Persian tales of *One Thousand and One Nights*, the history of *Sinbad the Sailor*, and even in the *Travels of Marco Polo*. This bird of prey, identified as the legendary *rukh* (or *roc*),[53] is given an eloquent and stirring description by the Castilian king:

"*The wise men tell in their books that when this bird flies no other bird dares to take off. Those birds hide in their trees and caves and do not dare to leave them; they strive to hide as well as they can. It is so large that it can carry an elephant or any other large beast it finds to its nest. It is a very beautiful bird. Its chest and neck shine like gold. Its side and wings are yellow. Its feet, eyes, and beak are scarlet and its claws are very black. On its head is a spiked crown like a diadem. This bird raises its young in the highest peaks for two reasons. First, it always wants clear and clean air and second, because it has short legs and long wings and so cannot take off from a low place. Whenever it wants to fly, it makes as if to jump and then flies straight to where it wants.*"[54]

Several researchers postulate that a now-extinct gigantic bird, such as the elephant-bird or "*vorompatra*" (*Aepyornis maximus*) from Madagascar, may have inspired the Oriental legend of the *rukh*. The extinction of this species occurred in the 17th century, and its enormous eggs continued to be traded for a long time.[55] The Arabs, who furrowed the Indian Ocean with their long-ranging dhow vessels as far as the Malagasy coasts, had a credible chance of hearing about, or even seeing, this impressive bird. Perhaps it is from the marvelous tales of such travelers that the Aanca finally arrived in Spain, on Alfonso X's great chessboard.

By asserting that this game originated in India, the Christian king clearly recognized the eastern origin of this grand chess. Two exotic menageries contend across a board which shows an obvious parenthood with other large variants described in the Oriental sphere of the Middle Ages. A parallel may be inferred between this large Castilian variant and Timur's or Turkish great chess, already presented—more than mere coincidence. From Samarkand to Toledo, the Muslim culture has been very fruitful, with the enduring traditions of zoological and fairy chess as admirable examples.

## Ten-Square Chess

In the same "book" of the Castilian codex dedicated to large games, instructions are given for manufacturing a special seven-sided die to play a form of chess on a 10 × 10 square chessboard ("*el acedrex de la diez casas*"). The additional pieces were two Judges accompanied by their respective Pawns. Alas, nothing is indicated regarding their moves or starting positions. Each number on the die was associated with a particular piece, in hierarchical order: 7 the King (*Rey*), 6 the Fers (*Alferza*), 5 the Rook (*Roque*), 4 the Horse (*Cavallo*), 3 the Judge (*Juyz*), 2 the Elephant (*Alffil*) and 1 the Pawn (*Peon*).

Apart from the royal couple, the text informs us that the pieces are numbered in order of their respective strengths. In this case, the Judge must be stronger than the Elephant but weaker than the Horse. This mysterious piece, not included in the *grant acedrex* but seemingly too trivial to garner a full explanation, must have had a relatively unremarkable move. Let's speculate that the Judge jumped two squares vertically or horizontally, a natural complement to the move of the Elephant. If this is correct, this 10 × 10 square chess is identical to the Muslim variant described by Firdawsi, Gaw's chess, mentioned in the first part of this book.[56]

The same seven-sided die was used in a curious form of tables with 14 stations and 17 pieces per player. This contrasts with standard games of tables (such as backgammon and tric-trac), which have 12 stations and 15 pieces, and are played with a pair of common six-sided dice.

Illustration of a game of seven-point tables using seven-sided dice and seventeen pieces on each side. Alfonso is named as one of the players here (*Libro de los Juegos*, f85v).

## Chess of the Four Seasons

Among the chess variants described by King Alfonso X was a game for four players. This Spanish game differs from the Indian chaturaji because here each contender is pitted against the other three. Powerfully symbolic, this chessboard reflects a world in which all things are derived from four primordial elements. Each player is identified with a certain color, a season, an element and a "humor"[57] (in medieval philosophy, these "humors" were literally considered to be fluids coursing through the body and determining the person's emotions, temperament and state of health):

| Color | Season | Element | Humor |
|---|---|---|---|
| Green | Spring | Air | Blood |
| Red | Summer | Fire | Choler |
| Black | Autumn | Earth | Melancholia |
| White | Winter | Water | Phlegm |

## *Material*

This game is played on an 8 × 8 square chessboard. The central 4 × 4 square area has its long diagonals marked in order to show the paths of the Pawns, which march in different directions.

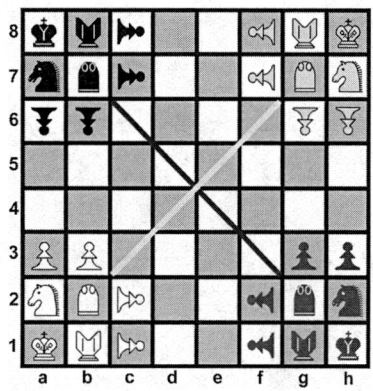

Initial array of Four Seasons Chess. From bottom right, counter-clockwise: Green, Red, Black and White.

Each player receives 8 pieces of one color: green, red, black or white. Each set includes: 1 King (*Rey*), 1 Elephant (*Alffil*),[58] 1 Horse (*Cavallo*), 1 Rook (*Roque*) and 4 Pawns (*Peon*). The initial setup shown in the manuscript's miniature does not have identical arrangements for each player. Green and Black show the King with a Horse at his right and Rook to his left; whereas Red and White have those positions reversed.

## *Rules*

Green begins the game, as befits the player of spring. The game takes place counterclockwise, following the natural order of the seasons. Each plays for himself, with no alliances. Players are instructed to attack the player to the right (the following season), and defend against the player to the left.

The pieces move as in medieval chess. In particular, the Elephant jumps two squares diagonally. The Pawn steps straight ahead and, when it reaches the far side of the board, is promoted to a Fers (*Alfferza*), a piece which is absent in the initial array. It then moves one square in any of the four diagonal directions.

END OF THE GAME. When a player mates a King, the mated player's pieces are withdrawn from the game. The winner is the owner of the last King standing on the board.

The original rules were played for stakes beginning with each player laying down an opening wager. An amount was then paid for each piece lost and for each check given to a King. The successively checkmated players left what they had won so far on the board, and paid their winner an amount for as many remaining pieces as they had. The final winner took all the money on the board.

DISCUSSION. The resemblance this medieval variant bears to chaturaji is unavoidable. It is possible that the Indian game, known to the Muslim world since al-Biruni described it in 1030, inspired the Castilian game.

However, the Spanish four-handed chess presents two major differences with the Indian game. First, the contest is between four individuals; whereas, the Indian game pits two pairs of allies against each other. Second, the pieces are set up in the corners of the board instead of being aligned along the sides. Consequently, four seasons chess offers frontal opposition of Pawns that does not exist in chaturaji.

Another game of tables accompanied this chess variant. Logically, it was designed as a four-handed backgammon. Named *el mundo* ("the world"), it was played over a circular board with six stations per quadrant. Using the same colors found in four seasons chess, each player has 12 playing pieces.

Illustration of a game of four seasons chess and of a game of the world (*Libro de los Juegos*, f88v, f89v).

## *Escaques*

With this word, which was a synonym of *acedrex,* and which indeed designates regular chess in other Romance languages, Alfonso X presented an astronomical game that has very little in common with chess.

Here, seven players sit around a circular board, formed of concentric circles that correspond to the moving heavenly bodies (those known at that time). From the center to the periphery, they are the Moon, Mercury, Venus, the Sun, Mars, Jupiter and Saturn. Each circle is divided into twelve sectors representing the constellations of the zodiac. The sectors themselves are divided into a number of squares varying from 1 (for the Moon) to 7 (for Saturn).

Each player moves a colored piece symbolizing his planet on its dedicated circle according to the result of a special seven-sided die. The text associates each piece with certain human characteristics.

| Planet | Color | Character |
|---|---|---|
| Saturn | Black | Old thin man. Sad and troubled |
| Jupiter | Green | Middle-aged man. Happy face |
| Mars | Red | Young man. Armored |
| Sun | Gold | Young king. Crowned |
| Venus | Purple | Young woman. Beautiful |
| Mercury | Many colors | Young man. Writing a book |
| Moon | White | Young woman. Hands over head |

A player may win or lose stakes according to the configuration his planet achieves with those of the other players: oppositions, conjunctions, etc., representing astrological patterns. This *escaques* is a board game of chance, a circular race around the board without captures. This game was probably similar to *al-falakiya*, "celestial chess," an astronomical game on an identical board described by the Muslim scholars, al-Mas'udi (c. 950) and al-Amuli (c. 1350). It can be seen that, except for the name, this game has little connection with chess variants as a whole.

Finally, here as well, the codex associated the game of *escaques* with a game of tables: this is a competition between seven players with seven pieces each, on a sort of heptagonal backgammon board divided into seven sectors forming seven points. With this game description, the book's theme of pairing chess and backgammon variants is complete.

Illustration of a game of escaques and a game of astrological tables (*Libro de los Juegos*, f96v, f97v).

## History

In 1283, the completion date of this codex, King Alphonse X reigned over Castile, the most powerful kingdom of the Iberian Peninsula. The victory of the Christian kingdoms over the Almohads[59] in Las Navas de Tolosa (1212) signaled the rise of the *Reconquista*. Within a few years, Aragón took Valencia and the Balearic Islands, Portugal seized the Algarve, while Castile, which had absorbed León in 1230, achieved the most important gains by seizing Córdoba, Murcia, Seville and Cadiz. Thereafter, the Arab dominion was reduced to a small emirate centered around Granada where it lasted until 1492. However, is spite of great military losses, the Muslim civilization, installed since the eighth century, had profoundly shaped the character of Spanish culture. The schools of Islamic knowledge provided the models and the context that made the Alfonso X codex possible. The intellectual illumination cultivated in the Islamic state of al-Andalus continued to shed its light through all sectors of the Iberian Peninsula, Christian and Muslim alike.

Not surprisingly, the chess games set forth in Alfonso's document trace their lineage directly to the Islamic world.

In spite of this comprehensive documentation by the Castilian king, none of these atypical variants, either those of chess or those of tables, seems to have caught on in wider European culture. There is no trace of these games in subsequent texts.

# 30. Courier Chess

This chess variant owes its celebrity to a painting by the young Lucas van Leyden (1494–1533), dated circa 1508.[60] Seated at the board are a man and woman, in a room full of kibitzers and onlookers. Although the origin of this game is unknown, the earliest trace dates from the very beginning of the 13th century in Germany. Several mentions of the game are sprinkled sparsely through texts of the following six centuries, until the game finally faded from popularity in its last stronghold—Ströbeck, Saxony, a German village famous for its passion for chess, in the early 19th century.

Coat of arms of Ströbeck.

Initial array of courier chess.

## Material

The board has a rectangular shape with 12 × 8 squares, checkered with two colors.[61]

Each player possesses 24 pieces: 1 King (*König*), 1 Queen (*Königin*), 1 Sage or Counselor (*Mann, Ratgeber*), 1 Jester or Sneak (*Schleich*), 2 Couriers (*Kurrier*), 2 Archers (*Schütze*), 2 Knights (*Reutter*), 2 Rooks (*Roche*) and 12 Pawns (*Soldat*).

Modern reconstitution of courier chess. KNOWLTON PHOTOGRAPH

## Rules

MOVES AND CAPTURES. The six standard pieces move and capture as they do in regular medieval chess; in particular, the Queen and the Archer (which is identical to the Aufin) retain their medieval moves.

*Queen:* steps diagonally only one square.

*Archer:* jumps diagonally to the second square, regardless of whether the intermediate square is free or occupied.

The other pieces are more original:

*Courier:* moves any number of squares in one of the four diagonal directions. It can cross only empty squares. This is exactly the move of the modern Bishop.

*Sage:* steps one square in any of the eight directions. It moves just like a King, but is unhindered by check.

*Jester:* moves one square orthogonally, i.e., one step forward, backward, left or right.

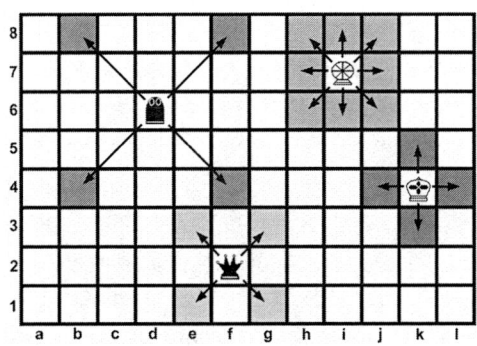

Moves of Archer, Queen, Sage and Jester.

INITIAL MOVE. The "joy leaps" (*Freudensprünge*): this was the German name given to the first moves, which are obligatory. Each player advances the Rooks' Pawns, the Queen's Pawn and the Queen herself two steps forward. Then, the game is played normally.

The King does not have a special leaping or castling move.

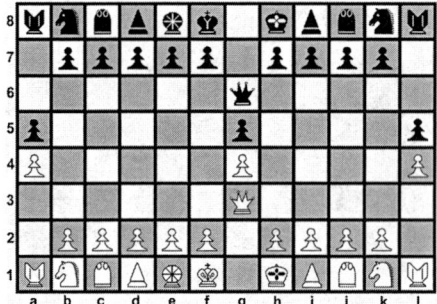

Starting position after the "joy leaps."

PAWN'S PROMOTION. The rules that reached us do not specify this particular point. Nevertheless, Murray supposed that the rules followed those in force for standard chess at the same epoch and place.[62]

- When reaching the eighth rank, the Pawn makes three "joy leaps" backward on the sixth, fourth and second rows on the same file. Each jump counts for one turn of play. It becomes a Queen on the second row.
- The Pawn cannot capture during these moves; therefore, it must jump to free squares. It also cannot jump over occupied squares.
- It is immune from capture on the eighth row but not on the squares reached with the joy leaps.
- The three joy leaps do not need to be taken in consecutive turns.

# Strategy

The relative strength of the pieces is as follows: Rook (5), Courier (3.1), Sage (3), Knight (2.5), Jester (1.6), Queen (1.4), Archer (1.1), Pawn (0.6).

The most remarkable new piece was, of course, the Courier, which leant its name to the game. It was a major novelty for Northern Europe, where the Bishop still had the limited move inherited from shatranj. The players dreaded this Courier, and they argued that it was the strongest piece on the board, even surpassing the Rook. Modern analysis proves their estimation to be rather exaggerated; nevertheless, it is clear that the players considered this long, diagonal move an unprecedented threat, piercing the defenses in new and powerful ways.

Could this Courier have been the origin of the modern Bishop? The connection appears doubtful at first, since the modern Bishop's and Queen's moves first emerged in Spain, far from this Germanic variant. However, there is a possible connection, which is discussed in the following chapter. For the moment, suffice it to say that the modern Bishop is designated in German by the word *Läufer*, meaning "runner," which carries precisely the etymological sense of *Courier*.[63]

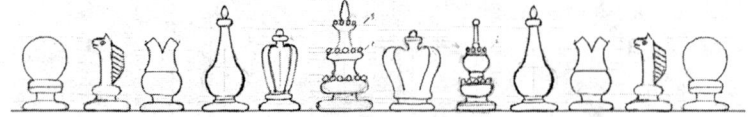

Sketch of the first rank from Lucas van Leyden's painting. KNOWLTON DRAWING

## History

The evidence of this game is spread over more than six centuries, making this an amazingly long-lived variant—especially in view of the limited region of its popularity, in and around Germany. Courier chess first emerges in the Middle Ages, mentioned in the *Wigalois*, a poem from Wirnt von Gravenberg which appeared toward 1205. There are mentions of the game in German translations of the *Moralities* and other 14th century Germanic works such as Heinrich von Beringen's *Schachbuch,* around 1300. Among these works, Kunrat von Ammenhausen reported seeing courier chess played in 1337 in Konstanz, and he enumerated the supplementary pieces it added to the standard game.

No one knows how or why courier chess arose as it did, found exclusively in the German sphere. It appears to be the first enlarged variant designed outside of Arabian influence—unless, of course, the anonymous inventor was a student or monk who had visited a Spanish university, or a Knight who had fought in the Crusades in the holy lands. Ideas circulated broadly throughout medieval Europe and any suitable hypothesis bears some consideration.

Despite the long trail of references to the game, no indication was given as to how to play with these novel pieces until a description by Gustavus Selenus, pen name of Duke Augustus of Brunswick-Lüneburg (1579–1666), appeared in his book *Das Schach- oder Königs-Spiel* in 1616. Selenus devoted an entire chapter to the strange chess passion carried on by the village of Ströbeck, in Sachsen-Anhalt, Germany. An extreme devotion to the game had been burning there since the High Middle Ages, and it inhabitants still carried on the "old" chess played by the medieval rules, the "Italian" chess played by modern rules, and the courier game, played on the long board of 96 squares.

*Top:* King, Queen, Sage, Jester, Courier; *bottom:* Archer, Knight, Rook, Pawn. Illustrations collected from Gustav Selenus's *Das Schach- oder Königs-Spiel* (1616).

The fame of this village attracted many visitors, including the King of Prussia, Frederick the Great, in 1744, and its draw continues to this day. A famous gift of a courier chess set was presented to the village of Ströbeck by the Elector-Prince Frederick William of Brandenburg in 1651, of which the board (but not the pieces) is still on display. The game was still played sporadically through the 18th century, but as the 19th century was underway, it began slipping into oblivion. There have been a few isolated attempts to revive it since then, sometimes updating the rules to resemble modern chess, such as the version offered by Albers in 1821, presented further in this book.

The drama and majesty of courier chess was passed on to posterity, thanks to the painting *The Chess Players* by the precocious Dutch master Lucas van Leyden. The long 12 × 8 board in the painting is unmistakable, and the scene surrounding the game serves as a unique testament to the enchanting excitement chess has generated through the ages. The painting itself had quite an eventful history, having been evacuated by Nazi troops from a besieged Berlin in 1945, then recovered by General Patton's army in a salt mine 2000 feet underground.

Returned to Germany after the war, the painting is now on display at the *Gemäldegalerie* of Berlin, where it continues to intrigue the attentive visitors who can't help noticing that this chessboard has "too many squares."

*Left:* Detail from the painting of Lucas van Leyden (n°574A) conserved at the Gemäldegalerie of Berlin, displaying the play of courier chess. *Right:* Drawing by Jan de Bray, 1661, possibly a self-portrait, showing a courier chess board and pieces.

But van Leyden's famous painting is not the only portrait of this unusual chess form. In 1661, the Dutch artist Jan de Bray (1627–1697) posed with a scattered set of courier chessmen as a prop for his own self-portrait. A review of de Bray's set reveals interesting similarities to the chessmen of van Leyden.

Courier chess stands as the very archetype of a successful chess variant. An altered board, a few simple added pieces, and a long existence punctuated by anecdotes and references. And the van Leyden painting capturing a game like a snapshot, projecting it into eternity. The fascination for courier chess continues. Several later attempts to rejuvenate the game are presented in the following section of this book. Also, a detailed reconstruction of van Leyden's chess set has been available since 2008 on http://courierchess.com.

# 31. Gala

Like courier chess, this variant appears to be of Germanic origin and, perhaps, medieval. First described in Schleswig-Holstein, a province of North Germany, long contested by Denmark, this very curious game could be a hybrid of chess and other Scandinavian board games. The main pieces undergo unexpected changes of direction, which give this game an intriguingly modern quality.

Initial array of gala.

## Material

This is a game for two players on a board of 10 × 10 squares, which is sectioned off in a particular pattern: each corner area of 4 × 4 squares is delineated by a heavy line, leaving a central cross area 10 squares long, 10 squares tall and 2 squares thick. This arrangement represents four castles, each surrounded by a moat (the heavy line), with common space between them. The four central squares of the board (e5, e6, f5 and f6) are known as the "holy place."

Each of the two players has 20 pieces: 2 Kings (*Gala*), 5 Heroes (*Korna*), 5 Horsemen (*Horsa*) and 8 Pawns or Warriors (*Kampa*).[64]

The pieces are shaped like small ninepins, white or black according to the camp. The Kings are the tallest; all others are of the same size. A strip of color painted on their upper half marks them: green for the Heroes, red for the Horsemen, gold for the Kings, with the Pawns remaining plain black and white.

## Rules

The goal of the game is twofold: either to capture the two opposing Kings or to place one's own Kings inside the central "holy place" square.

Arnold Mayer's work (available at www.chessvariants.com) has successfully clarified several points, and the rules given here follow his reconstruction. However, it is still uncertain whether it is compulsory to remove a King from check; whether the Warrior gets more possibilities of move after its first step, or after having crossed the moat; whether the Warrior is allowed to enter the central "holy place," etc.[65]

**INFLUENCE OF THE BOARD.** • *Moats:* the thick lines indicating the edge of each castle. When Heroes or Horsemen cross a moat, their moves change direction.

Mayer's reconstruction adds the following rules:

- If the first step of the Hero's or Horseman's move passes over the moat, the remainder of his move is wide ranging, as many squares as are available in his line of motion. But if they have taken more than one step to pass over the moat, the remainder of their move is limited to just one more square. A piece may pass over only one moat in a single move.

- Diagonal moves within the cross area, passing through the corners of the moats (e.g., d6–e7, f7–g6, e4–d5, f4–g5) are allowed; such moves are not considered to pass over the moats.

- *Central "holy place"*: only the Kings are allowed to land on these squares. Heroes and Horsemen can cross over that space without stopping in it. A King may capture an opposing King standing in the central holy place on a move in which he, himself, is entering the holy place. Once within the central four-square region, the King cannot make any captures.

MOVES AND CAPTURES. As in chess, captures are made by landing on the square of an opposing piece and removing it from the board. There are a few situations in which captures are forbidden, detailed below.

Black starts the game.

*Hero:* inside the castles, it moves orthogonally like a Rook but outside the castles, in the cross area, it moves diagonally like a Bishop. The Hero can capture while passing over a moat, without any restrictions.

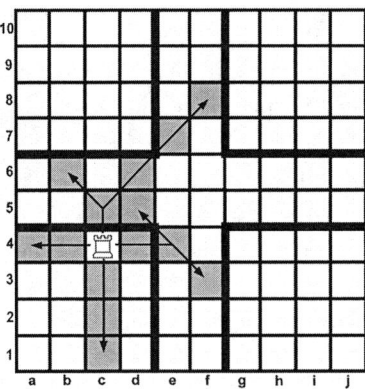 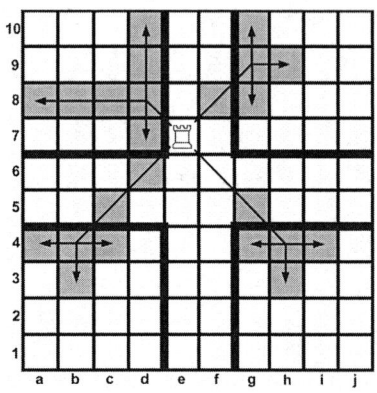

Moves of the Hero, according to Mayer's reconstruction.

*Horseman:* inside the castles, it moves diagonally like a Bishop but outside the castles, it moves orthogonally like a Rook. The Horseman can capture while passing over a moat with one stipulation: when moving into the cross area, it cannot capture a piece orthogonally adjacent to its point of departure, lying on the other side of a moat. For example, a Horseman on g3 cannot capture a piece on f3.

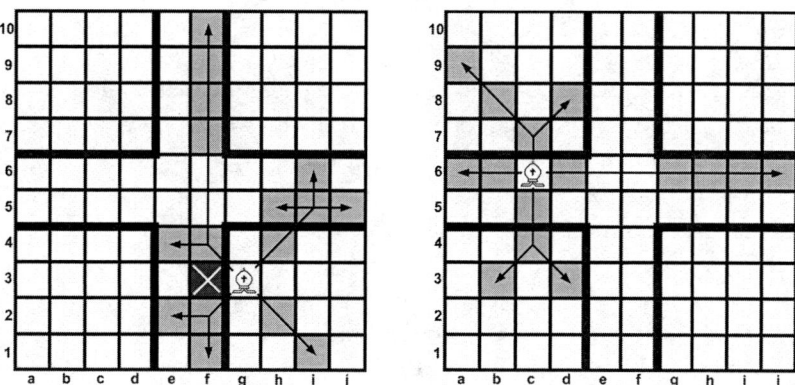

Moves of Horseman, according to Mayer's reconstruction. Note that the Horseman in the left diagram is restricted from making a capture on f3.

*Warrior:* starts with a diagonal step toward the center of the board. On its second move, it may move one square in any direction, orthogonal or diagonal, forward or backward. If, however, the Warrior lands on one of the four squares where the Warriors began in his own camp, his next move must be one diagonal step toward the center, like a first move. The Warrior can never capture while crossing a moat, in either direction.

*King:* always steps one square in any of the eight directions. The King may be captured like any other piece. A King starting his move on the four central "holy place" squares can be transported in a single move to any free square of the board except those squares occupied in the initial array (i.e., the 40 squares that form the corners of the board). The King cannot capture when starting a move from the central place; however, the King can capture while entering the central place.

END OF THE GAME. The original German rules specified that victory is attained by the first player who captures both opposite Kings. After play-testing with several partners, Mayer proposed allowing two kinds of victory:

- "Major Victory": for the first player who can bring his two Kings together inside the central "holy place."
- "Minor Victory": for a player who can put one of his Kings inside the central place after having captured both opposing Kings.

If both players each have one of their Kings in the central area and there are no more Kings on the board, the game is a draw.

All games ending in other configurations are draws.

## Tactics

The orthogonal moves are a lot stronger than the diagonal moves. Therefore, the Horseman is more powerful inside the cross than in the castles. Of course, the reverse is true of the Hero, which is stronger inside the castles.

## History

The exact origin of gala remains unknown. Murray did not mention it. It was revealed to the public by R.C. Bell, a British author of numerous board-game books in the 1960s and 1970s, but with some confusion in the rules. It is true that the principle of moves changing direction when crossing the moats is easily stated, but that the practical application raises numerous issues. Bell opined that gala must have been a medieval game.

Gala is also known as "peasant's chess" and Bell asserted that old boards could be found in some remote German farms. The German historian, Arnold Mayer, however, considers this nickname to be a mistranslation of the Latin word *paganus,* which also means *pagan*, implying that for some reason this game was not considered Christian or was played by non–Christians.

The original account of this game can be traced to a specific source. Bell learned of gala from the German publication *Das Hausbuch der Spiele und Hobbies* (1955) by Theodor Müller-Alfeld. The Danish historian Peter Michaelsen discovered an older German work, *Brettspiele,* by B. Arbeiter and W. Ruhnke, which appeared in Potsdam in 1937 and was the source used by Müller-Alfeld. According to Arbeiter and Ruhnke, gala came from the district of Dithmarschen in the German state of Schleswig-Holstein. Close to Denmark and the Frisian coasts, this provenance led Arnold Mayer to suggest a hypothetical filiation with the board game family of *hnefatafl* of the former Viking (and Celtic) culture. This is why his reconstruction insists on a strong influence on the board's topography, notably, a sacred center that only the King can penetrate; and a victory by bringing the King to a determined place. In tafl (table) games, however, the capture of an opposed piece is achieved by surrounding it ("custodian" capture) which is very different from the capture by displacement in the chess family.

In spite of their intensive research, neither Mayer nor Michaelsen could find any traces of gala, in Dithmarschen or elsewhere. Did this game indeed exist? Discovering this to be a 1930s invention, camouflaged under the aspect of an ancient game, would be very disappointing, but current research cannot rule out the possibility.

If gala is in fact an authentic ancient game, it may be the peculiarities of its rules that created a barrier to a wider diffusion. In any case, with its captures by substitution, this mysterious game is certainly related to chess, though perhaps a hybrid of other Nordic board games—which makes it uniquely fascinating.

# 32. European Chess

In a book like this, which explores the full diversity of the chess world, finding an appropriate epithet for this "regular old chess" game is unavoidable. But which one? "Modern" is too vague; "orthodox" is biased in favor of its Western roots, and "international" would not respect xiangqi and shogi which are also played well beyond their national borders. The term "Western" has often been used in these pages, which is better—but not perfect if one remembers that our planet is spherical...

# 32. European Chess

Chess, familiar to most of our readers, as it comes to us from modern Europe.
KNOWLTON PHOTOGRAPH

This form of chess was born in Spain just over 500 years ago, and was cultivated by the Italian masters, then treated at an entirely new theoretical level by François-André Danican Philidor in the 18th century. In 19th century England, the Staunton style of chessmen was designed, soon becoming the "universal" standard. Finally, the Russian schools spread chess out among the masses, making this game really "popular" for the very first time in its long history. So, although this game has been embraced and mastered in every part of the world, the present authors consider it by origin and culture to be the "European" variety.

Initial array of chess.

## Material

The game is played over an 8 × 8 square board, checkered black and white. The board is oriented so that each player has a white square in the right-hand corner. Each side has 16 chessmen, white for one and black for the other: 1 King, 1 Queen, 2 Bishops, 2 Knights, 2 Rooks and 8 Pawns. While actual chessmen and boards may vary in color, "black" and "white" remain the official designations of the dark and light chessmen and squares.

White starts to play the game.

Chessboard and standard "Staunton" type chessmen.
KNOWLTON PHOTOGRAPH

# Rules

MOVES AND CAPTURES. Each player moves one piece on his turn. Moves are made to vacant squares except when capturing an opponent's piece. Captures are made by substitution, the attacking piece taking the place of the captured piece which is withdrawn from the game. Capturing is not compulsory. All pieces, except the Pawn, capture as they move.

*King:* moves only one step onto any adjacent square, provided that this square is not under the threat of an adverse piece. The King is in check if he is threatened to be captured by one or more adverse pieces. The King is in check even if the pieces which threaten him cannot move without exposing their own King to check. Declaring check aloud is not compulsory, but failing to move out of check is considered an illegal move.

*Queen:* moves any number of free squares along the rank, file or diagonals on which she stands. She may not jump over any pieces in her way.

*Bishop:* moves any number of free squares diagonally. It may not jump over any pieces in its way.

*Knight:* moves with an L-shape of 2 squares in one orthogonal direction (that is, forward, backward or sideways) plus one step at a right angle. The Knight freely leaps over any pieces in its path.

*Rook:* moves any number of free squares along a rank or file (forward, backward, left or right). It may not jump over any pieces in its way.

*Pawn:* it normally steps one square forward, but for its first move it may go to the second square forward if the intermediate square is unoccupied. It does not capture that way. It may capture an enemy piece standing one square diagonally forward.

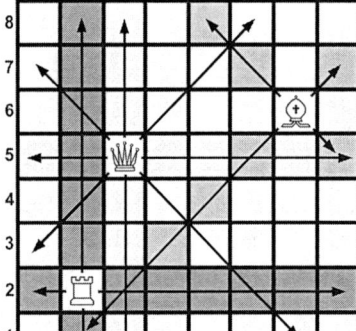 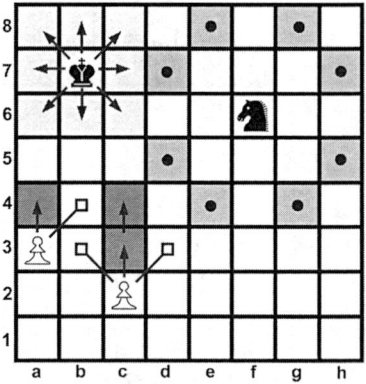

Moves of chessmen in chess, with the Pawn's capture ability marked by small squares.

PARTICULAR RULES. • *Pawn Promotion:* a Pawn reaching the last rank of the board is immediately replaced with a Queen, Bishop, Knight or Rook of the same color at the choice of the player. Promotional choice is not limited to pieces that have already been captured; for instance, a player can have more than one Queen by virtue of promotion.

- *Castling:* castling is a simultaneous movement of the King and a Rook which stand on the same rank.[66] The King moves two spaces toward the Rook and, in the same move, the Rook moves around the King to stand next to him on the opposite side. According to the selected side, one distinguishes a King's side castling ("castling short") and a Queen's side castling ("castling long").

Queen's side castling, annotated 0–0–0 (left) and King's side castling, annotated 0–0 (right).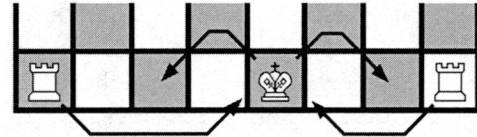

Castling is permitted only once per player per game and only if the following conditions are met:

- Neither the King nor the Rook has yet made any move.
- All squares between the King and the Rook are empty.
- Neither the King's arrival square, nor the square/s the King passes over is threatened by an enemy piece.
- The King is not presently in check.

• *"En Passant" Capture:* when a Pawn uses its double step to pass over a square that is threatened by an enemy Pawn, that enemy Pawn may capture it as if it had only moved one step. The enemy Pawn moves forward-diagonally as in a normal capture, and the captured Pawn is removed from the board. This *en passant* (French: "in passing") capture may only be done immediately following the Pawn's double step; afterward, the opportunity is lost.

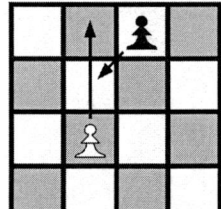 

The white Pawn moves two squares, and is taken *"en passant"* by the black Pawn.

END OF THE GAME. An attacked King must immediately be placed out of check. This can be done in three ways: moving the King to a non-attacked square, capturing the attacking piece, or interposing a friendly piece between the King and the attacking piece. If no possible move will save the King from capture, the player has lost the game: it is *checkmate*.

A player whose King is *not* in check but has no legal move (i.e., if any move would place the King in check) is *stalemated*. This is a drawn game.

When the same position of all pieces on the board is repeated three times, with the same player to move, the game may be declared drawn by repetition.

If the fighting forces on the board are reduced to the point that no checkmate is possible, the game is declared a draw.

If one player doubts that the opponent can make progress and create checkmate in a reasonable time, he may challenge the opponent to checkmate within 50 moves or accept a draw. If, however, any Pawn is moved or any piece is captured, this is considered progress, and the count must begin again. Only the opponent's moves are counted. If fifty moves are counted without a capture or Pawn move, the game is declared a draw.

The game may also end by the consent of the players. If a player declares that he is resigning the game, it is scored as a win for the other. If a player verbally offers a draw to his opponent, and the offer is accepted, then a draw is the official result.

## Tactics and Strategy

This familiar variety of chess has a rich tradition of literature and analysis far beyond any other board game ever created. Chess books fill numerous libraries and many are dedicated to the technical aspects of play with dense catalogs of openings and endgame studies. This book cannot even scratch the surface of the rich knowledge that has been accumulated regarding this game. The reader will easily find an endless supply of books, videos and computer programs leading to the highest imaginable levels of expertise.

RELATIVE VALUE OF THE PIECES. Numerical values for the various pieces are quite useful in estimating the relative power the two sides possess on the board; actual play, however, demonstrates that the functional strengths of the pieces change substantially as the board's configuration is transformed throughout the game. For example, a Knight loses strength as the board empties of pieces, while the Rook becomes more mobile and more dominant. Bishops, depending upon the structure of Pawns on the board, may have great mobility or may find themselves totally blocked from effective play. And mobility is only one factor, along with coordination between pieces, strengths and vulnerabilities on the board, and endless strategic positional considerations.

Nevertheless, a game of chess, more than most other variants, often does hinge on the sheer value of pieces on the board, and a simple tallying of their assigned points can hardly be avoided. In the present day, most beginners learn the values of pieces early, using simple whole numbers: Queen (9), Rook (5), Bishop (3), Knight (3) and Pawn (1). Some authors see a slight superiority of the Bishop over the Knight. Hans Berliner (World Correspondence Chess Champion 1965–1968) used a scale based on computer experimentation; it is often reported as Queen (8.8), Rook (5.1), Bishop (3.33), Knight (3.2) and Pawn (1).

## History

This form of chess first arose in the Catalan lands of Spain, the ancient heart of European chess. The medieval game was assuredly too slow to start, not quick and dynamic enough for Renaissance minds. In a time of great upheaval in the arts and sciences, chess in turn came due for a momentous revision. It was approximately the year 1475, in Valencia, Spain, among a circle of intellectuals associated with the *conversos*, Jewish families that had converted to Christianity to escape persecution, that the new laws of chess were first set forth.

Among those Valencian intellectuals were printers (heralding a new profession that would prove to be strategic) as well as poets, including Castellví, Vinyoles and Fenollar.[67] These three accomplices stand in the center of the *Scachs d'amor*, a Catalan poem framing them in an allegorical game of chess,[68] the first ever recorded of the modern era:

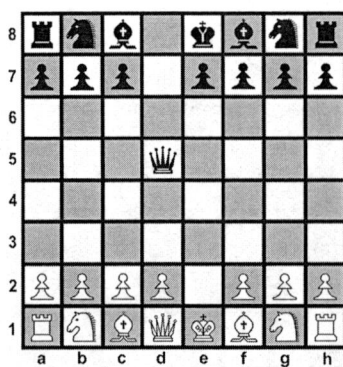

1. e4 d5
2. exd5 Qxd5

The newborn Queen has just revealed her mighty power …

3. Nc3 Qd8
4. Bc4
... and the new Bishop seizes the diagonals!

| 4. ... Nf6 | 13. Bb5+ Nxb5 |
|---|---|
| 5. Nf3 Bg4 | 14. Qxb5+ Nd7 |
| 6. h3 Bxf3 | 15. d5 exd5 |
| 7. Qxf3 e6 | 16. Be3 Bd6 |
| 8. Qxb7 Nbd7 | 17. Rd1 Qf6 |
| 9. Nb5 Rc8 | 18. Rxd5 Qg6 |
| 10. Nxa7 Nb6 | 19. Bf4 Bxf4 |
| 11. Nxc8 Nxc8 | 20. Qxd7+ Kf8 |
| 12. d4 Nd6 | 21. Qd8 mate |

The very first mate of the new Queen.

The new Queen was granted an unlimited move in all directions, perhaps inspired by the mighty Isabella I the Catholic (1451–1504) who had been crowned Queen of Castile in December 1474.[69]

The new Bishop complemented the Rook's move, with free range along the diagonals. The historian Morten Lilleøren has suggested that this change had perhaps been influenced by the German printers who were working in Valencia. They would have "imported" the mighty Courier, already known in their country, onto the Spanish chessboard.[70]

Chess would never be the same.[71] The first technical treatise of modern chess, *Libre dels jochs partits dels schacs en nombre de 100 (Book of 100 Chess Games)*, published in Catalan by Francesch Vicent—is now lost.[72] This incunabulum has a notable history. The book's colophon, which had been described in bibliographies of other texts, indicates that it was printed in May 1495 by Lope de Roca "Alemany" and Pere Trincher, two printers associated with Fenollar and Vinyoles. The last known copy was destroyed by the French Napoleonic troops during the sack of Montserrat's monastery in 1811. The soldiers used the paper to fabricate bullets.

Thereafter, the honor of being the most ancient extant manual passes to *Repeticion de amores & arte de acedrex (Repetition of Love and Art of Chess)*, printed in 1496 or (probably) 1497 in Salamanca and dedicated to Prince Don Juan (1478–1497), heir to the Spanish throne, by an obscure student and courtier, Lucena.[73] Unfortunately, the Prince's untimely death dashed Lucena's further ambitions at the royal court. This second treatise, printed by Sanz and Hutz (a companion of Lope de Roca, "Alemany," meaning "German") presented 75 problems of medieval chess and 75 problems according to the new rules. The Spanish historians, Ricardo Calvo and José Antonio Garzón, have concluded that those were most likely copied from Vicent. If so, this second book was merely a translation of the first modern chess book, from Catalan to Castilian.

But tensions were mounting under the *Catholic Kings* as the Inquisition brought more Jews and *conversos* to trial. The Valencians dispersed, fleeing to Italy and France. The new rules of chess, facilitated by the emergent printing profession, spread quickly and efficiently.

The so-called Da Vinci chessmen, recreated from a manuscript by the great mathematician, and friend of Leonardo, Luca Pacioli, c. 1500. KNOWLTON DESIGN AND PHOTOGRAPH

The game, soon known as "*alla rabbiosa*" in Italian or "*de la Dame enragée*" in French—chess of the rabid (or enraged) Queen,[74] became the chess of the entire European continent in less than a single century. At first, the old and new chess coexisted—but only for one generation. By 1510, the medieval game was essentially obsolete in Spain and Italy. Twenty years later, the new chess had conquered France and England, and by 1536, it had a strong foothold in Germany. While Europe stood poised to tear itself limb from limb in wars of religion, the old chess surrendered with barely a skirmish. Chess had successfully emerged from the Middle Ages, and the first pages of its modern history were written in Italian. In 1512, the first sophisticated treatise on the new chess was published to a wide and receptive audience; it was subsequently reprinted nine times. This book, *Questo libro e da imparare giocare a scachi (This Book Is to Learn How to Play Chess)*, was signed by Pedro Damiano, a Portuguese pharmacist who emigrated to Italy following the Jews' expulsion from his homeland. But today, it has been established that this name was a mere pseudonym. A recent study, advanced by the historian José Antonio Garzón, draws a striking conclusion: this great treatise was drafted by the quill of Vicent himself![75]

Leonardo "il Puttino" defeats Ruy Lopez under the eyes of Philip II, king of Spain, in Madrid in 1575 (painting by Luigi Mussini, 1883). WIKIMEDIA COMMONS PHOTOGRAPH

As early as 1560, the Spanish priest Ruy Lopez faced the best Italian masters of his day, and the history of chess became the history of its champions. Soon, the details of the rules evolved and stabilized. The Queen's initial leap became superfluous in light of her new powers, and the King's leap, when executed straight forward, appeared too dangerous. The lateral jumps over the Rook remained, with the Rook brought closer in order to control the center of the board. The Calabrian, Gioachino Greco, recommended making this maneuver in one move only—and castling was born. In the 1620s, he composed and printed his own manuscripts with which he retailed his study of the game. He traveled all through the European courts, selling his books and popularizing the rule of castling "*alla Calabrese*" (in the Calabrian style) throughout the continent.[76]

THE SOUL OF CHESS. In one stroke, the Valencian reform turned the value of Pawns on its head. Starting as the weakest chessman on the board (not even properly called a *piece* in modern parlance), the lowly Pawn now carried the potential of promoting to the strongest piece ever seen on the chessboard. The French champion François-André Danican Philidor, widely credited as the father of chess analysis, wrote in his famous book, *Analyse du jeu des Échecs* (1749): "*Les Pions sont l'âme des échecs*" ("*The Pawns are the soul of chess*").

But even in Philidor's time, a few details remained to be fixed. Philidor complained that some German players used to advance two Pawns simultaneously from the starting row, one square each in a single turn. On the other hand, Philidor deplored the idea that one could possess several Queens by virtue of promotion. In several countries, the convention held that the promoted Pawn had to select its new value from the lot of formerly captured pieces—a convention that is now long overruled. It was only in the second half of the 19th century that the rules converged and were officially adopted, which continue to the present day.

It was the right time, because chess had entered the era of international tournaments. The tournament of London in 1862 became the first to be regulated with hourglasses. In 1866, also in London, Wilhelm Steinitz of Austria defeated the reputed top player of the time, Adolf Andersen of Germany, and proclaimed himself "World Champion." That title was officially confirmed in 1886 after a match in the United States (20 games played in New York, St. Louis and New Orleans) against Johannes Zukertort.

In 1924, an international chess governing body was created, F.I.D.E.,[77] with the motto *Gens Una Sumus* (*We are all one family*). At that time, the Staunton style of chessmen (patented in 1849 by Nathaniel Cook) was officially selected as the F.I.D.E. standard.

**The mighty Pawn.**
KNOWLTON PHOTOGRAPH

Those rules and design of chessmen remain the standard to the present.

*Names of pieces in the dominant European languages. Meanings by number:*
*(1) Lady, (2) Fool, (3) Runner, (4) Standard Bearer, (5) Elephant, (6) Jumper,*
*(7) Horse, (8) Tower, (9) Boat, (10) Peasant, (11) no other meaning in the native*
*language. (Terms which are not numbered have the same meaning as*
*the English nomenclature.)*

| English | French | German | Italian | Spanish | Portuguese | Russian |
|---|---|---|---|---|---|---|
| King | *Roi* | *König* | *Re* | *Rey* | *Rei* | *Korol* |
| Queen | *Dame (1)* | *Dame (1)* | *Regina* | *Dama (1)* | *Dama (1)* | *Ferz (11)* |
| Bishop | *Fou (2)* | *Läufer (3)* | *Alfiere (4)* | *Alfil (11)* | *Bispo* | *Slon (5)* |
| Knight | *Cavalier* | *Springer (6)* | *Cavallo (7)* | *Caballo (7)* | *Cavalo (7)* | *Kon* |
| Rook | *Tour (8)* | *Türm (8)* | *Torre (8)* | *Torre (8)* | *Torre (8)* | *Ladya (9)* |

| English | French | German | Italian | Spanish | Portuguese | Russian |
|---|---|---|---|---|---|---|
| Pawn | *Pion* | *Bauer (10)* | *Pedone* | *Peón* | *Peão* | *Peshka* |
| Chess | *Échecs* | *Schach* | *Scacchi* | *Ajedrez* | *Xadrez* | *Shakhmaty* (Шахматы) |

# *Recreations*

## *The King and Pawns Game*

In the long and successful history of Western chess, various entertaining diversions have been tried by players of the standard game. We offer two pleasant samples here, which hail from historical sources. The following clever theme was already being practiced toward the end of the Middle Ages. It has been played with the modern moves since the 16th century. One player has only a King and the eight Pawns, but has the right to make two moves in each turn. In his double move, he is allowed to place his King in check in the first move, as long as he has removed it from check by the end of the turn. His opponent plays normally. Both players may promote Pawns according to the standard rules.

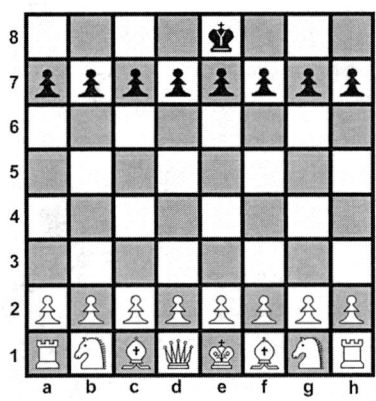

Initial array of the King and Pawns Game.

## *The Pawns Game*

In this game, attributed to Kermur Sire de Légal,[78] White gets eight additional Pawns instead of his Queen.

Initial array of the Pawns Game.

This game met with some success in France and several games have been recorded around 1850 between de la Bourdonnais and Deschapelles, two of the best chess players of their time.

The history of chess is very distinctly divided into three nearly equal periods of five hundred years. During the first, it was essentially unknown in Europe. In the second period, it spread throughout Europe, played by the Arab rules. Only in the last third was it played according to the modern rules with the Queen and the Bishop benefiting from much more powerful moves, bringing quicker engagement and heightened dynamics. This change intervened opportunely, at the right moment. It was fortuitous that chess was reborn just when the printing press was emerging. Without this lucky conjunction, this *chess of the mad Queen* may well have fallen into oblivion like so many variants.

◆ Part VI ◆

# Chess Out of the Box

The previous parts of this book have shown that chess is not a singular, uniquely conceived game, but a broad family of games which have developed quite differently throughout Asian and European civilizations. The game which is now recognized as "international" chess was born just over five hundred years ago as a new variant by a group of creative individuals, probably intent on making the game more fun to play.

As one might imagine, the creativity of chess enthusiasts did not stop there in Valencia, Spain, circa 1475. The quest for novelty, improvement and expansion was alive before the birth of modern chess, and was boosted into new realms of possibility when the modern game achieved its popularity. Beginning with augmented board sizes, possibilities progressed to alternative arrays, new board geometries, differently shaped cells, multiple players, and even expansions into the third dimension.

The world of chess variants is endless. Pritchard offers more than 1600 samples in his *Encyclopedia of Chess Variants*,[1] and the Chess Variants Pages on the Internet have several thousand entries. The quest for new chess creations lives on today, branching out into unlimited possibilities. Why not try inventing a six-player 3-D hexagonal shogi with some novel fairy chess pieces sprinkled in? Try it! It would be absolutely impossible to present all variations, even the most interesting, in the scope of this (or any) book. Indeed, new chess variants are created every day. While some players of the standard game shy away from the uncharted land of chess variants—or even view them with contempt as an intrinsically inferior distraction from the "real" game—significant changes are gradually taking hold. The active recreational variant, bughouse chess, can often be seen at chess clubs. The array-changing variant, Fischer Random (a.k.a., Chess960), has appeared in tournaments of the highest level. Rain Drop Chess, a commercial variant, has made inroads into the chess culture of Western Europe. And it should be noted that many excellent proprietary board games have appeared in the recent years, inspired by chess and rightly considered chess variants.[2]

Out of this ludic jungle, a few key developments deserve description. Some of these illustrate alternative directions that chess could have taken. Some are so often reinvented that it makes sense to show them in this book to give justice to the first creators and their string of recurrences. Finally, some must be included just because the authors find them truly exceptional.

# 33. Knighted Chess Variants

The mighty Queen combines Rook's and Bishop's powers. What if there were pieces combining the Rook and Knight on one hand and the Bishop and Knight on the other? This idea has repeatedly been proposed by a long succession of "inventors." The first documented case was an Italian, describing his novelty some 400 years ago.

## Carrera's Chess

In the 16th and 17th centuries, the world of chess was dominated by Italy. The peninsula hosted the very best players, who would fight over the board and over the printed page as well, each master publishing his own book, criticizing and disassembling the opinions held by his competitors. Among them was the priest of Syracuse, Pietro Carrera (1573–1647). He published *Il gioco degli scacchi (The Game of Chess)* in Militello, Sicily, in 1617, an enormous treatise compiling the full chess knowledge of his predecessors. In the last chapter of this treatise, he proposed a *gioco nuovo* ("new game") with a board extended to 80 squares and with the addition of two novel pieces. Here, little more than a century after the birth of a new *chess of the mad Queen*, was the first publicized variant to spin off from the new chess.

### Material

A rectangular 10 × 8 square board, each player's right-hand square being white. There are 20 pieces on each side: 1 King, 1 Queen, 1 Champion, 1 Centaur, 2 Bishops, 2 Knights, 2 Rooks and 10 Pawns.[3]

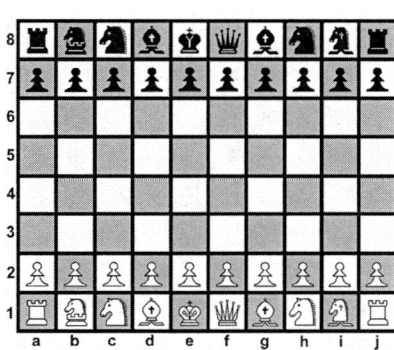

Initial array of Carrera's chess.

### Rules

The standard array is completed by two pieces standing between Rooks and Knights, a Champion on the King's side and a Centaur on the Queen's side.

*Centaur:* combines the powers of Bishop and Knight.

*Champion:* combines the powers of Rook and Knight.

In Carrera's time, the rules of castling, *en passant* capture and Pawn's promotion were not yet stabilized. Today, players are advised to follow all modern rules for this enlarged variant. In the case of castling, the King would always move two spaces toward the Rook.

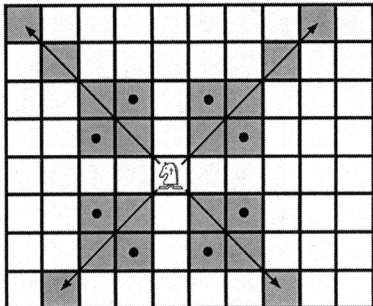 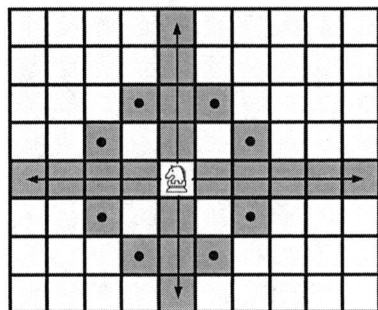

Moves of the Centaur (left) and the Champion (right).

The relative and normalized values of the pieces are: Queen (8.3), Champion (7.8), Centaur (6), Rook (5), Bishop (3.4), Knight (2.8), Pawn (1.2).

The Champion brings an elegant counterpoint to the Queen because it is nearly equal in power while allowing her to maintain her dominant position on the board. The Centaur is no less interesting: this piece alone has the unique ability to give mate without the assistance of other pieces.

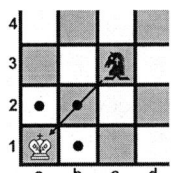

Better not to leave a King in the corner: the Centaur can mate him without any aid.

Apparently, Carrera's proposition did not meet with much success among contemporary players. Murray boldly wrote, "*The game never got beyond the book stage.*" For more than two centuries, the expanded board of ten files seemed to be forgotten. But things changed in the 19th century and Carrera's ideas resurfaced, with only slight modification or improvement. This has become the most-borrowed idea in the long history of chess, usually taken up with no knowledge or acknowledgment of its originator. Credit to Carrera is long overdue.

Sample realization of "knighted" Rook and Bishop (center), standing among standard Staunton chessmen.
KNOWLTON SPECIAL DESIGN AND PHOTOGRAPH

# *Related Early Chess Variants*

Other open-minded players followed Carrera, exploring further possibilities of an extended board and new forces in the lineup.

## Duke of Rutland's Chess

In 1747, John Manners, Third Duke of Rutland (1696–1779), proposed his own invention over a very large board of 10 × 14 squares. What is more, the best players of his time took an interest in trying and testing this new game. The English writer Richard Twiss reported that the game was presented in London to the French champion Philidor by Sir Abraham Janssen. In less than three months, Philidor was able to beat Stamma and Janssen, among other highly esteemed players, with a Knight handicap. In spite of its prestigious beginning, the Duke's grand variant did not last long, fading quickly in subsequent years.

For the Duke of Rutland's chess, each player has 28 chessmen including a Concubine, moving as Rook or Knight, and two Crowned Rooks, moving as Rook or King.

*Crowned Rook:* combines the moves of the Rook and the King.[4]

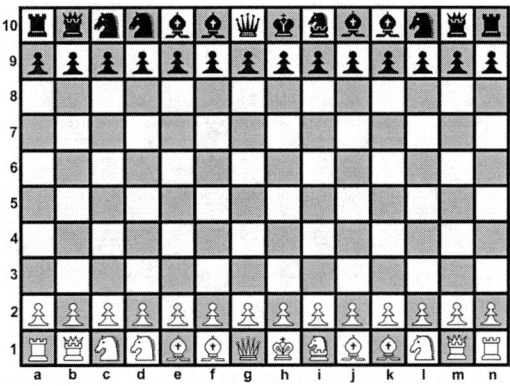

Initial array of Duke of Rutland's Chess (it is surprising to note the presence of four Bishops and three Knights in each camp whereas other combined pieces, such as Bishop + Knight, Bishop + King or Knight + King, are absent).

The Pawns may step one, two or three squares on their first moves. It is reasonable to assume that *en passant* capture was allowed when one Pawn moved through an opposing Pawn's square of capture. No more details such as Pawn promotion or castling rules (if they existed) have been recorded.

The piece value is as follows: Queen (8.1), Concubine (7.1), Crowned Rook (6.2), Rook (5), Bishop (3.3), Knight (2.2), Pawn (0.7).

## Gustav III Chess

If a Duke could invent a chess variant, then a King was all the more entitled to do so. Gustav III (1746–1792),[5] king of Sweden and prince of Finland, is credited with adding a seventh type of piece to the standard array. This magnificent piece combines the powers of Queen and Knight. Four of them—two on each side—are placed in the corners of the board. These "Adjutant-Generals" infused the field of battle with devastating power.

THE AMAZON. As the matter of fact, a piece combining the powers of Rook, Bishop and Knight (i.e., Queen + Knight) had already been investigated by early Italian masters. It is reported in a 16th century manuscript and also mentioned by Carrera who called the piece *Donnacavallo*. *Amazon* is another name under which this chess monster is widely known.

The apparition of the Amazon in a Swedish variant of the 18th century is perhaps not too surprising. Indeed, the existence of this piece on the eastern fringe of Europe was significantly documented during this epoch. The English historian, William Coxe, who traveled through Russia in 1772, reported that the players of that country added the Knight's power to that of the chess Queen. Richard Twiss (*Miscellanies*, London, 1805) mentioned a match between Philidor and the Turkish ambassador to London in 1795. The diplomat reportedly defeated the French champion because he was moving his Queen in the manner of the Knight "as in Russia." According to Coxe, Philidor declared that granting so much power to the Queen spoiled the game.[6] In 1821, Ivan Butrimov, author of the first technical chess manual, deplored this bad habit. King Gustav's Sweden was bordering Russia, and the shared idea of an enhanced Queen may have been more than coincidence.[7]

In order to play this historic Swedish game, four squares are added to the standard chessboard, beside the Rooks' squares. These squares get the new Adjutant-Generals or Amazons in the opening array.

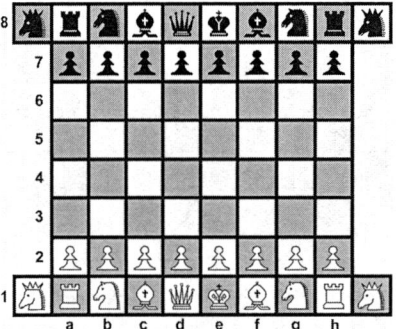

Initial array of Gustav III Chess.

All standard rules of chess are maintained. Pawns can be promoted to any piece, including Amazon, upon reaching the far side of the board.

 *Amazon:* combines the powers of Queen and Knight.

The relative value scale: Amazon (11.5), Queen (8.7), Rook (5), Bishop (3.1), Knight (2.9), Pawn (1.1).

The rules of this game, simply titled *Schackspel (chess game)*, appear in an ancient Swedish book of board games, *Hand-Bibliotek för sällskapsnöjen*, authored by Gustav Johan Billberg (1772–1844) and published in Stockholm in 1839.[8] Surprisingly, no historical testimony on this chess variant has come to light other than this one book that appeared so long after the King's death. The assertion of this game as an invention of the king himself is weakened by the lack of any boards, pieces or reports ever being discovered. Could Billberg, a scholar well aware of the pastimes of his own era, have "improvised" this historic recounting?

The Amazon has also been designated by other names in later times. It was an Angel for Louis P. d'Autremont (1918), a Commander for D. Trouillon (1953) or a Wyvern for Vernon Rylands Parton (1970)—only a few examples of this theme's enduring appeal.[9]

## *Tressau's Chess Variants*

A German book by Ludwig Tressau of Leipzig, *Das Schachspiel, seine Gattungen und Abarten* (*The Game of Chess, Its Types and Varieties*), appearing in 1840, has the distinction of being the first book ever dedicated entirely to chess variants. Its source was, no doubt, the book *Archiv der Spiele*, I–III, Berlin 1819–21, in which the rules of the Kaiser's Game were published in the first volume (1819). The anonymous author of *Archiv der Spiele* book did visit the inventor, a certain councilor Peguilhen in Berlin, who had invented this game a few years earlier, perhaps circa 1815. Peguilhen showed him both his original invention and a larger variant which was later to be named the Sultan's Game.[10] Both variants use the Knight-combined pieces.

THE KAISER'S GAME (*DAS KAISERSPIEL*). The *Kaiser's game* is played over a 10 × 10 square board with 20 pieces for each player. The pieces include the standard set augmented by an Adjutant (*Adjutant*) and a Commander (*Feldherr*).[11] The Adjutant combines Bishop's and Knight's powers. The Commander is an Amazon which combines powers of Queen and Knight.

Above: Das Schachspiel, seine Gattungen und Abarten (1840).

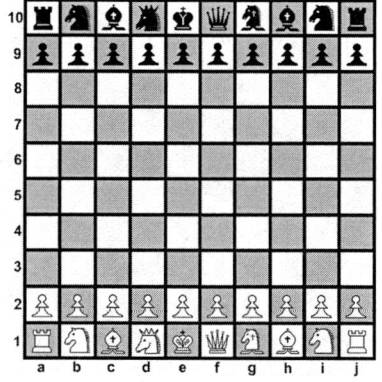

Initial array of Kaiser's Game.

Pawns may step up to three squares on their first move and *en passant* capture is extended accordingly, whenever a Pawn uses the double or triple step to pass through an opposing Pawn's square of capture. Pawns promote when reaching the opposite row of the board, but only to a piece which has previously been captured. The King castles by stepping three squares (King's side, landing on b1/b10) or four squares (Queen's side, landing on i1/i10) in the direction of the Rook, which moves itself the same number of squares toward the center of the row (landing on d1/d10 or f1/f10). Therefore, King and Rook do not finish castling on adjacent squares. Castling is subject to the standard restrictions.

Tressau places the Commander and the Adjutant respectively in d1/d10 and g1/g10; whereas, it seems that in the original source (*Archiv der Spiele*, 1819) the place of the Queen and the Commander were switched (Queen on d1/d10; Commander on f1/f10).

*The Sultan's Game (Das Sultanspiel)*. In order to incorporate a "Rook + Knight" piece, the Sultan's game has the board increased to 11 × 11 squares. Every corner square of the board is white. A Marshal (*Marschall*), combining the move of Rook and Knight, and an extra Pawn are added to the previously presented Kaiser's game. Because the board features an odd number of columns, the Bishop and the Knight at White's left (and Black's right) are inverted so the two Bishops are standing on differently colored squares. For castling, the King steps four squares in the direction of the Rook and the Rook steps four squares toward the center line (landing on e1, g1, e11 or g11). The other rules follow those of the aforementioned Kaiser's game.

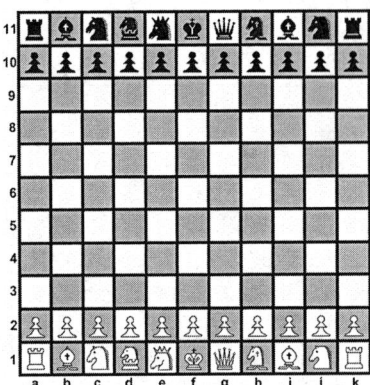

Initial array of Sultan's Game.

# In Carrera's Footsteps

Carrera chess contains a weakness which has been criticized by subsequent game developers: the Pawns in i2 and i7 are not protected in the starting array. This fact has motivated various schemes to alter the initial setup. In the following descriptions, unless indicated otherwise, the initial array for the White player is mirrored by the Black player.

## Bird's Chess

In the 1874 issue of the *City of London Chess Magazine*, the English chess player Henry E. Bird (1830–1908) proposed a 10 × 8 board with a "Rook + Knight," which he called a Guard, and a "Bishop + Knight," called an Equerry. At this point, Bird's idea was exactly like that of Carrera, except for the initial setup.

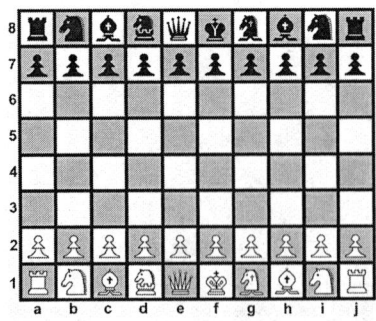

Initial array of Bird's chess.

Here, the new pieces are located near the royal pair. The Pawns on c2/c7 are still not protected in this arrangement; alas, Bird did not endeavor to correct the Pawn protection issue.

Pawns promote to any piece (other than King or Pawn). When castling, the King moves three squares toward the Rook and the Rook jumps over the King to stand beside him. All other rules follow those of regular chess.

Bird's purpose was to enhance the role of calculation and reduce the role of book analysis in play. He created several other variants in this vein, but did not make a great effort to promote any one in particular.[12] His lasting fame in the annals of chess history is derived from the development of the off-beat opening in standard chess, "Bird's opening": 1. f4.

## Chancellor Chess

Perhaps the introduction of two new pieces was too much. This is what the American Benjamin R. Foster thought when he announced, in the February 12, 1887, issue of the *St. Louis Globe-Democrat* newspaper, the creation of a new chess featuring a Chancellor which combined the moves of Rook and Knight, played over a 9 × 9 board (with black squares in the corners).

Two years later, he published a book simply titled *Chancellor Chess or the New Game of Chess*, dedicated to "*All Liberal-Minded Chess Players Throughout the World*" in which he detailed his new game and proposed a few problems. Foster made clear that he was aware of the "Chancellor" used by Carrera, the Duke of Rutland, Tressau,[13] and Bird. Foster's own conviction was that adding a piece combining the move of Rook and Knight would equalize the forces between the King's side and the Queen's side.[14]

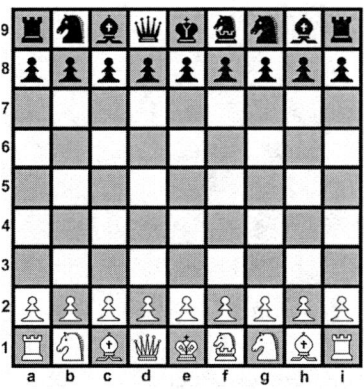

Initial array of Chancellor Chess.

All Pawns are protected in the initial array. To keep the Bishops on opposite-color squares, the Knight and Bishop positions in the g and h files are switched. Queens face Queens and Chancellors face Chancellors across the board. The King may castle to either side by moving two squares toward the Rook, which leaps over the King and stands beside him (e.g., White King goes to c1 or g1, Rook to d1 or f1). Pawns can also promote to Chancellor in addition to the standard options. All other standard chess rules apply.

## Capablanca's Chess

During his reign as world chess champion (1921–1927), the Cuban José Raúl Capablanca (1888–1942) was reported to publicly admit being concerned over too many draws in chess tournaments and, being really worried for the future of this sport—a sentiment often repeated by chess champions and spectators to the present day. Possibly inspired by H.E. Bird, Capablanca experimented with several setups with the "Rook + Knight" and "Bishop + Knight" in the early 1920s.

His first proposal was based on a 10 × 10 square board, but after play-testing with Edward Lasker[15] (1885–1981), he expressed preference for a 10 × 8 board, which offers a more rapid encounter. Capablanca and Lasker also tried several starting arrays, eventually selecting an arrangement in which the added pieces are placed between Bishops and Knights.[16]

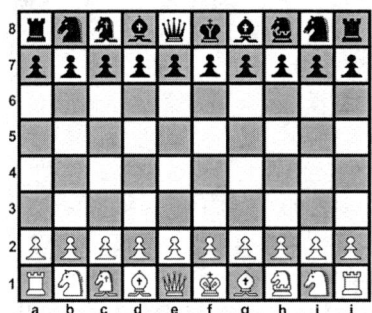

Initial array of Capablanca's chess.

The name adopted by Capablanca for the new pieces also evolved. The Bishop + Knight piece was at first a Chancellor but finally became an Archbishop. The Rook + Knight piece which began as a Marshal ended up designated as a Chancellor, a choice making it consistent with Foster's game (see above).

For castling, the King always moves three squares toward the Rook, with the Rook coming around to stand next to the King on the other side. Naturally, Pawns can also promote to Archbishop or Chancellor when reaching the last row of the board, along with the standard options. All other chess rules are kept.

This variant, carrying the gravity of Capablanca, the greatest natural chess genius ever known at that time, received widespread attention, but obviously failed in convincing the chess authorities to modify the standard game.

## Neo-Chess

Hugo Legler, several times California chess champion, picked up Capablanca's thread of chess game improvement, at about the same time. In 1923, he proposed "Neo-Chess"[17] with a Chancellor (Rook + Knight) and an Archbishop (Bishop + Knight) in place of the Queen-side Rook and Knight on a standard 8 × 8 square chessboard.

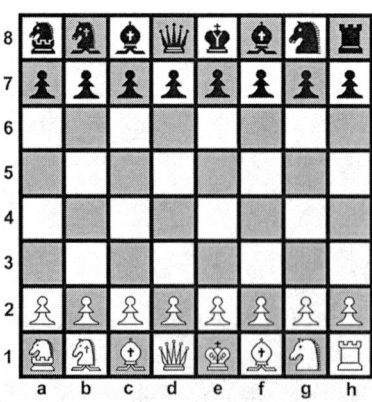

Initial array of Neo-Chess.

Pawn promotion is naturally extended to the two new pieces. It is not known whether the King was allowed to castle with the Chancellor, but it seems reasonable to allow that.

A tournament was organized and reported in the *American Chess Bulletin* of April 1923 by the journalist Leander Turney, who suggested placing the Archbishop on the King's side in order to balance the greatly empowered pieces.

## Coronation Chess

In the years 1924–1925, the American Frank Maus, invented several chess variants, seeking "the next permanent change in chess." His idea was to add the "knighted" pieces on the regular 8 × 8 chessboard by means of a specific move, the *coronation*, which consisted of moving an elementary piece (Rook, Bishop or Knight) onto the square of another one in order to meld them into a unique, stronger piece thus combining the powers of the two. For example, a player who has lost his Queen may "crown" a new one by combining a Rook and a Bishop.

Maus asserted that the coronation could become the main feature of the middle game, much as castling is associated with the opening and Pawn promotion with the end of the game. In developing his game, Maus experimented with several manners of play.

Curiously, what finally remained from Maus's work became his choice of names. He chose to call the Rook + Knight an *Empress* and the Bishop + Knight a *Princess*, maintaining a logical, feminine connection to the Queen. Chess problemists enthusiastically adopted this proposal, though it has been unaccountably ignored by subsequent chess variant inventors.

## Universal Chess

A game similar to Carrera's chess was again proposed in 1928 by Dr. Bruno Violet.[18] It makes use of the 10 × 10 square board and two possible opening arrays to offer some variety.

The names for the new pieces are Admiral (Rook + Knight) and Pilot (Bishop + Knight).

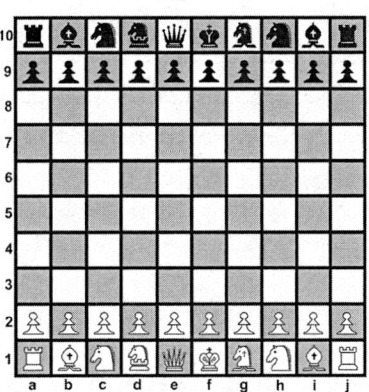

First option for Universal Chess initial array.

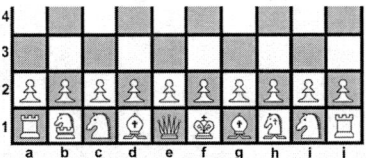

Second option for Universal chess initial array.

Remarkably, both initial arrays have all Pawns protected.

## Modern Chess

In 1980, a book appeared in Spain, *Evolución del Ajedrez* (*Evolution of Chess*), by the Puerto Rican author Gabriel Vicente Maura (1909–1990), which proved to be more than a mere presentation of chess history. In the first part of his book, the author reviews almost a hundred historic chess variants. In the second part, he presents a game of his own: "Modern Chess." His invention goes back to 1968, when he originally published a rather speculative mathematical "thesis" about chess which served to demonstrate that regular chess is not well balanced—a defect demonstrably corrected by Modern Chess.[19] Maura later noted that when he had devised Modern Chess he was not aware of Ben Foster's Chancellor Chess, invented in 1887 and presented above.

This variant experienced a degree of success, particularly in Spanish-speaking countries. The FEMDAM (*Federación Mundial de Ajedrez Moderno*, World Federation of Modern Chess) was founded in 1972 and international tournaments were organized in Spain (with the first world championship in Seville, 1976), Puerto-Rico, the Virgin Islands and Mexico until 1983, at which time the FEMDAM was dissolved, while Maura had fallen ill.

A 9 × 9 square board is used, with black squares at the four corners. The 18 pieces of each side are the standard set with the addition of a Minister, playing as a Bishop + Knight, and a complementary Pawn. Both players have a Queen to the King's right and a Minister to King's left. A Staunton-type design was invented for the Minister: tall as the Queen with a top hat. Sets were manufactured and commercialized.

Initial array of Modern Chess.

The rules are standard as much as possible. Pawns can naturally promote to a choice of Queen, Minister, Bishop, Knight or Rook. The Minister, which can give mate without assistance, represents a real alternative to the Queen. Castling is the same on both sides: the King moves two spaces toward the Rook, and the Rook moves around to stand next to the King. The resulting position is identical to "castling long" in standard chess. The conditions for castling are unchanged in regard to regular chess.

Federación Mundial de Ajedrez Moderno
World Federation of Modern Chess
Federation Mondiale des Échecs Modernes
Internationaler Moderner Schachverband
Всемирная Федерация Модных Шахмат

*Right:* The FEMDAM's official stamp (showing the shape given to the Minister).

BISHOP'S ADJUSTMENT. This is an original rule proposed as an option for players who do not wish to play with all Bishops on the same color of square as they are in the initial array. If both players agree prior to the start of the game, it is permitted during the game to switch the position of one Bishop with one adjacent piece (Queen, Minister or Knight)—only if neither of the switching pieces has yet been moved. This action can be performed only once for each player. It counts as one move.

## *Janus Chess*

This variant, also known as "*Super-Schach,*" was invented in 1978 by Werner Schöndorf. It met with noteworthy success, especially in Germany, as several chess grandmasters, including the great Viktor Korchnoi, played it and participated in some publicized tournaments.

The board has 10 × 8 squares with a white square in the corner to the players' right.

Each player has 20 pieces: the 16 standard ones plus 2 Janus pieces, moving as a Bishops or Knights, and 2 additional Pawns to complete the second row. In the marketed sets, the Janus was simply a Knight surmounted by a slotted Bishop's head.

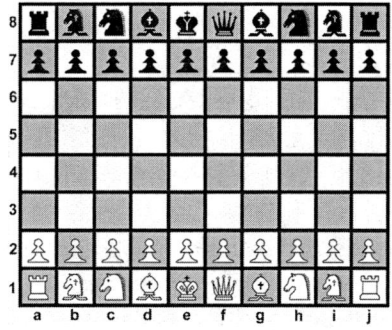

Initial array of Janus Chess.

The Queen starts on a square of her own color. Both Pawns standing before the Januses are unprotected in the initial array.

For castling, the King moves all the way to the square beside the Rook (moving 3 or 4 squares), and the Rook moves around to stand on the other side next to the King (the resulting position is the same as "castling short"). All standard rules of chess apply. The Pawn may promote to a Janus, in addition to the usual choices.

## *Tutti-Frutti Chess*

Curiously, Neo-Chess of the 1920s was nearly reinvented by two American chess-variants enthusiasts, Ralph Betza and Philip Cohen, in 1978 or 1979. Their "Tutti-frutti" or "Mixture" chess also includes the Amazon (Queen + Knight). Chancellor and Archbishop are respectively named Empress and Princess, agreeing with the preferred nomenclature of chess problemists. The array (a1 to h1 and a8 to h8) is Empress / Knight / Bishop / Amazon / King / Queen / Princess / Rook.

Pawns promote to any non–King non–Pawn piece of the same color. Kings may also castle with the Empress.

The normalized relative values of the pieces are: Amazon (11), Queen (8.2), Empress (7.8), Princess (6.3), Rook (5), Bishop (3.4), Knight (2.9), Pawn (1.4). The Pawn has a higher value relative to regular chess since it can be promoted into the powerful Amazon.

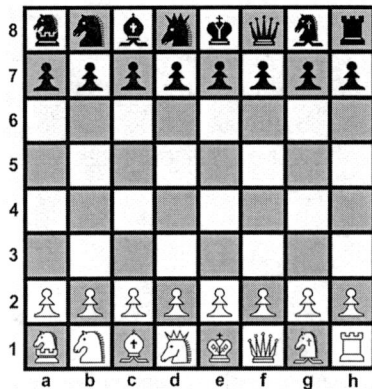

Initial array of Tutti-Frutti Chess.

Tutti-frutti chess has been played in postal competitions for several years following its invention.

## Grand Chess

In 1984, the prolific Dutch inventor Christian Freeling took a fresh look at this issue. Noting, with good cause, that none of the preceding variants was fully satisfactory, he proposed his own invention consisting of the Pawns' line starting one step forward, on the 3rd (for White) and 8th (for Black) rows of a 10 × 10 square board. All pieces except the Rooks also begin one step forward, leaving the Rooks in the back row, "connected" from the start of the game.

Here, the names chosen for the new pieces are Cardinal (Bishop + Knight) and Marshal (Rook + Knight)—avoiding the confusing name of Chancellor. Their given shape in a specially designed and commercialized set was simply a Knight surmounted by either a slotted Bishop's head or a crenelated Rook's top.

There is no castling because it would be useless in this game. The Pawn's initial double step and *en passant* capture are kept as in regular chess. Pawn promotion is optional on moving to the 8th or 9th rank and compulsory on moving to the 10th.

A Pawn can only promote to a piece of the same color which has already been captured. If no captured piece is available, a Pawn that has reached the 9th rank remains there, unable to move, until it can go on to the 10th rank and promote. While waiting for a possible promotion, the Pawn can still give check.

Initial array of Grand Chess.

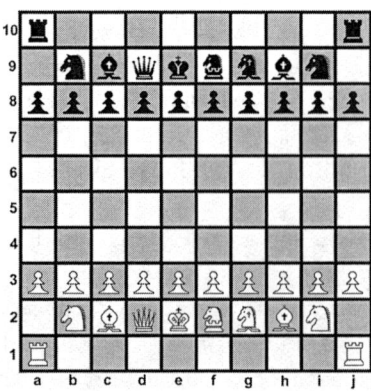

Grand Chess has genuinely renewed this family of variants, achieving notoriety in many books and magazines. An international tournament was organized on the occasion of the Chess Olympiad in Yerevan in Armenia in 1996. A "Grand Chess Corner" with games, problems and analysis was a regular feature of *Abstract Games*, an American magazine published by Kerry Handscomb, during the years 2000–2003.

## Gothic Chess

The American chess player Ed Trice also revisited Carrera's and Capablanca's chess in the years 1998–2000. In 2002, he patented his own creation, Gothic Chess.[20] A commercial development followed, with the creation of a specifically fashioned set and the organization of several international tournaments. A *Gothic Chess Computer World Championship* was organized in 2004. Ed Trice claimed to have solved several flaws present in previous setups; for instance, all Pawns are protected in the starting array, avoiding "Trice's mate," an equivalent of "fool's mate" transposed to Capablanca's chess.

The knighted pieces here are an Archbishop (Bishop + Knight) and a Chancellor (Rook + Knight).

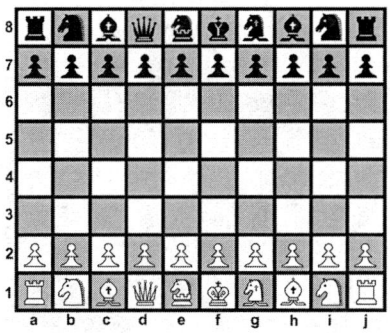

Initial array of Gothic Chess.

Castling is achieved by moving the King three squares toward either Rook and, on the same move, placing the Rook around next to the King. Pawns can promote to any piece other than Pawn or King when reaching the opposite side of the board. Basically, all standard chess rules are maintained.

The Hungarian-American woman world chess champion Susan Polgar has been reported playing Gothic Chess. In 2006, an improbable match between Fischer and Karpov in this variant was announced, but it never took place. Ed Trice claimed to have sold 50,000 boards and sets, but more recently, the interest in this game seems to have declined and the dedicated website was no longer available after 2012.

The elegant Staunton-derived pieces created for the Archbishop (left) and the Chancellor. REYKJAVIK II EDITION, HOUSE OF STAUNTON, © 2006 FRANK A. CAMARATTA, JR.

## Embassy Chess

Embassy chess, created in 2005 by Kevin Hill, is another variation of Capablanca's game. Played on a 10 × 8 square board, the starting array (White's side, also mirrored by Black) is Rook, Knight, Bishop, Queen, King, Marshal (Rook + Knight), Cardinal (Bishop + Knight), Bishop, Knight, Rook.

This arrangement has the same order as Freeling's Grand Chess, though adapted on a narrower board.

In castling, the King moves three spaces and the Rook comes around to stand beside him. This game can be played on the Internet at brainking.com.

## Seirawan Chess

Finally, the American chess grandmaster Yasser Seirawan also proposed a game he developed with his friend Bruce Harper in 2007. The novelty is that both knighted pieces are introduced to the chessboard in the course of play. This variant uses the standard 8 × 8 board and starts with the initial array of regular chess. The new pieces here are named the Hawk, for the Bishop + Knight, and the Elephant, for the Rook + Knight.[21] Among various promotional activities for this game, Yasser Seirawan has given simultaneous exhibitions.

RULES. Each player begins with one Elephant and one Hawk, which will be introduced while the game is in play. When a player moves any piece other than a Pawn, for the first time, either the Elephant or Hawk may immediately be placed in the vacated square.

Placement of the Elephant or Hawk may not be used to block check. When castling, the player may place an Elephant or Hawk on the space vacated by the King or Rook, but not both in the same turn. If all pieces in the back row have been moved, and the player has not seized the opportunity to place the Elephant or Hawk on the board, he forfeits the opportunity to place the special piece (or pieces) for the rest of the game.

Pawns may also promote to Hawk or Elephant when reaching the end of the board.

Seirawan pieces created to accommodate a standard Staunton style tournament chess set: the Elephant (left) and the Falcon (courtesy Yasser Seirawan).

Seirawan's and Harper's decision to keep their variant on a standard 8 × 8 board offers many advantages. The relative value of the pieces is not affected, no additional Pawns are needed and the structure of play remains familiar. And, of course, there is no need to procure a special 10 × 10 or 10 × 8 board and thus standard chess players are not so disoriented.

In the words of the inventors, *"the placement of the pieces on squares vacated by the existing pieces changes the game and creates innumerable possibilities which render all existing opening theory open to reexamination and opens up many new possibilities as well. Players who understand the principles of opening play will do well, while players who rely primarily on memorizing variations will find themselves in trouble."* A clever suggestion has been made to change the name of the game to "Sharper chess," a combination of the names Seirawan and Harper. However, the name Seirawan Chess is holding well, thanks to the grandmaster's widespread recognition.

## *Review of Knighted Variants*

The following table gives a quick review of the identities taken on by the Rook + Knight and Bishop + Knight pieces over the centuries. The list is far from exhaustive.

### *Four centuries of names given to the Rook + Knight and Bishop + Knight*

| Chess Variant | Year | Rook + Knight | Bishop + Knight | Queen + Knight |
|---|---|---|---|---|
| Carrera's | 1617 | Champion | Centaur | — |
| Duke of Rutland's | 1747 | Concubine | — | — |
| Gustav III's | 1839 | | | Adjutant-General |
| Sultan's Game | 1840 | Marshal | Adjutant | Commander |
| Bird's | 1874 | Guard | Equerry | — |
| Chancellor Chess | 1887 | Chancellor | — | — |
| Capablanca's (1) | 1920s | Marshal | Chancellor | |
| Capablanca's (2) | 1920s | Chancellor | Archbishop | |
| Neo-Chess | 1923 | Chancellor | Archbishop | |
| Coronation Chess | 1924 | Empress | Princess | — |
| Universal Chess | 1928 | Admiral | Pilot | — |
| Modern Chess | 1968 | — | Minister | — |
| Janus Chess | 1978 | — | Janus | — |
| Tutti-frutti Chess | 1978 | Empress | Princess | Amazon |
| Grand Chess | 1984 | Marshal | Cardinal | — |
| Gothic Chess | 2000 | Chancellor | Archbishop | — |
| Embassy Chess | 2005 | Marshal | Cardinal | — |
| Seirawan Chess | 2007 | Elephant | Hawk | — |

# 34. Fairy Pieces on Board

Possibly the largest category of game variants ever investigated is the realm of *fairy chess*. These games include pieces with entirely novel moves and move concepts. More than a hundred samples were patiently collected by Pritchard. Here are a few exemplary games, highlighting historic developments and modern possibilities.

## *Earliest European Augmented Chess*

### *Arciscacchiere*

Francesco Piacenza (1637–1687), doctor of law and diplomat from Naples, was a chess player of great renown—if one can judge his prowess by accounts in his treatise, *I campeggiamenti degli scacchi (The Basics of Chess),*[22] published in Turin in 1683. There he introduced his *arciscacchiere*, intent, like Carrera before him, on improving chess. The novel pieces betray a certain nostalgia for the Roman Empire.

The game is played on a decimal (10 × 10) chessboard, with a white square in each player's right-hand corner. Each side has 20 pieces: 1 King, 1 Queen, 1 Centurion, 1 Decurion, 2 Bishops, 2 Knights, 2 Rooks and 10 Pawns.

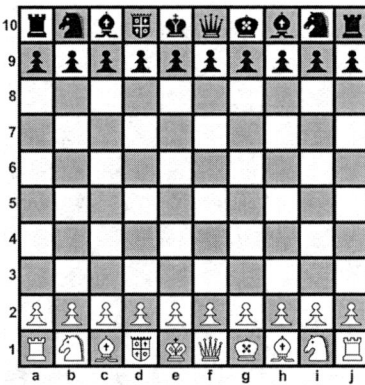

Initial array of arciscacchiere.

RULES. The additional pieces:

*Decurion:* steps diagonally one square, identical to the move of the medieval Queen.

*Centurion:* may step two squares horizontally, vertically or diagonally providing the intermediate square is free. In addition, it can leap like a Knight.[23]

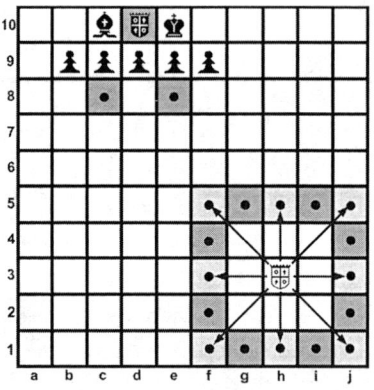

Moves of the Centurion.

The Centurion on h3 shows the full range of the Centurion's move, able to reach any of the light gray squares if unobstructed, or to leap to the dark gray squares, regardless of any piece standing in its way. The Centurion on d10 shows the piece as it is in the opening array, with only two possible moves.

Piacenza did not provide other rules specific to this game. It may be supposed that they follow those he gave for regular chess.[24] Castling is free according to the Italian fashion of the time in which the King may move to any of the vacant squares between King and Rook, and the Rook moves around the King to any spot up to the King's square of departure. Pawns promote only to Queens.

The normalized relative values of the pieces are: Queen (8.2), Rook (5), Centurion (3.9), Bishop (3.4), Knight (2.5), Decurion (1.4), Pawn (0.8). Like other Italian authors of the time, Piacenza could not resist the temptation of using his book to promote his own invention which could, he thought, renew the game. It is almost certain that Piacenza's variant was influenced by Carrera's example.

## "Enlarged and Improved" Chess

Perhaps because they found the standard game lacking in character, some inspired Northern European players also tried expanding the game as early as the end of the 17th century, when chess was barely approaching its adolescence.

The game that follows is anonymous but comes to us from a Dutch edition of a treatise by Greco, placing the date of its invention circa 1696.

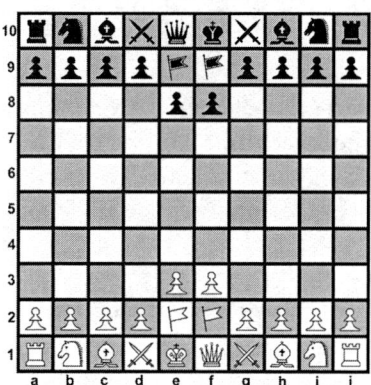

Initial array of "Enlarged and Improved Chess."

The board is the decimal 10 × 10 squares again and there are 22 pieces for each player. These are the novelties:

*Guard:* moves like a Rook but captures like a Bishop.

*Ensign*: moves like a Bishop but captures like a Rook.

The Kings do not face each other in the initial arrangement (standing on e1 and f10).

No details have been recorded about castling, the Pawn's initial move, *en passant* capture or promotion.

## So-Called "Spanish" Chess

This variant appeared in a German work dated 1739. It was said to have been played in Spain but the assertion has not been corroborated. The game may well have been invented in the Leipzig area, where the account of this game was first published.

The board has 10 × 8 squares. Each player has 20 pieces including two Archers, hybrids of the Rook and Bishop.

*Archer:* moves any number of free squares on three directions: straight forward or diagonally backward. It may not jump over any pieces in its way.

This new piece is slightly stronger (2.8) than the Knight (2.7).

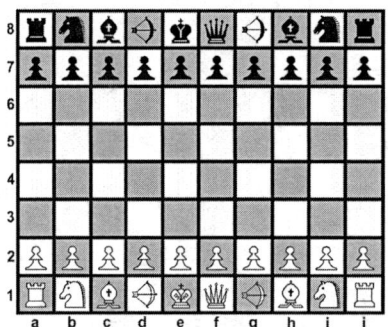

Initial array of "Spanish" chess.

Castling rules have not been recorded. It may be assumed that Pawns can promote to Archers as well as the standard choices.

## Ciccolini's Chess

In a book titled *Tentativo di un nuovo giuoco di scacchi* (*Attempt at a New Game of Chess*), printed in Rome in 1820, Giuseppe Ciccolini also proposed modifications to the game of chess.

On a 10 × 10 board (with a white square at each player's right corner) he added two Elephants, two Generals and two Pawns and removed the Bishops which, according to his judgment, didn't "have an activity enough to render the game proportioned" for this enlarged board.

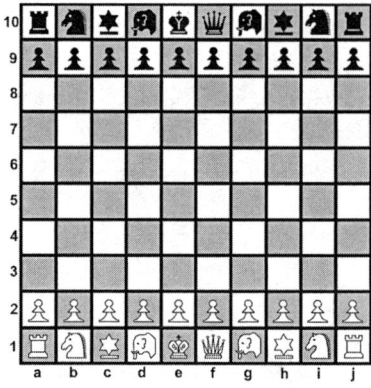

Initial array of Ciccolini's Chess.

*Elephant:* jumps like a Knight extended one further step diagonally, continuing along in the same direction. Like the Knight, this allows a move of eight possible directions and a change of square's color at every move.[25] It may leap over any pieces in its path.

*General:* moves like a Queen that is confined to a single color of squares. On the diagonals, its moves like a Bishop. On the rows and columns however, it is only allowed to land on a square of the same color as its starting square. The squares it passes over must all be vacant—it never leaps over other pieces.

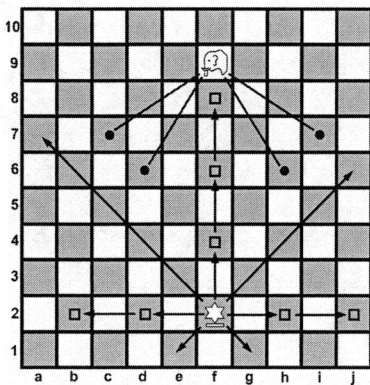

Move of the new pieces proposed by Ciccolini. The Elephant on f9 prevents the General from reaching f10.

White moves first. The Pawn can step up to three squares on its first move. It also maintains the right to step two squares if its first move took it only a single square forward. Ciccolini said that all other rules of the "antique game" were conserved.

In accordance with the conventions that prevailed in early 19th century Italy, it is supposed that the Pawns cannot capture *en passant*. Also, the Pawn that reaches the opposite side of the board promotes to a piece that has been previously captured. Castling is free, which means that the King can come to any square in the direction of the Rook while the Rook can go as far as the initial square of the King.

The relative values computed with Zillions-of-Games software are: Queen (8.2), General (5.3), Rook (5), Knight (2.5), Elephant (2), Pawn (0.7). Ciccolini had a different view: he overestimated the Elephant (judging it almost as valuable as the Rook) and slightly underestimated the General (valuing it at half a Queen).

## Courier-Spiel

In 1821, H.G. Albers of Lüneburg (Lower Saxony, Germany), proposed a reformation of the old courier chess by modernizing the moves of several pieces.

Albers introduced the modern Queen in place of the medieval one. He kept the Courier (which lends its name to the game) moving as the modern Bishop, but the old *Aufin,* or Archer, a diagonal jumper (essentially the medieval form of the Bishop), was renamed *Bishop* and had its power increased. On the Queen's side, the Jester (originally German *Schleich),* which moved one step orthogonally, was replaced by a Fool now moving one step in all directions. On the King's side, the old Sage (originally German *Mann*), which moved one step in all directions, was augmented to a Counselor that could also leap as a Knight.

Initial array of Courier-Spiel.

*Bishop:* different from the modern chess Bishop. This one steps diagonally one or two squares, leaping over the intermediate square if it is occupied.

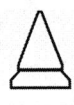 *Courier:* moves exactly like the modern Bishop.

 *Fool:* moves one step in every direction, like the King but is not limited by check.

 *Counselor:* moves one step in any direction (like the Fool) or leaps like a Knight.

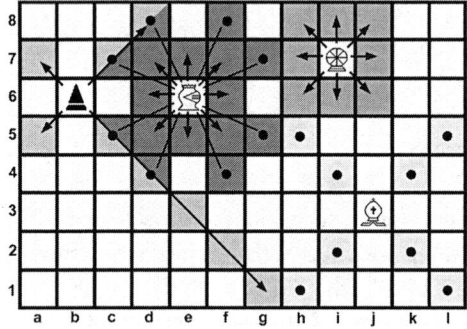

Moves of Courier, Counselor, Fool and Bishop.

Pawn, Rook, Knight, Queen and King keep their orthodox moves, including the double initial step for the Pawn.

The Pawn gets promoted to any piece (other than Pawn or King) when it reaches the far side of the board, but must remain on that square for two full turns. The promoted value is effective, and may move only on the third move and thereafter.

Castling is forbidden if the King is in check or if one of the squares between the King and the Rook is under threat, even if the King would not cross that square. For castling, the King moves three steps (to c1/c8) on the King's side) or four steps (to j1/j8) on the Queen's side, and the Rook comes around the King, landing in the square next to him (arriving in the d or i file).

The scale of relative values for the pieces is: Queen (7.9), Counselor (5.6), Rook (5), Courier (3.1), Fool (3), Bishop (2.5), Knight (2.5), Pawn (0.6).

The legacy of courier chess has fascinated more than one inventive chess player over the centuries. Albers was followed by several others who also introduced the modern Queen to the 8 × 12 board. Some have received a fair amount of attention in circles of chess variant enthusiasts.

The English FIDE Master Paul Byway proposed a "Modern Courier Chess" in 1971; it received regular coverage with reports of games and analysis in the British magazine *Variant Chess* from 1992 to 2010. In its final form, his variant has "Couriers" (c1 and j1) leaping two squares orthogonally or diagonally, modern Bishops (d1 and i1), a Fers (e1 and h1) stepping one square diagonally, a Queen (f1) and a King (g1). An unmoved Fers can leap like a Courier, but not to capture. An unmoved King can make a double move to a vacant square with the same restrictions as castling in chess. This move replaces the regular castling.

In 2011, this was reconsidered by the French Clément Begnis with his "Reformed Courier-Spiel." With valuable critiques of Byway's rules, Begnis proposed a return to Albers's game with only minor changes. Albers's Bishop was renamed an Archer, recalling that this was the German identity of this piece in the old courier chess; the Fool and the Counselor were now called Champion and Paladin respectively. Like Byway, he put the Kings on g1/g8 square (Albers had them on f1/f8). The Champion was enhanced with the move of a King (not subject to check) or a jump two squares orthogonally over anything intervening. All other pieces kept their moves according to Albers. Finally, castling and Pawn promotion were given modernized rules similar to those prevailing in standard chess (castling with King moving four squares toward the Rook, to c1 or k1 and Rook jumping over to d1 or j1). Begnis's Reformed Courier-Spiel is an excellent revision of the fascinating old courier chess.

*Comparison of the different courier chess adaptations, using Parlett's move notation*[26]

| Initial square (White side) | Historic Courier Chess | Albers's Courier-Spiel | Byway's Modern Courier Chess | Begnis's Reformed Courier-Spiel |
|---|---|---|---|---|
| f1 | King | King | Queen: n* | Queen: n* |
| g1 | Queen: 1x | Queen: n*  King | King | |
| e1 | Sage: 1* | Counselor: 1*, 1/2 | Fers: 1x | Champion: 1*, 2+ |
| h1 | Jester: 1+ | Fool: 1*  Fers: 1x | Paladin: 1*, 1/2 | |
| d1, i1 | Courier: nx | Courier: nx | Bishop: nx | Courier: nx |
| c1, j1 | Archer: 2x | Bishop: 1x, 2x | Courier: 2* | Archer: 1x, 2x |
| b1, k1 | Knight: 1/2 | Knight: 1/2 | Knight: 1/2 | Knight: 1/2 |
| a1, l1 | Rook: n+ | Rook: n+ | Rook: n+ | Rook: n+ |

# *Modern Fairy Chess*

Countless chess inventions have followed the pioneering variants presented above. It is the fate of chess variants to recede quickly into oblivion, unknown or even dismissed with ridicule by the following generation. Yet, new inventors continue to challenge the status quo, usually ignorant of the legacy of ingenious ideas that have gone before. Acquaintance with Pritchard's final work, *The Classified Encyclopedia of Chess Variants*, is recommended for a grand view of the many games that have come before. Following are a few selected games, chosen to illustrate the continuing surge of chess evolution.

## *Falconry*

This is a large variant played over the 10 × 10 square board, with a black square at each player's right corner. It was invented in Leningrad (now St. Petersburg again) in 1982 by four Russian authors: Boris Troshichev, Vasily Varkentin, Oleg Skaletsky and Yuri Rybakov.

Each player has 24 pieces. There are three pairs of new characters: the Princes, the Falcons and the Dolphins. In the mind of the creators, these were meant to bring representatives of air and water elements to the field. The Falcon gives the game its name: Falconery or стоклеточные (*Stokletochnye*) in Russian. In order to mark the new pieces distinctively, these novel chessmen are blue on the White side and red on the Black side.

 *Dolphin:* moves and captures orthogonally one, two or three squares (like a limited Rook). It may leap over occupied squares, but only when not capturing.

*Falcon:* may leap like an extended Knight's move, three squares in an orthogonal direction plus one step at a right angle (like the Camel in Timur's great chess). It may also move one, two or three squares diagonally, without jumping over occupied squares (like a limited Bishop). The Falcon is a color-bound piece (always landing on squares of the same color).

*Prince:* has an augmented Pawn's move. It steps one square in one of the three forward directions, straight forward or diagonally forward. On his first move, the Prince may advance two squares in the same three forward directions, provided the intervening square is unoccupied. The Prince captures like the Pawn, seizing an opposing piece standing one square diagonally forward. He promotes to Dolphin or Falcon.

Initial array of Falconry.

A Pawn may capture an opposing Pawn or Prince *en passant* which has just taken a double step through the Pawn's square of capture. Castling is possible only between the King and a Rook (never with a Dolphin), under the orthodox conditions.

When reaching the farthest row on the board, a Pawn is promoted to Queen, Bishop, Knight or Rook, at the choice of the player. A Prince that reaches the farthest row may be promoted to a choice of Falcon or Dolphin. There is no restriction on the number of pieces, so a player may have two Queens or three Falcons, etc.

The normalized scale value obtained with Zillions-of-Games is: Queen (8.2), Falcon (5), Rook (5), Dolphin (4.6), Bishop (3.4), Knight (2.6), Prince (1.2) and Pawn (0.8). However, Rybakov opined that the Dolphin should rank between the Bishop and the Knight. A curiosity is a very fast fool's mate in only two moves: 1 Fe5 f7 2. Fg7 mate.

Material for this game has been manufactured and sold on a scale of a few thousand sets. According to its promoters, Falconry achieved a remarkable success in Russia and neighboring countries.[27]

# Shako

Here is a game that deliberately incorporates several elements of the diverse heritage of chess into a single, modern game. All rules of orthodox chess are maintained, and the opening array allows players to follow nearly all of the openings used of standard chess. One new piece is borrowed from Chinese xiangqi, with the intention of joining the two branches of the chess family, east and west. A second new piece is derived from shatranj and medieval chess, bridging this game with its prestigious past. The design of Shako was completed in 1990.[28]

## 34. Fairy Pieces on Board

Initial array of Shako.

Shako is played on the "decimal" board of 10 × 10 squares. Each player commands 22 pieces: the standard set with two additional Pawns, two Cannons and two Elephants.

*Cannon:* when not capturing, it moves just like the Rook. But to capture a piece, there must be one additional piece in its path which the Cannon leaps over before landing on the piece being captured. This intervening piece may belong to either player. The cannon may not jump over more than one piece to make its capture, and may not jump over pieces when not capturing.[29]

*Elephant:* steps diagonally one or two squares, leaping over the intermediate square if it is occupied.[30]

All other pieces move as in orthodox chess, including castling. Pawns promote on the tenth row of the board to the player's choice of Queen, Rook, Knight, Bishop, Elephant, or Cannon. All other rules are precisely as in standard chess. White has the first move.

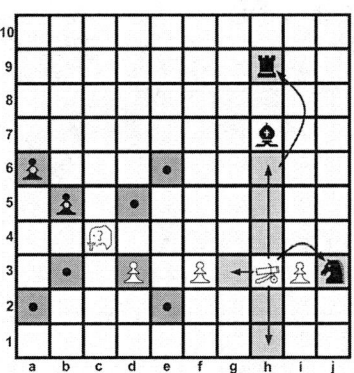

The Elephant (c4) may move to any of the squares shown with black dots. It may capture either of the black Pawns on b5 or a6. The Cannon (h3) may reach all grayed squares. It may capture the black Rook (h9) or the black Knight (j3).

The relative values are: Queen (8), Rook (5), Cannon (4.9), Bishop (3.2), Knight (2.7), Elephant (2.6), Pawn (0.9). It is possible that Zillions-of-Games software overestimates the Cannon's strength.

*Right:* A Shako set. CAZAUX PHOTOGRAPH

# Wildebeest Chess

In 1992, R. Wayne Schmittberger, strategy game expert and inventor of many, declared: "*This game is my attempt to balance the number of riders—pieces that move along open lines—with the number of leapers—pieces that jump directly to a square a certain distance away, regardless of what intervenes.*" Here is his chess variant, played over a large board of 11 × 10 squares with 22 pieces per player: the 16 standard ones, plus 2 Camels, 1 Wildebeest and 3 additional Pawns.[31]

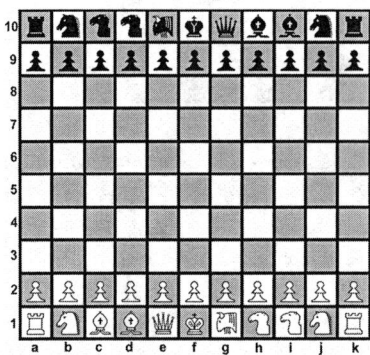

Initial array of Wildebeest Chess.

The classic pieces keep their orthodox powers, with the exception of the Pawn, which is allowed to move up to three squares on its first move. It also maintains the right to step two squares if it has stepped a single square or made a capture as its first move. A Pawn may be captured *en passant* if it uses its double or triple step to pass by an adverse Pawn's square of capture. Pawns can be promoted to either Queen or Wildebeest upon reaching the opposite side of the board. There are no other choices.

The large size of the board favors the efficiency of the long leapers. While the Camel is a historic piece, well known to ancient Persians and Arabs (see Timur's Great Chess), the Wildebeest is much less frequently encountered on the chessboard.

*Camel:* leaps three squares in an orthogonal direction, plus one step at a right angle, like an extended Knight's move. It may jump over any intervening pieces.

*Wildebeest:* combines the moves of the Knight and the Camel.

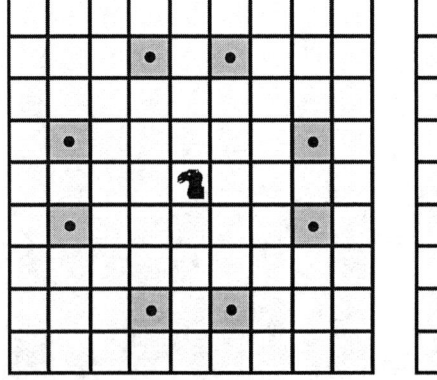 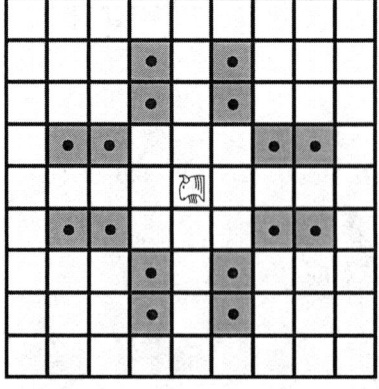

Moves of Camel and Wildebeest.

Castling obeys the same restrictions found in standard chess, but offers more flexibility. The King may step one, two, three or four squares toward either Rook, and the Rook moves around the King, landing on the square next to him.

The end-of-game rules are the same as those of standard chess.

The relative values are: Queen (8.2), Rook (5), Wildebeest (4.7), Bishop (3.3), Knight (2.4), Camel (2.1), Pawn (1). Schmittberger opined that the Wildebeest is stronger than the Rook. This would be true on an 8 × 8 board, but it is arguable here because the Rook gains in strength on the over-size 10 × 11 board.

Wildebeest Chess is a well-balanced game. Simple and logical, it remains a model of a judiciously conceived chess variant for all inventors.

## Omega Chess

Self-proclaimed as "the next evolution of chess," this variant was invented by Daniel C. MacDonald in 1998. It has garnered a degree of success with the organization of several international tournaments and the endorsement of International Grandmaster Michael Rohde, the Chess 'n Math Association, the Hungarian Chess Federation and Australia's Chess Central. Grandmaster Judit Polgár was recorded playing the game against Alex Sherzer in 1999. Specially designed boards and pieces have been marketed for this game.

The board is a specifically configured arrangement of 10 × 10 squares with four extra squares in the corners. All pieces can play on these extensions except the Rooks and the Pawns, which have no way of reaching them.

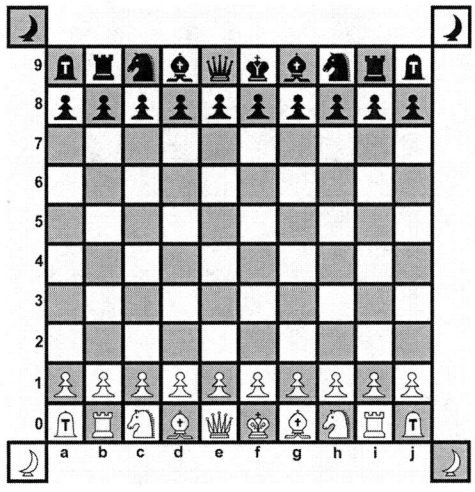

Initial array of Omega Chess. Note that MacDonald's choice for the notation of this game has the ranks numbered 0–9, rather than 1–10.

Each player has 22 pieces: the standard set plus two supplementary Pawns and two pairs of new pieces which have a combined move.

*Champion:* may step one square orthogonally (forward, backward or to either side) or it may leap two squares either orthogonally or diagonally in all eight directions.

*Wizard:* leaps like an extended Knight's move three squares in an orthogonal direction, plus one step at a right angle (like a Camel in Wildebeest Chess). It may also step one square diagonally. The Wizard is a color-bound piece.

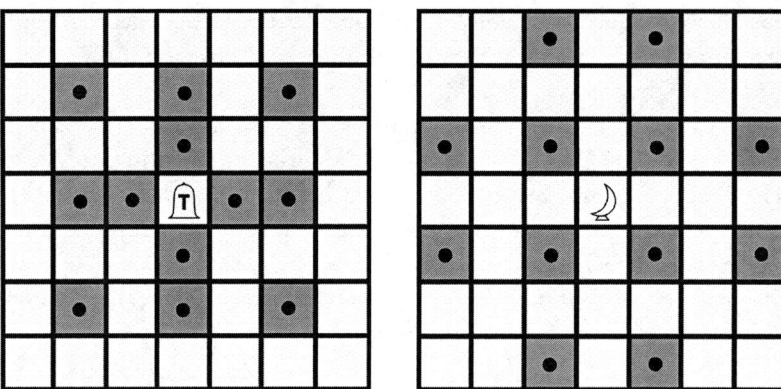

Moves of Champion and Wizard.

The other pieces move exactly as in classical chess except for the Pawn, which may step one, two or three squares forward on its first move; after that, only one square at a time. A Pawn cannot move one square initially and then two squares in a later move (as it does in some variants). *En passant* capture is possible whenever a Pawn passes through an opposing Pawn's capture square, either by a double or triple step. Apart from this, the Pawn's rules remain standard. A Pawn can be promoted to Wizard, Champion, Queen, Bishop, Knight or Rook.

The Champion (left) and the Wizard of Omega Chess.
CAZAUX PHOTOGRAPH

The piece value scale computed by Zillions-of-Games is Queen (8.3), Rook (5), Champion (4), Wizard (3.6), Bishop (3.5), Knight (2.4), Pawn (1). MacDonald disagrees and considers the Bishop slightly superior to the Champion and the Wizard. Time will tell whether Omega Chess can continue to gain popularity. An International Omega Chess Federation was founded in 2007.[32]

## *Metamachy*

In ancient times, the number twelve was a symbol of perfection. This number is omnipresent in this chess variant as it constitutes the number of rows, of lines, of Pawns, of different types of pieces and of possible starting arrays.

The name of this game comes from the Greek μετάμαχια, "beyond the battle." It is played on a 12 × 12 square checkered board. Three horizontal lines divide the board into four equal parts: the central line (the *equator*) and the lines marking the initial camps (the *tropics*). These marks do not affect the moves of the pieces, but they are convenient for setting up the pieces and incidentally enforcing the board's correct orientation with the white square in the right-hand corner. The lines also lend the board a unique aesthetic character.

## 34. Fairy Pieces on Board

There are 60 pieces of twelve different types: each player has 1 King, 1 Queen, 1 Eagle, 1 Lion, 2 Princes, 2 Bishops, 2 Elephants, 2 Knights, 2 Camels, 2 Rooks, 2 Cannons and 12 Pawns. The King is the main piece, whose forced capture is the goal of the game.

The twelve types of pieces used at metamachy. Back row: King, Queen, Lion, Eagle, Rook, Cannon; front row: Pawn, Camel, Knight, Elephant, Bishop, Prince.
CAZAUX PHOTOGRAPH

Kings, Queens, Bishops, Knights and Rooks move as in standard chess, except for castling, which is not allowed in metamachy. Elephants and Cannons move exactly as in Shako (see above). Camels move as in Wildebeest Chess (and Timur's chess). Pawns present a small, but essential difference. Eagles, Lions and Prince have not been described previously.

 *Pawn:* steps one or two squares forward. If it moves two squares, the first square must be empty. It may move two squares from any row on the board. The arrival square must be empty because the Pawn does not capture as it moves. It may capture an enemy piece standing one square diagonally forward, like a standard Pawn.

 *Eagle:* steps one square diagonally, and then continues any number of squares horizontally or vertically. It may not jump over any pieces in its way and must always start with the diagonal step.[33] The Eagle is a strange piece with a move full of surprises. In fact, to get back to the square where it started, it must take a different path.

 *Lion:* steps one or two squares in any direction. It may reach any of the eight squares that surround it or jump to the second square orthogonally, diagonally or as a Knight, leaping over any occupied squares. The Lion is a mighty piece, which can mate without assistance.

 *Prince:* may move one step to any of the eight surrounding squares, like a King but not limited by check. Also, like the Pawn, this Prince may step two squares forward if the first square and the arrival square are unoccupied. He may not capture with this double step.

 *Elephant:* steps diagonally one or two squares, leaping over the intermediate square if it is occupied.

 *Cannon:* when not capturing, it moves just like the Rook. But to capture a piece, there must be one additional piece in its path which the Cannon leaps over before landing on the piece being captured. This intervening piece may belong to either player. The Cannon may not jump over more than one piece to make its capture, and may not jump over pieces when not capturing.

 *Camel:* leaps three squares in an orthogonal direction, plus one step at a right angle, like an extended Knight's move. It may jump over any intervening pieces.

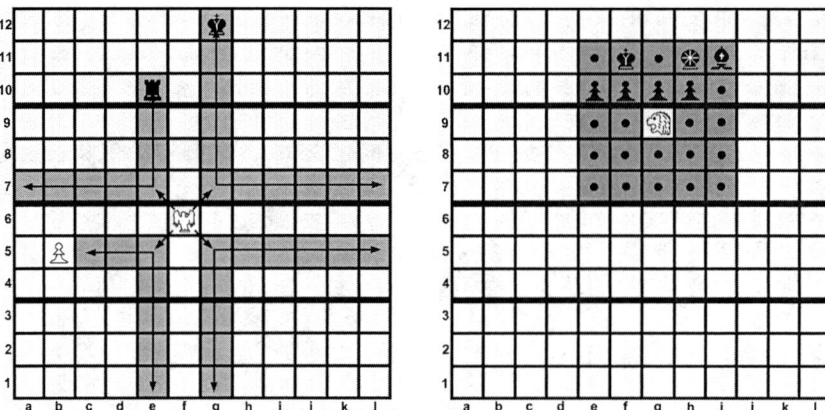

Moves of Eagle and Lion.

A CHOICE OF TWELVE STARTING ARRAYS. A fundamental characteristic of metamachy is the choice of opening arrays. The game begins in this manner:

- Black selects the starting array (detailed below) and places his pieces accordingly.
- White follows by placing his own pieces in position to mirror Black's.
- White then makes the first move.

The choice of a starting array is part of Black's strategy, intended to compensate for White's advantage of first move.

The starting position is fixed for the Pawns and the "Officers": Camels, Canons, Elephants, Rooks, Knights, Bishops and Princes. However, the arrangement in the center with the King and the three most powerful pieces—Eagle, Lion and Queen—is free for Black to choose. The four central squares on each side remain to be filled (f1, f2, g1, g2 for White; f12, f11, g11, g12 for Black). The King may be placed on any of these four squares. On his side, on the same row, one of the three major pieces, Queen, Eagle, Lion, can be placed. The two remaining pieces are placed on the other row. Therefore, there are $4 \times 3 \times 2 = 24$ possible starting positions.

Initial array of metamachy. The 4 x 4 center is vacant for the free setup of the King, Queen, Eagle and Lion.

White must follow Black's lead in the placement of the central pieces, with similar pieces facing each other in a mirror-like configuration. Note that, although there are 24 possible opening arrangements, half of these possibilities are simply left-right transpositions of the same thing—

so, theoretically, there are 12 possible opening configurations, not counting those which are simple mirror-image reversals.[34]

PARTICULAR RULES. • *Pawn and Prince Promotion:* a Pawn or a Prince reaching the last rank of the board is immediately replaced by a Queen, an Eagle or a Lion. Promotion to any other type of piece is not allowed. It is permitted to promote a Pawn or Prince to a type of piece already present on the same side; however; it is considered "good etiquette" to avoid choosing a piece which is not captured yet, if possible. Note that the Pawn must take at least five moves to reach promotion (taking double steps on rows 3–5–7–9–11–12), which is the same number of moves required for a Pawn in standard chess (rows 2–4–5–6–7–8).

- En Passant *capture:* Any time a Pawn or Prince takes a double step and passes through the capture square of an opposing Pawn, that Pawn may capture the Pawn or Prince as if it had only moved one square. This *en passant* capture must be made in the immediate move following the double step. Only a Pawn may capture *en passant*; the Prince does not have this option.

- *The King's jump:* as his first move, the King may jump to a free square at two squares' distance. For instance, from f2, it can jump to d1, d2, d3, d4, e4, f4, g4, h4, h3, h2 or h1). It does not matter if the square jumped over is occupied or not; however, the jump is forbidden if that intermediate square is threatened by an enemy piece. When jumping like a Knight, at least one of the two intermediate squares must be free of threat (e.g., if jumping from f2 to h3, either g2 or g3 must not be under attack). The King's jump is not permitted if the King is in check. This rule, which was once prevalent in medieval European chess, replaces castling.

The end-of-game rules, checkmate, stalemate, etc., are identical to standard chess.

RELATIVE VALUES OF THE PIECES. With the usual reservations regarding numerical values of pieces, the following scale of strengths can be observed as a guideline: Queen (9), Eagle (8), Lion (7.5), Rook (5), Cannon (3.5), Bishop (3.5), Prince (3), Knight (2.5), Elephant (2.5), Camel (2), Pawn (1).

The larger board benefits the Bishops, which have a longer range of penetration in contrast to Knights, whose scope proves to be relatively more restricted.

Metamachy ready to play.
CAZAUX PHOTOGRAPH

# 35. Chess and War

In earlier times, chess simulated a battle with foot soldiers, cavalry, elephants and war chariots. But with the presence of Rooks, Bishops and Queen, it lost some of that seminal military spirit. So, the idea has again crossed the minds of some creative players: how to simulate war over a board?

Not surprisingly, the first attempts appeared amidst a strong militaristic movement of 17th century. As early as 1644, Christoph Weickhmann presented, in the city of Ulm, a *Grosses Königs Spiel* (*Great King's Game*). Two players faced off over a huge board of 13 × 15 squares, engaging a total of 58 pieces with military names. This earliest attempt is so complex that its full description would exceed the capacity of this book.

## *Le Jeu de la Guerre*

A much simpler game was published for the first time in Prague (Czech Republic) in 1770, in French and in German, by a mysterious *M.M.*

The board has 11 × 11 squares with black corners. Each of the two players has 25 pieces whose names have been revised. There are 1 King, 2 King's Guards (Queens), 2 Dragoons (Bishops on white squares), 2 Hussars (Bishops on black squares), 2 Cuirassiers (Knights), 5 Cannons (Rooks) and 11 Fusiliers. The Fusilier is an improved Pawn, which steps one square orthogonally without capturing, or captures one square diagonally in any direction. The Fusilier has no initial double step, and does not promote. There is no castling. Except for these changes in names and specific rules, the game proceeds as in standard chess.

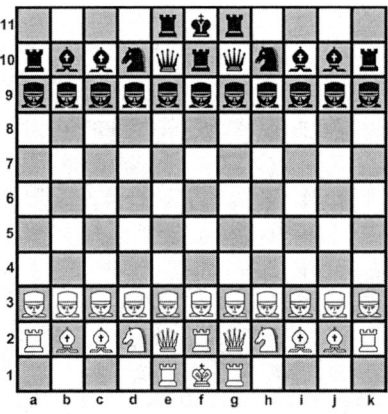
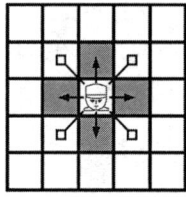

*Left:* Initial array of the "Jeu de la Guerre."

*Above:* Moves of the Fusilier (gray squares) and captures (marked by small squares).

## *Il Giuoco de la Guerra*

Ever more realistic and complex *Kriegsspiele* (war games) were developed by army officers, such as the *Kriegsspiel* of Johann Christian Ludwig Hellwig (1780), mathematician and advisor to the Duke of Brunswick. It was played on a giant 1617-square board of 49 ranks by 33 files with terrain features.

The *Giuoco de la Guerra* (*Game of War*) from the Italian Francesco Giacometti was a simplified version. Appearing in 1793, this game was played by two opponents over a board of 27 rows and 12 files (324 squares). Each side had 34 units that could be freely placed on the board

(1 King, 1 General, 1 Standard Bearer, 2 Commandants of Cavalry, 8 Knights, 3 Commanders of Infantry, 12 Soldiers, 4 Cannons and 2 Mortars), but also some immobile pieces (12 ditches, 6 bridges), to be disposed over the board before play commenced.

Later, Giacometti judged his game too long, and published a second version in Genoa in 1801, bearing a flattering dedication to the "Great general, First Consul of the French Republic, Napoléon Bonaparte"! This time, the board was reduced to 153 squares (17 × 9), plus two citadels whose capture constituted the goal of the game. With this revised objective, the game no longer included Kings. Each player had 26 units (1 Chief General, 1 Lieutenant-General, 1 General of Cavalry, 3 Generals of Infantry, 4 Knights, 10 Soldiers, 4 Cannons, 2 Mortars) and 16 immobile pieces (8 ditches, 4 bridges and 4 scales). Giacometti also proposed versions of the rules for three or four players in a booklet, with detailed handling of these features drawn out to 100 pages— as if it were an actual military manual.

It is not known if the future French Emperor paid any attention to these Italian or German martial games. Probably not. These creations pushed the desire to bridge chess and war nearly to the point of absurdity. Chess was certainly inspired by the battlefields in its debut, but the confrontation always remained symbolic, never realistic, and no chessboard can pretend to simulate any field of battle faithfully.

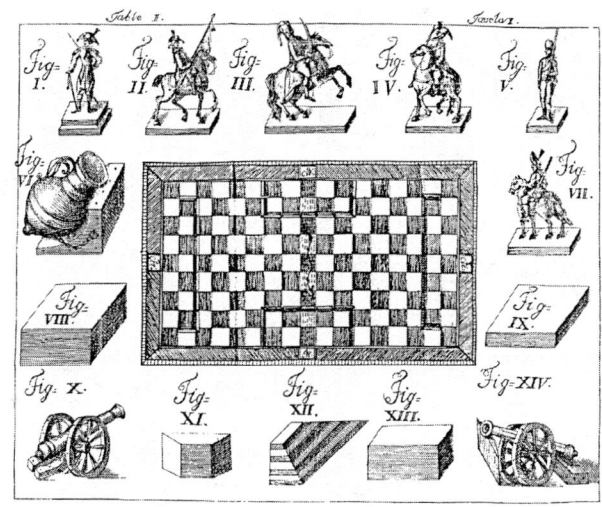

Artwork illustrating Giacometti's *Jeu de la Guerre* (1801).

## So-Called "Prussian National Chess"

In 1806, the General Baron Freyherr von Hoverbeck from Breslau (today Wrocław, Poland), modified M.M.'s "*Jeu de la Guerre.*" He inverted and reappointed the Hussars (Knights) and the Cuirassiers (Bishops on black squares). He removed three Cannons (Rooks) and replaced them with an additional Hussar (Knight) on f2 and two Batteries on e1 and g1.

Initial array of Prussian National Chess (the full board is 11 x 11).

The Battery moves like a limited Queen, up to three squares only. Its capture mode is original: it takes an enemy piece situated in the same direction and range of its move but it need not actually move to capture. It can land on the square of the captured piece or it may stop before it; it may even capture without moving from its position.

When one player puts the other in check, it is mandatory to clearly announce "check"; otherwise the attacking piece is removed as a penalty. There is no castling.

This "Prussian National Chess" was dedicated to the Prince Friedrich Wilhelm of Prussia.

## Silberschmidt's Game

Later, in 1827, Hans Silberschmidt presented this chess game, placing another type of Pawns on the front row that were less powerful than the Fusiliers. He restored the Knight's move to the Cuirassiers and the Hussar's identity to the piece moving as a black-square Bishop. The pieces on e1 and g1 became Royal Guards which play as Queen + Knight. The eleven Soldiers on the third row move one step forward or sideways and capture one square diagonally forward.

This third variation prolonged the success of German military chess for several more years.

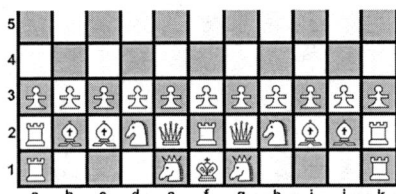
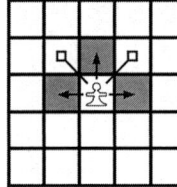

Left: Initial array of Silberschmidt's Game (the full board is 11 × 11).

Right: Moves of the Soldier (gray squares) and captures (on the marked squares).

It is interesting to draw a parallel between these chess variants and the creations of the Hindu Maharajahs, presented earlier in this book. Both were conceived at almost the same period. They maintain an unrivaled stature as precursors of the numerous war games that have flourished in our modern times.

# 20th Century Military Chess

Many subsequent chess variants were directly inspired by warfare. *Victrix,* invented by A.N. Petrov (1928), set two groups of 30 pieces opposing each other over a decimal (10 × 10) chessboard. In addition to the classic pieces, renamed according to a military vocabulary, it had Tanks, Batteries and Airplanes with new powers.

*Wehr-Schach* (a.k.a. *Tak-Tik*), by Rudolf Kuch (1938), had some success in Germany before and during World War II. The board had 11 × 11 squares representing a battlefield with a river, two lakes and a highway. The 18 pieces of each camp included Panzers, Artillery and Air Force.

*Chess-Battle* (A.S. Yurgelevitch, 1933, 128 squares, 2 sets of 24 pieces) and *Military Chess* (V.P. Grachev, 1958, revised in 1988, 12 × 12 squares, 2 sets of 24 pieces) are further examples.

*Commander Chess (Cờ Tư Lệnh),* by Vietnamese war colonel Nguyễn Quí Hải, is played on the intersections of a board of 11 × 12 interections, with markings distinguishing land, sea and a river. With disc-shaped pieces, similar to those of Chinese chess, this very complex game attempts to recall the military strategies gleaned from combat during the American-Vietnamese war of the 1960s and 1970s. With exceptional governmental support and media coverage, the game has been making its way into schools and military academies. Information can be found at ancientchess.com/commander-chess.

It is probably not fortuitous that these martial games appeared in countries and periods such as Third Reich Germany, Soviet Russia and post-war Vietnam, each in various stages of celebrating their military prowess.

Wehr-Schach Tak-Tik displayed in the Nuremberg Toy Museum.
CAZAUX PHOTOGRAPH

## *Stratomic*

This had to happen! Nuclear nonproliferation is a serious policy issue upon which the state of the world depends. But alas, among countries, and in the world of chess as well, dissemination of nuclear weaponry is the reality. It began very early, in 1947, only two years after the bombing of Hiroshima, that Transjordan's Minister of Agriculture, Nassah Bey Taher, invented "Atomic Chess." Upon promotion, the Pawn becomes an Atomic Bomb able to move in the eight directions, jumping over any number of pieces. The Bomb then explodes, destroying all pieces, friend or foe, at a distance of one to six squares (the board has 12 × 12 squares). If the opposing King appears among the victims, the bombed player may "crown" another piece to replace the deposed monarch. Tanks (playing twice as a Knight) and Aeroplanes (playing like a flying Queen) complete the lineup of this game's modern arsenal.

In 1973, the Canadian International Chess Grandmaster, Duncan Suttles, invented "Bomb Chess," a recreation in which Queens are Bombs, which move like Kings and destroy all pieces on the eight surrounding squares.

But the game that best symbolizes this terrifying invention is undoubtedly Stratomic, invented by the French player Robert Montay-Marsais in 1972.[35] A pair of *Nucleas* is added to the standard set on a 10 × 10 board.

Initial array of Stratomic.

*Nuclea:* moves like a King, can capture and give check in any direction, and can itself be captured by other pieces. It can also make a move called a "launch" which is detailed below.

All standard orthodox rules of chess are maintained, including castling and *en passant* capture. Pawn promotion is obtained on the 2nd and 9th row respectively, not on the 1st and 10th. Pawns may be promoted to any type of non–King pieces, including a Nuclea.

THE LAUNCH. The Nuclea may be "launched," which counts as one move: it is picked up and placed on any other square on the board, whether or not that square is occupied. The target square and all pieces adjacent to it (an entire 3 × 3 square) are "blown up"; all pieces being removed, friend and foe alike. This includes the Nuclea itself which has consummated its mission.

Only the Kings are immune to the explosion. A Nuclea may target the square occupied by the King itself, thus removing all pieces surrounding him. A Nuclea strike may create an immediate check or mate situation if it happens to remove the King's defenders or any other screening pieces.

There are two conditions which must be met in order to launch the Nuclea:

- The Nuclea must not be under threat. (If an opposing piece has a direct line of attack on it, it is assumed is that the launcher cannot be safely deployed.)
- The Nuclea launch must follow an "escalation" protocol: it cannot occur until the first capture of a piece other than a Pawn has been made.

The "nuclear threat" adds a subtle element to the game's strategy. One should pay attention not to group too much strength in one area and bear in mind the threat of a ballistic attack.

Stratomic set.
CAZAUX PHOTOGRAPH

# 36. Round Chess

This is a very old idea that flourished at the earliest stage of chess development in the Muslim lands, erroneously named Byzantine chess. It has been revived over the past century with modernized moves and has met with enviable success. The round board is sometimes manufactured as an elegant piece of furniture. It offers a pleasant game, quite different from standard chess.

# Circular Chess

## Material

The board is made of four concentric circles of sixteen "squares" each, with checkered colors. Kings and Queens are set in the inner circle, with Queens standing on squares of their own color. This detail establishes the main difference with the Byzantine setup in which both Kings would have been on white squares. The King's side is to White's left and Black's right.

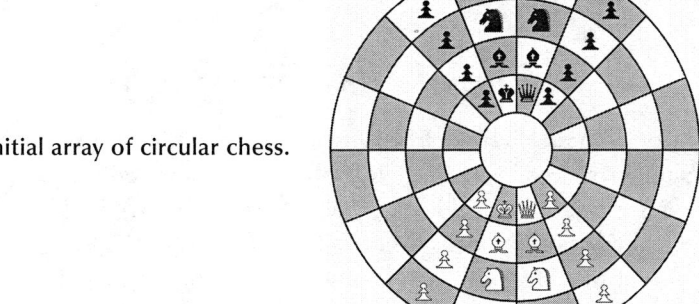

Initial array of circular chess.

It should be noted that this circular board is topologically equivalent to the surface of a deformed cylinder.

## Rules

All standard rules of chess are maintained on the circular board as much as possible. It is forbidden to move a piece around the board, landing on the same square from which it started. This rule prevents Queens or Rooks from making a null move by simply circling the board.

There is no castling. There is no *en passant* capture, although Pawns can make an initial double step. Pawns move straight forward, moving around the board. They get promoted when they reach the starting squares of the opposing King, Queen, Bishop, Knight or Rook, six steps away from their initial square, just as they do in standard chess.

The pieces' values are strongly affected by the form of the board. Rooks are empowered in comparison to Bishops which become less mobile. Keeping the Queen to 9 (roughly its value in standard chess), Zillions-of-Games software gives the following relative values: Queen (9), Rook (6.9), Knight (2.4), Bishop (2.2), Pawn (0.9).

## History

Circular chess is not a modern innovation. We have already described a 10th century round chess (*shatranj al-muddawara*) that Muslim authors formerly attributed to the Byzantines, although this game was likely of Persian origin. Though probably never rising beyond a mere curiosity, the circular board was not entirely unknown to medieval Europe: Forbes and Murray report a diagram drawn in a 13th century English manuscript.[36]

The 19th century saw a revival of interest for this board and the associated game, especially in Germany and England. George Hope Verney reported a round chess played with modern moves in his book *Chess Eccentricities* (1885), erroneously attributed to Timur by the German author Dr. Netto (*Das Schachspiel*, Berlin, 1827). Thereafter, it was briefly mentioned in several chess books up to modern times. Inspired by a drawing of Byzantine chess that he had seen in an old book,[37] the English author Dave Reynolds, defined and fixed a set of modern rules for circular chess in 1983. With the help of some friends, he began playing it regularly at a pub in Lincoln, England. In 1996, Reynolds founded the "Circular Chess Society," which has organized a World Championship since that date, in England.

The circular board has also been implemented in multiple-player variants (more than two opponents) which are presented further in this book.

# Cylinder Chess

The origin of cylinder chess is rather obscure. A cylindrical board was investigated by Teodoro Ciccolini, Marquee of Guardiagrele, who wrote a study book about the chess Knight, *Del Cavallo delli Schachi*, printed in Paris in 1836. Since then, the idea has resurfaced several times to the present day, notably with chess problemists.

The idea is quite simple. One has only to imagine that the chessboard is wrapped around a cylinder, with the a-file adjacent to the h-file.

## Material

Standard chess equipment is used. The players understand that moves proceeding off the right edge of the board continue by entering in on the left edge and vice-versa. So, a1 is understood to be adjacent to h1, a2 to h2, etc.

For instance, if White opens with 1. d4, Black may play 1. ... g5 and declare "check," since Black's Bishop has a clear path to h6, then continues over the edge of the board to a5 and all the way to e1.

An alternative representation, perhaps clearer because it embraces the full game's area in one glance (though with considerable distortion), is to flatten the cylinder in order to get a round board.

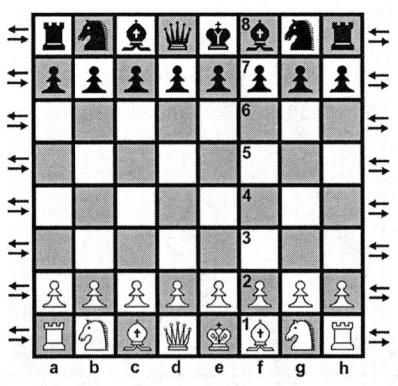
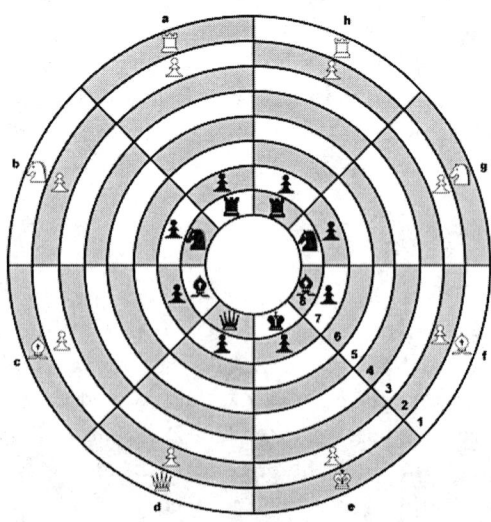

*Above:* Initial array of cylinder chess played on a square board. *Right:* Initial array of cylinder chess as it appears on a round board.

## Rules

All pieces move and capture as in standard chess.

A move that would not alter the overall situation on the board, i.e., starting and finishing in the same spot, is forbidden. This would occur, for instance, if a Queen or Rook were to completely circle the board.

All other rules, including castling, are maintained.

Knights lose power relative to the other pieces, in comparison to regular chess. Zillions-of-Games software gives: Queen (9), Rook (5.4), Bishop (3.7), Knight (2.8), Pawn (0.9).

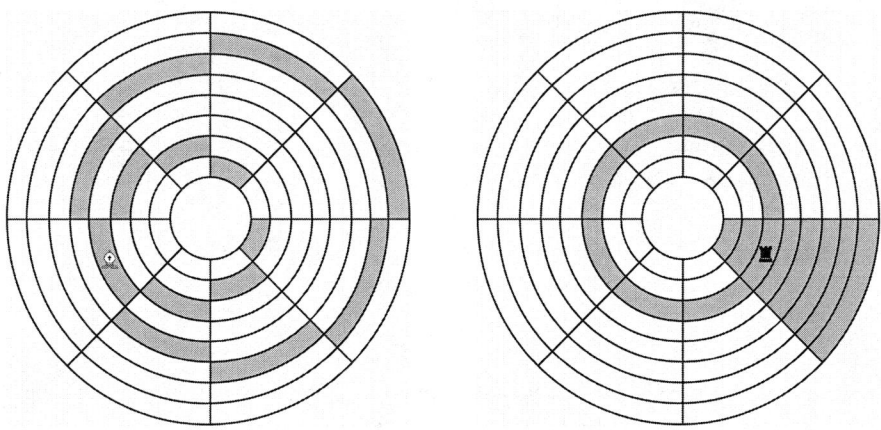

The Bishop's (left) and Rook's (right) path in cylinder chess.

The Bishop's move is particularly surprising. When observed on the round board, it looks like a spiral going from the outer ring to the center. A proprietary version of this game, *Noble Celts,* has a board with these spiraling diagonals actually drawn onto the playing surface. In this commercialized edition, the elongated, curved squares of the circular board are replaced by round dots. This gives the *Noble Celts* board a very different look, but it remains topologically the same as the circular boards shown in this chapter.

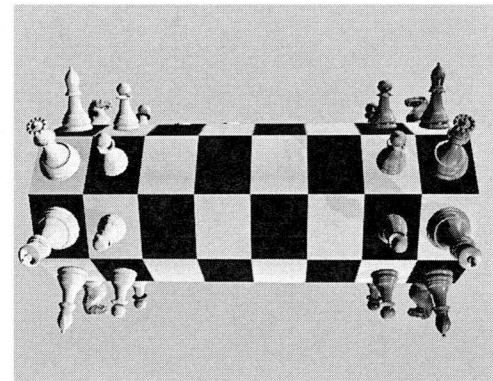

The most direct way to visualize the cylindrical board—though not very practical for actual play—is to imagine a standard chessboard curved around so that the right and left edges (a and h files) meet, thus creating a perfect cylinder. This computer-generated 3-D representation of the game can actually be played with at Jocly.com.

# 37. Hexagonal Chess

The hexagon is, along with the square and the equilateral triangle,[38] the other regular polygon that can uniformly tile a plane. This cell shape brings two major novelties: first, three colors instead of two are necessary to checker the board; second, the move possibilities are theoretically increased as the cells have now six faces and six corners instead of four.

A few years before World War II, Władysław Gliński established the basics of a comprehensive "hexagonal chess," opening this new dimension in chess possibilities. His initial investigations received little notice from subsequent inventors who, attracted by the increased possibilities of hexagons over squares, set out in their own directions. In the meantime, the hexagonal lattice became a standard feature for the development of many modern "war games" which certainly have a shared influence with chess variant creations. Pritchard reported about 40 different hexagonal chess variants in the second edition of his encyclopedia. In addition, the hexagonal tiling has turned out to be an excellent solution for three-player (and six-player) chess variants.

## *Gliński Hexagonal Chess*

Among all various hexagonal chess forms that have been proposed so far, the most successful is undoubtedly that invented by Gliński. It is presented here first, followed by other proposals with details as to how they differ from Gliński's game.

### *Material*

The board is of a hexagonal shape composed of 91 hexagonal cells (called "hexes"). Each side of the board has six cells. A hexagonal tiling needs three colors for its checkering. The most often used are black–white–red or black–white–gray.

Each player has 18 pieces: 1 King, 1 Queen, 3 Bishops, 2 Knights, 2 Rooks and 9 Pawns.

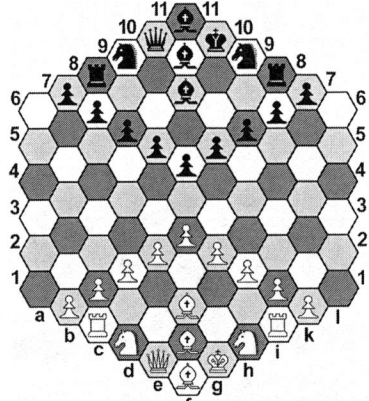

Initial array of Gliński's hexagonal chess.

### *Rules*

MOVES AND CAPTURES. By analogy with the classical squared chessboards, the orthogonal move is defined as a move crossing the sides of the hexes. The diagonal move travels along the

## 37. Hexagonal Chess

line between hexes, joining cells sharing the same color, which are not actually adjacent. Therefore, a piece moving diagonally is in fact leaping, not sliding.

*King:* moves only one hex toward one of the twelve possible directions: six orthogonal and six diagonal. The arrival cell must not be under the threat of an adverse piece. In the case of the diagonal step, the adjacent cells are not an obstacle. This diagonal step allows a rather fast pace for the King.

*Rook:* moves any number of free hexes in one of the six orthogonal directions (crossing the sides of the hexagons). It may not jump over any pieces in its way.

*Bishop:* moves any number of free cells in one of the six diagonal directions. Therefore, the Bishop leaps and always stands on hexes of the same color. It may not jump over any pieces on its path but the pieces located on adjacent hexes of different colors are not an obstacle.

*Queen:* moves any number of free cells in one of the six orthogonal or one of the six diagonal directions, combining the move of the Rook and the Bishop.

*Knight:* leaps chaining a diagonal step to an orthogonal step, continuing away from its hex of departure (see illustration). It always lands on a hex of a different color from its starting spot. The Knight freely leaps over any pieces in its path.

*Pawn:* it normally steps one hex forward. It may capture an enemy piece standing at one of the adjacent cells obliquely forward. It is important to notice that the Pawn's capturing move is also orthogonal (like a Rook's step) and not a diagonal Bishop's step (different, therefore, from regular chess).

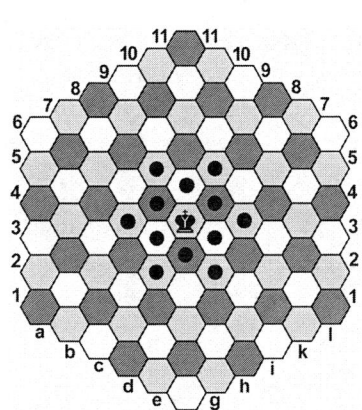
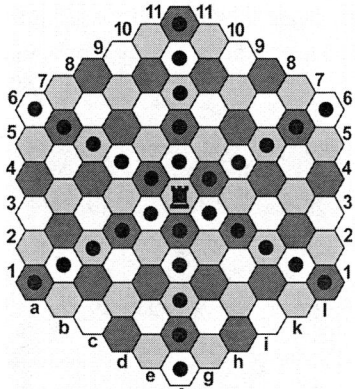

Moves of King and Rook.

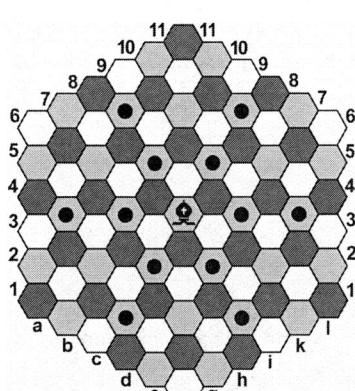
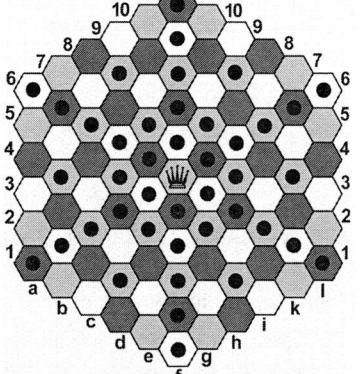

Moves of Bishop and Queen.

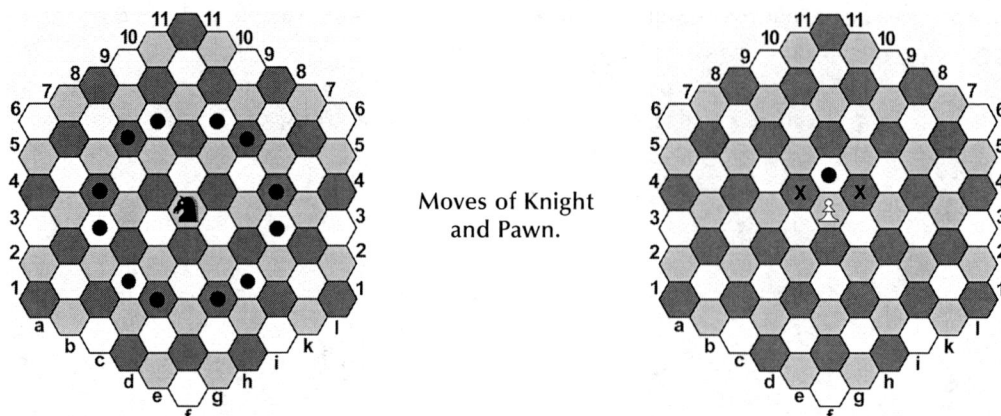

Moves of Knight and Pawn.

It may be noted that in the starting array, the Queen has one open line and the center Bishops (f2 and f10) have two.

Also remarkable is that the Knight is able to move and still threaten a cell that it was threatening before its move.

PARTICULAR RULES. • *Pawn Promotion:* a Pawn reaching the opposite side of the board (which includes 11 cells) can immediately be replaced by a Queen, Bishop, Knight or Rook of the same color at the choice of its player.

- *Pawn's Double Step:* a Pawn, standing on an initial Pawn's hex of its own side, can step one or two hexes, at the choice of its player, if the intermediate hex is unoccupied. This is the case for the Pawn's first move, but also applies when a Pawn is, after making a capture, on the initial hex of a neighboring Pawn. This rule prevents the players from having to remember whether a Pawn on such a cell has already moved or not.
- En Passant *Capture:* concerns a Pawn which has just moved two hexes forward. An opposing Pawn, which threatens to capture on the intermediate cell over which the Pawn has passed, can capture it as if it had moved only one cell. The *en passant* capture must be done immediately following the opponent's double step.

There is no castling in Gliński's hexagonal chess.

END OF THE GAME. An attacked King must immediately be placed out of check. If no possible move will save the King from capture, his owner has lost the game: it is *checkmate*.

A player whose King is not in check, but who has no possible move other than placing his King in check is in *stalemate*. This is not a drawn game in Gliński's hexagonal chess but a victory of lesser value. In a tournament, the stalemated player gets ¼ point and the player who delivers it gets ¾ point, instead of 1 and 0 in the case of checkmate.

If the same position of pieces on the board is repeated three times, with the same player to move, the game is declared a draw.

Gliński estimated the Bishop to be equal to 3 Pawns, the Knight to 4 Pawns, the Rook to 5 Pawns and the Queen to 10 Pawns. The IA of Zillions-of-Games software suggests a comparable scale, although with the Bishop stronger than the Knight: Queen (7.9), Rook (5), Bishop (3), Knight (2.9), Pawn (starting at center) (0.7).

# 37. Hexagonal Chess

## History

Curiously, the use of hexagonal cells is relatively recent in board games, despite the many examples found in nature, such as the wax alveoli of bee hives. Perhaps the earliest recorded board game using hexagonal cells is *Agon*, a very original strategic Pawn game first published in 1842.[39]

The earliest hexagon-based chess variant is credited to Thomas Hanmer Croughton, who presented a "hexagonal chess" in 1853. It was played over a 61-cell hexagonal board (sides of 5 hexes) with 11 pieces per player. Curiously, the winning player was the first to place his General, moving like a Queen, on the starting hex of the enemy General. Soon afterward, in 1864, the English company, John Jaques & Son, commercialized a game called *Hexagonia*, which appears to have been invented a few years earlier in New Zealand. *Hexagonia* is played on a hexagonal board of 127 hex cells (7 hexes on each side). Each player has 1 King, 2 Cannons, 4 Knights and 8 Pawns. Again, the player's task was not to checkmate but to be the first to bring the King to the center hex.[40]

The first hexagonal chess with checkmate was *Mars*, a commercial game invented by M. van Leeuwen and published in a 20-page booklet by F.H. Ayres in 1910. The board had 77 hexes arranged in a rectangular pattern of 9 files alternating 9 and 8 hexes each. Each player had 14 pieces with "astronomical" names (Sun, Moon, Astronomers, Observatory, Radium Tower and Telescope), the two sides representing Earth (White) against Mars (Black). The board was colored with only two colors, and several pieces were color-bound. This was followed by three-handed variants proposed by Sigmund Wellisch (1912) and then by Elizabeth Perry (1918), presented later in this book.

Finally, in 1929, Lord H.D. Baskerville invented a two-player hexagonal chess simply called "Hexagonal Chess." He used a rectangular-shaped board made of 83 hexagons of three colors (11 files of alternated 8 or 7 hexes, blue, red and white). Baskerville simply tried to adapt the standard "square" chess to the hexagonal pattern, therefore each player had the regular 16-piece set which only included two Bishops. The King was limited to the six adjacent cells; otherwise, the pieces, including the Pawn, moved as presented above. With some reasonable assertions, Władysław Gliński determined that Baskerville's game was flawed in several ways: the Bishops of the two camps stood on two different colors and could never attack each other. Moreover, one third of the board, the third color, was out of reach for any Bishop.

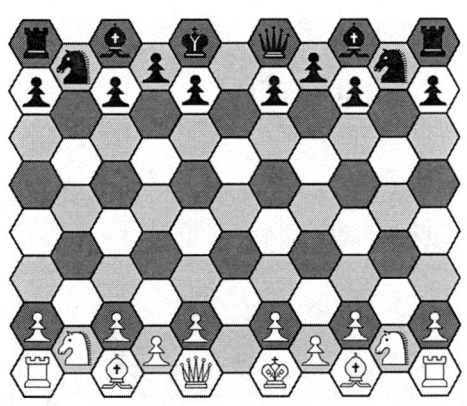

Initial array of Baskerville's hexagonal chess.

Gliński's hexagonal chess solved these issues and finally turned out to be the most famous among all variants of its category, thanks to the efforts and the lifelong enthusiasm of its creator.

His game was invented in 1936 and, remarkably, publicized only after World War II. According to the French writer, Joseph Boyer,[41] the first version proposed in 1949 was a bit complex and it was rightly simplified in 1953. It quickly reached a degree of popularity, notably in Poland, Gliński's homeland, where Pritchard reported that 130,000 games were sold in a few months. In the meantime, Gliński had moved to England where he lived until his death in 1990, promoting his game in his adopted country. His book, *Hexagonal Chess*, was published in English in 1973. Several organizations have been created, including an International Hexagonal Chess Federation, which organized a European Championship on a regular basis. This variant has been particularly popular in Central and Eastern Europe.

# Subsequent Hexagonal Chess

## Shafran's Hexagonal Chess

There is some uncertainty regarding the date at which this game was first devised by the geologist, Isaak Grigorevich Shafran.

Pritchard dates this game to 1953. The Chess Variant Pages report that it was first invented in 1939, then registered in 1956. It was publicly presented at the Worldwide Chess Exhibition in Leipzig (then in East Germany) in 1960. The invention of this game, which was essentially contemporary with Gliński's proposal, was intended to transfer regular chess to the hexagonal grid with a minimum of changes.

The board is an irregular hexagon (sides have 5, 5 and 6 hexes) with a total of 70 hex tiles.

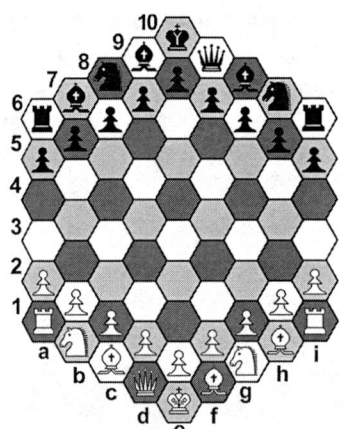

Initial array of Shafran's hexagonal chess. In Shafran's notation system, the files a through i run vertically, while the ranks, 1 through 10 descend diagonally, from left to right.

Non-Pawn pieces move as in Gliński's chess. It must be noted that all three Bishops and the Queen can move from the initial array.

The Pawn captures by making a Bishop's forward move, i.e., going onto a forward cell of the same color. In the starting array, the three central Pawns can advance 1, 2 or 3 steps at their first move. The b, c, g, and h Pawns can advance 2 steps. The Rooks' Pawns (a and i Pawns) can only step one hex forward. In this way, a Pawn's initial step may reach, but not cross, the central line of the board.

Regular chess rules are preserved. Pawns promote (to any piece other than Pawn or King) on the last hex of their files. *En passant* capture applies to any Pawn advancing 2 or 3 cells forward, passing over the capture hex of an opposing Pawn. Castling is possible either long or short with either Rook: in short castling, the Rook moves next to the King (i.e, to d1 or f2) and the King leaps over (to c1 or g3 respectively); in long castling the King moves all the way next to the Rook (i.e., to b1 or h4) and the Rook jumps over to land beside the King that is on c1 or g3.

## De Vasa's Hexagonal Chess

Helge Em. de Vasa, of Finland, invented a variant of his own in 1953 on a diamond-shaped board made of 72 hex cells (9 files and 8 ranks). The novelty was the orientation of the hexes, which permitted a horizontal move for the Rook, whereas previous variations had instead allowed a vertical move.

Here too, the driving idea is to have a close transfer of standard "square" chess onto the hexagonal lattice. All pieces but the Pawns proceed as in Gliński's game. The Pawn has a choice of two forward directions (except for the Pawn located at the extreme right of the players, which can only move toward the left) and three hexes of capture (on the three cells "diagonally" forward, including the one straight forward). On its first move, the Pawn also has the double-step option, which gives a choice of 4 cells.

In response to criticism deploring the exaggerated power given to the Pawn, de Vasa modified his game with a larger board of 81 cells (9 files and 9 ranks) and limited the Pawn's capture to the two sideways diagonals, eliminating the "diagonal" which was straight forward. Several variations have been subsequently proposed, keeping the same idea with a similar orientation of the hex cells.

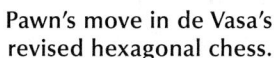

Pawn's move in de Vasa's revised hexagonal chess.

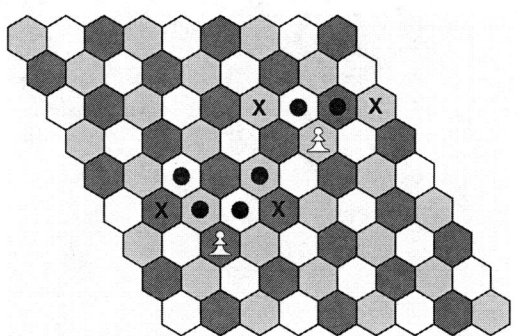

Castling is permitted with two options: short castling by moving the King two steps to the right and the right Rook jumping to the cell just left of the King, or long castling by moving the King three steps to the left and the left Rook jumping to the cell just to the right of the King. *En passant* capture is also permitted whenever a Pawn's double-step passes an opposing Pawn's hex of capture.

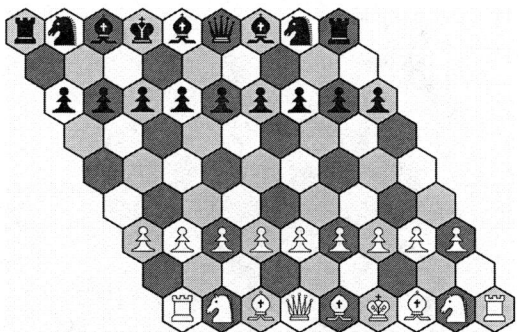

Initial array of de Vasa's hexagonal chess (2nd version). Note that each player places the King on his right and Queen on his left.

## Honeycomb Chess

This proprietary game was invented in 1972 by Douglas Graham Reid who published a book about it, edited by D.B. Pritchard. Also called *Hexabrain*, this game was an attempt to create more natural moves on the hexagonal grid, not necessarily augmenting the power of the pieces.

The board is similar to Gliński's, but the initial array and the moves are quite different. Each player has 22 pieces: 1 King, 2 Queens, 2 Castles (represented by Rooks on the diagram), 6 Hoppers (represented by Knights on the diagram) and 11 Pawns. Only the Pawn is identical to Gliński's. The King moves one step to adjacent cells only (a maximum of 6 possibilities); the Queen moves like Gliński's Rook; the Castle moves vertically like Gliński's Rook and horizontally like Gliński's Bishop; and the Hopper moves only one step diagonally (thus always staying on the same color).

All other classical chess rules (castling, Pawn's promotion, *en passant* capture, etc.) apply.

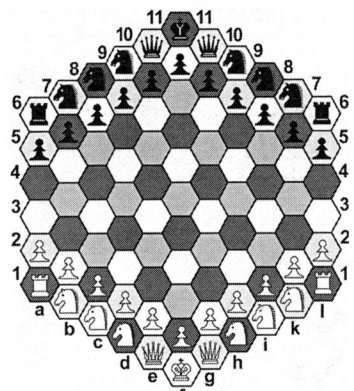

Initial array of Reid's Honeycomb Chess. This notation system was preferred by Gliński, and became the most common method of notating hexagonally shaped boards. Here, the files are simple vertical lines, a through i, but the ranks are envisioned as *descending* at an angle from the left edge to the center (a to f file) and then *ascending* at an angle from the center to the right edge (f to i file). So, for instance, White's Pawns are all considered to start on the second rank (a2, b2, c2, etc.); whereas Black's Pawns will be annotated as starting on several different ranks (a5, b6, c7, etc.).

## McCooey's Hexagonal Chess

This interesting variation was proposed by Dave McCooey and his friend Richard Honeycutt in 1978. Dave McCooey has stated that he was unaware of Gliński's hexagonal chess at the time of his own invention.[42]

Here, each player has (only) 16 pieces, as there are 7 Pawns instead of 9. The piece deployment in the initial array is more compact, allowing more space to unfold the forces.

Initial array of McCooey's hexagonal chess; notation is similar to Reid's Honeycomb.

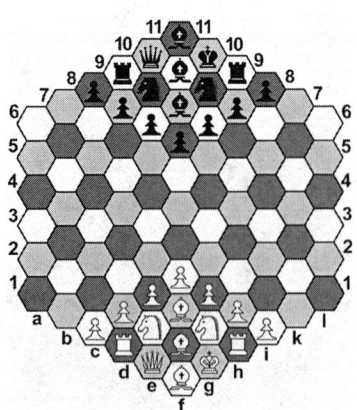

The game is designed to be as close as possible to standard chess. *En passant* capture is possible. Pawns promote on any of the 11 hexes at the opposite side of the board. There is no castling.

The other differences with Gliński's rules are:

- The center Pawn (in the f file) has no initial double step.
- The Pawn captures by moving one diagonal step forward, moving diagonally like a Bishop.[43]
- Stalemate is a draw.

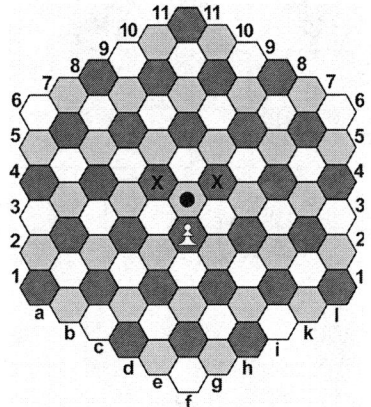

Move of Pawn at Shafran and McCooey's hexagonal chess.

McCooey's arrangement has enticed many hex chess players, who prefer it to Gliński's now "traditional" game.

Presented above are the hexagonal chess variants which we find most essential. Many more exist and will certainly exist in the future, each with its own advantages and drawbacks. As Pritchard remarked, it is possible that the ideal hexagonal chess still remains to be invented!

# 38. Four-Player Chess

Extend the number of players to four, as is done in many card games—the idea is definitely attractive, though it is not a recent development. Four-player chess games, as we know, were played since the Middle Ages in India (chaturaji) and in Spain ("four seasons" chess). They came back in vogue during the 19th century, notably in Germany and in England, practiced in clubs and tried out by some famous champions.

## *Cross-Shaped Board*

Of the many cross-shaped boards proposed for four players, the variant initiated by Verney and later refined by Hughes-Hughes garnered the greatest interest among players of its day.

The board looks like a wide cross. It contains 160 squares, arranged as a regular chessboard augmented by 8 × 3 square extensions on each of the four sides. Each player has the 16 classical chessmen, colored white, black, yellow and red. Each Queen stands at her King's left.

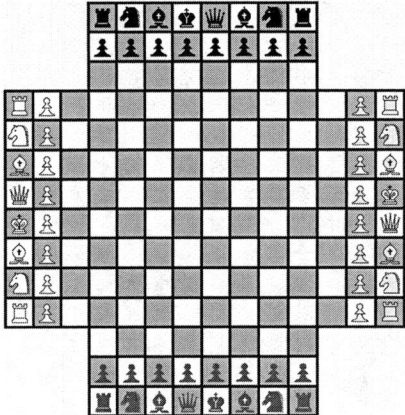

Hughes-Hughes's chessboard (1888).

# Rules

- The game is played between two teams of two, White and Yellow against Black and Red, with partners facing each other. White starts, followed by subsequent players passing in the clockwise direction. All pieces move and capture as in regular two-player chess. The Pawn's initial double step, castling and *en passant* capture are permitted.
- *The Pawn's Change of Direction:* when the Pawn reaches the last row (the partner's first row), it does not promote but makes its further moves heading back toward its original side. If it arrives on its own first row, it makes a 180° turn again, just going back and forth across the board. It is advised to somehow mark Pawns that have changed direction in order to clarify their orientation. Figurative Pawns with faces are convenient in this case because they can be simply turned around to face the new direction.
- *Meeting of Allied Pawns:* when a Pawn stands blocked by a partner's Pawn, it can jump over the other Pawn on condition that the square it lands upon is not occupied. This rule also applies when the two allied Pawns are progressing in the same direction. However, it is not permitted to jump over a Pawn of the same color.
- *Pawn's Promotion:* when a Pawn reaches the last row in one of the opposing camps, it is promoted to a Queen (exclusively). As at least three captures are necessary to perform this, promotion is quite rare.
- When a player is checkmated, his men become inert. They cannot move or check and cannot be taken. The player passes his turn as long as he stays checkmated.
- A checkmate can be released, generally by his partner, but also by one of the opponents. However, it is not allowed to release an opponent from mate while capturing one of his men in the same turn.
- The pieces of the partners have no influence over each other. For example, the two partner Kings can stand on adjacent squares. A player cannot capture his partner's pieces, nor can he check his partner's King. It is forbidden to make a move that would expose his partner's King to a check.
- *Victory:* the winning side is the one that has checkmated the two enemy Kings at the same time. All other situations are drawn.

The shape and the size of the board impact the relative value of the pieces. The Queen becomes very powerful. Bishops are as strong as Rooks, whereas the strength of Knights and Pawns is reduced in comparison to standard two-player chess.

## History

Christoph Weickhmann, already cited for warlike chess, presented another *Große Königs Spiel* (*Great King's Game*) in his book published in Ulm, Germany, in 1664. That game, involving 120 pieces (30 per player) over a cross-shaped board (with four extensions of 6 × 7 points around a 7 × 7 center), is the earliest known four-player chess in modern history. Weickhmann also proposed six-player and eight-player versions. They did not achieve any more success than the *Große Königs Spiel* for two players and fell into oblivion.

The English historian William Coxe (1747–1828) recorded a Russian four-player chess in his travel journal, observed in 1772.[44] Murray believed, without any argument, that it was a reference to the variant with fortresses (see following description). A cross-shaped board variant was explicitly described for the first time in 1779 in Gotha; then, in 1792 in Altenburg, near Leipzig, Germany. This invention is attributed to Duke Ernest II of Saxe-Gotha-Altenburg (1745–1804). The board has 8 × 2 extensions on the four sides of the 8 × 8 board. All Queens start on white squares. A rule forbids Pawns to capture each other from the starting position. In the same period, in 1784, another cross-shaped four-handed chess was reported in Leipzig, Germany by von K.E.G. Dessau. This early variation used a larger board with 8 × 3 extensions. All Queens were also deployed on the white squares.

In the 19th century, there was a proliferation of proposals which varied only in minor details. Pritchard enumerated four variants with 8 × 2 and 15 with 8 × 3 extensions up until 1882, all arising in Germany and England, except for two, which came from North America. Among them, one had an enviable destiny: Verney's four-handed chess.

The English captain George Hope Verney (1842–1896) wrote a small booklet dedicated to this variant in 1881. He chose the 8 × 3 extensions for the board and fixed most of the rules that are presented in this chapter, except that he recommended that all Queens be placed on white squares. Two years later, he founded a club in London that remained active until World War II. In 1885, the now *Major* Verney made the game a centerpiece of his book *Chess Eccentricities*.

The definitive rules were fixed by Verney's partner, M.E. Hughes-Hughes in 1888. He switched the Black and Red royal pieces to have the Queen at King's left for all four players. His new laws included the Pawn's double step (not allowed by Verney), *en passant* capture and castling. These rules (as given at the head of this chapter) were quickly adopted at the Four-Handed Chess Club of London.

## *Russian Fortress Chess*

For this variant, each player has a fortress on his right-hand side, where the King may seek shelter.

The board has 192 squares. It is made with a center, initially empty, of 64 squares, four extensions of 8 × 2 squares on the sides, and 4 × 4 square "fortresses" at the corners. Each corner is connected to the player's camp without obstacle; however, the border between the fortress and the camp to the player's right is an impassable boundary.

Each player commands a troop of the 16 standard men with three extra pieces—a Rook, a Bishop and a Knight—placed at the player's discretion inside the fortress. The partners face each other and play passes clockwise.

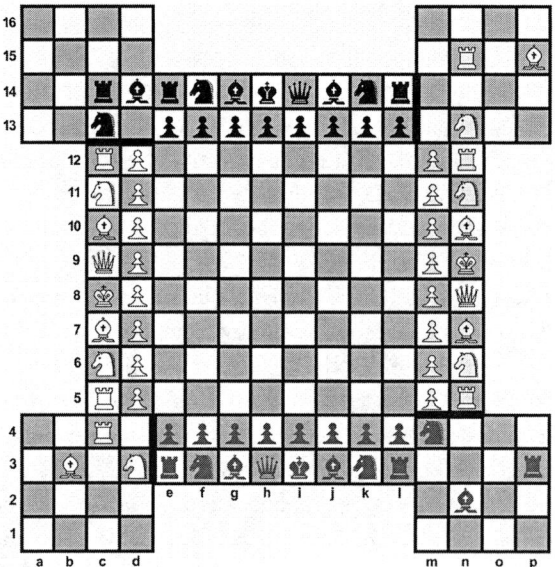

Example of initial position at Russian Fortress chess.

## Specific Rules

- All pieces may enter any of the fortresses.
- The diagonals touching fortress walls and board angles (e.g., d4–e5, or d5–e4) are impassable. This affects the move of the Knight, which is understood to consist of one square orthogonally and one diagonally, in any order (so a Knight in d3 cannot jump to e5; nor can it jump to f4 because of the barrier). A Knight at c4 may go to d6 (through c5 or d5) or to e5 (through d5). In the latter case, its move is considered to be one square diagonally followed by one orthogonally.
- The Rooks' Pawns may not capture each other from their starting squares.
- The most common castling is on the King's side in order to expedite his seeking refuge inside the fortress.
- The Pawn is promoted to any piece of the same color, other than King or Pawn, upon reaching any edge of the board, whether in his partner's or an enemy's starting area.
- *Meeting of allied Pawns:* when a Pawn is blocked by a partner's Pawn, they both remain immobile until one of them makes a capture or one is captured, freeing the path of the remaining Pawn.
- When a player is mated, his pieces are withdrawn from the board and his partner continues to fight alone. If this partner is stalemated, the game is drawn.[45]

## History

Fortress chess was briefly mentioned by Ivan Butrimov in the first Russian chess manual, published in 1821. The board was sketched but no details of the rules were given. The first description of the game came only in 1850 in an article published in Berlin by the Russian master, Alexander Petrov.[46]

## *Baltic Four-Player Chess*

Here, the board is more elaborate, with 128 diamond-shaped cells arranged in an eight-pointed star. Note that, by stretching out the inner points of the star, it is possible to form an octagon with varying quadrilateral cells. Topologically, the eight-pointed star is identical to the "stretched" octagonal board.

Each player has the full set of pieces. Classical rules are applied. The Pawn's initial double step and castling are permitted.

The players form two teams: White and Yellow play against Black and Red. The order of play is counterclockwise. The object is to mate both adversaries.

Initial array of Baltic Four-Player Chess.

## *History*

This game, *Das baltische Vierschach*, was presented in the German chess magazine *Schachzeitung* in 1865, in an article referring to a paper in a Latvian book authored by Leo Livonus in 1855. According to Murray, this variation is attributed to Lionel Kieseritzky,[47] said to have invented it about twenty years earlier. A strictly equivalent game on an octagonal board has been reinvented and marketed in 1994 under the name *Double Chess*.

Four-handed chess is continuously reinvented and often commercialized as a proprietary game. Two sorts are found: four-handed chess in which the players form two teams, and all-play-all chess in which every player is pitted against the others. In modern times, many new shapes of board have been explored, adding to an apparent originality in the eyes of the inventors, although the basics of the games have remained more or less the same.

# 39. Three-Player Chess

Alliances and betrayals on the board! Chess lovers have dreamed of a worthy three-handed variant for many years. Indeed, it is difficult to design a balanced game and the first variants were not entirely successful. However, following is a well-deserved exposition and comparison with more modern developments.

It is possible to play three-way chess on various board and cell shapes: square, quadrilateral, triangular, hexagonal, circular—and probably more.

## *Earliest Three-Handed Chess*

The first three-handed chess proposed in Europe involved square cells on an extended board, in an attempt to maintain most of the characteristics of two-player standard chess. But the square's four sides have posed a considerable difficulty for the design of a truly balanced three-player game. The three proposals described below have flaws that convincingly demonstrate these difficulties. Most of the proposals that appeared in the 19th century were only minor modifications of these rules. It was only at the end of that century that the research of a more equitable shape brought new board topologies.

### *Marinelli's Triple Chess*

This earliest version of three-player chess was proposed by Captain Filippo Marinelli in Naples in 1722. It must have been appreciated by Prince Eugene of Savoy, to whom it was dedicated.

The classic chessboard of 64 squares is augmented by 8 × 3 square extensions on three sides. The center player has the Black pieces. White and Red are facing each other.

Initial array of Marinelli's chess for three players. The Queens are placed at the King's left for all players.

Rules. • The moves of the pieces are the same as in standard two-player chess.
- The players agree on who starts. Then, the turn passes to the player at the right and continues counterclockwise.
- The Pawns achieve promotion by reaching the opposite side of the board. Obviously, Black has a shorter distance, but this advantage is balanced by a greater difficulty in crossing two enemy lines. White and red Pawns do not promote on the edges of Black's board extension. They end there with no future move (except those which have a possible diagonal capture).

- Checkmate or stalemate must be given by pieces of a single color. Placing a King in a position of checkmate or stalemate in which he is hemmed in by a combination of the other two players' pieces is not allowed.
- When a player is checkmated or stalemated, all of his pieces stay on the board. The adverse Kings cannot enter squares threatened by the "dead" pieces. These immobile pieces may be captured normally. The defeated King, however, stays on his square, invulnerable but inert until the end of the game.
- At the finish of the game, there are specific rules for settling the players' stakes. The winner is the player who succeeds in mating both of the opposing Kings. He is "paid" by both players. The player who mates one King and stalemates the second one gets nothing, but some glory. The player who mates the King of the one who had already mated the other is the winner and is also paid by both opponents. The player who has stalemated a King and then mates the second one wins nothing, but if he loses he must pay the stake if he is mated by the remaining player.

## Waidder's Three-Handed Chess

A new board, respecting the symmetry between the three players, was invented by S. Waidder, presented in a German book published in Vienna in 1837, *Das Schachspiel in seinem ganzen Umfange nach allen Schriftstellern auf eine leichtfaßliche Weise dargestellt* (*The Game of Chess in All Its Aspects According to All Authors in an Easy Presentation*).

The board has 120 squares resulting from joining and overlapping three 8 × 8 boards. Each player has a zone formed by 4 ranks of 8 files plus a rank of 6 (4 squares with 2 trapezoids on the ends) and a front rank of 2 trapezoidal cells. Those 3 sets of 2 cells join in the center point. Six spaces with a "kite" shape are ignored.

PARTICULAR RULES. • All Queens stand on white squares.
- The turn passes counterclockwise.
- Pawns promote when they reach the first row of either opponent.
- Pieces that cross a boundary between two zones are allowed to change direction in the same move.[48]
- Castling and the Pawn's initial double step are permitted.
- A checkmated player has his pieces frozen and immune to capture. If he becomes released from mate, he can resume playing.
- The game is won by the player who has checkmated the two other Kings.

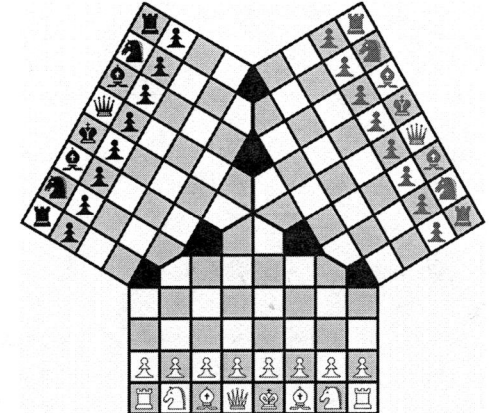

Initial array of Waidder's chess for three players.

Surprisingly, a chess variant with the same board configuration was marketed under the name *Interface* in 1972.[49]

## *Tesche's Three-Handed Chess*

Walter Tesche proposed a different version in 1843 in a book published in Vienna, *Theoretisch-praktische Anweisung zum Dreischachspiel (Theoretical and Practical Instruction of Three-Handed Chess)*.

PARTICULAR RULES. • Red and White Pawns move forward toward each other, and Black Pawns move forward between the other two.

- The turn passes counterclockwise. The colors are Black, Brown and White.
- The Pawns can take a double step on the first move.
- Pawns promote on the opposite side on the board, to any piece that has already been captured. If there is none available, the Pawn waits on the promotion square, immobile and immune to capture until it can promote. When such a piece is lost, the Pawn is immediately exchanged. This does not count as a move.
- Castling is not allowed in this variant.
- A checkmated player has his pieces frozen and immune to capture. If he is released from mate, he resumes playing.
- A King cannot stand next to a frozen (checkmated) King.

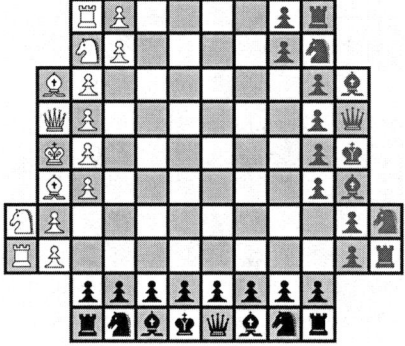

Initial array of Tesche's chess for three players.

## *Modern Three-Player Chess*

The definitive solution for a balanced three-player game came only at the end of the 19th century, with the use of non-squared boards.

## *Circular Three-Player Chess*

The large circular board, proposed by G.H. Verney in 1884, placed the three players in a satisfactory confrontation: each one faces his two opponents on his flanks. The board presents four concentric rings of 24 curved quadrilateral cells each, for a total of 96.

RULES. • The Queens are always placed beside the King, on a white square.

• The turn passes clockwise.

• Pawns can only move one square at a time, even from their starting positions. There is no Pawn promotion in this game; Pawns remain Pawns forever.

• Castling is only possible with the Rook that stands on the King's row. The King goes to the Knight's square and the Rook goes to the Bishop's square.

• Two players cannot unite their forces to checkmate the third King. Creating such a configuration would be considered an illegal move. A checkmate can only be given by the men of a single player.

• If a player is checkmated, his pieces remain on the board waiting for an eventual release from the mate, in which case the player can resume playing. The pieces of a checkmated player do not threaten the other pieces and a King can even move to a square adjacent to the frozen King.

• A player who checkmates both the opponents' Kings is victorious. If he checkmates one King and stalemates the second King, he only wins half a game.[50]

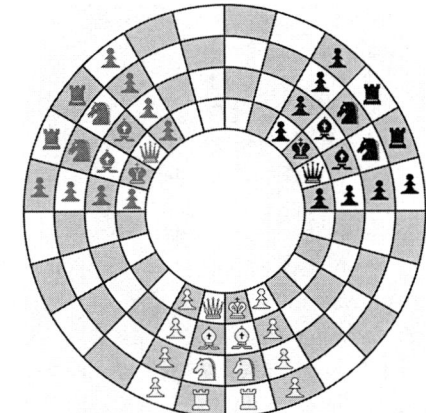

Initial array of Verney's three-handed circular chess.

The chess variants expert Joseph Boyer considered this game to be the best three-player chess. Verney also proposed a similar four-handed circular chess on a larger board with 128 cells, in four concentric circles of 32 cells each.

More recently, a new and original circular chess was created in 1999, by Clif King of Nashville, Tennessee. It has been marketed successfully by the creator as "3 Man Chess," and is easily available online.[51]

## Hexagonal Three-Handed Chess

With its six edges, the hexagon easily makes a perfect board to accommodate three players. This was first realized by Sigmund Wellisch in 1912, who published his invention in the Viennese chess journal (*Das Dreierschach* [Chess for Three], *Wiener Schachzeitung*, 1912, vol. 15, pp. 322–330). He proposed using a board of 91 hex cells with 15 pieces per player. Each player has 1 King, 1 Queen, 2 Rooks, 3 Knights and 8 Pawns. There is no Bishop. The colors of the chessmen are Yellow, Black and Red.

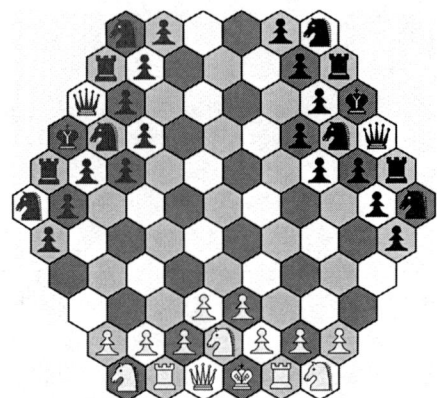

Initial array of Wellisch's three-handed hexagonal chess.

MOVES AND RULES. • The King moves to any adjacent hex. The Rook moves as in Gliński's chess. The Knight moves "diagonally" to the next hex of the same color. The Queen combines Rook and Knight's moves.

- The Pawn moves one hex forward (two possibilities) and captures the same way. There is no initial double step. The Pawn promotes when reaching the opposite side of the board to any piece previously captured.

- A checkmated player may at some point be released from checkmate, or his King may actually be captured (not necessarily by the player who delivered mate). A player who captures a checkmated King takes over all his men (the seized Pawns continue in their original direction). The winner is the player who defeats both his adversaries.

Many other three-player games have been invented and proposed on the hexagonal grid, with board shapes varying from simple to complex. Among the simplest, it deserves mentioning that McCooey's arrangement for two-player chess can be readily adapted for three players.[52] Also noteworthy is Tanigasaki Jisuke's *kokusai sannin shogi*, proposed circa 1930, based on the principles of Japanese shogi over a hexagonal *shogiban* composed of 127 cells.[53]

## 96-Diamonds Three-Player Chess

Ironically, when Waidder proposed his board in 1837 (see above), he was not far from a convenient solution to arranging a three-player game. The key was to accept a deformation of the cells, allowing them to deviate from the strictly square shape.

The result is a hexagonal board of 96 quadrilateral cells which, with 32 "squares" per player, presents a proportional spatial equivalent to that of the standard two-player arrangement. It appears that the earliest mention of this board is found in a U.S. Patent (3,652,091) filed by the American engineer Robert Zubrin in 1971, then a 19-year-old student at the University of Rochester.

This remains one of the most reinvented boards among modern three-player variants. Sometimes, the inventors come up with another shape, not necessarily realizing that their proposals are topologically the same use of space. Indeed, the hexagon is just a distortion: if the pattern is compressed on the three medians in order to obtain diamond cells, it becomes a six-pointed star. An intermediate fat Y-shape can also be obtained by stretching only three edges.

# 39. Three-Player Chess

These three boards appear different; however, they correspond to the same topology. They are strictly equivalent.

Whatever the board's final shape, the pieces move on it with identical principles. Hence, this three-player chess is known under many names, several of them being proprietary and commercial games. *Dreier Schach* was produced in Germany in the 1970s. There is a photograph with the former World Chess Champion Max Euwe playing it in a Dutch newspaper of 1976. In France, it has been popularized under the name of *Yalta,* beginning in 1975, by Pierre-Éric Splinder, and was still being sold in 2016. In the Netherlands, *Trioschaak* (*Triochess*) by Van der Laken and Buijtendorp has been marketed since 1979. George Dekle Sr. reintroduced it as *Three-Man Chess* in 1984.[54]

The list is long and has been boosted by the Internet. Since 2011, a related *Trichess* is available to play online.[55] Following are the general rules which apply to most of the best-known variations.

MATERIAL AND RULES. Each player possesses the standard set of 16 pieces. All Queens are placed at the King's left.

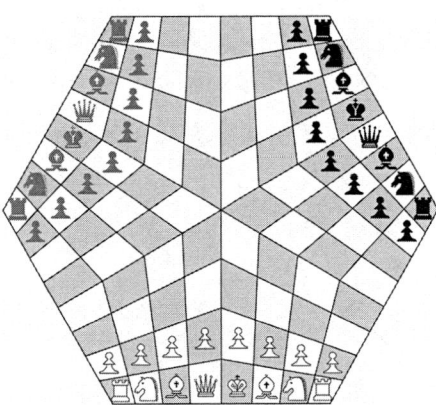

Initial array of 96-Diamonds Three-Player Chess.

The pieces keep their standard moves, but with special attention to the altered geometry of the board. When a piece moving diagonally, such as a Queen or Bishop, passes through the center point of the board, it continues on squares of the same color, with two possible directions.

The Rooks maintain a move that links the opposite edges of adjacent cells. The diagram below illustrates the moves of Bishop and Rook.

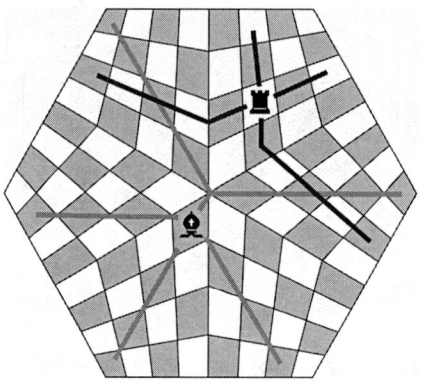

Moves of Rook and Bishop.

The King can go to any adjacent cell. Placed in a cell touching the center, he can reach nine cells instead of eight, since his diagonal move through the center point has two possibilities.

Moves of King.
(The King can reach all cells marked with circles. The King cannot reach the crossed cell.)

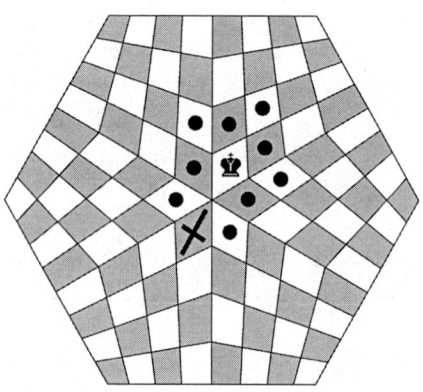

The Knight has a move which may be difficult to visualize. It is easiest to think of as making one step straight orthogonally to an adjacent cell, followed by two steps at a "right" angle; or two steps orthogonally followed by one step at "right" angle. Therefore, it can reach two cells when it is in a corner of the board and up to ten cells when it is close to the center.

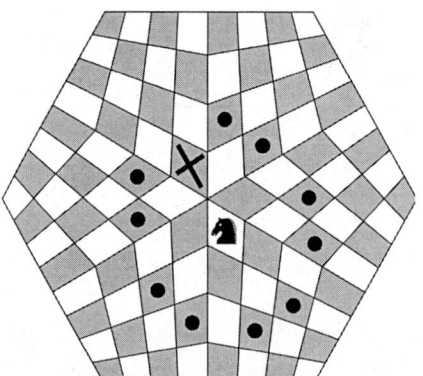

Moves of Knight
(The Knight can reach all cells marked with circles. It cannot reach the crossed cell.)

The Pawn steps one square straight ahead as it does in standard chess. After passing the fourth row, the four left white Pawns go toward the red camp and the four right white Pawns go toward the black camp. The Pawn captures one cell diagonally which means that it threatens two cells, and sometimes three.

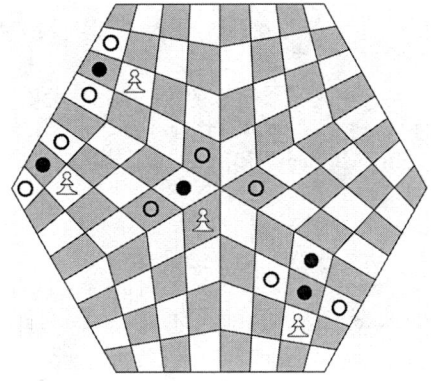

Moves of Pawns (step to solid circle; capture to open circle).

Castling, Pawn promotion and *en passant* captures are possible.

A checkmated or stalemated King is eliminated. The King is withdrawn and all pieces are placed under control of the player who has realized the checkmate or played the last stroke leading to stalemate. The reenlisted Pawns continue in their original direction. The player who takes control of the men of another player does not take the other's turn to play—he alternates turns with the remaining player.

When the game is down to two players, the winner is the one who checkmates the other remaining King.

Three-handed chess games have been invented everywhere. The Western variants are comparable to *sanguo qi*, or "Three Kingdoms chess," and other related Chinese games presented earlier in this book.

# 40. 3-D Chess

For many people, chess, with all of the intricacies of its pieces, moves and combinations, symbolizes intelligence. A chess champion is admired as someone who is able to think more deeply and more quickly than his peers. We are also amazed and spellbound by those with such spatial conceptual abilities that they actually think in three dimensions. It seems natural that taking the well-established two-dimensional game of chess and extending it into a third dimension would be widely regarded as the summit of complexity. That someone could actually "play" with such a monstrous thing seems at first highly unlikely. It is probably for this reason that 3-D chess has attained most of its popularity in science fiction books, film and television.

Nevertheless, the idea had its spark on Planet Earth in the second half of the 19th century and has been realized and developed in the following century. Chess is fundamentally a war game, and as balloons, airships and airplanes began appearing in the military arsenal, expectations grew that chess would soon conquer the third dimension as well. Dr. Ferdinand Maack, in particular, investigated numerous possible solutions to the question and finally proposed a 3-D chess that is really manufacturable, playable and enjoyable. This one is described here in detail.

# Space Chess or Raumschach

This variant deserves its success. Compared to monstrous stacks of eight chessboards that were first envisioned, the limited depth of the boards here eases the handling of the pieces that stand in the central cells. Also, with 125 cells and 40 pieces, the game remains within reasonable bounds.

## Material

Five boards of 5 × 5 squares each are stacked. The corner squares of each board are of alternating color from top to bottom. Dark squares appear in the top and bottom corners.

The boards are identified with capital letters, from A (bottom board) to E (top board). The full space is conceived as a cube of 125 cubic cells.

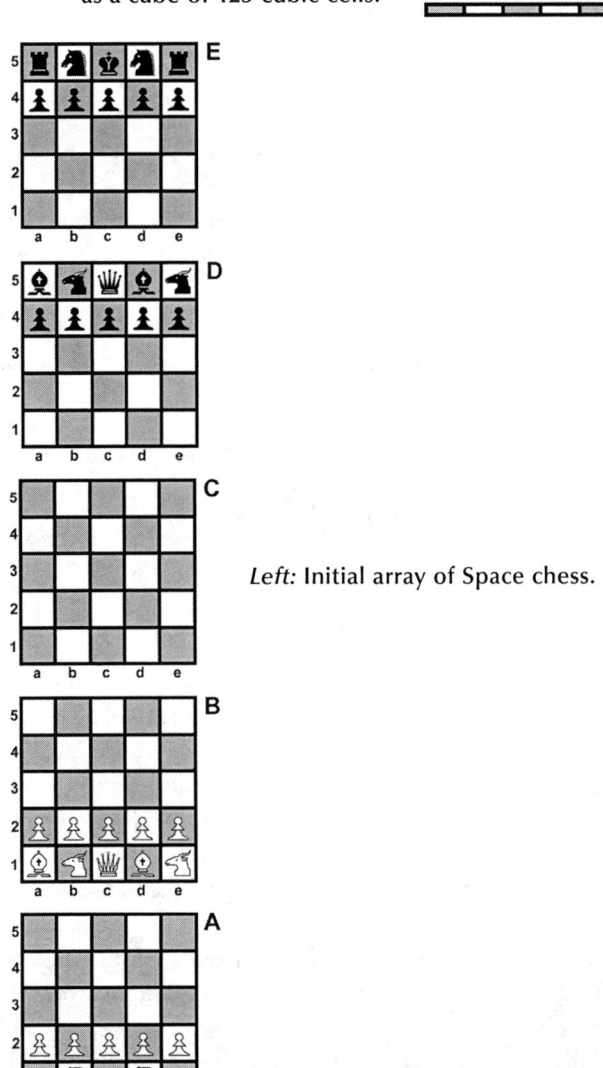

*Left:* Initial array of Space chess.

Each player has 20 pieces: 1 King, 1 Queen, 2 Rooks, 2 Bishops, 2 Unicorns, 2 Knights and 10 Pawns. White pieces start on the bottom boards, A and B; black pieces start on the upper boards, D and E. Board C is empty at the beginning.

## Rules

MOVES AND CAPTURES. The pieces move in combination of the three basic spatial directions which consist of crossing the cubic cells either by their faces, their edges or their vertices (corners). The latter move is sometimes designated as *triagonal*.

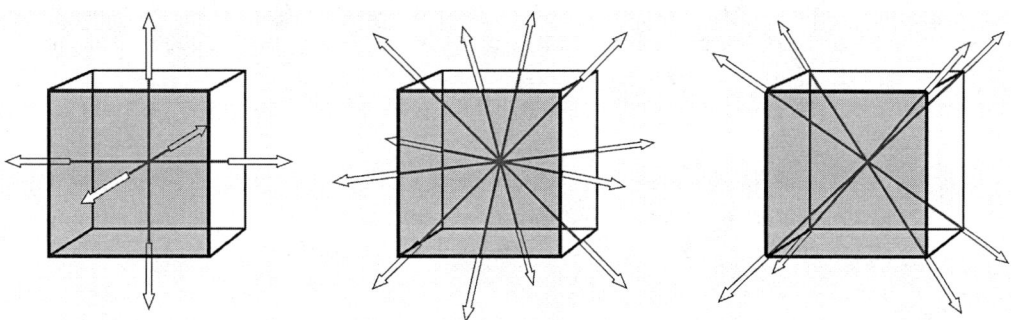

The three possible directions defined in cubic cell: Rook-type (through faces); Bishop-type (through edges) and Unicorn-type (through vertices).

*King:* moves only one step to any of the 26 adjacent cells (6 through the faces, 12 through the edges, 8 through the vertices) that surround it, provided that this cell is not under the threat of an adverse piece. The King is in check if he is attacked by one or more adverse pieces.

*Rook:* moves in a straight line, crossing the faces of any number of free cells. The Rook can go in six different directions. On a given board, it goes on the rank and column where it stands (forward, backward, left or right). On the third vertical dimension, the Rook moves straight up and down as if it were in an elevator. The Rook may not pass through any occupied cell in its way.

For example, from Aa1, the Rook may go to: Aa2, Aa3, Aa4, Aa5, Ab1, Ac1, Ad1, Ae1, Ba1, Ca1, Da1, Ea1.

*Bishop:* moves in a straight line perpendicularly to the edges of any number of free cells. At the maximum, the Bishop has a choice of twelve directions. However, it can only reach half of the cells, those which correspond to a same color of square on the five boards: the Bishop is color-bound. On a given board, it goes on the familiar diagonals (as it crosses the vertical edges of the cells). In the 3rd dimension it goes up and down as if it moved on the steps of a staircase. The Bishop may not pass through any occupied cell in its way.

For example, from Ba1, the Bishop may go to: Ab1, Aa2, Bb2, Bc3, Bd4, Be5, Ca2, Da3, Ea4, Cb1, Dc1, Ed1.

*Unicorn:* moves in a straight line, joining the vertices on any number of free cells. At the maximum, the Unicorn has a choice of eight directions and it changes floor, rank and file in every step. It should be noted that the Unicorn cannot reach all the cells of the space-board: the Unicorns starting on Bb1 and Db5 can only reach six cells of each floor; the Unicorns on Be1 and De5 can reach four cells on floors A, C, E and nine cells on floors B and D. Therefore, a Unicorn can only reach 30 cells on a total of 125. The Unicorn may not pass through any occupied cell in its way.

For example, from Bb1, the Unicorn may go on Aa2, Ac2, Ca2, Cc2, Dd3, Ee4. After the Pawn, it is the weakest piece of the game.

*Queen:* moves either like a Rook, a Bishop or a Unicorn. Therefore, from the central cell, she has a maximum choice of 26 directions. She may not pass through any occupied cell in her way.

*Knight:* moves with an L-shape of two cells like a Rook plus one step at a right angle like a Rook again. It may be noticed that this move is always inscribed in a single plane.[56] The Knight freely leaps over any pieces in its path. The Knight has a maximum choice of 24 possible cells.

For example, from Ab1, the Knight may go on Aa3, Ac3, Ad2, Bb3, Bd1, Cb2, Ca1, Cc1.

*Pawn:* it steps one cell straight forward or upward (for White) or downward (for Black). It does not capture that way. It may capture an enemy piece standing one cell at a Bishop's step forward/upward (for Whites) or forward/downward (for Blacks). That means that a Pawn controls five cells, two on the same floor where it stands and three on the next floor.

For example, from Ac2, the Pawn may go to Ac3 or Bc2 and may capture on Ab3, Ad3, Bb2, Bc3, Bd2.

PARTICULAR RULES. Because of the small size of the boards, there is no Pawn's initial double step, no *en passant* capture and no castling.

- *Pawn Promotion:* a Pawn reaching the last rank of the furthest floor (rank 5, level E for White; rank 1, level A for Black) is immediately replaced by a Queen, Bishop, Unicorn, Knight or Rook of the same color at the choice of the player.

END OF THE GAME. The goal of the game is to checkmate the opponent's King. The end-of-the-game rules of standard 2-D chess also apply here.

The estimated relative values for the pieces are: Queen (14.2), Knight (6.5), Bishop (6.5), Rook (5), Unicorn (3), Pawn (1.4).

# History

The first attempt at a three-dimensional chess is generally attributed to the chess player Lionel Kieseritzky, who is credited with *Cubic Chess* (*Kubicschach*) in London in 1851 (also credited with the invention of Baltic four-handed chess). However, no material trace of this has ever been found to confirm the invention. The idea was then borrowed by Dr. Ferdinand Maack, who detailed a first version of his *Raumschach* (space chess) in 1907. He published a book the following year to offer details on this game, then based on eight stacked 8 × 8 square boards. Each player had 24 pieces made of a standard set disposed on the first two rows of the bottom board in standard position. This was complemented by eight extra Pawns placed on the first row of the second board (just above the bottom board). All pieces had move possibilities in the third dimension, so they were gradually tempted to step up to the floors above. In a second variant, White had his pieces on the two lowest boards with Black on the two highest boards, which forced the game to dive into the third dimension.

But such a huge playing space of 512 cells was not practical, either to be conceptualized or to be played upon. Later, Maack experimented with different configurations such as 7 × 7 × 7, 6 × 6 × 6 and even 4 × 4 × 4 before preferring a 5 × 5 × 5 cell space. With this definitive version, he founded a Space Chess Club in Hamburg, Germany, in 1919 which continued operations for twenty years. It is this latest version that we have detailed in this chapter.

As usual, this did not stop other inspired minds from inventing and creating, with more or less success. The monstrous octuplet board was again adopted by Prof. William F.H. Godson in 1930 who published a book the following year entitled *Three-Dimensional Chess: History and Rules of the Game*. 3-D chess penetrated science fiction when it was mentioned by Isaac Asimov in his novel *Pebble in the Sky* (1950). It continued to attract the attention of the public when a series of articles appeared in *Time Magazine, Newsweek,* the *New Yorker,* and *Life Magazine* in 1952. The credited inventor this time was the American mathematician and Armenian-born Dr. Ervand Kogbetliantz (1888–1974). He filed a French patent on September 30, 1925 (N° 608.196) and stated that he had invented this game, *Space Chess,* in 1918 just before he left Russia. Each player had 64 pieces combining the different basic moves and placed on the 512 cells of a giant space made by eight superposed standard chessboards made of glass. This excessive size condemned the game rapidly to oblivion, with the sheer impracticality of manufacture and play. Pritchard reports that a demonstration had been stopped after three hours in which only ten moves had been played.[57]

A more reasonable attempt, *Total Chess,* invented in 1945 by the Englishman, Charles Beatty, also received a bit of publicity when it was launched. It used four 8 × 8 boards. A limited form with only 4 × 4 × 4 cells was established by Texas Instruments in 1966 under the name of TEDCO (Texas Educational Devices Corporation), to serve in psychological studies on the human ability to think in three dimensions.

Many chess variant inventors took an interest in the third dimension. Among the most influential, John Gollon (1968) proposed a game on 8 × 8 × 8 squares in which all pieces are initially placed on the lower chessboard, among several other versions. In Gollon's game, the pieces only start to conquer the upper levels after the first check. V.R. Parton[58] (1970) invented *Cubic Chess*[59] played on six 6 × 6 boards, with one of each standard piece, a Unicorn and twelve Pawns per side.

R. Wayne Schmittberger (1972) summed up the general critique of 3-D chess game that were widely available saying, "*Commercial three-dimensional chess sets come with many different rules, most of which have one thing in common: They're very bad.*" He proposed a 3-D chess on a smaller triple stack of 8 × 8 boards with "hook-moves" (inspired by some large shogis) for the Rooks, Bishops and Queens, an extended 2-D move for the Knight, and reduced 3-D moves for the King and the Pawn in order to present a reasonably playable game.

In modern times, the proposals of 3-D chess are indeed numerous: overall, Pritchard reported about 60 different games using the third dimension! Many games are proprietary and are sometimes commercialized. A popular solution to the expensiveness of the material has been to limit the space to three stacked boards only. The third dimension has inspired other creators, especially in the fields of science fiction and fantasy. The famous television series *Star Trek* popularized a peculiar chess having the shape of a space vessel and made of seven boards. Four of them are mobile and at each turn the players have the choice between moving one piece or one of these platforms. Each player has a familiar set of 16 pieces. In this case, the game was invented before the rules. The complete rules, obviously complex, were later written by Andrew Bartmess in 1976. They are still the object of refinement and clarification by several enthusiasts on the Internet.

Star Trek's "Tri-D Chess" ready to play. KNOWLTON PHOTOGRAPH

Another remarkable creation in this area should be credited to Gary Gygax (1938–2008), American writer and game designer and father of the role-playing game "Dungeons and Dragons." His *Dragonchess* was first published in Issue 100 of *Dragon Magazine* (August 1985). It pits two armies against each other consisting of 42 pieces each, gold and scarlet, inspired by the heroes and monsters from the fantasy universe of Dungeons & Dragons, on three superposed boards of 12 × 8 squares. The upper board, checkered blue and white, represents the skies; the middle floor, green and amber, is earth; and the one at the bottom, red and brown, is the underworld. The reader will easily find the rules of this 3-D chess variant, a fantastic modern creation.

There are also some hybrid variations. *Timur's Cubic Chess,* also invented by the prolific V.R. Parton (1971), adapts Timur's chess on a 6 × 6 × 6 board. *Space Hexchess* by John Stratford (1985, revised 1992) has three boards of 91 hexagonal cells each; *Space Shogi* from George R. Dekle, Sr. (1987), has nine superimposed *shogibans* (9 × 9 squares each).

Last but not least, the imaginations of chess inventors need not be confined to the ordinary realm of three spatial dimensions.[60] Conceptually, four or even more dimensions of "hyper-space" can be logically postulated and laid out in clear diagrams. Maack himself investigated a "four dimensions board" which was represented on the page by a 4 × 4 array of sixteen 4 × 4 chessboards. Maack's arrangement was studied by the English problemist Thomas Rayner Dawson (1889–1951), who published a paper about it in 1926. Parton also conceived of a *Sphinkian Chess* played on a 3 × 3 array of nine 4 × 4 chessboards, in 1970. Parton did not stop with 4-D chess. The same year, he also invented a 6-D Chess: *Ecila Chess*, represented by a cubic 2 × 2 × 2 array of 2 × 2 × 2 cubes.[61]

# *Alice Chess*

This is the most famous chess variant invented by V.R. Parton (1897–1974) in 1953.[62] It was thus baptized in honor of the Lewis Carroll heroine. Indeed, at every move, the pieces seem to pass on to the other side of a glass mirror separating two chessboards. This mechanism gives birth to very elegant situations that are greatly appreciated by chess problemists. The second board behaves like a virtual world and there is something magical in seeing the pieces disappear and rematerialize on the other board. There is a pertinent overlap between this game and the 3-D variants, each taking the standard game into another dimension.

# 40. 3-D Chess

## Material

Two regular boards are placed side by side. The pieces are set up on one board, the second remaining empty at the beginning of the game.

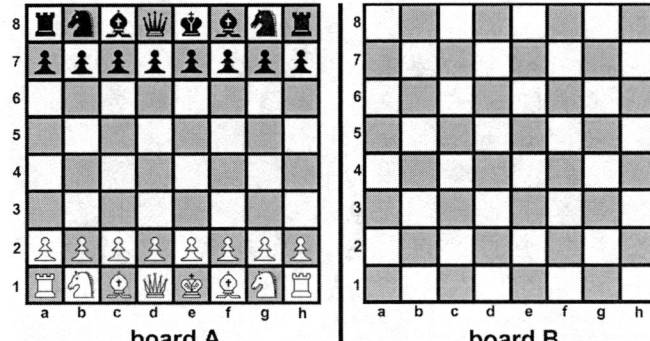

Initial array of Alice Chess.

## Rules

The basic rules are the following:

- The move must be legal on the board where it is initiated.
- Once the move is made, the piece must switch to the corresponding square (with the same coordinates) on the other board.
- The destination square on the arrival board must be free.

## Remarks

- For the first move, the pieces go from board A to board B. On the subsequent moves, the players have the choice of playing a piece from board A or a piece from board B, always ending the move on the other board.
- The corresponding squares of the two boards can never be occupied at the same time.
- A piece starting on one board cannot capture a piece standing on the other. A piece captures another piece which is standing on the same board; however, the capturing piece must then end its turn by being transposed to the other board.
- The King is very vulnerable, especially in the opening, as is shown in this three-move mate:
    1. e4(B)     d5(B)
    2. Be2(B)    d × e4(A)
    3. Bb5(A) mate

    Or, another example:
    1. e4(B)     e5(B)
    2. Qh5(B)    Nf6(B)
    3. Q × e5(A) mate

Despite the simple rules, Alice Chess is a very deep game.

A possible variation is to set up White's pieces on board A and Black's pieces on board B for the starting array.

Parton was convinced that this form of chess was the preferred alternative to the three-dimensional variants, which proved too difficult in actual play.

Lewis Carroll's "Alice," illustrated by John Tenniel.

# 41. Extraterrestrial Chess

If an alien race exists, do they play a game similar to chess? Some inspired Earthling minds have imagined that some chess-like games could have been played under other skies by aliens living exciting adventurous lives in popular science fiction stories. Two in particular have been quite successful, attracting a base of Earthly fans who play them regularly.

## *Jetan*

The American novelist Edgar Rice Burroughs (father of Tarzan and author of epics that have made him a legend of fantasy and science fiction literature) described a form of chess practiced by the Martians in the fifth volume of his *Barsoom* series, *The Chessmen of Mars*.[63]

While this could be taken as a puerile and naive fantasy, John Gollon, author of *Chess Variations: Ancient, Regional, and Modern* (1968), was curious enough to manufacture the game of Jetan and play it according to the rules given by Burroughs: the game is not only playable, it is also very enjoyable.

### *Material*

The game symbolizes the struggle between the Black and Yellow races of South and North Barsoom, the fictional name given to Planet Mars. Accordingly, the board has 10 × 10 squares alternating black and orange. The colors of the right and left corner squares were not specified by Burrough.

Each side commands 20 pieces of 8 different kinds: 1 Chief, 1 Princess, 2 Fliers, 2 Dwars, 2 Padwars, 2 Warriors, 2 Thoats and 8 Panthans.[64]

# 41. Extraterrestrial Chess

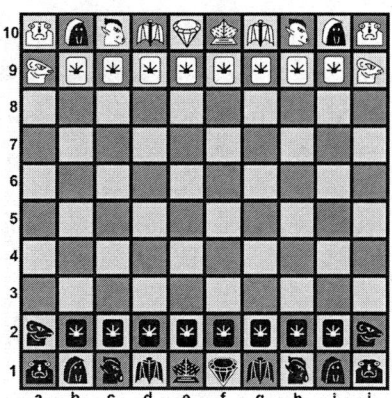

Initial array of Jetan.

## Rules

Burroughs presented the rules of Jetan in Chapter 2 and also summarized them at the end of his book. However, the two descriptions are minimal and sometimes contradictory, leaving the need for some interpretation.

MOVES AND CAPTURES. Except for the Princess, all pieces capture as they move. As in regular chess, a piece captures by landing on the square on which its target stands.

The pieces move in a combination of directions; that is, they are not forced to move in straight lines. They may change direction, but no piece can cross the same square twice in a single move.

The number of allowed squares for the move of a given piece is understood as an exact number; e.g., moving three squares means *exactly three*, not one or two.

 *Chief:* moves three squares in any direction or combination of directions, orthogonally or diagonally. It cannot jump over intervening pieces.

 *Princess:* moves three squares in any direction or combination of directions, orthogonally or diagonally, but can also jump over squares that are occupied. The Princess cannot take other pieces. Once during the game, the Princess may make a special escape move in which she moves directly to any unoccupied square on the board.

 *Flier:* sometimes called an *Odwar*, moves three squares diagonally or in a combination of diagonal directions. It may jump over intervening pieces.[65]

 *Dwar:* moves three squares horizontally or vertically or in a combination of these directions. It cannot jump.

 *Padwar:* moves two squares diagonally or a combination of diagonal directions. It cannot jump.

 *Warrior:* moves two squares horizontally or vertically or in a combination of these directions. It cannot jump.[66]

 *Thoat:* moves one space orthogonally (horizontally or vertically) and then one space diagonally in any direction. As clearly stated on Chapter 2 of Burroughs' book: it may jump over an intervening piece. Therefore, the Thoat may reach twelve squares at the maximum: eight like a Knight from orthodox chess and the four orthogonally adjacent to its square of departure.

*Panthan:* moves one square straight forward or diagonally forward or sideways (five directions). It is assumed that Panthans do not promote.[67]

The relative strength of the pieces is the following: Flier (9.5), Thoat (5.6), Dwar (4.9), Panthan (2), Warrior (1.9), Padwar (1.7).[68] The value of the Chief and the Princess are meaningless as their loss in this game is fatal. Curiously, the Panthan, positioned like a Pawn, is not the weakest piece of the Martian army. This is explained by its efficient mobility despite its short range. The Warrior and the Padwar are weakened, lacking the ability to leap over occupied squares in their paths.

FREE JETAN. As has been mentioned already, Burrough was prosaic in his account of Jetan's rules, allowing several possible interpretations. The rules given above have a sound logic and balance, though others are also plausible.

One alternate way of playing is called "free Jetan." In this variant, the number of allowed squares for the move of a given piece is understood as a *maximum*. A piece which moves three squares, for instance, could move one, two or three at the player's choosing. In this variant, the Panthan can move to the two rear diagonals, giving it a choice of seven directions. The Warrior can also move two squares diagonally in addition to its normal powers.

END OF THE GAME. The original rules state that a player may win either of two ways: capturing the opponent's Chief with his own Chief, or taking the opponent's Princess with any piece at all.

The game is a draw when a player takes the enemy's Chief with a non–Chief piece. It is also a draw when both sides are reduced to three pieces or fewer of equal value and the game is not won in the ensuing ten moves, counted as five moves by each player. Because a Chief capturing a Chief wins the game, any piece that a Chief protects is immune from capture by the opposing Chief. Therefore, the Chief has a defensive role, and it happens very seldom that the game is won by the Chief's capture.

Gollon opined that this rule gives too many draws. An alternative ending rule is the following: if the Chief is taken by a piece other than the opposing Chief, the game is not a draw. The captured Chief is simply lost and the game continues, leaving the capture of the Princess the ultimate goal of the game. Some players find this the best solution.

Cover of one edition of Edgar Rice Burroughs's *The Chessmen of Mars*.

# Klin Zha

Klin Zha is a *Klingon* game. The Klingons are mighty aliens, fierce and aggressive warriors, well known from the famous *Star Trek* television science fiction series. Klin Zha is to them what chess is to Humans. This game is described in *The Final Reflection*, the 16th book of *Star Trek:*

# 41. Extraterrestrial Chess

*The Original Series*, written by John Ford. Playable rules have been established by Leonard B. Loyd, Jr., in 1989.

## Material

This game is played over a triangular grid of 9 triangular cells per side, making a board of 81 cells.

Each of the two players commands nine pieces (Klingon terms given in parentheses): 1 Fencer (*yanwI'*), 1 Lancer, (*ghIntaq yanwI'*), 1 Swift (*qetwI'*), 2 Fliers (*puvwI'*), 3 Vanguards (*'avwI'*) and 1 Blockader (*botwI'*).

In addition, each player possesses a Goal (*ngoQ*), which should not be considered as a regular piece. The object of the game is to capture the opponent's Goal or to block it so its owner has no legal move.

The pieces may be figurines or mere discs which are marked with a symbol or a Klingon letter. The pieces are colored gold on one side and green on the other.

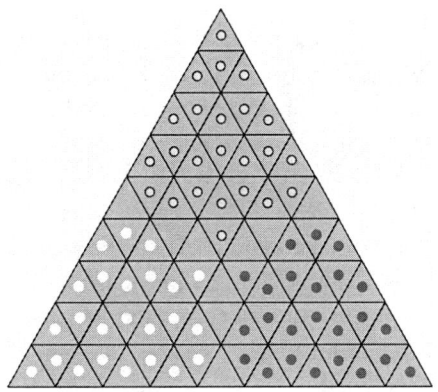

The Klin Zha board. The dots indicate the cells on which it is possible to place a piece at the beginning of the game.

## Rules

SETUP OF THE PIECES. At the beginning of the game, the board is empty. Two "spindles"—actually two hexagonal long rods whose sides are marked from 1 to 6—are thrown to determine the first player. Of course, regular dice can be used with the same result. The player who rolls the highest score plays first.

Playing first is considered to be a disadvantage. Therefore, the first player may offer the first move to his opponent, but the opponent may refuse.

The first player then chooses a corner of the board. His camp corresponds to 24 triangular cells shown in the diagram with dots of the same color. The player then places his nine pieces, one per triangular dotted cell, in his camp.

The second player then selects one of the two remaining corners of the board, and places his own pieces in the same manner. The third corner of the board is empty when the game starts.

After this disposal, the first player places his Goal over one of his "carrier pieces" (see rules below); the second player then does the same. The first player then makes the first move.

MOVES AND CAPTURES. The pieces move from one triangular cell to another one. The triangles are crossed from side to side, never by the corner points. Triangles joined at the corners are not considered to be adjacent.

A piece "kills" an enemy piece by landing on the cell it occupies.

*Fencer:* troop leader and most important piece of the game. It moves one, two or three cells in any direction or combination of directions. It cannot jump over intervening pieces.

*Lancer:* moves one, two or three spaces in a straight line. It cannot jump over intervening pieces.

*Swift:* moves two, three or four cells in any direction or combination of directions. It cannot jump over intervening pieces. It cannot carry the Goal.

*Flier:* moves three, four, five or six spaces, in straight line only. It can jump over interposed pieces, including those protected by the Blockader. It cannot carry the Goal.

*Vanguard:* moves only one cell in any direction.

*Blockader:* unit that carries a force field which can protect the pieces at its sides. Moves one or two spaces in any direction or combination of directions. It cannot jump. The Blockader cannot move to a cell adjacent to an enemy piece.

The cells adjacent to the Blockader's cell form its control zone. Enemy pieces cannot enter its control zone. The control zone of the two enemy Blockaders cannot overlap. When the Blockader moves, its force field is interrupted and its control zone is activated around its destination cell only. Therefore, by moving two squares, it can cross a cell adjacent to an enemy piece.

The Blockader cannot kill nor be killed but it can capture an abandoned enemy Goal by moving onto its cell. It cannot carry the Goal (otherwise, the Goal would be invulnerable).

*Goal:* it is not a piece; it represents the player's spirit. It cannot move by itself and must be carried by a Warrior: Fencer, Lancer or Vanguard. It cannot be carried by the Swift, Flier or Blockader. It can be left on a cell if the Warrior that carries it moves away alone, leaving the Goal on its cell of departure. If a Warrior begins his carrying the Goal, he must complete the move with it: it is forbidden to abandon the Goal on an intermediate space.

When the Goal is left alone on a cell, it does not obstruct pieces that may cross over that cell. A Goal can be transferred to an allied Warrior that just moves onto the cell where it stands alone.

It is forbidden to move the Goal inside the control zone of his Blockader (this would be a cowardly attitude, contrary to the Klingon spirit). However, it is permitted to carry the Goal through the control zone providing that the destination cell is outside that zone.

A player is forbidden from intentionally placing his own Goal in check.

No piece can move in such a way as to pass through the same triangle more than once in a single move (doubling back is not allowed).

**END OF THE GAME.** The Klin Zha winner is the player who succeeds in capturing the opposing Goal or in making it impossible for his opponent to move legally.

Note that the Goal may be captured by the enemy Blockader as well as by the other enemy pieces.

The winner concludes the game with this statement: *"Zha riest'n, teskas tal tai-kleon"* (*A pleasant game. My compliments to a worthy opponent*).

The green Flier threatens all dotted cells. The yellow Blockader protects all grayed cells. The yellow Vanguard, which carries the Goal, is in check. It has only one safe space: the cell marked X.

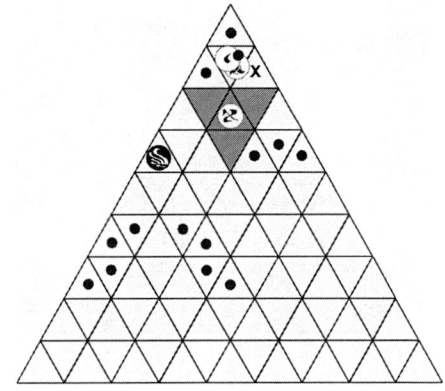

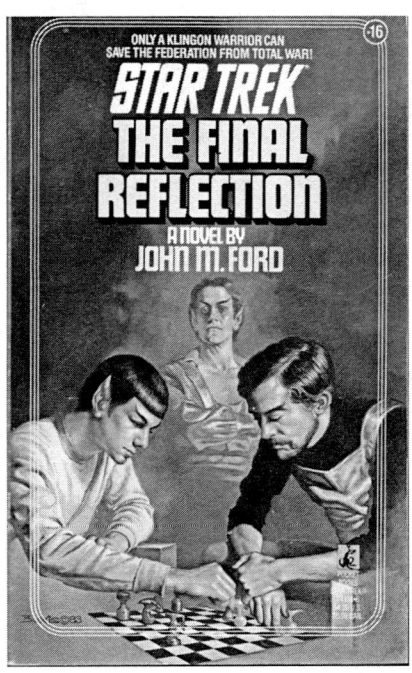

Klin Zha is an avatar of the Star Trek mania. The Klingon language has been constructed and there is a Klingon Language Institute and even a Klingon Wiki site. Kevin A. Geiselman is the webmaster of a very rich Authorized Klin Zha Homepage.[69] Klin Zha competitions and tournaments are organized among enthusiastic amateurs who go by Klingon names. For instance, Len Loyd is Admiral Korath and Kevin Geiselman is Kordite. Perhaps this game ventures further into fantasy than most, but it is probably the best chess variant ever devised on a board with triangular cells.

*Left:* Cover of John M. Ford's *Star Trek: The Final Reflection*.

# 42. Chess960

The board here is the familiar pattern of 64 checkered squares. The pieces are the 16 white and 16 black chessmen of standard chess. Nevertheless, this variation is certainly one of the most successful in the past few decades. According to some experts, it represents one of the possible future developments of competitive chess (along with the trend for shorter time limits in tournaments). No less than that prodigy Bobby Fischer (1943–2008), world champion in 1972 and considered by many to be the most brilliant chess player of all time, is credited as the inventor of this way of playing.

"Inventor" may be too strong a word, as the idea of modifying the initial array was investigated long before the American champion took an interest in it. But Fischer's contribution has been instrumental in fixing a set of rules that respect and maintain the essence of orthodox chess, allowing many enthusiastic chess players throughout the world to be drawn in to its possibilities.

This name refers to the number of possible starting arrays. The main advantage of this system resides in the fact that it dispenses with memorized openings. Fischer asserted that these rules considerably reduce the superiority of computers and encourage the return of creativity and talent by freeing players from an intensive course of memorization.

## *Rules*

The rules are orthodox except for the initial array and castling.

INITIAL SETUP. The initial array is randomly chosen, usually with the help of a computer program, coin tosses, dice or any sort of random generator, respecting the following conditions:

- All Pawns are placed normally, on the second row for each player (second rank for White; seventh for Black).
- The other pieces are placed on the first rank of each player (first rank for White, eighth for Black). Black pieces must mirror white pieces. For example, if the white Queen is on a1, black Queen is placed on a8.
- The King must be situated somewhere between the two Rooks.
- The two Bishops must be placed on squares of different color.

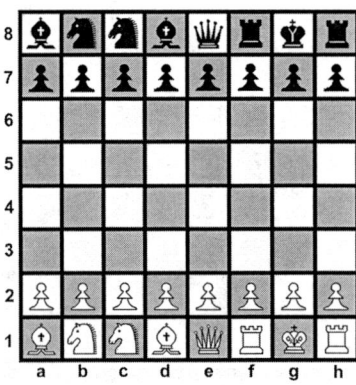

Example of a possible initial array of Chess960.

It can be demonstrated that there are 960 legal initial positions: starting with the white Bishop, there is a choice of 4 different white squares to host it. Then, there are 4 different black squares for the black Bishop. That means there are 16 (4 × 4) different ways to fix both Bishops. That leaves 6 squares from which to choose the Queen's placement. There are now 5 squares left to place the first Knight, then 4 squares to place the second. That gives 5 × 4 possibilities but in fact there are only 10 because both Knights are identical. There is then no more choice as only 3 squares remains free and it is compulsory to place the King in the middle one and both Rooks on the left and right. Overall, we have 16 × 6 × 10 = 960.

CASTLING. Castling must fulfill the usual prerequisites: the King must not be in check, the King and the Rook must not have been played yet, and the King must not cross a square threatened by an adverse piece. Whatever their initial squares, when the King castles on the a-side, he must come to c1 (c8 for Black) and the Rook must go on d1 (d8). This is noted 0–0–0. On h-side, the King goes to g1 (g8) and the Rook on f1(f8). This is noted 0–0. Therefore, the castled King and Rook land in the same positions that they would in orthodox chess.

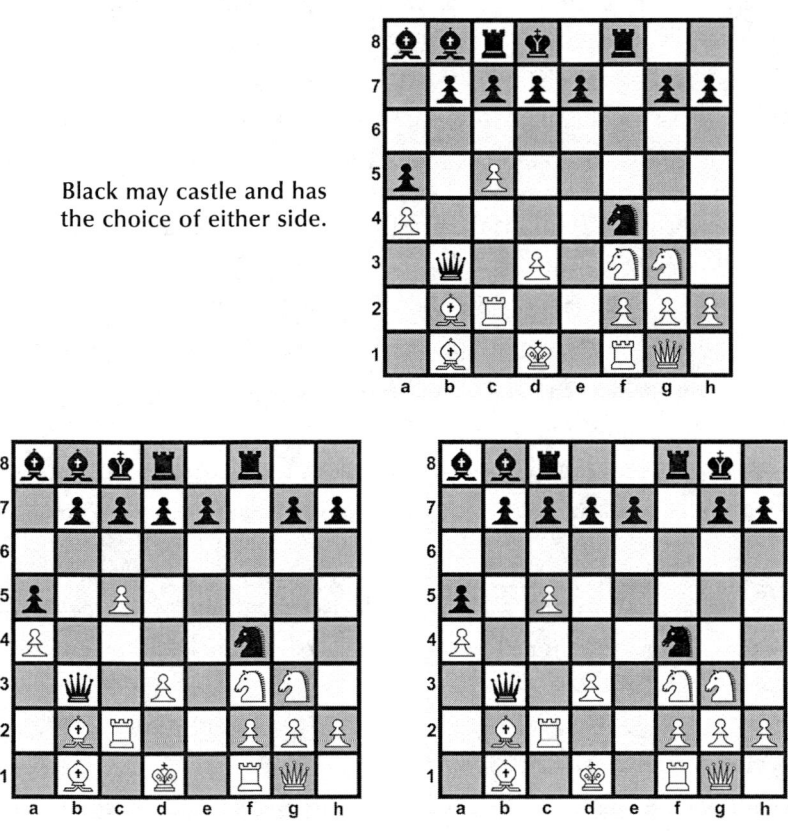

Black may castle and has the choice of either side.

Situation after castling when the King goes to either c8 (left) or g8 (right).

## Technical Matters

NUMBERING THE POSSIBLE ARRAYS. Are there really 960 different starting positions? One may pose the objection that mirrored positions are structurally the same (i.e., placing the piece on a1 is changed to h1, the piece on b1 is placed on g1, etc., creating the same arrangement in reverse order). In this view, there are only 480 unique configurations. However, the rules of castling, being inherently asymmetrical, invalidate that contention, since play does not proceed symmetrically even in symmetrical starting positions. Therefore, the contention of 960 unique starting arrays holds under scrutiny.

DRAWING THE ARRAY. In Chess960, the starting array is determined at random. Fischer spent a lot of time in designing an electronic "piece shuffler" that could draw an initial position and also offer other services such as printing score sheets and diagrams. Of course, with the rapid development of personal computers and similar devices, these efforts became quickly outdated. Nowadays, there are plenty of convenient ways to shuffle a Chess960 initial array.

At the same time, several aficionados have conceived methods for creating starting positions with equal probability with simple objects such as coins or dice.

The following method was proposed by Ingo Althöfer in 1998. It simply requires a single die. The position of White's pieces is determined as follows:

- Roll the die and place a Bishop on the black square indicated by the die, counting from the left, a through g. Thus, 1 indicates a1, 2 indicates c1, 3 indicates e1, and 4 indicates g1. If a 5 or 6 is rolled, simply roll again until a usable number appears.
- Roll the die and place a Bishop on the indicated white square. 1 indicates b1, 2 indicates d1, and so on. Re-roll a 5 or 6.
- Roll the die and place the Queen on the empty square indicated, not counting the squares occupied by the Bishops. Thus, 1 is the first (leftmost) empty square, while 6 is the sixth (rightmost) empty square.
- Roll the die and place a Knight on one of the 5 available squares. Re-roll if a 6 appears.
- Roll the die and place a Knight on the empty position indicated. Re-roll a 5 or 6.
- This leaves three empty squares. Place the King on the middle empty square, and the Rooks on the remaining two squares.

Note this method leads to 1920 possible combinations. Every Chess960 initial array is given by two different dice combinations. For instance, the standard chess setup is given by either the rolls 2–3–3–2–3 or the rolls 2–3–3–4–2. Nevertheless, it meets the criterion of Chess960 perfectly since every possible opening position can be rolled with equal probability.

Another elegant method employs a set of polyhedral dice shaped like each of the five Platonic solids. With this method, there is no need to re-roll any dice. Roll all the dice in one throw, and place White's pieces as follows:

- Place a Bishop on one of the eight squares (counting from the left, a through h) as indicated by the octahedron (eight-sided die).
- Place the other Bishop on one of the four squares of opposite color as indicated by the tetrahedron (four-sided die).
- Place the Queen on one of the remaining six squares as indicated by the cube (six-sided die).
- Place the first Knight according to the value of the icosahedron (twenty-sided die), by counting the five empty squares and looping back to the left when necessary after reaching the rightmost empty square.
- Then with four empty squares remaining, do the same for the other Knight, but using the value of the dodecahedron (twelve-sided) die.
- Place the King between the Rooks on the remaining three squares.

DOUBLETS. One admitted weakness of Chess960 is that some starting arrays may offer an exaggerated advantage to White. For example, there are initial positions in which not every Pawn is protected, allowing White to attack the unguarded point in the first few moves.

A suggested method to overcome this drawback is to play two games from each initial position with each player taking a turn playing the black and the white side.

## Variants

Chess960 has developed its own variants:

*Double Fischer Random Chess* allows White and Black to have starting positions not mirroring each other. Thus, there are 921,600 (960 × 960) different initial arrangements. Many are substantially unbalanced, as not all the 960 positions are of equal strength. Once again, playing two games each round with the same starting array, but switching sides, can even out the discrepancy.

*Shuffle Chess, Baseline Chess* or *Randomized Chess* are generic names for variants in which there is no restriction as to how the pieces are placed in the back row. Keeping a mirrored symmetry between White and Black setups, there are 5040 possible different positions. If the Bishops are forced to be on squares of different colors, that number is reduced to 2880. As a matter of fact, many variants of this sort were invented prior to the development of Chess960. The most influential among them are presented in the following historic review.

## History

The idea of corrupting the chess rules by randomly shuffling the pieces in the back row is fairly old. The earliest proposal on record was that promoted by Philippus Julius van Zuylen van Nyevelt, a Dutch officer who penned the French book *La supériorité aux échecs* (*Superiority at Chess*), in 1792. His goal was to fight monotony and inject diversity, restoring the chances to common players who might meet "a player who knows five or six moves in advance."

Gligorić reports a game played in 1842 in Mannheim (Germany) between the Baron Von der Hoeven and Aaron Alexandre.[70] Except for the advanced position of the b- and g-Pawns, the starting array would have been legal in Chess960.

Starting position for the game between Von der Hoeven (White) and Aaron Alexandre (Black) in Mannheim, 1842. Alexandre won.

Two other games were also recorded, also lost by the Baron Von der Hoeven, against Von der Lasa in 1851. Pieces were freely shuffled, with mirrored positions for Black and White. However, in those two games, the players' Bishops were not on different colors of square and, in one game, the King was standing in a corner. These completely free positions are not allowed in Chess960.[71]

In the early years of the 20th century, many good chess players contended to invent a new system that would both diminish White's advantage of first move and invalidate the tenets of opening theory.

In 1911, a tournament was organized at the Patent Office Chess Club in London, on the instigation of H. Mountcastle, with the initial position of pieces on the back row determined by lot. If both Bishops were on the same square color, the right one (from White's view) exchanged its place with the piece to its left. Both players had symmetrical arrays. There was no castling.

Drawing the positions at random is not the only way to change the initial setup of the pieces. It can also be achieved by allowing the players to place their pieces at will. In this case, the initial setup can be decided independently of the opponent by concealing the chosen array until the game starts, or the disposal of the pieces can constitute a first phase of the game. This last idea goes back to the early 1920s when the Swiss problemist Erich Anselm Brunner (1885–1938), deploring the way opening theory was transforming the game into an exercise in brute memorization, invented *Free Chess*. In Brunner's system, White first places a piece of his choice on any square of the back row; then Black places the same piece on the symmetric square. He has the choice between respecting bilateral ("mirror") symmetry (e.g., a8 corresponds to a1, b8 corresponds to b1 etc.) or point symmetry (where each player has the same arrangement from his own left-to-right, so g8 corresponds to b1, etc.). Then, Black puts a second piece on his back row and White places the same piece on the symmetrical square (keeping the mode of symmetry chosen by Black). Then, White places a third piece and so on. Observing this dual-symmetry system, with no constraint on the Bishops, 10,080 starting positions are permitted. Castling is possible.

Going one step further toward full freedom, Karl Kaiser proposed *Funkschach* in 1926, in which players were invited to place their pieces one by one, starting by the Kings, then Queens, Rooks, Bishops and Knights, in that order. There was no obligation of symmetry, leading to very high number of possible arrays: 5040 × 5040, more than 25 million. It is fortunate the game was not named Chess25401600.

In 1934, *Real Chess* by the Hungarian, E.I. Csaszar, accepted a fully free arrangement of the pieces on the back row (Pawns were still set on the second row). Players simply took turns placing a piece of their choice on the back row. This system is the most open: there is no restriction of any sort, nor any determined symmetry between the two sides. Castling is possible between the King and a Rook under the classical conditions (unmoved King and Rook, unobstructed path, no check or passing through check): the King goes up to the square adjacent to the Rook and the Rook leaps over the King onto the next square. If the King is already on a square adjacent to the Rook, the King does not move and only the Rook jumps on the other side of the King.

A similar concept was advocated by E. Slater in the 1950s under the name of *Free Chess* (again). Unlike Csaszar, Slater did not permit castling. This ancient concept was once again presented and newly accredited under the name *Pre-Chess*, in a 1978 article in *Chess Life & Review* magazine, endorsed by two American grandmasters, Arthur Bisguier and Pal Benko—who credited the idea to Russian champion David Bronstein (1924–2006). This game begins with the Pawns placed on the second row. Then, each player in turn places one piece at a time on his back row. Bishops are required to be on opposite color squares. Castling is allowed only if the King and the Rook are disposed in their standard chess positions (King on e-square, Rook on a- or h-square). Max Euwe, former world chess champion and former president of FIDE, judged the idea "interesting and worth trying."

*Transcendental chess*, often abridged as "TC," was invented by Maxwell Lawrence in 1978. Each player arranges the pieces on his first row at random. The Bishops must be on different colors; therefore, there are 8,294,400 (2880 × 2880) possible starting positions. No castling is permitted. Because many starting arrays present a disadvantage to Black, match games are played in pairs: two games are played with the same initial array but with the players alternating sides for the second game. Also, both players have the right, on the first turn only, to transpose two pieces in their array instead of moving. Tournaments have been held in the U.S. by correspondence play.

*Comparative summary of the different proposed systems.*

| Name | Year | Starting positions | Setup | Symmetry | Bishops | Castling |
|---|---|---|---|---|---|---|
| Van Nyevelt | 1792 | ? | Random | Mirror | Free | ? |
| Von der Hoeven | 1851 | 5040 | Random | Mirror | Free | ? |
| Mountcastle | 1911 | 2880 | Random | Mirror | Colored | No |
| Free Chess (Brunner) | 1921 | 10080 | Alternate choice | Mirror or Diagonal | Free | Yes |
| Funkschach (Kaiser) | 1926 | $(5040)^2$ | Alternate, ordered | None | Free? | ? |
| Real Chess (Csaszar) | 1934 | $(5040)^2$ | Alternate choice | No | Free | Yes |
| Free Chess (Slater) | 1950s | $(5040)^2$ | Alternate choice | No | Free | No |
| Pre-Chess (Bronstein) | 1978 | $(2880)^2$ | Alternate choice | No | Colored | Yes |
| TC (Lawrence) | 1978 | $(2880)^2$ | Random + switching 2 pieces | No | Colored | No |
| Chess960 (Fischer) | 1993 | 960 | Random | Mirror | Colored | Yes |

Then, Bobby Fischer, the famous and mysterious American World Chess Champion who had disappeared for years after 1976, returned to the limelight in 1992, promoting a new system. Fischer opined that the number of legal positions in "shuffle chess" had to be reduced. He suggested imposing different colored squares to the two Bishops and forcing the King to stand between the two Rooks in order to allow castling. In 1993, the rules of "*Fischerandom Chess*" were formulated. In July 1995, Karpov tried this system and, in the spring of 1996, a first tournament was won in Kanjiza (then in Yugoslavia) by the Hungarian grandmaster Péter Lékó.

The resurrection of the elusive champion lent considerable momentum to the game's enthusiastic reception. A high-level match was organized in Germany on the occasion of the Mainz Chess Classic 2001, between the English champion, Michael Adams (then the number 4 player in the FIDE ratings), and, again, Péter Lékó (then the number 7). The match was played in eight games and the Hungarian won 4½ : 3½. Further Chess960 tournaments have been organized at the Mainz Chess Classic up through 2009, with several first-class world players.

Naming this variant has been an issue. Also known as Shuffle Chess, it was first named in honor of its famous promoter, Fischer Random Chess or, sometimes, Fischerandom Chess. Some players preferred not to peg this variant to its famous patron, and some felt that the term "random" was too vague. So, *Chess960*, referring to the number of possible starting arrays, has been selected and finally adopted by many chess players worldwide.

In 2008, FIDE added Chess960 to an appendix of the laws of chess. Chess960 is more than a variant now: it is an officially recognized game.

# ♦ Part VII ♦

# The Origins of Chess

## *Looking for a Common Ancestor*

A review of the many games we have presented here can leave no doubt that they share a common origin. These games are considered indigenous to the diverse regions of Persia, India, Mongolia, Burma, Thailand, Cambodia, Vietnam, Malaysia, China, Korea, Japan and Europe; however, each one could well be a re-working of a game that came before it. As scholars look back into the fascinating histories of the chess variants, the historic evidence becomes scarcer with every passed century. Finally, we are left with the task of using our best evidence and best judgment to surmise the possible *prehistory* of chess.

For many decades, authors have relied heavily on the Indian origins model advocated by H.J.R. Murray's *A History of Chess (1913),* but an objective examination of the available source materials reveals the fragility of this widespread thesis. A final, tangible proof is sorely lacking. It is of value, therefore, to reassess and clarify what is and is not known—and to reconsider possible interpretations of the evidence.

The game of chess has a fascinating history, but the study of chess history itself has a history all its own, imaginative and rich with surprises. Our oldest confirmed record of the game, telling of its arrival in Persia from an Indian envoy, already mixes history with legend. Centuries later, as European scholars delved into the subject, a tantalizing new myth took hold: the origin of chess as the Indian game *chaturaji* (sometimes known as *chaturanga*), a game for four players with dice. In this game, each player had eight playing pieces. When the four armies of eight were combined into two armies of sixteen, and the dice discarded—*voilà*—the two-player form of ancient chess was born. It is a tempting hypothesis, in its logic and simplicity, but it can be said with near certainty that it is a false lead. The present authors intend to demonstrate why.

The following is a brief, up-to-date account of what is now known regarding the origin of chess. Many chess enthusiasts and authors have worked tirelessly for many years uncovering the mysterious birth of this King of Games. The present review branches into diverse fields of study, all of which have made significant progress in the past several decades. It is an endeavor to present the fundamental questions along with the most telling evidence, piece by piece, inviting the reader to develop an informed and appreciative view of this historical mystery.

The invention of nard, in response to the arrival of chess at the Persian court. Persian miniature dated 1536.
BRITISH LIBRARY, ADD. 15531, FOLIO 445B

# 43. Legends of the Creation

*Who invented chess? When? Where? How? Why?*

## *The Persian and Arabic Legends*

The oldest known text written specifically about chess immediately addresses some of the above fundamental questions. With the Persian epic *Wizarishn i chatrang*, chess made its entrance onto the stage of history. It tells of the arrival of chess at the court of King Khusraw I (a.k.a. Chosroes, 531–579), known in Persian as *Anosharwan*, "the Immortal Soul." According to this ancient legend, a magnificent envoy had come from Dewisharm, king of the Hind,[1] with a caravan of 90 elephants and 1,200 camels. All were laden with gold, silver, pearls and splendid fabrics, all guided by the emissary, Tataritos.

Within a great treasury of gifts, there appeared one particular game, with pieces of ruby and emerald, and this game came with a grave challenge: "*As your name is King of Kings, it is said that your sages are wiser than the wisest among us. If you discover the secrets of this game, it will prove that this is truth; otherwise, you will pay us a tribute in return.*" After three grueling days of study and deliberation, the Persian sage Wuzurgmihr succeeded in piercing the enigma. He told his king, "*Be immortal! I am going to explain chatrang and to force Dewisharm to give you twice that which he asked because there is not any doubt that your sages are wiser than his.*"

Wuzurgmihr summoned Tataritos and explained everything in detail: "*Dewisharm made this game like a battlefield. There are the kings, like two overlords, the ministers essential for the right and left flanks, the general as chief of the warriors, the elephants that resemble the royal bodyguards, the horses like commanders of the cavalry and the foot soldiers identical to those that lead the battle.*" Tataritos then put the chatrang set on the table challenging Wuzurgmihr to play with him and Wuzurgmihr won three times. Wuzurgmihr then proposed to the King of Kings that he take his own invention back to the Hind king. Wuzurgmihr's invention was the game of *new-ardakhshir* (later known as *nard*), named in honor of Ardakhshir I, founder of the Persian Sassanid Empire. This game comprised 15 black pieces ("like the night") and 15 white pieces ("like the day"), on a board inspired by the movement of the stars and planets. But in India, no one could guess the rules of this game, even after days of contemplation. Dewisharm conceded, paid tribute to the Persians, and Wuzurgmihr was highly honored upon his return.

This tale of chess, arriving at the court of Sassanid Persia, made a lasting impression on Islamic literature. Four hundred years later, the famous Iranian poet Firdawsi adopted this legend in his monumental epic of ancient Persia, the *Shahnama* (*Book of Kings*). In Firdawsi's retelling, the envoy was representing the Indian raja of Kannauj (formerly, Kanyakubja), then the preeminent city on the Ganges River. It seems that this tale, implying the superiority of Persia over India, carried some political leverage, just as Islam was asserting its power in Northern India. Countless artistic representations of this legendary event have come to us from the Middle East, including drawings, watercolors, wall paintings, and illustrated manuscripts.

But this is not the only legend of chess's origin to circulate in the ancient Muslim texts. Most notable are the accounts given by Baghdad's famous historians and geographers Ya'qubi and al-Mas'udi.[2] The most common of these diverse tales, often attributed to al-'Adli, is cast in the court of the legendary Indian king, Balhait. According to one account, the king asked Sassa (a.k.a. Sissa), son of the Brahmin Dahir, to invent a new game exalting the qualities of good government. The king wanted a game morally superior to nard—which was considered to run against the prevailing religious precepts against gambling. Another account has the king simply desiring to alleviate his boredom after defeating all of his enemies. Other versions have the king wishing to occupy his vassals, steering them clear of bloody rivalries, or to provide a means of educating the prince in the art of military strategy.

While theories of the exact motives in this scenario are plentiful, the theme is consistent with the king, Balhait, requesting a new game of Sassa, and Sassa inventing the game of chess. As the story continues, the king asks Sassa what he would have as his reward. His reply sounds modest at first: he would like one grain of wheat on the first square of the chessboard, two grains on the next square, four grains on the next ... and so on, doubling each time all the way to the sixty-fourth square.

While Sassa's request might seem quite modest at a casual glance, a mathematician will see at once that it sets up an explosive mathematical progression. By the time the 64th square was covered, Sassa would have amassed an incredible 18,446,744, 073,709,551,615[3] grains of wheat! That's two thousand times the current annual worldwide production of wheat—or approximately enough wheat to cover the United States four inches deep. Or, if the grains could be laid end-to-end, they would make a line of about two light-years! According to the legend, the equivalent value in gold was calculated and duly paid—a worthy fee indeed for the invention of chess!

Firdawsi was not necessarily committed to the legend given above. He conveyed this chess origin legend as well: Jamhur, king of Kashmir, had died, leaving his kingdom and his son, Gaw, in the care of his brother, Mai. Mai married Jamhur's widow and they had another son, Talhand. But Mai shortly followed Jamhur to the grave. While growing, Talhand grew to hate his elder half-brother, Gaw, and ultimately declare war on him. A bad decision, because Talhand perished on the battlefield. But then Gaw was beset with the terrible obligation to tell his mother what had happened. For this, he invented chess. While the bereaved mother was learning to play, she came to understand how two kings may be pitted against one another—and only one may prevail.

Some Arabic texts pushed the invention of chess back further still: Adam was said to have invented chess to console himself over the death of Abel. Sem, Japhet and Solomon were reported to be chess players, as were the Greek philosophers Aristotle, Galen and Hippocrates.

The Persian and Arabic texts gave a good variety of legends to explain the origins of chess. But, after the year 1000, the Europeans spun tales of their own.

## *The European Legends*

As chess spread into European society, so did new legends of its originator take hold. Pyrrhus, king of Epirus, was one—famed for his victorious assault against the Romans and its ill-fated aftermath. Attalus, king of Pergamon and friend of the Romans, also joined the long list of proclaimed inventors. One report had chess invented during the Trojan War, by "divine birth." Odysseus and Diomedes were named as its creator—but then, Palamedes, shrewder and more artful than Odysseus, was also given credit.

Jacobus de Cessolis, Dominican friar, had a quite different idea. Around 1270 he wrote *Liber de moribus hominum et officiis nobilium super ludo scacchorum (Book of the Customs of Men and the Duties of Nobles or the Book of Chess)*. Translated into nine languages, it was nearly the most popularly copied book, second only to the Bible, of the 14th and 15th centuries. Cessolis claimed that the Greeks received the game from Babylon, under the reign of the dread king Evilmerodach, son of Nabuchadnezzar. This notorious tyrant began his reign by cutting his own father into three hundred pieces, and feeding them to as many vultures. With unparalleled courage and wisdom, knowing that Evilmerodach was prone to murdering all who crossed him, the noble advisor Xerxes invented the game of chess in order to teach the values befitting a righteous king.

Image from the first illustrated text printed in the English language, *Game and Playe of the Chesse* (1480), printed by William Caxton, after Jacobus de Cessolis's manuscript, *… the Book of Chess*.

Xerxes first tantalized the king by introducing chess to the noblemen, who openly displayed their enjoyment of the game at the royal court. When the king begged Xerxes to teach him the game, Xerxes did so with great care, delivering a moral message with the introduction of each piece. Finally, with the king's dedicated interest and attention, Xerxes was able to reform Evilmerodach by instructing him on the exact virtues required of an honorable monarch.

It can be seen that this Xerxes is a reinvention of the character Sassa[4] in the Arabic tales, a very clever advisor who invented the game to teach the king a most essential lesson. By making a comparative review of ancient manuscripts, one can see the pattern of stories mutating over time as they pass from one civilization to another. The Indian king of the Arabic tale becomes the Babylonian king in the European telling, merging the details of this old story with the legendary personalities of the new setting. Chess is deeply embedded in this amazing process of cultural evolution.

Similarly, another Palamedes appeared in the Arthurian cycle as a knight of the Round Table. First a rival, then a friend of Tristan, he was a Saracen, son of the sultan of Babylon. From the Orient, he brought back this game which he taught to his friends. He became the "checkered knight" of sable and silver, so recognized by his shield, which is how Évrard of Espingues painted him in a 1463 manuscript. Here, we have a unique meeting of Oriental and Celtic legend.

## The Chinese Legends

Far away, in China, an entirely different set of legends was brewing. Around the year 1100, the scholar Chao Buzhi attributed the invention of chess to the Huangdi, the Yellow Emperor, who ruled in the third millennium B.C.E.[5] But in the 14th century, Huangdi's legendary predecessor, Shennong, revered father of Chinese civilization, was cited as the inventor by the monk, Nianchang.[6]

A more realistic—but still questionable—account of a Chinese chess inventor surfaced in the 18th century. According to this report, Liu Bang (the future Emperor Gaozu, 202–195 B.C.E., and founder of the Han Dynasty) sent out his troops to fight Xiang Yu, the king of Chu. As winter approached, the chief general, Han Xin, established a base on one side of the river. To keep his men from drink, debauchery and disputes, he invented this absorbing game of war. With their minds keen and strategically alert, Han Xin's troops marched to victory the following spring. According to this telling, the Chinese chess form, *xiangqi*, was originally known as "the game to capture Xiang Yu." This tale explains the xiangqi boards, which have a "river" between the two sides with Chinese characters indicating the border between Han and Chu.[7]

Tales of Sassa, Gaw, Adam, Palamedes, Xerxes, Huangdi, Shennong, Han Xin well represent some of the heroic "founders" of chess in world legend. But let us move on from these tales as we consider chess origins in the light of modern historic research.

---

# 44. The Modern Search Begins

## Thomas Hyde: The First Modern Chess Historian

Illustration from *De Ludis Orientalibus* by Thomas Hyde (1694), the foundational work of modern chess history.

The end of the 17th century marks a turning point in the study of chess history. Thomas Hyde, professor of Oriental languages at Oxford and official interpreter to the English court, is credited as the first scholar to hold the question under the rigorous scrutiny of science. His first compilation of studies of Asian games, *Mandragorias seu Historia Shahiludii*, was published in 1689. It was followed in 1694 by a study of the game of nard, *De Historia Nerdiludii*, and the two volumes were combined that same year, under the title *De Ludis Orientalibus*. This work was composed in an unlikely mixture of Latin, Hebrew, Greek, Arabic and Persian, and drew much of its information from the ancient

Muslim manuscripts. Firmly rejecting the legends of chess attributed to Palamedes or Xerxes, Hyde was finally convinced that chess must have been invented by an Indian philosopher named Sissa.

Today, we can see limitations and errors in Hyde's work based on a few incorrect assumptions. For instance, Hyde found a natural association between the word for chess, *shatrang*, and the word *satrang*, which indicates a mandrake plant. He speculated that the curious roots of these plants, which sometimes resemble human figures, could have some connection with the design of chessmen. But we should consider his work in the context of the times. Sanskrit texts were virtually inaccessible to European scholars in Hyde's day.

Among Hyde's contributions was the first complete description of xiangqi, Chinese chess, to appear in a Western publication. A former Chinese mandarin, Michel Fen Fu-Tsung, had reported on the game after being converted by Jesuit missionaries and brought back to Europe.[8]

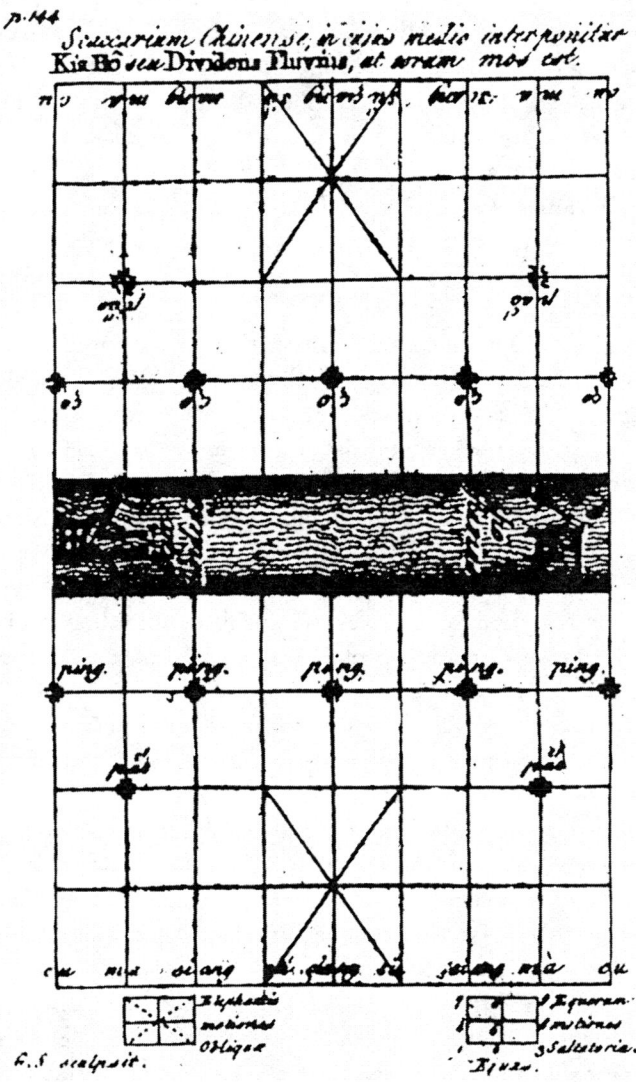

Hyde's original drawing of Chinese chess (1694)—introduced to Western literature for the first time. His diagram features Latin text with phonetic adaptations of the pieces' names and details regarding directions of movement. Note that this is the same as the modern xiangqi board.

# The False Trail of Four-Handed Chaturanga

About a century later, the brilliant linguist Sir William Jones turned his attention to chess origins. Famous for observing the kinship among the Sanskrit, old Persian, Greek and Latin languages, he was in a unique position to postulate the Asian roots of chess. In an essay of 1790, "On the Indian Game of Chess," he explained the sense of the word *chaturanga*, now generally accepted, as referring to the four (*chatur*) arms (*anga*) of the classic Indian army. He also transcribed the rules of four-handed chaturanga, designating it as *chaturaji*, which was then played in India and had been described in the sacred Sanskrit text the *Bhavishya Purana*. Jones told the traditional story, given to him by an Indian Brahmin named Radhakant, that chess had been invented by the wife of Ravana, king of Lanka, capital of Ceylon (now Sri Lanka). She had created the game to distract her husband during the unpleasant time in which his city was under siege by the god Rama. Although Jones did not take the Indian myth literally, and doubted that the four-handed game preceded the game for two players, he did come away convinced that all types of chess had originated in India.

In 1799, Captain Hiram Cox (mentioned previously, regarding the Burmese game of sittu-yin) sent a somewhat convoluted letter to the respected Asiatic Society.[9] He claimed that the four-handed variant predated the two-handed chaturanga—setting in motion a tempting thesis that would be echoed for centuries to come.

With the consensus of Indian origins of chess gaining momentum, the lone voice of one English Orientalist, Nathaniel Bland, begged to differ. In his 1851 book, *On the Persian Game of Chess*, Bland argued for a Persian origin of the game, citing the noteworthy absence of chess in the old Sanskrit texts, and the lack of Sanskrit roots in the nomenclature of the pieces. But this perspective received little notice in its day.

It was in 1860 that the British linguist Duncan Forbes produced a comprehensive and methodical treatise on the origins of chess, encompassing the most significant aspects of chess history into a unified theory in his book, *The History of Chess*. He seized upon Cox's idea that chess first came about as a game for four players using dice. According to this thesis, the four-handed game was gradually adapted to two players. Then, in obedience to a religious ban on games of dice, chess went on as a game of pure strategy with nothing left to chance. Forbes did not extend his view back to the god Rama's siege of Lanka, but he did accept the assertion that the rules of the four-handed game had appeared in the *Bhavishya Purana*, a text he estimated to be about 5,000 years old.

This ancient date however, was soon rebutted by the German Indologist Albrecht Weber and the Dutch historian Anton van der Linde. In 1874, Weber and van der Linde argued that texts of the *Bhavishya Purana* could not be as old as had been claimed, and probably did not contain actual references to chess. (These points of rebuttal have since been confirmed as the texts became available to European scholars.)

Accordingly, in the 1898 publication *Chess and Playing-Cards*, an impressive exhibition catalog of almost all known games at the time, the American ethnologist and game specialist Stewart Culin presented chaturanga for four players with dice, but recognized that "*The theory that modern chess had its origin in chaturanga* [i.e., the four-player game with dice], *suggested by Capt. Hiram Cox in 1799, and upheld and developed by Prof. Duncan Forbes has not been accepted by students of the game generally. The antiquity of the Purana in which it is described, has been questioned, and the game asserted to be a comparatively modern adaptation of the primal Hindu game."* Nevertheless, he put forth the hypothesis that most board games, such as chess, were preceded by race games in which the pieces were animated by dice, cowries or knuckle bones. He insisted that the relationship between chess and pachisi, an Indian race game for four players, was *"very evident."*

In 1900, the outstanding American ethnologist and Icelandic games historian Willard Fiske put forth this pertinent assessment: *"Before the seventh century of our era, the existence of Chess in any land is not demonstrable by a single shred of contemporary or trustworthy documentary evidence.... Down to that date, it is all impenetrable darkness."*

Then came H.J.R. Murray. In 900 dense pages of careful research and detailed discussion, including passages in many languages and copious footnotes, Murray, with his *A History of Chess* (1913), created the monument to chess history that has become the standard reference work for all scholars. According to Murray's analysis, dice were never forbidden or discouraged for religious reasons in India. On the contrary, representations of gods and goddesses playing such games are numerous. Murray confirmed that neither the *Bhavishya Purana* (composed at the earliest in the third century B.C.E. and finally available to Westerners in the late 19th century), nor any other such text, contained any references to chess.

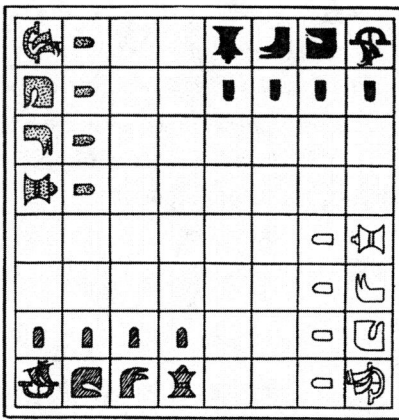

Murray's illustration of "four-handed chess" (1913).

Murray concluded that *"The silence of all other Sanskrit works before 600 A.D. makes Radhakant's assertion improbable in the highest degree."* The so-called "Cox-Forbes" theory had just been demolished. Concerning Culin's argument about chess evolving out of a race game, Murray revised it politely and, finally, wrote the definitive sentence, *"I find this hypothesis incredible."*

Actually, three Indian texts do allude to the passage mentioned by Jones and Forbes. All three refer back to the same two Bengalese texts from the late 15th or early 16th century: the *Tithitattva* by Raghunandana, and the *Chaturangadipika* by Shulapani. So, Forbes was badly mistaken. The details upon which all modern descriptions rely, for the four-handed *chaturaji*, barely reach back 500 years. Finally, the earliest reference to this game remains an Arabic manuscript, the *Tahqiq ma li-l-Hind*, a travel journal of the north of India, written around 1030 by the Persian, al-Biruni.[10] The first certain mention of a chess game for two (clarified because a General stands next to the King) dates from the beginning of the seventh century, four hundred years earlier.

Since Murray's centenary work, no historic or scientific evidence has arisen to modify the conclusion that the story of a game for four players ruled by luck and evolving toward a game of pure strategy for two is attractive but totally unfounded. Unfortunately, many chess writers perpetuate this simplistic tale in books, magazines, newspapers and, of course, the Internet.

# 45. Approaching the Question from Several Angles

Where and when did chess first appear? Three vast geographical zones can still claim the title of cradle to the King of Games:

- The North of India: All the earliest Sanskrit references to chess—disputed or not—are concentrated in Kashmir or the Ganges valley, with a special mention of Kannauj (home to the Kanyakubja Brahmins). This zone can be extended to Sindh, Punjab, Gandhara and the entire Indus basin, including parts of modern-day Pakistan.
- Historic China: specifically, the Huang He (Yellow River) basin and, perhaps, also the Yangtze River valley to the South.
- The great Persian sphere: all countries crossed by the antique Silk Road, centered in Persia but also including Arachosia, Bactria, Khwarezm, Sogdiana, and Serindia. Essentially, Central Asia, from modern Iran to Xinjiang, through Afghanistan, Turkmenistan, Uzbekistan, Tajikistan, Kyrgyzstan. All these regions were related to the Persians by language and culture at the height of the Persian Empire.

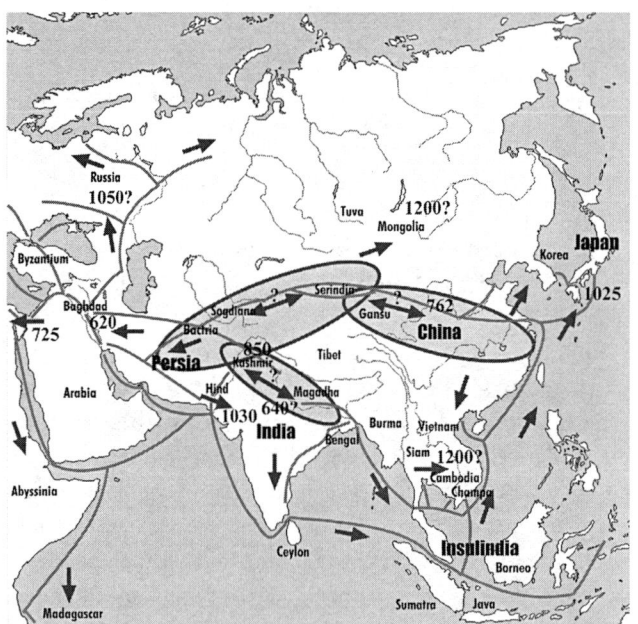

Candidates for to the birth of chess, showing its diffusion throughout Asia.

Is there an answer? Most people, familiar with the question, will maintain the view defended by Murray that chess was born in India, in or around the fifth century. Almost every available book or article on the subject repeats this well-worn hypothesis, spread by countless scholars (mostly English), from the time when England ruled the Indies. To view the question objectively requires one to consider that the power and profusion of these accounts may have carried a certain bias. The other two regions postulated deserve a fresh look.

Viewing chess as a broad-based world phenomenon appearing differently in different lands leaves one well poised to consider the question anew—and from several angles.

## 45. Approaching the Question from Several Angles

What do we learn from:

- Ancient texts?
- Archeology?
- Philology and nomenclature?
- Comparisons of game structure?

First, a review of the peoples and countries of the Silk Road:

Map of Central Asia crossed by the Silk Road.

**Gandhāra** occupied the area of modern-day northern Pakistan and eastern Afghanistan, along the valleys of the Swat and the Kabul rivers, which merge into the Indus. This kingdom, a part of the Kushan Empire, is renowned for its art, a fusion of the Hellenistic and Indian influences. Its main cities were Peshawar and Taxila, an influential center for Buddhist studies.

**Khorasan** draws its name from an Old Persian expression meaning "land of the sunrise." This area constituted an eastern region of the Sassanid Empire, essentially encompassing Nishapur (Iran), Merv (Turkmenistan) and Herat (Afghanistan). For Arab geographers, the *Great Khorasan* also included Bactria and Sogdiana. The Merv region was also known as Margiana.

**Bactria** was situated between the Hindu Kush Mountains and the Amu Darya River. It was centered in the northern tip of modern-day Afghanistan, around the city of Balkh (old Bactra) and spread into areas now known as Pakistan, Tajikistan and Uzbekistan. Central to several powerful kingdoms and empires (the Greco-Bactrians, the Kushans and the Hephtalite Huns) it finally became the easternmost extension of the Sassanid Persian Empire.

**Khwarezm** (Greek, Chorasmia), the Persian "land of the sun," spread from the south of the Aral Sea to the Western regions of Uzbekistan and Turkmenistan, east of Iran, around the Uzbek city of Khiva. The Khwarezmians were active tradesmen on the Silk Road.

**Sogdiana** covered the eastern area of Uzbekistan and parts of Tajikistan and Kyrgyzstan, around the prestigious cities of Samarkand and Bukhara. Situated along the rich Fergana Valley and Kokand, it controlled the passage through the Pamir Mountains, which led to the oasis of Serindia. The Sogdians developed a brilliant and original civilization, based more on trade and diplomacy than on war and conflict. Sogdian merchants established many trading posts along the roads, extending to the great cities of China. The Sogdian language became the *lingua franca* of the Silk Road, and it is this language, adopted by Persian and Turkish ambassadors, in which the Silk Road's history is written. The impartial Sogdians facilitated the circulation of all religions—Buddhism, Zoroastrianism, Manichaeism and even Nestorianism.

**Transoxiana** was a term used by Persian and Arab writers to indicate the land beyond the Oxus River (modern-day Amu Darya), essentially corresponding to Khwarezm, Sogdiana and Bactria.

**Serindia** corresponds to the Tarim Basin, a long stream of 2000 km (1,240 miles) that crosses the dangerous Taklamakan desert to dry, with no outlet, in the Lop Nor swamps. To avoid this inhospitable pan, surrounded by high mountains, the Silk Road divided into two branches, between Kashgar to the west and Dunhuang to the East, reconvening at various oases.[11] Occupied by the Yuezhis, an Indo-European people who may have used the Tokharian languages, its strategically enviable position made it subject to the assaults of Tibetans, Göktürks and, of course, the Chinese. A campaign of Emperor Taizong in 648 to seize the oasis put an end to the brilliant Serindian civilization. Repopulated with the Uighurs in the tenth century, it became a part of eastern Turkestan that the Chinese authorities renamed Xinjiang, meaning "new border," indicating that it would be a land of immigration for the Han people.

## *Ancient Texts*

Seeking evidence in ancient texts, we must bear in mind the limitations which are always present. Foremost, we should remember that the texts available to us are copies of copies, usually in a long line of written or verbal reports, which may have undergone centuries of subtle (or not so subtle) alterations before arriving as the text we finally access. The possibility is always present that copyists may have updated or "improved" the texts along the way. It is only through cross-checking, analyzing and comparing various versions of related documents that historians are able to attribute dates and authenticity to particular manuscripts or passages. Any modern theory of chess origins should take on the same academic rigor assumed in all historic disciplines.

THE PERSIAN EPICS OF THE SASSANID EMPERORS. Our game enters the stream of history in the heart of medieval Iran. Here, appearing in three Pahlavi (Middle Persian) texts, dating to the late sixth or early seventh century, we find descriptions of a game for two players, each commanding an army of 16 pieces.

The oldest of these three, which we have previously mentioned, is the *Wizarishn i chatrang ud nihishn i new-ardakhshir* (*Explanation of Chatrang and the Invention of Nard*), estimated to have been written around 600 C.E.[12] This text presents the scene already described in which chess arrives at the court of the Sassanid emperors, their wise men decipher its mystery, and return the challenge of deciphering nard to the Indian court—at which the Indians fail. As a result, the Indians pay a tribute to the Persian King of Kings. Six sorts of pieces are named, with varying degrees of description. The pieces are a King (*shah*), a General (*frazen*), Ministers (*madayar*) "on the right and left flanks," Elephants (*pil*), Horses (*asp*) and Soldiers (*payadag*). The

Pahlavi word for flank is *rokh*, and this is the most plausible etymology for this word which, through Arabic (*rukhkh*) and then Latin (*rochus*), leads to the English *Rook*.

So, what is to be made of this account? It is interesting that, before the Arab conquest (636–651), the Persians attributed chess to Hind, situated on the banks of the Indus River, at the footstep of India. As a result of this early assertion, all of the following Islamic and classic historians have adopted this view of chess as a Hindu invention.

In any case, this early account does establish a few things firmly. This game of chatrang is almost certainly the game of chess, and the names of the pieces are clearly given. While the Persians laid no claim to chess's invention, the passage does credit them with the game *new-ardakhshir*, understood to be nard, a predecessor of backgammon. We now know that that race game actually has a much deeper history, dating back before the fifth century, found in both Oriental and Roman sources.[13] This discrepancy should caution the reader not to take the tale too literally. Another interesting aspect of the story is that the Persians credited themselves with a game of chance, rather than chess, a game purely of reason, in a book composed to enhance their national pride. By claiming nard as a Persian invention, it is clear that the Persians of the late sixth century had a view quite different from our own. They valued the roll of the dice, considered a means of divine intervention, above the decisions drawn by mere mortals.

This legend, placing India as the original source of the game, has been a source of conjecture for many centuries. In more recent times, the German chess historian Dr. Renate Syed has suggested that the envoy in the legend, Dewisharm, could be the historic Deva Sharvavarman of the Maukhari Dynasty, which ruled Kannauj (560–585).[14] A tempting hypothesis, but it must be admitted that the legend itself remains historically unverified.

The vast Sassanid Persian Empire spread eastward from its capital Ctesiphon (near present-day Baghdad) all the way to the banks of the Indus River, and reached into Central Asia as far as the Amu Darya River. India, to the Persians, represented an exotic world, a source of mystery and the setting for many elaborate stories. So, when considering this earliest account of chess, we must allow the possibility that Persia, like many civilizations after it, attributed chess to its neighboring land of marvels, and painted a lovely picture of elephants with precious stones to complete the tale. Though this story has been told and retold for centuries, it remains lacking in corroborative evidence.

The next Persian text to mention chess is the *Karnamag i Ardakhshir i Pabagan* (*Book of the Deeds of Ardakhshir, Son of Pabag*), composed under Khusraw II Parwez (reigned 590–628).[15] This is the glorious tale of Ardakhshir, founder of the Sassanid Dynasty (reigned 226–241). It reports that Ardakhshir was "more victorious and warlike than all princes, at *chobagan* [polo], at *aswarih* [horse dressage], at *chatrang*, at *new-ardakhshir* [nard], and in several other arts."

The third text, written at the same period, but unknown to Murray, is the *Khusraw i Kawadan ud Redag* (*Khusraw, Son of Kawad, and His Page*). In it, the young prince is quoted saying, "...and in playing *chatrang*, *new-ardakhshir* and *hashtpay*,[16] I am superior to my comrades." We gather from this context that the Persian court held chess in the highest esteem at the beginning of the seventh century.

SOME CONTROVERSIAL SANSKRIT TEXTS. Contrary to what one might expect, chess does not make a strong appearance in the ancient texts of India.[17] Although the words *ashtapada* and *chaturanga* have a very old Sanskrit origin, it is difficult to correlate the uses of those words with something resembling chess. *Ashtapada*, which transliterates as "eight feet," first appears in the sense of gaming board in the Buddhist text *Vinayapitaka*,[18] dated between the third and fourth centuries B.C.E. The ashtapada designates a game board of 8 × 8 squares, as distinguished from the *dasapada*, which has a 10 × 10 square surface. But details of this ashtapada game do not seem to indicate chess. We know only that the game used a board with dice. There is no indication of any gaming pieces.[19]

The word *chaturanga* also appears in the Hindu epic *Ramayana*, dated back to the fourth or fifth century B.C.E. In this context, *chaturanga* was a military term, signifying the four arms of the army: infantry, cavalry, elephants and war chariots.[20] Clearly, this four-fold division suggests a correlation between the Indian army and the pieces on the chessboard, and many authors have taken it as proof of an ancient Indian origin of chess. But caution is needed in taking on that assertion. By the time of the first certain evidence of chess as a game, the four-limbed Indian army was long obsolete.

It should be noted that one of Murray's main pieces of evidence for chess in ancient India is no longer considered relevant. The Sanskrit classic *Vasavadatta* is credited to Subandhu, who historians generally placed in the second half of the fifth century, at the court of the Gupta Empire.[21] It contains a pleasant poem of green and yellow game pieces leaping about a colorful board. Modern scholars do not find any terms or actions in the text that would denote chess or chessmen.[22]

However, another Sanskrit text, the *Harshacharita*, written shortly after 643, suggests chess more strongly. This excerpt appears in the context of an official history of the King Harshavardhana of Kannauj,[23] written by Bana, the court poet. Here, Bana praises the peaceful reign of this great Buddhist king: "*Under this monarch, [...] only among earthen objects were fights of kings, only the bees quarreled to collect the dew, the only cut feet were those of measurements, and only from the ashtapada one could learn the positions of chaturanga, no one cut the four limbs of the convicted....*" Bana was a master at word play, here giving a series of lines with double meanings. The line regarding chaturanga seems to allude to the original meaning—the four divisions (or limbs) of the army—but in this peaceful land, chaturanga (the game) is practiced only on the 8 × 8 board. The suggestion of chess is very strong.

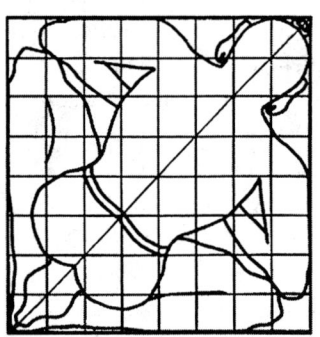

The giant, Purusha, on an ashtapada board.

But, even this strong evidence of chess has its detractors. Some experts see Bana's pun in reference to the mythic giant, Purusha. The Vedas tell us that the gods captured Purusha with a net, sacrificed him, and created the world while dismembering him. He is often represented with legs and arms bent on a square diagram, a mandala, similar to the traditional ashtapada,[24] and the text would evoke this picture as well. It could be that this was the nature of Bana's word play—or it could be that all of these associations were intended at once, puns and double puns! All viewpoints considered, the argument that chess, chaturanga, was played in Kannauj at Harsha's court maintains its validity.

It should be noted that India possesses a rich literary tradition, going back many centuries, with frequent discussions of dice games. By contrast, there are only a few chess reverences to be found predating the 12th century.

The three following allusions to chess come from Kashmir. First, there is the *Haravijaya* (*The Victory of Shiva*), composed around 850 by the poet Ratnakara. This work describes the *ashtapada* in connection with the four limbs of the army: soldiers, chariots, horses and elephants (*patti, ratha, ashva* and *dvipa*). Although the word *chaturanga* is not used, the board, together with the constituents of the army, makes a strong enough case for chess.

The second reference comes from the *Kavyalamkara* (*Ornaments of Poetry*) by Rudrata, also dated to the ninth century. This ingenious text contains verses with syllables arranged to indicate the "Knight's tour"; that is, the pattern the Horse (*turaga*) makes as it lands only once on each square of the chessboard. The tour of the Chariot (*ratha*) and Elephant (*gaja*) are also given, although the latter is difficult to interpret.

Around the year 970, Kashmir offers us one more chess allusion. A phrase appears in Halayudha Bhatta's mathematical treatise *Mritasañjivini*, which is a commentary of Pingala's ancient classic *Chandahsutra*. It states, "Draw an *ashtapada* as in *chaturanga*...." Finally, in the last years of the tenth century, the *Nitivakyamurta* contains the passage, "in *chaturanga* one does not have a King without an Advisor,"[25] indicating that the *Nitivakyamurta* clearly dealt with two-handed chess.

The first complete description of chess from an Indian source finally appears at the beginning of the 12th century with the *Manasollasa* (*Refresher of the Mind*) of King Someshvara III. By that late date, the Arabs had well established themselves as the world's leading chess masters and the game had been mentioned in many European works. The trail of Indian chess references in the first millennium comes up surprisingly sparse. Tantalizing, yet disappointing to the chess historian.

GAMES AND ASTROLOGY IN ANCIENT CHINA. Chinese authors are in unanimous agreement that the race game *shuanglu* (similar to Persian nard) came from the West along the Silk Road, but the traditional account of chess is another story altogether. Most Chinese literature attests that xiangqi, Chinese chess, was created by mythical emperors or demiurges at the dawn of the Han Dynasty.

The two characters, *xiang* (象) and *qi* (棋), written together and indicating a game, appear in some very old texts. The anthology, *Chu Ci*, dating to the third or second century B.C.E., mentions "xiangqi" in the poem *Zhaohun* (*The Recall of the Soul*) by Song Yu. The characters of *xiangqi* also appear in the *Shuo Yuan* (*Collection of Explanations*), presented to the royal court by the Confucian scholar, Liu Xiang, in 17 B.C.E. Unfortunately, the texts give no indication of the sort of game being discussed.[26] According to ancient Chinese commentators, it may be related to the mysterious *liubo*, a race game popular during the Han Dynasty. Numerous liubo boards have been recovered, though the rules of play are lost.

In the sixth century C.E., there is an interesting discussion in the classic, *Xiangjing* (*Game of Symbols*), attributed to Emperor Wu of the Northern Zhou Dynasty. This work has been lost but its preface, written by Wang Bao (died 576 or 581), has been preserved. It discusses an enigmatic description of something that may have been a board game, while expounding upon astrology and moral precepts.[27] Bao's preface explains that the pieces were moved on a board and that both strategy and military concepts played a role in the game.

A contemporary of Wang Bao, the general Yu Xin, composed a piece entitled *Xiangxi Fu* (*Poetic Exposition of Xiangxi*).[28] Yu Xin praises Emperor Wu's creation, declaring that he has succeeded in representing the order of the world in this game. It is possible that xiangjing or xiangxi may have preceded or inspired the modern game of xiangqi. With scant evidence, we can only speculate about the relationships among these games.

Finally, toward the beginning of the ninth century, we find the first indisputable mention of the game xiangqi. The *Xuanguai Lu* (*Accounts of the Mysterious Marvels*), is a compilation of supernatural tales written by the Tang Dynasty official Niu Sengru (780–849). In one episode, the hero, Cen Shun, was living in an old residence in spite of being advised not to do so. This mansion was haunted and one night he dreamed that a military chief revealed the secrets of an upcoming battle: *"the celestial horse springs aslant over three, the commanders go sideways and attack on all four sides, the chariots go straight forward and never backward, the six men in armor go in file but not backward [...] on both sides material was unpacked, stones and arrows flew across...."* In the nights that followed, Cen Shun helped defeat the attackers from a foreign kingdom and was rewarded with a treasure of precious gems and pearls. But then he was profoundly changed and he refused to leave the supernatural house. One day, while drunk, he confessed to his friend how he had become rich and how this had affected his behavior. The two dug up the floor of the room he was sleeping in and found an old grave on which stood a xiangqi board with bronze and golden pieces.

Cen Shun's battle was reported to have occurred during the short-lived Baoying Era (762) and, for this reason, the game described has come to be known as Baoying xiangqi. The moves of the pieces can be understood to varying degrees, and do not entirely coincide with the moves of the modern game.[29] We can surmise that pieces included a Commander, a Celestial Horse, Chariots and Soldiers. Crossbows and Catapults may also be implied. The gold and bronze pieces discovered leave open the question of whether the gaming pieces were standing figures or simply disks like modern xiangqi pieces. One could draw many lessons; nevertheless, prudence is advised as this source is unique and rather obscure.

At this point in the collective scholarly research into the origins of chess, it must be admitted that the ancient texts of Persia give the earliest accounts of a game we can call chess with much certainty. Arguments for chess in early Indian literature have been eroded over the past century, leaving the question more open and mysterious than it had appeared in Murray's time. The Chinese texts which strongly evoke chess are late in the game, though they offer tantalizing hints that chess may have roots that are much more ancient.

## *Archeology*

The oldest known chessmen are seven artifacts found together in 1977 by Professor Yuriy F. Buryakov in Afrasiab, near Samarkand, Uzbekistan. They are small, ivory figurines, three to four centimeters in height. Included are two foot soldiers with swords and shields, a similarly armed horseman, an elephant rider, a rider on an unidentified animal,[30] and apparently two different sorts of chariots—one possibly of a royal order whose chariot section is broken off. These pieces were found in the same layer of sediment as a coin dated 712 C.E.

Reconstructed models of the Afrasiab chessmen. The original fragments were found by Yuriy Buryakov in 1977 and dated to the seventh or eighth century C.E.
KNOWLTON SCULPTING AND PHOTOGRAPH

## 45. Approaching the Question from Several Angles

EXCAVATIONS ALONG THE SILK ROAD. Additional pieces of similar design have also been found along the stage cities of the Silk Road. In these areas, the famous trade route passed through areas inhabited by peoples generally conversant in Iranian dialects. Sogdians, Khwarezmians and Bactrians controlled extensive parts of the east-west passage, with stations as far east as Chang'an (Xi'an) and Luoyang, two of China's ancient capitals. In the sixth century, Sogdian merchants came under the protection of the mighty Göktürks, the Tujues of the Chinese chronicles, who had just built a powerful empire from the Caspian Sea to the Tarim Basin.[31] The Sogdians were instrumental in establishing diplomatic relations between the Göktürks, Persians, Byzantines and Chinese, and the Silk Road became a channel of cultural and political exchange as well as commerce.

The list of the artifacts found on this road is long indeed: a chariot in Gaochang found by Albert von Le Coq[32]; another rider, a third soldier and another king or vizier[33] in Afrasiab; other chariots, elephants and riders in Samarkand, Nishapur, Western Iran, and Iraq, to name a few. All are estimated to date from the sixth to eighth centuries.

More recently, in 2006, a new set of five pieces appeared miraculously at an antiquarian shop, with the simple information that they had originated in Afghanistan.[34] The identification of these large and somewhat damaged pieces remains a difficult task. One can make out two jointly harnessed horses, a carriage on horseback, a horseman, an elephant with headless rider, and some sort of great feline ridden by a warrior.

Set of chessmen, probably one of the oldest ever recovered. Afghan origin, dates still undetermined. CAZAUX PHOTOGRAPH

In all, more than 25 figurative pieces of this genre have been uncovered in Central Asia. All share the same "Afrasiab" style, and may therefore be from the same period.[35] It has proved to be a very fertile region indeed for chess archeology.

In addition to these pieces, all strongly associated with a unified style of chessmen, many isolated figures have been uncovered with less certainty as to their original use. A magnificent elephant in black stone, seven centimeters high, dated from the sixth or seventh century, is kept at the Metropolitan Museum of Art in New York. Another elephant and a piece vaguely resembling a bull (or possibly a camel) were discovered in 1972 in Dalverzin Tepe, a former Bactrian citadel of the Kushan Empire, today a part of Uzbekistan. Of course, there is no bull in the typical ancient chess menagerie, but that piece bears a vague resemblance to the apparently feline mounted figures of the Afrasiab and Afghan variety, so they may be a part of the same tradition. These pieces, each about two centimeters high, are estimated to date from the second century C.E., which would set a new record of chess antiquity—if only it could be proven that they were chessmen!

Elephant and bull found in Dalverzin Tepe (Uzbekistan, second century): chessmen or not?

SEARCHING FOR THE MISSING LINK IN INDIA. India however, has turned up very few ancient archeological clues. A considerable limitation is India's humid climate. The moist earth, combined with the abundance of perishable materials, such as wood, for carving pieces, leave less chance of artifacts' lasting for centuries underground. A series of game pieces has been discovered from the Harappan period, from a mysterious civilization which flourished in the Indus Valley around 1900 B.C.E. The pieces are truly intriguing, and may well be a sort of game pieces, but cannot be firmly correlated with chess. Though some writers have hurried to draw the connection, the lack of similarity to known chessmen and distance in time makes a chess-related interpretation highly improbable.

There are also famous bas reliefs on the Buddhist stupas of Bodhgaya and Bharhut, dating to the first century B.C.E. Although some show a game played on a board of 8 × 8 squares, recent studies have shown that they depict a game of dice, having nothing to do with chess.[36]

Another isolated piece is an ivory chariot from Mantai, an old harbor in Sri Lanka. Dated to the second or third century, it has sometimes been thought to be the earliest known chess piece. But in fact, its connection to chess remains unsubstantiated.

The chess historian Dr. Renate Syed, has given much theoretical consideration to the possible use of the small terracotta figures held in the basements of several museums across Northern India. She postulates that such figures were used by early Hindu strategists to create simulated military conflicts on sandbox landscapes. Then, around the fifth century C.E., some ingenious mind would have placed these miniatures onto the familiar 8 × 8 ashtapada board, assigned the pieces specific moves and, essentially, invented chess. But, while the Sanskrit literature does mention diagrams (*vyuha*) used by the Indian generals, there is no indication in the texts of using model forces in sandboxes to represent the battles. Dr. Syed's hypothesis is in fact a part of a broader vision, emphasizing the city of Kannauj and its kings, Sharvavarman and Harshavardhana. Syed proposes this as the explanation of Bana's verse: *"only among earthen objects were fights of kings."* According to the poet, as King Harsha propagated an era of peace and harmony, war theoreticians could teach strategy and battle tactics only with miniature terracotta maneuvers in sandboxes. Based on an expert knowledge of Sanskrit and of the old Indian civilization, her scholarly statements carry an authority which can be quite convincing.

Some other Indologists, however, are not so sure. Micaela Soar,[37] for example, points out that the many terracotta chariots, horses and elephants, which date from the early centuries C.E., remain independent pieces with no discernible connection to each other or to any particular game. Moreover, other figures, including bulls, dogs, rams, donkeys, lions and birds from the same epoch and the same places, have been found with even less potential association to an early form of chess. It seems that this doubt will remain, until and unless a more cohesive group of pieces is uncovered.[38]

In 2007, a group of German historians toured the museums of North India specifically to identify chess pieces that remained unknown. Although no conclusive new evidence was revealed, there was clearly much more material yet to be reviewed in future investigations. Many new figures were added to the lists of possible chessmen by this expedition, yet the question of positively identifying these figures remains open.

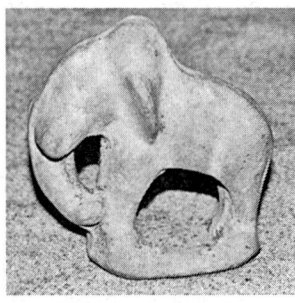
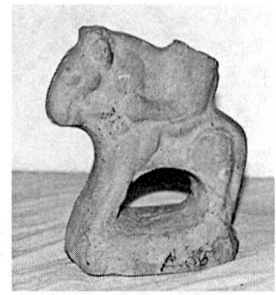

Terracotta elephant (left) and horse (fourth–seventh centuries) which could have been used for a sort of proto-chess.
M.A.J. EDER PHOTOGRAPHS

THE OVERLOOKED MATERIAL OF CHINA. To our knowledge, no three-dimensional standing chess pieces, either figurative or abstract, have ever been found in Chinese excavations.[39] The earliest known xiangqi pieces look surprisingly similar to pieces of today. Several xiangqi sets of copper and bronze, and even a few rare sets of porcelain, are kept in Chinese museums. The oldest of these sets date to the Northern Song dynasty, in the Chongning era (1102–1106). This is a later date in early chess history; however, these are not necessarily representative of the antiquity of the game. With few exceptions, the artifacts that have been publicized and made accessible to the West are complete sets. Incomplete sets and odd discoveries of pieces have rarely been reported, though they must exist. Much archeological evidence is clearly still unexamined.

The traditional Chinese chess pieces, simple disks with Chinese characters, are so similar to old Chinese coins that many old, worn or damaged pieces may well have worked themselves into collections of ancient currency. An extensive review of many collections of such objects throughout the world remains to be undertaken.

Often, these old xiangqi pieces show a Chinese character on the top and a stylized drawing on the bottom. For example, a dressed character on the back of the Advisor piece, and a catapult's image on the flip slide of the Cannon. The Soldier holds a spear. It is remarkable how these centuries-old pieces from disparate regions and eras resemble each other so strongly—almost as if they were all made from the same pattern.

It is likely that many pieces were made of a more perishable material, usually wood, giving them almost no chance to last through the centuries. There is one exceptionally lucky find which attests to ancient wooden Chinese pieces. A shipwreck found in the Quanzhou Bay, dating to the end of the Southern Song Dynasty (late 13th century) has yielded 20 wooden pieces marked with red and black ink. Fortunately preserved in salt water, and protectively encased within the ship, this set is a rare example of the sort of pieces that would never have survived under normal conditions. There is no way of knowing how widespread such pieces were in their time.

Ancient Chinese chessmen were probably made of simple material and formed in a very common disk shape—factors making it hard to find and hard to identify very old specimens. One interesting exception is a single Chariot piece (the Rook of Chinese chess), found in Chongqing in 2001, and dated to the third century C.E.[40] This tantalizing discovery is tempered by the fact that it is only one piece, and the date has not been independently confirmed.

Still, it is difficult to make a strong argument, based on archeology, for an early beginning of xiangqi. The finds in India have also been disappointing, yielding many specimens, but thin evidence of actual chessmen. The arid steppes of Central Asia lay claim to the most ancient pieces.

## Philology and Nomenclature

The people of ancient Iran, Central Asia and India spoke varieties of Indo-European languages which were all closely related to each other. Linguists suppose that the Persian Pahlavi word *chatrang* is borrowed from the Indian Sanskrit *chaturanga*. This in itself is a worthy argument that the game of chess has an Indian origin.

It is also possible that chess was invented in a region outside of India which was influenced by the Indian civilization. As an example, in Sogdiana, wall frescos have been discovered in Panjakent depicting scenes borrowed from the Sanskrit epic *Mahabharata*. With this cultural borrowing, one can imagine that a Sogdian board game, inspired by war and the four military units of the epics, would naturally have been called *chaturanga*.

But the Sanskrit influence does not extend into other aspects of the early references to the game. The names of the pieces and the vocabulary describing the manner of play prove to be of Persian origin. The Chinese nomenclature of xiangqi is removed from both the Persian and Sanskrit terms for chess and chessmen. So, while the linguistic study of early chess terms shows some interesting connections, its value as a determinant of chess origins remains inconclusive.

THE ELEPHANT SUGGESTS INDIA. The earliest known forms of chess in India, Persia and China all include a playing piece distinctly identified as an Elephant. Here is another strong suggestion of Indian culture. The domestication of the Asian elephant stems from the Indus valley, dated to the third millennium B.C.E., and the great beasts had a longstanding role in the Indian armies. The elephant is featured as a prominent image in Hindu spiritual iconography as the deity Ganesha.

However, by the middle of the first millennium C.E., elephants were spread widely throughout the subcontinent. For example, armored elephants constituted one of the bodies of the Sassanid army—but these Persian elephants were often attended by Hindu mahouts.

The elephant was also a familiar figure on the Chinese battlefield, especially in the southern regions. It should be noted that xiangqi has two characters for this piece, displaying the figure for elephant (象) on one side but another character (相) on the opposing side. Both are pronounced the same, "xiang." This is consistent with a broader difference between the two sides. While they are composed of equal opposing forces, the characters of the opposing camps are decidedly different. The first one has a commander-in-chief (帥 *shuai*), while the second is under a general (將 *jiang*). The first employs soldiers (兵 *bing*), the second enrolls mercenaries (卒 *zhu*). The first benefits from the early Chinese fire (火) power with a Cannon, while the second uses a less elaborated catapult that throws stones (石). These political and military differences are also conveyed by other pieces in the first camp which sometimes carry the character for "man" (亻 *ren*), as a distinction to honor the national side (that is, the side with 相 in the place of the elephant). In all, the game represents the opposition of inner central forces head-to-head with an outer provincial or foreign army vying for dominance. In this recurring struggle, the character for the Minister was mirrored across the river by the relatively exotic Elephant.

*Comparison of the Chinese characters used for both sides shows an opposition between national and foreign forces.*

| Red | Black | |
|---|---|---|
| 帥 | 將 | A Governor versus a General |
| 兵 | 卒 | A common Soldier versus a private, a mercenary |
| 炮 | 砲 | A Cannon versus a mere Catapult |
| 仕, 偶, 俥 | 士, 馬, 車 | First character for Red stands for "man" |
| 相 | 象 | A Minister versus an Elephant |

The suggestion that these pieces originated in a characteristically Chinese battle scenario certainly deserves further research. In the meantime, the question remains: If China did adopt chess from India or Persia, why did it add a "Minister" in opposition to the "Elephant"? Even if the two sides were not distinguished by color, these pieces would not need special differentiation, since they never cross over the river.

Considering the importance of elephants in India's culture and military history, the existence of elephants in the earliest chess forms suggests that the game may have originated there. Nevertheless, it remains quite possible that China or Persia could have invented a military game in which elephants played a role.

## 45. Approaching the Question from Several Angles

THE PRESENCE OF THE CHARIOT IN INDIA AND CHINA. The presence of Chariots on the early Chinese and Indian chessboards presents an interesting puzzle. It should be noted that the first mention of chess in Persian texts does not designate this piece as a Chariot (*rah*), but rather as an officer controlling the flanks (*rokh*) of the army. But Chariots are certainly common among the pieces uncovered in Persian areas, as shown by the Afrasiab pieces.

When the Persian texts first mention chess, war chariots had not been part of the standard army for several centuries, though they were still used by officers to review the troops. With its powerful command of the chessboard, the Chariot could be seen as a commanding official, or could recall the ancient warring chariots as depicted in the legend of *Ramayana*. Chariots had a similar history in China, reported as vehicles of warfare as late as the fifth century B.C.E., but used thereafter only for ceremonial and official purposes.

With the widespread familiarity of chariots throughout Eurasia, and the agreed obsolescence of chariots as warring vehicles during the times that chess first appeared, it would be hard to guess when they began to be used as gaming pieces, and for exactly what purpose.

While India has long been considered the birthplace of chess, a close look at the philological evidence does not eliminate China and Persia as reasonable candidates. In fact, we are left with more tantalizing speculations than authoritative answers.

## Comparison of Game Structure

While the early descriptions of chess in Persia and India were very much the same, the early chess of China shows several striking differences. Nevertheless, the two contrasted chess forms have some remarkable similarities. Both games have two equal, opposing armies of 16 pieces each. With the exception of the Chinese Cannons, both games feature a front row of Pawns and a back row of pieces that correspond to each other as a central "royal" King (or Commander), a Counselor (or two), beside a pair of Elephants (or Ministers), followed by Horses, completed by two Chariots in the corners. The objective in each case is to force capture of the central royal piece.

The moves of the pieces on this back row seem to have a certain logic. Each one fills in an aspect of the possible moves to places just one or two steps away:

- One orthogonal step: this is the General's move, the central piece in xiangqi. Elsewhere, this piece is a King, and may move diagonally as well.
- One diagonal step: this is the move of the Counselor, Advisor or Assistant, the same in all Indian, Persian and Chinese forms.
- Two diagonal steps: this is the move of the Elephant (or Minister), also present in all forms.
- One orthogonal step followed by one diagonal step: this is the Horse's move in all forms of chess.

There has been speculation, noted particularly by the Spanish historian Ricardo Calvo, that the moves of chess may derive from magic squares, or some other mathematical principles of the ancient Asian civilizations. This curious line of thought, sometimes overlapping with theories of numerology, has sparked some interest over time, and would deserve further research.

Considering the logical geometry of the moves just mentioned, one may notice a particular omission. A piece which moves just two steps orthogonally would complete the pattern perfectly, filling in the square of all possible one- or two-step moves. Indeed, it has been speculated that the Chariot may have started out as that two-step orthogonally moving piece. Even the Chinese

Catapult has been suspected as once being the perfect two-step leaper, to fill in the puzzle. But alas, research finds no evidence whatsoever of an early piece moving in this way, leaving that geometric ideal still wanting for historic support.[41]

Squares reached from the central position by the King, the Counselor, the Elephant and the Horse.

To complete the pattern, the gray squares could correspond to the hypothetical primitive move of the Chariot or the Catapult: two squares orthogonally from the central white square.

Though the similarities between the games are indisputable, the process by which one game may have evolved from the other is difficult to grasp. To address this question, we must consider the differences between the Indo-Persian and the Chinese games to postulate possible channels of game "genealogy." By investigating the games' overall structures and rules, we hope to gather clues as to which may have preceded the other.

The Indo-Persian game presents an asymmetrical array with a "King side" and a "Counselor side" (King and Queen sides in modern chess), whereas the xiangqi array is perfectly symmetrical, with a royal General standing in the center of his troops, flanked by Advisors on both right and left.

Indo-Persian chess has eight larger pieces and eight Pawns on each side, set on the squares of a uniform 8 × 8 board. Those pieces are sculpted figurines, either representational or abstract. On the other hand, xiangqi is played on a board endowed with specific topological markings, including a river and two palaces, which decisively affect the mobility of the pieces. The xiangqi pieces are simple disks with Chinese characters including only five Pawns, leaving 11 stronger pieces in each camp. They move on the points marked by the intersections of 9 × 10 lines.

Near the western ends of the Silk Road, the game seems to represent an orderly battlefield while, toward the eastern end, the challenge appears to be the siege of the enemy fortress.

THE GREEK INFLUENCE: A BOLD HYPOTHESIS FOR THE ORIGIN OF THE INDO-PERSIAN PAWN. Our view of chess history can be greatly broadened by examining earlier board games which may have influenced or led to the development of chess.

- The Indian ashtapada, a board of 8 × 8 squares, predates all known accounts of chess by several centuries, yet the exact nature of the earlier game (or games) played on this board is still unknown. Modern research indicates that it may have been a board game using the squares with dice, but no account of this game mentions any playing piece.[42] There has been no evidence to confirm Murray's assertion that it was a spiral race game.[43] This leaves the board itself as the only link to chess.
- Central Asia may have been home to a game more relevant to chess. These lands, now bruised by modern conflicts, were once the basin of a fertile convergence of several civilizations. This region's successor to the rule of Alexander the Great, the Greco-Bactrian Kingdom and the Kushan Empire, developed a Hellenistic, Iranian and Buddhist syncretism as original

## 45. Approaching the Question from Several Angles

as it was brilliant, lasting for several centuries. There is a strong possibility that games of pawn capture were played there. The ancient Greeks played *polis*, in which two Pawns were used to "trap" an opponent's Pawn between them. In this game, it can be seen that, prior to capture, the opponent's Pawn is just a step diagonally forward of the attacking piece. Though the correlation is tenuous, it is conceivable that this Greek rule, or some minor variation, could have been the source of the diagonal Pawn capture in Persian, Indian—and modern Western chess.[44]

The Greek game of *polis*: As the White Pawn advances, the Black Pawn is surrounded and therefore captured. Could this be the inspiration of the strange rule which has the chess Pawn capturing diagonally?

IN CHINA, THE OBSCURE ROLE OF LIUBO. The Chinese Soldier seems more primitive than the Indo-Persian Pawn. It captures just as it moves: straight ahead at first, then forward or directly to the right or left after crossing the river. In addition, there is no Pawn promotion at the end of the board. Could it be that this simpler move of the Chinese Soldier is older than the Indo-Persian Pawn?

In general, it can be seen that almost every piece in the Chinese game has a more limited move than its counterpart in the Central Asian variant. The xiangqi pieces are variously confined to the fortress, unable to cross the river, or blocked by intervening pieces (i.e., the Horse and Elephant), while the pieces of chatrang or chaturanga know no such limitations. Perhaps the fact that the Chinese pieces are played on the intersections, rather than the squares, causes an interposing piece to be perceived as more of a barrier. It can be seen that standing on the line of a piece that moves point-to-point poses a more definite obstacle than standing amid a row of squares.

Since the nine-line board width of the Chinese game and the eight-square width of the Indo-Persian game are essentially identical, a common origin is strongly suggested. It can be debated whether the topographical marks of the xiangqi board are a later refinement, or whether they preceded the simplified board of plain squares. One can imagine a game played on intersections with limiting board markings and restrictive rules of move giving way to a game where those limitations and restrictions are forgotten. But the opposite case—a freer game being made more restrictive—is also plausible.

But while the widths of both boards are visually similar, the respective lengths are different: ten horizontal lines on the xiangqi board versus eight rows of squares for chaturanga. The xiangqi board is split into two halves by a river. At this point, it must be noted that the Korean game, janggi, which seems to have been a later development, has no river. In this case, the river appears to be a primitive characteristic which was abandoned when chess spread west (to Persia and India) and east (to Korea). The alternative theory—that chess was imported into China from the West—requires an acceptance of the theory that the river was added when coming into China and then eliminated as it traveled further eastward.

In the Chinese Empire, two great games existed probably well before xiangqi: *weiqi* (the game of go) and *liubo*. Both games are reported to have been evoked by Confucius around 500 B.C.E., and both were certainly known long before the beginning of the Han dynasty (207 B.C.E.– 220 C.E.). The first is still very well known, and is played on the intersections of lines, as is xiangqi. The second, whose name means "six sticks," declined under the Tang (618–907) before disappearing completely. Many archeological specimens of playing boards have been recovered, but the comprehensive rules of the game are lost. Only a few literary clues survive, dating from the Zhanguo period (Warring States period, 480–221 B.C.E.) and the Han Dynasty.

Based on the available evidence, one can establish that liubo was a competition between two players, having six game pieces each, a kind of race game involving captures. One piece seems to have been allowed to become a sort of a chief. The pieces progressed according to the result of six sticks with two faces thrown like dice. The board possessed numerous angled lines and markings arranged in the "TLV" pattern, so called because they somewhat resemble the letters T, L and V. This pattern is well known from many artifacts, particularly the backs of mirrors, which date to the Han Dynasty (206 B.C.E.–220 C.E.). More interesting in this context, the board incorporated a central square which was called "water." Recently, a study from the Japanese historian Yasuji Shimizu has shown that the most ancient boards, such as the one excavated in Jicheng, presented a north-south symmetry with a neat separation between the two sides made by five vertical segments. From all these elements, it is tempting to see an association with the five Soldiers, the General and the river of xiangqi, especially because, as mentioned previously, the characters *xiang* and *qi* are found in the company of the characters *liu* and *bo* in a very early Chinese text (from the third or second century B.C.E.), well before the confirmed appearance of chess in China.

Could liubo have evolved to become the xiangqi we know today? Another pertinent question left for further research.

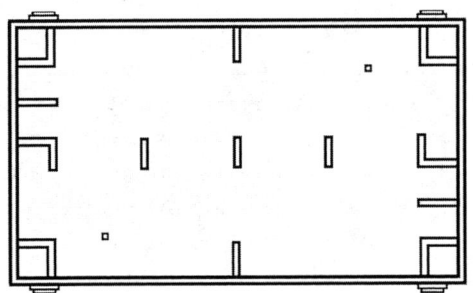

Liubo board excavated at Jicheng (Hubei province, China, Mid Warring States period, about 350–300 B.C.E.)

A VERY WEAK ELEPHANT. The Elephant's peculiar two-step diagonal move poses additional questions. As has been shown, this move on the 8 × 8 square board proves to be very weak, reaching only eight of the board's 64 squares. These Elephants, each running its own circuit, never defend each other nor confront the Elephants of the opponent's camp. This weak and disjointed move has since been replaced by more powerful moves in Southeast Asia and Europe, and has even undergone many variations in India, confirming that players have had a long-standing dissatisfaction with the two-square leaper. On the other hand, the Elephant's/Minister's move on the xiangqi board has a clear logic and symmetry. Though it only reaches a few points, these are key posts for defending the General and strongly placed pieces. On the Chinese chessboard, these "Elephants" naturally defend each other as they bolster the central line along with the Advisors. Their move, though limited to only seven points, reaches the furthest lines right, left and forward of their own territory. Following this reasoning, it can be argued that the Elephant's move first appeared as a logical defender on the Chinese chessboard, only to have its strength and symmetrical integrity broken as it adapted to the 8 × 8 board of Persia and India.

THE MYSTERY OF THE SHAPE OF THE PIECES. The pieces of Persian or Indian chess are sculpted or carved standing figures. In China, playing pieces are flat disks with a Chinese character or a distinctive sign inscribed on the top surface of each one. Do the inscribed disks result from a simplification of the standing figurines or do the figurines represent an improvement on the flat pieces? If the first hypothesis is correct, why did this simplification occur only in the direction of China and Japan? Why was this transformation not repeated in other regions conquered by chess, such as Mongolia, Southeast Asia and especially Europe, whose peoples were well acquainted with other games using flat disks, such as games of *tables*,[45] merels and checkers?

The opposite theory would imply a birth of the chess pieces in China as flat disks, taking on a sculpted three-dimensional shape, for easier identification, in Central Asia or in India.

THE KING NEVER DIES. Finally, there is a point of formality which deserves some attention. Several authors and historians have remarked on the fact that the King is captured but not killed in chess; he merely surrenders. This has been called "the inviolability of the King" and highlighted as the very essence of the game, with an assertion that this is a purely Indian characteristic and therefore a strong argument that chess was born in India. But this argument is weakened by further investigation. There are actually several kings who die at war in ancient Indian literature. One example is the tale of Chandragupta Maurya who conquers the kingdom of Magadha in 313 B.C.E. by seizing Pataliputra and killing the last Nanda king. Or, for instance, the last Maurya king, Brihadratha, who was killed in 180 B.C.E. on the order of his chief general, Pushyamitra. Even king Bana's history has many kings slaughtered or killed on the battle field. Also, there are Indian chess variants in which the King is killed. Chaturaji, four-handed chess, is a good example. Looking at the further evolution of the game, if the King's inviolability was exclusively Indian, one would wonder why Persians, Arabs and Europeans also persisted with the practice. The king was not sacrosanct in those civilizations, but this did not affect the rules of the game. Simple characterizations of cultural histories often make pleasant and memorable tales, but frequently fail to explain all of the available evidence.

Two players sitting at a liubo board (top) and a carpet showing 6 sticks thrown in the manner of dice.

Drawing after an engraving on an Eastern Han (25–220 C.E.) tomb in Shandong province, China. CAZAUX DRAWING

## From West to East or from East to West?

At this point, two conflicting scenarios establish themselves to explain the birth and the first diffusion of chess:

The first scenario can be expressed as follows: From a game inspired by astrological diagrams, possibly related to liubo, the Chinese invented a game simulating battle which involved Generals,

Counselors, Officers, Horses, War Chariots, Catapults and Foot Soldiers. The board bore topological marks (perhaps derived from a more ancient game such as liubo). With the exception of the move of the Catapult (which may have varied over time), this game was very similar to present-day xiangqi.

Before the end of the sixth century, this game was transmitted[46] to the peoples of the West who traveled and traded along the Silk Road, such as the Serindians, Göktürks, Sogdians, Bactrians and other Kwarezmians. They roughly understood the meaning of the game and reproduced it in a way suited to their languages and cultures.

For the flat pieces bearing Chinese characters, they substituted more easily identifiable figures, independent of language and cultural symbols. The board was rudely drawn and, necessarily, simplified: only lines were kept. Nine vertical lines gave the board eight columns. The river was omitted, making a square board identical to the old 8 × 8 square board already familiar in games of ashtapada and hashtpay, among others. Sixteen pieces neatly filled the ranks of each side. The five Soldiers and the two Catapults which were seated in front in the Chinese arrangement were put on the first line, leaving one vacancy. The other pieces were placed as they should be: Chariots in the corners, beside the Horses, beside the Elephants, and finally the Chief, understood as a King, in the center. There was only one place next to the King, so one Counselor fit there. The extra Counselor naturally joined the line of the Soldiers.

Movement rules were kept more or less the same except that, in the absence of palaces and a river, the associated restrictions also disappeared. Kings, Counselors and Elephants could now go everywhere. However, the symmetry of the two Advisors was broken, and the Elephants could no longer protect each other.

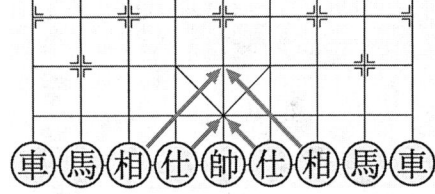 

The symmetry has been broken.

The Soldiers, no longer affected by a river, underwent the most important change. Perhaps under the influence of a previous game of pawns in the region, they were allowed to promote upon reaching the opposite side of the chessboard. And an original diagonal capture move was established, which was more convenient now that the Pawn's line was complete. By 650 C.E., the game had reached both Ctesiphon in Persia and Kannauj in India.

The second and opposing scenario has the Indo-Persian game inspired by the Indian epics: The four arms of the mythical Hindu army were represented by the pieces: Chariots, Horses, Elephants and Soldiers, and the name of the game, *chaturanga*, means just that—the four-limbed army. Perhaps the first pieces used to play this game were originally created for army strategists to diagram actual battle scenarios.

By the end of the sixth century then, this game would have been standardized for play on the popular 64 squares of the ashtapada board, already in use in much of India and Iran. Then, this game spread into China, following the spread of Buddhism via the Silk Road. During that time, many missionaries—Indians, Kashemiris, Kushans, Bactrians and Sogdians—traveled to China to teach the wisdom of the Buddha, the "Awakened One." They met Chinese sages and pilgrims who had been sent westward by the emperors to collect sacred books and relics (and also to spy upon those kingdoms raising horses, so precious to the fight against the Barbarians).[47]

Thus, chess spread into China, brought by travelers and merchants, by the same road from which the secrets of silk and paper escaped in the other direction.

But then, perhaps in a violent wave of xenophobia,[48] the game was suddenly converted to established Chinese conventions. Pieces slipped from the center of the squares to the intersections of the lines, being inspired by other Chinese games like weiqi (go). Now, the chessboard offered nine points at each end, allowing the addition of another Counselor, taken from among the troop of Pawns. Seven Soldiers remained, not enough to form a complete line, but five fit well with spaces between them. The two remaining Soldiers filled in the missing aspect of warfare, ballistics. They were Catapults and, later, Cannons. These pieces were set back one row from the Soldiers, as befits a heavy attacking weapon.

A river was added to separate the two sides, in accordance with the historic war between the kingdoms of Han and Chu. In this way, the xiangqi board reached its present dimensions and the moves of the pieces were adjusted to reflect the constraints brought on by the topography of this new battlefield. Jumps were forbidden and the Elephant could not cross the river. The five Pawns were now too far from each other and the diagonal capture had become impractical. So, Pawns began capturing with their normal move, just like other pieces. They were promoted with increased power of move when crossing the river, making further promotion at the end of the board unnecessary. To make things more realistic, palaces were added. The King, now a General as was proper to a Chinese war game, was confined along with his Counselors to this nine-point fortress.

For practical reasons—expedited manufacturing, easy transportation—the sculpted three-dimensional pieces were replaced by flat disks, inscribed with symbols designating their values with a different color for each side. In case these colors faded over time and also perhaps to increase the realism of the conflict, several pieces took different names from their counterparts across the board. The Elephant, for instance, became a Minister in the opposing camp, making use of the different writings and meanings of the word *xiang*. With these transformations, the game also changed its nature: the game of the elites and the nobles in the West had become a game of the people in the East. By the eighth century, this transformed game had conquered all of China.

The reader is invited to consider which of these scenarios appears most plausible. Of course, it may also be that the truth involves some variation of these possibilities or the game may even have been invented partly in the East and partly in the West, with each game influenced and transformed by the other. Chess may be a hybrid of related "proto-chess" games, now long extinct. Though the research has brought much to light, there is so much still to consider.

## Conclusions—and Open Questions

So, did chess first arise in India, Persia or China? Each hypothesis has credible support, but each one also leaves quite reasonable doubts.

The dominant theory, supported by research, but intertwined with a heavy dose of myth and tenacious legend, assigns the birth of chess to India, North India more precisely, around 500 C.E. It would then have spread first through Central Asia, then into China following Buddhism along the Silk Road. This hypothesis is attractive. It still maintains its long-standing credibility and a good probability of truth—but it must be recognized that the hypothesis fails to explain all available evidence. Indeed, the majority of recent archeological discoveries point to a birth in Central Asia—Eastern Iran and Afghanistan, Pakistan, Uzbekistan, Tajikistan, Turkmenistan,

Kyrgyzstan and Eastern Turkestan (all of those countries ending in "-stan") which, in that remote time, were inhabited by peoples mostly speaking Iranian languages.[49]

But Central Asia still constitutes too broad an area to be satisfactory. Even if their languages were related, these diverse groups—Persians, Bactrians, Sogdians or other Serindians—lived in different states and adhered to different religions.

Another objection arises from the persistent, unanswered questions around Chinese chess. Several features of xiangqi seem more primitive than those of its Western cousins. In this view, it seems most logical that, when the game was first invented, it would have been most aesthetically pleasing to begin with the King or General in the center, flanked symmetrically on his left and right. Furthermore, it seems most likely that the complicated board—with the river and fortresses, the limited range of non-jumping pieces, and the broken line of Pawns of xiangqi—would have been an original design, later simplified in the West as an undifferentiated board and unrestricted moves of pieces, rather than the other way around—in which case, someone would have made everything more complex. These complexities would have been carried to the entire Chinese empire without exception and with an unlikely unanimity.

Xiangqi bears several characteristics so deeply Chinese (engraved characters on the pieces, the Han-Chu river border, etc.) that it would have been nearly impossible to export it outside the cultural limits of the Chinese civilization without a transformation. But, if the game was transferred from West to East, the need for a transformation is not obvious and does not seem so compulsory. The possibility of a transmission of chaturanga or chatrang toward China is weakened by the complete absence of traces, textual or archeological, of the Indo-Persian game existing in ancient China.

The culmination of the archeological evidence and the decoding of the ancient texts are far from finished in China.[50] In fact, any future discovery of a solid piece of evidence could sweep aside decades of carefully crafted hypotheses. Moreover, the truth of chess's origin may be much more complex, with multiple influences of various successive civilizations, each one influenced by its existing board game traditions.

THE PRASENA MYSTERY. We offer one final example of just how confounding the clues of ancient chess can be. Our quote here is from the Buddhist monk Fazang (643–712), also known as Dharmakara, as he summarizes the characteristics of a game known as *prasena* or *prasaka* in Sanskrit and as *boluo saixi* in Chinese: "*Prasena was a military game played in the Western region, and two players each have more than twenty small jade tokens which serve as elephants or horses and these must take strategic command of all roads on the board.*"[51]

Fazang was a major proponent of Buddhism in China. He served under the mighty empress, Wu Zetian, during the Tang Dynasty, and is known as the third patriarch of the Huayan Buddhist tradition. Of special interest is the fact that although he was born in the Chinese capital, Chang'an, he was actually Sogdian.

It is known that *boluo saixi* designated a variant of liubo, played without dice, during the Han Dynasty (207 B.C.E.–220 C.E.), and that this game was known as *shuanglu*, which is similar to nard, by Yan Shu (991–1055), a scholar of the Northern Song Dynasty. Yan Shu attributed this game to India. Later, the term *boluo saixi* became a synonym of the word *xiangqi*, according to the monk Yuxiang, whose writings are dated before 1162.

But what was this enigmatic game under the Tang Dynasty, in Fazang's times? His description strongly suggests a chess game—but which one? Elephants and Horses appeared in both the Indo-Persian chatrang and the Chinese xiangqi. The allusion to tokens of jade appears more suitable to describe the flat Chinese playing pieces than the carved figures that have been excavated along the Silk Road. Would the need to "control all roads" be more apt to indicate a game played along lines than one played in squares? If so, this could be the first ever reference to xiangqi. Speculating further, we can surmise that if Fazang was introducing this game to inhabitants of the Chinese capital, it was not already generally known in that country. On the other hand, the "Western region" Fazang describes must have meant the Gansu or the Tarim oasis of Serindia. This quote brings us tantalizingly close to grasping a new bit of information we are seeking—but without further corroboration and cross-referencing, the exact meaning of the passage escapes us.

We can only assume that the cradle of chess and its primordial history still lie hidden somewhere in Asia. Our investigation into this enigma, raising more questions than it has answered, is still, necessarily, unresolved. Perhaps it is best that the exact birth of the royal game remains clouded in mystery.

It is one of humanity's greatest inventions, a gift the mind of mankind has given to itself. Its astonishing diversity carries the influence of the various civilizations that have carried it along, running in parallel currents, diverging, and recombining over time. The internationalization of the modern world has shortened the distances, and makes all of these games available to know and to play, through the Internet.

Who knows if the modern and future heirs to the chess legacy will recombine it into new and unforeseeable forms, breeding an entirely new game yet to be unveiled? The final chapter of this book remains to be written.

# Timeline

*This is a chess history timeline. Several dates are approximate or "at the latest," when they refer to a text of which only the year of the author's death is known.*

**569:** A game, *xiangxi*, is mentioned in the Chinese Emperor Wu's *Xiangjing*. Xiangxi is inspired by astrology, and is possibly a predecessor of xiangqi.

**620:** Earliest mentions of chatrang in three Pahlavi (Middle Persian) epics of the Sassanid kings. One of them, the *Wizarishn i chatrang*, names the types of chess pieces.

**640:** *Chaturanga* is mentioned in the *Harshacharita* by the poet Bana, in Kannauj, Northern India. Chaturanga in this context may be a reference to chess.

**712:** Earliest possible burial date of the earliest known chess pieces, found in Afrasiab close to Samarkand (Uzbekistan).

**728:** Earliest Arabic evidence with an allusion to the Pawn of shatranj, by the Arabic poet al-Farazdaq.

**822:** Date the Kurdish musician, Ziryab, was reported to have brought chess to Córdoba, then in Muslim Spain.

**830:** The *Xuanguai lu*, written by the Chinese diplomat, Niu Sengru, contains a tale of a battle, supposed to have occurred in 762, which is the earliest description of xiangqi.

**840:** The rules of shatranj are given in a chess book by al-'Adli, known from later manuscripts.

**850:** Two poems from Kashmir present a probable allusion to chess: the Ratnakara's *Haravijaya* which connects the four limbs of the army (soldiers, chariots, horses and elephants) with the ashtapada board; and Rudrata's *Kavyalamkara* which evokes the famous "Knight's tour."

**900:** Dating of the most ancient European chess pieces, found in Spain.

**947:** Rules of several chess variants given in the *Muruj adh-dhahab* of the Arab historian al-Mas'udi.

**997:** First description of chess in Europe, in the Latin poem *Versus de Schachis*. For the first time the chessboard has checkered squares and a Queen replaces the Arabic General.

**1027:** Evocation of shogi in the *Kirinsho*, composed by the Japanese poet Fujiwara no Yukinari.

**1030:** Description of chaturanga for two and four players (earliest description of the four-handed game) played in India, according to the Persian scholar and traveler al-Biruni.

**1030:** Earliest description of rithmomachy in South Germany, by the clerk Asilo.

**1059:** Dating of the earliest extant shogi pieces, found in Nara (Japan).

**1075:** The *Xiangxi shiguang*, a Chinese poem from Cheng Hao evokes a "river" in xiangqi for the first time.

**1085:** The imperial minister, Sima Guang, writes

the rules of qiguo xiangxi, seven-player Chinese chess, which includes a Catapult and a piece that moves like the modern chess Queen.

**1090:** Dating of the figurative set wrongly named Charlemagne's chessmen. The pieces are of Italian origin.

**1106:** Date of the earliest extant xiangqi pieces found in China. They are made of copper. The set includes Catapults.

**1129:** Rules of chaturanga for two and four players in the *Manasollasa*, written by the Indian king Someshvara III.

**1141:** Li Qingzhao inserted a drawing of a xiangqi board in her work, the *Dama Tujing*.

**1150:** Dating of the oldest pieces of the figurative set, probably of Norwegian origin, found in the Isle of Lewis (Scotland).

**1200:** Engraving of chess players on the Angkor temples in Cambodia.

**1205:** Allusion to courier chess in a German text, the *Wigalois*. This variant had a piece moving like the modern Bishop.

**1210:** A Chinese poem by Liu Kezhuang gives the complete rules of xiangqi.

**1221:** A short description of a small shogi appears in the *Nichureki* in Japan. Rook and Bishop are absent. The board is not described. The same text contains the mention of a large shogi on 13 × 13 squares, including the Bishop and, possibly, the Rook.

**1283:** Description of several chess variants in the *Libro del Acedrex* of King Alfonso X of Castile, including Grant Acedrex over 12 × 12 squares (with a piece moving like the modern Bishop) and Chess of the Four Seasons, for four players.

**1300:** Complete descriptions are given of sho shogi (including a Drunk Elephant piece, played on a 9 × 9 square board), and of dai shogi (played on a 15 × 15 square board) in the *Futsu Shodoshu*, by the monk Ryoki.

**1342:** Description of several chess variants in the *Nafa'is al-funun*, by al-Amuli, including "citadel chess," with a piece similar to the modern Bishop, and the variant later known as Timur's chess.

**1424:** The Japanese diary, *Hanasakai Sandaikai*, commented on a large shogi game (chu shogi?) in which a player had a Free King handicap. The Free King moves as the modern Queen.

**1443:** Earliest date for the description of several large shogis, up to tai shogi on 25 × 25 squares, in a lost Japanese book, *Shogi Shushu no Zu*, according to Minase Kanenari, who wrote this in **1591**.

**1475:** Invention of new moving rules for the Queen and the Bishop. These novelties are set in the scene of a Catalan poem, the *Scachs d'amor*.

**1495:** Supposed date for the publishing of a Catalan treatise, Francesch Vicent's *Libre dels jochs partits dels schacs en nombre de 100*, today lost. That would be the first chess book with the modern moves of Queens and Bishops.

**1497:** Publishing of the Spanish book, Lucena's *Repeticion de Amores e Arte de Acedrex*, most ancient extant treatise using the modern rules of European chess.

**1540:** Description of a giant chess variant (board of 14 × 14 squares) in India, in Godavaramishra's *Hariharachaturanga*.

**1560:** Earliest appearance of castling in France and Italy, with various rules from place to place.

**1577:** Short mention of chess in a Korean text by Yu Hui-Chun.

**1587:** Earliest publication of a shogi diagram that shows a game as today.

**1602:** The Japanese craftsman, Minase Kanenari, writes an inventory with the 735 shogi sets he has manufactured: 618 sho shogi, 106 chu, 2 dai, 2 dai dai, 3 maka dai dai and 4 tai shogi.

**1607:** Earliest record of a complete game of shogi, between Honinbo Sansa (1558–1623) and Ohashi Sokei (1555–1634).

**1612:** Foundation of a professional Academy for go and shogi in Japan.

**1617:** Earliest proposal of a chess variant over a 10 × 10 board with pieces combining Rook + Knight and Bishop + Knight. By the Italian author and player, Pietro Carrera.

**1636:** Publication of the definitive rules of shogi by Ohashi Soko in the *Shogi Zushiki*. Included is the first mention of dropping pieces into play. There is no Drunk Elephant among the pieces.

# Timeline

**1638:** Full description of Korean janggi in an essay by Jang Yu.

**1689:** Publication of *Mandragorias seu Historia Shahiludii* by Thomas Hyde, professor of Oriental languages at the University of Oxford, England, and first modern chess historian.

**1697:** Invention of a three-player version of Chinese xiangqi by Zheng Jinde.

**1722:** Invention of a three-player version of European chess by Filippo Marinelli.

**1772:** Travel journal in Russia by the English historian William Coxe, who reports a version of chess for four players and the addition of the Knight's move to the Queen's power.

**1792:** Earliest recorded attempt to revitalize chess by shuffling the pieces in the back row. This is credited to a Dutch officier, Philippus Julius van Zuylen van Nyevelt.

**1849:** Design of chessmen patented by Nathaniel Cook and John Jaques of London, baptized "Staunton" in honor of the British chess champion.

**1851:** First international chess tournament, organized in London by Howard Staunton and won by Adolf Anderssen (Germany).

**1853:** Earliest hexagon-based chess variant proposed by Thomas Hanmer Croughton.

**1866:** Earliest use of the clock in an international chess tournament (London).

**1886:** First official chess world championship held in the United States, won by Wilhem Steinitz (Austria).

**1907:** Earliest record of a three-dimensional chess variant, Ferdinand Maack's Raumschach. An earlier version, by Lionel Kieseritzky (Kubicschach), in **1851,** was not fully recorded.

**1913:** Publication of the monumental *A History of Chess* by the English professor Harold James Ruthven Murray.

**1924:** Foundation of the F.I.D.E., *Fédération Internationale des Échecs*, in Paris, France.

**1996:** The American chess champion, Bobby Fischer, presents his rules for *Random Chess* or *Chess960* in Buenos Aires, Argentina.

**1997:** The super-computer Deep Blue beats the Russian chess world champion Garry Kasparov in a six-game chess match.

**2008:** F.I.D.E. adds Chess960 to an appendix in the *Laws of Chess*.

# Notes

## Introduction

1. As an excellent example of new research in chess history, readers are directed to Peter J. Monté's *The Classical Era of Modern Chess* (2014), a virtually exhaustive examination of early modern European chess literature.

## Part I

1. This Arabic word for chess can also be transliterated as *shitranj*.
2. Our word "Rook" derives directly from the Persian *Rukh* (with a guttural "k"). The original meaning of this word remains a mystery. The most ancient written reference to this piece calls it a minister (*madayar*) ruling one flank (*rokh*) of the army; and among the very earliest pieces found (at Afrasiab), in a land which was then Persia, the piece is apparently indicated by a man riding in a cart. This image, as a charioteer, was the common depiction in ancient India. In Arabic and in Persian, this word *Rukh* referred to the chess piece and had no other specific meaning.
3. Although the ancient Arabic manuscripts showed the King that is at the bottom of the board to be on d1, it was usually the side across the top of the board that moved first. In this way, the game was set up very similarly to the modern convention in which the player who moves first has his King standing to the right of his Queen.
4. The British scholar, Harold James Ruthven Murray (1868–1955), is the author of the monumental book *A History of Chess*. It comprises 900 pages, with footnotes and line drawings. This work, published in 1913, remains the unsurpassed reference work for chess historians today.
5. Descending from a Turkish prince reigning on Gorgan, in the southeast Caspian Sea, as-Suli arrived at the court of caliph al-Muktafi (902–908) where he became the official champion after his victory against al-Mawardi. Fallen into disgrace because of his Shiite leanings, he finished his life miserably, exiled to Bassora. However, his name grew to the status of legend after his death. He was even sometimes reputed to be the inventor of chess.
6. Presumed to be a native of the Byzantine lands in the West, because of his nickname—ar-Rumi, the great champion—al-'Adli became the best player in the courts of the caliphs of al-Wathiq (842–847) and al-Mutawakkil (847–861) in Baghdad. He was finally defeated by ar-Razi.
7. Al-Lajlaj was the most celebrated student of the great master, as-Suli. Although his name means simply "the stutterer," al-Lajlaj became a major contributor to the theory and analysis of shatranj. He is known to have lived in Baghdad, and later in Shiraz at the court of the Buyid dynasty under emir Azad od-Dowleh. He died there in 970 and is now legendary among the Persians, Turks and Indians. As a twist in the fabric of history, he later became identified in India as the legendary Lilaj, the Hindu ambassador credited with bringing chess to Persia.
8. According to modern Iranologists, the *Wizarishn i Chatrang ud Nihishn i New-ardakhshir (Explanation of Chatrang and the Invention of Nard)* was written around 600 C.E. We discuss this text further when examining the origins of chess, in the final part of this book.
9. Al-Farazdaq's verse states, "*I keep you from your inheritance and from the royal crown so that, hindered by my arm, you remain a* baidaq *(Pawn) among the* bayadiq *(Pawns).*" Such a reference strongly suggests that the game was already well known.
10. The Sunni schools condemned carved chessmen that actually reproduce the King and other figures as *'ansab*, "images." Persian scholars however, considered that this condemnation was only valid for idols, so the Shiite players had no restrictions on using representational chessmen.
11. His name indicates that he was probably born in Cathay, a word designating the north of China for Arabian chroniclers in that time period.

12. The Madagascan game *fanorona* is probably derived from an Arab game *al-qirq*. *Al-qirq* is mentioned in a tenth century book, the *Kitab al-aghani* (*Book of songs*) by Abu al-Faraj. This game was transmitted by the Moors to the Spanish Christians, who baptized it *alquerque*. It is a direct ancestor of merels and also of the game of checkers which appeared in 15th century Valencia, Spain.

13. The African continent has been a major contributor to the games of the world. It must be credited for the race games of the Pharaonic Egypt (*mehen*, *senet*, game of the fifty-eight holes, etc.) and for the numerous North African games of the Berber, or Tuareg, peoples. Other African games involve races and captures, such as *tab* and *sig*, and the spiral of *li'b el-merafib* (the "Hyena game"), played by the Arabs of Sudan. Of great significance is the family of sowing games of the *oware* type (2 or 3 rows) that spread into Asia with merchants and into America on slave ships. Even more complex are the *mancalas* of the *bao* type (4 rows), still practiced in all Bantu lands in East Africa. The continent is also home to games of capture, such as *yoté* from Senegal and Mali, and *zamma*, or *srand*, from the Sahara desert. With such a wealth of strategy games, it is not surprising that chess found a limited role in Africa.

14. This word, *Dabbaba*, designates a siege engine of the medieval Arabic military arts. In the universe of chess, it may cause some confusion because it refers to completely different sorts of chessmen depending on the particular variant. For clarity, the present work uses different symbols depending upon the nature of the chess piece.

15. The original sources do not specify which citadels were concerned; it is assumed that the rule applied to the citadels on the opponent's side only.

16. Again, the original Arabic rule was vague and did not specify which citadel was concerned. The proposed rule here is a logical assumption.

17. Cited by Murray.

18. *Rumiya* literally means Roman; this is how the Arabs designated their Byzantine rivals.

19. Giafar al Barmeki, *A Tale of the Court of Haroun al Raschit* (New York: Harper & Brothers, 1836).

20. The legacy of games in the Byzantine Empire (330–1453) remains to be written; very little has been added to the information compiled by Murray in 1913.

21. *Tali'a* means scout, vanguard, outpost, picket, advanced post, spy, a group of soldiers or troops placed on a line forward of a position to warn against an enemy advance.

22. This rule is given by Murray. Forbes, who is less reliable, has this piece moving exactly like the modern Bishop.

23. If the Scout could stop on the first square like the Bishop, its value would be (3.3).

24. The English Orientalist Thomas Hyde was the first to reveal this game to Western scholars in his book *Mandragorias, seu, Historia shahiludii*, first published in 1694. Hyde reported a board bearing the Arabic names of the pieces. Curiously, this board was checkered and has 12 rows of 11 columns and no citadel.

25. Indeed, they are subject to many interpretations from modern authors who do not agree on every point.

26. *Kashshaf* was translated as *Sentinel* by Forbes and also by Murray. This is contested by modern linguists because the root of the word refers to *search* and *discover*, which differs from the idea of *keeping* or *watching*. *Explorer* or *Tracker* would be a better translation.

27. This Forbes and Murray translate as *crocodile*. But the word also applies to the shark and the barracuda.

28. Forbes had also made his own speculation: a Lion moving like the Rukh + Giraffe, a Bull moving like the Scout (= Bishop for him) + Giraffe and an Explorer moving like the Scout + Rukh, being "*precisely the power of our modern Queen.*" This choice was explained thus: "*it very aptly happens that these three pieces admit of just three distinct combinations of pairs or twos*" [of Rukh, Giraffe and Scout, the three strongest pieces of regular Timur's chess]. This hypothesis seems to yield too many powerful pieces. They are typical of 19th century chess variant experimentation in Europe but they do not match very well with the spirit of the game in its historic context.

29. According to Verney (1885), but Gollon (1968) places a Counselor at the King's right side for both players.

30. Neither Verney (1885) nor Murray (1913) stated whether the modern moves of the Queen and Bishop applied to this game, in place of the moves of the Counselor and Elephant. The Turkish encyclopedia that described this variant used the modernized moves for most shatranj problems—but did keep the old moves in one case. It is, therefore, difficult to determine.

31. The presence of the *Rhinoceros*, half-diagonal and half-equestrian, leads one to think of the *grant acedrex*, which appeared in Spain in the 13th century. It was played on a board of (only!) 144 squares. A link between both games—tenuous, but supported by a common Muslim influence—could suggest an explanation.

32. What is meant here is probably *roc* or *rokh*, a fabulous giant bird, able to seize an elephant, which is encountered in several Oriental tales including *Sinbad the Sailor*.

33. Shatar is the name under which this game has been described in Western literature; however, the literal rendering from the original Mongolian script is *sitar-a*.

34. Known as *ulzin*, it is the most frequently used abstract symbol. It looks like a long ribbon forming a complex knot and closing on itself. It is a symbol of happiness.

35. In this context, the swastika is a traditional Tibetan symbol, indicating the sun.

36. The testimonies vary. Murray reports an account from E.K. Yakovlef in 1880 which states: "*the K and Q do not occupy a fixed position but always stand side by side on the middle squares of the border line, yet invariably so that the K stood [sic] opposite K, and the Q opposite Q.*"

37. In nature, the Snow Leopard is an animal in danger of extinction. So it is in shatar as well. According to E.K. Yakovlef (1880, cited by Murray), this move was the standard. But according to Assia Popova (1974), the Mongolians used this move only in periods of mourning. The rest of the time, they adopt the modern move of the chess Queen.

38. Citing N.V. Kocheshkov (1972).

39. The authors are indebted to Peter Michaelsen for this information.

40. Kalmykia is an autonomous republic of the Russian Federation, located at the northwest shores of the Caspian Sea. It is the only European territory of Mongolian language and Buddhist faith. It was ruled with an iron hand between 1993 and 2010 by Kirsan Ilyumzhinov, who also was president of the Fédération Internationale des Échecs from 1995 to 2015! This eccentric autocrat raised a "City of Chess" in the capital, Elista, where the 2006 World Chess Championship saw Vladimir Kramnik defeat Veselin Topalov. As of 2010 evidence shows that traditional shatar remains alive and well in Kalmykia.

41. The Mongolians dominated Tibet in the 13th century. In return, the Tibetans exercised a strong cultural influence on Mongolia to the point that the dominant religion in Mongolia today is Lamaism, a form of Tibetan Buddhism. In the area of games, Mongolians commonly play *dörvölzh*, a form of go (or *weiqi*) on a board of 17 × 17 intersections (instead of the usual 19 × 19). This board is said to be precisely the same as that used in this great game in Tibet. Thus, the hypothesis has been advanced that shatar was brought by the Tibetan Lamas who converted Mongolia. But the absence of a popular chess game in Tibet makes this a fragile thesis. All recent testimonies of chess in Tibet describe the Chinese game, *xiangqi*. It is true that the situation in the historical Tibet (Tibet Autonomous Region or Xizang; parts of Qinghai and Sichuan) has dramatically changed since 1913, when Murray published his *magnum opus*.

42. The rules given here are the best logical composite drawn from a variety of sources, each of which has its own omissions and inconsistencies. It is also likely that there was some variation in how the game was played at different locations. For instance, some reports have the Bodyguard only arresting the moves of the enemy pieces; others have the Bodyguard capturing using his normal move.

# Part II

1. The sources do not tell which piece was on the left or on the right. Kings were presumably put face-to-face. (Murray opined that the Indian habit for crosswise setup did not begin before the end of the 18th century.)

2. This precision in parentheses is given because the statement of the original source is ambiguous and somewhat open to interpretation: "*When [the foot soldier] has moved across 4 rows of squares it will become a Minister. It [will be] a Minister on the 4 squares if it returns.*" Thus, according to A. Bock-Raming, the Pawn wins its promotion in three steps: it may jump to the second square on its first move (from 2nd row to 4th row), then it must first arrive on the last row (so, four steps from 4th to 8th row), then it is promoted to a Minister and repositioned on its original departure square. Bock-Raming asserts that this description had some similarities to the rules applied to Malay chess (*catur*), as well as the "joy leaps" long practiced in Ströbeck, Germany. However, they are not quite the same and there is no objective confirmation of such a relationship.

3. Someshvara III (reigned 1126–1138) was king of the Western Chalukya Empire, which ruled most of the western Deccan between the 10th and the 12th centuries. His domination was a time of intense literary activity in Sanskrit and in Kannada (the Dravidian language of Karnataka, the land of Mysore). The *Manasollasa* was a Sanskrit encyclopedia of daily life at the royal court, written by the king himself, which covered many subjects including architecture, medicine, cuisine, magic, ornaments, sports, painting, music, dance, games, etc.

4. In addition, the Indian scholar Siddharth Y. Wakankar affirmed that there is another text from the same period that details the chessboard, the arrangement of the pieces and their movements. This text is the *Balakahita Buddhibala Kridanam*, a small anonymous work of seven verses intended for children and appended to the end of the Marathi edition of *Chaturanga Vilasamanimañjari*. According to Wakankar, it had not a single Persian word, suggesting that it was composed prior to the Muslim period. It was therefore dated from circa the 10th to the 12th century. Bock-Raming added that this short text is about two-handed chaturanga and that its dating remains uncertain.

5. The pieces are Prince (*nripa*), Counselor (*mantri*), Elephants (*hasti*), Horse (*ashva*), Forerunner (*agresara*) and Foot Soldiers (*padati*).

6. Information from C. Rajendran (professor of Sanskrit at Calicut University, Kerala, India). The Chariot (*ratha*) moved like a Rook, the Elephant (*danti*) jumped one square diagonally and the Minister (*mantri*) moved one step diagonally. Other pieces were King (*deva*), Horse (*turaga*) and Footmen (*patti*). All pieces were arrayed as in shatranj, i.e., Chariots in the corners and Elephants close to King and Minister.

7. This work was ordered by Bhagavantadeva, chieftain of Bhareha in Uttar Pradesh. His literary activity is dated between 1610 and 1645, according to S.C. Banerji's *A Brief History of Dharmasastra*, Abhinav Publications, New Delhi, 1999.

8. Other terms were often used instead of the word *chaturanga*. The regions dominated by the Persian or Muslim laws use the word *shatranj* or *shatrang*. In the South, words based on the Sanskrit root *buddhi*, meaning intellect, like *buddhibala* (intellect army), are used. During the same period, the word chaturanga or its derivative (*chaturamga, saturankam*, etc.) started to designate race games played until recently on a spiral path over a 7 × 7 or a 9 × 9 squares board in South India and Sri Lanka.

9. It is not easy to determine the exact time modern European moves of the Queen and Bishop were adopted in India. According to Murray (1913), it must have been a "recent" introduction. Bock-Raming has remarked that these moves were in use in the game treatise *Kridakaushalya* (1871).

10. According to K.R. Banerjee on the Internet (http://www.hinduwisdom.info/articles_hinduism/164.htm).

11. The Kashmiri nomenclature is similar to that of Punjabi. The pieces are Shah, Wazir, Fil, Ghor, Rukh, Piyada (in order, K, Q, B, N, R, P). The game is known as shatranj.

12. This word has no other meaning in Punjabi. It is obviously derived from Arabic *fil* (elephant) but, as an Elephant is also used for the Rook with its local name, it is probable that *Fila* is just the name of the piece.

13. English domination has broadly influenced the modern Sinhala or Sinhalese nomenclature in both meanings of names—*Rajana* (Queen), *Dewagathi* (Churchman), *Maligawa* (Castle)—and through phonetics: *Naytwaraya* (Knight), *Pon* (Pawn) and *ches* (chess). However, chess is also called shatranj in Sri Lanka.

14. The cross-wise arrangement, as opposed to the mirror arrangement, is a change first recorded in India in 19th century treatises.

15. A rule not always applied. In the *Kridakaushalya* (1871) the King can escape a check by leaping.

16. Some players allow the double step for the Pawns on the files a, d, e and h, files which have an "x" marking on the board, providing that the piece behind the Pawn has not yet been moved.

17. Notation: K (King), C (Camel), E (Elephant).

18. Dice were used in this way: A throw of 6 moves the King, 5 the Minister, 4 an Elephant, 3 a Horse, 2 a Chariot, and 1 a Pawn. In each turn, the player throws two or more dice. It is supposed that this gave some choice of possibilities to the player. The player of the Maharaja was forced to adopt one of the moves indicated by the dice.

19. *Rumi* chess had one more peculiarity: In his first move, the Minister could jump to the 3rd row, passing over the Pawn in front of him if necessary. This same Pawn could, on its first move, leap to the 4th row, jumping over the Minister. However, if they are chosen, these two moves must be the first two moves executed.

20. This term for the game, *chaturaji*, was first proposed by Sir William Jones in 1790. The word originally designated the supreme victory rather than the game itself. However, it is still used here to avoid misunderstanding since the word *chaturanga* means "chess" in general, and more often designated the two-player game than the four-player game in original Indian sources.

21. A Boat is named in the rules reported from Bengal. Al-Biruni had a Chariot for this piece.

22. The interested reader will find other reconstructions in Murray, Bell or Gollon. (See bibliography.)

23. Al-Biruni clearly indicated the use of two dice, whereas the Bengali poem did not mention how many were employed. In practice, two dice (instead of one) bring much flexibility to the game.

24 Murray's rendition of the translation of the *Tithitattva* contains a contradiction. On verse 25, it is said that promotion is not possible in the corner and on the King's square, and then on verse 25 it is said that promotion is forbidden on King's and Elephant's square. But the corner is not the Elephant's square! The corner is the Boat's square. As "corner" is explicitly mentioned, we assume, as Forbes did, that there is a mistake here, and consequently that promotion is possible on Horse's and Elephant's square and impossible on King's and Boat's square.

25. Apparently, a rule of exchange of Boats also existed (*naukakrishta*), but the details are lost.

26. This thesis was primarily put forth by Captain Hiram Cox, Governor of Bengal, who conveyed the idea from Calcutta in 1799, later adopted, developed and strengthened with the authority of the linguist Duncan Forbes in 1860.

27. The *Rajatarangini* from Kalhana was a chronicle of Kashmiri kings written in 1148-49. It alludes briefly but clearly to the four-handed chaturanga: "*The king, though he had taken two kings (Lothana and Vigraharaja), was helpless and perplexed about the attack on the remaining one, just as a player of chess (who had taken two kings and is perplexed about taking the third). He had no hidden plan to give up for its sake. Yet he did not pay any regard to his antagonists who were taking his horsemen, peons and the rest*" (translated by M.A.Stein, Westminster, 1900, cited by H.J.R. Murray, 1913, p, 68).

28. This story is part of the famous Indian epic the *Mahabharata*. In the original version, the King was simply playing and betting at a dice game.

29. This story is told by Forbes (1860). The officer belonged to Colonel Baillie's detachment which had been massacred by Hyder Ali at the Battle of Pollilur, among the most severe British losses in the subcontinent. The officer, who was captured, kept a journal which was published in London, 1789, under the title, "Memoirs of the War in Asia from 1780 to 1784." He wrote, "*In India there are three kinds of chess: two of these are much more complex than the game of that name played in Europe. In one of them, the men, or fig-*

ures, amount to sixty; and the movements are proportionally various."

30. Details from this manuscript have been borrowed from Murray (1913).

31. Murray is again the source for Lala Raja Babu's work, written in Persian and published in Delhi in 1901. It appears that this treatise described many variants including *shatranj diwana shah*, the game of Pawns (each player having his King and his eight Pawns on their original squares), and several variants copied from Duncan Forbes and his *The History of Chess* (1860). Those are circular chess, Timur's chess and even chaturaji, which Forbes detailed from Indian sources! Lala Raja Babu also presented a four-handed chess on a cruciform-shaped board (adding three rows of eight squares on each edge of the 8 × 8 board), very similar to the games existing at that time in England.

32. Baroda is the former name of Vadodara, considered the cultural capital of Gujarat in Western India.

33. However, Gollon's account contained many mistakes. He reports that it is impossible to tell exactly when this variant was played, and that it came from "the region of Turkey." Gollon gives a Pawn promotion rule (to a Vizier) that was probably his own invention.

34. Murray indicates the native names only for the Vizier (*Wazir*) and Giraffe (*Zurafa*), in addition to the *Dabbaba*.

35. The source for this game is Pritchard (1994) citing *Indian Chess* by S.R. Iyer (Nag Publisher, Delhi, 1982).

36. Murray could not identify those three pieces. A reasonable guess would be *Mantri* (Minister) for M, and *Shahzada* (Prince) for Shh. For Wkh, we still have no explanation.

37. Lala Raja Babu had *Rukh* on a1 and l1, *Ghora* (Horse) on b1 and k1, *Dahja* (Standard) on c1 and j1, *Ratha* (Chariot) on d1 and i1, *Fil* (Elephant) on e1 and h1, *Wazir* (Minister) on f1, *Padshah* (King) on g1, and *Paidal* (Pawns) in the second row. Vasantha's rendition of Krishnaraja Wodeyar indicates Indian names only for the *Raja* (King), *Mantri* (Minister) and *Ratha* (Chariot).

38. Note that the Minister (*Wazir*) holds the central position here, and it is the Indian "Queen" (*Rani*) who is off to one side. This bears some logic, as the Minister has the power of the western Queen and this game's Queen is a less powerful piece.

39. Note that the strongest piece is the Prince (*Shahzada*) which, strangely, stands two squares away from the King (*Raja*).

40. A diagram dated 1871 is reproduced in Pritchard (1994). His source is *Indian Chess* by S.R. Iyer (Nag Publisher, Delhi, 1982). We have had no access to the latter book. Giving the date 1871, we understand that the original source should be Harikrishna's *Kridakaushalya*. However, Bock-Raming (1995) has pointed out that Iyer's rendition of the *Kridakaushalya* is incomplete and in more than one case gives faulty translations.

41. In addition, each player has four Musicians whose roles remain obscure.

42. *Khun* means "lord," an abbreviation of *khun luang*, "king."

43. Literally, *Met* means a seed, and a clitoris in colloquial use. That term would relate to the feminine symbolism of this piece. Murray had suggested another explanation: It could be a word deriving from Sanskrit *mantri*, minister. This idea was probably inspired by James Low, who translated *met* as minister in his 1836 article. But, it is not a solid etymology, as the Thai word for minister is *montri*, a word of obvious Indian roots. In that case, it is difficult to understand why the chess piece is not called *montri* instead of *met* if the sense was that of a minister. If one considers that there are many *met* in the course of the game, as several Pawns quickly promote, and that a promoted Pawn is often a flipped cowry shell showing its slot, the first explanation appears the most plausible.

44. *Neang* is a "young lady," a term also denoting a female character for this piece.

45. *Koul* designates a pillar, a border post. The word is used here with the meaning of "guard."

46. From an interview of Vladimir Kramnik by German columnist Dr. René Gralla, May 2004 (available on the Internet).

47. Transcribing the Khmer language into the Roman alphabet is a challenging task, as the language has a very difficult pronunciation for foreigners. The first three names from this table are obscure even with the help of a dictionary. The three other terms are recognizable, as they are similar to the names of these chessmen in *ouk*, the traditional Cambodian chess.

48. *Variant Chess* (Issue 55, September 2007 and issue 64, August 2010).

49. With the help of a Japanese chess researcher, Yasuji Shimizu, who got in touch with Umebayashi Isao.

50. Last and not least, John Beasley (who has published a correction to his *Variant Chess* articles on his website) has demonstrated that shattrong would be a flawed game: if Black mirrors White's play, he gets a material advantage as soon as White moves a Fish forward.

51. We here follow the most complete edition of Marco Polo's travels by Pierre-Yves Badel: *La description du Monde*, Le Livre de poche, Lettres gothiques, Paris, 1998. The original text says, "*Il y a olifans assez en ce royaulme et si ont aussi lingaloes assez et si ont moult grant planté de grans bois et si ont fust noir que l'en appelle ybenus et dont l'en fait les eschiez noirs.*" Note that the text refers specifically to "black chessmen," a point that is lost in most popular English renditions.

52. Concerning the Cambodian name of this game, it appears that *ouk* designates a check by Boat or Horse. As far as Thai language is concerned, a check by Seed, Nobleman or Pawn is called *ruk*. *Mak* has the meaning of a (board) game. So, *makruk* can be interpretated as the check-game.

53. La Loubère's description of xiangqi is astonishingly precise and shows no difference at all from the modern Chinese rules. Only a few years separate this account from Thomas Hyde's description of xiangqi, the earliest complete publication available to Western scholars. La Loubère's book was published in 1691 and Hyde's first edition appeared in 1689.

54. Low's report indicates that the counting rules were already in place and that the Counselor was allowed to move two steps straight forward on his first move. Low's text was written in 1829 and revised in 1836.

55. Pronounced "sit-too-rin."

56. As presented by Maung Maung Lwin, president of the Myanmar Chess Federation and author of a book on traditional sit-tu-yin (2011).

57. Pieces other than the Chariots can be placed on the first rank squares but this is usually avoided except, in rare cases, for the King.

58. Supplementary rules are sometimes found which have not been selected by the Myanmar Chess Federation: (1) Black has an extra constraint. If Red does not allow him to do so, he may not put a Chariot in the same column as a Red Chariot if there is not at least one red piece other than a Pawn between them. (2) The player may replace one (or several) of his Pawns with another piece, then freely redeploy this (or these) Pawn(s) in his camp.

59. This book's title is *Myanmar Sit Ba-Yin Lam-Nyun Sar-Oak Gyi* (*Burmese Chess Guide*) by Shwe Kyin U Ba, 1924.

60. It might appear superfluous to specify the color of the promoted piece; however, this precision does not exist for ASEAN chess alone; it is stated exactly like this in the official FIDE chess rules. There is a famous historical puzzle in which one side could only play a Pawn and get it promoted—but doing so led to stalemate. The astute player then promoted his Pawn to a piece *of the opposing color*, avoiding the stalemate, and checkmate became possible. Since that historic case, the official chess rules have stated that promotion is for a piece of the same color.

61. Hiram Cox (letter written May 28, 1799, published posthumously in 1801 and 1803), "On the Burmha [*sic*] Game of Chess, compared with the Indian, Chinese, and Persian Game of the same denomination," *Asiatic Researches*, Calcutta, 1801, vii. 488–511; reprinted verbatim in *Asiatic Researches; or, Transactions of the Society, Instituted in Bengal...*, London, 1803, vii. 480–504.

62. There is a tradition which affirms that chess arrived at the kingdoms of Arakan and of the Mons in the ninth century, or even before, and that it was in vogue in the court of the Burmese kingdom of Pagan in the 11th to 13th centuries. See for instance, Peter Nicolaus (sources not cited) on www.chessvariants.org.

63. Pronounce "chatoor." Murray used the expression *main chator*, literally "chess game" where *main* means "game" and *chator* uses the old Malay spelling system, before the 1972 reform.

64. According to Thomas Stamford Raffle's account (1817).

65. Elcum (1907) affirmed that the Pawn can promote to any piece which is no longer present on the board. Robinson (1904) did not indicate any restriction. Raffles (1817), regarding Javanese rules, was clear in saying that the Pawn promotes to a Queen and there can be any number of Queens on the board.

66. Example: White has a Pawn on e7, Black has a Chariot on f7. White plays e7–e8–f7, capturing the black Chariot and completing its promotion. However, if Black has his King on f7 instead, White plays e7–e8 and stops. Black is in check and the White Pawn is not yet promoted.

67. Private communication from Jiří Jákl. This text originates from a collection of Sanskrit tales compiled in the sixth century C.E., first translated into Persian in the beginning of the 14th century, then into Malay by Kadi Hassan in 1371, according to traditional sources.

68. The Czech historian, Jiří Jákl, is convinced that a race game is meant, and not chess. Indeed, in some occasions, derivations of the Indian word *chaturanga* have been used to indicate race board games. For example, *saturankam*, a race game following a spiral path over a 7 × 7 square board is practiced in Southern India and Sri Lanka. The present authors find his argument, particularly the fact that stakes and dice are evoked, not convincing enough to discount chess, which has also been played with dice for stakes in many places. One may leave the point to further investigation.

69. Country of the former president of the F.I.D.E., Florencio Campomanes (1927–2010), who organized a Chess World Championship in Baguio City in 1978, where Anatoly Karpov defeated Viktor Korchnoi.

# Part III

1. Pronounce "shyang chee." This word is most often translated as "elephants' game" but "game of symbols" is probably a better etymological interpretation.

2. Pronounced approximatively as "cutwong," said rapidly. It means "generals' game."

3. See Marc-Antoine Nguyen (Praxeo, 2009).

4. *Yitong* means "big river" in the Manchu language.

5. The authors of this book are indebted to Peter Michaelsen who has drawn their attention to the Pawn's promotion rule. This rule was omitted in Pritchard's books. The reference is to an Italian article by Giuseppe Baggio in *Eteroscacco*, 86/87/88; April–December 1999, p. 31.

6. The first Toronto Undercover Xiangqi Open in January, 2012.

7. The details of these texts, as well as those which follow, are given in the last part of this book, which discusses the origins of chess.

8. The poems are the *Xiangjing* "Classic of the Game of Symbols" of Emperor Wu (Northern Zhou dynasty), now lost, but known by its extant preface written by Wang Bao (fl. 552–581), and the *Xiangxi Fu* of Yu Xin, written before 569.

9. "The Celestial Cavalry should advance aslant over three squares. The General should travel everywhere and control the four directions. The Chariots should move straight forward and not retreat. The six infantry units [or 'The Soldiers with six weapons...'] should advance in an orderly manner." This leaves some room for interpretation and, as pointed out by Peter Banaschak, these moves can be deduced from the text, but not with certainty.

10. These ranks were official titles in use during the Han dynasty, in descending order: general in chief (*jiang*), deputy general (*pian*) and assistant general (*bai*). It is possible that those chess pieces were playing the role of *Jiang*, *Shi* and *Xiang* chessmen of common xiangqi.

11. This intriguing game, chess for seven players over a 19 × 19 point board, is described further in the text. Interestingly, in addition to the Catapult, it also utilizes the *Jiang*, *Pian* and *Bai* pieces, although with very different moves than those of regular xiangqi.

12. The German historian, Karl Himly, presented a reconstruction with 32 pieces over an 11 × 11 board, without a "river," in the 1890s. Several further reconstructions followed which are presented in Li (*Genealogy of Chess*, 1998).

13. *Ji* means *basis* and was probably interchangeable with *qi*, meaning *piece*.

14. Li Qingzhao inserted a drawing of a xiangqi board in her work the *Dama Tujing*. This board is similar to the present xiangqi with its palaces and river, and the same number of rows and columns. A few years later, Xiao Zhao painted a scene from the Story of Prince Kang, who used a xiangqi General to predict the future of his son (who became Emperor Gaozong). That painting clearly shows the correct board, with 16 black and 16 red pieces.

15. Liu Kezhuang (1187–1269) wrote a poem entitled *Xiangyi yi shou, cheng Ye Qianzhong (Poem on the Elephant Game, to Show Ye Qianzhong).* "Xiangyi" should be read as xiangqi. It describes all of the various pieces, General, Advisor, Elephant, Chariot, Horse, Catapult, and Soldier, and the board is as in modern xiangqi.

16. This title, sometimes also translated as "The Secret Inside the Orange," is a fable from the Sui (589–617) or Tang (618–907) period, first narrated by Niu Sengru, which inspired many Chinese poets.

17. Pronounced "jang-ghi." We follow here the *Revised Romanization of Korean* system, official since 2000. Depending on the adopted transliteration system, one can also find *jangki* or *changgi*. Culin (1895) had *tjyang-keui*, which was borrowed by Murray (1913).

18. For instance, in the "janggi" Korean Wikipedia page on the Internet.

19. Nam Yu-Yong (1698–1773) was a Joseon (or Chosun) official who has passed the very demanding literary examination called *mun-gwa* in 1740. He served under King Yeongjo from 1754 to 1767 as tutor to the king's grandson and successor, Jeongjo. Soon after becoming king, Jeongjo ordered the publication of the *Noeyonjip*, the collection of all the works of his old tutor, which was edited and printed in 1783.

20. The passage of the *Noeyonjip* can be tentatively translated as follows : "*Gwangsanghui is derived from the game of janggi but is more extended. Its board is composed of 15 columns and 14 rows, totaling 210 points. The pieces are disposed on 90 points on North and South, forming three army corps. The central corps lies on 45 points, 21 forming the inner camp, counting 7 columns and 3 lines in the North, with a 9-point palace in the middle, where the Marshal is placed in the center. The two Counsellors, who are Advisors, are placed behind, at left and right of the Marshal. The two Elephants, elite troops, are placed at left and right of the Advisors. The two Chariots, pounding units, are placed at left and right of the Elephants. The two Cannons, strong charging units, lie on two of the palace's corners. The two Horses, rapid executing units, are placed before the Elephants with one step in between. The 24 points that encompass the inner camp form the outer camp; one Vanguard, protecting the front, keeps the South. One rear general, a Rearguard, keeps the North. The two Elite officers, fantastic doorkeepers, are placed one at the East, the other at the West. At South-East and South-West, the two travelers, Mobile units; at North-East and North-West lie two concealed Units which are Ambush units. At one step distance from the Vanguard is the palace's door; Infantry and Cavalry units are posted separately, by groups of three, on the columns on the left and on the right of the doors, keeping the East and the West. Cavalry pieces are the cavalry troops; Infantry pieces are the infantry soldiers; there are six for each category. On each left and right side of the army, there are 15 points with a 9-point palace, always with a General in its center. An Advisor sits behind each General. A Chariot and an Elephant are placed on both Advisors' sides. A Horse and a Cannon stay on the 9-palace's East and West corners. For the right camp, the Chariot stays on the right with the Horse being on the West, this is the organization of the lines.*

*The first Marshal moves inside the 9-palace with no constraint, but cannot go out of it. The left and right Generals are like the first Marshal, they stay in the middle of their troops, helping them, and cannot go out from there. The Vanguard stays outside without entering inside, and moves without constraint. The Rearguard stays inside without going out, and moves without constraint. The Advisor moves like the General. The Chariot moves vertically and horizontally without constraint. The Cannon shall move with another piece's help, except from another Cannon, and cannot capture a Cannon. The Horse moves one oblique step, the Elephant moves three oblique steps, however the Horse must have a free shoulder and the Elephant must have a free shoulder and belly, or it cannot move [note: "shoulder" and "belly" apparently refer to intermediate points; this seems to describe the moves still used by the modern janggi Horse and Elephant]. The Cavalry moves half an oblique step. The Infantry moves one step. Cavalry and Infantry may move sideways but cannot retreat. The Mobile unit moves two oblique steps, it must have a free heart [intermediate point] or it cannot move. The Ambush unit moves an oblique step and half; the Ambush unit cannot capture; after being captured it remains an Ambush [perhaps indicating that the piece is not removed from the board; this is not clear].*

*The Elite unit moves as a square, it can enter any palace without constraint, however it cannot leave the three lines of the palaces. Capturing the first Marshal achieves victory; it is not possible to have a draw. This is a great feature. The danger comes from the General's left and right sides, the prisoners belong to their winner's camp, they may be kept as hostages. Both armies mobilize; before the soldiers' lines have crossed each other, no capture can be made, this is the end of the rules.* The diagram has been reconstructed from those elements, taking into account that South was always at the bottom of the maps in ancient China.

21. Jang Yu was a Joseon dynasty civil bureaucrat and father of Korean Queen Inseon (1619–1674). "Gyegok" was his pen name.

22. Conserved at the National Research Institute of Maritime Cultural Heritage, Jeonnam, Republic of Korea.

23. The current form of janggi dates, at the latest, from the second half of the 19th century. Culin (1895) already had octagonal pieces varying in size according to their values. He also noted that two sets in the U.S. National Museum in Washington were octagonal, and that the pieces exhibited by the Korean Government at the Columbian Exposition in Chicago (1893), in the Museum of the University of Pennsylvania, were circular, but with variable sizes according to the chessmen's values.

24. The move of this piece has an intriguing similarity to that of the Elephant in the Korean janggi, though having a longer range.

25. We follow here Dennis Leventhal, author of *The Chess of China,* published in 1978 in Taiwan. This work contains translations of the most fundamental historic texts related to Chinese chess.

26. According to Leventhal, the preface and colophon of Sima Guang's essay are written by Wang Yimin, dated 1206. This essay is found in Tao Zongyi's *Shuo Fu* (*Environs of Fiction*). Tao Zongyi was a writer and scholar born in 1316 and the edition of *Shuo Fu* referred to is from 1647.

27. Qin is pronounced "chin," a word adopted first by Persians and Indians, then by Europeans, as the name of the country, China.

28. Yan is represented at northwest on the board, although the State of Yan was actually located at the northeast. It seems that the original Chinese rules mixed up Yan and Zhao.

29. Dennis A. Leventhal, 1978.

30. This recalls the peculiar move given to the regular xiangqi Soldier by Cheng Hao in the 11th century.

31. Two other moves have been attributed to the Flag once it has penetrated enemy lines: moving like a Chariot according to some, like a Horse according to others.

32. The banner system combined both civil and military administrative functions, and provided the means of governing the Chinese and Mongol peoples, as well as the Manchu tribesmen.

33. The detailed rules of the *sanyou qi* are available in Cui Yuequan's book *Tushui Zhongguo Gudai Youyi* (*Ancient Chinese Recreation Including Figures*), published in 2002. The *Zhongguo Xiangqishi Congkao* (*Chinese Chess History Book*), by the scholar Zhu Nanxian (1916–1970), also recorded this board, but lacked the detailed rules. Mr. Yu Ren Dong from Hsinchu, Taiwan, is gratefully acknowledged for his communication of the details reported in this chapter.

34. Most inventions of *siguo xiangqi* use a regular set of 16 xiangqi chessmen per player. The board is generally organized around a 9 × 9 point central area with extensions at each of the four sides, representing the players' camps. Extensions can have 9 × 4 points and be directly connected to the central area or have 9 × 5 points and be separated from the central area by a river strip. The four players comprise two teams of two players each. In some versions, the allies are seated opposite each others, while in other games, the allies are seated side-by-side. One reported game shows a "forbidden city" inside the center area; another makes use of 25 chessmen per side, with supplementary Soldiers and Cannons. Variations are endless.

35. This is the order in use in Hong Kong and Guangdong province. In northern mainland China, the ranking is General ⇒ Advisor ⇒ Elephant ⇒ Chariot ⇒ Horse ⇒ Cannon ⇒ Soldier.

36. Many players are surprised that the Dog is superior to the Wolf; moreover, this does not seem in agreement with their respective positions on the board. But some versions of the rules reverse these and play with the Wolf stronger than the Dog. Some sources replace the Wolf with a Fox, eliminating the doubts, as a Dog is perceived as stronger than a Fox. In any case, this has practically no impact on the game, as those pieces seldom meet each other.

37. There are variations on this point. Other sources allow the Rat to capture another Rat from land to lake or from lake to land.

38. This game is described here for the very first time in a Western language. The instructions were included as a leaflet written in traditional Chinese, included in the game box. The Chinese text rules, however, lack precision on several points and, consequently, the translation by the present authors does not produce a perfectly definitive set of rules.

A second set of rules, brought to the authors' attention by Peter Blommers, appears in a Chinese boardgames booklet published in 1987. It shows a few differences from the first source. Here, the Wild Beasts are Lion / Tiger / Bear / Wolf; the Insects are Bee / Butterfly / Ant; and the Birds have a different order: Eagle / Swallow / Sparrow.

Any reader having more information is invited to contact the authors at the publisher's address or through the Internet. Lisha Bai, Samuer Shao, Marc-Antoine Nguyen and Gaëtan Prigent are kindly acknowledged for their help in translating the rules of this game.

39. This game was not competely forgotten. A color photograph of some pieces and a strip from the board are displayed in the *"Jungle"* (doushouqi) chapter of Jack Botermans's *The Book of Games* (Sterling, 2008). The caption reads, *"A Korean variation on the game of Jungle. The game uses many more pieces, and the board consists of 11 × 12 squares with no special markings."* The text gives no further information. The present evidence casts doubt on Boterman's assertion of the game having a Korean origin; it is quite likely he received the game with some misinformation.

40. At the time of this writing, further research on this family of games (L'Attaque, Stratego, doushouqi, luzhanqi, gunjin shogi, etc.) is being conducted, by the game historians, Fred Horn and Michel Boutin.

41. Pronounced "loo tsahn chee."

42. In the northern areas of China, the Landmine is not removed when attacked by another piece—except when attacked by the Sapper, who defeats it entirely.

43. See www.tanken.com/gunjin.html.

44. This rule is similar to the rule of capture that is applied in Luzhanqi, Stratego and all other games in the family. However, this rule has been changed in some later editions. For example, in the English edition by H.P. Gibson & Sons Ltd. (not dated, probably 1970s), it is specified, "Pieces attack each other back to back only, by moving on the square in front of the opponent and saying 'attack.'" This is surprisingly different from all other related games.

45. This patent (N° 379.625) was filed on June 24, 1907, delivered on September 13, and published in November (France) and December (U.K.) of the same year, 1907. Entitled *"Jeu de la Guerre"* (Wargame), it says: *"Le jeu consiste essentiellement en ce que des cartes à jouer, pliées au milieu et ne portant des images que sur la face antérieure, sont placées de façon telle, sur une feuille à jouer divisée en carrés et représentant une mer rétrécie en son milieu par des îles en passes étroites traversées par une ligne de démarcation, que l'adversaire ne voit que le côté de la carte ne présentant pas d'image, de sorte qu'il peut déduire seulement de la manoeuvre de ses coups de son adversaire le genre et la valeur des différents vaisseaux ou similaires représentés sur les cartes à jouer"* (The game consists essentially in playing cards, folded in the middle and not bearing images on the front side, which are placed on a playing sheet divided into squares and representing a sea, narrowed in its middle by islands separated by narrow passes and crossed by a demarcation line. The opponent sees only the side of the card having no image, so that he may deduce only from his opponent's moves the identities and the relative values of the different vessels or similar units represented on the playing cards.). This game has a board with two camps of 7 × 5 squares each, separated by four two-square-long rivers; therefore the full board has 12 rows. There were 35 pieces on each side, which were not detailed.

46. Although the origin of banqi is a matter of conjecture, it appears to be a simple game that could have been invented before luzhanqi.

47. Michel Boutin, "L'Attaque, un jeu français issu du Gunjin Shogi," *Art et Savoir de l'Inde*, Les Éditions HEB, 2015. This paper cites Matsura Masayasu (*Games of the World*, Tokyo, 1907, in Japanese) and Sumire Shoshi (*Book containing numerous interesting games*, Tokyo, 1913, in Japanese).

## Part IV

1. Pronounced with a hard "g" as in "geese." This word literally means general's (*sho*) game (*gi*).

2. Actually, shogi has different names for the two players, according to whether they play even games or handicap games. Black is called *Sente* in even games, and *Shitate* (lower hand) in handicap games. White is called *Gote* in even games, and *Uwate* (upper hand) in handicap games.

3. Also translated as Laurel, Cinnamon or Cassia, the exact meaning is Katsura, a Japanese tree (*cercidiphyllum japonicum*) whose leaves have a caramel scent.

4. Also translated Fragrant or Perfumed. Japanese scholars have noted that jewel, gold, silver, katsura and incense correspond to the Five Buddhist Treasures.

5. It should be noted, however, that a Pawn already on the board is allowed to mate by simply moving.

6. Referred to here is the Gold General, who has the same role of first advisor as the General in sit-tuyin, or the Seed in makruk.

7. This was first noted by the Japanese historian, Koichi Masukawa (see the bibliography), in 1994. He wrote *"From ancient times the ocean current, called Kuro-Shio in Japanese, has flowed, and still flows today, from South-East Asia to Japan. The old Japanese envoys to China (from AD 630–894 approximately) regularly made use of this current to return home, and a noted Chinese bishop came to Japan from ports in southern China using this ocean current (AD 753). There was a close connection between South China and Japan."*

8. A traditional account tells us that shogi was brought from China by Kibi Makibi (695-775), a famous Japanese scholar who visited the Tang Court for 17 years, but the available evidence indicates this tale was created at the start of the Edo period (early 17th century). Koichi Masukawa has noted that there are a few works describing games and pastimes in Japan before the 11th century (for example, the catalog of

properties of Emperor Shomu (756) and Japan's first encyclopedia, the *Wamyo ruiju-sho,* published circa 931–938); none of them mention shogi or any chess form, though they do mention the game of go and *sugoruku,* the Japanese form of backgammon; both games were imported from China.

9. The *Kirinsho* is attributed to Fujiwara no Yukinari (972–1027). Its title evokes the *kirin,* a mythical animal that was a kind of monstrous winged unicorn. Fujiwara no Yukinari, also known by his court title, *Gonseki,* was an important civil servant and a remarkable calligrapher. He was part of the *Sanseki* ("the Three Traces"), a group of three very famous calligraphers during the Heian period (794–1185). Of the seven volumes that compose this work, only this chapter is dedicated to shogi. The text is written in *Kanbun* (classical Chinese annotated with Japanese indicators) and was translated into French specifically for this book from the Japanese manuscript *Shogi Zushiki,* by Erwann Le Pelleter: "*Pour ce qui est des pièces de shôgi, il faut peindre en faisant onduler le pinceau, sans simplement effleurer la pièce, en style régulier ou en style régulier proche du style semi-cursif. Le caractère du haut doit être écrit distinctement et exactement comme dans un carré et les traits du caractère doivent être amples. Les caractères du narikin sont écrits dans un style cursif très prononcé. Ils sont presque semblables à des kana. Comme les pièces sont petites et difficiles à tenir, il faut les insérer dans un support tout en les tenant en main quand on écrit.*" (As far as shogi pieces are concerned, it is necessary to paint them waving the brush, without skimming the piece, in regular style or a style close to the semi-cursive style. The top character must be distinctly written and precisely inscribed within a square and the strokes must be ample. The characters of the narikin are written in a very pronounced cursive style. They are almost similar to kana. Since the pieces are small and difficult to hold, it is necessary to insert them in a support to hold them in hand when writing.) It is then explained that promotion to Gold (*narikin*) was already in use. It is also established that there is more than one character written on the piece, and that the top one is the most difficult to write. This could be understood if the pieces already had the pentagonal shape that they have today in which space is narrower for the upper character.

10. The *Shinsarugakuki* is a comic work of the theater *sarugaku* (later known as *Noh* Theater), written during the Kohei era (1058–1065) by Fujiwara no Akihira (989?–1066), a high ranking minister and important scholar of the Heian period. The story takes place during a night carnival in Kyoto featuring various entertainments of the time. Shogi is mentioned among them, along with several musical instruments, *sugoroku,* the game of go, *dangi* (a sort of billiard) and *kemari* (a ball game): "The lover of the eleventh girl is Kakinomoto Tsuneyuki, first rank Master of poetry of the Imperial Prince. He is very skillful for waka and musical instruments, either wind instruments or percussions. His deep knowledge of *koto, kin, biwa, wagon, hokyo, shakuhachi, go, sugoroku, shogi, dangi, kemari,* archery, cooking knife slicing, waka and ancient poems makes him an impressive person." *Koto, kin, biwa* and *wagon* were string instruments, *hikyo* a percussion instrument, *shakuhachi* a wind instrument, *sugoroku* a kind of backgammon, *dangi* a billiard game, and *kemari* a ball game.

11. The pieces were discovered in a structure shaped like a well. This site was once close to a warehouse of the Kofuku-ji shrine, one of the two most important Buddhist temples of the Heian era. The structure was probably dug as a well but later became a sort of refuse heap where a craftsman would throw away shogi pieces of poor quality. The pieces are made of *hinoki* (Japanese cypress) and are only painted, not engraved. Twelve pieces are almost complete, one piece is blank, and two are fragmented halves of pieces. A sixteenth artifact is unfinished and actually constitutes two pieces.

12. Exactly from the second year of the Jotoku era, which means 1098 C.E. (http://www.ajw.asahi.com/article/behind_news/social_affairs/AJ201310250064).

13. Actually, one of the *mokkan* found in the Kofuku-ji stock in Nara (dated 1058) could corroborate this finding. This piece of wood is full of graffiti, very difficult to decipher because the characters are not complete and overlap each other. It appears to include the words *kinsho* (Gold General), *fuhyo* (Soldier) and *suizo* (Drunk Elephant). It is not possible to confirm that those three characters refer to shogi but, if they do, it constitutes another apparition of the Drunk Elephant in the end of the 11th century.

14. It is not known whether the passage about shogi was present in the *Shochureki* or the *Kaichureki.* It is possible that this passage was only added when the *Nichureki* was compiled in the period 1210–1221.

15. The first known depiction of shogi players is dated to the same period. It is a detail from the *Choju jinbutsu giga* (*Scrolls of Frolicking with Animals*), a scroll dated 1252 and conserved at Kozanji Temple, Kyoto. It shows a group of four monks engaged in a shogi game. It is not possible to distinguish the exact size of the board which seems drawn either on paper or directly on the ground.

16. In his *Futsu Shodoshu,* the monk Ryoki collected funeral words destined to help those who had passed on to the "other world." There are prayers for every person, including the gambler, the *sugoroku* player and the shogi player. The mention of shogi is rather short: "To the attention of *sho shogi* player, a Pawn (*Fuhyo*) which goes up becomes Gold (*Kin*). By coming into the sacred points, it is close to making it. A Katsura Horse (*Keima*) which springs may be changed with Silver (*Gin*). It is interesting to surprise the enemy." The promotion of the Knight to Silver is a possible interpretation. This passage could also refer to a mere exchange by mutual captures.

17. This is reported in the 1696 edition of the *Sho Shogi Zushiki* (*Illustrated Small Shogi*) from Nishizawa

Teichin. A diagram is given with a Drunk Elephant placed on 5h, and the text indicates that it was removed on order of Emperor Go-Nara (reigning 1536–1557).

18. Matsudaira Ietada's diary diagram of 1587 and the Honinbo Sansa versus Ohashi Sokei game of 1607 are both reported by Tony Hosking (*The Art of Shogi*, 1997).

19. The Kirin (or Kylin, Qilin) is an East Asian mythical animal, similar to a large unicorn, perhaps inspired by the giraffe. It reigns over the hairy animals as the phoenix reigns over the feathered animals, the dragon over the scaled animals and the turtle over the shelled animals. It lends its name to a famous Japanese brand of beer.

20. The literal meaning is "unfettered" king.

21. This is the rule followed by the Japanese Chu Shogi Association.

22. This was translated into French for us by Erwann Le Pelleter from the Japanese manuscript *Shogi Zushiki*; the present authors then translated Le Pelleter's version into English. The text says: *"There is also the dai shogi. Its size is of thirteen spaces. Jewel Generals [Gyokusho] are placed in the center. There is a Gold General [Kinsho] on both sides [of the Jewel General]. The Silver Generals [Ginsho] are after the Gold Generals. After, there are the Silver Generals. [This is probably a mistake in the text. It would be surprising to have a second pair of Silvers and it can be safely assumed that the Knights were meant]. After, there are the Copper Generals [Dosho]. After, there are the Iron Generals [Tessho]. After, there are the Lances [Kyosha]. The Copper Generals cannot move in diagonal. The Iron Generals cannot move in the three backward directions. There is also the Side Mover [Ogyo] before the King. Forward, it moves one square. Also, it can move without limit. There is also the Ferocious Tiger [Moko] before the Silver General. It can move one step diagonally. The Flying Dragon [Hiryu] is before the Katsura Horse [Keima]. It can fly in the four diagonals. A Running Chariot [Honsha] is before the Lance. It moves forward and backward without limit. An Armed Workman [Chunin] stands before the center Soldier. It can move one step forward or backward."* According to this description, the Copper General, the Iron General, the Side Mover and the Rook seem to have different moves than are later attributed to these pieces at dai shogi.

23. The *Futsu Shodoshu* says: *"To the attention of dai shogi player: if the Reverse Chariot (*Hensha*) and the Incense Chariot (*Kyosha*) attack the ear [perhaps meaning flank], the Flying Chariot (*Hisha*) flees and they get the victory. If the Go-Between (*Chunin*) and Ferocious Boar (*Shincho*) stand side-by-side and if the Katsura Horse goes up, that becomes a very efficient defense."* This is a very short description in which neither the board size nor the total number of pieces is mentioned, contrary to what has been mistakenly asserted by several authors. Those details were known much later.

24. This 15 × 15 square form would have been presented in the *Shogi Shushu no Zu* (*Illustrations of Shogi Varieties*), a 1443 work, now lost but known from subsequent copies (see later in this book), which would have also mentioned other giant shogis described further in this book.

25. According to the Japanese historian Yoshinori Kimura, this text (as translated by Le Pelleter into French and then by the authors—see note above) says: *"Games of dai shogi and chu shogi, kemari, wind or string instruments, renku, classic poems, composition, etc., are subject to gambling for many people"* (*renku* means series of poems composed by two people or more; *kemari* is a ball game). This dating is contested by Masukawa, who believes the text to be from the 15th century.

26. Banaschak (2000) cites a reference to Yamashina Tokitsugu who played "108 games of shogi, 82 of chu shogi and 27 of sho shogi"; and Yamashina Tokitsune who played "32 games of shogi, 55 of chu shogi and 19 of sho shogi." Both were living in the second half of the 15th century. In the early 16th century, Ise Sayadori, a poet from the end of the Muromachi period (1392–1573), gave the following protocol in his *Sogo Ozoshi*: *"When you face your shogi opponent, open the box containing the pieces and put the pieces on the board. [...] [T]o finish setting them up too quickly is a breach of politeness. It is also impolite to be too slow and to make the opponent wait. Practice therefore, so that you can set up the pieces in just the right time. This applies also to both middle shogi and little shogi"* (this reference indicates that the word "shogi" by itself presumably meant large shogi [dai shogi] at that time). The translation from Japanese to English is by Peter Banaschak. It can be found in Banaschak's article "On the History of Chu Shogi" (2000), available at www.banaschak.net, menu selection "Zu einer Auswahl von Texten zur Schachgeschichte," and "A few Notes on the History of Chu Shogi."

27. For example, Masukawa (2004) names Kanroji Chikanaga (d. 1500), Sanjonishi Sanetaka (d. 1537) and Yamashina Tokitsugu (d. 1579).

28. The "Four Heavenly Tetrarchs" are major Buddhist deities adored in Japan. These mythological kings are guardians of the horizons at the four cardinal points. The plural is recommended for naming this piece.

29. The vertical aspects of this move are found only in Japanese sources, not previously conveyed by Western sources.

30. There is an uncertainty regarding this move since the Edo Japanese source (*Shogi Zushiki*) indicates that it moves like a Free King (i.e., like a Queen) or like "twice a Cat Sword." The Cat Sword is a dai shogi piece which moves one diagonal step. A logical interpretation is that the Lion, upon promotion, gains the diagonal moves of the Free King, and the Free King gains the diagonal moves of the Lion.

31. According to the *Shogi Zushiki*, it moves like a Rook horizontally but does not move forward or back-

ward. This seems logical, since it is a promoted Water Buffalo. Nevertheless, we follow the rule here, from another historical Japanese source, which is followed by modern players.

32. This is the rule followed by the Shogi Association (founded in 1975 by George Hodges). The Japanese version of Wikipedia allows this jumping even if it does not lead to a capture.

33. According to Colin Adams (*The Struggle for Survival*, available on the Internet) and some software that play tenjiku shogi, all other adjacent enemy pieces are withdrawn as well.

34. The word *maka* is a corruption of Sanskrit *maha*, meaning "large."

35. A Buddhist deity.

36. These are essentially the moves indicated by the *Sho Shogi Zushiki* and, to a lesser extent, by the *Shogi Zushiki*. The account in the *Shogi Rokushu no Zushiki* has many differences, and the source is less certain.

37. These new pieces are the Furious Fiend (from the Lion); the Bat (from the Old Rat); the Square Mover (from the Prancing Stag); the Fragrant Elephant (from the Northern Barbarian, but there is some doubt here); the Wizard Stork (from the Chinese Cock); the Mountain Witch (from the Old Monkey or the Blind Monkey—there is some doubt here); the Teaching King (from the Deva); and the Buddhist Spirit (from the Dark Spirit).

38. This text is known by several copies, the most ancient being dated 1386. It was probably composed a few years earlier. Its authorship is uncertain. It has been attributed to Gene (died in 1350), a Tendai (Buddhist Japanese school) monk or to Kokan Shiren (1278–1347), a Zen poet.

39. We are very grateful to Erwann Le Pelleter, whose help has been instrumental in establishing the filiation of those ancient Japanese texts.

40. *Yamato* is a traditional term meaning Japan. It is written with the same character as *wa*.

41. This work, whose author is unknown, also contains descriptions of sho shogi, chu shogi, dai shogi, dai dai shogi, maka dai dai shogi and tai shogi. It also mentions Korean chess, as well as two otherwise unknown shogi varieties: *shiho shogi* (four-direction shogi) and *sei shogi* (fair shogi). Unfortunately, the text is too short to permit a description of those games. (Private communication from Erwann Le Pelleter).

42. *Yokaï no mori* is another proprietary game, sold in Germany and France in 2013, which includes two minishogi variants: Dobutsu Shogi and goro-goro shogi (further presented in this chapter), but with renewed illustrations for the pieces, on the theme of *anime* characters. In Poland, the game Robotow is published as an adaptation of Dobutsu Shogi in a world of small robots. (http://www.acebo.pl/instrukcje/pojedynek_robotow.pdf).

43. The drop restrictions that are found in shogi, such as forbidding two Pawns on the same column or immediately checkmating with a Pawn drop, do not apply to Dobutsu Shogi.

44. The other openings are moving the Lion diagonally forward either left or right, or moving the Giraffe forward. The Elephant cannot move on the initial array.

45. Actually, the Japanese name is "Go-Li" (Five-li) in which a *li*, a Chinese measurement, is approximately 2.4 miles; therefore, 5 li equals about 12 miles.

46. It is assumed that the different Guns, Cannons and Bows are allowed to stay in place and shoot. The Japanese source is not explicit about this.

47. Another Buddhist deity.

48. Only 14 pieces do not promote. Among the 194 that do promote, 92 promote to a new type of piece.

# Part V

1. There have been several attempts to prevent the presence of two Queens on the chessboard, but they were often ignored. A way of reducing the cultural disdain for more than one ruling Queen was to adopt a different name for the promoted Pawn. This was particularly the case in manuscripts of French origin in which a *Fierce* or a *Fierge* was made by promotion, whereas the *Reine* was the original Queen. A similar practice in England differentiated the two words, *Fers* and *Queen*. The Latin word *Domina* was also introduced for the promoted Pawn (instead of *Regina*). It became *Dame* in later Anglo-French manuscripts from the 14th–15th centuries, a term which remains in present-day French to name the Queen.

2. The Queen's leap rule is first given by Abraham ibn Ezra (c. 1089–1167) in a poem of his famous *Songs of Exile*. Ezra was an influent Jewish philosopher, poet and mathematician born in Tudela, Spain, and who visited Italy, France, England and Egypt.

3. The Pawn's double step is first attested in the 13th century, in the works of the Lombard Jacobus de Cessolis and the Castilian King Alfonso X.

4. The date of the adoption of the *en passant* rule remains obscure. It was certainly in use in England and in Spain in the 15th century, before the great reform that modified the Queen and the Bishop.

5. The King's leap is a rule which is also given in the earliest didactic works of Jacobus de Cessolis and Alfonso X.

6. This rule was gradually abandoned. It was no longer in use in the 14th century.

7. This rule survived in some parts of Italy until the end of the 19th century.

8. The French historian Wilfrid Fauquet denies the existence of a short assize. According to him, this advanced setup is only justified by the need of the romance tale.

9. Or possibly only 11 pieces disappeared, since the poem mentions the presence of a second black Bishop, which the author of the prose would have omitted in the diagram. Fauquet imagines it on d6, which has no bearing on the rest of the game.

10. Beyond the allegory, this rare example of a me-

dieval chess game demonstrates that the art of chess play had not made any progress since the Arabic times. The opening was probably adapted from a shatranj *ta'biya* (it is very close to the one called "the old woman") and the end bears a striking resemblance to a *mansuba*.

11. This thesis was proposed in 1993 by the Spanish historian Ricardo Calvo (1943–2002). Calvo won the title of International Chess Master in 1973.

12. This word designates the Christians living in al-Andalus in the 8th to 11th centuries. They formed autonomous communities, paying tribute to the Muslim authorities. While keeping their separate religion and following the code of Visigothic law, they adopted the Arabic language and culture. Sometimes persecuted, they were driven to settling on the deserted lands, buffers between the Christian kingdoms and the caliphate, which they repopulated over time. They contributed to the spread of Cordoban civilization beyond its original borders.

13. The Fatimid dynasty was ruling over the Maghreb in the early tenth century, before conquering Egypt in 969, and establishing Cairo. The crystal rock workshops from this city were famous all over the Mediterranean, illustrating a shining example of the circulation of precious goods. The Fatimid caliphate declined quickly at the end of the 12th century.

14. Such a spectacular announcement again occurred in 2002, when a team of British archeologists claimed to have exhumed, in Butrint (Albania), the oldest extant chess piece ever found. Just the thing to grab headline news in the media! This turned-ivory piece of four centimeters, surmounted by an apparently chipped cross, vaguely resembled a modern King. It was dated to approximately 465 C.E. The overly-zealous announcement has no chance of withstanding serious analysis. Chess Kings with cross are modern designs. This isolated object remains unidentified but there is no objective reason to associate it with chess.

15. The Einsiedeln manuscripts with its *Versus de scachis* has attracted much attention from historians. A very deep and detailed study was published in 1954 by the Chicagoan Helena M. Gamer ("The Earliest Evidence of Chess in Western Literature: The Einsiedeln Verses," *Speculum*, vol. 29, no. 4 [October 1954], pp. 734-750) in which she demonstrates that this work, safely dated about 997, is the first instance of chess in Western literature. She argued, rather convincingly, that this text betrays an Arabic transmission of the game to German lands "*by way of Italy and not Spain, or not only Spain.*" This issue is still subject to debate.

16. For example, in Fréteval, Loisy, Pineuilh or Charavines, France.

17. A city renamed Carignan in 1662, located at the present-day French-Belgian border in the Ardennes Mountains.

18. The "Chancellor of the Exchequer" remains the title borne by the British Minister of Finance today.

19. That boardgame family includes *hnefatafl, alea evangelii, fidchell (or gwyddbwyll), brandubh, tawlbwrdd, tablut*, etc. These Nordic games may be derived from Roman board games such as *ludus latrunculorum*, which may itself be descended from the Greek game of *polis*.

20. These sagas are the *Tristrams saga ok Ísondar (The saga of Tristram and Isond)*, written by Brother Robert and finished in 1226, and the *Ólaf saga ins Helga (The saga of Saint Olaf)*, written by the Icelandic poet Snorri Sturluson (1179–1241). The latter evokes an incident of a chess game supposedly played between King Cnut and the earl Ulf in Denmark. Those sagas were written in Old West Norse, the language then spoken in Norway and Iceland.

21. This contact explains why the Queen and Bishop are, respectively, a *Ferz* and a *Slon* (an Elephant) in Russia, to the present day.

22. A Turkic people dwelling at the north shore of the Black Sea after a long migration. Its elites were converted to Judaism.

23. The Byzantine Greeks, as was previously mentioned, employed the word *zatrikion*, borrowed from the Persians. However, chess is known as *skaki* (Σκάκι) in Modern Greek.

24. The word *pawn* follows the same etymology. Pawn comes from Anglo-Norman *payn* or *poun* (Old French *paon*), from Late Latin *pedonem*, "foot soldier."

25. From *rock* to *tower* was a small leap. The connection may have been reinforced by the abstract design of the piece with a V-shaped cut (inherited from the Arabs) that could evoke a style of battlements around castle walls. In 1524, the fifth edition of Damiano's book *Questo Libro e da Imparare Giocare a Scachi et de li Partiti* represented the Rook as a small tower. However, it is not until 1669 that we see *Tour* replacing *Roc* in the French nomenclature. The *Roc* has not fully disappeared in French as the verb *roquer* means *to castle* (an English term which evokes a tower).

The V-shape of the piece may be the reason this piece was identified as a Boat (*Ladya*) in Russia, where chess penetrated the road following the strands of the Caspian sea and the Volga river. It is remarkable that the same meaning is given to that piece in Bengal, Thailand, Cambodia and Java.

26. This led to the modern French *Fou*.

27. A Bishop appears in the Lewis chess set (second half of the 12th century). The word Episcopus is used in the chess passage of *De Vetula* ("On the Old Woman"), a 13th century French romance written in Latin, and Old Icelandic "*biskup*" is found in a saga (*Mágus saga jarls*) towards 1300. In the early 12th century, the bishop's miter had a different shape than it did in subsequent eras. These earlier miters featured two puffs or small horns on the upper part of the cap, on the left and right sides of the head, showing a noteworthy resemblance to the stylized chess piece of that time. Also worth mentioning is an ivory Bishop from the Collection Marquet de Vassalot (now in the musée of Cluny, Paris) that presents such a miter with two puffs. Although its ivory has been dated, with 95 per-

cent accuracy, to 790–990, the carving itself dates to the first half of the 12th century and is believed to come from Northwest Europe. Curiously, the chess term Bishop is not evident in English before 1562 (see Robert Nedoma, "Old West Norse Chess Terminology and the Introduction of Chess into Scandinavia," in D. Caldwell and M.A. Hall (eds.), *The Lewis Chessmen: New Perspectives*, 2014).

28. Accompanying these pieces, there is an additional ivory mounted elephant that remains controversial. It is a very finely carved and massive piece bearing the signature of Yusuf al-Bahili, a known Indian carver from the eighth or ninth century, but is comparable in style to some 15th century art. Some experts think it may be the most antique chess piece conserved in Europe; others doubt that it is a chess piece at all.

29. Therefore, these pieces cannot have been owned by Charlemagne (748–814). Chess was never reported in the Frankish Empire in that era, and there is no reason to think that Charlemagne would have played chess. This is a tantalizing legend, but lacking in any historical basis.

30. According the Norwegian chess historian, Morten Lilleøren, "*hròkr*" is an old Norse male name that could mean "big and strong man" or "brave warrior." It may be the meaning behind this design of the Rooks as warriors.

31. Cited by H.J.R. Murray (*A History of Chess*). Needless to say, the present authors do not share this view.

32. According to Jean-Michel Mehl (1995).

33. This title is, in fact, the pseudonym taken by the anonymous author, perhaps a monk from Picardy (Northern France). "*Socius*" was a term used by the professors of Lombard universities to refer to themselves.

34. This is the most common case, but some historic authors recommended playing on boards of 9, 10, 12 or 14 ranks, always with 8 columns. The first boards were monochromatic but bicolor checkered boards quickly dominated, as they did in European chess.

35. Presented in his treatise of 1563. This way of playing was recommended by Claude de Boissière in 1556.

36. From the detailed tables given by Parlett (*The Oxford History of Board Games*).

37. A similar rule was used in draughts/checkers. Since the 1910s, it is no longer in force in international draughts.

38. A historic region in the center of South Germany, today forming Northern Bavaria. Its main cities are Nuremberg and Würzburg. The German historian Menso Folkerts asserted that the invention of rithmomachy was probably a consequence of a competition between the cathedral schools of Worms and Würzburg.

39. The principle of this game was to select a *virtue* by roll of the dice. With three dice, there were 56 possibilities, each virtue being associated to one combination. From "charity" to "humility," passing by "faith" or "poverty" the clerks first shared all available virtues, then tried to pair them according to precise rules. The winner was the one reaching the highest score by summing the highest virtue of every realized pair.

40. This Latin romance, wrongly attributed to Ovid, may have been composed by Richard de Fournival (1201–1260?), physician of the French kings Philip II Augustus and Louis VII. It evoked several indoor games: tables, chess, merels, and rithmomachy.

41. Titled *In hoc opere contenta Arithmetica decem libris demonstrata. Musica libris demonstrata quattuor. Epitome in libros arithmeticos divi Severini Boetti. Rithmimachiae ludus qui repugna numerorum appelatur.*

42. *Ouranomachia* in 1571 and *Metromachia* in 1578. The first, inspired by astrology, involved two players each commanding seven astral bodies (sun, moon and the five known planets: Mercury, Venus, Mars, Jupiter, Saturn) over a board representing the twelve signs of the zodiac. Fulke admitted he was not the inventor of this game and that he had developed it from a former incomplete manuscript. On the contrary, the second game was his own: a huge battle of 120 mobile pieces (Soldiers and Cannons)—24 fixed ones that could be destroyed (Towers and Dungeons), and 32 armaments (Barrels, Scales and Beams), played over 33 × 52 squares in which moves and captures depended on the mathematical properties of the geometric shapes of the pieces.

43. Only the "books" of chess (*acedrex*), dice (*dados*), "tables" (*tablas*) and merels (*alquerque*) have particular headings in the Spanish codex. This is the reason the other "books" are identified here under English titles.

44. See http://historicgames.com/alphonso/index.html.

45. The *Cocatriz* is a cockatrice, a monster of the medieval bestiary, a sort of dragon with a lion's head. The original illustration of the codex shows a quadruped whose shape strongly resembles a crocodile. The text specifies that it is "half beast half fish" and that it looks like a lizard. The aquatic reptile probably inspired the creation of the mythical monster.

46. These rules have been the subject of a fruitful collaboration and correspondence between the American language professor Sonja Musser, while she was writing her doctoral thesis, and the senior author of the present work, Jean-Louis Cazaux. The interested reader can find more details in Musser's doctoral thesis; see bibliography.

47. The Castilian codex says: "*ante que comience a correr faze un salto en traviesso. & a semeianca deste su andamiento esta puesto su juego en este acedrex. & anda a quarta casa en sosquino assi que quando sale dela blanca va a la negra. & quando sale dela negra va a la blanca.*" (*Before it begins to run it gives a sideways jump and so this piece plays in this chess. It goes to the fourth square in corner and therefore from a white square it goes to a black one. And from a black it goes on a white square*). The counting included the departure square, therefore the move is a three-square jump.

48. The Castilian codex says: "*el Leon es bestia otros si muy fuerte & salta mucho en traviesso o en derecho; mas que otra bestia quando quiere tomar alguna cosa. E a essa semeianca lo pusieron aquí & salta a quarta casa la una en derecho & las dos en traviesso.*" (*The Lion is another very strong beast and it jumps a lot to the sides or straight, more than any other beast when it wants to capture something. And so they place this piece here and it leaps to the fourth square, the one straight and the two aslant*). Again, it is a jump to a third square, according to our modern way of counting.

49. The Castilian codex says: "*corre mucho des que comienca & faze ante en salto en traviesso como cavallo & assi lo establecieron en este acedrex que anda el primer salto como cavallo & depues en sosquino como la cocatriz fata do quisiere; o que tome. E da quella casa o salta non puede tornar a tras si non yr siempre adelante.*" (*It runs a lot and begins with a sideward jump like a Horse and so does its piece in this chess. It goes the first jump like a Horse and then goes in corner like the Crocodile does where it wants to go or take. And from that square where it jumps, it may not turn back, it shall always go forward*). It is the second part of the move which presents a difficulty. In a strict interpretation, the word "forward" may be understood relative to the orientation of the board, toward the opponent. In this case, it seems logical that the backward prohibition is only valid for the diagonal part of the move; otherwise, that piece would finish immobile on the opposite side of the board. This is the interpretation proposed by Jean-Louis Cazaux and adopted by Dr. Musser for her doctoral dissertation (2007). It constitutes the present authors' second interpretation in this book. The first option is a relative interpretation in which "forward" is understood as "continuing away from its square of departure" which is a forward direction from that square. It is possible that this is what the Spanish text intended to convey, considering how frequently compound moves are imprecisely described, even today. For example, many authors say the Knight takes one step like a Rook followed by a step like a Bishop, assuming the learner will not think of moving back at an acute angle. Saying "forward" may imply a compound move continuing away from the square of departure, and this reasoning can be applied to the Rhinoceros here. The result would give a symmetric move very well in agreement with the other long-range pieces of this large chess, such as the Giant Birds.

50. The text does not specify if he may jump to escape a check or pass over a square controlled by the opponent. It is presumed that this was forbidden.

51. According to Sonja Musser, the Lion would jump three squares forward or sideways, never backward. This Lion would then be even weaker than Murray's interpretation. This is the only piece for which the present authors disagree with Sonja Musser.

52. It should be stressed that Murray treated this Spanish game with uncharacteristic brevity. He dedicated only half a page (p. 348), with an error on the explanation of the dice (He gave 6 to the Rook—instead of 5—and gave both 5 and 4 to the Lion, omitting the Rhinoceros). This reinforces the idea that Murray did not pay a great deal of attention to this variant.

53. From the Persian *rokh*, this word is homonymous with the one naming the Rook in shatranj, which has sometimes been a source of error. For instance, an ivory statuette, excavated in the Fergana valley (Uzbekistan) and kept in the State Hermitage Museum of St. Petersburg (Russia), representing a bird of prey, has been denoted as a *rukh* and presented as a chess piece in several works. Actually, this artifact is probably meant for the end of a cane or the cork of a vial.

54. From this vivid description, the text explains the move of that piece: "*& dessa guisa ordenaron aqui so iuego que desque salta como Alfferza; en postpunta a una casa; va depues en derecho quanto puede yr & en traviesso. Fata cabo del tablero; o hata que falle que tome. E el departimiento de como salta; es este que si estudiere en casa prieta yra a la primera prieta en sosquino como alfferza & en essa carrera en derecho quanto quisiere. & si estudiere en blanca faze esso mismo. & si estudiere en casa prieta departenlo las quatro casas blancas que estan en derredor della que non puede entrar en ellas. E si estudiere en blanca departen lo otrossi las quatro casas prietas que estan cerca della.*" (*Thus they ordered that its move is composed of two different steps. First, like the Fers, it makes one step of one single square to any adjoining square on the diagonal(s) on which it stands. It can remain on that square or may also continue to any square on the file or rank of that square, maintaining its movement in the same direction away from its starting square. Its jumping movement is such that if it begins on a black square, then it will move one step of one square of the same color along the diagonal like the Fers and then continue straight ahead as far as it likes. And if it begins on a white square, it moves in the same way. Starting on a black square, then it may not enter the four white squares that surround its starting square and likewise if it begins on a white square it may not enter those four surrounding black squares.*)

55. Looking like a giant ostrich, three meters (10 ft.) high and weighing up to 400 kilograms (880 lb.), it was the largest bird that ever existed. It is still possible to find fossil eggs (more than 30 cm in length) in Madagascar and, occasionally, even on sale over the Internet!

56. The Spanish historian Ricardo Calvo had offered the same idea in 1987. In 2007, Sonja Musser suggested that the Judge could rather move one square in all directions, like a King. Such a piece existed in the Muslim "complete chess." But in her reasoning, she mistakenly thought that this piece would be less powerful than a Horse. (It would be worth 3.1, as opposed to 2.6 for the Horse.) The Judge (leaping orthogonally) is worth 1.4. The Elephant is worth 1.1. In this light, Calvo's hypothesis fits better with the order on the die than Musser's proposal.

57. Sonja Musser has demonstrated that Isidore of

Seville (d. 636) and Aristotle were the sources for this theory of interrelationships among the four seasons, the elements and the humors.

58. This is the Arabic word (still maintained in modern Spanish), and King Alfonso X is quite clear on this point: this piece is *"the elephant that the kings used to bring at that time because no one dared to stand in front of them."*

59. The Almohads were a Berber dynasty that first developed in modern Morocco. They crossed the Strait of Gibraltar and seized al-Andalus from the Almoravids between 1146 and 1173. Interestingly, their flag, the oldest known for Morocco, was red with a black and white chessboard placed in the middle.

60. The exact age of van Leyden is controversial. He was regarded as extremely precocious, and 1494 is the date traditionally held for his birth in Leiden, the Netherlands. However, some more recent studies have questioned that, noting that his family made a special issue of his high skill at an early age—they may have exaggerated. According to these assertions, he may have been born five years earlier. There is also some uncertainty regarding the date of his chess painting, which is generally dated 1508 or 1509. Therefore, van Leyden would have painted this masterpiece between the ages of 14 and 20, truly very young to achieve such a fine work.

61. A board kept in a museum in Ströbeck has a white square for the corner at player's left hand (a1). This is consistent with Selenus's description. However, van Leyden's painting shows a1 as dark. Board orientation, regarding square color, did not have a widespread uniform convention at that time.

62. That is to say Ströbeck, Germany, at the beginning of the 17th century. In 1616, medieval chess was still played in this village, and the games always started with a "joy leap" of the Rook Pawns, Queen Pawn and the Queen. Since this was practiced there in courier chess as well, it is likely that Ströbeck players also practiced the joy-leaps in the promotion process of both games. The English travel journalist William Lewis reported that in his 1831 trip to Ströbeck, that modern chess players still observed the same mandatory joy-leaps at the start of the game, and in promotion of Pawns.

63. From Latin *currere* "to run." The use of *Läufer* for the Bishop begins in the 18th century. Before that time, Germans called that piece the "Old One" (*der Alte*) or Archer (*Schütze*).

64. The *Korna* is literally a bull but by metaphor that word designates a furious warrior here. The *Horsa* is a mounted warrior, a Knight. We have avoided using the word Knight which can be confusing for chess players in this context.

65. The Swedish chess expert Mats Winther has published a set of rules on the Internet (available on www.zillions-of-games.com/games/), which claims to follow Arnold Mayer's reconstitution as well. Mats Winther also made a playable gala file with Zillions-of-Games software. His interpretation differs from the rules presented in the present work in the following ways: (1) the central zone can be entered by a Warrior if that zone is already occupied by a Gala or an enemy Warrior; (2) the restriction for the Horseman's capture does not apply if the adjacent piece is in the vertical direction (for instance, the Horseman on h4 can take a piece on h5). This rule only applies to a horizontally adjacent piece.

66. A precision officially added in 1972 following a joke chess problem (composed by Tim Krabbé) containing a castling between a King on e1 and a promoted Rook on e8. Although absurd, this case was not specifically forbidden by the former wording of the rules.

67. The "*cavaller*" Francesc Castellví, member of a distinguished Valencian family (his mother was a "*conversa*"), acted as a close advisor in the Aragonese court of King Ferdinand. As a poet, Castellví appears mostly in minor poems in collaboration with the other two companions. He died in 1506.

Narcís Vinyoles was an important politician and writer in Valencia in the last quarter of the 15th century. Appointed a member of the City Council, he enjoyed the favor of King Ferdinand as a reliable servant. Vinyoles had to rescue his wife, Brianda de Santangel, a *conversa* and niece of the great banker who financed the first expedition of Columbus, from the Inquisition. He died in Valencia in 1517, at an age estimated to be between 70 and 75 years.

"*Mossèn*" Bernat Fenollar (c. 1435/1440–1516) also belonged to a notable Valencian family. He was King Ferdinand's secretary, chapel man and choir director. As a priest, he held a post in the cathedral of Valencia, but later was a married layman. The organizer of cultural contests in Valencia, he was the soul of the group, and he played an active role in promoting the first books printed in Spain.

68. The exact title of the poem is "*Scachs d'Amor, feta per don Francí de Castelví e Narcís Vinyoles e Mossèn Fenollar, sots nom de tres planetas, ço es Març, Venus e Mercuri, per conjunccio e influencia dels quals fon inventada*" (*The Chess Game of Love, written by Don Francí de Castelví and Narcís Vinyoles and Mossèn Fenollar, under the names of three planets: Mars, Venus, and Mercury, by conjunction and influence of which the work was devised*). In the allegory, Castelvi is Mars playing against Vinyoles who is Venus. Fenollar watches them as a referee and is Mercury. The Spanish historian Garzón has pointed out that the curious astrological reference in the title might be an indication of the exact date of the composition of this text. Indeed, in June 1475 the three planets, Mercury, Mars and Venus were in conjunction in the sky of Valence.

69. This opinion is supported by a stanza in the poem which reads: "*But our game now wants to adorn itself / With a new and strange style for whom is well watching it / Taking the orb, sceptre, and throne / Because, above everything, the Queen requests her honor.*"

70. Indeed this era was the beginning of printing in Spain, whereas much of Europe considered printing

a German affair. Several German printers, seeking fortune in this part of Spain, have passed to posterity: Lope de Roca "Alemany," who had probably transformed his original name of Stein into Spanish (*Roca* = *Stein*), Pere Trincher, a Catalonian of German ancestry, Petrus Hagenbach, Leonhard Hutz (who worked with Lope Sanz from Navarra), Nicolaus Spindeler, Lambert Palmart from Cologne, and Paul Hurus from Constance—all connected with the intellectual circle of Valencia.

71. The same Valencian poets and their circle also improved the game of draughts by allowing the promoted man, the "king" (which is a *dama*, lady, in Roman languages) to move freely, no longer limited to one square.

72. Francesch Vicent was born in Segorbe, near Valencia, around 1455. There is a theory developed by the Spanish historians Ricardo Calvo and José Antonio Garzón which explains that, after several difficulties with the Spanish authorities (Vicent was imprisoned in 1487 and withstood trial in 1500), Vicent finally fled to Italy. This would make him the likely chess instructor of Lucrezia Borgia and, very probably, the real author hidden behind the pseudonym of Damiano in his book of 1512. It is almost certain that Francesch Vicent died before 1524.

73. Lucena's first name is unknown. His family members were Aragonese *conversos*. His father, Juan de Lucena, was an ambassador and member of the Council of the King and Queen, often travelling from Valencia to France and Italy. Juan de Lucena was prosecuted by the Inquisition in 1504. It is presumed that the younger Lucena went into exile in Burgundy or France. Calvo ascribes several chess manuscripts to him, which are among the first to promote the newly reformed rules, including the "Göttingen Manuscript" (c. 1500) and the "Paris Manuscript" (c. 1530–1550).

74. It is written as "partito a la rabiosa" in several Italian codexes, using a Spanish orthography. These nicknames were obviously inspired by the Queen's new power which surprised and shocked many players.

75. In addition, Calvo has demonstrated that a chess book written by the physician, astrologer and humanist, Gerolamo Cardano (1501–1576), was referring to Vicent's work. And the Italian historian, Andriano Chicco, proved that the Catalan book was still known by Alessandro Salvio (c. 1570–c. 1640) in Naples in the early 17th century.

76. If Greco was an efficient promoter of the modern castling, he was not its inventor. This simultaneous move of the King and the Rook appeared in France in the 1560s. In his fifth book, published posthumously, Rabelais testified while speaking of the King on the chessboard: "*À la première démarche, si leur filière estoyt trouvée vuide d'aultres officiers, fors les Custodes, ils peuvent les mettre en leur siège, et à costé de luy se retirer.*" ("At the first move, if their rank is empty of other officers, except the Rooks, they can put them in their throne, and retire beside it.") But the rule took a long time to be fixed. Players were still practicing a "free castling at the Italian manner," in which the King could land on any square on the first rank and the Rook could come as far as the King's initial square, in Rome, in 1877.

77. *Fédération Internationale des Échecs*, or the International Chess Federation, in English.

78. François-Antoine Kermur Sire de Légal (1702–1792) was a famous player from the Café de la Régence in Paris. The teacher of Philidor, he was considered the best French player until he was defeated by his pupil.

## Part VI

1. David Brine Pritchard (1919–2005) was a British writer, chess player and expert of indoor games. His master work is still the *The Encyclopedia of Chess Variants*, first published in 1994. A second edition, fully revised and completed, *The Classified Encyclopedia of Chess Variants*, edited after his death by John Beasley, is an unsurpassed monument gathering more than 1600 different chess varieties! Despite obvious common material, both editions are complementary and constitute a must-have for any person passionate about board games. The present authors are deeply indebted to D.B. Pritchard.

2. A first example is Arimaa, a two-player strategic game invented in 2003 by Omar Syed, inspired by Garry Kasparov's loss to the chess computer Deep Blue. Arimaa was designed to be resistant to computer analysis. Arimaa uses an 8 × 8 square board and 16 pieces per player. It can be played with a standard chess set although the pieces have different (animal) names. The goal of the game is to move one of the player's Rabbits (Pawns) to the home rank of the opponent. A second example is Hive in which there is no board, the flat, hexagonal pieces tiling a hive in permanent evolution. Hive was designed by John Yianni and published in 2001 by Gen42 Games. The two players have pieces with differentiated powers and moves. The goal is to trap a central piece, a Queen Bee. Randy Ingersoll has written a book on Hive (see the Bibliography). Arimaa and Hive have been ported to electronic format, and hold their own world championships.

3. Carrera used Italian names for the pieces: *Rè*, *Donna*, *Alfino*, *Cavallo*, *Rocco*, *Pedone* for the six standard ones and *Centauro*, *Campione* for the new ones.

4. Coincidently, this piece moves like the Dragon King, i.e., the promoted Rook of Japanese shogi. This move also occurs with the Bers, i.e., the Queen in shatar, Mongolian chess.

5. Gustave III began his reign in 1771. He ruled as an absolute monarch, committed to the predominance of his nation. He established the Swedish presence in Saint-Barthélémy in the Antilles and was considering colonizing Australia when a futile war (which he had provoked) against Russia annulled that project. In the cultural sphere, his actions presented a more favorable balance: he encouraged theater, ballet and

opera, and founded the Swedish Academy. A learned admirer of Voltaire, a despot and a Freemason, he granted the equality of rights to all Swedes and fought against the power of the nobility. He paid a heavy price: the hostile nobles plotted and succeeded in assassinating him in 1792.

6. Coxe wrote: "*Chess is so common in Russia that during our continuance at Moscow I scarcely entered into any company where parties were not engaged in that diversion and I very frequently observed in my passage through the streets the tradesmen and common people playing it before the doors of their shops or houses. The Russians are esteemed great proficients in chess. With them the queen has in addition to the other moves that of the knight which according to Phillidor spoils the game but which certainly renders it more complicated and difficult and of course more interesting.*"

7. Similar attempts of replacing the Queen with a more powerful Amazon have also been found in the Ottoman Empire during the same period. In addition, a German description of 1874, reported by Murray, about chess practiced in Georgia (Caucasus) affirmed that the Queen could also be played like a Knight.

8. This information has been communicated to the present authors by Peter Michaelsen, an historian specializing in Scandinavian games.

9. The Amazon has been the central idea of many chess variants in the 20th century. Louis P. d'Autremont created *Angel Chess* (1918) on a 9 × 8 board with RNBQKABNR (Amazon = Angel, starting on the right side of the King, on f1 and d8). D. Trouillon proposed *Power Chess* (1953) on a 10 × 10 board with RNBQKAQBNR (Amazon = Commander on f1 and f10). V.R. Parton invented *Wyvern Chess* (1970) on the same board with RNABQKBANR (two Amazons = Wyverns, Queen on e1 and e10).

10. The full title of this three-volume work is *Archiv der Spiele oder fortlaufende Beschreibung aller Spiele der Vorwelt und Mitwelt*. The Kaiserspiel is described on pp. 63–69, and the enlarged variant, later named the Sultanspiel, on pp. 68–69. (Peter Michaelsen is gratefully acknowledged for these precisions.)

11. The German names used by Tressau for the standard pieces were: *König, Königin, Läufer, Springer, Thurm, Bauer*.

12. Bird also tried an asymmetrical setup, i.e., with the black Queen facing the white King, and so on. According to Pritchard, Bird also proposed a 9 × 8 board with an extra piece jumping like the Camel of Timur's chess placed between King and Queen. He also experimented with a 10 × 8 board with two pieces per side playing as Rook + Knight. That supplementary piece was then called a Chancellor.

13. Foster wrote "L. Tressan of Leipsic." Tressau's book was written with a gothic script which made it nearly impossible to distinguish "u" from "n."

14. Another idea would have simply been to add a second Queen. This has been proposed by D.Trouillon for Ultra Chess (early 1970s) on a 9 × 8 board and by Michael Corinthios for Ministers Chess (1975), a commercialized game on a 9 × 9 board (www.corinthiangames.com).

15. Edward Lasker (1885–1981) was an American International Chess Master, born in Prussia and living in the U.S.A. since 1914. He was also a fan of the game of go and cofounder of the American Go Association. He wrote several books, among them, *The Adventure of Chess* (1949), in which he claimed to have played many test games with Capablanca. He is not to be confused with Emanuel Lasker (1868–1941), German and World Chess Champion from 1894 to 1921. It happened that the two Laskers played against each other and were friends.

16. Detractors have criticized this initial setting because the i2/i7 Pawns are not protected.

17. Not to be confused with the proprietary game, Neo-Chess, invented by Alex Randolf and published by 3M in 1972, which combines standard chess and shogi. It uses the usual material adapted to be able to change color so the captured pieces change side and can be dropped on the board against their former owner. This game was also known as "mad mate" or "chessgi." It attracted the attention of several grandmasters including Larsen, Spassky, Petrosian, Keene and Chandler.

18. Published in a booklet titled "*Das Grosskampfschach oder Universalschach.*"

19. Maura's thesis consists in summing the maximum mobility of every piece, in terms of reachable squares on an empty board. For example a King has 8, a Queen has 27 on an 8 × 8 board. With a debatable 2 for the Pawn, the result is 121 for one side of a standard chess set. Then Maura stated that a player had only the half of this number because he has to share with his opponent. Thus, 60.5 in our case. The comparison with the number of squares on the board, 64, led Maura to conclude that chess is not well balanced. In the case of Modern Chess, the calculation gives 81 for the half-mobility of the full set of one color and 9 × 9 = 81. The reader is free to question the soundness of this mathematical method.

20. The patent (U.S. 6,481,716 B2) lapsed in 2006 because of nonpayment of maintenance fees.

21. The choice of the word *Elephant* is debatable for a piece playing partly as a Rook rather than a Bishop. Indeed, in chess history that animal was associated with the piece that became the Bishop. Even today, the Elephant (*Slon*) is the Bishop for Russians who foster perhaps the world's greatest chess-playing culture. On the other hand, Elephants are broadly known by chess collectors and Indian nationals to figure as Rooks in the modern Indian tradition. Perhaps this is the reason for the creators' choice.

22. The complete title is *I campeggiamenti degli scacchi, o sia, nuova disciplina d'attacchi, difese e partiti del giuoco degli scacchi si nello stile antico, che nel nuovo arcischacchiere* (The basics of chess, or new discipline of attacks, defenses and game of chess plays in the old style and in the new "*arcischacchiere*"). Note that Piacenza used the orthography "*arcischacchiere*" on the

book cover only. Everywhere within his book, he called his game "*arciscacchiere*."

23. The moves given to the Centurion deserve some examination. It is obvious that Piacenza's seminal idea was to reintroduce the ancient Queen and Bishop to the board. But, while he kept the former unchanged, he revisited the latter to give it a totally new character. Piacenza started by declaring: "I thought to move it as the Queen does, but not more than two squares, according to the nature of the Rook, on straight lines, or obliquely like the Bishop, on empty squares, without obstacle coming from other pieces." We therefore understand that the Centurion cannot leap occupied squares along rows, columns and diagonals and Piacenza insisted on this point in the games he gave as examples. However, Murray did not understand correctly and described the Centurion as a jumper in the eight directions. Pritchard repeated the definition given by Murray and added the Knight's leap that Murray had forgotten. Indeed, Piacenza confessed to having spoken with a certain Battista Fantone, royal librarian in Turin, which would easily have allowed him to have seen a chess book in which a Centaur also had the Knight's power. Piacenza decided to adapt this idea in order to allow his new piece to reach any square on the board (otherwise the Centurion would have been color-bound and limited to a quarter of the board). So, Piacenza's Centurion jumps when moving like a Knight but does not leap on the rows, columns and diagonals. To the understanding of the present authors, this is the first time that the rules of this curious game of chess are correctly presented in an English book.

24. Francesco Piacenza remains a privileged witness to the history of chess in Italy because his book described the good and bad uses of the rules of the game by his compatriots. Thus, he denounced the fanciful interpretations that prevailed here and there for castling or Pawn's promotion.

25. Curiously, Ciccolini's Elephant moves as the Korean Elephant does (though the Korean Elephant does not leap over other pieces). This intriguing resemblance is very likely a mere coincidence.

26. A very compact and intuitive system: 1* means 1 step in every direction; 2+ means leaping two steps in orthogonal directions; nx means sliding any number of free squares in diagonal directions; 1/2 means leaping like a Knight, and so on.

27. The first Falconry championship was organized in Leningrad in 1990. The game, patented in Russia, won several medals and awards in that country. Authors claim 15,000 players in Russia and 5,000 in neighboring countries (Belarus, Ukraine, e.g.).

28. Shako means "chess" in Esperanto, a kind of nonconformist utopian world language invented in 1887. Shako was created by Jean-Louis Cazaux, first described in his French book *Guide des échecs exotiques et insolites* (2000), and later on the Internet. Shako has an entry on Pritchard's book (second edition, 2007).

29. The Cannon is identical to the Cannon of xiangqi.

30. Therefore, the Elephant combines the moves of the shatranj *Firzan* (Counselor) and *Fil* (Elephant), ancestors of the modern Queen and Bishop, respectively.

31. The wildebeest, also called *gnu*, is an African antelope.

32. Moreover, MacDonald has presented an extension of this game called Omega Chess Advanced in 2008, with a sort of castling for the Queen (the "guarding") and the introduction of a new piece, the Fool, which may enter the game in the opening moves on a vacated square. The Fool plays as the piece that was most recently moved by the opponent. Some optional rules were also proposed, such as the replacement of the Knight by a Templar Knight, which has an augmented power. This new sophistication probably detracted from the "regular" Omega Chess and it has been removed from the official website (omegachess.com).

33. The Eagle is identical to the Giant Bird of medieval Spanish Grant Acedrex. It is also reminiscent of the Giraffe of Timur's chess, though with a simplified and more powerful move.

34. As a clarifying example, when the Kings are placed on g2 and g11 or on g1 and g12, it is equivalent to positions in which the Kings are placed on f2 and f11 or on f1 and f12.

35. Robert Montay-Marsais met Jean-Louis Cazaux in the early 2000s and kindly gave him a copy of his booklet in order to correct and complete the existing Stratomic page on chessvariants.com. Some details were not correctly reported previously in Pritchard's book.

36. Conserved in Cotton Manuscripts, Cleopatra, B. ix, f.9, in the British Library, London.

37. According to *Variant Chess* magazine, that book would probably have been Joseph Strutt's *Sports and Pastimes of the People of England*, 1801.

38. Chess forms based on triangular cells have been proposed rather recently. "Triangular Chess" and "Tri-Chess" by George R. Dekle, Sr., used a hexagon-shaped board with 96 triangular cells in 1986. The triangles offer 12 natural directions of move. Another game is Klin Zha which is popular among the fans of the Star Trek series. It is the abstract game of the Klingons, the fictive alien race described in John M. Ford's novel *The Final Reflection*. The board is triangular and made of 81 triangular cells. See page 316 for complete rules, codified by Leonard Loyd in 1989.

39. Agon is a two-player strategy game that uses a hexagonal board (made of 91 hexagons, 6 on each side). Each player has 1 Queen and 6 Guards starting on the outer ring and the goal is to bring the Queen to the center of the board (the throne), surrounded by her Guards. A piece is captured when two enemy pieces are surrounding it in a straight line and the captured pieces are not removed from the board but placed on the outer ring (Guards) or any vacant square (Queen).

40. We do not know what the moves were. The text

that has been conserved says, "*The last game which we have to notice is undoubtedly the most scientific of the lot, and somewhat resembles chess. It is called "Hexagonia," and is published by Mr. Jaques, of Hatton Garden. The board is in the shape of a hexagon, and contains hexagonal figures, painted red, blue, or white. Two play at this game. To each combatant is given a king, four knights, and two pieces in the shape of cannon, called artillery, and eight pawns, or pieces of infantry. Each piece has a different mode of moving, and can capture an enemy; and the object is to place the king on a gold square in the centre of the board. This sovereign can never be taken, but can be checked as in chess. The reader will gather from this that much head-work and tact can be brought into play in this game, and that a knowledge of chess is often highly advantageous. We have endeavoured somewhat briefly to state the chief points of the new in-door games. We feel sure that they are varied enough to please the tastes of everybody, and we sincerely hope that our young friends may enjoy many a pleasant hour in the enjoyment of the intricate manoeuvres that these games involve*" (Edmund Routledge, "The New Winter In-door Games," *Routledge's Every Boy's Annual, an Entertaining Miscellany of Original Literature*, George Routledge and Sons, 1866, New York, p. 35).

41. In the 1950s, the French author Joseph Boyer collected and presented several dozen "unorthodox" chess forms in self-published booklets, which resonated surprisingly well among curious amateur chess enthusiasts.

42. Dave McCooey's declaration on the Chess Variants Pages can be viewed on the Internet (http://www.chessvariants.org/hexagonal.dir/hexchess2.html).

43. This rule makes the Pawn's move more consistent with its move in standard chess. However, a direct consequence is that f-Pawns are not protected in the initial array (the Knights shown have a more far-reaching move and do not protect those Pawns). A Knight capturing that Pawn would immediately mate. Also, it has been criticized that the Pawns advance too rapidly toward the opposite side when they capture.

44. Coxe wrote: "*The Russians have also another method of playing at chess, namely, with four persons at the same time, two against two; and for this purpose the board is larger than usual, contains more men, and is provided with a greater number of squares. I was informed, that this method is more difficult, but far more agreeable, than the common game.*"

45. The original rules did not indicate what happens if a player is stalemated with his partner still in play. Georgi Markov (2015) suggested that it would be an immediate draw, in the spirit and logic of Russian fortress chess.

46. A. von Petroff, "Das Vierschach mit Festungen" in the *Berliner Schachzeitung*, May 1850. The article was translated from Russian to German by Carl Jaenisch.

47. Lionel Kieseritzky (1806–1853) was a German chess master born in Livonia (today Estonia). He moved to Paris, France, in 1839, where he became a chess professional, one of the best players of his time. In 1851, he lost the famous "Immortal Game" against Adolf Anderssen. Kieseritzky is credited with invention of the first three-dimensional chess, Kubicschach ("Cubic Chess") in 1851. He died in Paris.

48. Clearly, this rule has not been explained with sufficient detail, considering the specific topology of the board. The explanations given by former authors are either erroneous (Verney) or not fully explanatory (Pritchard).

49. Source: http://boardgamegeek.com/boardgame/8289/interface.

50. Verney failed to mention what happens if a player mates one King and is then mated by his remaining opponent.

51. See www.3manchess.com. The board is composed of six concentric rings of 24 curved quadrilateral cells each, for a total of 144. The three sets of pieces are arranged on the two outermost rings, so that each player's Rooks stand next to another player's Rooks on both sides. Thick lines temporarily block interaction between the opponents' Rooks, Pawns and Knights. Spiraling diagonal lines of varying colors and textures, swoop through the circle in the center of the board. While diagonal movers (Bishops) follow these lines inward and (helped by the color coding) re-emerge on another point from the inner circle, the orthogonal movers (Rooks) move straight through the center in a literally straight path.

52. In 1998, a three-player hexagonal chess named *Echexs* was proposed by Jean-Louis Cazaux. It is played over a hexagonal board of 91 hexes (sides of 6 hexes). *Echexs* was also presented in a six-player version over a hexagonal board of 217 hexes (sides of 9 hexes).

53. The interested reader will find the detailed rules on a dedicated web page on Wikipedia: http://en.wikipedia.org/wiki/Sannin_shogi.

54. With alternate rules for diagonal moves: a Bishop or a Queen that crosses the center point of the board can only go straight (instead of having the choice of two directions) and therefore changes to the opposite color squares.

55. On www.trichess.com. Invented by Christophe Langronier. This variation includes a non-aggression rule that protects a player from being attacked by another player who has a material superiority (according to a system of points per piece lost).

56. It corresponds to a Rook's step followed by a Bishop's step but it must be noted that not all Rook-then-Bishop moves stay in a single plane. Those which do not are not permitted for the Knight. For example, going from Ab1 to Ba2 is not permitted.

57. Under the title "Three-Dimensional Headache," the June 9, 1952, edition of *Life* magazine reported, "Whereas in ordinary chess there are 400 possible positions resulting from White's first move and Black's response, in three-dimensional chess there are 47,524 positions. After two moves in the three-

dimensional chess the figure jumps to 1,500,000, which may explain why the Western Hemisphere contains only eight players. Six are pupils of Dr. Kogbetliantz, one is his daughter, the last and best is the doctor himself."

58. Chess variant enthusiasts are familiar with the name of Vernon Rylands Parton (1897–1974). Born in Cannock, Stadffordshire, England, he lived there until 1960, when he moved to Liverpool. He was a very active chess variant promoter and invented some of the most famous and most remarkable games. His interests were wide and he was a great believer in Esperanto. He was particularly passionate about Lewis Carroll's imaginary world. He collaborated with Joseph Boyer, author of self-published books on unorthodox chess. Parton composed nine monographs in the 1960s and 1970s; seven are accessible on the Chess Variant Pages on the Internet, on a page written by Jean-Louis Cazaux.

59. Not to be confused with Cubic Chess by Vladimír Pribylinec (2003), a two-dimensional chess in which the pieces are replaced by cubes having the different chess pieces on their six sides. The players may roll the cubes under some conditions, thus changing the value of the piece. This game has evolved from a first version named Echo (1977) and, after several alterations, it has been manufactured in 2013, in Slovakia.

60. Extra spatial (or hyperspatial) dimensions have been studied by philosophers and mathematicians for over two centuries. More recently, the concept has taken off in the public imagination, spurred on by popular science fiction literature and theories of particle physics. A good introduction to the concept of the fourth dimension and beyond can be found on Wikipedia at https://en.wikipedia.org/wiki/Four-dimensional_space.

61. Both games are described in Parton's monograph titled *"Chessical Cubism for Chess in Space"* (1971). Note that Ecila is Alice read backward. Parton was fascinated by Lewis Carroll's heroine.

62. This game was included in Parton's first monograph entitled *"Curiouser & Curiouser"* which was published a few years later (1961).

63. This text first appeared in 1922. Following U.S. copyright law, the book is now in the public domain, and can be read at the website of the Gutenberg project (gutenberg.org).

64. Fliers are generals, Dwars are captains, Padwars are lieutenants, Thoats are mounted warriors and Panthans are mercenaries.

65. Some Martian-chess players reportedly aver that the Odwar was the ancestor of the Flier although the Flier flies while the Odwar, present in an older version of Jetan, is not able to jump over occupied squares.

66. The text is ambiguous, stating in chapter 2, *"straight in any direction, or diagonally, two spaces"* and in the appendix, *"2 spaces straight in any direction or combination."* A diagonal move is then mentioned in chapter 2 but not in the appendix. A combination of two straight steps at 90° makes a diagonal move. That is perhaps the best explanation of this apparent discrepancy.

67. The text says in chapter 2, "... *moves one space in any direction except backward*" and in the appendix: "*1 space, forward, side, or diagonal, but not backward.*" This is understood as one square straight forward or diagonally forward or sideways (five directions). Some other sources also allow the two backward diagonals. However, playing with Zillions of Games has demonstrated that the Panthan would be superior to other pieces if allowed to go diagonally backward. It is therefore unlikely that this was what Burroughs meant.

68. Normalized to 5 for the value of a Rook if it were introduced to a Jetan board. A Rook is considered to have the strength of "5," and the numbers indicating the strength of other pieces are adjusted relative to that standard. This standard is used in comparing the Jetan pieces, although the game does not actually employ a piece that has the Rook's move.

69. http://www.tasigh.org/takzh/

70. Aaron Alexandre (1765/8–1850), Bavarian, then French, then English, was a famous chess player and writer of chess books. He introduced the 0–0 and 0–0–0 notation for castling in chess texts. Boyer, citing Kraitchik, reports that his adversaries used to impose a fancy setup in order to "detour" him.

71. Tassilo von Heydebrand und von der Lasa (1818–1899) was a German diplomat, chess master and chess historian. He encouraged H.J.R. Murray to research chess history. For these two games between Von der Hoeven and Von der Lasa, the starting positions were (a1 to h1 for White; a8 to h8 for Black): B-R-K-R-B-N-N-Q for the first game and K-B-N-N-R-B-R-Q for the second game.

# Part VII

1. The Hind was the country on the banks of the Indus River, then separating the Hindu world from the Persian world. It corresponds to the modern province of Sindh, now part of Pakistan, bordering India. The word comes from Sanskrit *sindhu* meaning "river." The words Indus and Hindu are also derived from this root.

2. They were two of the most talented Islamic historians and geographers. Al-Ya'qubi was working for the Tahirids, an Iranian dynasty. He traveled in India, Maghreb and Egypt, where he died in 897 or 898. Even more important was al-Mas'udi (896–956). Born in Baghdad, he spent his life visiting still more countries, from East Africa to the Mediterranean and Caspian seas, and to India. He compiled all that was known from ancient times and other countries such as China or Western Europe. He also died in Egypt.

3. The number of grains on the 64th square would be $2^{63}$ and the total of all grains would be $2^{64}$ minus 1.

4. The name Xerxes in this passage is probably phonetically derived from the Arabic Sassa through Greek or Latin.

5. Only the preface of Chao Buzhi's *Guang Xiangxi Ge Xu* (*Rules for Wide Xiangxi*) has been preserved. It contains this passage: "*Xiangxi is a game of strategy; Huangdi in his wars used fierce animals in his battle array; as Elephants (*xiang*) are the strongest of wild animals, the game is called xiangxi according to this strategy.*" Huangdi is a legendary emperor, traditionally dated 2697 to 2597 B.C.E.

6. The monk, Nianchang (1282–1342), wrote in the *Fozu Lidai Tongzai* (*Buddha in Passing Generations and All the Years*) that xiangqi was created by the legendary Emperor Shennong (traditionally, reigned 2737–2697 B.C.E.). "*In old times Shennong used the sun, the moon, the stars and the planets as symbols (*xiang*). Niu Sengru replaced them by chariots, horses, scholars, soldiers and catapults as ustensils in the game.*" Niu Sengru was a State minister in the Tang Dynasty.

7. This legend was expressed by Eyles Irwin, author of an article read to the Royal Academy of Dublin in 1793, related by a Chinese informant, Pan Zhenguan. It was revived and imaginatively, extensively embellished, by the American David Li in *Genealogy of Chess* (1998), a noted but controversial book. The German historian Peter Banaschak has decisively revealed this energetically promoted thesis to be a mere fable.

8. Michel Shen Fu-Tsung himself became a Jesuit. Hyde made use of descriptions drawn from the travel narratives of other Jesuits who had lived in China a few generations earlier: Matteo Ricci (1552–1610), Nicolas Trigault (1577–1628) and Alvarez of Semedo (1585–1658).

9. The Asiatic Society was founded in 1784 by Sir William Jones. Still active, it is based in Kolkata (formerly Calcutta), India.

10. This precious testimony of the great Persian poet travelling through Punjab has already been cited. Murray provides extensive detail on al-Biruni's text. First, al-Biruni described the move of the Elephant stepping to five squares as "*the trunk and the four feet*" of the animal, which was a probable reference to the move of this piece in two-handed chess. Then he added, "*They play chess, four persons at a time, with a pair of dice. Their arrangement of the figures on the chessboard is the following. As this kind of chess is not known to us, I shall explain what I know of it.*" And he continued by giving the rules that have been detailed above in the chapter dedicated to chaturaji.

11. The most famous oases were Aksu, Kucha, Karasahr, Turpan to the north, Yarkand, Hotan, Niya, Cherchen, Miran to the south.

12. This date is sometimes contested. Followed here is the rigorous study led by the Italian Iranologist Antonio Panaino, published in 1999, which has reestablished the historical importance of this fundamental text, also known as *Chatrang-Namak* or *Matigan-i-Chatrang*.

13. Race games claim the title of humanity's oldest board games. Indeed this family of games existed in Iran, Mesopotamia and Egypt as early as the 3rd millennium B.C.E. Before the third century C.E., boards evolved to adopt a 2 × 12 format, dice were reduced from 3 to 2, and that game—called *nard* by Muslim authors—spread through Byzantium, the Middle East and India. Though its place of birth is disputed (even more than that of chess), it is certain that nard was invented well before the reign of Khusraw I.

14. At the end of the fifth or the beginning of the sixth century, the Gupta Empire disintegrated and Harivarman, founder of the Maukhari Dynasty, seized the city of Kanyakubja (today Kannauj). The Maukhari Empire reached its furthest extension, dominating the Gangetic plain, under the reign of Sarvavarman, who held the title of *Maharajadhiraja* (Supreme King of the Great Kings), from 560 or 565 until 585. He was succeeded by his son, then by his grandson Grahavarman, who was killed at war in 605 or 606. Kanyakubja was then ruled by his brother-in-law, Harshavardhana, founder of the Pushyabhuti Dynasty.

15. This text was first mentioned in a manuscript from 943 or 944.

16. According to Antonio Panaino, the *Khusraw i Kawadan ud Redag* was a small text, probably written in the early seventh century under the Sassanids. *Hashtpay* is borrowed from the Sanskrit *ashtapada*, meaning "eight feet." Therefore, it is known that the Persians also were familiar with the *ashtapada*. (See Antonio Panaino, *Hashtpây*, date and place of publication unknown, paper available on http://history.chess.free.fr/library.htm).

17. Modern historians, including Panduranga Bhatta and Andreas Bock-Raming, have shown that texts like Kautilya's *Arthashastra* (completed before the second century B.C.E.), Vatsyayana's *Kamasutra* (completed second century C.E.), Kalidasa's *Kumarasambhava* (fifth century C.E.), the *Harivamsha* (a supplement to the *Mahabharata* completed before the fifth century C.E.), as well as the great epics, *Ramayana* and *Mahabharata*, mention gambling, dice games and even sometimes game boards but do not contain any reference to chess—despite many assertions to the contrary.

18. It says, "*The shameless, sinful monks play on [boards with] ashtapada and on dasapada.*" This was explained by Buddhaghosa (between 370 and 450 C.E.) in his commentary *Samantapasadika* to refer to gaming boards. Also, the grammarian, Patanjali (second century B.C.E.), in his *Mahabhasya,* indicated that "*ashtapada is called [a board with] eight fields in each row,*" without saying what sort of game it was used for. (We follow here Bock-Raming's extensive study of the use of the word *ashtapada* in old Indian texts.)

19. It may have been a kind of lottery game. Nothing has ever confirmed Murray's hypothesis that it could have been a race game on a spiral board.

20. The word *chaturanga* is even found in Vedic texts (composed earlier than the sixth century B.C.E.) such as the *Rigveda* or the *Satapatha Brahmana*, in the sense of having four limbs or parts.

21. Subandhu, author of the *Vasavadatta*, is now identified as a courtier of Emperor Kumaragupta I (414–455) and his son Skandagupta (455–467). At the time Murray wrote his *History of Chess*, Subandhu was thought to have lived in the early seventh century, which made it easier to accept that his text was referring to chess.

22. That Indian romance tells the story of the princess of Ujjayini, and contains a short, intriguing passage: "*the time of the rains played its game with frogs for 'chessmen,' which, yellow and green in color, as if mottled with lacquer, leapt up on the black field squares.*" Murray accepted it for a chess reference. However, the assertion is very weak. The world translated as "chessmen" more accurately refers to "game pieces" (*nayadyutair*), not specific to chess, but can indicate the pieces of any board game. The colors are not those of the two camps, but mean that the frogs have a mottled yellow and green coloring. Finally, "black field squares" can also be translated as "black edges of the irrigated fields." In any case, chessboards used by the Indians were uncheckered, the alternate black and white squares being a medieval European invention.

23. Harshavardhana was the brother of Rajyasri, who was married to the last Maukhari king, Grahavarman. Harsha succeeded him in 606, after a war against neighboring kingdoms, and reigned until his death in 647. This king built a powerful Buddhist empire, from the Himalayas to Odisha, in bloody campaigns lasting until 642. Bana's poem, praising the peace of his reign, appears today to be flattery toward a mighty sovereign. His kingdom was visited by Xuanzang, a Chinese Buddhist pilgrim, who gave an account of his long trip (from 629 to 644) in this region.

24. The diagram superimposed on the figure of Purusha is not always an ashtapada, an 8 × 8 square board; often it is a navapada, a board of 9 × 9 squares.

25. This passage was first revealed by the German indianist Dr. Renate Syed.

26. Song Yu's *Zhaohun* has this sentence (as reported by Banaschak): "*The castor shrubs hide the xiangqi, but there still is the liubo!* (or: *... there it is, the liubo!*)." Peter Banaschak adds that from this sentence it cannot be determined for certain whether one game (liubo alone) or two games (liubo and xiangqi) are indicated. The *Shuo Yuan* also presents translation difficulties. It has a passage saying "*If you have leisure, then fight at xiangqi or dance with the women from Zheng.*" However, other meanings are possible and it cannot be said with certainty what game this text refers to.

27. This text was evoked in other writings such as the *Zhoushu* (*Book of the Zhou Dynasty*), written by Linghu Defen (583–666); the *Suishu* (*Book of the Sui Dynasty*), by Wei Zheng (580–643); and the *Beishi* (*History of the Northern Dynasties*), by Li Yanshou (612–678). In the *Suishu* it is written (as reported by Banaschak), "*When Zhou Wudi created the* xiangjing, *the now deceased emperor casually asked Zheng: What is the place of the ruler of mankind, should he unify heaven and earth, should he move the ghosts and spirits, like in the* xiangjing *with many binding rules, how shall I govern?*" Was this game identical to xiangqi? Unfortunately, this *xiangjing* is no longer extant; a preface written by Wang Bao has, however, been preserved. It says that the game was supposed to represent the 12 phenomena: Earth and Heaven, the Yin and Yang principles, the passing of seasons, the eight trigrams, the musical scale, loyalty and filial piety, lord and vassal, civil and military, rites and virtues. All this refers to several philosophical Chinese schools of the time. Wang Bao added, "*Some (of the pieces) are moved outward as if in response to good advice. This signifies changing to a better position. Some (pieces) are demoted and withdrawn as if in punishment for faults. This is a matter of penalizing wrongs. Some (players) consider thoughtful action of value (and so they) rectify their appearances. Some regard aggressive action as of merit (and they thus) manifest their accurate observations.*"

28. According to Banaschak, the *Xiangxi Fu* was written during or shortly before 569. This prosaic poem affirmed: "*the game pieces are comparable to horses, each worth a thousand pieces of silver; the tallies shine like the tallies of the six spirits [in the command of the heavenly emperor]; carrying out in the south the tallies from Red River; carrying out in the north the tactics from Black Mountain; the green dragon in the eastern path; the white horse leaves the western pass,*" (according to Lo and Wang, 2004).

29. The Chariot described in this passage is very limited and tends to recall the Lance from Japanese shogi (some authors suggest there is a direct connection). The count of six Soldiers is uncertain as the text may also be interpreted, "... the men armed with six weapons" (Private communication from Peter Banaschak).

30. The face of this animal is flat with two large, circular eyes. Buryakov suggested it may represent a lion. This could correspond to a Sogdian tradition of depicting a hero riding a lion, found in artifacts of the same period. Even more surprising, the rider of this strange animal shows a similar face as if he too wears a "lion" mask. The top of his skull is flat, a characteristic also observed in a seventh or eighth century piece found in Saqqizabad (Iran), conserved in the Metropolitan Museum of Art in New York and assumed to be a Firzan (Advisor). Buryakov believed that this piece was an Advisor. Manfred Eder, a German chess collector, suggests that it represents an alternative design of a Knight. It is worth considering that this representation may be related to one of the creatures that populate the Mazdean mythology as it is narrated in the *Shahnama*.

31. The Göktürks were the first Turkic people in these regions. Other waves followed which ultimately shaped the Central Asia of today, where Turkish languages dominate.

32. Making this discovery all the more intriguing, this Chariot was found beside a xiangqi metallic piece, bearing the Chinese Pao character on one side and a

representation of a catapult on the back. The pieces were uncovered in 1913.

33. Pieces of this sort which represent a King or Vizier show a carriage on or behind a team of horses, and this carriage contains two riders. Based on these various finds, Yuriy Buryakov's "Afrasiab" King has been reconstructed with two riders, although the original fragment now shows only one rider, with the back of the piece (presumably including the second rider) broken off.

34. These pieces were acquired by a neutral party, who sent the photographs to J.L. Cazaux. They belong today to a private collector.

35. Details and photographs of these pieces may be found on http://history.chess.free.fr.

36. A study was conducted by Andreas Bock-Raming, founded by the *Förderkreis Schach-Geschichtsforschung e.V. (FSG)*, a German private institution supporting research into the origins of chess.

37. See Micaela Soar's paper in the book *Ancient Board Games in Perspective*, a collection of papers from the 1990 British Museum colloquium of same title.

38. This uncertainty also holds for the two early pieces from Dalverzin Tepe.

39. This does not apply to Xinjiang of course, which was long populated by Indo-European peoples (Tokharians), and then by Turkic peoples (mainly Uighurs). Similarly, no game piece, flat and inscribed with a character or drawing, has ever been excavated outside of China.

40. Mentioned by Andrew Lo and Tzi-Cheng Wang in the article "The Earthworms Tame the Dragon: The Game of Xiangqi," in *Asian Games: The Art of Contest*, Asia Society, 2004.

41. Such an orthogonal leaper has appeared in chess history however, in later times. That move was ascribed to the Elephant in India by the Arab chess master al-'Adli in the mid ninth century. It also corresponds to the Camel described by Firdawsi in the early 11th century in his "complete chess" on 10 × 10 board. Finally, such a chessman was called a Dabbaba in Timur's chess in the 14th century.

42. See Bock-Raming (1999) for a deep analysis of occurrences of *ashtapada* in Sanskrit texts.

43. Spiral race games are common in India. In his *A History of Chess* (1913), Murray wrote (pp. 40–41), "*The existing board-games of this special type in Southern India and Ceylon are all played on boards with an odd number of squares, so that there is a single central square which serves as point of exit for all four players alike. In* Pachisi *on the other hand, each player has his own point of exit, and there seems no reason why a similar arrangement should not have been tried upon a square board. In this case the square would obviously be one with an even number of points, and the four central points would serve as the four points of exit for the four players.*" Murray was not necessarily right. As the matter of fact, the situation is very different in Pachisi, with its cruciform board. The four players share the same central square—the *char-koni*—as point of exit. In Pachisi, the path of every player is very clear, as opposed to a race along four different spirals on an even-square board which could be very confusing, maybe unplayable. This is probably the reason all documented spiral race games are played over an odd-square board: *thayam siga, sadurangam, gavalata*, and *ashta-changa* on 5 × 5 squares; *ashta-kashte* on 7 × 7 squares; *saturankam* and another *siga* on 9 × 9 squares. *Sadurangam* and *saturankam* obviously derive from the word *chaturanga*, indicating the tendency of common people to confuse the names of board-games.

44. This interesting idea was first advanced by the Canadian Myron Samsin, in the collective book, *Anatomy of Chess* (2003).

45. The game of tables was derived either from the old Roman race game, *duodecim scripta*, or from nard. Through Byzantine influence, the games of tables exploded in Europe in several dozens of variants. Among them, the *todas tablas* depicted and detailed in the 1283 codex of the king of Castile Alphonse X was strikingly similar to a description dated 1129 and included in the *Manasollasa* of the Indian prince Someshvara III. A Chinese engraving of a game of *shuanglu* from the Yuan time (1279–1367) also shows the same array of the 30 playing pieces. Surprisingly, this array is precisely the same as that of modern backgammon, a name that first appeared in 17th century England. The invention of the doubling cube, in New York City in the 1920s, changed the game radically and brought it to a new (and well deserved) level of popularity.

46. Perhaps intermarriage played a role in the game's dissemination. Examples of "matrimonial diplomacy" can be found all along the history of the Silk Road. In this way, the daughter of Istämi, king of the Western Göktürks, was married to Khusraw I, emperor of Persia. Several Chinese princesses were offered to the Khans of nomadic tribes. A game of chess would have easily found its place in the suitcases of a bartered bride.

47. Many missionaries left Central Asia to teach Buddhism in China. Examples are Dharmaraksha (265–313), originally a Kushan from Dunhuang; Kumarajiva (344–413), another Kushan; Bodhidharma (440–528), Indian or Persian, founder of the *Zen* school; Jñanagupta (561–592) and Shikshananda (652–710), both monks from Gandhara; Prajña (circa 810) from Kabul. In the other direction, there are several examples of Chinese pilgrims travelling to Central Asia and India. In the period of concern, one can cite Faxian (traveled 339–412); Song Yun and his companions (traveled 518–522); Xuanzang (traveled 629–645); and Hyecho, from Korea (traveled 723–729), among the most famous.

48. China suffered several attacks of xenophobic fever in which everything foreign had to be eliminated. Buddhism, Manichaeism and Nestorianism have been regularly subjected to persecutions. The

Chinese reaction following the An Lushan rebellion (755–763) was especially violent with the massacre of Sogdians and Turks living in China.

49. The situation is different today. With the exception of Iran and Tajikistan, the Turkic languages have become most widespread.

50. For instance, there are tens of thousands of scrolls, written in Chinese, in Sogdian and in Serindian Tokharian idioms (Kuchean, Agnean), discovered in the cave of Mogao, close to Dunhuang, in the Gansu, at the Eastern entrance of the Silk Road. These Buddhist texts from the first millennium, found by archeologists Aurel Stein and Paul Peliot in the early 20th century, have not been yet analyzed for content related to the history of games.

51. This excerpt is taken from an academic paper authored by Dong Li, from the Museum of History of Shaanxi (1999, English translation 2002). Fazang's work is the *Fanwang fazang shu* "Commentary on the *Fanwang jing* by Fazang." The *Fanwang jing* was an important Buddhist text from the mid–fifth century C.E. Its original Sanskrit title is *Brahmajala Sutra (Brahma's Net Sutra)*. Its 33rd precept ("On Watching Improper Activities") says: *"A disciple of the Buddha must not, with evil intentions, watch people fighting or the battling of armies, rebels, gangs and the like. He should not listen to the sounds of conch shells, drums, horns, guitars, flutes, lutes, songs or other music, nor should he be party to any form of gambling, whether dice or games. Furthermore, he should not practice fortune-telling or divination nor should he be an accomplice to thieves and bandits. He must not participate in any of these activities. If however, he intentionally does so, he commits a secondary offense."* This passage is inspired from the *Daban niepan jing* (*Nirvana Sutra*, composed in India before the second century C.E. and translated into Chinese in the fifth century C.E. about 415–420) which cites *prasaka* among the list of forbidden leisures. This is a recurring precept in Buddhist thoughts since the *Vinayapitaka* (fourth or third century B.C.E.).

# Bibliography

## Books

*Archiv der Spiele.* Berlin, 1819.

*Art du jeu, jeu dans l'art, de Babylone à l'Occident médiéval.* Exhibition catalog, Musée de Cluny—Musée National du Moyen Âge, Paris, 2012.

Badel, Pierre-Yves. *La Description du Monde.* Le Livre de poche, Lettres Gothiques, Paris, 1998.

Bell, Robert Charles. *Board and Table Games from Many Civilizations.* Oxford, England: Oxford University Press, 1960 and 1969; reprint, New York: Dover, 1979.

_____. *Old Board Games.* 1973, Shire Publications, reprint, Bucks, UK: Shire, 1980.

Botermans, Jack. *The Book of Games; Strategy, Tactics and History.* New York: Sterling, 2008.

Boyer, Joseph. *Les Jeux d'échecs non orthodoxes.* Paris, 1951.

_____. *Nouveux Jeux d'échecs non orthodoxes.* Paris, 1954.

Brunet y Bellet, José. *El Ajedrez, Investigaciones sobre su origen.* Barcelona, 1890.

Caldwell, David H., and Mark A. Hall (eds.). *The Lewis Chessmen: New Perspectives.* Edinburgh: NMS Publishing/SAS, 2014.

Carrera, Pietro. *Il Gioco de gli scacchi.* N. Militello: Per G. de'Rossi da Trento, 1617.

Cazaux, Jean-Louis. *Guide des échecs exotiques et insolites.* Paris: Chiron, 2000.

_____. *L'Odyssée des jeux d'échecs.* Paris: Praxeo, 2010.

_____. *Traité pratique de métamachie.* Pionissimo: TheBookEdition.com, 2012.

_____. Gerhard Josten and Myron Samsin. *The Anatomy of Chess.* Pfullingen: Promos-Verlag, 2003.

Cessoles, Jacques de. *Le livre du jeu d'échecs ou la société idéale au Moyen Âge, XIII<sup>e</sup> siècle.* Translated and presented by Jean-Michel Mehl. Paris: Stock/Moyen Âge, 1995.

Ciccolini, Giuseppe. *Tentativo di un nuovo giuoco di Scacchi.* Rome: Preso Franceso Bourlié, 1820.

Coxe, William. *Travels into Poland, Russia, Sweden and Denmark.* Vol. 1. Dublin, 1784.

Culin, Stewart. *Chess and Playing-Cards, Catalogue of Games and Implements for Divination Exhibited by the United States National Museum in Connection with the Department of Archæology and Palæontology of the University of Pennsylvania at the Cotton States and International Exposition, Atlanta, Georgia, 1895.* Washington, D.C.: Government Printing Office, 1898.

_____. *Korean Games: With Notes on the Corresponding Games from China and Japan.* Philadelphia: University of Pennsylvania Press, 1895; reprint, New York: Dover, 1991.

Davidson, Henry A. *A Short History of Chess.* New York: D. McKay, 1949.

Dickins, Anthony. *A Guide to Fairy Chess.* Richmond, Surrey, England: The Q Press, 1969; reprint, New York: Dover, 1971.

Eales, Richard. *Chess: The History of a Game.* New York: Facts on File, 1985; reprint, Glasgow: Hardinge Simpole, 2002.

*An Easy Introduction to the Game of Chess Containing One Hundred Examples of Games, and a Great Variety of Critical Situations and Conclusions.* London: Printed for Baldwin, Cradock, and Joy, 1816.

Falkener, Edward. *Games Ancient and Oriental and How to Play Them.* London: Longmans, Green, 1892; reprint, New York: Dover, 1961.

Finkel, Irving L. *Asian Games: The Art of Contest.* New York: Asia Society, 2004.

_____, ed. *Ancient Board Games in Perspective.* London: British Museum Press, 2007.

Fiske, Willard. *Chess in Iceland and in Icelandic Literature.* Florence: Florentine Typographical Society, 1905.

Forbes, Duncan. *Observations of the Origin and Progress of Chess.* London: Sercombe and Jack, 1855.

_____. *History of Chess.* London: Allen, 1860; reprint, Olomouc: Publishing House Moravian Chess, CAISSA-90, 2000.

Foster, Benjamin R. *Chancellor Chess or the New Game of Chess.* St. Louis, MO, 1889; reprint, Kessinger Legacy Reprints.

*The Game of Chesse by William Caxton: A Facsimile Reproduction of the First Work Printed in England from the Copy in the British Museum.* London: Trübner, 1862.

Giacometti, Francesco. *Nuovo giuoco di scacchi ossia il giuoco della guerra.* Genova: Stamperia Scionico, 1801.

Gifford, Gary. *Thai Chess and Cambodian Chess.* Raleigh, NC: Lulu Publishing, 2010.

Gini, Gianni and Roldolfo Pozzi. *Scacchi, giocchi da tutto il mondo.* Milano: Casa Editrice Stefanoni, 2007.

Giżycki, Jerzy. *A History of Chess.* London: Abbey Library, 1972.

Gligorić, Svetozar. *Shall We Play Fischerandom Chess?* London: Batsford, 2002.

Gliński, Władysław. *Rules of Hexagonal Chess with Examples of First Openings.* London: Hexagonal Chess Publications, 1973.

Gollon, John. *Chess Variations, Ancient, Regional, Modern.* Rutland, VT: Charles E. Tuttle, 1968.

Golombek, Harry. *A History of Chess.* London: Routledge & Kegan Paul, 1976.

Gotha-Altenburg, Ernst II von. *Gesetze des Schachs zu Vieren.* Altenburg, 1792.

Haebler, Konrad. *The Early Printers of Spain and Portugal.* London: Chiswick Press, 1896.

Hooper, David, and Kenneth Whyld. *The Oxford Companion to Chess.* Oxford, England: Oxford University Press, 1984.

Hosking, Tony. *The Art of Shogi.* Stratford-upon-Avon: Shogi Foundation, 1997.

Huc, Évariste Régis. *Souvenirs d'un voyage dans la Tartarie, le Thibet et la Chine pendant les années 1844, 1845 et 1846, par M.Huc, prêtre-missionnaire de la Congrégation de Saint-Lazare.* Vol. 2. Paris, 1850.

Ingersoll, Randy. *Play Hive Like a Champion*, 2d ed. Port Orange, FL, 2013.

Jones, Sir William. *On the Indian Game of Chess*, 1790. In *The Works of Sir William Jones*, Vol. IV, by Lord Teignmouth, London, 1807.

Kitao, Madoka. *The Book of Dobutsu Shogi.* Tokyo: Nekomado, 2013.

La Loubère, Simon de. *Du Royaume de Siam.* Amsterdam, 1691.

Lau, H.T. *Chinese Chess.* Rutland, VT: Charles E. Tuttle, 1985.

Lemmonier, de la Bissachère, Pierre-Jacques. *État actuel du Tunkin, de la Cochinchine, et des royaumes de Camboge, Laos et Lac-Tho*, Vol. 2. Paris, 1812.

Leventhal, Dennis A. *The Chess of China.* Taipei, Republic of China: Mei Ya, 1978.

Lhôte, Jean-Marie. *Dictionnaire des Jeux de Société.* Paris: Flammarion, 1996.

_____. *Histoire des jeux de société.* Paris: Flammarion, 1994.

Li, David H. *The Genealogy of Chess.* Bethesda, MD: Premier Publishing, 1998. See http://www.banaschak.net/schach/ligenealogyofchess.htm for a critical and informative review.

Linder, Isaac. *The Art of Chess Pieces.* Moscow: H.G.S. Publishers, 1994.

Lwin, Maung Maung. *How to Play Myanmar Traditional Chess (Sit-Tu-Yin).* Yangon, Myanmar: Ma Khin Mya Sar Pay, 2011.

Marinelli, Filippo. *Il Giuoco degli Schacchi Fra Tre.* Naples, 1722.

Markham, Clements R. *Narratives of the Mission of George Bogle to Tibet, and the Journey of Thomas Manning to Lhasa.* London, 1876.

Markov, Georgi. "Russian four-handed chess: myths and misconceptions," *Board Games Studies Journal*, online, number 9, pp. 41–49, bgsj.ludusopuscula.org, 2015.

Marsden, William. *The History of Sumatra Containing an Account of the Government, Laws, Customs and Manners of the Native Inhabitants.* London, 1811.

Maura, Gabriel Vicente. *Evolución del ajedrez, 40 siglos.* Madrid: Ricardo Aguilera, 1980.

Monté, Peter J. *The Classical Era of Modern Chess.* Jefferson, NC: McFarland, 2014.

Moyer, Ann E. *The Philosophers' Game: Rithmomachia in Medieval and Renaissance Europe.* Ann Arbor: University of Michigan Press, 2001.

Müllers, Fabian, and Sylvestre Jonquay. *Les Jeux au Moyen-Âge.* Auvilliers en Gâtinais: Editions La Muse, 2016.

Murray, H.J.R. *A History of Chess.* Oxford, England: Oxford University Press, 1913; reprint, 1962, 2012.

_____. *A History Of Board-Games Other Than Chess.* Oxford, England: Oxford University Press, 1951; reprint, Oxbow Books, 2002.

Musser, Sonja. *Los Libros de acedrex dados a tablas: Historical, Artistic and Metaphysical Dimensions of Alfonso X's Book of Games.* Ph.D. dissertation, University of Arizona, 2007.

Needham, Joseph. *Science and Civilisation in China: Physics and Physical Technology, Part I: Physics*, "The Magnet, Divination, and Chess." Cambridge, England: Cambridge University Press, 1962.

Netto, Dr. *Shatranj oder das Schachspiel unter Zweien, und dessen Geheimnisse; ferner das Courierspiel, Rundschach des Tamerlan, und das Kriegesspiel.* Berlin, 1827.

Nguyen, Marc-Antoine. *Xiang qi, l'univers des échecs chinois.* Paris: Praxeo, 2009.

Panaino, Antonio. *La Novella degli scacchi e della tavola reale.* Milan: Mimesis, 1999.

Parlett, David. *The Oxford History of Board Games.* Oxford: Oxford University Press, 1999.

Piacenza, Francesco. *I Campeggiamenti degli scacchi.* Turin, 1683

*Pièces d'échecs.* Exhibition catalog, Bibliothèque nationale de France, Cabinet des Médailles et Antiques. Paris, 1990.

Png, Jim Hau Cheng. *Understanding the Elephant, a Xiangqi Primer, Part 1: History of Xiangqi.* Published by the author, New Taipei City, Taiwan, 2016.

Pritchard, D.B. *The Encyclopedia of Chess Variants.* Godalming, UK: Games & Puzzles Publications, 1994.

_____. *The Classified Encyclopedia of Chess Variants.* Edited by John Beasley. Harpenden, UK: 2007 (available at http://www.jsbeasley.co.uk/encyc.htm).
Raffles, Thomas Stanford. *The History of Java.* Vol. 1. London: Black, Parbury and Allen, 1817.
Schmittberger, R. Wayne. *New Rules for Classic Games.* New York: John Wiley & Sons, 1992.
Semedo, Père Alvarez. *Histoire universelle de la Chine.* Lyon: Chez Hierosme Prost, 1667.
Stratford, Neil. *The Lewis Chessmen and the Enigma of the Hoard.* London: British Museum Press, 1997.
Symes, Michael. *Account of an Embassy to the Kingdom of Ava, Sent by the Governor-General of India in the Year 1795.* London: Printed for J. Debrett, Piccadilly, by Wilson and Co. at the Oriental Press, Wild Court, Lincoln's Inn Fields, 1800.
Tesche, Walter. *Theoretisch—praktische Anweisung zum Dreischachspiel.* Vienna: Pfautsch, 1843.
Tressau, Ludwig. *Das Schachspiel, seine Gattungen und Abarten.* Quedlinburg und Leipzig, 1840.
Turner, Captain Samuel. *An Account of an Embassy to the Court of the Teshoo Lama, in Tibet.* London: W. Bulmer, 1800.
Twiss, Richard. *Chess.* London: Printed for G.G.J. & J. Robinson in Paternoster Row and T. & J. Egerton Whitehall, 1787.
Van Langendonckt, Michel, ed. *Art et Savoir de l'Inde: Actes du colloque "Jeux indiens et originaires de l'Inde" organisés dans le cadre d'Europalia India.* Brussels: Les Éditions HEB, 2015.
Vasantha, Rangachar. *Maharaja's Games and Puzzles.* Kelkheim: Förderkreis Schach-Geschichtsforschung e.V., 2006.
Verney, Major George Hope. *Chess Eccentricities.* London: Longmans, Green, 1885.
Waidder, S. *Das Schachspiel in seinem ganzen Umfange nach allen Schriftstellern auf eine leicht faßliche Weise dargestellt.* Vienna, 1837.
Weickhmann, Christoph. *New-erfundenes Grosses Königs Spiel.* Ulm: Kühne, 1664.
Williams, Gareth. *Master Pieces.* London: Apple Press, 2000.
Yalom, Marilyn. *Birth of the Chess Queen: A History.* New York: HarperCollins, 2004.
Yi, I-Hwa. *Korea's Pastimes and Customs—A Social History.* 1937. English translation by Ju-Hee Park. Paramus, NJ: Homa & Sekey Books, 2006.

## Articles

Baggio, Giuseppe. "Giochi orientali—Oriental Games." *Eteroscacco.* 86/87/88, April–December 1999.
Banaschak, Peter. "Early East Asian Chess Pieces: An overview." www.banaschak.net. August 1999.
_____. "Facts on the origin of Chinese chess (Xiangqi)." *4th Symposium of the Initiative Gruppe Königstein.* Wiesbaden, August 1997.
Bhatta, C. Panduranga. "Antiquity of Indian Board Games—A New Approach." *New Approaches to Board Games Research, Asian Origin and Future Perspective.* IIAS Working Papers Series 3, Leiden, 1995.
Bland, Nathaniel. "On the Persian Game of Chess." *Journal of the Royal Asiatic Society.* Part I, Vol. XIII, London, 1851.
Bock-Raming, Andreas. "The Literary Sources of Indian Chess and Related Board Games." *New Approaches to Board Games Research, Asian Origin and Future Perspective.* IIAS Working Papers Series 3, Leiden, 1995.
_____. "The Varieties of Indian Chess through the Ages." *Asiatische Studien—Études Asiatiques,* XLIX, 2, 1995.
_____. "The Gaming Board in Indian Chess and Related Board Games: A Terminological Investigation." *Board Games Studies,* no. 2, 1999.
_____. "The Gambling Scenes of Bharhut and Bodhgaya: A Critical Assessment of Their Previous Interpretations and Some New Suggestions." *Asiatische Studien—Études Asiatiques,* LIV, 1, 2000.
_____. "Das 8. Kapitel des *Hariharacaturanga*: ein spätmittelalterlicher Sanskrittext über eine Form des "Großen Schachs." *Board Games Studies,* no. 4, 2001.
Boutin, Michel. "Histoire d'un jeu particulier (Stratego). Les jeux de pions et l'education. Les apports de la classification formelle des jeux." In *Art et Savoir de l'Inde,* Vol. 2, ed. Michel Van Langendonckt. Brussels: Les Editions HEB, 2015. Available on http://www.euskomedia.org/PDFAnlt/lankidetzan/51/51149165.pdf.
_____. "L'Attaque, un jeu français issu du *Gunjin Shogi.*" In *Art et Savoir de l'Inde,* Vol. 2, ed. Michel Van Langedonckt. Brussels: Les Éditions HEB, 2015.
_____, and Pierre Parlebas. "Rithmomachie, Ouranomachie et Metromachie," *Art et Savoir de l'Inde,* Vol. 2, ed. Michel Van Langendonckt. Brussels: Les Éditions HEB, 2015.
Buryakov, Yuriy. "Chess in Ancient Afrasiab." *Journal of the Academy of Arts of Uzbekistan.* San'At 4/2000.
Calvo, Ricardo. "Der Musiker, der das Schachspiel brachte." *Schach-journal.* Berlin, 3. jg., N1/1993, pp. 86–93.
_____. "Valencia Spain: The Cradle of European Chess." *Colloquium Chess Collector International.* Vienna, Austria, May 1998.
_____. "The Oldest Chess Pieces in Europe." *Colloquium IGK—Amsterdam,* December 2001.
Cazaux, Jean-Louis. "We Played Liubo Last Night!" *Abstract Games.* Issue 15, Autumn 2003.
Chicco, Adriano. "Il Giuoco di Pitagora." Genoa: Edizione privata a cura dell'Autore, 1979.
Dong, Li. "Suspicions Regarding What Are Alleged to Be Sui Dynasty Glass and Agate *Weiqi* Chess Pieces." *China Archaelogy and Art Digest,* "Fortune, Games and Gaming." Vol. 4, no. 4, April–May 2002.
Eder, Manfred. "Bagdad—Bergkristall—Benediktiner Zum Ex-oriente des Schachspiels." *Begleitschrift mit Katalog Schach zur "Ex-oriente"–Ausstellung in*

*Aachen 2003*. Förderkreis Schach-Geschichtsforschung e.V., Kelkheim/Taunus, June 2003.

_____. "Early Terracotta-Figures from Kanauj Chessmen?, Chapter II: Half an Answer and More Questions." 19th International Congress of South Asian Archaeology, Ravenna, Italy, July 2007.

Elcum, John Bowen. "Malay Chess." *Journal of Straits Branch of the Royal Asiatic Society*. No. 49, 1907, pp. 87–92.

Fairbairn, John. "Shogi History and the Variants." *Shogi Magazine*, no. 27, September 1980.

Fauquet, Wilfrid. "Le Giu parti d'Evrart de Conty, une version échiquéenne du Roman de la rose." *Romania*, Vol. 123, no. 491, Paris 2005, pp. 486–522.

Ferlito, Gianfelice. "Old Islamic Chessmen. Historical, Religious and Artistic Considerations about Their Shape and Design." *Homo Ludens der spielende Mensch IV* (Munich-Salzburg), band 4, 1994, pp. 81–89.

_____. "Riflessioni sulla storia e le origini degli scacchi." *Scacchitalia—Organo Ufficiale della Federazione Scacchistica Italiana*. No. 11, 2010.

_____, and Alessandro Sanvito. "Origins of Chess, Protochess, 400 B.C. to 400 A.D." *The Pergamon Chess Monthly*. No. 6, Vol. 55, September 1990.

Folkerts, Menso. "'Rithmomachia,' a Mathematical Game from the Middle Ages." In his *Essays on Early Medieval Mathematics: The Latin Tradition*. Ashgate Variorum, 2003.

Gamer, Helena M. "The Earliest Evidence of Chess in Western Literature: The Einsiedeln Verses." *Speculum*, Vol. 29, No. 4 (Oct. 1954), pp. 734–750.

Garzón, José Antonio. "El regreso de Francesch Vicent: la historia del nacimiento y expansión del ajedrez moderno." www.ajedrezmoderno.com, 2005.

Horn, Fred. "L'Histoire du Stratego, faits, témoignages, anecdotes et petits mensonges." In *Art et Savoir de l'Inde*, Vol. 2, ed. Michel Van Langendonckt. Brussels: Les Éditions HEB, 2015.

_____, and Alex de Voogt. "The Development and Dispersal of L'Attaque Games." *Proceedings of Board Game Studies Colloquium XI*. pp. 43–52, 2008.

Irwin, Eyles. "An Account of the Game of Chess, as Played by the Chinese." *The Transactions of the Royal Irish Academy*, Vol. 5 (1793/1794), pp. 53–63.

Jákl, Jiří. "Yudhisthira the Chessplayer? *Caturanga* Game of the Old Javanese *Wirataparwa*." Expanded version of a paper prepared for the 14th Colloquium of Board Games Studies held in Bruges, Belgium, May 2011.

Lilleøren, Morten. "The Courier from Constance." Unpublished article based on a lecture at Board Game Studies Colloquium XVIII, Swiss Museum of Games/Musée Suisse du Jeu La Tour-de-Peilz, Switzerland, April 15–18, 2015. (With the author's permission.)

_____. "Theses on Chess in Scandinavia in the Middle Ages." *The Chess Stalker Quarterly*. Vol. 1, No. 4, June 2011.

Lo, Andrew, and Tzi-Cheng Wang. "The Earthworms Tame the Dragon: The Game of Xiangqi." *Asian Games: The Art of Contest*. Asia Society, 2004.

Low, Captain James. "On Siamese Literature." *Asiatic Researches; or, Transactions of the Society, Instituted in Bengal*, 1836, Vol. 20, Part 1, pp. 338–392.

Makariou, Sophie. "Le Jeu d'échecs, une pratique de l'aristocratie entre islam et chrétienté des IX$^e$–XIII$^e$ siècles." *Les Cahiers de Saint-Michel de Cuxa*. XXXVI, 2005.

Masukawa, Koichi. "The Origin of Japanese Chess." *Variant Chess*. Oct.–Dec. 1994.

_____. "*Shogi*: Japan's Game of Generals." *Asian Games: The Art of Contest*. Asia Society, 2004.

Popova, Assia. "Analyse formelle et classification des jeux de calculs mongols." *Cahier nº 5, Études mongoles*. Université de Paris X, Nanterre, 1974.

Pozzi, Rodolfo. "I Giochi di scacchi mongoli riflesso della cultura nomade delle steppe/The Mongolian chess reflecting the nomadic culture of the steppes." *Chess Collectors International, 10th Biennal Convention*. Philadelphia, May 2002.

Rajendran, Chettiarthodi. "Traditional Caturanga as Preserved in Kerala," followed by "The 'Caturangastaka' of Melputtur Narayana Bhattathiri." *Working Papers, Indian Views*. Förderkreis Schach-Geschichtsforschung e.V., 2001.

Robinson, H.O. "Malay Chess." *Cheltenham Examiner*. July 27, 1904. (Also in *Papers on Malay Subjects, Life and Customs Part III, Malay Amusements*, edited by R.J. Wilkinson. Kuala Lumpur, 1910.)

Röllicke, Hermann-Josef. "Von 'Winkelwegen,' 'Eulen' und 'Fischziehern'—Liubo: ein altenchinesisches Brettspiel für Geister und Menschen." *Board Games Studies*, no. 2, 1999.

Shimizu, Yasuji. "The Development and Regional Variations of Liubo." *Board Game Studies Journal online 8*, pp. 81–105. bgsj.ludus-opuscula.org, 2014.

_____, and Shin'ichi Miyahara. "The Chinese Chess Pieces in Song Era and Their Characteristics." *Schach-Forschungen*, No. 26. Seevetal, 2004.

Slobodchikof, Léon A. F, "Cò' tuô'ng: le jeu d'échecs des Vietnamiens," *Bulletin de la Société des Études Indochinoises*. N.s., XXVIII, no. 4, 1953.

Soar, Micaela. "Board Games and Backgammon in Ancient Indian Sculpture." *Ancient Board Games in Perspective*. British Museum Press, 2007.

Stigter, Jurgen. "Rithmomachia, the Philosophers' Game: An Introduction to its History and Rules." *Ancient Board Games in Perspective*. British Museum Press, 2007.

Syed, Renate. "Early Terracottas from Kanauj: Chessmen?" *Asiatische Studien—Études Asiatiques*. Vol. 55, no. 2, 2001.

_____. "War, Peace and Chess. Bana's References to 'Terracotta Chessmen' and 'Discourse on War' in the Harsacarita," *Asiatische Studien—Études Asiatiques*. Vol. 62, no. 2, 2008.

Wakankar, Siddharth. "A Survey of Sanskrit Works

on the Game of Chess," *Journal of the Oriental Institute.* Vol. 35, Nos., 3–4, March–June 1986.

Zeng, Lanying (Lillian L. Tseng). "Divining from the Game Liubo: An Explanation of a Han Wooden Slip." *China Archaelogy and Art Digest,* "Fortune, Games and Gaming." Vol. 4, no. 4, October–December 1999.

## Web Sites

*All Internet addresses listed below were checked on February 1, 2017.*

http://history.chess.free.fr: Jean-Louis Cazaux's website, dedicated to history of chess and all chess variants.

http://ancientchess.com: Rick Knowlton's website presenting a wide variety of chessmen and chess variants.

www.chessvariants.com: the very rich *Chess Variant Pages*, founded by Hans Bodlaender and then edited by David Howe and other editors.

www.zillions-of-games.com: the software Zillions-of-Games allows to play more than 300 board games. It embeds a language with which it is possible to describe almost any rule.

www.boardgamegeek.com

www.schachquellen.de: the website of the *Initiative Group Königstein,* a group of scholars working on the origins of chess.

www.boardgamestudies.info: the very scholarly *Board Games Studies* review.

www.cci-italia.it/indcol.htm: website of the *Chess Collector International—Italy* where several articles are available.

http://historicgames.com/alphonso/index.html: for a translation of Alfonso X's codex, many colorful illustrations.

www.goddesschess.com

www.fide.com: website of the International Federation of Chess.

www.yutopian.com/games: a lot of information about Chinese board games.

www.wxf.org: website of the *World Xiangqi Federation.*

www.banaschak.net: Peter Banaschak's page (Ph.D. in Oriental chess history).

http://praxeo-fr.blogspot.com

# *Index*

Numbers in ***bold italics*** indicate pages with illustrations

Aaron Alexandre 323
Abu'n-Na'am 17
al-'Adli 11, 14, 17, 29, 50, 328, 382$n$41
Afrasiab ***340–341***, 345, 359$n$2
Africa, chess in 7, 17, 21; *see also* samantsy; senterej
Albers, H.G. *see Courier-Spiel*
Alfonso X 28, 72, 210–***211***, 223–232, ***223–225***, ***228–232***, 370$n$3, 370$n$5
Alice chess 312–314, ***313–314***
Alquerque 223, 360$n$12
Amazon (chessman) 58, 66–67, 69, 72–73, 253–255, 261, 265
al-Amuli, ibn Mahmud 21, 30, 35, 231
anatomic chess 28
Andersen, Adolf 247
*Angel Chess* 376$n$9
Angkor Wat ***84***
Annan shogi 151
Arabian chess *see* shatranj
ibn 'Arabshah 30, 32, 35–36
*Arciscacchiere see* Piacenza
Ardant du Picq, Charles Paul 20
area move 164–165, 167
*Arimaa* (game) 375$n$2
*Aro Kassen, Monogatari* 162
*Arthashastra see* Kautilya
ASEAN chess ***90***, 91
ashtapada 48, 50, 337–339, ***338***, 342, 346, 350, 380$n$16
Asilo 220
assize 200–203, 226
*Atomic Chess* 283
atranj 65, ***67–68***; second version 68
*L'Attaque* ***137***–141, 367$n$40; *see also* Stratego
Aufin (chessman) ***199***, 208–***209***, ***233***, 269; *see also* Elephant, Bishop

backgammon 16, 24, 50, 64, 210, 223, ***228***, 230–232, ***230–231***, 240, 337, 349, 368$n$8, 368$n$10

*baduk see* weiqi
Bai Juyi 107
Baltic four-handed chess *see* Kieseritzky
Bana 50, ***338***, 342, 349
*banqi* ***123***, 124, ***125***, 130, 139
Baroda chess 65, 68–70, ***69–70***
Baskerville, Lord H.D. ***291***
Bataks' chess 93, 95–96
Beasley, John 83, 375$n$1
Begnis, Clément *see Courier-Spiel*
Bell, Robert Charles 130, 139, 240, 362$n$22
Berg Moller, Julie 138, 140–141
Betza, Ralph 261
Billberg, Gustav Johan 253–***254***
Bird's chess ***256***–257, 265
al-Biruni 50, 59–60, 62–63, 92, 230, 333
Bishop + Knight (chessman) ***66***, ***251***, ***253***, ***256–260***, 262–265
Bishop: predecessor 24, 30, 32, 52, 118, 120, 145, 153, 161, ***199–200***, 209, 224, 227, ***233–234***, 245, 360n22
Bland, Nathaniel 31, 332
Boat (chessman) 2, 52–54, 59–62, 78–79, 81–82, 93–94, 247
Bock-Raming, Andreas 49, 63, 77, 361$n$4, 362$n$9, 363$n$40, 380$n$17, 380$n$18, 382$n$36, 382$n$42
de Boissière, Claude 222, 372$n$35
*boluo saixi* 108, 352; *see also* liubo
*Bonus Socius* 210
Boutin, Michel 138, 141, 367$n$40
Boyer, Joseph 292, 303, 379$n$58, 379$n$70
de Bray, Jan ***236***
Brunner, Anselm *see* free chess
Brunswick-Lüneburg, Duke Augustus of *see* Selenus
*buddhi* chess 51–52, 54
*burj* 55–56
Burmese chess *see* sit-tu-yin
burning power 164–165, 167, 196

391

Burroughs, Edgar Rice *see* Jetan
Burton, Robert 222
Burtrimov, Ivan 254, 298
Buryakov, Yuriy **340**, 381*n*30, 382*n*33; *see also* Afrasiab
Byway, Paul *see* Modern Courier Chess
Byzantine chess 27, 29, 58, 285, 371*n*23; *see also* circular chess

Calvo, Ricardo 245, 345, 371n11, 373*n*56, 375*n*72, 375*n*73, 375*n*75
Cambodian chess (ouk) *see* makruk
Camel (chessman) 2–3, 23, 29, 31–36, 38, 40–42, **45**, 52–56, 69–73, 121, 272, **274**–275, **277**–279, 376*n*12, 382*n*41
*I campeggiamenti degli scacchi (The Basics of Chess) see* Piacenza
Cannon (chessman) 98–104, 107–108, 110–111, 113–114, 118–119, 193, 273, **277**, 279, 343–345, 351, 377*n*29
Capablanca, José Raúl 257–**258**, 263–265
Carrera, Pietro 23, **251**–**252**, 253, 256–257, 259, 263, 265–266
Castellví, Francesc *see Scachs d'amor*
castling 9, 18, 42, 45, 54, 78, 86, 91, 95, 201, 242–**243**, 247, 252, 379*n*70; in shogi **149**
Catapult (chessman) *see* Cannon
catur 93–97 (**93**–**94**), 361*n*2
Caxton, William **329**
celestial chess *see escaques*
de Cessolis, Jacobus 199, 210, 329, 370*n*3, 370*n*5
chancellor chess **257**, 260, 265
chandaraki *see* Tibetan chess
Chao Buzhi 107, 193, 330
Chao Gongwu 107, **108**
Chariot (chessman) as a Rook 16, 47–49, 51–54, 63, 66–67, 86–87, 92–95, 100, 102–104, 107, 110–111, 144–146, 152–153, 161–162, 209, 221, **340**, 343, 345, 350, 362*n*21; *see also* Rukh
Charlemagne **200**, 209
Charts *see* names (of chessmen, compared)
chatrang 15–16, 29, **327**, 337, 343, 347, 352
chaturaji 59–64, **59**, **61**, **64**, 77, 228, 326, 332–**333**, 349, 363*n*31; *see also* four-player chess
chaturanga **16**, 47–57, **48**–**50**, **52**–**53**, **55**–**56**, **59**, 63–64, 85, 92, 96, 106, 326, 332, 337–339, 343, 346–347, 350, 352
*Chaturangadipika (The Light of Chess)* 63, 333
checkered board 30, 39, 46, 90, **199**, 207, **241**, 288, **329**, 381*n*22
checkers 223, 349, 372*n*37
Cheng Hao 107, 366*n*30
*Chess-Battle* 282
chess rules **241**–**243**
chessmen (identities) *see* names (of chessmen, compared)
chessmen (photographs): Afrasiab (replica) **340**; Charlemagne (so-called)(replica) **200**; courier chess (replica) **233**; Da Vinci (so-called) **246**; doushouqi **131**; Gothic **263**; hiashatar **45**; Indian **55**–**56**, **58**; janggi **113**; "knighted" **252**; Lewis (replica) **209**; Medieval (replica) **206**; Metamachy **277**; Moro **97**; Muslim style **18**; Omega **276**; Seirawan **264**; shatar **40**–**41**, **44**–**46**; shogi **142**, **152**, **197**; xiangqi **101**, **105**
Chess960 89, 250, 319–325 (**320**–**321**, **323**)
Chinese chess *see* xiangqi
*Choju jinbutsu giga (Scrolls of Frolicking with Animals)* 368*n*15
Chu Ci 339
chu shogi 153–164, **154**–**155**, **158**, 166, 176–181, 183, 189–190, 192
Ciccolini, Giuseppe **268**–**269**
Ciccolini, Teodoro 286
circular chess 27–30, 230, **285**–287, 302–303, 363*n*31
citadel chess 23, **24**, 27–28, 30–35
*Civis Bononiæ ("Citizen of Bologna")* 210
*Cờ Tư Lệnh see* Commander Chess
cờ tướng 99; *see also* xiangqi
Cohen, Philip 81, 261
*Commander Chess* 282
complete chess 21, **22**, 24, 28–30, 70, 373*n*56, 382*n*41; *see also* decimal chess
Contractus, Hermannus 220
coronation chess 259, 265
Counselor (chessman) Queen forerunner 8–9, 11–12, 18, 48, 51, **79**, 101, 345–**346**, 350–351; leap 18, 79, 86
counting rule 79–80, 88, 91, 364*n*54
courier chess **232**–**236**, 270–271
*Courier-Spiel* 269–271, **269**–**270**
Cox, Hiram 91, 332–333, 362*n*26, 364*n*61
Coxe, William 254, 297
cubic chess 310–312
cylinder chess **286**–**287**

Dabbaba (chessman) 22, 24, 31–34, 66–67
dai dai shogi 167–170, **167**–**169**, 172, 176–177
dai shogi 153, 159–163, **159**–**161**, 167–168, 173, 176
Dalverzin Tepe **341**, 382*n*38
*Dama Tujing see* Li Qingzhao
Damiani, Petrus 207
Damiano, Pedro 246, 371*n*25
decimal chess 21, 23, 29–30, **70**, 228, 252, **266**–**267**, **273**, 282; (hyperabad) 65–67, **66**; *see also* complete chess
Da Vinci chessmen (so-called) **246**
Dekle, George 305, 312, 377*n*38
*De Vetula* 221, 371*n*27
dice (use of) 24, 26, 29, 38, 51, 57, 59–60, 62–63, 221, 228, 320, 322, 326, 332–333, 337–338, 346
Dilaram (legend) 12–14
Dobutsu Shogi 183–186, **184**, 188
*dongwuqi* 127, **128**, 130; modern version **135**
Double Chess 299
doushouqi 125–131, **125**–**126**, **130**, 135, 367*n*39
Dragonchess 312

*Dreier Schach* 303, 305
drops 142, 146–147, 149–*150*, 153, 158–160, 162–163, 170–171, 175, 180–183, 185–188, 193, 196, 250, 376n17
Drunk Elephant (chessman) 152–153, 155, 157, 159, *171*–174, 176, 178, 181, 190, 193, 195, 368n13

Ecila chess 312
Edan, Hermance 138–139, 141
Einsiedeln manuscripts *see Versus de scachis*
Elcum, John Bowen 95
Elephant (chessman) 3; as a Bishop 18–19, 54, 66, 93–94, 191, 247; Bishop forerunner 8–9, 11–12, *16*, 100–102, 104, 107, 120, 208–209, 228–229, 336, 339, 344–348, *350*–351; "five legs" *50*, 83, 78–79, 86–87, 90–92, 151–*152*; other moves *49*, 50, *75*, 82–83, 110–114, 116, *264*–265, 268–*269*, *273*, 277–279, *342*, *350*, 382n41; as a Rook 48–49, *50*, 52–54, 59–60, 69, 71–73
*Embassy Chess* 264–265
Emperor (chessman) 170–176
*Enlarged and Improved Chess* 267
en passant capture 9, 42, 45, 54, 91, 94–95, 201–202, *243*, 252–253, 255, 269, 279, 290
Ermengol *206*
*escaques* 28, 30, 230–*231*
*Eschez amoureux* 202–204, *203*–*204*
Ethiopian chess *see* senterej
European chess (standard, international) 240–248, *241*–*248*; recreations *248*–249
*Explanation of Chatrang and the Invention of Nard see Wizarishn*
ibn Ezra, Abraham 370n2

Fairbairn, John 180, 183
*Falconry* 271–*272*
Falkener, Edward 58
*fanorona* 20
al-Farazdaq 16
Fazang *see prasena*
Fenollar, Bernat *see Scachs d'amor*
Ferz (or Fers, Ferzia, Firz, chessman) *8*, 19–21, 38, 44, *199*, 201, 208, 228–229, 247, 270–271; *see also* Counselor
Firdawsi *23*, 29, 228, 328, 382n41
Fischer, Bobby 89, 263, *320*
Fischerandom chess *see* Chess960
five minute poppy shogi *see* gofun maka shogi
Forbes, Duncan 34, 62–63, 97, 285, 332–333, 360n22, 360n26, 360n27, 360n28, 362n26, 362n29, 363n31
Ford, John *see* Klin Zha
Foster, Benjamin *see* chancellor chess
4-D chess 312
four-player chess 50, 57, *59*, 63–*64*, 117, 123, 129, *134*, 139, 223, 228–230, *229*–*230*, 295–*299*, 310, 332–*333*, 349, 363n31, 366n34
four seasons (chess of the) 228–230, *229*–*230*, 295
free chess 324–325; *see also* Chess960

Freeling, Christian 262, 264
Fujita, Maiko *see* Dubutsu Shogi
Fulke, William 212–215, *213*, *222*
*Funkschach* 324–325
*furigoma* 148
*Futsu Shodoshu (Collection of Sermons for Everyday Use)* 153, 161

Gala 237–240, *237*–*239*
galactic chess 65, *71*–*72*
*Game and Playe of the Chesse see* Caxton
Gaw (legend) *23*, 228, 328, 330
*gelong* 95–96; *see also* Pawn (promotion)
"The Generals" (game) *136*
Generals facing each other 101, *103*, 108, 112
Gerbert of Aurillac 220–221
Giacometti, Francesco 280–*281*
giant chess 64–65, 72–77, *73*, 114–115, *167*–*177*, 188–197, *280*, 311
gidongcha janggi *114*
*Il gioco degli scacchi (The Game of Chess) see* Carrera
*giog* 125
Giraffe (chessman) 31–34, 38, 66–67, *224*–*227*, 369n19, 377n33; illustration *330*
Giżycki, Jerzy 38
Gliński, Władysław 288–295, *288*–*290*, 304
go (game of) *see* weiqi
Godavaramishra *see* Harihara Chaturanga
Godson, William 311
gofun maka shogi *187*–188
gogo shogi *see* minishogi
Gollon, John 65, 81–83, 311, 314, 316, 360n29, 362n22
Gontier, Samuel-Alexandre 129
goro-goro shogi 185–*186*, 188, 370n42
*Gothic Chess 263*, 265
*Grand Chess 262*–265
*grant acedrex* 72, 223–228, *223*–*225*, 360n31, 377n33
great chess *see shatranj al-kabir*
Greco, Giachino 247, *267*
*Grosses Königs Spiel (Great King's Game) see* Weickhmann
*Guangxiangxi Tu (Widened Xiangxi with Illustrations) see* Zhao Buzhi
gunjin shogi 136, *140*–*141*
Gustav III chess 253–*254*, 265
*gwangsanghui* 114–115
*Gyegokjip* 116

*haijunqi* 134
half-victory 22, 51
Han Xin 330
*Hanasakai Sandaikai* 162
handicap 148–149, 162, 253, 367n2
*Haravijaya* 50, 338
Harihara Chaturanga text 64–65, 77; game 73–77, *75*–*76*
Harikrishna *see Kridakaushalya*
al-Harrani 29

*Harshacharita see* Bana
Harun al-Rashid 29
*hashtpay* 337, 350; *see also ashtapada*
Heian shogi 152–153, *161*, 176
Hellwig, Johann Christian Ludwig *see* Kriegspiel
hexagonal chess 120, *288–295*, 300, 303–*304*, 312
hexagonal shogi *see* kokusai sannin shogi
*Hexagonia* 291
*hiashatar* 23, *44–45*
*Hikayat Bayan Budiman (Seventy Tales of the Parrot)* 96
Hill, P.A. 81–82
Himly, Karl 365*n*12
*Hive* (game) 375*n*2
*hnefatafl* 207, 223, 240
Hodges, George 162, 177, 196, 370*n*32
*Honeycomb Chess* 294
Honinbo Sansa 153
Horn, Fred 139, 367*n*40
Horse (chessman) Knight forerunner 8–11, *16*, 247, 336, *342*, 345; checkmate with 20, 42; special moves 21, 43, 75
Hughes-Hughes, M.E. 295–297, *296*
*hunheqi* 106
Hyde, Thomas *330–331*, 360*n*24, 364*n*53

*igui* 156–157, 164, 169, 189–192
Indian chess *see chaturanga*
*Interface* (game) 302
international chess (standard, modern) *see* European chess
*Isei Teikin'orai (Correspondence Manual for Family Teaching)* 176

Jabir al-Kufi 17
Jákl, Jiří 96
Jang Yu *see Gyegokjip*
janggi 85, 105, 109–116, *109*, *111*, *112–115*, 366*n*24
*Janus Chess* *261*, 265
Japan Shogi Association 188
Japanese chess *see* shogi
Javanese chess *see* catur
Jetan 314–316, *315–316*
Jeu de la Guerre *280–281*, 367*n*45; *see also* Kriegsspiel
*jieqi* 106
*jishogi* 147
*jitto* 156–157, 164–165, 189–191
*joara-joari see maddat mari*
Jones, Sir Williams 332–333, 362*n*20, 380*n*9
"joy leaps" *234*, 361*n*2, 374*n*62
*Ju Zhongmi (The Secret Inside the Tangerines)* 108

*Kaiser's game see* Tressau
Kalhana *see Rajatarangini*
Kanyakubja (Kannauj) 50, 328, 334, 337–338, 342, 350
*kar ouk* 81
Kautilya 48, 380*n*17
*Kavyalamkara* 50, 339
Kermur Sire de Légal, François-Antoine 248–249

Khalifa, Hajji *see* ash-Shatranji
al-Khalil 28
Khusraw 16, *327*, 337, 382*n*46
Kieseritzky, Lionel *299*, 310
Kimura, Yoshinori 369*n*25
King: bare King 10, 15, 18, 22, 34, 49, 62, 76, 80, 88, 91, 95, 159, 166, 201–202; escape 24, 26, 28, 34, 94–95, 202, 362*n*15, 373*n*50; leap 18, 55, 79, 86, 94–96, 201, 226, 247, 279
*Kings and Pawns Game* 248
Kirin (chessman) 156–157, 159, *168*, 170–172, *174*, 189, 195
*Kirinsho (Notes about the Kirin)* 151
*Kitab al-aghani (Book of songs) see* al-Faraj
*Kitab al-Fihrist see* an-Nadim
*Kitab ash-shatranj see* al-'Adli
Kitao, Madoka *see* Dobutsu Shogi
Klin Zha 316–319, *317*, *319*
ko shogi 176, 188–193, *189*
Kogbetlianz, Ervand 311; *see* 3-D chess
kogun shogi *see* gunjin shogi
*Kokon Shogi Zui (Illustrations of Past and Present Shogi Styles)* 180
kokusai sannin shogi 304
*komadai 143*, 146
Komnene, Anna 29
Korean chess *see* janggi
*Kridakaushalya* 58, 65, *71*, 362*n*9, 362*n*15, 363*n*40
Kriegsspiel 280
Kyoto shogi *187*–188

al-Lajlaj 11, 15, 17
Lala Raja Babu 58, 65, 67, 71, 73
de La Loubère, Simon 85
large chess *see* grant acedrex; shatranj al-kabir
large shogi *see* dai shogi
large xiangqi *see* gwangsanghui; ko shogi; qiguo xiangxi
Lasker, Edward *258*
"leap of joy" *see* "joy leaps"
Lefèvre d'Étaples, Jacques (Faber) 215, 221–222
legends 12, 16–17, *23*, 28, 35, 108, 194, 209, 327–331, *327*, *329*, 337, 359*n*7
Legler, Hugo *see* Neo-Chess
Le Pelleter, Erwann 368*n*9, 369*n*22, 369*n*25, 370*n*39, 370*n*41
*Let's Catch the Lion see* Dobutsu Shogi
Leventhal, Dennis 122, 366*n*25, 366*n*26, 366*n*29
Lewis (set of Isle of) 209
*Liber de Moribus Hominum see* de Cessolis
*Libre dels jochs partits dels schacs en nombre de 100 see* Vicent
*Libro de los juegos see* Alfonso X
Lilleøren, Morten 245, 372*n*30
Linder, Isaac 207
Lion (chessman) 35–38, *40*, 70, 154, 156–159, 161–162, 166, 224–226 (*224–225*), 277–279 (*279*), 369*n*30
Li Qingzhao 108

Liu Kezhuang 108
Liu Xiang 339
*liubo* 98, 107, 125, 339, 347–350, *348–349*, 352
Lopez, Diego 96
Low, Captain James 85, 363*n*43
Loyd, Leonard B., Jr. *see* Klin Zha
Lucena 245
*ludus latrunculorum* 223, 371*n*19
*ludus philosophorum see* rithmomachy
*ludus regularis seu clericalis* 221
*luhaikong zhanqi* **135**
*luzhanqi* 89, 130–136, ***131***, ***134***, 139–141
Lwin, Maung Maung 89, 364*n*56

Maack, Ferdinand 307, 310–312; *see also* 3-D chess
*madayar* 336, 359*n*2; *see also* Rukh
*maddat mari* 57
*Mahabharata* 96, 343, 362*n*28, 380*n*17
Maharaja and the Sepoys *see* sarvatobhadra
mahjong 125, 129, 139
*main chator see* catur
maka dai dai shogi ***170–172***, 176–178, 182–183, 370*n*41
makruk 77–86, ***77–79***, ***81***, ***85***, 90, 151
Malagasy chess *see* samantsy
*Malat* 96
Malay chess *see* catur
al-Ma'mun 17
*Manasollasa (Joy of the Mind)* **48**–51, 57, 63, 339, 382*n*45
Manchu chess *see* yitong
*Mandragorias, seu, Historia shahiludii see* Hyde
*mansuba* 12–15, 28, 371*n*10
maps: Asia (diffusion) ***334***; China, Warring States 260 B.C.E ***119***; Europe (diffusion)***208***; Indian subcontinent ***53***; Islam and Byzantium 900 C.E. ***17***; Silk Road ***335***; Southeast Asia 1000 C.E. ***84***; Spain 912–961 C.E. ***205***
Marinelli, Filippo **300**
*Mars* (game) 291; *see also* Jetan
al Mas'udi 17, 21, 28–30
Masukawa, Koichi 367*n*7, 367*n*8, 369*n*25, 369*n*27
Maura, Gabriel Vicente *see* Modern Chess
Maus, Frank *see* coronation chess
Mayer, Arnold 237–240
McCooey, Dave ***294–295***, 304
medieval chess 199–210, ***199–200***, 214, 217, ***224***, 226, ***229***, ***233–235***, 244–246, 272, 279, 381*n*22
metamachy 276–279, ***277–279***
metromachy 372*n*42
Michaelsen, Peter 240, 361*n*39, 364*n*5, 376*n*8, 376*n*10
middle shogi *see* chu shogi
Minase Kanenari 162, 176–177
minishogi 183, ***186***, 188, 370*n*42
minixiangqi 105, ***106***
*Mo'allim ul shatranj see* Lala Raja Babu
*Modern Chess* (Maura's) ***260***, 265
*Modern Courier Chess* 270–271
Mogendorff, Jacques Johan 139

*mokkan* 152
Mongolian chess *see* shatar
Montay-Marsais, Robert *see* Stratomic
*Moralities* 209–210
*Mritasañjivini* 339
mujo dai shogi *see* tai shogi
*el mundo* **230**
Murray, Harold James Ruthven 4, 12, 17, 19, 24, 29, 35, 43–44, 63, 70, 72, 95–97, 139, 208–209, 224, 226–227, 234, 240, 252, 285, 297, 299, 326, ***333–334***, 337–338, 340, 346, 360*n*17, 360*n*20, 360*n*22, 360*n*27, 360*n*30, 361*n*36, 361*n*37, 361*n*1, 362*n*9, 362*n*22, 362*n*24, 362*n*27, 363*n*30, 363*n*31, 363*n*34, 363*n*36, 363*n*43, 364*n*63, 365*n*17, 372*n*31, 376*n*7, 377*n*23, 379*n*71, 380*n*10, 380*n*19, 381*n*21, 381*n*22
*Muruj adh- dhahab (The Meadows of Gold) see* al-Mas'udi
Musser, Sonja 227, 372*n*46, 373*n*49, 373*n*51, 373*n*56, 373*n*57
Mussini, Luigi (painting) **246**

ibn an-Nadim 17
*Nafa'is al- funun (Treasury of science) see* al-Amuli
Nam Yu-yong *see Noeyonjip*
names (of chessmen, compared) 8, 19, 21, 31, 41, 54, 78, 82, 86, 94, 100, 110, 126, 132, 144, 208–209, 247, 265
nard 16, 24, 327–328, ***327***, 330, 336–337, 339, 352, 382*n*45; *see also* backgammon
Navoï, Alisher 38
*Neo-Chess* **258**, 261, 265
*Nichureki (From the Two Chureki)* 152–153, 161
*Nifu* 147
Nilakantha, Bhatta *see Nitimayukha*
Nishizawa Teichin *see* zushiki
*Nitimayukha* 51–52
Niu Sengru *see Xuanguai Lu*
*Noble Celts* 287
*Noeyonjip (Collected works)* 114

oblong chess 24–26, ***24–25***, 28–30
Ogyu Sorai 193
Ohashi Soei 183
Ohashi Sokei 153
Ohashi Soko 153, 176; *see also* zushiki
Okano Shin 83
*Omega Chess* **275–276**
*Othello* 223
*ouk see* makruk
ouranomachy **222**

pachisi 62, 64–65, 333, 382*n*43
Palamedes 329–331
*Pañcha Danda Chattra Prabandha* 51
*pancha keliya* 62
Parlett, David 221, 271, 372*n*36
Parton, Vernon Rylands 254, 311–312, 314
patent 129, ***137***–138, ***140***–141, 247, 263, 304, 311, 324, 377*n*27

Pawn: earliest 9–11; Asian forms 102, 112, 146; promotion 9–11, 16, 18, 22, 26–27, 33–34, 49, 54–56, 60, 82, 86–88, 90–91, 95–96, 102, 112, 146, 201, 226, 234, 242, 247, 252, 259, 262, 279, 283–284, 290, 296, 300, 302, 310, *347*, 351
*Pawns Game* **248**–249
*Payyannur Pattu* 51
peasant's chess *see* gala
Persian chess *see* chatrang
Petrov, Alexander 299
Philidor, François-André Danican 241, 247, 253–254, 375*n*78
Piacenza 23, 265–**266**
Plowden, Walter 19
Polo, Marco 83, 227
Popova, Assia 41, 43–44, 361*n*37
*Power Chess* 376*n*9
Pozzi, Rodolfo 43, 91–92
*prasena* 352–353
*Pre-Chess* 324–325
Pritchard, David Brine 56, 68, 81, 83, 89, 91, 250, 265, 271, 288, 292, 294–295, 297, 311, 363*n*35, 363*n*40, 364*n*5, 376*n*12, 377*n*23, 377*n*28, 377*n*35
Prussian National Chess (so-called) **281**–282

qiguo xiangxi **107**, 116–120, **119–120**, 176, 193
*al-qirq see* alquerque
Queen: earliest modern 18, 74, 77, 96, 118, 120, 156, 162, 164, 172, 190, 198–200, **203–204**, 207–209, 222, 360*n*28, 362*n*9; leap 201, 234, 247
*Questo libro e da imparare giocare a scachi see* Damiano

Rabrab Khata'i, Zairab 17
Raghunandana *see Tithitattva*
*Rain Drop Chess* 250
*Rajatarangini (The River of Kings)* 63
*Ramayana* 85, 92, 338, 345, 380*n*17
range jumping 164–165, 167
Ratnakara *see Haravijaya*
*Raumschach see* 3-D chess
ar-Razi 17, 359*n*6
*Real Chess* 324–325
referee 103, 133–134, *136*, 374*n*68
Reid, Douglas Graham *see* Honeycomb Chess
*Repeticion de amores & arte de acedrex see* Lucena
*Reversi see* Othello
Reynolds, Dave 30, 286
Rhinoceros (chessman) 38, 224–227, **224–225**
rithmomachy 211–223, **212–215**, **217–219**
Robinson, H.O. 94–95
*Robotow see* Dobutsu Shogi
*Roman de la Rose* 202
Rook + Knight (chessman) **66**, **251**, **253**, **256–259**, 262–265, **262–263**
Rook: earliest European **199**, 208–**210**, 337, 359*n*2
Rudrata *see Kavyalamkara*
Rukh (chessman) 2, 8–12, *16*, 208, 337; bird 227, 360*n*32

Rumi chess 19, 58–59
*Ruodlieb* 207
Russian fortress chess 297–299, **298**
Rutland, Duke of **253**, 257, 265
Ruy Lopez **246**–247
Ryoki, monk *see Futsu Shodoshu*

*Salpakan (Game of the Generals)* **136**
Salt, Henry 19
samantsy **20**, 21
San Genadio 205
sanguo qi **120–123**, 307
sanyou qi *see* sanguo qi
*Sardarnama (Book of Commanders)* 65, 70
sarvatobhadra 50, **57**, 58, 77, 363*n*31
Sassa (inventor) 35, 328–330
*Scachs d'amor* **244–245**
*Schach- oder Königs-Spiel see* Selenus
Schmittberger, R. Wayne 180, 183, **274–275**, 311
Schöndorf, Werner *see* Janus Chess
Seirawan, Yasser **264**–265
*Sejarah Melayu* 96
Selenus, Gustavus 215, 222, **235**, 374*n*61
*sennichite* 147, 166
senterej *19*, 21
Seongho Yi Ik 115
seven-player chess *see* escaques; qiguo xiangxi
Shafran, Isaak Grigorevich **292**, **295**
*shah masnu'a* 34
*shah mat* 7, 10, 96
*shah munfarid see* King (bare)
*Shahnama* 381*n*30; *see also* Firdawsi
*Shako* 272–**273**, 277
shape (of chessmen) *16*, 19, **40**, 52, *78*, 86, 94, 100, 110, 116, **123**, **144**, **151**, **209**, 211, **213**, **222**, **234–235**, 237, **260**, 262, 349, 371*n*25, 378*n*40; *see also* chessmen (photographs)
shatar 23, 39–46, **39–42**, **44–46**, 375*n*4
shataranja 54, 67–68
shatranj 7–21, **8–18**, **21**, 51, 54, 58, 67–68, 200, 204, 207–208, 234, 272–273, 371*n*10, 373*n*53
shatranj al-falakiya *see* escaques
shatranj al-husun *see* citadel chess
shatranj al-jawarhiya *see* anatomic chess
shatranj al-kabir 30–31, 35, 37–39, 65, **70**, 228
shatranj al-mamduda *see* oblong chess
shatranj al-muddawara *see* circular chess
shatranj al-mustatila *see* oblong chess
shatranj ar-rumiya *see* circular chess
shatranj as-su'diya 28
shatranj at-tamma *see* complete chess
shatranj at-tawila *see* oblong chess
shatranj diwana shah *see* sarvatobhadra
as-Shatranji, Ali 18, 35
*shattrong* 81–83, **82**
Shennong 330
Sherwood, John 215, 221
*Shinsarugakuki (An Account of the New Comic Entertainment)* 151

shitranj 359*n*1; *see also* shatranj
sho shogi 153, 161–162, 176, 180
sho-chan shogi **186**
shogi 3, 85, 105, 136, 142–154, ***142–144***, ***146***, ***149–152***, ***154***, ***161***–162, 176, 185, 188, 223, 240, 250, 312, 375*n*4, 376*n*17
*Shogi Koma no Nikki see* Minase Kanenari
*Shogi zushiki (Illustrated Explanations of Shogi) see* zushiki
*shuanglu* 339, 352, 382*n*45; *see also* backgammon
shuffle chess *see* Chess960
Shulapani *see Chaturangadipika*
*Shuo Yuan see* Liu Xiang
Shwe Kyin U Ba 91, 364*n*59
siguo xiangqi 123; *see also* four-player chess
siguodazhan **134**
Silberschmidt, Hans **282**
Sim Su-Gyeong 116
Sima Guang 107, 119–120; *see also* qiguo xiangxi
sit-tu-yin 85–93, ***87–90***, ***92–93***, 151, 332
6-D chess 312
Someshvara III *see Manasollasa*
space chess (*raumschach*) *see* 3-D chess
space hexchess 312
space shogi 312
Spanish chess (so-called) 267–**268**
Sphinkian chess 312
spiral race game 62, 346, 360*n*13, 362*n*8, 364*n*68, 380*n*19
stalemate specific rules 10, 22, 43, 49–50, 52, 55, 88, 103, 112, 121, 147, 201, 243, 290, 364*n*60
*Star Trek* chess 311–312, 316, ***319***, 377*n*38; *see also* Klin Zha
Staunton (design) 97, 100–101, ***241***, ***247***, ***252***, 260, 263–264
Steinitz, Wilhelm 247
stem 59, 94
*Stratego* 89, 130, 137–139, ***138***, 141
*Stratomic* **283–284**
Ströbeck **232**, 235–236, 361*n*2, 374*n*62
Subandhu 338, 381*n*21
*Suizo see* Drunk Elephant
ibn Sukaikir ad-Dimashqa 18
as-Suli 11–13, 17, 359*n*7
Sultan Khan, Mir 48
*Sultan's game see* Tressau
Symes, Michael 91

at-Tabari 17, 29
*ta'biya* ***11–12***, 20, 28, 48, 371*n*10
tables (game of) *see* backgammon
Tahir ibn Husayn 29
*Tahqiq ma li- l-Hind see* al-Biruni
Taï-Hou 128–130, ***129***
tai shogi 173–177, ***173***, ***175***, 194, 370*n*41
Taiki 161
taikyoku shogi 176, ***194***–197
*Tali'a* (chessman) 31–32; *see also* Bishop
Tang shogi 176

Tattersfield, James 20
TEDCO 311
ten-square chess 228
tenjiku shogi 163–168, ***163***, ***166***, 176, 178, 190, 193
*Tentativo di un nuovo giuoco di scacchi (Attempt at a New Game of Chess) see* Ciccolini
Tesche, Walter **302**
Thai chess *see* makruk
thayam 62, 383*n*50
3-D chess 307–313, ***308–309***, ***312–313***
*3 Man Chess* 303, 305
three-player chess 98, 117, ***120–123***, 129, 288, 291, ***300–307***
Tibetan chess 43
Timur (the Lame) 18, 30–31, 35, 37; portrait **35**
Timur's great chess 30–38, ***31–33***, ***36–38***, 69, 121, 228, 272, 274, 277, 286, 312, 363*n*31, 376*n*12, 377*n*33, 382*n*41
*Tithitattva* 59, 63, 333, 362*n*24
Tokyo janggi 115
tori shogi 180–183, ***180–182***
*Total Chess* 311; *see* 3-D chess
Toyota Genryu *see* Ohashi Soei
*Transcendental Chess* 324–325
Tressau, Ludwig 254–256, ***255–256***, 257
*Trichess* 305–306
*Trioschaak* 305
*tsume shogi* **150**
Turkish chess 18–19, 37–38, 44, 58, 65, 228, 363*n*33
Tutti-Frutti Chess 261–**262**, 265

U Pe Hsaung 89
*uchifuzume* 147
Umebayashi, Isao 83, 196
*Undang-undang Melaka* 96
Unicorn (chessman) 38, 224, 227, 309–311, 369*n*19
*Universal Chess* **259**, 265

Vaidyanatha Payagunda *see Chaturangavinoda*
van Leyden, Lucas 232–234, ***233***, ***236***
van Zuylen van Nyevelt, Philippus Julius **323**
Varchi, Benedetto 215, 222
de Vasa, Helge Em **293**
Vasantha, Rangachar 65, 71
*Vasavadatta see* Subhandu
Venafro 206
Vérin, Pierre 20
Verney, Major George Hope 285, 295, 297, 302–**303**, 360*n*29, 360*n*30, 378*n*48
*Versus de Scachis* 207
Vicent, Francesch 245–246
*Victrix* **282**
Vietnamese chess *see* cờ tướng
*Vinayapitaka* 337, 383*n*51
Vinyoles, Narcís *see Scachs d'amor*
Violet, Bruno *see* universal chess
von Ammenhausen 235
von der Lasa, Tassilo 323
von Le Coq, Albert 341

von Öfele, Armin 95
*vyuha* 48, 71–72, 74, 92, 342; *see also* ta'biya

Waidder, S. **301**, 304
wa shogi 176–180, ***177***, ***179***, 183
Wang Bao *see* Xiangjing
*Wehr-Schach* 282–***283***
Weickhmann, Christoph 280, 297
*weiqi* (game of go) 98–99, 109, 116–117, 125, 142, 144, 154, 188, 348, 351, 361$n$41, 368$n$8, 368$n$10, 376$n$15
Wellisch, Sigmund 291, 303–***304***
*werera* 20; *see also* ta'biya
whale shogi ***182***–183
Whater Wheel (problem) 15
*Wigalois* 235
*Wildebeest Chess* ***274***–275, 277; *see also* Schmittberger
*Winchester Poem* 207
*Wirataparwa* 96
*Wizarishn i Chatrang ud Nihishn i New-ardakhshir* 16, ***327***, 336
Wodeyar III *see* galactic chess
Wu, Emperor *see* Xiangjing
*wuhuqi* 105
*Wyvern Chess see* Parton

Xerxes ***329***–331
*Xiangjing (Classic of the Game of Symbols)* 339, 365$n$8
xiangqi 43, **82–83**, 85, 97–109, ***99***, ***101–103***, ***108–109***, 119, 125, 188, 240, 272–273, 330–***331***, 339–340, 343–353, 361$n$41, 381$n$32

xiangxi 107, 114, 116, 122, 339, 380$n$5
*Xiangxi Fu (Poetic Expression of Xiangxi)* 339, 365
Xiao Zhao 108
*Xuanguai Lu (Accounts of the Mysterious Marvels)* 107, 339, 365$n$16, 380$n$6

*Yalta* (game) 305
Yamato shogi 180; *see also* wa shogi
yan xiangqi *see* ko shogi
al-Ya'qubi 17, 328
*yitong* 105
*Yokaï no mori see* Dobutsu Shogi
Yu Hui-Chun 116
Yu Xin *see Xiangxi Fu*
*Yugaku Orai* 162
*yut* 116
Yuxian 108, 352

*za'id see* stalemate
zatrikion 29, 371$n$23
*Zhaohun* 339
Zheng Jinde 122–123
Zhu Jinzhen *see* Ju Zhongmi
Zillions-of-Games© 4, 11, 159, 269, 272–273, 276, 285, 287, 290, 374$n$65, 379$n$67
Ziryab 204
Zorzi, Alessandro 19
Zubrin, Robert 304
*zushiki* 153, 162, 166, 176, 180, 196, 368$n$9, 368$n$17, 369$n$22, 369$n$30, 369$n$31, 370$n$36